# FUNNY MAN

## MEL BROOKS

ALSO BY PATRICK MCGILLIGAN

*Young Orson: The Years of Luck and Genius on the Path to* Citizen Kane

*Nicholas Ray: The Glorious Failure of an American Director*

*Oscar Micheaux: The Great and Only*

*Alfred Hitchcock: A Life in Darkness and Light*

*Clint: The Life and Legend*

*Fritz Lang: The Nature of the Beast*

*Jack's Life: A Biography of Jack Nicholson*

*George Cukor: A Double Life*

*Robert Altman: Jumping Off the Cliff*

*Cagney: The Actor as Auteur*


EDITED BY PATRICK MCGILLIGAN

*Backstory: Interviews with Screenwriters of Hollywood's Golden Age*

*Backstory 2: Interviews with Screenwriters of the 1940s and 1950s*

*Backstory 3: Interviews with Screenwriters of the 1960s*

*Backstory 4: Interviews with Screenwriters of the 1970s and 1980s*

*Backstory 5: Interviews with Screenwriters of the 1990s*

*Tender Comrades: A Backstory of the Hollywood Blacklist* (with Paul Buhle)

*Six Screenplays by Robert Riskin*

*Film Crazy: Interviews with Hollywood Legends*

# FUNNY MAN

## MEL BROOKS

Patrick McGilligan

HARPER

*An Imprint of* HarperCollins*Publishers*

HarperCollins books may be purchased for educational, business, or sales promotional use. For information, please email the Special Markets Department at SPsales@harpercollins.com.

FIRST EDITION

Library of Congress Cataloging-in-Publication Data has been applied for.

ISBN 978-0-06-256099-5

19 20 21 22 23    LSC    10 9 8 7 6 5 4 3 2 1

FOR CLANCY, BOWIE, AND SKY

My mind is a raging torrent flooded with rivulets of thought cascading into a waterfall of creative alternatives.

—Hedley Lamarr, *Blazing Saddles*

# Contents

# FUNNY MAN

## MEL BROOKS

# CHAPTER 1

# 1926

=========

## Little World

What made Melvin, the youngest of the Kaminsky kids, so darn funny? Later people said—he himself said—it was Brooklyn, the Depression, being Jewish and growing up in the shadow of Hitler. But there was also something about birth order and the family genes that contributed to "the strange amalgam, the marvelous pastiche that is me."

Before there was Mel Brooks there were the Kaminskys. The Kaminsky family formed their own little world in Brooklyn, the mother and four brothers living in humble circumstances, the brothers sharing the same bed and crawling over one another like a litter of adorable puppies in a cardboard box, as Brooks often said in interviews.

The oldest, Irving, was almost ten when his youngest brother was born. Intelligent and wholesome, Irving acted more like a father than an older brother when Melvin was growing up. He was the only Kaminsky brother to get his college diploma.

Leonard was older than baby Melvin by seven years. Unassuming Lenny was interested in machines and science. As time would tell, he had the stuff of a war hero.

Bernard, only four years older, was closest in age and perhaps also in jaunty-jolly spirit. He was also the best athlete among the brothers. In his youth Bernard was "a great softball pitcher" (in Brooks's words) and a star of Brooklyn bowling leagues.

His older brothers held regular jobs and helped out with household expenses long before Melvin finished high school. Each played a different role inside the family and in life, but birth order—being the youngest—benefited Melvin, just as the B for Brooks alphabetically advantaged the sequence of his later writing credits. Melvin was still in diapers when his father passed away; his older brothers mentored and shielded him.

Being the youngest, most pampered brother with the least responsibility in the family, Melvin found that his role from infancy was to make people laugh. His family tossed baby "Melb'n" (as his mother called him in her fractured English) into the air, he made funny sounds, and they all cracked up. Everyone indulged the last born, Brooks recalled in many interviews, so much so "my feet never touched the floor until I was two."

Making people laugh—forging a career out of laughter—became his lifelong quest. In time millions of people would find the youngest Kaminsky hilarious, whether they experienced his comedy on television or in stage plays, recordings, advertisements, or motion pictures. Eventually he'd make several hundred times as much money from his comedy as all his brothers combined—or, for that matter, most of his famous show business friends.

The mother of the four boys had to be a miracle woman, and Kitty Kaminsky was: "a little Jewish rhino," in Brooks's words, and as good-humored as she was hard-charging. Shorter than her boys, which was really short—"so short she could walk under a coffee table with a high hat on," Brooks liked to say—Kitty worked like a slave day and night, stretching the dollars and pushing her boys through school, dividing the love and *matzah* ball soup equally. She was the heart and soul of the family and the supreme boss.

As a boy Irwin Alan Kniberg, who later changed his name to Alan King when he, too, grew up to become a comedian, lived in Williamsburg, a Brooklyn neighborhood, at the same time as the

Kaminskys. He remembered the formidable sight of the family as they arrived as one to pick up the youngest of the bunch after the school bell, the three older boys surrounding Kitty in a phalanx as the Kaminskys swept across the playground and swooped down on little Melvin. They were a tight-knit, fierce, single-minded unit.

Before Brooklyn there was Manhattan, where the Kaminsky clan, the paternal side of the family, turned up on Henry Street in the 1900 census amid the tidal wave of European and Russian Jews flooding into the Lower East Side of New York City. Many immigrant Jews came to the United States to escape religious pogroms in their native lands, while others were seeking economic opportunity. Persecution and opportunity were the yin and yang of Jewish identity, and they were fused in the bloodline of the Kaminskys.

Most Henry Street denizens were Russian Jews. Their number included thirty-two-year-old Abraham Kaminsky and his wife, Bertha, who arrived in America in about 1896, with their eldest child, Martha, and her brother Maximilian James, called Max. Max was born on January 8, 1893; some records say in Grodno, an ancient city near the onetime western border of Poland and Lithuania; others say in Danzig, then a region encompassing the city now known as Gdansk. Grodno was part of the Russian Empire before remapping, and Gdansk was a Baltic Sea industrial port within imperial Germany.

In Russia, Abraham Kaminsky had been a traveling merchant who specialized in sewing and knitting supplies. He had learned to read and write in English by the time of the 1900 census, although his wife relied upon Yiddish for most of her long life. Kaminsky also knew enough Norwegian to strike deals with the Norse captains who arrived in New York with their ship holds filled with herring—the coveted silver of the sea. Selling herring to Eastern

European Jews on the Lower East Side in the early twentieth century was akin to selling white rice to Chinese. The Kaminsky herring business boomed with, at its height, a storefront on Henry Street, a warehouse close by on Essex, and reportedly a hundred neighborhood pushcarts. Eight Kaminsky children were born in New York following Martha and Max: ten siblings in all.

The Kaminskys were as good-hearted as they were prosperous. Even with twelve members in his own household, Abraham, whom everyone called "Shloimy," made room for relatives arriving from Russia. He donated generously to Jewish charities. Perhaps that was how the Kaminskys became acquainted with the Brookmans, who came to the United States in about 1899, initially living on Norfolk Street, a few blocks north of the herring dealer.

Their surname, first reported as "Brockman" in the 1905 New York census, became "Bruckman" a few years later. The spelling changes might be ascribed to the family's imperfect English, or perhaps, later, a desire to shed the name of the patriarch, Isaac Bruckman, a tailor from Kiev who arrived in 1899 with his wife, Minnie, and three children, including the last to be born in Kiev, two-year-old Kate or Katie, called "Kitty." Three more Brookman children followed. But the Brookman side of the family—the "Brooks" in Mel Brooks—experienced setbacks and did not flourish like the Kaminskys.

Isaac "absconded" from his wife and six children in early 1906, according to documents, and was never seen nor heard from again. Minnie did not matriculate beyond primary school and only ever spoke Yiddish; she did not boast a profession. Throughout the ordeal of her abandonment the mother of six kept her two youngest children, four-year-old Dora and one-year-old Sadie, at home. Kitty and one or more of her siblings were sent uptown to the main building of the Hebrew Orphan Asylum of New York on Amsterdam Avenue between 136th and 138th Streets. The Hebrew

Benevolent Society paid Minnie's rent starting in 1906, and immigrant neighbors pitched in to help out the family.

The original surname disappeared from records for five or ten years, reemerging as "Brookman" by World War I. The five Brookman sisters and their brother were devoted to one another as a result of this early family rupture—especially the sisters, who were close to their mother and keenly felt Minnie's hardships and humiliation. The weeks if not months that Kitty spent as a young girl in Jewish charity homes fortified her survival skills in preparation for life's later tribulations and made her a tenacious mother.

The Kaminskys were not dependent on the garment industry, which employed thousands of immigrant Jews in New York City, but the Brookmans may have had a familial foothold in women's wear. The sisters took their first jobs as floor girls and milliners, while Joseph, the only boy and oldest sibling, started as a cap-maker. One way or another, nineteen-year-old Kitty Brookman met and fell in love with twenty-two-year-old Max Kaminsky by late 1915. Both already had passed the US citizenship test and been naturalized. Their marriage took place on January 31, 1916, after which Mrs. Max Kaminsky briefly moved in with her husband at the family's crowded 200 Henry Street address.

Within the year, however, the newlyweds joined the swelling exodus of Jews from the Lower East Side that moved to Brooklyn, one of the five New York City boroughs, across the nearby Williamsburg Bridge; they initially took up residence on Stone Avenue in Brownsville. Brooklyn was an enclave separate from Manhattan, with its own unique character, then as now comprising distinct neighborhoods, thickly populated by people with a common ethnicity, religion, national origin, or income level. Brownsville was an eastern district packed with poor Eastern European Jews, tenements, and synagogues.

Max Kaminsky, who bore the high expectations for the oldest

Kaminsky son, was a catch: short and wiry, with brown eyes and a full head of black hair. He could read and write English, and he had bookkeeping skills. He had an auspicious job as a general factotum for an attorney, Jacob W. Hartman, whose offices were situated on Broadway in lower Manhattan; his varied duties included serving as an investigator for insurance cases, knocking on doors as a process server, and acting as a public notary.

As for Kitty, a striking redhead with pop eyes, she had a commanding personality from girlhood. Soon after marriage she devoted herself to motherhood, giving birth to her first son, Irving, in late 1916, then to Leonard in 1919 and Bernard in 1922. By the time her fourth baby came along on a muggy summer day, June 28, 1926, the Kaminskys were ensconced in 515 Powell Street, still in Brownsville, sharing a building with a hundred other people, the vast majority Jewish, listing Russia or Poland as birthplaces. A great number of the occupants were unable to read or write English; Yiddish was their language.

The Kaminsky family was so poor, Mel Brooks liked to say, that his mother couldn't afford the medical expenses—so "the lady next door gave birth to me." Actually, Kitty gave birth while lying on the kitchen table, which was standard in that era, especially among the lower classes. The couple named the newborn Melvin with no middle name.

By now Max, the father of four sons, was toiling round the clock for Joseph J. Jacobs, the law partner of Jacob Hartman, who had died in the postwar flu epidemic. Mel Brooks said in later interviews his father had sometimes delivered writs and summonses to celebrities such as the Broadway musical headliner Marilyn Miller, "and he'd often get into the picture with them. He was known at the courthouse as 'Process Server to the Stars.'" But this is hand-me-down family lore, and little evidence of Max's brushes with celebrities can be found. Much of Max's work was as a paralegal for court filings.

Over the next three years the Kaminsky family moved several times, first to an apartment on South 4th Street in Williamsburg, which lay northeast of Brownsville, adjoining the East River where the Williamsburg Bridge penetrated Brooklyn; then to another multifamily dwelling at nearby 145 South 3rd. The Brookman sisters, who helped Kitty out, lived in the same Williamsburg neighborhood, as did Grandma Minnie.

3rd Street was the family's address when Max Kaminsky was admitted to Kings County Hospital two days before Christmas 1928, suffering from chronic pulmonary tuberculosis, which was a pandemic ailment among immigrants living in unhealthy crowded conditions. Max died on January 14, 1929, having marked his thirty-sixth birthday as he lay dying in hospital. Curiously, his death certificate lists as his address 16th Avenue in New Utrecht, a distant Brooklyn neighborhood within Bensonhurst, probably because that was where his parents now lived and Abraham Kaminsky had footed the hospital bills.

A temporary estrangement between Max and Kitty cannot be ruled out, however. One relative interviewed for this book depicted Max Kaminsky as a secretive, brooding, hard-wired personality. Max spent most of his time busy at work and at home was often tense and moody. He left the parenting to Kitty, that relative said.

The family lived frugally. Radio ownership was considered one measure of affluence, and the Kaminskys did not own a radio set, according to the 1930 census. But another curious detail surrounding his death suggests that Max possessed hidden resources.

From 1917, New York State corporation records list Max Kaminsky as a founding shareholder in a surprising number of business enterprises, including the D. Wald Mfg. Co., which marketed food products and glassware; the K. & C. Dress Company, Inc., which manufactured and sold dress apparel; the Abraham Pomerantz Company, Inc., which collected and traded woolen rags and remnants;

and Hygienic Hot Salt Water Baths, Inc., which specialized in hot-water baths.

Mel Brooks's father may have been a nominal signatory fronting for lawyers, but his business shares were sometimes valued as high as $100 each and in number might run to ten. The various entities were launched, in certain instances, with as much capital as $10,000; some appear to have been going concerns at the time of Max's death.

Devastated by the loss of their golden child, Abraham and Bertha Kaminsky unstintingly assisted Kitty and her four boys in the years ahead. "He gave us money sometimes or gobs of herring," Brooks recalled. "Lenny used to collect the herring." (His beloved firstborn son was the only member of his immediate family to have predeceased Abraham when the Kaminsky patriarch passed away in 1948; his wife, Bertha, survived Abraham, as did their nine other offspring—then still alive and well.)

The Brookmans were just as profoundly committed to helping the bereaved mother raise four sons on her own. Grandma Minnie helped out with babysitting and cooking. Aunt Sadie always lived close by Kitty (sometimes in the same building) and tithed out of her garment industry paycheck to her sister's family. Sadie also arranged piecework for Kitty when the children were asleep, at relatives', or in school. She remained a spinster and after retirement shared a condo with Kitty in Florida.

Mel Brooks was two and a half years old when his father passed away; all he would ever know about Max Kaminsky was what family members told him; that included the faint notion his father was "lively, peppy, sang well." Melvin shrugged off that heartache as a boy, saying he never even thought about not having a father until later in time. But subconsciously it must have influenced him, he subsequently realized; for one thing, it affected how he dealt with his own family responsibilities as an adult and father. "There's a side of Mel that will never be fulfilled, no matter how hard he drives himself," his friend novelist Joseph Heller once said, "and it all goes back to his father's death."

Brownsville, where Max and Kitty Kaminsky started out after their marriage, was probably the most densely populated, most Jewish section of Brooklyn in the early 1920s—the most religious, Orthodox, Old World neighborhood. Gentiles were neither common in nor alien to Williamsburg, which was more polyglot and fluid than Brownsville, its jammed, low-rent housing and slum dwellings broken up by occasional fields and parks.

Not long after Max's death, Kitty moved the family one more time, just a couple of blocks north, to the home of first memories for Melvin, now a toddler. This cheaper apartment house stood at 365 South 3rd, "close to the corner of Hooper and Keith," in Mel Brooks's words, and the Kaminskys lived on "the top floor of a five-story building."

South 3rd in Williamsburg became the first crucible of his humor. The neighborhood was tough and impoverished, in ways both good and bad, and Brooks could recall boyhood memories of a suicide victim, for example, a despondent building jumper, whose broken body lay on the sidewalk amid the police and ambulances. Little Melvin suffered a fright, noticing that the dead woman wore the same brand of shoes as his mother.

Almost from the cradle, it seemed, Melvin could make jokes out of his terrors and pitfalls. Kitty Kaminsky, rarely interviewed, said once that her youngest son's special knack for drawing laughter had first become obvious to her when Melvin was about five years old—around the time the family settled on South 3rd Street. "He was very talented," she said. "He showed signs of it. He was a lively boy. He was never a quiet boy."

The first targets of his comedy were undoubtedly his Jewish

neighbors in the crowded 3rd Street tenements, "a hotbed of artistic intellectuality," in his words. They "filled their daily lives with assorted expressions of art, particularly with theater, music and dance. Above all they loved theater. And these tenement Jews loved books and serious plays—Boris Thomashefsky–type plays.* They loved information so much they could read a dental manual with fierce appreciation, as if it was a comic book."

Kitty's lively boy drew from his observations of the other inhabitants of his building. "My very first impressions were of Mrs. Bloom and Mrs. Rosenthal," Brooks remembered. "We had Mr. Katz on the third floor. He had a fierce stutter. For me, he was like an ace in the hole. And the guy who lived in apartment 9B had this crazy walk."

Another early fount of imagination for him was actors and the fictional characters they portrayed in motion pictures. Sometimes on weekends, his mother took the boys to Feldman's, a beer garden restaurant on Coney Island, which offered free silent pictures to customers along with its beloved hot dogs. There for the first time little Melvin watched Charlie Chaplin and Buster Keaton while eating "a frankfurter, a root beer and a boiled-to-death ear of corn." Later in life Brooks would express varying opinions about Chaplin and Keaton, telling the *New York Times* in 1976 that *Modern Times* "isn't all that funny" and *The General* was "dreadful," while pointedly siding with the zanier comedians whom many critics viewed as less artistic. Never mind. "I fell in love with movies right there," Brooks recalled. "This was much better than real life. Who needs real life?"

Closer to home, on Broadway as it wove through Williamsburg, were "many movie houses" offering "three features for ten cents or a

---

* Actor and singer Boris Thomashefsky was a star of the Yiddish theater in New York City, performing classical drama as well as follies in the late nineteenth and early twentieth centuries. He was also a pioneering Borscht Belt entertainer.

double feature and a 'chapter' [in a serial] and Fox Movietone News, the races, where if you chose the right one you got a stick of gum for free." On Fridays his mother would "put out three milk bottles," Brooks recalled; she would "get nine cents back and then borrow a penny from somewhere so she could give me ten cents to go to the movies." Sometimes, if Kitty had other things to do, Melvin would go hand in hand with one of his grandmothers to the theater at the corner of Marcy and Broadway; just as often one of his older brothers took him to a matinee.

Around Hanukkah in 1931, it must have been, he saw director James Whale's version of Mary Shelley's *Frankenstein*, starring Boris Karloff as the Monster. Little Melvin was not yet six; no wonder that at home afterward, he had recurring nightmares of the Monster climbing up the fire escape toward his bedroom window; and no surprise, forty years on, that he recalled the classic horror film so vividly when sending up its scary story, its spooky milieu and atmospherics in *Young Frankenstein*.

As a nonagenarian, Brooks could reel off favorite stars and scenes from movies he had first watched in boyhood, those that had afforded escape from the "outside" world, where "life was dirty and hard." He relished *The Adventures of Robin Hood* with the dauntless Errol Flynn; *Flash Gordon* and other boy-oriented fantasy adventures; carefree musicals, especially the series starring Fred Astaire and Ginger Rogers; and the slapstick of the reigning comedy teams, many of them Jewish, such as the Three Stooges, but especially those that were made up of brothers—the surreal Marxes, the goofy Ritzes.

The Ritz brothers, Al, Jimmy, and Harry, were former Brooklynites, of whom the youngest brother, Harry, was "the sire of mugging," in Brooks's view. Pure clowns who made stupid puns with manic eye-rolling, the Ritzes were also comedic song-and-dance artists. The boy loved their wacky number "The Horror Boys from Hollywood" from *One in a Million* in 1936, with Al as a singing-dancing

Frankenstein's Monster. Brooks would incorporate a lot of mugging into his career, and "The Horror Boys from Hollywood" was an example of how he frequently drew from youthful favorites later, to inspire and to create memorable scenes such as "Puttin' on the Ritz" in *Young Frankenstein*.

The boy began to follow the films of Alfred Hitchcock, dating to a reissue of *The Lodger*, a silent thriller he saw at a Brooklyn theater with his brother Irving, and he'd rush to any picture featuring Cary Grant in the lead—or, for that matter, any glossy British production with a tall handsome leading man and lady with perfect diction and teeth.

His own teeth? A dentist looked into his mouth, diagnosed cavities, and pulled four teeth out for fifty cents each after Kitty balked at a dollar each for fillings. The surprise of the anecdote may be that he even visited a dentist, but for the rest of his life he had "tooth problems because of that," his son Max Brooks told an interviewer decades later.

When he was seven going on eight years of age, Melvin physically escaped Williamsburg for the first time. He left behind his brothers and mother and New York and felt the first pangs of insecurity, and he learned to defend himself by making strangers laugh.

The boy spent part of the summer of 1934 at Camp Sussex in New Jersey, spread over one hundred scenic acres on the shore of Lake Glenwood in Sussex County. Although it was run by a Jewish welfare organization and underwritten by comedian Eddie Cantor, Camp Sussex was open and free to all orphans and poor children. The goal was to provide needy children with a respite from the city's sweltering summers and its dismal slum conditions while immersing them in nature and outdoor activities.

Melvin rose with the other kids early every morning to boom out the camp ditty ("We welcome you to Sussex Camp/We're mighty glad you're here/We'll send the air reverberating/With a mighty cheer!") and to eat crabapples until his belly ached.

At Camp Sussex Melvin found his first audience outside the neighborhood. Whatever dictum the camp counselors issued to the boys, he would promptly subvert for laughs. ("Stay at the shallow end of the pool until you learn to drown!") At one weekend show the boy took center stage to offer his devastating imitation of a counselor. "I brought the house down," he recalled years later, "and I understood then that if you take comedy from life instead of repeating Henny Youngman jokes it works even better."

Jokes protected him, he learned. "They were afraid of my tongue . . . words were my equalizer." His antics preempted the counselors and made a nonathlete feel as though he belonged with the other boys. "'Who said that? Kaminsky! Grab him! Hold him!' Slap!" Brooks recalled. "But the other kids liked it and I was a success. I needed a success. I was short, I was scrawny. I was the last one they picked to be on the team."

He loved singing and dancing and clowning more than sports. When relatives gathered, he did animal impressions ("As a boy, I could make the greatest cat sounds in the world") and sang favorite songs, shuffling his feet in time with the music, which was not uncommon, even among Brooklyn kids, in an era that exalted song and dance on Broadway and radio and in movies. "I always got 'em at family parties," Brooks said years later, "with [Al] Jolson's 'Toot, Toot, Tootsie,' and Eddie Cantor's 'If You Knew Susie.'"

After his Camp Sussex summer, toward the end of 1934, Joe Brookman, Kitty's older brother, arranged a special outing for the eight-year-old that proved as influential as any experience—good, bad, or indifferent—that Melvin notched in his boyhood.

Cherished Uncle Joe, now a taxi driver, was a "character" with peculiar mannerisms and maxims; sometimes he was mock wise ("Marry a fat girl, don't marry a face"); sometimes he made head-scratching pronouncements ("Never eat chocolate after chicken"). The diminutive Joe wore Adler's elevator shoes and drove a Parmelee cab sitting on a stack of phone books with a special apparatus that allowed him to shift gears and operate the pedals and brakes. "When you saw a cab coming down the street with no driver at the wheel," Brooks said, "that was Uncle Joe." Uncle Joe was absorbed into the boy's repertoire, and years later there would be a little of him in the 2000 Year Old Man.

Uncle Joe had done a *mitzvah* for a Manhattan doorman who thanked the taxi man with a pair of tickets for *Anything Goes*, the hottest show on Broadway after its opening in late November 1934. The Cole Porter musical starred the electrifying Ethel Merman. Uncle Joe in his taxi chauffeured his nephew to the Alvin Theatre. The two sat "in the next to the last row at the top of the balcony," Brooks recalled with writerly exaggeration. The performers weren't using microphones in those days. Still, "all these Russian Jewish melodies that came from Cole Porter . . . Ethel Merman started to sing, and I had to hold my ears—she had a big voice. It was the most thrilling experience of my life."

"That day infected me with the virus of the theater," he recalled in Michael Kantor's documentary *Broadway: The American Musical* seventy years later. Cole Porter became "my all-time favorite composer," he said, but over time Uncle Joe took his nephew to other Broadway musicals that impressed the boy, including *Hellzapoppin'* in 1938, a hectic revue stuffed with slapstick and sight gags, written by and starring the *goyish* comedy duo of John "Ole" Olsen and Harold "Chic" Johnson. "A musical not only transports you, but stays in your brain because of the songs," Brooks told Kantor. "The musical blows the dust off your soul, like no other phenomenon in the history of show business."

Even before he saw his first musical the stage-struck boy already knew "the tunes and lyrics to a whole bunch of the numbers," because there was "music in the air, music everywhere," in his Brooklyn neighborhood, as he wrote in a piece he bylined more than half a century later for *The Times* of London. "Bing Crosby singing 'From Monday On' on the radio, the Millers in the next apartment playing Russ Columbo records on their wind-up Victrola, a wannabe Benny Goodman practicing 'Don't Be That Way' on his squeaky clarinet in the apartment across the backyard, a piano player in the open window of Heller's Music Emporium down the street knocking out Broadway tunes as a come-on to peddle street music."

When music wasn't in the air, there were plenty of other things for a boy to see and do all day long on crowded 3rd Street. The backyards and front steps were clogged with kids from big Jewish families. The Kaminskys played stickball, stoopball, and bottle-cap checkers and invented card games "with dirty old, very thick cards." With precious pennies they bought egg creams delicious enough to make you "swoon with ecstasy."

Somehow the pennies always stretched. "We were really poor but so was everybody else," Brooks said. "We always had enough to eat. Our poverty didn't really bother us emotionally." He added, "Being poor was good! It was a good thing for me."

The older brothers chipped in money from their small jobs. Before Melvin was a teenager, Kitty convened a family meeting. The Kaminskys lived in a fifth-floor back apartment with a view of fluttering clotheslines and prowling cats, which cost about sixteen dollars monthly; it had a kitchen, a living room, Kitty's bedroom, and another room for the boys. "One big bed for us, and we slept across the mattress," Brooks said. "I loved it because I loved my brothers, and I loved the action, and I loved being warm."

Kitty made sure of the warmth. "On cold winter mornings," Brooks recalled, she "put my underwear, my socks, my shirt and trousers on the radiator, and she dressed me under the covers. And she gave me kisses and whistled while she was doing it. When I go onstage or write something, I want my clothes from the radiator. I want my mother whistling."

The space was okay, but Kitty yearned for a front apartment

with a big window overlooking busy 3rd Street. Such an apartment had just been vacated and was available for a few more dollars per month. Irving and Leonard agreed to squeeze the extra money out of their earnings, and the family moved again from inside the building.

Until he was about ten Melvin went to grade school at P.S. 19, and then it was J.H.S. 50 for junior high—both schools located on different nearby blocks of South 3rd. Junior high was a shock to the system, Brooks said later, because it introduced the concept of homework into his life. He remembered struggling with a test calling for him to memorize the names of the signers of the Declaration of Independence. Irving had just returned home from Brooklyn College, where he was studying pharmacy and chemistry at night after "working at a ten-hour job during the day to help pay the rent." His older brother sat down to help and asked Melvin where he played punchball. On Rutledge Street, he replied. Where else? Rodney Street. On and on through all the familiar streets of their turf, even Williamsburg itself the name of a Declaration of Independence signer, William Williams, Irving pointed out. "I got an A on the exam," Brooks recalled.

Not the best student, by his own admission, since he couldn't sit still for very long, Melvin was less an avid reader than "an avid talker and doer." If he read at all, it was more likely to be comics than book-books. Yet like his brothers he easily got good grades in science classes, and perhaps for that reason Kitty did not worry too much about her youngest son. Kitty was really something: "the best cook in the world," a person with an "exuberant joy of living," in Brooks's memory. Melvin could say virtually anything at all and get a smile or a chuckle out of his mother. He was encouraged, coddled. Among his tales of growing up there was not one of Kitty spanking him.

As Melvin became a teenager, he hung out with friends in daytime and darkness, honing his wisecracks. He regarded himself as the "undisputed champ of corner shtick." Street-corner shtick was "a kind of rudimentary stand-up comedy," as his first biographer, William Holtzman, explained, "an unruly verbal slapstick." Brooks recalled: "The corner was tough. You had to score on the corner—no bullshit routines, no slick laminated crap . . . and you really had to be good on your feet. . . . Real stories of tragedy we screamed at."

By junior high he was roaming freely across Williamsburg, and he and his friends even took twenty-minute walks across the long suspension bridge to the Lower East Side for knishes and root beer. "That was okay, there were a lot of Jews there," he recalled. "However, when we'd go any farther uptown it became very scary and very exciting."

He and his pals experienced a few close calls. They hung out at the neighborhood Woolworth's and were known to pocket the yo-yos and cap pistols. One time Melvin was making his getaway with a cap pistol when he felt the manager clutch his shoulder. "Without thinking I turned the cap gun on him and said, 'Lemme go or I'll blow your head off,'" Brooks recalled. "He was so surprised that he stepped back, and I ran around him and out the door." Brooks told variations of that yarn in many interviews in later years, but the incident must have happened in some way; an uproarious re-imagining of it occurs in *Blazing Saddles* when Black Bart (Cleavon Little), threatened by the racist townsfolk of Rock Ridge, turns his own gun around and threatens to shoot himself.

By that time in his young life, admittedly, Melvin was watching "a big diet of Western movies" either with his best friend, Eugene Cohen—later a Broadway press agent under the name Eugene Cogen—or alone at some "dump neighborhood theater. My mother was always sending an older brother to drag me out. Sometimes I went there when it opened at 11:30 in the morning and stayed until nightfall starved to death, a splitting headache, but I couldn't take my eyes off the screen." As boys will do, he'd watch all those cowboys sitting around the campfire eating beans and wonder about farting. "How many beans could you eat and how much black coffee could you drink out of those tin cups without letting one go?"

On the Williamsburg Bridge he and Cohen smoked a pack of Sensations for the first time. The young teenagers had a contagious-laughter friendship. The pair had begun to sneak into neighborhood movies rather than fork over their pennies, and one time they were caught at it and dragged into the manager's office. They just couldn't stop laughing. "You have your choice," the manager barked. "I could call the police or give you a beating." Melvin shouted, "Beating!" at the same time that Cogan yelled, "The police!" The youths burst into more helpless laughter. The manager glared. "Just get out of here!"

By the mid-1930s, Kitty had decided to move yet again, this time across Brooklyn, as far southwest as one could go before splashing into the Lower New York Bay: to Brighton Beach, named for the English resort town, one of several shore-adjacent communities leading to Coney Island. Once the westernmost barrier island of Long Island, Coney Island was by now a fabled sandbar destination of fairgrounds and amusement rides for New Yorkers.

Brighton Beach was densely populated and heavily Jewish, but perhaps Kitty moved the family there to be close to the ocean and Bensonhurst, where Abraham and Bertha Kaminsky still maintained their residence. There were vague Kaminsky relatives sprinkled all over the borough, synagogue leaders and public officials, including a radical state assemblyman who probably accounted for Brooks's later remarks about "my Labor Party beginnings in Brooklyn." Kitty's family usually celebrated holidays with Kaminsky aunts, uncles, and cousins; some served fancy melon balls and lived in luxury buildings with elevators, at which Melvin and his brothers, the shabby relatives, gawked. Passover was always held at Grandfather

Shloimy's, with the elder statesman presiding over the rituals of the Seder. Max's youngest brother, Leon, a teacher, sat closest to the children's table and regaled them with play-by-plays of Mel Ott at bat—going, going, gone!

Perhaps Melvin's family moved to the larger Brighton Beach apartment because the household now boasted a lodger, Kitty's boyfriend, Anthony Lombardi. Born in Italy and a few years older than Kitty, Tony was "a pal" to take the place of her deceased spouse (that is how Lainie Kazan, playing Belle Carroca, describes her second husband, who acts as stepfather to the Mel Brooks character in *My Favorite Year*). The brothers called their mother's boyfriend "Uncle Tony" or "T." Brooks didn't often mention Uncle Tony in interviews, but one time he described him as a trash collector who gave the boys and their friends rides to Coney Island in his garbage truck. ("The garbage trucks were big . . . people got out of the way!") Probably Uncle Tony held several jobs; the 1940 census lists him, like Aunt Sadie, as working in the garment industry—a presser of ladies' coats.

Some days in those Brighton Beach summers Melvin and his friends headed to Ebbets Field in Flatbush, scrounging Brooklyn Dodgers tickets. If they couldn't get their hands on extra tickets or couldn't afford the scalped ones, they'd sneak through cracks in the gate, St. Louis outfielder Joe "Ducky" Medwick waving to them as they grabbed seats.

Most summer days they spent at the beach: their place on Brighton's 6th Street and Mostmere was three blocks from the boardwalk. Forever after, saltwater ran in Brooks's veins. "Right near the sea and I loved that," he recalled, "loved the smell of the ocean."

Irving, by then in his early twenties, was working as a shipping clerk for a shirt factory while still taking night courses at Brooklyn College. Leonard was a runner for a novelty company. Bernard sold newspapers and magazines for a newsstand dealer. And now, only twelve, Melvin was earning his first nickels and dimes running errands for elderly people and relaying phone messages to neighbors from the corner pharmacy.

Saintly Aunt Sadie continued to toil in leisurewear in the garment center, and she brought home "bathing suit sashes," Brooks recalled, for his mother to turn "inside out with a long metal rod." His mother was often surrounded by "enormous bags" of such homework from the garment trade, working late into the night, he said. But such work was almost always at home and off the books; resourceful about money, Kitty "lived on welfare checks," Brooks insisted in interviews. She is listed in every public record, through his high school years, as unemployed, without a profession, or simply as "mother."

The family paid regular visits to Williamsburg, where they still claimed close relatives on the Brookman side, and after dark the teenager hung out near a shop that sold candy and soda. Melvin and his friends traded wisecracks as they waited for a school acquaintance of Lenny's—Lenny's age—to pass by on his way home late at night.

That friend of Lenny's stood out on 3rd Street not only because he was dark and handsome and resembled John Garfield in a gauzy light. He was homosexual—not that the teenagers realized that right away, nor was it ever mentioned. And he was an actor who aspired to be a writer and director. Born Daniel Appel, the son of a Russian ballet dancer, that neighborhood acquaintance even already had a stage name: Don Appell.

A warmhearted, exuberant person, Appell was friendly to all the 3rd Street kids, who regarded him as "our show business god," in Mel Brooks's words. Appell always paused to chat with the youths, sharing gossip about the famous people he had crossed paths with backstage on his engagements—mostly small parts in Yiddish theater and summer stock. But Appell had also done a few walk-ons with the celebrated Group Theatre and had understudied Garfield himself, who was also Jewish, a Brooklyn hero.

The teenagers tried out their jokes and bits on him. Appell encouraged them with his laughter. He took a particular liking to Melvin, the most persistent if not the funniest of the bunch, who asked half-jokingly if Appell might help him get into show business. Appell was about to go to work, in the summer of 1940, as the social director of the Avon Lodge near Woodridge, New York, in the Catskill Mountains. About ten miles down the road from the Avon Lodge, near Hurleyville, was another, smaller operation, the Butler Lodge, which every summer needed a supply of teenagers to fill lowly staff positions. Appell told Melvin that he could put in a good word for him with the Butler Lodge owner; Appell himself would be close by, organizing the entertainment for Avon Lodge guests. Melvin could draw a summer paycheck and perhaps moonlight in the Avon Lodge shows, as resorts in the same areas shared guest activities. Fourteen-year-old Melvin leaped at the chance.

The Catskill Mountains in southern New York State, about a hundred miles northwest of Manhattan, hosted a constellation of hotels, boardinghouses, and bungalow colonies that catered primarily to immigrant Jews, frequently Yiddish-speaking and largely from the Lower East Side and Brooklyn. Some of the estimated one thousand hotels were palatial resorts; others were humble cabin camps. Almost uniformly they offered a kosher diet—hence the "Borscht Belt" nickname—and a *hamish* feeling for their clientele, who swam in pools or lakes, played golf, went on hayrides, and enjoyed country hikes. Fresh air and outdoor life were the attractions, with daily activities and entertainment. Most big venues had a social director who acted as master of ceremonies and staged theatricals with a core group of professionals hired for the summer; some of the biggest hotels presented as many as three shows a week: one dramatic, one comedy, one revue.

Both the Avon Lodge and the Butler Lodge were located in

Sullivan County. Neither ranked high in the Catskills hierarchy; neither lodge was as magnificent, sprawling, or expensive as the fabled Grossinger's, with its (eventually) several dozen buildings, twelve hundred acres, and one hundred and fifty thousand guests annually.

Even so, the Butler Lodge boasted spacious grounds with a swimming pool and handball courts and a dining room that a band could transform nightly into a ballroom dance paradise. First Melvin had to pass muster with Joseph Dolphin, a stalwart of the Yiddish theater who was the summer social director of the Butler. Once hired, the teenager was obliged to perform all kinds of menial tasks as a busboy, waiter, and swimming pool and rowboat attendant ("Mrs. Bloom, if you don't bring that rowboat in, by God, you'll never see another one!"). For that the teenager was paid a munificent sum on the order of $8 weekly. Meanwhile, he watched for any opportunity in the weekend programs.

Everyone on the staff thought of themselves as *tummler*s, from the Yiddish word *tummel*, meaning "make a noise." The Yiddish lexicographer Leo Rosten defined the consummate hotel *tummler* as an individual forever traversing the grounds and buildings of a vacation spot, "in an uninterrupted exhibition of joking, jollying, baiting, burlesquing, heckling and clowning to force every paying customer to have fun."

The new kid was hardly the *tummler*-in-chief of the Butler Lodge, although he did as much as could be expected of a young employee. His daily routine included stimulating the logy vacationers after a heavy lunch as they lolled around the pool. He'd don a derby and alpaca coat (props in a suspicious number of his anecdotes) and "go to the diving board with two heavy suitcases and I'd say, 'Business is bad, I don't want to live' and I'd jump in the pool and everyone would laugh." (His rescuer in these anecdotes was "often a tall, blond Gentile," another biographer, James Robert Parish, noted.)

On occasion the teenager visited the Avon Lodge, where Don

Appell introduced him to a recent high school graduate, not yet eighteen, named Sidney Caesar, who played sax in the house band. Appell had noticed Caesar's knack for mugging and quipping and found parts for him in his busy slate of staged drama, comedy, and revues for Avon guests.

Six foot two with lush dark blond hair and the shoulders of a lifeguard, "Sid" didn't look like the usual Jewish boy from Yonkers. Years later, writer Mel Tolkin, who met Caesar when they worked together on their first television show, *Admiral Broadway Revue*, said Caesar looked so *goyish* it took him a while to realize that they were coreligionists. Younger than Caesar by four years and shorter by six or eight inches, Melvin was instantly smitten by such a physical specimen. "Sid was the Apollo of the mountains, the best-looking guy since silent movies," Brooks recollected in one interview. "He would stretch himself out on a rock near the lake and we'd all stand and look at him."

At the time they had only a passing acquaintance, but Caesar was magnetic as a performer and Melvin noted his impressive saxophone jazz work in the band as well as his cavorting in smallish parts in the Saturday-night entertainments staged by Appell. Those varied from a cycle of Clifford Odets dramas, performed reverently, to radio comedy skits with everyone standing around onstage reading into microphones. This time and place may be where a certain factoid originates: that Mel Brooks entered show business with a walk-on in an Odets play, according to some early published reports, or with bit roles in *Counterattack* and *Junior Miss*, according to other accounts listing Brooks's first stage appearances in the Catskills. Many Borscht Belt hotels staged similar established fare, and Joseph Dolphin's playbill at the Butler was also ambitious.

The teenager did attain one milestone that summer, landing his first big break at the Butler. Dolphin was directing *Uncle Harry*, written by Thomas Job, a melodrama involving a small-town perfect crime gone awry; Job's play was inching toward its Broadway premiere in 1942 (it would be filmed as *The Strange Affair of Uncle Harry* in 1945). One of *Uncle Harry*'s pivotal characters was the governor, who at the climax considers a reprieve of the convicted killer. A summer member of the troupe, playing the governor, took ill and had to be replaced for one performance. Melvin, who like all the staff was an understudy and walk-on, knew the lines and waved his hand to volunteer.

The nervous fourteen-year-old was garbed in "gray wig, gray beard, period clothes," he later recalled. In the final minutes of the play Uncle Harry, shaking with emotion, confesses to the governor, hoping to save his innocent sister from hanging for his crime. The governor hands Uncle Harry a glass of water, telling him to drink it and calm himself.

"The glass slips out of my hand and breaks," as Brooks told the tale, "the water goes all over the desk and stage, and I'm mortified. I don't know what to do. So I walk down to the floodlights, and I say to the audience, 'Hey, this is my first job as an actor, I'm really only 14,' and I take off my wig and beard, and the audience gets hysterical."

"Joe Dolphin," Brooks finished, embellishing the anecdote with details that would make it even more colorful, as was his lifelong wont, "leaped on the stage in a rage, I think he had a knife in his hand, and he chased me through three Catskills resorts."


Often, in subsequent interviews, Brooks explained why, dating from his youth, he had felt impelled toward a life of comedy. "You hear about the people who become comedians because they had unhappy childhoods," he said repeatedly, "but a lot of us go into it for the opposite reason. We got so much adoration and love and attention that when we left the nests and didn't get it we started to ask, 'Where is it, the throwing in the air?'"

By high school the throwing in the air had evanesced. Gradually leaving behind the little world of his automatically supportive family, the teenager discovered unhappiness in what he sorely missed, lacked, envied, or felt deprived of. The needs and anxieties, fears, hostilities, and resentments would fuel and sharpen his comedy.

If he had ever been happy-go-lucky, that changed after his first Catskills summer. By 1940, no longer was Melvin such an adorable puppy. He noticed taller, handsomer people and felt short and ugly. In later interviews he frequently gave his height as five feet, seven inches, which is not really *that* short. But any height can be psychologically short, and a person who adds knives and desperate chases to anecdotes also might add inches to his height.

The youngest Kaminsky brother was already the tallest, taller than Irving, Lenny, and Bernie. But outside the little world of his family he was not tall and handsome. Nor was he an athlete, and much of his psychology was formed around what he was *not*. Although he was okay at sports, he did not enjoy the same athletic reputation as his brothers; repeatedly in interviews Brooks complained about being picked last for sports teams. He became a "court jester" to the jocks, he said, chronologically his first acknowledgment of that role. Wearing the fool's cap only added to his bitterness, however. "Pretty soon, I came to hate them [the jocks] all. I really hated them for what they made me be."

A nonathlete was no babe magnet, and Melvin wasn't a Romeo, either. For one thing, Kitty didn't discuss the facts of life with him. "Never," Brooks told *Playboy* with unusual candor on the subject in 1975. "Completely taboo." He had his "first affair" on the roof of 365 South 3rd around the start of high school. But "there was never any unzipping," he said, "everything in pants, in dresses, never showing. Just a lot of pain and torture. Going home and unable to walk. Struggling into your bed and crying. Terrible. And it's hard to masturbate because your brothers are in bed with you. You're in between Bernie and Lenny, and four in the morning even Lenny looked pretty good!"

In many ways Mel Brooks's screen comedies would be suffused with a young teenage boy's sensibility, and what passes for sexual byplay in his films was usually leering and naughty with little actual nudity or sex. There'd never be more than a mock romance in a Brooks film—with the exception of *My Favorite Year*, which Brooks produced but did not write or direct—the exception for tenderness and in other regards.

After his summer in the Catskills, in the fall of 1940, Melvin joined the freshman class at Abraham Lincoln High School, a half mile from home in Brighton Beach. "Roughly a year," Brooks said of his stint at Lincoln. "Did well there." That included joining the school band and learning to play drums, a move inspired by Borscht Belt combos such as Sid Caesar's. It helped that the Kaminskys lived around the corner from the Rich family and that Bernard "Buddy" Rich, who drummed in Bunny Berigan's and Artie Shaw's big bands, was the older brother of Mickey Rich, another Lincoln high schooler. When Buddy Rich came home to visit, practicing on a spare drum set in the basement, the neighborhood kids flocked around to watch the famous musician, and fourteen-year-old Melvin got pointers: one time he said Rich taught him drumming "for six months"; more likely, as he said another time, it was "half a lesson" or "rudimentary paradiddles." Just as important, Rich invited his brother and friends to Shaw's recording sessions in Manhattan, launching Brooks's lifelong habit of haunting music studios.

The Kaminskys still lived frugally (his mother served coffee to friends in *yahrzeit* glasses, he told interviewers, and tea in jelly jars). But long before he entered high school the family had acquired a radio, a big wooden Philco. The brothers squabbled and fought to control the dial. In boyhood Melvin was an unabashed fan of *The Lone Ranger* and *Jack Armstrong, the All-American Boy*, but he also listened to comedy programs, especially Jack Benny and Fred Allen, *The Yiddish Philosopher* and *The Eddie Cantor Show* ("very influential on my work," he recalled, "along with his timing was [Cantor's] particular delivery. He took his time, didn't rush."). In time he added big-band music to his enthusiasms. Asked to list his ten favorite recordings for the BBC's *Desert Island Discs* in 1978, Brooks named "one of my favorite swing recordings," Cole Porter's "Begin the Beguine"; he specified the Artie Shaw Orchestra version, which was popularized around the time the Kaminskys took up quarters in Brighton Beach.

Drumming would come in handy down the road; improving his musicianship opened up a means of income for the teenager, and drumming also helped him hone his nascent comedy skills. Drumming had a lot in common with achieving the proper joke-telling rhythm, he often told interviewers. "Some punch lines should be on the offbeat," he'd say, "they shouldn't be right on the beat because they'll sour. There's a thing called syncopation, in which you feature the offbeat instead of the beat itself. The offbeat is the after-beat. And you wait, and hit it on the after-beat. So I was a real big fan of syncopation and it carried on into my movies—into my writing and my direction."

On television talk shows in years to come, Brooks would guide the house drummer into a rim shot—which *The Complete Idiot's Guide to Playing Drums* defines as simultaneously striking the rim and head of a snare drum, creating a sound that is "part normal snare and part loud, woody accent"—accentuating the punch lines of his jokes.

When school let out for the summer in June 1941, fifteen-year-old Melvin returned to the Butler Lodge, this time appearing in "the first sketch I ever wrote" for one of the Saturday theatricals. He persuaded a young female staffer to walk out from the wings and join him in the center of the stage for the debut of Mel Brooks–style comedy:

**He:** I am a masochist.
**She:** I am a sadist.
**He:** Hit me.

(She does, very hard in the face.)

**He:** Wait a minute, wait a minute, hold it. I think I'm a sadist.

Don Appell and Sid Caesar were still knocking around in nearby Catskills venues, and after the summer Appell made another crucial connection for the teenager, hooking him up after school hours with the low-level impresario Benjamin F. Kutcher.

Melvin ran errands and handed out flyers for Kutcher, formerly a photographer and theatrical agent in Philadelphia. Now operating out of a modest office in the theater district, Kutcher booked music acts including the jazz pianist-singer Hazel Scott and the Mexican balladeer Tito Guízar. Kutcher invested money in little theater while dreaming of Broadway hits. According to Brooks, Kutcher wore a "charcoal-gray thick Alpaca coat" and a felt homburg in all weathers, hung laundry in his office, and slept on the office couch, with cans of Bumble Bee tuna stacked beneath it. Upon that couch he seduced rich elderly women who showed their gratitude by writing checks to bankroll his disparate ventures. "I was his sixteen-year-old assistant, his Man Thursday (I wasn't important enough to be his Friday)," Brooks recalled. "He had about one hundred little old ladies in the New York area. Once I blundered in on him and said, 'Sorry I caught you with the old lady.' And he said, 'Thank you Mr. Tact.'"—an exchange that would find its way into the scene where Leo Bloom meets Max Bialystock in *The Producers*.

Although Kutcher would inspire the character of Bialystock, he was probably not a seedy type, and there is no way to know if he really dallied with numerous white-haired lady investors. Kutcher's many interests included opera, black music and theater, and serious message drama. That was his connection with Appell, who still wore his social conscience on his sleeve and who, in the spring of 1940 in a Greenwich Village showcase, played a lawyer defending a Negro accused of rape. Kutcher was one backer.

By the fall of 1941, the Kaminskys had shifted back to Williamsburg, moving into 111 Lee Avenue, less than a mile south of their former South 3rd Street neighborhood. "I think my mother missed her mother and her friends," Brooks explained later. But relocating also made it easier for Kitty's youngest son to attend Eastern District High School, one of Brooklyn's oldest and finest comprehensive schools, which was located on Marcy Avenue between Keap and Rodney. Two of his brothers had graduated from Eastern District, including Bernie, who was out of school by the time Melvin joined the tenth grade.

The sophomore class of roughly 450 students reflected the evolving demographics of Williamsburg. Still predominantly Jewish, since Melvin's birth in 1926 Eastern District had added a liberal sprinkling of Italians and blacks to the student body (there was even a Negro Culture Club). The curriculum promoted writing, dance, music, and graphic arts over sports. Eulalie Spence, an actress and playwright from the West Indies, who had been a major figure in the Harlem Renaissance involved with W.E.B. Du Bois's Krigwa Players, ran the drama program. (An earlier student, Joseph Papp, had sung in the Eastern District Glee Club, acted in the school's Gilbert and Sullivan operettas, and served as president of its Dramatic Society; Papp, who went on to found New York's Public Theater, credited the drama coach from the West Indies, Spence, as "having the greatest influence on me than any teacher's had.")

Melvin continued steady in math and the sciences while showing aptitude and a good pronunciation in French; in other classes he mainly got by. After Pearl Harbor on December 7, 1941, when the United States entered World War II, aviation fever swept the nation, and Kitty pushed for him to switch to a technical school—the Herron High School for Aviation in Manhattan. He tested the waters, joining Eastern District's Aviation Club, aka the "Balsa Bugs," and with a pal went up in a biplane for his maiden fly-round at Brooklyn's Floyd Bennett Field. The teenager crafted one of his first songs for the occasion ("We're a bunch of Balsa Bugs, Balsa Bugs are we . . ."), but he also vomited during the flight and afterward said no to aviation. At home, his brother Irving stuck up for him and told their mother, "This kid is special. We have got to give him a chance."

Instead Kitty bought Melvin a set of drums, and he began to play at weddings and bar mitzvahs and on subway platforms, he claimed later, with a small unit dubbed Melvin Brooks and the Wife Beaters. Chronologically, this is the first appearance of "Brooks" in his life story—his mother's maiden name shortened with the addition of an "s" for professional purposes. The change had been necessary, he often said in interviews, because the longer words "Kaminsky" and "Brookman" did not fit on the front head of his bass drum. He didn't say that many Jewish immigrants to the United States anglicized their surnames to make them sound "less Jewish" and "more American." As Carl Reiner once explained forthrightly, with the change from Kaminsky to Brooks his friend Mel had "made himself more Gentile." Mel's own brother Irving eventually changed his surname to Kaye.

Although Brooks could rattle off the Wife Beaters ("two Italians, two Jews, and me"), the local press contains no record of their performances. The most important thing, though, may have been the band's summer engagement at the Butler Lodge before Melvin's senior year in high school, when the veteran comic headliner took ill. The drummer, who knew all the routines, took the microphone for the next show. Later Brooks told many variations of this milestone: how he had aped the veteran comic's clichés ("You can't keep Jews in jail, they eat the lox!") while improvising his own permutations. Already he had developed the habit of borrowing from and tweaking other people's most entertaining bits, a penchant that would sustain him in his future as a comedy writer, performer, and filmmaker. Comics stole from other comics all the time, reinventing the jokes as their own; there was a very long and contentious tradition of theft in the comedy profession.

The teenager also imitated the proprietor of the Butler Lodge, Pincus Cohen, and a hotel maid who, after accidentally locking herself in a room, had screamed her panic in a mockable dialect. He may or may not have hung a star on his dressing room door after his debut as a stand-up comic, as he claimed in one interview; he may or may not, at that time, have introduced his signature song ("Please love . . . Melvin Brooks!"). His debut as a funnyman was less than auspicious, and the true headliner returned after his recovery.

Melvin's presence was certainly underwhelming in the arts programs on offer at Eastern District High School. His high school years, 1941–44, are something of a black hole in his résumé. Official records, including the high school newspaper and the complete yearbook for his senior year, cannot be found in any archives. His senior class portrait surfaced decades later in the *New York Times*, courtesy of a classmate, and under his jacket-and-tie photograph were listed these activities: Class Day Committee, Senior Council, Dean's Assistant, and (following his brothers' example) the Fencing Team.

His future ambition, according to the caption adorning his senior class photograph: "Kaminsky—To be President of the U.S." But such captions under the names of classmates were often intended as jibes, and that is probably the more accurate reading.

His teachers did not spare the rod, he often said in interviews. "The class would laugh and I'd get hit. But by then I'd be laughing so hard I couldn't stop. Slapped, grabbed by the hair, down to the principal's office, couldn't stop laughing," he recalled. He was the class clown, he said more than once. But not officially: he was not mentioned among the forty honors accorded to graduating classmates, ranging from "Brightest" and "Personality Plus" to "Best All-Round" and "Best Class Writers."

Over time few classmates have come forward with colorful reminiscences about Melvin. No evidence exists that he had the slightest involvement in Eulalie Spence's vaunted dramatic society. Most likely he kept to himself and his small circle, at least one of whom—Mark Nelson, whom James Robert Parish tracked down for his 2007 biography of Brooks—noted that his friend was "always on. Mel really commanded an audience. He mesmerized all the boys. But it was only the boys, the girls never paid him much attention."

From the point of view of most of his classmates, while at Eastern District Melvin Kaminsky was—in the words of Lester Persky, another graduate of the class of '44 who went on to produce such films as *Taxi Driver* and *Shampoo*—"the class *shmendrick*."*

Maybe high school plays just weren't cool and Melvin had set his sights higher, circling the theater district, seeing every show for which he could wangle tickets, breathing the same rarefied air as Benjamin Kutcher and Don Appell. Just before joining the army in the spring of 1944, he may even have gone before the footlights, fleetingly, on Broadway.

Appell had returned from military service by the spring and was hovering backstage during rehearsals for a new show called *Bright Boy*. Preparing to direct his first Broadway play, *Career Angel*, Appell would pluck several cast members from *Bright Boy*, a prep school drama, after the show closed within two weeks. *Bright Boy*'s first-time producer was David Merrick; its director was Arthur J. Beckhard,

---

* Leo Rosten's *The Joys of Yiddish* provides several definitions of *shmendrick*, including "a Caspar Milquetoast; a kind of schlemiel—but weak and thin"; "a pipsqueak; a no-account; the opposite of a *mensch*"; and "someone who can't succeed but thinks he can, and persists in acting as though he might."

who resided in frowsy hotels and seduced aspiring actresses. "A somewhat disreputable Broadway 'character,'" roly-poly with a soup-strainer mustache, Beckhard became another "model for Max Bialystock" for a certain Brooklyn teenager helping out backstage at the Playhouse Theatre, according to drama critic and Merrick biographer Howard Kissel.

One of *Bright Boy*'s lead juveniles, Carleton Carpenter—who was among those who segued into *Career Angel*—recalled a teenager who may have "edged onto stage" now and then. Carpenter, who went on to a lengthy Broadway and Hollywood career, said he remembered the kid, a standby, "because I always suspected him of putting thumbtacks in my shoes" as a practical joke. Melvin Kaminsky "very well may have been that kid." Certainly he was not billed, and he exaggerated his appearance, as his army stint wound down, in the *Fort Dix Post*: "I had three lines, was on the stage about two minutes, what a part!"

Brooks paid a return visit to the Playhouse Theatre, incidentally, when he staged the big musical number "Springtime for Hitler" there for *The Producers*. And Liam Dunn was an actor in the cast of *Bright Boy*, playing one of the prep school professors. Brooks always remembered Dunn fondly and reached back to cast the veteran character actor in several later comedies, starting with the sanctimonious Reverend Johnson in *Blazing Saddles*.

# CHAPTER 2

# 1944

## Big World

Around the same time that Melvin Kaminsky anglicized his name to Melvin Brooks for billing purposes, he embraced his Jewish religion and heritage on a deeper level.

World War II disrupted the entire world, but it also rocked the little world of his family. The Selective Training and Service Act conscripted Leonard among Brooklyn's first sixty draftees in late 1940, and soon after Pearl Harbor and the United States' subsequent declaration of war, Leonard started aviation training in Texas. The next year, Irving, who could have been deferred because he was still in college and also working to support his dependent mother, enlisted in the Signal Corps. Bernard joined the army soon after his twentieth birthday in early 1943, leaving Melvin home alone with Kitty.

Seventeen-year-old Melvin was in his senior year in early November 1943, when Leonard, an engineer/gunner in the waist of a B-17 Flying Fortress, took part in a large force of US heavy bombers dispatched from Britain over northwest Germany and Austria. During a raid on a German Messerschmitt factory at Wiener Neustadt near Vienna, as enemy planes assailed the bombers, Leonard's machine gun jammed. At a height of some five miles and in a temperature of thirty-two degrees below zero Fahrenheit, his hands froze "almost immediately," the *Brooklyn Daily Eagle* reported, "as he knew they would. His fingers swelled to twice their normal size and the skin of his hands stuck to the steel as he worked. But he repaired the gun and went back into action."

Shot down during a similar air battle over Austria six months later, Leonard was first reported as missing in action, then described as a prisoner being held in an unknown location. Jews in US uniform bore an *H* for *Hebrew* on their military IDs, noting their religious preference, but many, like Leonard, ripped their dog tags off before possible capture to lessen the threat of torture or removal to a concentration camp under Adolf Hitler's anti-Semitic regime. Leonard remained a POW for the duration of the war.

Hitler, World War II, and his brothers' exemplary military service bolstered the Jewishness that, although firmly rooted in the family, Melvin had largely taken for granted.

A synagogue had sponsored his time at Camp Sussex, and a mezuzah always hung by the Kaminskys' front door. Kitty's mother, Minnie, was omnipresent on the Sabbath, a handkerchief over her head, lighting the candles, reciting the blessings. But ironically—for a comedian later famous for wearing his Jewishness on his sleeve— the Kaminskys were secular religionists. Melvin's Jewish upbringing was "very Reformed," he noted in interviews. Kitty might pore over the Yiddish-language *Jewish Daily Forward*, but there were no anecdotes of her scrutinizing the Torah. Nor did the boys frequent *shul*. "I went for a little while" with his brothers, Brooks recalled. "About forty-five minutes. They told us religious life was important, so we bought what they told us. We faked it, nodded like we were praying. Learned enough Hebrew to get through a bar mitzvah."

The capture of Leonard sealed Melvin's determination to follow his brothers into the army, and he enlisted in April, the week Leonard made headlines as missing in action somewhere in Europe. Melvin was tested for intelligence, and it says something about his aptitude—not reflected in his high school grades—that he was promptly channeled into the Army Specialized Training Program

(ASTP), which was intended to develop the technical skills of junior officers and personnel. In early May he was sent to the Virginia Military Institute (VMI), located in Lexington, Virginia, about sixty miles east of the West Virginia border. Skipping his formal high school graduation ceremony, the new VMI student arrived in time for D-Day (June 6) and his eighteenth birthday (June 26).

"I knew what Hitler was doing to Jews, so I really did feel this was a proper and just war," he said later. "I could have gotten out of it but I was gung ho to be a soldier."

Listening to President Franklin Delano Roosevelt on the radio—FDR, in fireside chats, spoke fervently about the war as the battleground of civilization—also affected him. "For years I thought Roosevelt was Jewish," Brooks said. "No kidding. I mean the Nazis called him a Jew bastard, right? I loved him. I thought of him as my father."

Popularly known as the "West Point of the South," the Virginia Military Institute was one of dozens of US colleges training Army Specialized Training Program soldiers alongside their regular pupils. ASTP recruits, some 348 strong arriving at VMI that May, wore their army uniforms, while the VMI "rats" were clad in traditional gray. Dining on rations in the mess halls, the ASTP soldiers underwent twelve-week cycles of classroom instruction that included traditional cadet drills and skills—saber use and horsemanship—along with a grounding in civil, electrical, and mechanical engineering.

One local perk was invitations to the cotillions sprinkled with chaperones and "the flowers of Virginia," in Brooks's words. "The most beautiful girls, Southern belles," he recalled, "but I was just this Jew from New York and not so good-looking."

In Brooklyn, he had encountered anti-Semitic taunts from gangs of young toughs when, a few times, he had ventured into Gentile fiefdoms. While standing in the commissary line at VMI, however, a fellow serviceman growled, "Come on, you dirty Jew, move it!" Melvin lunged at the GI, swinging his mess kit, and was dragged off to quarantine, as he recalled, until a lieutenant asked for his side of the story and released him with a caution. Melvin was proud of being "a tough Jew from Brooklyn."

By the first of August, Melvin had completed his twelve-week orientation, and then, partly because the ASTP was being phased out nationally, he was transferred to Fort Sill, a longtime army installation the size of a small city located near Lawton, Oklahoma, about eighty-five miles southwest of Oklahoma City. A headquarters for officer and artillery training, Fort Sill groomed fresh army troops to support infantry advances in both the European and Pacific theaters of war.

At Fort Sill, Melvin Kaminsky, along with thousands of other raw GIs, received his standard-issue supplies, a buzz haircut, and vaccinations. He underwent eight weeks of basic physical training for toughening up, followed by, in his case, another eight weeks of schooling in combat engineering practices, which would prepare him for the post–D-Day infusion of US personnel into Europe that loomed on the horizon.

The Oklahoma weather was blistering. A mere cog in the army, Melvin didn't make the *Lawton Constitution* or *Fort Sill Army News*. He kept his head down, marching to the refrain "Beans, beans, the musical fruit! The more you eat, the more you toot!" while chuckling at the signs proclaiming the Field Artillery Replacement Training Center: F.A.R.T.C. "Somewhere in my head I said, 'I will. I will use this,'" he later recalled. "You know, because it was too crazy. It was all over the place. You saw F.A.R.T. everywhere at Fort Sill and I said, 'Don't they know this? Can't they see this?'"

Anywhere west of Brooklyn was "John Wayne country," the way he saw it, and Virginia and Oklahoma were his first far-flung adventures. But Oklahoma was too far away; it got him down. As the

Waco Kid (Gene Wilder) asks Black Bart (Cleavon Little) in *Blazing Saddles*, "What's a dazzling urbanite like you doing in a rustic setting like this?" Cheering themselves up as much as their audience (Brooks recalled that he felt like a fish out of water, "near suicidal," at Fort Sill), he and another displaced urbanite performed an Army Club skit lampooning the differences between East Coast sophisticates and heartland rubes. Just as in Brooklyn, the army recruit roamed far and freely whenever he could slip the leash, including to Dallas, Texas, two hundred miles southeast of Sill, where the nightlife beckoned. Dallas felt like "Brooklyn-in-the-West," Brooks recalled. "Every weekend," he said. "It was great. It was still foreign to me. It was still Texas. But it was a big jump from Oklahoma in terms of elegance and sophistication. So Dallas was important to me every weekend for four months."

In December, the Fort Sill soldiers were packed onto a train, the windows blacked out to minimize any fifth-column surveillance; they headed east to Fort Dix, New Jersey, near Trenton. While waiting for overseas orders, Melvin could visit his mother and friends in Brooklyn. The Battle of the Bulge, the German counteroffensive against Allied forces, was bogging down in the hilly, densely forested Ardennes, located primarily in Belgium and Luxembourg but stretching into eastern France and southern Germany.

The reinforcements would not depart the United States until midwinter, transported on troop ships carrying upward of eight thousand servicemen, the officers in staterooms and the enlisted men quartered in the hold and cramped bottom decks. Through rough winter seas the convoy-guarded ships zigzagged across the Atlantic, avoiding enemy threat. Most of the ships were routed from Bermuda around UK-friendly Northern Ireland, a ten- or twelve-day trip ending with Red Cross doughnuts and coffee in Liverpool. Upon landfall, Melvin and the other soldiers were crammed into a train, making stops across the English countryside, including at Nottingham, the mythical home of Robin

Hood—the future subject of a Mel Brooks comedy—before grinding to a halt at Southampton port.

By the time they crossed the English Channel to Le Havre, France, arriving sometime in early February 1945, the fiercest battles in the Ardennes had concluded, Germany was in retreat and fighting rearguard actions, and the winter temperatures had turned frigid.

Briefly Melvin Kaminsky was pressed into duties as a forward observer/radio operator, helping to call in aerial support for the advancing forces, but soon he and his unit were handed daily assignments as part of the 1104th Engineer Combat Group. The 1104th was attached to the 78th Infantry Division, one of multiple divisions and numerous battalions, both US and British troops, under command of the Supreme Headquarters Allied Expeditionary Force, which joined together the soldiers of both countries in the drive to the Rhine River.

The combat engineers were tasked with rebuilding mountain roads and supply routes in the rugged Ardennes terrain, which had gone to pieces under dismal weather and the constant pounding of artillery and trucks. They erected vehicular bridges and footbridges across the Roer and lesser rivers; tore out wire barriers and cleared minefields; removed rubble and demolitions and destroyed German pillboxes to assist forward movement.

By late March, moving closely with the assault forces, the 1104th crossed the Rhine and marched with the main army toward northern Germany, from Magdeburg to Goslar in the Harz Mountains, a grueling advance of more than two hundred miles in fourteen days, during which time Brooks and the 1104th were reposted multiple times.

The work was dangerous, especially early in the advance. From June 11, 1944, to May 8, 1945, when the 1104th Engineer Combat Group entered the hostilities on the continent, 329 engineers were slain and hundreds more wounded. Dozens of Bronze and Silver Stars were bestowed on the 1104th for gallant action against the enemy.

Death, destruction, and a constant atmosphere of fear surrounded Melvin Kaminsky. The daily news and talk among the GIs revolved around the common goal to vanquish Hitler and his hate-filled Nazi regime. Brooks said his character was forged when a bomb hit his unit one day and he crouched under a desk, debris tumbling all around him. He thought, "Okay, if I get through this, I'll get through anything."

The end was in sight. Hitler committed suicide on April 30, 1945, less than two months after the 1104th landed at Le Havre. May 8 was V-E Day. Brooks spent the momentous occasion holed up in a wine cellar in a small town in western Germany, pickled in May wine. Long-serving veterans were promptly demobilized, but the Brooklynite would stay in uniform for almost another year and remain in Germany.

That lost year is but one of the intriguing gaps in Mel Brooks's early life. In numerous later interviews, he reminisced about his World War II experiences, often recounting an anecdote about the night he had heard German music wafting from entrenched lines and in response imitated Al Jolson at the top of his lungs, aiming his "Toot, Toot, Tootsie (Goo'bye!)" across no-man's-land toward the enemy. Another favorite story told of the Camel cigarettes Melvin stuffed into his ears ("I might be the first man to die of emphysema of the inner ear") to muffle the constant thudding of trucks and bombs.

Although Brooks later said his unit had been "fired on by a lot of kids and old men who were left in the villages," not in any interview did he say he had witnessed any fatalities. Under "Battle and Campaigns" on his discharge papers is plainly typed "NONE." Under "Wounds Received in Action," also "NONE." Under "Decorations and Citations" are listed a "Good Conduct Medal," "American

Campaign Medal," "EAME Campaign Medal," and "World War II Victory Medal"—all standard issue for dutiful GIs.

In books, articles, oral histories, and official documents, there are as few sightings of him in the army and World War II as fond reminiscences by his high school classmates. That personal lack of colorful wartime incident might have inhibited him when he considered, in the 1970s, making a semiautobiographical film about World War II, a combat comedy with Dom DeLuise and Marty Feldman as wacky tail gunners.

Yet if he was a *shmendrick* in high school, in the army he helped make a difference alongside millions of fellow *shmendricks*. Melvin bonded with his unit, contributed to the push for victory, and in later years often took time to revisit northern France, where the 1104th had been billeted. He'd collaborate with Ronny Graham on a funny song called "Retreat," with lyrics that encapsulated his attitude: "Run away!/Run away!/If you run away you live to fight another day!" A half century later, nearing ninety, he'd don his old full-dress uniform with medals for the documentary *GI Jews*, reciting his serial number automatically and recalling his World War II service with bittersweet pride.

In Hitler and the Nazis he found lifelong nemeses, and he'd channel "that molten ball of hatred for Nazis and Hitler" into his comedy. The army hardened him physically, made him tough and wiry, and added a layer of outer shell to his personality. But he also admitted to having suffered "a lot of conscious and unconscious frustration and hatred" during his time in uniform. In the end, opportunistically, the war assisted his professional goals.

Already the "barracks character," in his words, shortly after the war officially ended in Europe Melvin Kaminsky migrated into the Special Services branch of the army, which produced entertainment of every sort and variety for servicemen in the German encampments. The German section had its hands full after the armistice because such a huge number of soldiers remained behind for rebuilding and occupation. Reassigned to the 1262nd Service Command Unit, Kaminsky was reclassified as not a writer, playwright, or artist, three of the four categories, but "entertainment specialist."

One of his jobs was squiring around visitors such as the army comedian Harvey Stone or even bigger celebrities. "Every time Bob Hope came by," Brooks recalled, he sat up close to "write down all his jokes and use them." The GI from Brooklyn grabbed at Hope's pants cuff, pleading for an autograph as the star tried to exit the stage after one performance near Wiesbaden in August 1945. Brooks reminded Hope of that encounter when they crossed paths backstage years later on Johnny Carson's *Tonight Show*.

According to his Separation Qualification Record, Brooks scheduled the touring entertainment supplied by the United Service Organizations (USO) and also the amateur productions staged by servicemen. He "directed shows for military personnel. Wrote dialogue . . . acted in capacity of master of ceremonies and comedian during presentation of shows. Arranged schedules of dance orchestra[s] for musical revues and concerts."

Many army shows were vaudeville-type revues featuring GIs in skits, with singing and dancing. While it was too soon for the entertainment specialist to think of Bob Hope as any kind of role model, by the end of his time overseas Melvin Kaminsky, though still just a private, rose to noncommissioned officer in charge of Special Services, serving under a sergeant and lieutenant, producing big events for the officers' clubs and entire divisions. He was furnished with a Mercedes-Benz for transportation, he later boasted, and "a German fiddle player named Helga" as his "chauffeuse." With a special pass to Frankfurt, he obtained "certain rare cognacs" and indulged in even rarer, admitted debauchery. "There wasn't a nineteen-year-old soldier who got drunker than I did," he recalled.

The noncommissioned officer in charge increasingly took the stage himself, introducing acts or making patter. He donned a

German uniform and toothbrush mustache to offer his first public impersonation of Hitler, screaming unintelligible "Deutsch."

By the time Melvin Kaminsky returned to the United States in April 1946, he had been promoted to "head of the entertainment crew for Special Services" for the army's main separation center at Fort Dix in New Jersey. The former combat engineer was a familiar emcee of the Fort Dix shows he organized, telling jokes between the acts and parodying popular songs, including a version of Cole Porter's "Begin the Beguine" that was bound to resonate with his audience ("When you begin/To clean the latrine . . ."). "Nothing frightened me," he recalled. "I sang like Al Jolson. Everybody could do the low Jolson, but I did the high Jolson . . . " With "two friends," according to William Holtzman's dual biography of Brooks and Anne Bancroft, Melvin also "wowed the troops with a raunchy rendition of the Andrews Sisters—Patti, LaVerne, and Maxine—in army drab and five o'clock shadow."

Consciously or otherwise, the soldier absorbed comedy lessons that he would bring to his filmmaking years later. "I had a wide audience from all over the country," he explained, "so I had to find enough ubiquitous stuff to make them all laugh, enough universal ideas. It helped me a lot in forming my own kind of humor."

On the base he billed himself as the "atomic comedian," according to the first known profile of the Special Services entertainer in the *Fort Dix Post*. A series of photographs in the *Post* showed a wildly mugging "first sergeant" displaying the same array of funny faces he'd proffer throughout his career: "Determination" (sporting a steel helmet, gritting his teeth); "Man of the World" (a zany look, half effete, half doltish); "Happiness" (a toothy grin); and "Confusion" (crossed eyes and lolling tongue). Already his own best salesman, the first sergeant himself arranged the *Post* publicity, hired the photographer, and later passed out the one-sheet when applying for show business jobs.

Importantly, by the end of the war he'd also officially chosen his stage name: "Melvyn Brooks," according to the *Post*. (The "y" would come and go over the next few years.)

The "atomic" side of the nascent comedian reflected the tensions of his personality: at times his humor was too explosive, belligerent, or crude. At least one campmate thought that too many of Brooks's onstage jokes landed with a thud, a problem sometimes in the years ahead, too. Close up and personal, he was usually funnier.

"In the barracks there was a funny guy," recalled infantryman Stanley Kaplan. "Terrible as a comedian, but around the barracks he was very funny"—so funny that Kaplan, a budding comic strip artist, borrowed off-kilter ideas from Brooks for his cartoons. "He would jump from footlocker to footlocker acting like an ape, swing from the rafters, and make up the most fantastic images and stories. I thought this guy is funny!"

Elevated to the rank of corporal just before his discharge, the newly christened Melvyn Brooks was released from the army on June 27, 1946, just one day before celebrating his twentieth birthday. His discharge records show him at five feet, three and a half inches and 125 pounds.

The war, which he had entered as a high school graduate, reshaped him like a bullet. Now he was a man. Probably he had lost his virginity somewhere in Europe. One anecdote he told friends was about "the time he was approached by a comely French hooker," in William Holtzman's words, "with the businesslike query: 'Fuck, no?'" Brooks would evade probing sexual interrogatories by the press later in his career, but he did say, once, that he preferred dark-haired women, but not Jewish princesses and not the busty, cartoon-ish *shiksa*s that cropped up in his films as joke fodder. He told *Playboy* that he relished "dirty" lovemaking. "Only when it's dirty and when there's a lot of yelling and cursing and filth and all the other things

that I thought were taboo—then it's very sexy and very hot for me."
(Albeit any kind of lovemaking, clean or dirty, would be sparse in
his films.)

Upon release, his ambitions recharged, Brooks launched himself
back into show business with a gig as social director at his old
summer stomping grounds, the Butler Lodge, according to Charles
Cohen, whose family operated the Catskills resort.

He may have hopscotched around several area resorts in the
summer of 1946, as he performed as a stand-up comic, drawing on
*Joe Miller's Joke Book* ("Puns, Quips, Gags and Jokes") and what had
clicked in Special Services. Hearing something he liked, Brooks
would throw it into the repertoire. His act was heavy on impersonations: giving the audience his solemn Thomas Jefferson (striking
a rigid, statesmanlike pose); his Cagney—not Jimmy Cagney—but
"Jimmy Cagney's Aunt Hilda"; and his Man of a Thousand Faces
("... and now 'Face 27'!"), which took up where the *Fort Dix Post*'s
rubber faces left off.

That summer of 1946 was probably when the future illustrator
and graphic designer Bob Gill, leading a small house band at a
Sullivan County resort, saw the act of the twenty-year-old "atomic
comedian." On his own, Brooks was still an acquired taste and not
clearly destined for greatness. "He slept in one dressing room just off
the stage," Gill said, "and my trio slept in the other one. I remember
thinking he was not very funny."

His act was sprinkled with imitative songs, and Al Jolson was
almost as much of an obsession for Brooks, in his salad days, as was
Adolf Hitler. But probably he performed his own original, amusing,
and oddly touching signature song for the first time in the army
before taking it to the Catskills that summer. The song ended à
la Jolson with Brooks on bended knee. The number became en-
shrined in his career repertoire. More than one journalist in the
years ahead, when he burst into the song during interviews, agreed
with the *Saturday Evening Post* reporter who described it, in 1978, as "a

pithier metaphor of all he [Brooks] was and all he has become than anything anyone has ever said about him."

> Here I am, I'm Melvin Brooks!
> I've come to stop the show.
> Just a ham who's minus looks
> But in your heart I'll grow!
> I'll tell you gags, I'll sing you songs
> (Just happy little snappy songs that roll along)
> Out of my mind. Won't you be kind?
> And please love Melvin Brooks!

Brooks had left the army with an inner fury never glimpsed in his anecdotes about his boyhood. Hitler, the Nazis, death, and destruction: he saw life now as a battle like those he had survived, with himself as the underdog leader of a personal mission seeking victory and vindication. Slights and drawbacks, both real and exaggerated, became increasingly crucial to his psychology, his drive and willpower, his persona, his brand of comedy.

Back home with his mother in the fall, he pondered a vague future. Many veterans were signing up for college on the GI Bill. That was his mother's wish for him. Although according to some accounts in the fall of 1946 Brooks registered at Brooklyn College, where his brother Irving had matriculated, the college has no record of his enrollment or attendance. Later, in 1947, he did turn up in a New School for Social Research course, solemnly intoning Keats and Job 28 from the Bible on a recording that was included in the DVD box set *The Incredible Mel Brooks*. The minute-and-a-half-long recording might have been for a night course on diction. Again, the New School has no records of him.

When Brooks said he accumulated about one year of college study over time, he was inflating the two months he had spent at Virginia Military Institute. His lack of higher education always touched a nerve with him; it added to his insecurity as a writer and sympathetically explained why so many of his interviews—and interviews with his friends—insist upon his being a funnyman with the breadth and depth of an intellectual.

Sitting in a classroom was not for him, and besides, what would he study?

For a while he drew a regular paycheck as a courier for the US Post Office, working out of the mail department at Penn Station. His brother Lenny was now a postal clerk, working for the same employer. Yet one job was never enough for Brooks, and soon he took another position with flexible hours at Abalene Blouse & Sportswear, a retail and wholesale clothier on Seventh Avenue in the Garment District. He was a born salesman, and, he liked to boast in interviews, "I'm a better salesman than I am anything else."

Selling clothing was useful in developing his communication skills, and he didn't have to learn the cocky, often aggressive manner of the profession, which was his natural demeanor. Beneath it all he was anxious to get something going in show business. He was acutely aware that his father, Max Brooks, had died young, the very week he turned thirty-six.

To that end, in the late fall, Brooks reconnected with Don Appell, who had established himself after military service as the playwright and director of two Broadway plays. *This, Too, Shall Pass*, his recent tolerance drama, told the story of a war veteran coping with anti-Semitism. The irrepressible Benjamin Kutcher was an investor, and onetime Butler Lodge social director Joseph Dolphin was involved behind the scenes.

Appell brought Brooks to the Copacabana nightclub on East 60th Street early in 1947 to see the revue everyone in New York was raving about; and afterward he took him backstage to greet

Sid Caesar, the saxophonist of the Avon Lodge house band back in the pre–World War II era, who had become (as the advertising proclaimed) a "comedy star."

Caesar was more than just a comedian who could mimic all kinds of funny sound effects, including involuntary bodily functions; he could sing, dance, play the saxophone; he had chameleonic acting skills. The impresario Max Liebman had launched the strapping, charismatic performer in a Coast Guard variety show during World War II, called *Tars and Spars*, which was later filmed in Hollywood with Caesar making his screen debut. Even as the Copacabana revue drew crowds, *Tars and Spars* was still playing in theaters.

The watershed moment of Brooks's career came backstage at the Copacabana when he was reunited with Caesar, who was now Caesar the budding phenomenon. Caesar remembered Brooks; they took to each other instantly with banter and joking.

Realizing that fame and fortune were descending on Caesar, Brooks attached himself as a "sort of groupie," in Caesar's words. "He was funny and ingenious and he liked my type of humor, so he hung around me." Brooks began to visit Caesar backstage frequently at the Copacabana and Roxy, where the star headlined later in 1947, and each time Caesar opened a new show, Brooks lingered longer after the curtain rang down.

Meanwhile, his old boss Benjamin Kutcher offered him a promising job for the summer of 1947. The New Jersey Atlantic shore was a summer magnet for entertainers as well as vacationers, and Kutcher planned to launch a theatrical stock company in Red Bank, a picturesque Podunk about fifty miles south of Brooklyn on the Navesink River, an estuary that flowed into the Shrewsbury River and ultimately into the Atlantic Ocean. Joseph Dolphin was on board as one of the stage directors, and Dolphin said he could work with the onetime pool boy he had chased through the Catskills with a knife.

The Manhattan-based Kutcher needed a proxy in Red Bank to

supervise the ambitious playbill, which promised a new show every week, supplemented with weekend magician and clown acts for children. Kutcher had leased the premises of the Mechanic Street School from the Board of Education, and downtown department stores were already selling tickets. The twenty-one-year-old veteran of Special Services would serve as Kutcher's Johnny-on-the-spot, and for the first time his name would be proclaimed as "Mel Brooks" in Red Bank Players programs and publicity. (His name fluctuated between "Mel" and "Melvin" over the next several years, but "Melvyn" was gone forever.)

Brooks would manage the stock company and represent it to merchants, civic officials, and the local newspapers. He would also take the stage to introduce the shows and perform walk-ons in the plays. That summer he roomed with two young members of the troupe: an actor and aspiring comedian named Wilbur Roach and Roach's cousin John Roney, a townie known as "Red Bank's Barrymore," in William Holtzman's words.

Sprinkling in Red Bank residents with an ensemble of low-wattage New York professionals, the Players opened the season in mid-June with *Hell-Bent fer Heaven*, a Pulitzer Prize–winning melodrama from 1924 about feuding Blue Ridge Mountain clans. Things went swiftly downhill from there. The Red Bankers did not turn out in droves, and ticket prices had to be slashed. Guest celebrity performers were jettisoned, and plays were trimmed from the calendar to extend the up-and-running shows and save money. Strapped for cash, Kutcher fell behind on the Mechanic Street School rent, and then the Red Bank Board of Education—already alarmed by reports of cigarette butts and empty soda bottles strewn all over the public grounds—tried to cancel the Players' lease.

Onstage blunders and miscues only added to the negative publicity. The curtain was so tardy one night that Roney had to take the stage in his dressing gown and wave Roach and Brooks on from the wings. The roommates improvised "with close to sixty minutes of mimicry," William Holtzman wrote, with Roach offering an "admirable" Charles Laughton while Brooks did a "regrettable" Al Jolson that closed with his trademark song, "Mammy."

There was a gray area of authority between the stage director and the producer's surrogate, and more than once, according to another biographer, James Robert Parish, Brooks clashed with Dolphin's successor, director Percy Montague, who took over in midsummer. Montague tongue-lashed Brooks in front of the company for a "minor infraction," at which Brooks "burst into a tirade filled with enough big words and erudite references to convince everyone in earshot that he was not a man to be taken lightly."

Wilbur Roach remembered a roommate who was keen at the time on nasal Jolson impersonations and sophomoric clowning. Brooks was "flirtatious and grabby" with women, Holtzman wrote in his book, but also "awkward and almost adolescent."

Red Bank also occasioned the first glimpse of the wishful wordsmith. Brooks spent part of the summer crafting a short story, Roach recalled, "an allegory really, about two cats at opposite ends of the social ladder, one patrician, the other plebeian. When they finally come to words, the alley cat lectures the fat cat: 'You may have this beautiful home, but I have my freedom of being able to go from trash can to trash can.'"

After their problem-plagued summer, the Players limped across the finish line in late August, barely making it to the sixth and final production of the season with *Separate Rooms*, a comedy revolving around the love life of a self-centered actress. A week or two before the comedy opened, director Percy Montague either quit in a pique or was fired by Kutcher. Either way, the "atomic" Mel Brooks was poised to assume the reins.

The twenty-one-year-old oversaw a furious scramble of last-minute casting and rehearsal. The professionals had dwindled, but Cathy Clayton, as the self-centered actress, and John Dennis, as her man-about-town husband, had played leads all summer. Brooks's roommates Roney and Roach took bigger parts, and so did local thespians.

For himself, Brooks set aside the eighth-billed role of Scoop Davis, a press agent for the self-centered actress, his only listed role of the summer. "Not the typical blustering sort," the script describes Scoop, "a natural comedian and a little screwy."

With assistance from Roney and Roach, however, Brooks really "blossomed" as a director, Holtzman wrote. "If Mel's directorial style had few niceties (he once corrected [Roach's] interpretation of a British character: 'Too much swish,' neither did he have any pretensions. They were all having fun, they were experimenting and learning."

The *Asbury Park Press*, reviewing the premiere of *Separate Rooms*, wasn't sure how much fun the show really was, however. The largest-circulation paper in the county said the cast suffered from "a lapse of memory" and "the play lost some of its best scenes thru dialog bungling." The production was "not up to the standards" of "earlier efforts."

Even so, for the first time that summer the turnout was strong, the applause and laughter loud. Wilbur Roach would go on to become the comedian Will Jordan, famed as an Ed Sullivan impressionist. He stayed in touch with Brooks for decades and on more than one occasion, in interviews, traced Brooks's borrowings, especially his Hitler riffs, from Jordan's own earliest stand-up comedy bits. John Dennis moved on to a long career in Hollywood, and his onetime Red Bank director remembered Dennis fondly, years later, by giving him some moments in *Young Frankenstein* and *High Anxiety*.

Chaos fed Brooks's energy and imagination. In war and summer stock he prevailed, and he blasted through all the obstacles, in the summer of 1947, for the Red Bank Players and himself.

Was he an aspiring comedian, actor, writer, or director? All of the above? Or was he condemned to forever be a ladies' wear salesman with colorful summer jobs?

Returning in the fall of 1947 to work at Abalene Blouse & Sportswear (which he'd "use as a stopgap when money was tight," in Holtzman's words), Brooks looked for the occasional gig as a comic or fill-in drummer. In one interview he said a friend recommended him once as a substitute for an ailing drummer with Charlie Spivak's big band, which was performing at Bill Miller's Riviera at the foot of the George Washington Bridge in Fort Lee, New Jersey. If true, he had just reached his pinnacle as a musician.

But he had treaded water for two years since leaving the army, making only haphazard progress in his show business aspirations. His brothers, no longer such an integral part of his life, held good-paying jobs and were married now. His mother worried about her youngest son. Brooks's answer was to move, in the fall, into a flat on Horatio Street in Greenwich Village, which had become his favorite neighborhood, sharing the modest space with another escapee from Brooklyn.

Brooks was burning with ambition by the time he visited Sid Caesar backstage in the spring of 1948, following performances of Caesar's latest triumph, *Make Mine Manhattan*, a musical revue of songs and skits playing at the Broadhurst Theatre. By now Caesar's reputation was in steep ascent. Besides *Manhattan*, which had been filling seats since January, Caesar boasted a new Hollywood movie, a straight melodrama, *The Guilt of Janet Ames*, which was playing in Times Square at the same time as his hit musical.

Reviewing *Make Mine Manhattan* in the *New York Times*, Brooks Atkinson had grumbled that most of the performers were "still in the junior class" but that was not true of Caesar, for he was "the most original item in the program. An amiable product of the local habitat, he can mimic anything from a subway vending machine to a dial telephone or a taxi driver, and rush through it with tremendous speed. Mr. Caesar is imaginative and clever."

Ever since *Tars and Spars*, Caesar had been under personal contract to Max Liebman, who had discovered him and paved the way to his breakthrough in the Coast Guard show. Liebman had helped devise *Make Mine Manhattan* and now was in talks with the National Broadcasting Corporation (NBC) about a television variety series to star Caesar.

Brooks learned that NBC had come through with an offer for a midseason TV series, beginning early in 1949 after *Manhattan* would close its expected run. The live one-hour program, aired simultaneously by NBC and the Dumont Network and sponsored by Admiral, a television manufacturing company, would give Caesar a revue format similar to the one he and Liebman had developed for *Tars and Spars* and successive stage shows.

Brooks saw Caesar as a role model for everything he dreamed of being and as the mentor who might light the path ahead for him. Caesar saw Brooks as an entertaining sidekick; Brooks's smart-aleck remarks, his off-beat sense of humor, distracted the rising star from his many other preoccupations. Yet Caesar also had an eagle eye for talent and saw possibilities in Brooks before anyone else did. He loved pulling people into a room and calling on Brooks to sing his signature tune, "Please love Melvin Brooks!" Caesar always chortled over that song. In the last few years their friendship had really grown.

Backstage at the Broadhurst, Caesar spoke about the new television series he and Liebman were planning, saying that maybe Brooks could tag along, help out with the jokes.

But first Brooks would have to pass muster with Max Liebman, and at first he didn't make the grade.

A Jewish native of Vienna transplanted to Brooklyn, where he had graduated from Boys High School, Liebman was a hunched, owlish man who customarily wore a neat bow tie and a dead-animal hairpiece. ("It looked like a family of birds that just left," Brooks said.) Born in 1902, Liebman had begun his career as a sketch writer for revues in the 1930s. Before linking up with Caesar during World

War II, he was already a vaunted name in show business for having launched an array of talent, most famously Danny Kaye, out of Camp Tamiment in the Pocono Mountains of Pennsylvania. The Poconos belonged to a more politically progressive tradition than the Catskills, and Tamiment in Pike County was a resort well known for its show business training and entertainment. For much of the 1930s and again after World War II, Liebman ran Tamiment's theater workshop and staged the shows for its playhouse. His weekly revues blended character-driven satire with songs, pantomime, and highbrow ballet and opera.

One day in the summer of 1948, Harry Kalcheim from the William Morris Agency, which represented Liebman, brought NBC executive Sylvester "Pat" Weaver to Tamiment to watch the shows and meet Liebman, setting into motion *Admiral Broadway Revue*, the new Liebman/Caesar series that NBC had scheduled for liftoff in January 1949.

Caesar needed supporting players for the projected series, and Liebman's hand was manifest in the casting. The two lead actresses the producer hired were Mary McCarty, a former child performer who was now a reliable character actress, and, from Tamiment, Imogene Coca, "a lovely little lady with big brown eyes," in Caesar's words, in whom Liebman had great confidence. Coca had starred with Danny Kaye in *The Straw Hat Revue*, a Liebman/Tamiment show that had been "transferred in toto" (in Liebman's words) to Broadway back in 1940. After the success of *Straw Hat*, Coca had been languishing except for other Tamiment bookings. Caesar knew Coca in passing, but now, reintroduced, they clicked. "I always called [Coca] Immy because she was so little," Caesar said. "We had chemistry right away and liked each other immediately."

Liebman also reached back to Tamiment for the team he engaged to write the *Admiral Broadway Revue* series. Initially the producer had put Mel Tolkin and Lucille Kallen together to write the summer camp shows. Tolkin was the senior partner not only by dint of age.

Jewish, born Shmuel Tolchinsky in the Ukraine in 1913, he had been raised in Canada. An infinitely resourceful comedy writer, Tolkin was also thoughtful to the point of being angst-ridden with "more tics than a flophouse mattress," as Larry Gelbart once described him. (The theater critic Kenneth Tynan said that Tolkin was "a harassed looking man," while Brooks said he evoked "a stork that dropped a baby and broke it and is coming to explain to the parents.") Kallen had also grown up in Canada, although she, too, was Jewish and a native of Los Angeles. Younger (born in 1922), Kallen was a brunette as attractive as she was brainy. She complemented Tolkin with her savvy and sensibility; she had a feminine but also feminist sensibility—"out of her guts," in Tolkin's words.

Both had written songs as well as satirical sketches for Tamiment, as they would also do for Sid Caesar down the years. (Tolkin wrote the theme song introducing *Your Show of Shows*: "Stars over Broadway/ See them glow . . .") Tolkin had clocked time as a jazz pianist in nightclubs and could imitate the style of any composer, popular or classical. Kallen was Juilliard-trained as a pianist and had performed in nightclub revues.

The same decidedly elaborate and sophisticated template that Liebman had developed for the Tamiment shows would be carried over to *Admiral Broadway Revue*—only everything would revolve around Caesar, who had never been to Tamiment. That was the plan of action as Brooks trailed Caesar to production meetings in the fall of 1948.

Except that Brooks could not get past Liebman. Caesar introduced them backstage at the Broadhurst one night, urging Brooks into his signature song: "Do it for Max!" As always, Brooks went down on the close à la Jolson. Liebman was unmoved. "Who is this *meshuganah*?" he demanded. ("He didn't know how right he was," Caesar recalled.) Caesar touted Brooks as a prospective gagman, but Liebman, notoriously thrifty, did not want more writers on the payroll. Apart from himself (he'd started as a writer) and

Caesar (who always contributed), he had the gifted duo of Tolkin and Kallen.

Brooks had to wait outside in the corridor and then race to catch up with Caesar as the star left meetings, fuming and in long stride. Brooks would throw out jokes and ideas—which from the get-go usually came in the form of icing on the cake—his verbal spin on other people's lame finishes, "topping" the comedy to Caesar's satisfaction.

Inside the room, the proven scribes—the older, taller Tolkin, always billed first, and Kallen—paid little heed to Brooks, at least initially. But Tolkin's family had fled Russia and anti-Semitic pogroms; he was a sensitive man who was always in dialogue with his own conscience, and gradually he and then Kallen took sympathetic note of Brooks.

Caesar decided to pay Brooks a little money out of his own pocket, thereby making him his personal gagman. The scowling Liebman looked the other way. Brooks remained persona non grata and had trouble talking his way into the rehearsals and live broadcasts at the International Theatre on Columbus Circle, which served as the NBC broadcasting studio. "He would make catlike noises and scratch at the door in order to be let in," Caesar recalled. "My manager, Leo Pillot, refused to believe that Mel knew me, and had two ushers grab him and literally toss him into the alley. When I found out about it, I told them that we were friends and it was okay to let him in."

When *Admiral Broadway Revue* premiered on Friday, January 28, 1949, it made an instant impression. Caesar was "[as] great on TV as he's been in other branches of showbiz," *Billboard* enthused, and the star was sublimely matched with Coca in the sketches. (Coca, a deft light comedienne, singer, and pantomimist, quickly outshone Mary McCarty, who would not last into the next year's *Your Show of Shows.*) The versatile singers and dancers behind the stars included the young Bob Fosse and the married smoothies Marge and Gower Champion, who were catapulted onto the cover of *Life.*

Much of the *Revue* was borrowed from Tamiment, Caesar's nightclub act, and his previous stage shows, but for the first time a national television audience was exposed to his specialties: the foreign-language gibberish and bits such as "Nonentities in the News," where he played a know-it-all ignoramus professor. Ratings soared, and sales of Admiral TV sets emptied out the warehouses. Liebman was hailed as "the new Ziegfeld of TV."

Brooks made small, targeted contributions, including to a skit for Caesar called "Bomba, the Jungle Boy." Caesar was "a boy from the African jungles, who had been discovered wearing a lion skin roaming the streets of midtown Manhattan," in the words of comedian Steve Allen, who published this excerpt from the skit in his book *Funny People*:

**Interviewer:** Sir, how do you survive in New York City? What do you eat?
**Caesar:** Pigeon.
**Interviewer:** Don't the pigeons object?
**Caesar:** Only for a minute.
**Interviewer:** What are you afraid of more than anything?
**Caesar:** Buick.
**Interviewer:** You're afraid of a Buick?
**Caesar:** Yes. Buick can win in a death struggle. Must sneak up on parked Buick, punch grill hard. Buick die.

A proper ending to that exchange stumped the salaried writers: Tolkin and Kallen—Caesar and Liebman, too—were all credited as writers in the early days. "Something was missing from the piece," James Robert Parish wrote in *It's Good to Be the King*. "No one could quite put his or her finger on what new funny ingredient needed to be introduced." Caesar summoned Brooks, commanding him, "Do something. Write!" Brooks improvised "a few off-the-wall ideas," according to Parish, which went nowhere, until he suggested "a bizarre noise," which the gagman dubbed "The Cry of the Crazy Cow," a "strange, harsh cawing sound" that indicated how Bomba, the Jungle Boy, ordered breakfast in the jungle. That was something Caesar had in common with Brooks: both loved weird noises. The star guffawed. "It worked," Parish wrote. The crazy cawing went into the sketch.

To most people he was the Kid, the *schlepper*, Caesar's jester. "I belonged to Sid," Brooks recalled. "Sid called me night or day, sometimes three in the morning. 'I need a joke.'" But Brooks began to think of himself as a gagman—a bona fide species in show business. Not once, however, was he screen-credited for *Admiral Broadway Revue*. And the twenty-two-year-old wannabe was still shut out of all the important meetings.

When, surprisingly, *Admiral Broadway Revue* was canceled in June 1949—for the remarkable reason that Admiral executives had decided to channel their allocation for the series into stepped-up factory production to meet the surge in demand for new TV sets—the hurt was only temporary. NBC quickly authorized a new series starring Sid Caesar and Imogene Coca, produced by Max Liebman, to be introduced in the midseason of 1950. The new series raised the production budget and everyone's salaries, and Caesar was allowed to take over several floors of office and rehearsal space at NBC's City Center facility on West 55th Street.

Over the summer, Brooks continued to juggle day jobs and moonlight in the Catskills while never, not for the next ten years, straying far from Caesar's side.

Brooks recognized that "his relationship with Sid Caesar was that of a child clamoring for the attention and approval of a father," as Kenneth Tynan wrote, although the new television star was only four years older than he. (Brooks was hardly alone; other writers for Caesar, even those who were older such as Mel Tolkin, loved and admired Caesar. Several were wont to refer to him, only half jokingly, as "Papa" or "Daddy.")

"I lost my father when I was only two," Brooks explained once in an interview. "I can't even remember him. There's something big, you know, emotionally missing in my life. [Making] alliances with father figures was always very important to me. Like Sid Caesar— he was very important to me, emotionally as well as professionally."

Caesar treated Brooks in fatherly fashion sometimes, taking Brooks along with him on the road to Chicago, for example, in late June after *Admiral Broadway Revue* went off the air. Caesar was booked into the Empire Room of the Palmer House, and he wanted refinements in his nightclub act, in which Caesar convulsed audiences with what were already evergreens from his repertoire, giving impersonations, according to a *Chicago Tribune* columnist, of "slot machines, aerial dogfights, condensed movie plots, a callow youth at his first prom, and French and British casts enacting the same playlet."

Caesar's two-week engagement at the Empire Room stretched into a triumphant eight-week stand. Brooks was there for much of that time, getting to know and love Chicago, as was another one of Caesar's close companions—his older brother and chief lieutenant, Dave—"the funniest, the most good-hearted and finest man I ever knew," in Caesar's words. Savvy about show business, Dave was the one who coined the phrase "Funny is money." ("Exec is dreck," Dave would add, especially in later years after Caesar became his own producer.) Brooks had long since begun to collect such little sayings, adopting them as his own, popularizing them for his own purposes. Another was something Adolphe Menjou said to Eleanor Powell in some forgotten movie: "Tops in taps!"

Dave sided with his brother on the subject of Brooks; both liked the younger man. At night after performances the Caesar brothers and Brooks all hung out with lead dancer Bob Fosse, who'd been on *Admiral Broadway Revue* and now was part of the stage act.

The William Morris Agency was helping to package the new NBC series for Caesar. The popular dance bands of the 1930s and '40s had begun to lose their luster. The agency had begun to gravitate toward nightclub and hotel bookings with comedians, more and more, as the top attractions of the future. Through Liebman, Caesar had the benefit of agency resources, and at his Chicago opening, Brooks sat at a front table with Lou Weiss from the William Morris Agency, who'd come from New York to stroke the ego of the agency's hottest new star. Brooks did not have an agent yet; he lusted after such powerful representation and did his best to ingratiate himself with the William Morris man.

# CHAPTER 3

# 1949

## Funny Is Money

*Your Show of Shows* would never have come to pass without Max Liebman, although it was Sid Caesar who stood center stage, with everything depending on him and his exploding talent. If Liebman rejected a joke or an idea, there might be wiggle room; if Caesar rejected a joke or an idea, it was dead. But Caesar had huge mood swings; he could be very calm and businesslike at one moment and other times extremely volatile or tricky to read. Among Liebman's many gifts was his ability to handle Caesar.

At the outset of *Your Show of Shows*, Liebman was essential as its producer, Caesar was indebted to him, and they had a close partnership. Drawing on lessons from Tamiment and previous shows they had done, Liebman took the lead in organizing the new series around the brilliance of Caesar and Imogene Coca; the skits, mime, comedy, and songs—Caesar and Coca together, alone, and with guest stars—would be interspersed with jazz, opera, and a corps de ballet capable of any style of dance. "What we did, every night, in Max's mind," Brooks said later, "was a Broadway revue."

Liebman signed backstage personnel for the series that would guarantee not only a high production gloss but also continuity with his and Caesar's mutual past. There were key holdovers from *Admiral Broadway Revue*, many dating back to *Make Mine Manhattan* or Tamiment, including set designer Frederick Fox, costumer Paul duPont, choreographer James Starbuck, musical supervisor Charles Sanford, and director Hal Keith.

Liebman also brought back the nonpareil writing twosome of Mel Tolkin and Lucille Kallen. They'd pen every script for the first half season of *Your Show of Shows*, although Liebman and Caesar were also often credited on the screen. And many specialty writers passed through the revolving door to help out with spot material.

A nonentity from Liebman's point of view, at the start of the first half season of *Your Show of Shows*, Brooks was still shut out of the meetings that mattered. A composer waiting outside Liebman's office at NBC, hoping for a job writing song and dance numbers, recalled his first sight of Brooks racing up the stairs one day, yanking open Liebman's door, shouting "Fuck!," slamming it, then running back down the stairs.

"Fuck!" meant it was an important meeting and Liebman had waved at the gagman to go away. Enemies caffeinated Brooks, and he took relish in irritating the boss with his cockiness, his arrogance, his bursting into rooms and rehearsals where he wasn't welcome. Caesar was usually his best audience, laughing at such shenanigans, but "I was not entertained," Liebman recalled, "when, on several occasions, I came upon [Brooks] in my chair, smoking my cigar, with his feet on my desk wearing my shoes."

However, for *Your Show of Shows* Brooks was admitted to the interim writers' room, which was rented space at the Malin Studios on West 46th Street. The "closet sized cubbyhole," in Tolkin's words, had previously been used as the male dancers' changing room; hence its nickname, the Jockstrap Room. Over time Tolkin and Kallen had surrendered to Brooks, recognizing his occasional valuable contributions, even if Little Mel—as he was dubbed to distinguish him from the older, taller Big Mel—often irritated them, too.

When there were story conferences, Caesar and Liebman also congregated in the Jockstrap Room with Tolkin, Kallen, and Brooks, and Liebman's cigar figured in the arguments that could turn fierce. The producer liked to quote a supposed Goldwynism to explain his theory about script conferences ("From a polite conference comes a polite script"), but Brooks made an art of impoliteness; irrepressibly rude and crude, he'd pop off with jokes so out of context that Liebman would whip his burning stogie out of his mouth and hurl it at him. "That to me was more than the playful rejection of an idea," Tolkin recalled. "It was the rejection of Mel as a person, someone to be taken seriously."

Tolkin and Kallen were the stable personalities. They were not spontaneous, or shouters. Shouting made them uncomfortable. Tolkin was inarguably the lead writer, and Kallen was generally the only woman in the room, the only sitter, the person taking notes, capturing lines as the sketches evolved. Most of the time the stable writers had come in before the conferences with drafts of the sketches. Then the shouting started.

People knew (he compulsively confessed it) that Brooks suffered from insomnia and roamed shows, cafés, bars, and the streets until late at night. He usually fell asleep while watching TV; that was one reason why he often burst into the middle of meetings and story conferences and was especially cantankerous and discombobulated in the morning.

His expected job—his role as gagman—was to top off what someone else had already written with a better joke or stronger finish. Everyone else in the room might be trying hard to solve the same problem. Brooks would do anything to grab attention; he'd shout insults or jump onto a desk, waving his arms. His proffered toppers were often flabbergasting non sequiturs, but other times he really hit the bull's-eye. "He always had a joke," Kallen recalled. "Nine out of ten were 'forget it,' and the tenth was brilliant." (Later, Carl Reiner was fond of saying "To get one good idea you have to have ten lousy ones.")

His lateness, his rudeness and crudeness, his screaming fits worried

Tolkin, who took him aside and related an incident from his youth that had made an impression on him. As a boy Tolkin had been practicing the piano one day, diligently working on his scales, attempting to apply equal graceful pressure to each note in spite of a sluggish thumb. A younger kid from his neighborhood had appeared, slid next to him at the piano, and started banging away with his fist, shouting rapturously "Look, I can play! I can play!"

Brooks nodded as he listened to Tolkin's anecdote. He understood that the story underlined the differences between the two Mels. Big Mel lived a structured existence, agonizing over his ability to do anything serious or artistic with his talent. "The one enjoying the sounds he makes at the piano," in Tolkin's words, that was Little Mel.

Tolkin perceived the hidden depths of anger and angst in Brooks, and he empathized with anger and angst. He took Brooks under his wing, urging him to read Gogol, Tolstoy, and Dostoevsky and to exhibit more patience and decorum if he wanted to be a writer. "The Russian novelists made me realize it's a bigger ballpark than the *Bilko* show," Brooks said later. "Right from the moment I read them, I knew I wanted to achieve more than Doc [Neil] Simon and Abe Burrows did. I wanted to be the American Molière, the new Aristophanes." Everyone noticed how "an ancient Jewish respect for literature," in Kallen's words, began to improve Brooks's behavior—if only a tad.

In numerous interviews Brooks said Tolkin was not just an early paragon of the profession for him; he was the Caesar writer who more than any other took the show into the realm of "the human condition." "He was never Bob Hope contemporary," Brooks said; Tolkin wrote about "what happened in the human heart, and he taught me that." More crucially, Tolkin was another father figure, an older man who treated him sympathetically at a time in his life and career when Brooks needed the touch of love.

Tolkin and Kallen worked like Trojans. Liebman gradually yielded to other responsibilities. Caesar increasingly reigned, making emendations to scripts as they evolved, as well as in performance. Often enough, Brooks slid in with his brilliance.

Although the talent, power, and maturity were not equally dispersed in the Jockstrap Room, a rhythm and teamwork soon emerged that would produce fabled scripts. The machinery of the team needed constant oil and grease, there were continual crises, eruptions, and breakdowns, but for as long as it lasted it was a beautiful machine.

*Your Show of Shows* premiered on February 25, 1950, shooting fireworks into the sky for thirteen weeks. The one-and-a-half-hour-long program was presented as part of a two-and-a-half-hour-long live block of time called *The NBC Saturday Night Revue.* As was true of *Admiral Broadway Revue*, the new Sid Caesar series was performed and broadcast live before a studio audience without taped applause, cue cards, or teleprompters. Caesar's share of the time block was preceded by one hour of *The Jack Carter Hour*, also transmitted live from Chicago from 8:00 to 9:00 p.m. Eastern Standard Time; that led into the hour-and-a-half-long *Your Show of Shows* from 9:00 to 10:30 p.m., beamed from Rockefeller Center. The rapid-fire Carter was more of a traditional stand-up comedian, but the two variety programs overlapped with peculiarly similar formats (Carter's also featured a recurring German professor, for example). The great difference really was Caesar.

Actor Burgess Meredith emceed the *Your Show of Shows* premiere and joined in the sketches with Caesar and another guest star, the stage doyenne Gertrude Lawrence. Caesar and Imogene Coca teamed up to parody silent pictures; Caesar played Columbus quelling a mutiny while en route to America; and Coca warbled a beguiling

"Smorgasbord Song." The Metropolitan Opera baritone Robert Merrill performed a duet with the soprano Marguerite Piazza, and Nelle Fisher and Jerry Ross demonstrated ballet and folk dances.

Though critical reaction to *The Jack Carter Show* was mixed ("not good," the *New York Times* declared), reviewers rhapsodized over *Your Show of Shows*. *Variety*, the show business bible, said Caesar's new showcase was adult and imaginative, magnificently produced— "big time entertainment and sales potential." Caesar was the "standout," but Coca, long "a comedienne of much promise," had found her natural groove as his female counterpart and foil. The influential television critic Jack Gould of the *Times* said Caesar's maturing artistry now ranked him "with the genuine clowns of the day."

Again Brooks's name never once appeared on the screen during the debut half season of *Your Show of Shows*. Max Liebman's resistance to Brooks was linked to his faith in the Tolkin-Kallen combo and to his reluctance to pay for a third writer. Moreover, Liebman viewed Brooks as a "talking writer," not a "writing writer." His spin and toppers were great, but Tolkin and Kallen—and he and Caesar— were writing writers.

With Liebman still refusing to hire him, Caesar continued to dole out $40 weekly to Brooks, which got pushed up to $45 or $50 when Brooks dragged the star down to Horatio Street, showing him his humble digs and impressing Caesar with his poverty.

NBC was overjoyed at the show's success and ordered up a full season for 1950–1951: thirty-nine hour-and-a-half-long episodes. ("We were too stupid to know it was impossible," Tolkin said later.) Liebman and Caesar immediately began looking to augment the ensemble and take pressure off the stars—Caesar and Imogene Coca—meeting with Carl Reiner, an "all around utility man," in *Variety*'s words, who had appeared in other Max Liebman ventures, and the high-strung, priggish Howard Morris, whose short height made him the natural butt of physical humor. Reiner and Morris were compatible with the show and each other; they had crossed paths in radio and army shows.

Classically trained, Morris had played Rosencrantz in Maurice Evans's most recent *Hamlet* and made his comedy debut on television the previous spring, doing small parts on *Admiral Broadway Revue*. Currently he had a billed role on Broadway in *Gentlemen Prefer Blondes*, Anita Loos's 1926 comedy revamped as a musical for Carol Channing.

Caesar took one look at Morris and lifted the short actor up by the lapels until their eyes locked; Caesar's head swiveled to Liebman: *Him. Get!* Brooks, who was also in the room, proceeded to pose as a visiting Parisian scholar, speaking mangled French to Morris for ensuing hours, days, or weeks—depending on versions of the anecdote.

While the TV world was fixated on *Your Show of Shows* in early 1950, New York theater mavens were more focused on *Gentlemen Prefer Blondes*, which had become a sensation after its celebrity-studded December 8, 1949, opening at the newly renovated Ziegfeld Theatre.

*Gentlemen Prefer Blondes* boasted the prettiest chorus of singers and dancers in memory, and an army of stage door Johnnys pursued them. Brooks began to turn up, ostensibly visiting Morris. Not all the chorus girls were blondes; many were dark beauties of the type Brooks confessed to preferring. This group included Polly Ward, one of triplet sisters, a short, cute midwesterner, and Mary Katherine Martinet, whom everyone called "M.K."—she hailed from Baltimore and had short brown hair and a gorgeous body. Ward and Martinet were strong, athletic types, while another chorine, their friend Florence Baum, a nineteen-year-old from Brooklyn, was more elegant and graceful and was ballet trained.

A number of the nonstars often went out on the town after the final curtain, and Brooks, looking almost as dapper as Howard Morris, palled along. He put a successful full-court press first on

Polly Ward, then on M.K. M.K. hypnotized men: her personality was electric, her body sinuous. Brooks thought he might be in love with the dancer, eight years older than he, and M.K. made no secret of their intense sexual chemistry.

The third dancer in the trio of friends had just sat down to a scrambled eggs supper with Morris in his Greenwich Village apartment one Sunday night when the doorbell rang. Morris nursed a crush on Florence Baum, although they would only ever be platonic friends. Morris had just separated from his first wife, and Baum was playing hard to get with Herman Levin, the roly-poly producer of *Gentlemen Prefer Blondes*, while trying to decide what to do about the heavy come-hither signals she was getting from the much handsomer Dean Martin. On Sundays, her *Blondes* night off, Baum often danced on NBC's *The Colgate Comedy Hour*, where Martin did his act with Jerry Lewis.

Two men strolled in the door when Morris opened it. One, Brooks's Horatio Street roommate, was pleasant looking; the other, bristling like a porcupine, not so much, Baum thought. That was her first close-up of Mel Brooks, who frowned when Morris introduced everyone, mentioning that Baum and Dean Martin were a romantic item. Brooks seemed to radiate hostility. Making a rude comment about her bright red lipstick, the visitor reached over with one finger, traced it across her lower lip, and smeared the lipstick across Baum's face. Outraged, Morris threw Brooks and his roommate out.

Brooks never intimidated the scrappy Morris, then or later. Partly for that reason—in addition to his classical training and their age difference (Morris was almost seven years older than Brooks)—Morris held a peculiar edge in their lifelong friendship.


Brooks put a different full-court press on Max Liebman. Mel Tolkin and Lucille Kallen needed help for a full season of *Your Show of Shows*, and Liebman finally consented to a work-for-hire salary in the fall and a screen credit for Brooks if the show used any of his ideas.

If you didn't have a powerful agent, you were doubly powerless in negotiations with Liebman. By early 1950, Brooks had finally wangled his first representation: a small-timer working out of his own theater district office named Fred Wolfe. Wolfe advertised Brooks as a "special material writer for Sid Caesar." But the small-timer had little clout, and the only job he could finagle for Brooks was Brooks's first stab at acting on television: a part as a brash window washer in pitchman Sid Stone's regular segment on Milton Berle's *Texaco Star Theater.* That *Star Theater* was packaged by the William Morris Agency, where Brooks boasted contacts via Caesar, didn't hurt.

**Stone:** So, you're a window washer, and you're working on the Empire State Building. What's your biggest fear?
**Brooks** (foreshadowing *High Anxiety*): Pigeons!

This early proof of Brooks's willingness to try anything aired in 1950. He performed dynamically in his fleeting turn at a point in time when the Milton Berle show was top rated ("I was the king of Williamsburg," Brooks recalled). But it was a one-off, no miracle followed, and a decade would pass before his face was again glimpsed on national TV.

In June, meanwhile, Caesar opened a new stage show at the Roxy Theatre, featuring Imogene Coca along with Faye Emerson. Brooks was ubiquitous in the greenroom. But after that he had to spend the rest of the summer scrounging for work: more drumming, a few Catskills dates as a comic. The summer of 1950 is probably when he traded on his Caesar connections for a few weeks as social director at Grossinger's, producing the midweek entertainment.

"Brooks was on the staff to write a show—the staff show," recalled Bill Persky, then serving in a lowly capacity at Grossinger's.

(Persky and collaborator Sam Denoff would go on to write several hit TV comedies and create *That Girl* starring Marlo Thomas.) "He entertained at the midweek variety show. On the weekends, they'd have big stars, but during the week they'd have lesser people. And Mel got to do stand-up and insulted everyone to the point that they ran him off the grounds the next day."

Much of the summer, however, Brooks spent traipsing after Caesar and M. K. Martinet. By September, he was firmly ensconced in better, jockstrap-less writers' offices at NBC, however, working on a daily basis with Mel Tolkin, Lucille Kallen, and Caesar, with Max Liebman increasingly preoccupied with demanding production chores.

When *The NBC Saturday Night Revue* premiered in the fall of 1950, again the allotted time was divided between the one-hour *Jack Carter Show*, which had been moved from Chicago to NBC headquarters in New York, and the one-and-a-half-hour *Your Show of Shows*, with its broadcast following Carter's in the same studio. Carter continued to lose ground—his series was canceled after that second season—while the first thirty-nine-week season of *Your Show of Shows* was lionized as the best and most sophisticated on television, thanks to the "remarkably gifted" Caesar, as Jack Gould wrote in the *New York Times*. "There can no longer be any doubt that Sid," he proclaimed, "is now a star."

The "sock mature" entertainment, in *Variety*'s words, continued to revolve around Caesar and his genius: his engaging pantomimes, dialect takeoffs and double-talk, his recurring characters. But Coca was a vital adjunct as his pixyish leading lady; she had solo flights that were just as mesmerizing, and together they hit "expert comedic stride," said *Variety*. Their regular sketches together as the squabbling Hickenloopers would fast become a beloved fixture of the show; they were a strong suit of Tolkin and Kallen's, who drew on vignettes from their own (separate) marriages. The variegated format of the show stayed basically the same, although Caesar and Liebman persistently tinkered with the mix and the regular performers, partly because of incessant budget issues.

The longhair singers Robert Merrill and Marguerite Piazza were among the people in the original ensemble who returned for the first full season; so did Bill Hayes, a popular vocalist (it would not be long before he reached number one on the charts with "The Ballad of Davy Crockett"), who could also be counted on to act in sketches. The Billy Williams Quartet supplied rhythm and blues and jazz. The Hamilton Trio of Bob Hamilton, Gloria Stevens (Mrs. Hamilton), and Patricia "Pat" Horn performed novelty dance numbers.

*Your Show of Shows* still opened with a celebrity guest who joined the sketches, but the extra celebrity or two from the opening half season was dropped because of budget concerns and a growing belief that Caesar himself could carry the program on his lifeguard-broad shoulders. Behind the scenes, the $40,000 weekly costs were the highest in prime time, along with Milton Berle's number one–rated *Texaco Star Theater.* (By comparison, Arthur Godfrey's series, also in the top ten, cost about half as much.) The top dollar paid to guest stars on *Your Show of Shows*—as much as $5,000 per episode—didn't help.

The talent portion of the weekly nut, which included the guest stars along with the salaries of Caesar and Coca—both now under exclusive contract to Liebman—also ranked among TV's highest: $32,000. Caesar had built-in hikes to boost his weekly paycheck from $7,500 to $10,000 over 1950–1951, while Coca was already demanding similar escalation clauses. Liebman added similar incentives to his producer's salary with raises he paid to himself out of the overall budget furnished by the network.

Those economic imperatives impelled Liebman to eliminate celebrity frills and solidify the stock company. Partly to stabilize the rising talent costs, Carl Reiner joined *Your Show of Shows* midway through the 1950–51 season, soon followed by Howard Morris.

Serendipitously, the budget issues also helped to solidify Brooks's position as third man on the totem pole. The pace of production was punishing for the writers; a new script had to be served up every week for thirty-nine weeks, translating into a six-day workweek of furious writing and rewriting, extending through the rehearsals leading up to Saturday night's live broadcast. Sunday was the only day off, and then Monday started the pressure cooker all over again. Even Sunday was only a half day for Tolkin and Kallen, who always arrived on Monday morning having roughed out the next Hicken-loopers vignette. (By midseason, the exhausted Caesar and Coca had begun to take episodes off, a pattern that would grow.) Numerous spot writers cycled in and out, helping to ease the burden on Tolkin and Kallen. But Brooks was always around, pitching jokes and ideas.

At last Liebman surrendered, awarding Brooks his first credit on the screen early in the 1950–51 season. Brooks proposed a setup for "Nonentities in the News," with Caesar as a "Stanislavski disciple, Ivano Ivanovich, who expounds upon Method acting," as William Holtzman wrote, "and, by way of illustration, does an impression of a pinball caroming its way around a pinball machine (with bounds, clangs, and choreography) as well as his rendition of *Romeo and Juliet* (both parts, in alternately basso and falsetto Russian gibberish)." For the Stanislavski skit and other contributions in 1950–1951, Brooks was listed under "Additional Material," sharing that peripheral credit with other writers.

Even so, Brooks finally managed to attract the attention of the William Morris Agency. Harry Kalcheim, a wheeler-dealer of the all-powerful talent agency, had been Liebman's agent since Tamiment days, and he also represented many of the other *Your Show of Shows* performers, including Carl Reiner. Kalcheim took Brooks on as a client. With Brooks looking over his shoulder attentively, Kalcheim ironed out the details of his contract when Liebman—like all the principals, exhausted by the rigors of thirty-nine weekly shows—finally agreed to add Brooks to the official staff for the upcoming 1951–52 season.

Once again, after the last broadcast in June 1951, Caesar and his brother Dave and Brooks headed to Chicago for another two-week stand. Though they bunked at the Palmer House, this time their booking was at the bigger Chicago Theatre in the Loop. Caesar's revue accommodated many from the cast of *Your Show of Shows* with most of the comedy and music also recycled from the TV series, the whole extravaganza produced by Liebman. Heartland viewers of the TV series were important to NBC, and Caesar had played Chicago regularly since 1946. That was where the idea of a success beyond New York—success in "John Wayne country"—became rooted in Brooks's professional psychology.

The visiting troupe from New York included Imogene Coca, Carl Reiner, Bill Hayes, and the Billy Williams Quartet, but ofttimes in the wee hours the socializing came down to just the Caesar brothers and Brooks. Sid was always wired after delivering an adrenaline-charged performance, and after a show he liked to retreat to his hotel room, where he customarily downed several whiskeys. Offstage, the dynamic Caesar ceased to exist. ("Without a character to hide behind," Larry Gelbart said later, "Sid was lost.")

One night, they relaxed after the show in Caesar's suite on the twelfth or eighteenth floor ("as retold by many persons over the years," James Robert Parish wrote in his biography, "the setting of the incident kept moving up to higher floors"). Caesar drank steadily, saying little, as was his custom. Brother Dave watched warily. Brooks was not a heavy drinker, but wired was also his natural state after dark, and as always he was restless; he yearned to go outside and do something—anything! Brooks paced the room, repeatedly mentioning favorite nightspots. Caesar didn't have the same roaming instincts. "Let's go somewhere and do something!" Brooks kept insisting. "Let's see the nightlife!"

Finally tired of his jabber, Caesar shoved open a window, grabbed the smaller man, lifted Brooks up by the seat of his pants, and thrust him out into the cool night air, holding him by his feet upside down, dangling from some manner of height. "How far do you want to go? Is that far enough?" he shouted. Dave was on his feet in a flash, pulling at his brother. "*In* would be nice," Brooks is said to have quipped. "In is good."

That might be the enduring image of their friendship in the early years, symbolic of the disparity in their relationship: Caesar dangling his personal jester out of a hotel window. Mel Tolkin, reflecting on Brooks's career in later years, thought the jester's voluntary clowning in the early 1950s had enabled Caesar's alcoholism, his womanizing, and other self-destructive habits that worsened over time. Tolkin couldn't understand why Brooks permitted the "humiliation of being held by his feet out of the eighteenth floor of a hotel, by Sid," in Tolkin's words, in order to score brownie points with the star.

After the dangling incident, Brooks followed Caesar and his wife, Florence, to Grossinger's for a visit in early July. One of the advantages of traveling with Caesar was that doors opened up to people of importance. At Grossinger's they mingled with other visiting celebrities, including Jerry Lewis, whom Brooks met for the first time. Brooks worshipped Lewis, who was already a major star on television and in motion pictures with his partner, Dean Martin, and envied his success. A demented comedian with a naive, bratty persona and a stock in trade heavy on rubber faces and weird noises, Lewis was also a surprisingly endearing singer and dancer. Though evoking Harry Ritz, another comedian Brooks loved, it was clear that Lewis had it all over Ritz and would go further.

While in Chicago, Carl Reiner had invited Brooks to come to Fire Island in August. Reiner and his wife, Estelle, had leased a small cottage in Ocean Beach, Fire Island's de facto capital. New York artists and entertainers flocked to Ocean Beach in the summer.

Besides the Reiners, the *Your Show of Shows* contingent included Sid Caesar and Florence, who was pregnant, and Mel Tolkin, his wife, Edith, and her parents. The Reiners would be vacating their place before Labor Day weekend. Brooks could move in.

In the middle of the night Brooks woke up Tolkin and everyone else, pounding on the Tolkin front door in a panic, clutching, to defend himself, a kitchen utensil. He was "incoherent with fear," Tolkin recalled, and refused to spend the night alone in the Reiners' vacation cottage. He insisted that only Caesar could protect him and pleaded for Florence to sleep out on the enclosed porch while he took over the couple's bedroom with Caesar.

It took some time to calm him down. Displacing Florence was out of the question, Big Mel told Little Mel, finally convincing him to take the couch on the Tolkin porch, where Brooks fell asleep clutching his culinary weapon. "I've always thought of Mel's visit as a search for security, for a safe haven," Tolkin recalled, "a fear of abandonment."

All his friends knew that behind Brooks's bravado—his genuine comedic courage—was profound insecurity. Behind his facade as a perpetual *amusant* were depths of self-loathing and a fury at the world. Friends believed that his negativity often got in the way of his positivity, his obnoxiousness in the way of his likability. Fears and neuroses limited Brooks's potential; they needed to be tempered, brought under control.

Big Mel, his friend and father figure, took him aside. Brooks was a staff writer now; his new position had enabled him to move into his first apartment of his own, a fourth-floor walk-up on West 68th off Central Park. Maybe, considering all the problems he was having, Tolkin said, he ought to see a psychologist. He could afford that now, too.

Most of the *Your Show of Shows* leads were also seeing therapists, and talk of Freud and Jung was commonplace among them. Tolkin and Carl Reiner shared the same analyst, and Tolkin sent Brooks first to that practitioner, who listened to Brooks recite a slew of hang-ups before shrugging helplessly and referring him to Dr. Clement Staff, a former student of Dr. Theodor Reik, who had been one of Sigmund Freud's early disciples in Vienna. Dr. Staff was the editor of *Psychoanalysis*, the quarterly of the National Psychological Association for Psychoanalysis, founded by Reik, and Dr. Staff still communed with Reik in New York. Dr. Staff saw patients in his office on East 94th Street.

The second full season of *Your Show of Shows* in 1951–1952 was the first with the linked-arms quartet that most people associate with the series: Sid Caesar, Imogene Coca, Carl Reiner, and Howard Morris.* Caesar and Coca fired on all cylinders, Reiner came into his own as a world-class straight man, and Morris proved a wondrous fourth wheel.

Bill Hayes, Jack Russell, and Judy Johnson completed the shifting troupe of performers, and the opera star Marguerite Piazza appeared intermittently, as she did throughout the series' five-year run. Bambi Lynn and Rod Alexander upheld the Marge and Gower Champion tradition of a cultivated dance duo, and another new team, Mata (Meta Krahn) and (Otto Ulbricht) Hari, offered their singular mix of mime and choreography. The Hamilton Trio continued on the show with terpsichorean novelties and vignettes.

It was a banner year: millions and millions of people tuned in, and *Your Show of Shows* made Nielsen's top ten (number ten) for the first time in October. (It would close the year at number eight.) Television's Emmy Awards were only four years old, but at the January 1952 ceremony *Your Show of Shows* was named Best Variety

---

* *Gentlemen Prefer Blondes* had closed in September 1951, freeing Morris up for the 1951–52 season.

Show, Caesar won Best Actor, and Coca won Best Actress. (All three had been nominated the previous year and lost.)

The 1951–52 season was also a landmark for "Melvin Brooks," his name scrolling thusly every week on the screen, third among the regular writing credits after Mel Tolkin and Lucille Kallen. "I wanted credit," Brooks told Albert Goldman in 1968, linking his salary and writer's credit to his identity crisis. "I wanted money. I wanted to be a man." Getting credit was "part of the whole business of affirming yourself," he told *Newsweek* in 1975.

Tolkin and Kallen were making $300 weekly by now, and Brooks earned only half as much: $150, later bumped up to $200. But he was no longer a gagman—he was a writer! He began introducing himself, in his first salaried season on the staff, as "Sid Caesar's writer," sometimes even (jokingly planting the idea), a "genius writer."

But was he really a writer? Did he deserve his big salary?—more dough than even his beloved brother Irving was earning, just for being a "talking writer"? Brooks was defensive about that disparity between himself and "writing writers" at the outset of his career. "I wished they'd changed my billing on the show, so that it said 'Funny Talking by Mel Brooks,'" he told Kenneth Tynan years later. "Have they found out yet?" his mother, Kitty, liked to tease him about his new status as a professional wordsmith.

Many of Brooks's early sessions with Dr. Clement Staff revolved around the dubious nature of his writing credit. Everyone working on *Your Show of Shows* knew about Brooks's frequent appointments with Dr. Staff: "four days a week," sometimes. "Instead of letting us do our work he would tell us everything that had happened to him during his session," recalled series composer Earl Wild, "from the beginning."

His many appointments with Dr. Staff gave Brooks another excuse for turning up late to work. When he wasn't arriving late and talking about his therapy, he was a notorious procrastinator—

hardly an unusual trait among writers. "He was constantly on the phone, even during our meetings," recalled Wild, often "placing a trade with his stockbroker."

Often Brooks wouldn't arrive at NBC until lunchtime, thereby avoiding the morning pool for bagels and cream cheese and positioning himself to grab the leftovers for free. Brooks was sensitive about this chronic lateness in later years, once sitting on a panel with other Sid Caesar writers and hearing them good-naturedly complain about his habits. "I'd show up by 10:45!" he'd protest to general groans from the others on the panel. No way: Brooks arrived persistently late, especially Mondays, after the weekends, when the writers and stars were laying down important foundations for the show to come.

Everyone was irked by his lateness, but no one, not even Caesar or Liebman, seemed capable of doing very much about it. Brooks was evasive, unapologetic, belligerent. Neil Simon, soon to join the writing staff, insisted in a later interview that four hours of Mel Brooks was equal to eight hours of most other people. "Mel coming in at one was a better commodity to have than a bum who came in early," Carl Reiner echoed. Still, "I always resented the fact that he would come in at noon, or past noon," said Lucille Kallen, "when we'd been there since nine o'clock in the morning."

They would draw straws to phone him, knowing they were stirring a hornet's nest.

"Mel!" the furious Caesar ordered Tolkin one day. "Call Mel!"

Lunchtime was past. The group was struggling with a sketch. Caesar kept pointing to his watch, waiting for Brooks. Finally Tolkin dialed Brooks at home, wondering desperately how he could convey Caesar's mounting exasperation without triggering one of Brooks's "towering" rages. His screaming was as feared as his sarcasm ("He used to bare his teeth like a rodent if you crossed him," Tolkin recalled). Brooks was proud of that terrifying weapon in his arsenal and later would sprinkle jokes about shouting through most of his films, even, with sight gags, in the soundless *Silent Movie*.

When Brooks eventually picked up the phone, Tolkin reluctantly mumbled something like "It's kind of late, Mel . . . Sid's kind of mad . . . how about . . . ?"

"You cocksucker!" Brooks screamed back so loud everyone could hear him in the meeting room. "Just because you come earlier doesn't make you a general!"

Tolkin was not alone in attributing Brooks's persistent lateness, much less his latent hostility and crudeness, to his fears that the newborn writer could not "rise to the standard he had set himself: to come in with a laugh-getter at entrance, be hilarious through the day, and exit with a laugh." His spontaneity was always partly a charade, Tolkin and others believed. Brooks pondered and practiced many of his bits at home.

Often enough, when Brooks finally did show up, he'd make funny, spectacular entrances designed to distract people from how late he was arriving. Once, without so much as a hello, Brooks dashed into the writers' room, froze in midstride, and then went into the studied pose of a suffering poet. "I have this great idea for a limerick," he announced grandly. "Beautiful. An inspiration. But I'm having trouble with a rhyme . . ."

There was a young lady named Rocksucker, [he recited]
Who lived in a town called Docksucker.
She was lively and gay,
And I've heard people say,
She was quite a . . .

"And here's where I get in trouble," he continued. "I can't think of the third rhyme . . ."

"Cocksucker" was among his favorite words, and Brooks's coarse vernacular in any setting could be as off-putting as it was humorous.

*Your Show of Shows* was a classy program, and nobody said "cocksucker" on television in the 1950s; nobody talked quite like that at work on the program, either. Some, like Tolkin—who said "Pole," not "Polack"—never used expletives. That was Brooks incarnate: blurting out expletives, never mind the ladylike Lucille Kallen, typically the only woman surrounded by a half-dozen men, herself five feet, one inch, with the rest either big, tall, and loud or (with the exception of Tolkin) acting big, tall, and loud. Kallen endured the rituals—the manly men (Tolkin excepted), their smelly cigars, the side-of-the-mouth talk about the broads they'd nailed over the weekend.

Brooks's crudeness went beyond the boundaries of good taste for most of the other Caesar writers, the big, tall men included, but that didn't stop them from often finding his antics very funny. Years later, watching *Blazing Saddles*, Caesar alum Neil Simon doubled over watching a scene he would not have dreamed of writing: cowboys sitting around the campfire, eating beans, and farting. "When something was funny to [Simon], he enjoyed it full out, scatological humor especially," his then wife, actress Marsha Mason, recalled. The farting scene "brought Neil to his knees, literally. He finally got up and ran up the aisle to the men's room, not being able to contain himself."

The regular salary and official screen credit turned the onetime "talking writer" into even more of a "performing writer." Always quick to talk, now Brooks had a small captive audience, and in script conferences he was fast to leap to his feet and launch into shtick, briefly nabbing the spotlight and in the process of his performance often topping the sketch at hand. "He performs brilliantly and it's very difficult to compete with that," Tolkin conceded.

Mocking imitations was one specialty: Hitler was already a go-to, behind closed doors. (Herman Raucher's novel *There Should Have Been Castles*, set partly in the 1950s, depicts a Jewish writer on "a weekly Saturday night TV show," a stand-in for Brooks named Monty

Rivers, who breaks up rehearsals with uproarious tirades about Hitler and Fats Göring.) U-boat commanders were also regulars in his gallery of types. Following his appointments with Dr. Staff he added psychiatrists. One was an accented psychiatrist who cured patients of aberrant behavior by exhorting them "Don't do that!"

Caesar's writers were the first to experience the roughhewn side of his personality as a form of performance art. The bad habits were uninhibited and studious at the same time. They were part of his persona. "You have to distinguish between Mel the entertainer and Mel the private person," novelist Joseph Heller said once. "He puts on this manic public performance, but it's an act, it's something sought for and worked on."

Inevitably, when Brooks performed, everyone else in the room became his straight men, yet certain people were more willing and able to play that role. One late afternoon the group was stuck on a joke that hadn't quite jelled. Glancing at his watch, one of the scribblers remarked dolefully, "Three-fifteen p.m. on a Friday. The last joke in the world has been written. There is nothing left to laugh at." Brooks whipped out a roll of Scotch tape and began slapping pieces across "his nose to his cheek," Tolkin said, "his lower lip to his chin, an eyebrow to his forehead. His face looked cruelly disfigured."

Without missing a beat, Carl Reiner popped up beside Brooks, assuming the guise of Intrepid Reporter. "Oh, how did this terrible thing happen? Who did it to you?"

"The Nazis," wailed Brooks. "They did it to me. Threw me in a ditch and did it."

"Oh, they beat you, eh? Disfigured you?"

"Oh no! No-o-o. They took Scotch tape and stuck it all over my face . . ."

The room dissolved in laughter. His performances, like his rudeness and crudeness, were never entirely for work purposes. Sometimes they were just Mel being Mel.

• • •

The willing and able straight men had the best odds of maintaining a long-term friendship with Brooks. Carl Reiner had the straight-man qualification, and more.

Born in the Bronx in 1922, Reiner had been trained in theater under the Works Progress Administration (WPA). After serving in the air force during World War II (he produced a Molière play in French during language training), Reiner performed in Broadway musicals, including the lead in the postwar GI hit revue *Call Me Mister*, in which Max Liebman noticed him and began casting him in other revues and television shows.

Reiner checked all the boxes for Brooks. He was tall, handsome, and Jewish to boot. A consummate performer, he seemed able to handle any silliness or depth. Also he was a closet writer, witty and adept as such, as he soon proved. As Reiner sat in on *Your Show of Shows* script sessions, he made an increasing contribution and, over time, became an arbiter of taste in the room; partly that was because everyone liked him but also because they trusted his judgment. An impossibly nice, earnest guy, Reiner was just as nice and wholesome as the writer Rob Petrie (the character played by Dick Van Dyke) in the television series Reiner later created, *The Dick Van Dyke Show*, which also had a character, Buddy Sorrell (Morey Amsterdam), who was a softened-up version of Brooks.

When it came to indulging Brooks, Reiner vied with Caesar, and early on the straight man became the number one fan of the talking/performing writer. Reiner reliably guffawed at Brooks's toppers and his writers' room impersonations, like the one of the Jewish pirate, Reiner often recalled fondly in interviews, who had trouble getting sailcloth at a good price. Reiner always looked past Brooks's anger, vulgarity, and piques, seeing only the positive side of his friend, just as Rob Petrie has only love and regard for Buddy Sorrell.

"I instantly knew Mel Brooks was the funniest man I ever met,"

Reiner reminisced later. The straight man "recognized that performing talent in me," Brooks recalled, at a time, lasting a decade, when his performances were all behind closed doors, at the office, or at parties. "What he secretly wanted was to perform himself," Reiner realized.

The 2000 Year Old Man had its roots in office byplay between Brooks and Reiner, originating one day when Reiner tried arguing for a Caesar segment in which the star would interview a plumber who has overheard Josef Stalin make newsworthy comments while fixing a faucet in the dictator's bathroom. The piece would parody the Sunday-night TV show *We, the People*, in which famous people were interviewed. Jumping up to demonstrate how the sketch might work with other historical figures, Reiner teased in Brooks. "Here with us today, ladies and gentlemen," Reiner declared sonorously, mimicking Dan Seymour, the on-air announcer of *We, the People*, "is a man who was actually at the scene of the Crucifixion, two thousand years ago. Isn't that true, sir?"

Aging before his very eyes, as Reiner recalled, Brooks allowed a long, sorrowful sigh to escape his puckered lips. "Oooooh, boy!"

"So, you knew Jesus?" Reiner prompted.

"Jesus . . . yes, yes," Brooks answered, his brow furrowing. "Thin lad . . . wore sandals . . . always walked around with twelve other guys . . . yes, yes, they used to come into the store a lot . . . never bought anything . . . they came in for water . . . I gave it to them . . . nice boys, well behaved . . ."

Everyone collapsed helplessly "for a good part of an hour," Reiner recalled, with—it was always key to the contagious quality of the 2000 Year Old Man—the straight man laughing longest and hardest. Their impromptu skit didn't get onto the air, but no matter: they began to bring the routine into living rooms and dinner parties, with Brooks channeling his mother, Uncle Joe, *The Yiddish Philosopher*, and the way older-generation Jews had of pronouncing and expert-opinionating about "anything and everything."

• • •

No one can separate out who wrote what tidbits of comedy amid the tangled web of collaboration on *Your Show of Shows*. The dynamism that reigned in the writers' room has become legendary. Lucille Kallen said that writing the scripts was like throwing a magnetized piece of a puzzle into a room with all the other pieces racing toward it.

Every *Your Show of Shows* writer and a few of the performers made contributions to nearly every comedy sketch. Once, when pressed to say who had written the riotous send-up of *This Is Your Life*, in which Sid Caesar played a man who is plucked from the audience and literally has to be dragged, kicking and screaming, onstage to rehash the highs and lows of his life, Brooks said, "Even if I remembered to the line, I would never tell you because that is a secret code of comedy writers." However, that secret code of never boasting "*I* wrote that joke" was—as Mel Tolkin once dryly noted, referring to all of Caesar's writers, not only Brooks—"a rule observed more in the breach than in the observance."

With Brooks, sometimes even his solo writing claims had a suspect provenance. That may be true of his first celebrated work independent of *Your Show of Shows*, which came toward the end of the 1951–52 television season and which raised the bar for his future.

Originally Brooks wrote that major breakthrough for a Broadway-bound show called *Curtain Going Up!*, another William Morris Agency package, with the head man, William Morris, among the chief investors. Other backers included Milton Berle, Jimmy Durante, Catskills resort owner Jennie Grossinger, and, making his first appearance in Brooks's life story, a young, aspiring producer named Daniel Melnick.

*Curtain Going Up!* was touted by insiders as a sure thing: a revue with up-and-coming comics, pretty soubrettes who danced, and jazz dancers who sang, all the sketches and music wrapped around the marquee attraction of Marilyn Cantor, the youngest of Eddie

Cantor's "famous five" children. Included in the large ensemble of principals and chorus were M. K. Martinet and her new dance partner, Charles Basile, another veteran of *Gentlemen Prefer Blondes*; the two performed a skit about a ballerina in a dime-a-dance hall.

The William Morris Agency initially took Brooks on as a client "probably as a favor to Sid," in the words of his agent Lester Colodny, who handled Brooks for the agency for several years in the 1950s. Despite his *Your Show of Shows* contract, the agency did not work too hard on Brooks's behalf, partly because writers ranked "at the bottom of the status totem pole," in Colodny's words. Still, writers were a necessary evil, and in late 1951, the agency sent around word that it was looking for fresh material for *Curtain Going Up!*

What Brooks came up with was a savage takeoff on Arthur Miller's *Death of a Salesman*, which he titled "Of Fathers and Sons"—echoing Ivan Turgenev, one of the Russian authors he had learned to love. Unlike Arthur Miller's Pulitzer Prize–winning drama, in which the goods Willy Loman is selling are never specified, Brooks's version featured a second-story man exhorting his son to follow in the family footsteps of petty thievery. The son is a failure as a no-goodnik; he gets A's on his report card and dreams of being a violinist.

"Of Fathers and Sons" was one of the few bright spots in *Curtain Going Up!*'s late-February tryout at the Forrest Theatre in Philadelphia. Local papers singled out Brooks's sketch for praise, and *Billboard* acclaimed it as a "sock sample" of satire. Unfortunately, the rest of the revue did not live up to the same high standard, Marilyn Cantor disappointed critics and audiences alike, and *Curtain Going Up!* rang down—forever—in Philly.

Another Broadway-bound musical revue, *Leonard Sillman's New Faces of 1952*, was scheduled to take over the Forrest after *Curtain Going Up!*, however. Among the new faces behind the scenes and cavorting onstage was a multitalent named Ronny Graham, who dragged producer Sillman to one of the last performances of *Curtain*, so he could meet Brooks backstage. When *Curtain* folded, Sillman scooped up two of its better set pieces—the "Lizzie Borden" hoedown and "Of Fathers and Sons"—for his *New Faces*.

A native Philadelphian seven years older than Brooks, born in a trunk to vaudevillians, Graham had been trying to make headway in New York and New Jersey clubs for a year, playing piano, singing jazz, and performing bent comedy before small audiences. After Brooks saw Graham's act, they began to hang out together. Their shared sense of humor led them one night to a New Jersey truck stop, where, famously, they entertained themselves and others by staging a "berserk faggot row" (Brooks's words).

"A grinning wag," as one critic dubbed him, Graham had a steeplechase grin that telegraphed his inner sweetness. In performance he was as nutty and nonsensical as Brooks, although in private—as close friends knew—he also harbored inner demons.

Sillman hired Graham as a composer, lyricist, and lead performer for his *New Faces of 1952*. Sillman had been producing variations of *New Faces* ever since its first Broadway manifestation, in 1934, which launched "new faces" Henry Fonda and a former child acrobat named Imogene Coca. That first edition was followed by 1936 and 1943 renditions; Brooks must have seen the 1936 show, which had the through line of a Broadway producer who thrives on surefire flops and was filmed as *New Faces of 1937*.

When *New Faces of 1952* acquired "Of Fathers and Sons," in effect Brooks traded up, and with his friend Graham he began to rework the entire book for Broadway.

The Broadway veteran John Murray Anderson was the director, and Sillman's team of sketch writers and songwriters included Peter De Vries and future *Fiddler on the Roof* lyricist Sheldon Harnick. Besides Ronny Graham, the "new faces" in the production included the French-American comic and singer Robert Clary; lyricist, singer, and actress June Carroll (Sillman's sister); the droll comedienne Alice Ghostley; singer-actress Carol Lawrence (later the original

Maria in *West Side Story*); and Eartha Kitt, an ex–Katherine Dunham Company dancer, whose sexy purring of "Monotonous" (lyrics by Carroll) was a showstopper.

Another up-and-comer, the campy comic Paul Lynde, played the patriarch in "Of Fathers and Sons," while Ghostley was the mother of the wayward son. According to Brooks, he was allowed to go onstage and help guide the actors during final rehearsals at the Royale Theatre in New York, before *New Faces* opened on Broadway on May 16, 1952.

Sillman's revue easily won over critics and audiences, ultimately running for ten months. Brooks Atkinson of the *New York Times* hailed it as "one of the pleasantest events of the year" and praised "Of Fathers and Sons" as "triumphantly sharp and satirical, both in the writing and the performances." (From one Brooks to another, the writer also named Brooks liked to say.) Arthur Miller himself attended *New Faces*, columnists reported, and had a good laugh, sending Brooks a nice note about his sketch afterward.

Although the revue had a thin continuity, and multiple writers and lyricists were involved in the patchwork script, Graham and Brooks shared the main book credit for *New Faces*. "Of Fathers and Sons" was always attributed solely to Brooks, however—a rare solo credit for him during those salad days (and just as rare later in his career).

But did Brooks really write that breakthrough alone? He was already known in show business circles as a talking writer who could not and did not actually write complete sketches, never without a collaborator. Not knowing how to type was his usual excuse, and for a long time he refused to learn. If he did scratch something out by hand, he wrote laboriously with pencil on lined yellow paper, then and for most of the rest of his career; usually, early on, the pages ended up jumbled with notes, circled lines, and arrows.

Brooks sorely needed another person in the room: someone to listen to his stream-of-consciousness talking, react to his nonstop performance, and edit his jokes and ideas. Ultimately, as well, he needed someone to type up the script, and that was how he was known to coax his ghost collaborators in the 1950s: Please, help me out, I need a typist!

That was what happened once in the early 1950s when Brooks approached a freelance specialty writer for *Your Show of Shows*, asking for assistance with some comedy sketches he was trying to write in his free time. He handed over some lined yellow pages. They were lengthy, repetitive. His sketches zigged and zagged, but the material was also promising and funny. The writer went home and turned the pages into coherent form. Several were incorporated into another musical revue, not *New Faces*. When the ghostwriter showed up for the opening, he saw only Brooks's name on the playbill.

"I wasn't surprised that my name did not appear," recalled the ghostwriter, "I hadn't really any creative input to the sketches. Still, if I hadn't written them down . . ." That writer, who later became well known in his field, asked to remain anonymous; no matter what had transpired between them, he liked Brooks personally, admired him professionally, and thought that much of his comedy— then and later—was funny.

Some people who knew Brooks well wondered if Ronny Graham had lent an invisible hand to "Of Fathers and Sons" while shrugging off any credit. It turned out exceedingly well for Brooks: *New Faces of 1952* had what in show business is called "legs," with multiple remunerative iterations over the years. Shortly, in 1954, the revue became the second *New Faces* to be re-created as a Hollywood picture.* A road version of the Broadway show toured the nation, and an original cast recording sold briskly. *New Faces* was revived on

---

* Brooks had nothing to do with the screenplay, which hewed close to the stage script. The camera stodgily framed the action as though the audience were seated in the front row of a theater. Yet "Of Fathers and Sons" was filmed faithfully and remains, on DVD today, as wild and woolly as when it was first seen on Broadway.

Broadway for its thirtieth anniversary in 1982, and no one could argue with including Brooks's sketch that year in a book entitled *The Greatest Revue Sketches*.

"Of Fathers and Sons" was indeed a great sketch and a bright feather in Brooks's cap as the television season wound down in 1952. He was no longer "just a TV writer."

One of the first times Brooks and Carl Reiner entertained people outside NBC and the *Your Show of Shows* writers' room with their 2000 Year Old Man routine was at an early-1952 dinner party convened in the flat of the married actors Gene Saks and Bea Arthur. Reiner's wife accompanied him, but Brooks's date surprised everyone: Florence Baum.

Though it had never been quite a love match between him and M. K. Martinet, Brooks had been hot and heavy with the dancer for months before *Gentlemen Prefer Blondes* closed and her interest faded. M.K. played the field and didn't want a steady boyfriend. All the dancers knew the story—M.K. made sure they did—of the time she had been in bed with the tall, athletically proportioned Wall Street stockbroker Edward Dunay, another stage-door Johnny pursuing the *Blondes* chorus. Brooks came around late that night to M.K.'s apartment, tossing pebbles at her window, which was one of his cute ploys. M.K. and Dunay continued to make love, pretending not to hear anything, until he slunk away.

Now that M.K. was immersed in her new dance team career with Charles Basile, she made it clear to Brooks that she was moving on. Neurotic and a heavy drinker, M.K. was not the easiest person to be around, and Brooks would not miss that part of the relationship.

Almost imperceptibly, in the late fall of 1951, Florence Baum began to find herself sitting next to Brooks or standing outside clubs alone with him after others in their group of friends had drifted home at night. For many of the stage-door Johnnys, Baum was the most beautiful of the chorus girls, the prize of the lot. She had blue eyes, full lips, perfect teeth, and short dark hair pulled back into a chignon. Men rhapsodized about her lithe body and "the most unbelievable insteps in town, a straight line from her knee to her toe tips," in the words of the author Herman Raucher, who also wooed Baum and later fictionalized her as "Florrie" in his novel *There Should Have Been Castles.*

Without thinking much about it at first, because Brooks was always the last to say good night and she'd be alone with him, he began accompanying her on long walks home, ending where she lived in her parents' apartment on West 81st Street, between Ninth and Tenth Avenues.

Baum was now dancing in a new Broadway musical—*Top Banana* starring Phil Silvers—that had held previews in the fall and opened in November 1951. *Gentlemen Prefer Blondes* producer Herman Levin was still trying very hard to get the leggy dancer into bed, as was true of Dean Martin, the handsomest man she had ever laid eyes on, who unfortunately—the way she saw it—had just married his second wife.

Baum began to wonder if Brooks was courting her. She didn't mind. When not talking morosely about losing M.K., he was an entertaining, thoughtful companion.

He appealed to her as different from the many other men who pursued her. For one thing, he was short and ugly with a face like a "Hebrew chipmunk"; that was how he often described himself, as though to remind people and lessen the impact of that impression. Baum was in fact slightly taller than Brooks; she was five feet, five inches and inclined to wear heels besides. Brooks was obsessed with his height, his looks, and his religion, in that order, Baum thought. He was overly critical of himself in that regard. Actually, she decided, Brooks often dressed snappily and could look strikingly handsome.

He, too, had beautiful blue eyes, and they seemed to flash with hidden depths. When Brooks wasn't "on" with other people, he could be a quiet, attentive listener. He pondered the eternal verities with what seemed, to her, a profound curiosity and intelligence. They both prized literature, and when he praised the Russians she countered with Stendhal, and then they started in talking about all the other great books they loved. Both adored modern art, especially van Gogh, and they began to rendezvous at museums on Sundays. Going to foreign films was another pastime, and early on the two friends dedicated themselves to the Italian Neorealist films being booked into the Little Carnegie Theatre.

Brooks saw all types of films incessantly, often going alone to kill an afternoon or evening, but the Italian Neorealist masterpieces were the kind of significant filmmaking he admired and dreamed of doing himself one day. Foreign pictures were a staple of the skewering on *Your Show of Shows*. The writers skipped work for afternoon screenings at the Museum of Modern Art, and one time, for example, they transformed Vittorio De Sica's *Bicycle Thieves* into "La Bicicletta," a fake-Italian parody with Sid Caesar at his finest. In private Brooks would never poke fun at De Sica, and he and Baum spent hours talking about movies, books, and paintings. She felt Brooks illuminated the masterworks for her.

By the spring of 1952, they had become a stealth couple, who didn't know yet whether to call themselves a couple, although they began to sneak nights together at Brooks's place on West 68th. "He is the ugliest man I've ever known, but I think I love him," Baum wrote her friend, singer Betsy Holland, who was also in the cast of *Top Banana*.

Their blossoming relationship was a dilemma for Brooks, who, unusually for him, was planning to splurge on a summer-long European trip with *Your Show of Shows* friends and associates. Brooks was thrilled to have been invited along with the elite group, which included Imogene Coca, Lucille Kallen, and another lady behind the scenes, Max Liebman's assistant, Estelle Jacoby—the three most important women on Caesar's show.

The trip was another sign of his acceptance and rising status. He debated asking Baum to come. He knew he had hit the jackpot with her. She was beauty and brains, personality and character, and multifaceted. They were kindred souls, both former Brooklyn kids who might have passed each other on the street when growing up. Brooks joked with Baum that she was exactly the kind of Brooklyn girl he could take home to his mother—a nice Jewish girl, but not too nice and not too Jewish. ("Not too Jewish," because although Baum had been born to a Jewish mother, her father practiced no religion and her mother had converted to Christian Science. Baum herself was an atheist.)

But Brooks was not ready for that commitment, nor was Baum. He did not take her home to meet his mother, and the dancer would never have quit *Top Banana*, now a Broadway hit, for a brief summer fling in Europe. The invitation went unspoken.

# CHAPTER 4

# 1952

## Dreams and Nightmares

As the *Nieuw Amsterdam*, the massive flagship of the Holland America Line, left New York Harbor in festive fashion on June 6, 1952, on deck Brooks was feeling less than buoyant. Despite his watershed success—breakthroughs on *Your Show of Shows* and *New Faces of 1952*—he felt apprehensive about leaving his new girlfriend behind.

Among the eleven hundred passengers were his group of friends from *Your Show of Shows*: the contingent included Lucille Kallen, Max Liebman's associate Estelle Jacoby, and Peter Goode, who acted as Sid Caesar's assistant and also designed settings for the show. Goode and Brooks had agreed to share a cabin. Imogene Coca was sailing separately later in the month, with plans for everyone to meet up on the French Riviera.

Kallen noticed that at the departure Brooks was more subdued than usual. Afterward he spent much of the crossing alone in his cabin, writing long letters daily to Florence Baum. The voyagers enjoyed blue skies and clear weather, but life on board the ship was horribly dull, Brooks wrote Baum, ending many of his letters with the same refrain: "Oh, my sweetheart, my baby, why did I leave you? Why did I ever leave you?"

At Southampton, already familiar to Brooks from his military service, the Americans passed through customs and immigration, then separated. Kallen and Jacoby departed for Paris, while Brooks and Goode took the boat train to London, where in the afternoon they checked into a regal but antiquated hotel, which was even duller than the boat, as Brooks wrote to friends at home. That night he hurried off to see comedian Harvey Stone, who was closing at the Palladium. Stone, whom Brooks knew from Special Services, had carved a career out of comic, sure-loser monologues about army life that he had perfected in uniform during World War II, giving many shows to Brooklyn-based reinforcements heading overseas at the point of embarkation.

London was gray and wet, but Brooks roamed it with pleasure. He and Goode made the museum circuit and saw West End shows for several days before heading to Normandy, where Brooks re-united with wartime acquaintances. In Paris in early July, he and Goode hooked up with Ernie Anderson, Harvey Stone's agent, who was passing through Paris. Anderson took the two Americans to clubs, shows, and parties. They ended up visiting the set of a Hollywood production being shot on location in the City of Light, *Moulin Rouge*, whose director was John Huston; the film starred José Ferrer, whom Brooks knew from his guest stints on *Your Show of Shows*.

He and Ferrer greeted each other warmly as colleagues, and the Hollywood star took the handoff from Anderson, escorting Brooks on another Cook's tour of Paris haunts. Ferrer tried to coax Brooks into writing a humorous monologue for him so he might play London's Palladium one day, and Brooks had to keep reminding himself he was on vacation. If Brooks never forgave a slight, he never forgot a mitzvah, either; years later he would go back to Ferrer—"a sweet guy," in his words—at a time when Ferrer was no longer in quite the same demand, giving the actor a juicy role late in his career: as the duplicitous Professor Siletski in Brooks's remake of Ernst Lubitsch's *To Be or Not to Be*.

Brooks kept up his daily correspondence with Baum, lamenting her absence and praising her exquisite face and body. He wrote, though less often, to his mother and New York friends. His *billets-doux* to Baum were frequently incidental and jokey, but other times he confessed he was feeling unfunny and disconsolate without her by his side.

Baum wrote back less effusively, in care of American Express offices, telling Brooks she felt comfortable with him because of their similar backgrounds, confessing an almost "brotherly love" for him, a phrase that plunged Brooks into depths of despair. What a schnook he was for not bringing her to Paris, which was a city with so many romantic inflections that even Romeo might be forgiven for forgetting Juliet, Brooks wrote; but he could not forget Baum, no, especially late at night. In Paris he had encountered several "fabulous broads" with big knockers, he wrote, but none of them could compare to Baum. The two shared a mutual lust as well as mere affection for each other, Brooks wrote; he urged Baum to reread Theodore Reik on the matter of sex and not deny their profound physical connection nor dismiss their relationship as transient.

From Paris, Brooks and Goode took the express to Nice, and he wrote more letters from their soot- and smoke-filled compartment. In Nice, where it was very hot and dry, they stayed in a *pension* near a nightclub. In Paris, they had reconnoitered with Coca, Kallen, and Jacoby, but Coca did not follow them to the south of France. Now they were a foursome: Kallen, Jacoby, Goode, and Brooks, motoring around Provence and Monaco.

One night, as the Americans wound along the Grand Corniche between Nice and Monte Carlo, one of them remarked on the narrow, dangerous road they were traveling on with cars hurtling toward them that could spell sudden disaster. Brooks "envisioned his death in headlines," in Kallen's words. "Lifting his hand to the Mediterranean stars," she recalled, "Brooks shouted, 'Caesar Writer Plunges to Death in Mediterranean!'"

Everyone shared in the laughter, although the joke had special implications for Brooks: He didn't want to be "just a writer," much less "just a TV writer." He realized that writers were less than dust in the hierarchy of show business, and that with his new calling he had attached himself to another oppressed minority. He feared that he would meet an untimely death and that Melvin Kaminsky, aka Melvin Brooks, would be remembered—credited—as "just another Caesar writer."

From the French Riviera, Brooks and Goode soldiered on alone—by bus and train—to Rapallo, Portofino, Florence, Capri outside Naples, and finally Rome. Sharing hotel rooms, Brooks and Goode had to make constant personal adjustments. Goode was homosexual, and he sought out European men as assiduously as Brooks chatted up the women. Goode was early to bed, while Brooks did not come home until extremely late, just as Goode was waking up. Goode had to tiptoe around in the morning for fear of rousing the sleeping monster. (In Paris Goode had had to borrow Kallen's nearby room for his morning toilette.)

Brooks's letters home were peppered with their joint and disparate adventures—"the fun-loving Melvin Brooks and hard-hitting Peter Goode," as he put it. In Venice, besides riding gondolas, the two spent a long, pleasant evening at the castle of a handsome gay count they met, who was eye candy to Goode. First Don Appell, now Peter Goode: even before achieving fame and fortune, Brooks boasted a number of intimate friends who were homosexual. Satirizing male homosexuals and their mannerisms would become a fixture of his films, and his over-the-top comedy was not always politically correct. That was not the case in his 1952 letters, either, in which the count was described "as queer as a bedbug."

Brooks's comedy was always personal, however, revolving around his own little world—his experiences, his views, his colorations. Show business was rife with homosexuals, and Brooks felt entitled to mock homosexual men because he did have homosexual friends and because the mocking aped the ways they mocked themselves.

His primary relationships, with the exceptions of those with his mother and wives, were usually with men. He was like an addict in his need for intimacy with men. Often smitten with handsome male WASPs, he was still more comfortable with Jewish men. Brooks would make jokes of his own physical attraction to men, kissing male friends hello on television shows, then discouraging any raised eyebrows. He himself, he'd wink, was manly. "You never see," he'd say in private, "a homosexual man smoking a cigar."

The letters home continued. He wore his heart on his sleeve in his missives to Baum. He said his ambition was to write serious plays or novels. After becoming fabulously wealthy as a playwright and novelist, he'd retire to a European villa, probably in Italy, he wrote. For Brooks, already a budding Anglophile, France and Italy would be other touchstones for him for the rest of his life. Brooks made it a mission for his films to conquer foreign countries, especially the English, French, and Italian markets.

His Italian villa would be desolate without Baum, however, he wrote to his girlfriend. When he returned, he promised, he'd remedy his faults. He'd dine alone with her (it was a bugaboo of his, never dining alone as a couple). He'd get started on making enough money to banish all thought of the rich-as-Croesus Herman Levin, his romantic rival. He missed the dancer terribly, and his letters hinted at marriage and children.

When Brooks returned by boat from Italy on August 13, he brought lavish gifts for the leggy dancer, including a stunning white summer coat and a gold bracelet from Florence, the city for which she had been named. They fell into each other's arms.

*Your Show of Shows* was not an agency package nor a single-product show but an independent program owned totally by Max Liebman, with top-brand advertisers excitedly bidding against one another in its first three seasons. In the 1951–52 season sixteen sponsors, an unusually high number, made the show profitable. The series offered "a field day for video sales buys," according to trade papers, to such an extent that the flow of entertainment was marred by what sometimes seemed "a commercial holocaust."

Already by its third full season, 1952–1953, however, sponsors had begun to defect from the Saturday night show. Audience numbers dipped and the critics were less enthusiastic. The cast and crew did not realize it in September, but the acclaimed series had peaked.

Brooks resumed his routine in the fall of 1952, reporting to NBC daily except for on Sundays and when keeping appointments with his psychoanalyst Dr. Clement Staff. *Top Banana* gave its final performances in October, and Baum went away for the rest of the fall, dancing in out-of-town tryouts for the musical *Two's Company*, which starred Bette Davis and was due to arrive on Broadway in mid-December.

Neither romance nor therapy yielded drastic changes in Brooks's workplace demeanor, however, and if anything the pressure to maintain the high quality of the show aggravated his behavior. He continued to arrive late; he was brusque to the point of being offensive; and he was the same scattershot writer—a talking/performing writer.

Even with a guaranteed credit and salary, he was still viewed by some people more as Sid Caesar's jester. Greg Garrison, who directed *Your Show of Shows* episodes, had no compunction about describing Brooks as merely "a *tummler*. He would pull the camera boom [mike] down and pretend he was using a periscope. He was there to amuse Sid."

Everyone realized that the volatile Caesar was more easily humored when Brooks was around. Caesar knew it, too, and on those occasions when the star abandoned New York for East Coast publicity appearances or when he went farther afield, for weekends in Miami Beach, for example, Brooks continued to tag along to keep the star company.

The grind of the series and the continued expectations for greatness exerted a tremendous burden on Caesar. It was five days of script work and preparation for each show, frenetic dress rehearsals on Saturday afternoons followed by the live performance in front of a studio audience—really a mass national audience—without cue cards or teleprompters. However godlike he might have seemed, Caesar was not superhuman.

Caesar had begun to subsist on booze and pills. He developed an incessant nervous cough that was like a red warning light, flashing sometimes even during a broadcast, when he was unsure or unsteady. Depression stalked him. Yet he never missed a day of work or slacked off at rehearsals, and he rose to the occasion every Saturday night.

Brooks, Mel Tolkin, and Lucille Kallen underwent similar stress. As the pressure built and his star burned brighter, Caesar became more imperious with the writers, carrying an imaginary rifle and whipping it out to shoot any writer's bad idea out of the air; he'd take aim at Brooks as often as anyone else and hurl objects at him, too, just as Max Liebman once had. They'd get into weird Mexican standoffs. Once Brooks jabbed his finger into Caesar's chest and demanded: "Do the joke!" Caesar looked down at him from his lofty height and said, "I let you live!" (Another time Brooks got so mad that he hauled off and slugged the star. Caesar, taken aback, shrugged. "Okay, if you feel that strongly!")

Tolkin and Kallen thought Brooks's jollying of Caesar, his performing antics and smart-aleck comments, gave him a sly advantage in the script conferences. All three writers saw their names on the screen now—Tolkin, Kallen, and Brooks, in that order, with the freelancers listed afterward as additional contributors—but there was also a subtle jockeying, a taking of credit *within* the room, of which Brooks was the master.

Even when Brooks thought someone else's idea was funny, he might sit with his arms crossed, unsmiling. "That's funny, that's funny," he'd say noncommittally. One couldn't be sure, though, that he wasn't just about to jump up and add his two cents. It was only when he exploded in sudden laughter that he could not control, when he didn't have any topper at the ready, that people knew he thought something was really funny.

Inside the room Brooks was brilliant about getting the nod and laughs from Caesar when he had shirked the hard work. He'd "add two jokes and get all the applause from the stars and actors," Tolkin wrote Kallen, still complaining, forty years later. Brooks has "a very, very funny mind," Tolkin explained another time, "he'd hit on a couple of classic lines and bits. That would get extreme laughter from the audience [in the room] and from Sid—papa. They're roaring with laughter. While we knocked our brains out."

As good as *Your Show of Shows* still was—for Caesar, Imogene Coca, Carl Reiner, and Howard Morris continued to sparkle as performers—already, in the 1952–53 season, some critics noticed that too many situations and setups were comfortable retreads. The cast members noticed it, too. Actor-singer Bill Hayes, for one, sniffed "strange vibes." The sketches and musical numbers kept gravitating to familiar ground. Hayes asked Tolkin if he was imagining that, and Tolkin told him that nobody wanted to mess with a "winning formula."

"Was Sid's cough the result of too heavy a load of responsibility?" Hayes wondered. "Did I hear him begin to argue with Max's decision and taste? Were the production people getting a little testy when final decisions were held off longer than before? Was Max slowing with weariness? . . . Sometime late in 1952, the gears began to slip."

Adding to the strain, the show's acclaimed variety format was now being intelligently imitated by several new television series. By midseason, *Your Show of Shows* was hemorrhaging advertisers and profits were tumbling even as the talent costs rose on the program that won the Emmy Award for Best Variety Show for the second year in a row.[*]

Behind the scenes, NBC recognized the ominous portents. The network was committed to Caesar, so officials looked to lay blame on the scripts. Max Liebman was pressured to hire the proverbial "fresh writer," only the fourth staff writer after Tolkin, Kallen, and Brooks. He engaged Tony Webster, who had cut his teeth working for the radio comedians Bob and Ray. Webster went on staff in April, becoming, in Brooks's words, the first of the writers not from "the same background, a second-generation Russian Ukrainian–Jewish intellectual heritage." Webster was from Middle America besides—Missouri.

But that was not enough of a fix. There were going to be "drastic changes" ahead for next year's *Your Show of Shows*, according to the national entertainment columnist Erskine Johnson.

With those dark auguries looming over the summer of 1953, Brooks did not take another prolonged vacation, as he had the previous summer in England, France, and Italy.

Sid Caesar and Imogene Coca had announced they were going to team up and star in their first motion picture, probably for Columbia Pictures, that summer. Partly for that reason, Brooks met with Columbia producer Fred Kohlmar in New York in early June, agreeing to a short-term summer contract. The studio would decide his assignment.

When Caesar visited Hollywood in the spring with Mel Tolkin, however, he made an unimpressive pitch to Harry Cohn, the mogul of Columbia, and the dream of a Caesar-Coca movie began to

---

[*]  Sid Caesar and Imogene Coca lost in their Emmy Award categories, however, to Jimmy Durante and Lucille Ball.

fade. Caesar returned to New York, read the tea leaves, and decided to take it easy over the summer. Only Coca elected to pursue the assault on Hollywood, accompanied by Max Liebman, who was ostensibly organizing guest stars for the next season of *Your Show of Shows*. Brooks, flying with them to Los Angeles, made three.

Hollywood during the sleepy summer of 1953, when Brooks made his first visit to the film capital, was introducing Cinemascope to theaters. The anti-Communist blacklist was in full cry, with the House Un-American Activities Committee (HUAC) launching a new round of hearings with subpoenas to Lillian Hellman, Dorothy Parker, and twenty-three other "pink" artists, mostly scenarists. The Los Angeles Archdiocese was busily urging Catholics to boycott Otto Preminger's "indecent" *The Moon Is Blue*.

Coca splurged on a rented Brentwood mansion with swimming pool, where she hosted admirers and met with producers, talking up future motion picture air castles. Brooks bunked at the Chateau Marmont, the hip hillside hotel on Sunset Boulevard; it had no swimming pool, but Columbia Pictures was paying his tab. As a close student of Caesar's career, watching the money when he traveled with the star, Brooks had picked up many business tips, including the advantages of demanding such perks in contracts.

A few miles to the east of Chateau Marmont lay the vast studio complex that included the Columbia soundstages and buildings. On his first day on the lot, Brooks was allocated an office and secretary in the four-story writers' building and assigned to slog away on a projected Rita Hayworth musical based on a 1919 Somerset Maugham play. His supervisor was Jonie Taps, a producer who specialized in light musicals.

On his second day, however, Jerry Wald, who supervised Taps, Kohlmar, and other staff producers for Harry Cohn, Columbia's top boss, walked in and tossed a different script at Brooks— voilà! "It's another Rita Hayworth movie, but the script is a little lousy," said Wald. "Jazz it up, boy! Jazz it up!" The little-lousy script was *Pal Joey*, more important than the Maugham adaptation. The Broadway hit musical had been optioned for somewhere down the road for Hayworth and Frank Sinatra: Double dynamite! Very exciting! Hayworth therefore might not be appearing in the Maugham project. Probably her part would go to Betty Grable. Give me your thoughts on *Pal Joey*, Wald urged, adding with a wagging finger that the Betty Grable script came first!

Love at first sight it was not for Brooks and Hollywood. Columbia was a dizzying merry-go-round. Brooks liked to tell the story of Wald taking him over to meet Harry Cohn in the studio barbershop, where the Hollywood monarch was laid out flat getting a foamy shave from an Italian barber. He was encircled by yes-men and eminences, including some A-list directors, sitting in chairs; among the latter group was Fred Zinnemann, whose *From Here to Eternity* earned thirteen Oscar nominations that year.

As the barber shaved Cohn, he spun him like a gun turret so his subordinates were rotated into his line of sight. The group was debating a picture in the works that needed a certain something to juice it up. The barber chair swiveled to Brooks. "I think it might need two or three more block comedy sequences," he volunteered. That TV terminology was met with a deafening silence. The mogul sat up straight, eyeing Brooks. "Who's the kid?" "I'm not here," Brooks said quickly. "I'm simply not here." "Good," said Cohn.

Cohn paid no more attention to the newcomer until later that same day or the next, according to Brooks. When Brooks's new office was fitted with a nameplate, he watched in horror as another nameplate was ripped off—that of writer Alfred Hayes. Realizing that Hayes had just been cashiered, Brooks went a little crazy over the lunch break, switching all the nameplates in the writers' unit: shuffling around the names on the first and third floors, scrambling those on the second and fourth. Called onto the carpet by Cohn, Wald pleaded for Brooks: "He's a good kid. I'll dock his pay. Give him another chance!"

Maybe true, maybe not. You never knew with Brooks, who embroidered stories and confabulated so much that there were usually multiple variations of favorite anecdotes, with Brooks sometimes making himself the hero in other people's vignettes.

Meanwhile at night, Brooks wrote abject letters home. Sure, the California weather was gorgeous. "So were the girls," Brooks told Conan O'Brien sixty years later. Thanks to the secretarial pool, there was no problem with his "typing." And not just the girls: everyone in Hollywood was physically beautiful; beautiful people, beautiful place—but empty and phony. And writers ranked lowest of the low in the studio caste system.

Brooks hated, hated, *hated* Hollywood.

He suffered the same terrible anxiety and fears as he'd suffered in New York, but his sleepless nights were accompanied by aching homesickness. He was too busy, he wrote home, even to visit Imogene Coca at her mansion with a swimming pool, except on a few Sundays. He yearned for Florence Baum and repeatedly wrote to the dancer, who had various engagements that summer, including a stint at the Texas State Fair. He begged for letters from her, snapshots ("the one in the turtleneck"), and any New York gossip.

The one surprising bright spot, he wrote, was Jerry Wald. According to the intimidating legend that wafted around him, Wald was the living embodiment of the producer Sammy Glick—the lead character of Budd Schulberg's quintessential Hollywood novel *What Makes Sammy Run?*—"crass . . . conniving . . . despicable," in the words of Robert Alan Aurthur, another writer who worked under Wald. But the real Wald was quite different, as Aurthur and Brooks both discovered. Brooks had expected a terrifying Jewish maniac like himself. But he found Wald to be a pudgy fellow with a butterball face and an irresistible smile and grin—"a nice man," which was the ultimate compliment Brooks might pay to someone. Expecting Sammy Glick, Brooks instead encountered a *mensch* who treated him like a fair-haired genius from TV-land.

True, Wald threw out story ideas and shuffled scripts in front of him faster than a Las Vegas card dealer, and there seemed to be an endless list of iffy projects and weary scripts that needed jazzing up. New assignments were lobbed at Brooks almost daily. On the Friday of his very first week, Wald convened a daylong assessment of ongoing projects in his office. According to the studio logs, staff producer Jonie Taps was summoned after 6:00 p.m. to discuss "problems" with Brooks's compatibility with the Maugham musical, now called "The Pleasure Is All Mine." The fair-haired TV genius was promptly switched over to full-time on a remake of the 1942 film *My Sister Eileen*, with Fred Kohlmar producing.

Kohlmar was simultaneously preparing *Pal Joey*, and Wald thought it might be convenient for the same writer to be working on both films. However, another meeting after the weekend was convened to decide on the senior writer of the more important—the all-important—*Pal Joey*. The studio decided it needed a consummate Hollywood pro to satisfy Rita Hayworth and Frank Sinatra, and eventually Wald found one in Dorothy Kingsley. But the upshot was that Kohlmar also confessed misgivings about Brooks, and on Tuesday the fair-haired TV genius was sent back to "The Pleasure Is All Mine," once more under Taps, whom Brooks always recalled as an amiable guy in black-and-white wingtips.

Telling tales of his first brush with Hollywood, Brooks always emphasized the Hayworth-Sinatra musical. But the studio relegated *Pal Joey* to the back burner almost immediately after his arrival, and that film would not show up in theaters for another three years. Brooks barely crossed paths with *Pal Joey* and spent most of July ping-ponging between the *My Sister Eileen* remake and "The Pleasure Is All Mine." He was taken off *Eileen* indefinitely in mid-July in favor of Richard Quine and Blake Edwards, who took the remake across the finish line, while "The Pleasure Is All Mine"— the script Brooks worked on most of the time—evolved into *Three for the Show*, both released in 1955.

The finishing writer for *Three for the Show*, incidentally, was Leonard Stern, a veteran of Abbott and Costello comedies who crossed paths with Brooks for the first time at Columbia. Little or nothing remained of Brooks's contribution, and he was not credited. As was the case later with *Get Smart*, which he also polished to a glow, Stern—another New Yorker, three years older—was not then or ever Brooks's close collaborator or friend.

California was beautiful, but Hollywood was empty, Brooks ruefully wrote home. What is to become of me out here? Enough! I pine for New York, he wrote to friends.

Brooks, however, also experienced a revelation in Hollywood. Back east on Fire Island by the end of summer, he warned Sid Caesar that the future was motion pictures. Television was ephemeral; if he made movies, Caesar could be a Matisse in a museum. "On kinescope you will die," he told Caesar. "On celluloid you can live forever."

That conversation may or may not have happened in quite that way, but a lot of people were whispering into Caesar's ear in the fall of 1953. *Your Show of Shows* held its 1953–54 season premiere with anxiety spreading among NBC officials. Along with the salaries of the stars, the production costs had skyrocketed. Ratings and advertising revenue had gone into freefall. Imogene Coca was agitating for her own series. Insiders predicted that it would be Coca's last season with Caesar and probably the last for the series.

The midwestern *goy* Tony Webster had been hired as the fourth staff writer the previous spring because the network and Caesar blamed the downward trend of ratings and profits largely on weak scripts. The 1953–54 writing staff continued to expand, at times including Joseph Stein, the future playwright of *Fiddler on the Roof*, and Danny Simon and his younger brother Neil, or "Doc," as he was nicknamed since boyhood. All three New Yorkers had been freelancing for the show, but now they were salaried for extended periods and the Simon brothers filled in for Kallen when she was in the latter stages of a pregnancy.

At work or out and about, Brooks wore his customary suit of armor, grinning and firing off jokes like silver bullets. In private with certain intimates, though, he was decidedly less effervescent and never more so than in the fall of 1953; his ongoing struggle to affirm his identity as a writer, his failure to do something worthwhile in Hollywood, and the seemingly inevitable fate of *Your Show of Shows* darkened his mood.

His closest intimate was Florence Baum, and alone with his girlfriend he cursed the artificiality of television and society in general; indeed, he railed at the overall futility of life. He had turned twenty-eight at the beginning of the summer, and all his birthdays renewed his obsession with the morbid idea that he would die before fulfilling his promise, just as his own father, Max Kaminsky, had at age thirty-six. Sleepless at night on West 68th Street, Brooks read fitfully, turning the pages of Gogol and Tolstoy, identifying with their bleakness and fatalism, their shrewd, morally superior peasants, and, in the case of *The Twelve Chairs* by Ilya Ilf and Evgeny Petrov, another novel Mel Tolkin urged upon him, the Russian black humor.

Baum was a frequent visitor, but in the wee hours she usually returned to her parents' new apartment, which was about thirty blocks away. Baum was Brooks's lifeline to positivism; many people thought she possessed a kind of inner Zen. The lovers had immediately reconnected when he had returned from Hollywood; they saw each other almost daily, although not always in a romantic context. With Howard Morris's connivance more than Brooks's, Baum had joined the Hamilton Trio when an original member, Pat ("the blonde") Horn, had quit and Mrs. Hamilton had left the act for motherhood. Now the trio was Bob Hamilton, newcomer Helena Seroy, and Baum, briefly dyeing her hair blond to evoke Horn.

Brooks and Baum had such divergent involvement on the Caesar series that they sometimes waved to each other as they rushed down the corridors of the NBC building in opposite directions. By now they were sort of going steady, but not officially. Marriage was a touchy subject they avoided. When Brooks suddenly popped the question in late November, however, Baum just as impulsively said yes, and Brooks arranged the whole ceremony in a whirlwind of time. In fact, Baum had a lunch date on the very day of her nuptials that she forgot to cancel with Herman Raucher, another Brooklynite and Fire Islander who was a professional rival of Brooks's and, because he was friendly with Baum, a seemingly romantic one. (In time Raucher would marry Mary Katherine Martinet.)

More than once Brooks had told Baum that she was the kind of woman he could take home to his mother: beautiful, brainy, ethnically Jewish (albeit personally irreligious). Yet characteristic of the distance, literal as well as emotional, that he kept from his Brooklyn family, Brooks had actually never taken the dancer home to meet Kitty Kaminsky. For the very first time at their marriage ceremony on Thanksgiving Day, November 26, 1953, Brooks introduced the bride-to-be to his mother and three brothers, Leonard, Irving, and Bernard. The first sight of the Kaminsky clan took Baum aback, according to friends. They all resembled shorter, less prepossessing versions of the groom. Brooks compulsively wisecracked about his own ugliness and short stature, but by comparison, Baum thought with amusement, she had snared the tall, handsome member of the family.

Yet Baum harbored misgivings about Brooks, and she wept hysterically when her mother woke her on her wedding day. Scolding her, her mother said it was too late and would be too embarrassing to cancel. She'd help Baum get an annulment if it became necessary.

Typical of Brooks, he arranged a status touch for the ceremony: Their vows were exchanged in the Central Park West home of Rabbi Louis I. Newman, a leading Reform Zionist, who was also a celebrated author of cantatas, stage plays, and Talmudic anthologies.

Brooks's *Your Show of Shows* friend, "third banana" Howard Morris, who had more or less brought the couple together, and Morris's first wife, Helen, were the official witnesses among a small party of friends and family hastily rounded up for the occasion.

The bride and groom were both so busy with *Your Show of Shows*— and Baum continued to hold dance spots on Sunday TV, too— that they agreed to delay their honeymoon.

After a small reception at Baum's mother and father's flat, the couple took a taxi to Brooks's place on West 68th, Baum toting one small suitcase. Dust balls lay everywhere, as usual. The floor was seemingly carpeted with torn royalty stubs from *New Faces* and other bachelor signs of grunge. The heavy ocher drape covering the windows, which had been designed by Peter Goode, sagged amid the detritus.

A self-confessed neatnik, Baum felt overwhelmed and confused. She knew Brooks's place well, but the fourth-floor walk-up was now going to be her home, too. The first thing she wanted to do was clean. But Brooks wouldn't let her. He even seemed reluctant to divide his tiny closet and give her space in his small chest of drawers for her personal items.

Before that moment, whenever the two had been together, most of the time it had been at night, usually out among a bunch of friends. Brooks still had a phobia about dining alone with Baum, at home or in restaurants. Now they were stuck with each other—alone.

Baum always felt that Brooks had a kind of Jekyll-Hyde personality. In public, he could be counted on to function as a one-man roller coaster: "a happening," as one friend described him. In public, he was constantly, compulsively entertaining. He had no "off" button. In private, though, he could turn glum, or worse, sullen, with no "on" button.

Jokes were his way of warding off emotional intimacy, she believed. And she loved the jokester who sometimes went too far, but she treasured more the Jekyll side of him. The Jekyll-Brooks began to vanish almost from the moment the two crossed the threshold that day. The ebullient humor, the tender affection, the thoughtfulness evaporated.

Just a few days more was all it took for them to start bickering and for the miserable Baum to pack up and move out, back in with her parents. Brooks phoned her parents, demanding "Send back my wife!" Tearfully, she returned, and they made up.

Then the couple went out with friends, and Brooks performed his already familiar shtick of putting a napkin over his arm and roaming tables, pretending to be an obsequious French waiter. Everyone laughed, including Baum. Baum hoped that all marriages had rough starts and her husband would return to being thoughtful and caring.

Along with hiring several new writers, producer Max Liebman had refreshed the format of *Your Show of Shows* for what was fated to be its last season, adding a surfeit of music and dance numbers to alleviate the burden on Sid Caesar and shift the spotlight to Imogene Coca.

Accordingly, the September premiere featured guest stars Nat "King" Cole; Lily Pons, who sang opera and a duet with Coca; the prima ballerina Tamara Toumanova, making her television debut, who danced to a tango; and a lavish musical finale entitled "Love Never Went to College," with the nightclub singer Robert Monet. Florence Baum danced with the Hamilton Trio in the premiere and in many other episodes in the 1953–54 season.

Although he was still very much the star of the series, Caesar's comedy was rationed. Along with his "Dentist's Apprentice" pantomime and a Hickenloopers outdoor barbecue with Coca, the main sketch of the season premiere was the Caesar-Coca takeoff of the famous love-on-the-beach scene between Burt Lancaster and Deborah Kerr in *From Here to Eternity*, Fred Zinnemann's Oscar-winning Best Picture that was fresh in Brooks's mind after his stint in Hollywood. Caesar and Coca's romancing on the beach as waves surged over them is one of the show's famous sketches to this day.

Critics, watching the premiere, tolled the series' end, however. "Curiously unsatisfying," said the *New York Journal-American*. "Considerably uneven," agreed the *Washington Post*. No "real pep or imaginative verve," Jack Gould wrote in the *New York Times*, partly blaming "the horrendous number of commercials" needed to support costs.

It hardly helped that once every fourth Saturday night, all season long, Caesar and Coca took desperately needed time off while another NBC show, *All-Star Revue*, filled the time slot. *Your Show of Shows*' cancellation was officially announced in February, and the 160-episode run of the acclaimed series ended on June 5, 1954, with a huge after-party, as it had most Saturday nights during the four and a half years, this last time at the Rainbow Room. Amid muttering about the unfairness of critics, the party celebrated the remarkable achievement. But it was also a funeral for the momentous time past. "There has never been a program before or since the natal day of February 25, 1950," *Variety* eulogized *Your Show of Shows* in the last week it was broadcast, "that embodied so many show business elements with such skill, imagination and truly big league touch."

NBC was anxious to try again with Caesar, though, and the network threw so much money at the star, giving him a ten-year deal with extraordinary financial guarantees and creative freedoms, that he didn't give any thought to Brooks's admonitions about the future lying in Hollywood. The network doled out several new contracts that divided *Your Show of Shows*, like Gaul, into three parts: Caesar, Coca, and Liebman.

Caesar got professionally divorced from Liebman, whom he no longer needed, and he was announced as the star and producer of *Caesar's Hour*, planned for the fall. NBC was amenable to Carl Reiner and Howard Morris rejoining Caesar with a new actress replacing Coca in the linked-arms quartet. Liebman accepted a long-term contract for producing network telefilms and "spectaculars" (soon to be renamed "specials"). Cleaved from Caesar, Coca was awarded with her own eponymous half-hour series also for 1955–1956.

The writers, too, had to be apportioned. One can imagine Caesar and Coca dividing the staff up as though they were choosing players for a neighborhood baseball game, a scenario that had rarely bene-fited Melvin Kaminsky in the past. Caesar got first pick, and the star took Mel Tolkin, the man he trusted above all for his mingling of comedy and wisdom. Big Mel would continue as the senior writer of *Caesar's Hour*.

Coca took Lucille Kallen, the only woman in the writers' room and the writer best attuned to Coca's talent. Caesar then picked Tony Webster, maybe because Brooks had preemptively chosen to strike out on his own and prove he was no longer Caesar's sidekick. Brooks had received overtures from comedian Red Buttons, who needed a head writer for his television variety show. Also, Brooks had plans to collaborate again with Ronny Graham, this time on a full-blown Broadway musical. Coca and Kallen, who both valued Brooks, said he could join *The Imogene Coca Show* if and when he became available.

In time Brooks would become the Matisse in a museum, but he'd keep *Your Show of Shows* alive in his films. The silent-picture spoofs, the genre parodies, the visits to random historical epochs—all those were staples of Sid Caesar's series. Even off-camera stuff from the Caesar years crept into Mel Brooks comedies, such as the scene in *Blazing Saddles* inspired by a fabled incident, perhaps apocryphal, that had supposedly occurred when Caesar decked a rented horse in Central Park after the animal had the gall to throw his wife, Florence, to the ground. Many of the "wonderful bits" rejected by

TV censors, which "were considered too vulgar or too insulting to certain groups at the time," said composer Earl Wild, "Mel later recycled. In all of Mel Brooks' cinematic efforts," he wrote admiringly in his memoir, "it's easy to recognize the crumbs from Caesar's table."

Summer came and with it the annual retreat to Fire Island, the thirty-two-mile-long spit of beach and dunes lying off Long Island's south shore about forty-five miles from Manhattan. Brooks leased a bungalow near the Reiners in Ocean Beach. Everyone was sanguine. Perhaps *Your Show of Shows* had to die, but they all believed in a television afterlife.

The previous summer, the weekend population of Fire Island had ballooned to a record eight thousand people. Vacationing yachtsmen and fishermen, sun worshippers, and partyers thronged the main walk of Ocean Beach, especially on Saturday nights.

This was Florence Baum's coming out as Mrs. Brooks, her first summer on Fire Island. People stopped by and knocked on their door simply to say hello and meet her. "I just wanted to see what the person looked like who married Mel!" Brooks took weekday trips into the city for meetings on his projects. The only way onto or off of the island was by ferry; the last one left nightly for mainland Bayshore at 7:15 p.m., and the train filled up with Fire Islanders coming and going, including Nora Kaye, a pretty garment district showroom model.* Brooks chatted with Kaye and told her to stop by his Ocean Beach cottage and meet his wife with the message "Hi! Mel said we should be friends!"

The writers and artists who mingled in Ocean Beach that summer included the radio and television announcer Ken Roberts, who introduced NBC soap operas; budding actors Robert Loggia and James Coburn; acting teacher Stella Adler; and authors Herman

---

* Not the American dramatic ballerina of the same name, Nora Kaye (1920–1987), who was married to the stage and screen director Herbert Ross.

Wouk and James Jones. (The last took perverse pleasure in his friendship with people connected with *Your Show of Shows,* which had satirized the film of his book *From Here to Eternity,* offending Columbia executives to the extent that the studio even filed a short-lived lawsuit against NBC.) The future novelist Herman Raucher, who would later write the best-selling *Summer of '42,* was also part of the Ocean Beach scene.

The Carl Reiners, the Mel Tolkins, and the Norman Lears were among the many vacationers who were associated with either Sid Caesar (who continued to spend part of every summer with his family on Fire Island), *The Colgate Comedy Hour,* or both.

The partying of the television crowd was pretty tame compared to the revels taking place at many island bars and clubs. Apart from Caesar, the *Your Show of Shows* folks were not heavy drinkers. Modest drinking was part of Brooks's paradox—self-control despite being a wild man. He'd take one Scotch, often with a dash of milk and ice, as he rushed out the door to a dinner or gathering. And no marijuana, then or ever.

Brooks loved the solitary walks he took on Fire Island beaches, and he enjoyed surf casting alone for hours, time that afforded him calm and inspiration. He and other *Your Show of Shows* friends whiled away the nighttime hours playing parlor games that involved words, songs, or playacting. He and Carl Reiner brought out the 2000 Year Old Man, polishing the repartee and introducing new bits, and many people first saw the act on Fire Island.

Fire Island was a status marker, and Brooks was never happier or more at ease than in the summers when he was among like-minded show business sophisticates. And in general, things always went better in his marriage when other people were around.

Though he bragged about his new wife, telling people how beautiful and smart Florence was, he also suffered fits of jealousy. One night Baum went to the island's small movie theater with her new girlfriend Nora Kaye, who met up with a man who was accompanied by another friend they all knew, Herman Raucher. Raucher sat next to Baum and stole his arm around her at the end of the movie. When the lights went up, Brooks was in the back row, staring stonily. He had followed them. He exchanged sharp words with Raucher. Baum said it was all a silly misunderstanding, but Brooks fumed.

Brooks had at least one paying summer job along with his other projects, and some of the train trips into Manhattan were for *The Colgate Summer Comedy Hour.* Collaborating with Ronny Graham, he contributed to sketches for an episode featuring New York Giants star Willie Mays singing his novelty "Say Hey!" Still an unabashed baseball fan, Brooks befriended the outfielder, who returned the favor with guest tickets for a Yankees game played against their bitter rivals, the Brooklyn Dodgers—Brooks's team—in August.

Together Brooks and Graham were also involved in a planned musical called "Samson and Lila Dee," which was intended as an "all-black retelling of the biblical Samson and Delilah story," according to Howard Pollack, the biographer of lyricist John Latouche. Latouche, a celebrated songwriter who had written lyrics to Vernon Duke's music for the 1940 film *Cabin in the Sky,* had conceived the story, but despite a series of collaborators—most recently Edward Chodorov—he had failed to produce a viable book.

Partly because Latouche had trouble landing an important black star, "Samson and Lila Dee" morphed into *Delilah: The Vamp,* a vehicle for Carol Channing, instead. No longer was there any black-Bible angle. Channing would play "a vamp enamored of a cinematic cowboy" in the pre–World War I era of East Coast silent-picture making, a spoof category already on Brooks's vitae from *Your Show of Shows.* There was talk of Graham, besides sharing book duties with Brooks, playing a lead role opposite Channing.

Brooks and Graham found it difficult to get their ideas past Latouche, however. Brooks tried a power play with Latouche and the nervous producers, telling them he and Graham might work better alone. Brooks "nailed me down over the phone," Latouche wrote in his journal, "finally getting rather triumphant as he sensed my confusion, and attempting to force a situation that would rule me out utterly." The producers proved "unexpectedly sympathetic" to Latouche, however, according to his biographer, and Brooks and Graham were dismissed. (Later in 1955, retitled *The Vamp*, the musical had a brief Broadway run, with Latouche solely credited for the story, book, and lyrics.)

The future still looked so good, however, that Carl Reiner and Howard Morris convinced Brooks to take a larger apartment for himself and his wife in the fall. They moved into a one-bedroom Strauss town house on West 70th Street. Their only roommate: an orange tomcat they named Chichikov in honor of the main character in *Dead Souls*. Brooks liked dogs but loved cats and did cat impressions at the drop of a hat.

One of the positive auguries was Red Buttons, whose revamped television variety show was now being produced by Brooks's old friend Don Appell. *The Red Buttons Show* had a phenomenal early success, starting out on CBS in 1951 and peaking at number eleven in the Nielsen ratings; the next year, however, the show began to sag in audience size, and after two seasons it had moved to NBC. Brooks met with Buttons, a New York comic with stubby red hair and freckles, and Buttons offered him upgrades and provisos in a contract that would, for the first time, let Brooks direct episodes he wrote. The William Morris Agency outdid itself on the details.

Puckish and (albeit a matter of taste) mirthful as he was on-screen, it was no secret in the television industry that off camera Buttons was an unpleasant egomaniac who blamed writers for show problems and went through writers like breath mints. At one time or another he employed many Caesar writers, including the Simon brothers—Danny and Neil—Joseph Stein, and Larry Gelbart, who had just joined the staff of the new Sid Caesar series.

Could Buttons be tougher to work for than Caesar at his worst? The answer: yes. Brooks later claimed he had written the premiere of Buttons's series that fall and was scheduled to direct the second episode before he quit in the first week of October. (For the record, *Variety* credited only Danny Simon and Milt Rosen with the premiere.)

Privately this is the tale Brooks told: He arrived for a high-level meeting at NBC with Buttons presiding. He listened with growing dismay as the freckle-faced comic spoke long and obstreperously about the quality he demanded from his writers. "None of that Caesar-Coca stuff," Buttons, who had a chip on his shoulder about *Your Show of Shows*, proclaimed, staring accusingly at Brooks. "None of that garbage. I want *good* writing." Buttons also reminded Brooks that he always sang his signature pop hit, "The Ho Ho Song," in each and every program. Besides grimacing when Buttons attacked *Your Show of Shows*, Brooks detested "The Ho Ho Song," and now, he decided, he detested Buttons, too. He excused himself to go to the bathroom, slipped out the door and away from the building, racing home to phone the William Morris Agency and beg out of his contract.

He still had positive options, and the most expeditious one was *The Imogene Coca Show*, which had premiered the same week as the retooled Red Buttons series. But Coca's new show was already looking like a loser. The decision had been made to present Coca in a situation comedy variant, playing a version of herself, an actress with sundry crises, interspersed with singing and dancing. The first reviews had been harsh ("A hapless occasion," *Variety* said), and director Marc Daniels, who had championed the original premise, was let go. The endless adjustments began, along with a parade of new producer-directors.

Lucille Kallen, famous for her ability to "handle" Brooks with tact and composure, needed him badly, even if inwardly Brooks felt growingly panicked at having chosen Coca over *Caesar's Hour*—which was doing better with both audiences and reviewers.

Ernest Kinoy and Max Wilk were the other Coca staff writers; they and Kallen showed up for work at 9:00 a.m. at the William Morris offices, then located in the Mutual of New York Building in midtown Manhattan, and sweated over the scripts. Brooks, same as ever, would turn up around lunchtime, proclaiming "I feel terrible. Send out for chicken soup!" His habit of lateness had been grandfathered in on *Your Show of Shows*, and there he had had a safety net of supporters including Sid Caesar and Carl Reiner—absent here.

The latecomer would read the progress and begin shouting "That's not funny! You don't know what's funny! I know funny!" The Wrecker, Wilk dubbed him. "He just takes everything and says, 'Forget that! We'll do this instead.' And he walks up and down screaming and yelling about what he is gonna do . . . it never happens very much."

The situation wasn't helped by the fact that Brooks already had a pattern of filling his plate with so many extracurricular jobs and prospects that it was hard to know how he divided his time or which had priority. Probably it was hard for Brooks himself to know.

With his days theoretically devoted to Coca's series, he filled his nights, from late 1954 into early 1955, with preparations for another, less ambitious (off-Broadway) revue, again in collaboration with Ronny Graham, called *Once Over Lightly*. This time, suggesting that Brooks had gained the upper hand in their partnership, the credits would read, "Sketches mostly by MELVIN BROOKS . . ." (his name in caps), trailed by another writer's name, Ira Wallach, then "Ronny Graham" in third position, upper- and lowercase. *New Faces of 1952* had had the order reversed: "Sketches mostly by Ronny Graham and Melvin Brooks."

*Once Over Lightly* might have been overlooked as the usual mélange of song, dances, and skits except for the involvement of actors Jack Gilford and Zero Mostel and a thespian turned director, Stanley Prager. Brooks had mingled with the three and a businessman friend of theirs named Irving "Speed" Vogel at Greenwich Village parties.

Mostel and Prager were left-wing refugees from Hollywood, looking warily over their shoulders after being cited in *Red Channels* and other blacklisting guides drawn up by anti-Communist zealots who targeted subversives in the film industry. Mostel got his official blacklisting later in 1955 after he was summoned before HUAC, the House Un-American Activities Committee, and invoked the Fifth Amendment, refusing to testify. Although Gilford was not as politically engaged as his wife, actress Madeline Lee Gilford (who was also blacklisted ultimately), he traveled in the same circles.

Brooks liked to say that if he had been born ten years earlier he might have become a radical; then he, too, would have been vulnerable when HUAC swooped down first on Hollywood in 1947 and later on the New York stage world. The *Your Show of Shows* writers, who were mostly Jewish, like the majority of the blacklist victims, were keenly aware of the anti-Red witch hunts. In the spring of the final season Caesar's writers compulsively watched the Army-McCarthy Hearings. Because of their heightened paranoia, the TV material they wrote was rarely topical and almost never infused with political messages. "We were political people, but we rarely did anything political," Larry Gelbart said later. Brooks's comedy, throughout his career, would likewise play down topicality and politics.

Despite his dominant credit, *Once Over Lightly* was one revue for which Brooks enlisted an uncredited ghostwriter. He required help on a sketch that overlapped the similar-sounding short story about cats he had started years earlier in Red Bank, New Jersey. That became a pattern in his career; certain signature ideas of his could be traced back over years of germination and evolution, taking an almost inordinate time to reach fruition. The ones that took the longest, arguably, ultimately worked out best.

Brooks's *pièce de résistance* for *Once Over Lightly*, in the words of the ballerina Sono Osato, who was also in the revue, was a particularly "zany but touching vignette" featuring "an alley cat whose mother had just been run over by a Chock Full o'Nuts truck and was now hopelessly enamored of an obstreperous stray dog." Osato impersonated the cat; Gilford was the gentle squirrel philosophizing about starvation in Central Park; and Mostel, who stomped around rehearsals like "a petulant child in a miniature operetta about the making of Kreplach," was the howling, growling, barking, panting, and ogling stray dog.

Although they were comradely at parties, Brooks clashed with the director, Stanley Prager, whom everyone called "Stash" and who was "a gifted comedian in his own right," in Osato's words. Watching the cat, dog, and squirrel sketch being rehearsed one day, Brooks jumped up and pronounced it shit, shit, shit! Prager and Brooks went chin to chin heatedly before their expletive-filled argument was defused by general all-around laughter at its absurdity. Another time Brooks intervened, and "Stash" simply threw him out.

Nobody felt very optimistic on opening night, which had been preceded earlier in the day by a long, tension-filled run-through. The only happy note in the run-through had been another one of Brooks's interruptions—this one calculated to break the prevailing mood of gloom. He had abruptly taken center stage and delivered "an extemporaneous one-man operetta version of *Anna Karenina*, complete with howling wolves chasing Anna in her troika across the frozen steppes of Russia," in Osato's words, reducing the cast and crew to hysterical guffaws. Someone suggested that Brooks go on instead of the company, performing his one-man Tolstoy, and all of a sudden people's spirits lifted.

When *Once Over Lightly* opened in late February at the Barbizon-Plaza Theatre, however, the revue went over like a lead sinker with critics. Its run was brief. Then it was back to the limping Coca series, Brooks's main job, which had become a writer's nightmare.

• • •

With his erratic hours and insulting manner, Brooks quickly alienated Ernest Kinoy and Max Wilk, and finally he also ran afoul of
Lucille Kallen, once his champion, by treating her as a mere "typist"
in their increasingly strained arguments over what *The Imogene Coca
Show* scripts lacked in the way of comedy. "That's very funny, Mel,
but we can't use it," she told him one day. "Don't you tell me what's
funny," he retorted. "You just type!"

First Wilk and Kinoy were let go; then Kallen left, asking to have
her contract settled. Brooks stayed. The producers flew in a couple
of "name" writers from Hollywood, trying to fix the series, then
flew them back when they failed. To be fair, Coca was clueless
without Sid Caesar, and she rejected scripts at the eleventh hour
without providing constructive feedback. During that difficult
season she was also coping with her husband's serious illness, ending in his death, and the passing of her mother. The frazzled actress
began to skip episodes of the half-hour program; NBC ran "kine-
scopes," 16-millimeter prints made from the broadcasts and used
for different time slots and reruns.

With Kallen gone, Brooks briefly became the head writer. He
had a good contract: $1,750 per episode, second only to Kallen's.
Producer Don Appell brought in Tony Webster to help with the
scripts. But the series kept vacillating between situation comedy
and revue. The revolving door of writers had neither the power nor
the imagination to reinvent it.

Brooks couldn't save the show, not with his lateness and absences
and impracticable suggestions, often "substituting energy and noise
for any ideas," in the words of another writer in the rotation. He
and Webster were both closed out in late March along with Appell.
Obviously, as even his William Morris representative conceded,
Brooks was ill suited to be head writer of the series. He was a decided
"eccentric," according to his agent, Lester Colodny, "and, I'm guessing, ADD to the *n*th degree in a world that didn't even know what
attention deficit disorder meant."

Brooks had come home every day from the Coca series in a darker mood. The show was a stinker, and his contribution had been negative. His misery mounting, he thought wistfully of Sid Caesar. The precise format of *Caesar's Hour* had been a trade secret until its premiere that September, but the new program had come roaring out of the gate with splendid reviews and robust ratings. The reduced one-hour structure made the show easier on the star and writers; variety numbers were deemphasized in favor of comedy and sketches. "No small credit," *Variety* wrote, "belongs to the quartet of writers," naming Mel Tolkin, Tony Webster, and Joe Stein, all Caesar veterans, along with Aaron Ruben, "fugitive from the Milton Berle show . . . anything but a slouch."

"Mel," Brooks's wife urged him, "call Sid. He loves you. He'll take you back."

"No," he replied dismally, "I can't. I'm saving face."

"Just dial the number."

"He'll turn me down."

"He won't turn you down."

Brooks finally phoned, telling Caesar "I want to come back." Caesar said, "Okay, fine." Seven words—five from Brooks, two from Caesar—and he was set for the fall.


Florence Brooks danced intermittently on both *The Imogene Coca Show* and *Caesar's Hour*. Because her husband made at least $1,750 weekly, and she was making about $300, he paid the rent, and she covered household expenses, laundry, and all else. He was secretive about money. The honeymoon he had promised her never transpired.

Despite the rocky year he had undergone with Red Buttons, *Once Over Lightly*, and Imogene Coca, Brooks's income continued to rise. He had *Caesar's Hour* banked for the fall and as usual many other irons in the fire. Once again, over the summer of 1955, he could afford a bungalow in Ocean Beach, and the couple sunbathed, read books, and hobnobbed with Fire Island friends, some of them already prominent in show business circles, others destined for fame. Again the 2000 Year Old Man was a hit at parties among the NBC and Sid Caesar circle. With Carl Reiner softening Brooks's edges, the act was never in bad taste. Everybody loved it, and word began to spread.

At the end of the summer, Mr. and Mrs. Brooks moved their household once again, this time to a spacious, fashionable Upper East Side apartment on Fifth Avenue.

# CHAPTER 5

# 1955

## Club Caesar

A half hour shorter than *Your Show of Shows*, *Caesar's Hour* used three times as many staff writers. A small army contributed to the second-season premiere in the fall of 1955. Credited for the script were Mel Tolkin, Larry Gelbart, Melvin Brooks, Neil ("Doc," the credits say in parenthesis) Simon, Sheldon Keller, Michael Stewart, and Gary Belkin, in that order. Danny Simon pitched in frequently during the season, as did actress-writer Selma Diamond, who had contributed occasionally to *Your Show of Shows*; informally she replaced Lucille Kallen as the only distaff writer. (Diamond, not Kallen, inspired the Sally Rogers character played by Rose Marie on *The Dick Van Dyke Show*.)

Tony Webster had been sent packing (and over to the *Red Buttons Show*) midway through the first season after he had returned from a multiple-martini lunch one day and insulted Sid Caesar. Numerous other writers checked in for individual episodes. At one point *Variety* ran an eye-catching publicity item noting that "nine cleffers" had composed a single song for the show: in order were credited Caesar, Bernard Green (musical director), Tolkin, Gelbart, Brooks, Keller, Neil Simon, Stewart, and Belkin.

Taking the place of Imogene Coca was Nanette Fabray as the leading lady of *Caesar's Hour*. Carl Reiner and Howard Morris were still the second and third bananas, celebrities still made guest appearances, and the singers, musicians, and dancers rotated. The new series borrowed heavily from what had worked best on *Your Show of Shows*. "The Hickenloopers," for example, became the kindred "The Commuters" with Caesar and Fabray. The "hour" may have been shorter, but the comedy sketches tended to run longer and be more elaborate: for example, "Aggravation Boulevard," which was among the most fondly remembered of the silent era send-ups, featuring Caesar as a John Gilbert type whose high-pitched voice dooms his transition to talkies. Without Max Liebman pushing highbrow musical interludes, the show's song and dance numbers also trended toward humor, such as the memorable spoof with Caesar, Reiner, and Morris as The Three Haircuts, teen-idol crooners rocking and bopping to "You Are So Rare to Me."

Without Liebman or Coca, the show was truly Caesar's. The star was remarkably canny about what worked for him and, above all, canny about the writers he needed to make the show hum, hiring the best available and paying them as well as possible, goading them in story conferences ("Show me the brilliance!" he'd proclaim upon arrival in the morning), sprinkling their names into interviews, and touting them in trade advertisements. (That tradition began with *Your Show of Shows*: "You mean the show is not AD LIB? No, it's written by—MEL TOLKIN, LUCILLE KALLEN, MEL BROOKS.")

The *Caesar's Hour* writers' room, bigger and with more writers than in the past, was rented space in the Milgram Building on West 57th Street and Fifth Avenue. Even more than before, it was a battlefield of competitors vying for Caesar's attention and approval. They told proud war stories afterward. "We became our own fan club," Neil Simon once said.

Arriving late to the series, after its first season, nonetheless Brooks was a senior writer, slightly older than some of them but senior also from having been present, more or less, at the creation of *Your Show of Shows*. Although two years younger than the red-haired Michael Stewart, Brooks called Stewart "the Kid" or "the typist," because Brooks had seniority with Caesar. (Stewart, in his early thirties, was at the typewriter partly because he had been to college and been awarded an MFA by the Yale School of Drama. He could spell, punctuate, and type.) But when Brooks referred to Stewart as "the typist"at the Writers Guild reunion of Caesar writers in 1996, there was murmuring from the panel and Carl Reiner gently reminded Brooks that no, not in the first year of the series—*then* the typist had been Aaron Ruben. The writers from the first season of the series were sensitive to being overlooked, as they—not Brooks—had laid the foundations of *Caesar's Hour.*

They may have been the most illustrious writers ever assembled in one place since Shakespeare wrote alone, as someone wisecracked at the 1996 reunion. (Albeit that the shifting aggregation was not always actually in the same room at the same time.) Admittedly the *Caesar's Hour* writers' room was even more of a shout fest, although not everybody was a shouter. Mel Tolkin rarely shouted. Stewart was inclined toward quiet thoughtfulness. Larry Gelbart, originally from Chicago, raised in Los Angeles, was the gentleman of the lot, arguably the wittiest and least contentious. Neil Simon was quiet as a mouse and never in the least aggressive, as Brooks said in one interview. "[Simon] would have to tell Carl Reiner, who was aggressive, what his ideas were."

They went to work as gladiators, however, their words weapons as they pitched shtick, jokes, characters, and sketches. They fought for the privilege of one-upping one another and pleasing Caesar. They threw pencils at the walls and at one another. "We nearly got to punching each other," Brooks remembered. Caesar decided who the losers were in every confrontation, and each of the writers—the best of the best—was bloodied in turn.

One often had to shout just to get Caesar's attention, and Big Mel had long before noted Little Mel's penchant for shouting loudest or last, jumping up, and taking the floor, "adding jokes to our pages," in Tolkin's words. "He'd start ad-libbing, as if he were searching for some idea, some humorous angle. Then he'd warm up and soon be on a roll." "Mel's performance," Tolkin noted, was always shrewdly directed at Sid, the Boss.

Tolkin recalled the time the group had labored to solve the problem of how to finish a sketch that took place in an Irish saloon. It involved a fey leprechaun, played by Howard Morris, who is confronted by a skeptic: "If you have magical powers, prove it. Make it rain." Leprechaun: "It will rain!" Skeptic: "In the middle of July from a cloudless sky?"

What should the punch line be? The writers were stumped. One of them spoke mildly from his seated position behind Brooks, who was up and pacing. "It will rain—*inside* the saloon." Brooks, wheeling around for attention, shouted, "It will *RAIN INSIDE* the saloon!" Brooks, not the other writer, got "the approval, the laugh, the love," Tolkin recalled.

That practice of Brooks stealing from other writers never ceased to bother Tolkin, and it took him decades to forgive it. Brooks realized that, and one time after a similar "performance" he sat quietly beside Tolkin, throwing his arm around Big Mel. "I'm a counterpuncher," he confessed. "I come in after you and others have done your work."

Carl Reiner, by now in the script room as a writer as well as a performer—often credited separately for both—became Brooks's most sympathetic explainer. "[Brooks] wasn't writing," Reiner told an interviewer decades later. "He was talking words. He was writing with his mouth. He still writes better with his mouth than anybody I know. What is writing? Writing is thinking, talking. Then writing it down is something else."

In large part thanks to the internecine rivalry, *Caesar's Hour* was initially as magnificent a series as *Your Show of Shows*. With their ever-growing numbers, it was no less difficult to unravel which writer had written what remembered highlight. Someone would suggest a scene, Caesar would nod with approval, and Michael Stewart would begin to type. Then there would be step-by-step enrichment: emendations and embroidery, twists and turns, with Caesar adding his final touches and editing, often in front of the television camera.

To a person the writers of *Caesar's Hour*, Emmy nominated as a group for Best Comedy Writing for every season in which the show was broadcast, forged distinguished careers. Neil Simon became America's most recognized Broadway playwright. Larry Gelbart triumphed with *M\*A\*S\*H* on television and twice was Oscar nominated for his screenplays. Michael Stewart, "the typist," wrote the librettos for the stage musicals *Bye Bye Birdie* and *Hello, Dolly!* While not quite the same household names, the others were known inside the business as kings of comedy—the creators of many successful sitcoms.

The only way one could belong to that privileged club was to have written for Sid Caesar in the 1950s. Except for Lucille Kallen and Selma Diamond, the membership was men only. They belonged to an elite fraternity—Club Caesar. Mel Brooks's future screen comedies would never evidence a single female name among the writing credits.

Club Caesar worked by day and socialized at night throughout the 1950s, and then the group did much the same for the rest of their lives, often collaborating with one another on other projects, congregating in New York and Hollywood. There was always *schadenfreude* among the competitors but also permanent bonds of shared affection and respect. They had fought in the same war to make the best possible television show for Sid Caesar. With Caesar as their patriarch, they were more than a club; they were a professional family. One couldn't resign. Outsiders need not apply.


One day Florence Brooks felt stomach pangs during the dance rehearsals for *Caesar's Hour* and went to a doctor on her lunch hour, learning that she was pregnant. On February 21, 1956, she gave birth to a girl the couple named Stefanie ("Stefanie with an 'F,'" Brooks always emphasized). The *New York Times* published a news item, "Mrs. Melvin Brooks Has Child," which was another sign of Brooks's rising recognition.

Now Brooks was a father as well as a husband. Florence had experienced an earlier pregnancy in their relationship, but she had insisted upon an abortion because she had not wanted to box them into a premature marriage. Yet Brooks had wanted children, always.

New fatherhood and returning to the Caesar fold, combined with turning thirty in 1956, led him to end psychoanalysis after six years of appointments with Dr. Clement Staff. In interviews in later years, especially when he was promoting *High Anxiety*, the comedy in which he played a psychiatrist warding off real and imagined fears, Brooks recalled Dr. Staff as "kind and warm and bright," a doctor who had done his best to heal him.

For years Brooks was afraid of dying before the age when his father had passed. Ironically, although a genuine hypochondriac, physically he seemed built of India rubber and rarely took sick even for a day. He used his hypochondria to learn all he could about illnesses and diseases from books and medical journals; often he volunteered plausible medical advice to friends. He and his wife kept a floor-to-waist-high medicine chest in their apartment, crammed with prescription bottles. Where Florence's health was involved, Brooks showed a heartfelt concern not often manifest in their marriage.

Dr. Staff had diagnosed him as having "anxiety hysteria," Brooks said, which Merriam-Webster defines as "an anxiety disorder and especially a phobia when the mental aspects of anxiety are emphasized over any accompanying physical symptoms (as heart palpitations and breathlessness)—used especially in Freudian psychoanalytic theory."

Very early in the 1950s, he was a "psychological mess," according to Brooks, and suffered "real physical debilitation. To wit: low blood sugar and under-active thyroid." Insecure about his status as a well-paid television writer ("Writer! I'm not a writer. Terrible penmanship."), he ran "miles through city streets," underwent dizzy spells, was "nauseated for days," and vomited "between parked Plymouths" on his way to various places.

"The main thing I remember from [those days]," Brooks told *Playboy* in 1975, "is bouts of grief for no apparent reason. Deep melancholy, incredible grief where you'd think that somebody very close to me had died. You couldn't grieve any more than I was grieving."

More than once he told interviewers that analysis had saved him from thoughts of suicide.

In his sessions with Dr. Staff, Brooks could not really build the standard case against Freud's typical patsy: his mother. Kitty Kaminsky had been the greatest mother possible, the greatest cook and nurturer. She had a tremendous sense of humor. "All I could say was, 'She was swell.'" Brooks had enjoyed more alone time with Kitty than his brothers had, and his mother "was really responsible for the growth of my imagination." Nonetheless he felt "multiple guilt on every level," including guilt that maybe he had "failed my mother" and for collecting a higher weekly salary than his hardworking older brother Irving. He also felt guilty about never having really known his father.

Dr. Staff helped him link his feelings about his father's early passing to his apprehensions about fatherhood. His "anxiety hysteria" revolved around "accepting the mantle of being a person, a mature person," Brooks told one interviewer. "And deep down I felt I would die if I ever did that. Because as long as I was metamorphosing as a green shoot and not a tree there was no chance of dying: I was still growing. The minute I stopped and became an adult, soon I would become a father and I would die. Because my father was dead. Men die. Boys do not. That's how primitive and deep it was . . .

"And the other thing was that I didn't think I was capable of doing the job I was doing, really, and they would find me out."

Again and again in interviews Brooks said he had learned from Dr. Staff that his aggressive personality and sometimes crude comedic impulses sprang mainly from defense mechanisms: trying desperately to please his absent father, getting even with people who hadn't picked him for the neighborhood sports teams in boyhood, bitterness over the girls who had looked past him in his youth, and resentment for having been born short, poor, and Jewish, not resembling—by any stretch of the imagination—FDR or Cary Grant.

Jewish himself, Dr. Staff discussed the Jewish comedy heritage with Brooks. Freud had written about humor and especially Jewish humor; so had Theodor Reik in a famous paper called "Jewish Wit," in which the renowned analyst even approved of jokes about "bodily functions," one of Brooks's comedy mainstays. As Stefan Kanfer summarized Reik's beliefs in *A Summer World*, his book about the Catskills, Jewish jokes served a variety of purposes, including, at their most desperate, "the Jew sharpens, so to speak, the dagger which he takes out of his enemy's hand, stabs himself, then returns it gallantly to the Anti-Semite with the silent approach, 'Now see whether you can do it half as well.'"

According to Reik, Jewish humor could bring "relaxation in the ardor of battle with the seen and with the invisible enemy; to attract as well as to repel him; and last . . . to conceal oneself behind them. Jewish wit hides as much as it discloses. Like the seraph in the Temple of the Lord it covers its face with two of its wings."

Dr. Staff could explain why so many of the comedians Brooks loved—the Marx and Ritz brothers, the Three Stooges—were Jewish. He talked with Brooks about Nazism and the role of Jewish comedy in the post-Hitler world. *Your Show of Shows* and *Caesar's Hour* were subliminally Jewish in many ways, but they couldn't be explicitly

Jewish in that era. The 2000 Year Old Man setup had begun to draw on Brooks's Jewishness, this wellspring of his imagination, in private performances. Dr. Staff, citing Reik, could validate that emerging side of Brooks's comedy. It was natural, Dr. Staff said, for a Jew to be preoccupied with anti-Semitism, Hitler, the Nazis, and the Holocaust.

Freud also wrote extensively about the id, the ego, and the super-ego, and Brooks learned that terminology and used it a decade later to describe the naive Leopold Bloom (the ego) and the Falstaffian Max Bialystock (the id) in *The Producers*. Comedians, Freud believed, expressed the thoughts society forbade. A benevolent superego created a lighthearted, comforting humor, while the harsher super-ego created sarcastic humor. The ego and the id might be seen as the Jekyll and Hyde sides of behavior in a person.

In effect, according to Dr. Staff's analysis, there were a Nice Mel and a Rude Crude Mel. The Nice Mel loved people and wanted people to love him. The Nice Mel bore deep humanistic feelings and was attuned to literature and the arts. The Rude Crude Mel defended himself psychologically against possible slights and prej-udices by uncivil behavior and offensive humor. Though the two Mels coexisted, they also vied for supremacy within him. Neither of the Mels could ever be extinguished, so Brooks's struggle—for the rest of his life—would be to strike the right balance in his char-acter and his comedy.

Even though Brooks told *Playboy* that "most of my symptoms disappeared in the first year, and then we got into much deeper stuff," that was probably gilding the lily; it served hindsight and publicity. No one detected a dramatic change in his personality or professional comportment when he quit analysis—nor for years to come. Brooks still couldn't sleep at night and arrived late to work; his anger continued to seethe beneath the surface and revealed itself in bizarre, seemingly hostile, sometimes hilarious outbursts.

But he never returned to psychoanalysis, nor could he have done so with Dr. Staff, who was struck with a sudden illness and died only two years later, in 1958. Colleagues mourned the forty-seven-year-old analyst as an "ecstatic visionary" in his field.

Curiously, in all the many interviews he gave that touched on his six years of therapy—exploring the influence of his mother and father, his fears of illness and death, his conflicted identity as a writer, and his role as a Jewish writer of comedy—Brooks never once mentioned having discussed his wife or his marriage with Dr. Staff. About all he ever said on the record about his first marriage were variations on (per *Playboy*) "we had married too young. I expected I would marry my mother, and she expected she would marry her father." Or "the word 'more' comes into it. I think my first wife needed more. I needed more attention from the world, and less attention from a wife."

The only people Mrs. Brooks discussed her marriage with, apart from her own therapist, were close girlfriends. To the men in Club Caesar the Brooks marriage looked—on the surface—to be a perfect one. The writers and their spouses dominated the Brookses' social circle; there were many informal get-togethers at one another's houses. The couple also socialized frequently with Ronny Graham and his wife, singer Ellen Hanley, and comedian Alan King, who had grown up in Williamsburg with Brooks. A few times a year, Sid Caesar invited the Brookses to his Fifth Avenue apartment.

Brooks was careful around other couples to give the best impression of the marriage. Florence was the beautiful young mother, and he was the perpetual funnyman. In fact, Florence had grown increasingly uneasy since the first day of their marriage. Dancing jobs had alleviated her unhappiness, but with new motherhood her misery grew.

She knew her husband to be a different and less amusing man when their show business friends were not around. He saved his worst tantrums for her friends and relatives, it seemed. Coming home fuming from work, he'd grab her visitors and physically throw them out the door. Alone with her, the verbally gifted writer was often taciturn and gloomy, treading heavily around their apartment as though slogging through snowdrifts. He'd punch walls and doors in anger, leaving behind cracks or holes. Novelist James Jones, visiting the couple once in their apartment, wondered aloud at the peculiar blemishes on the walls and remarked at how barren the place appeared of personal items, furniture, and adornments. Their apartment seemed, he said, more like a rented space than a family home. Brooks chuckled, but Florence silently agreed.

His despondence was another kind of performance, she felt. One time, claiming to be overcome with despair, he vaulted out of their car at Morningside Heights and threatened to jump over a black iron fence into the roaring traffic below. His wife talked him back into the car, but she brooded over the incident with her girlfriends. They agreed with her that Brooks was, in today's parlance, a drama queen, always saying "Look at me!"

Florence tried to empathize. Brooks was under constant pressure to prove himself; his wife knew better than anyone else that he really did have trouble "typing," i.e., writing alone without a collaborator. At times, he complained, Caesar rejected his best stuff. He was earning the only paycheck in the family, and with fatherhood his burden intensified.

Florence, however, had sacrificed her career to motherhood; she had made no big decision about it—it just happened. Without any independent source of income, she no longer contributed to the household expenses. Brooks wanted her to concentrate on being a mother. She might have accepted jobs, but when the phone rang with offers Brooks would rush to answer, shouting "My wife is not going to shake her naked ass in Macy's windows!" then slam the receiver down. Later, crafting his semiautobiographical script

"Marriage Is a Dirty Rotten Fraud," Brooks wrote variations of that dialogue into scenes.

At home Brooks was penurious with Florence, making a ritual of slapping three one-dollar bills on the dresser every morning and telling her the three dollars were her daily allowance. She had no access to his bank account or investments, no real idea of his financial worth. Although he allowed her a few charge accounts for household and personal belongings, he watched the bills like a hawk, exploding at "unnecessary expenses."

Florence was afraid to ask him for money because of his sharp-tempered rebukes, which cut her like knives. Once he yelled at her, "Who do you think you are, a diva like Marguerite Piazza?" before storming off. His standard insult when she brought up money: "You should never marry a woman who is either poor or Jewish, and I did both!"

He was hardly a homebody; he was always out and about or stuck at NBC or hanging out at Danny's Hideaway with Caesar and the other writers talking after the workday, frequently coming home very late, saying the script had needed extra attention. But Florence knew that the work couldn't have gone on that late because she had just gotten off the phone with Pat Gelbart, Joan Simon, or another Club Caesar spouse and knew that the other writers had been home for hours. Florence had suspicions but tried to put them out of her mind. It was a peaceful blessing when Brooks wasn't home. He'd often arrive in a sour mood, and even after finally nodding off he might jump up suddenly and begin sleepwalking, noisily taking down the odd painting or framed certificate from the walls.

Most of the time Florence felt helpless and alone. Most of the time she *was* alone, at home with the baby, while Brooks roamed the streets until late. And if one of her female friends happened to be visiting when he did show up, he was especially gruff and unpleasant, because he suspected his wife of sharing confidences with her girlfriends.

In the past the couple had often visited museums together. On weekends now, Brooks was more likely to traipse around New York galleries and museums with Zero Mostel and the painter Robert Gwathmey. Another new acquaintance was the Columbia Records press agent Walter "Wally" Robinson, with whom Brooks played long, intense chess matches. Robinson facilitated entrées to clubs and music recording sessions.

Passive and insecure, Florence never confronted her husband; she let her unhappiness slide. She feared his explosions. Busy being a new mother, she did not have time to think very much about their estrangement, and she kept hoping the marriage would improve. By early 1957, besides, she was pregnant with their second child.

The third year of *Caesar's Hour* was destined to be its last. Although the cancellation was not announced until the end of the 1956–57 season, everyone foresaw the descent of the guillotine.

Nanette Fabray had left the show in a pay dispute, and NBC had switched the series from Monday nights to Saturdays opposite *The Lawrence Welk Show* on ABC. To the everlasting consternation of Club Caesar, famous later as the crème de la crème among writers, Lawrence Welk topped Caesar in the ratings. The sponsors began to flee, while the production costs, bloated by the talent and writers' fees, rose to $110,000 weekly by September 1956.

In those days the bland bandleader reigned in Middle America, where many more Americans owned television sets now than in the heyday of *Your Show of Shows*. The first TVs had belonged mainly to affluent, well-educated Americans on the East Coast.

Once upon a time Caesar had prided himself on presenting the most sophisticated comedy and variety format on television.

Sophistication was no longer as viable. Nobody thought *Caesar's Hour* had become guarded or stale, but the episodes varied in quality, and critics complained about its unevenness. Caesar, in spite of the booze and pills, was still superb much of the time. The show was still superb. That was the tragedy of it.

*Caesar's Hour* was Emmy nominated for Best Variety Show each of the three years it was aired and it won in 1956. Caesar himself was nominated every year in his category of lead performer, and he also won in 1956. In that second season of 1955–56, the year Brooks joined the writing staff, the show garnered multiple Emmys: Best Series, Best Continuing Performance by a Comedian in a Series (Caesar), Best Continuing Performance by a Comedienne (Nanette Fabray), Best Supporting Performance by an Actor (Carl Reiner).

For three years in a row the writing staff, including Brooks for two of those years, was nominated for Best Comedy Writing. In the first two years Club Caesar lost to Nat Hiken's similarly lauded troop of scribes for *The Phil Silvers Show* (a group now including former Caesar colleague Tony Webster). By the third and last year of the show, when the contenders assembled for the annual dinner at the Waldorf-Astoria, *Caesar's Hour* had been off the air for months, and the writers prayed to beat Phil Silvers, who was seated at a nearby table.

That was an anecdote Brooks loved to recount, embroidering the facts with fancy. When the Phil Silvers staff was announced as winners for the third consecutive year, a livid Brooks stood on his chair, or table—accounts differ—screaming "Nietzsche was right! There is no God! There is no God!" In one interview he said his rage did not abate: on the way home in a taxi with his wife, he claimed, he grabbed a manicure scissors from her purse and proceeded to cut his tuxedo into strips. According to Mel Tolkin in his unpublished memoir, Brooks merely reached for the mike that sat at each table for the winners and shouted into it. Still, Brooks and Tolkin—all of Caesar's writers—felt crushed.

• • •

At the outset of the third and final season of *Caesar's Hour,* most of the writers were already taking side jobs when they could, anticipating a future without Sid Caesar.

Brooks certainly moonlighted, as he always had. Besides his responsibilities for the Caesar show, he was immersed in yet another Broadway musical, called *archy and mehitabel,* based on the popular World War I–era stories of *New York Sun* columnist Don Marquis, who had imagined a friendship between a slinky back-alley cat named mehitabel and a philosophical cockroach named archy. A poet and storyteller, archy can type only one letter at a time and can't manage the shift key; hence the names in lowercase.

Composer George Kleinsinger and lyricist Joe Darion had developed *archy and mehitabel* over years. They presented a Town Hall concert version in 1954, and that same year Columbia Records produced a "concept album" of *archy and mehitabel: A Back Alley Opera,* which broadened its jazz stylings and featured Eddie Bracken and Carol Channing as archy and mehitabel. Bracken had committed to a Broadway adaptation, while Channing's involvement depended on how the scheduling panned out. The momentum of the Broadway musical slowed down because Darion, who could not be faulted as a lyricist (he would go on to write *Man of La Mancha* and its signature anthem, "The Impossible Dream"), struggled to complete a satisfactory book on his own.

In late December 1956, the planned musical got a boost when Eartha Kitt agreed to play mehitabel. But Darion needed a collaborator. Brooks knew several key people behind the scenes of the production, and he boasted an especially close friendship with Kitt, the breakout star of *New Faces of 1952.* Also, Brooks loved cats; he already had cat short stories and sketches in his background and could relate to a cockroach that typed badly.

Involved early on in the packaging of *archy and mehitabel,* in January 1957 the William Morris Agency arranged for Brooks to come to

Darion's aid on the libretto. His contract guaranteed he would share the book credit, his name listed second and for the first time (in a departure from the ongoing *Caesar's Hour*) as "Mel Brooks." Darion and Kleinsinger's *archy and mehitabel* got a spiffy new title: *Shinbone Alley*.

The indefatigable writer stole time away from *Caesar's Hour* and labored nights and weekends to get *Shinbone Alley* ready for its April 13, 1957, opening at the Broadway Theatre. Differences with the writers led the director, Norman Lloyd, to leave the musical a week before its premiere, adding to the unease surrounding the show. The producer, Peter Lawrence, took over for the final rehearsals. For that and other reasons *Shinbone Alley* failed to live up to the high expectations for it. Many critics singled out problems with the libretto: John McClain of the *New York Journal-American* lamented the book's "long lapses," and Thomas R. Dash in *Women's Wear Daily* likewise bemoaned the "languid patches." Brooks Atkinson in the *New York Times* said that the musical "does not really come alive."

Although Brooks's disaffection with critics had begun with those who had hastened the demises of *Your Show of Shows* and *Caesar's Hour*, it was here, with *Shinbone Alley*, that the animus hardened and they became lifelong foes. Brooks Atkinson (who had hailed *New Faces of 1952*) and other New York reviewers betrayed him with their negative notices.

"We thought we were bringing happiness and joy to people, and I was just sitting on top of the world," Brooks recalled angrily four decades later. "It didn't get one good review," he continued, exaggerating the negativity of the notices, "and closed in a week."

*Shinbone Alley* actually managed to last for forty-nine performances and, like *New Faces of 1952*, it had a robust afterlife. A cast recording was released. Eddie Bracken and Tammy Grimes starred in a television version in 1960. It was animated in 1971 with the voices of Eddie Bracken and Carol Channing. And to this day regional theaters across the United States and around the world occasionally revive the odd musical about a cat and cockroach.

The best reviews for the 1957 musical went to its two stars, Eddie Bracken and Eartha Kitt. The latter was especially otherworldly, Atkinson wrote in the *Times*. Her husky singing was "electric with personality," her dance numbers transfixing and positively catlike.

Florence Brooks, who was newly pregnant, rented a white mink stole to drape over her best evening dress and took a taxi alone to the opening. Afterward Mrs. Brooks wove backstage and glimpsed her husband through the open door to Kitt's dressing room. The two were exchanging heated words and struggling physically. Kitt refused to come out to meet the writer's wife. As Brooks finally emerged with a stone face, Bracken took him aside. Florence overheard the *Shinbone Alley* star's admonishment: "Mel, what are you doing? You have a nice, beautiful, pregnant wife. Why are you fooling around?"

Brooks quickly explained to Florence that he had to attend the opening-night cast party, where wives were not welcome. Ushering Florence outside, he escorted her down the street, trying to hail a cab. "Wait!" he said, then dashed into the Stage Deli and emerged with a bag containing a corned beef sandwich. He handed it to her and thrust her into a taxi. That night he came home very late— not all that unusual—at 5:00 a.m.

Florence had danced in Broadway shows, however, and knew her husband was lying about the cast party. Spouses and intimates were always welcome. She realized that he and Kitt were having an affair. But she didn't bring it up to his face; she was too passive and felt humiliated and wondered if, in some way, her own shortcomings were to blame. She told only a few girlfriends. She continued to hope for changes in their marriage. Pregnant with their second child, she had no other choice—no means of earning an income.

Soon enough it was summer anyway. Both *Caesar's Hour* and *Shinbone Alley* ended, and as usual the couple went off, this time by limousine, to Fire Island, where they had leased their biggest cottage yet. They sunbathed and swam and socialized with old and new friends also taking beach vacations. The 2000 Year Old Man was in increasing demand, and the parties expanded to include elder statesmen of Broadway and Hollywood, who laughed and applauded alongside the younger crowd. Carl Reiner lugged around a portable reel-to-reel recorder and taped the living room performances, "concerned that my probing questions and Mel's brilliant ad-lib answers might be lost to posterity," according to Reiner. The tapes might be useful in polishing the act.

One of their enthralled new fans was Fire Island summer denizen Joseph "Joe" Fields, who belonged to a famous family of stage producers (his father, Lew Fields) and librettists (his sister, Dorothy, and brother, Herbert). In his sixties, Fields was a prolific author of hit plays and musicals, often in collaboration with Jerome Chodorov, including *My Sister Eileen* (the second screen version of which Brooks had toiled on briefly in Hollywood) and *Wonderful Town*. Most recently Fields had written the *Gentlemen Prefer Blondes* musical with Jule Styne in which Florence Baum had been dancing when she met Brooks. Fields became "our number one benefactor," in Reiner's words, promising to arrange a New York dinner party where the duo could perform for the royalty of Broadway: Billy Rose, Alan Jay Lerner, Frederick Loewe, Harold Rome, and Moss Hart.

As was true when they were home in Manhattan, the Brookses' summer cottage often filled with friends and acquaintances, although they rarely if ever hosted private dinners with just one other couple. "We lived next door to them [on Fire Island] for a while," recalled their neighbor Hope Holiday, a singer-dancer who was friends with Mrs. Brooks. (Holiday had performed in *Gentlemen Prefer Blondes* and *Top Banana*, and her husband was Sandy Glass, the William Morris talent agent now representing Brooks.) "[Mel] always used to say, 'When are you going to come over and have dinner?' But whenever we tried to nail him to a date it didn't work out, so we never did have dinner with them."

• • •

Club Caesar—the "name" writers who had been Emmy nominated as a group and whose close bonds had been forged in daily creative strife and prime-time triumph—would stay loyal to Caesar and stick together on non-Caesar projects for decades to come. Caesar united them professionally and deeply influenced their work and their approaches to comedy.

The majority of Brooks's projects in the immediate post–*Caesar's Hour* years were, one way or another, referrals or collaborations with members in good standing of this band of brothers. Often Brooks's partner was Mel Tolkin, but other projects had links to Michael Stewart, "the typist," who was equally friendly with both Mr. and Mrs. Brooks.

*The Polly Bergen Show* was almost an Upper East Side neighborhood thing. A popular actress, singer, and television host, Bergen was getting ready to launch a half-hour variety show on NBC, airing on alternate Saturdays in the fall of 1957. Howard Morris was set as one of her costars, and Stewart had been enlisted as a writer. The Brookses lived next door to Bergen and her husband, the talent agent Freddie Fields, who'd started out at the Music Corporation of America (MCA) booking Dean Martin and Jerry Lewis. Bergen and Mrs. Brooks strolled through Central Park together with their young children.

Brooks joined up to write for Bergen's new show, with options for directing episodes that didn't interest Stewart. However, Brooks's deal was not worked out in time for him to impact the premiere in September, which was poorly reviewed; the original producer was then dismissed, and Brooks became a "writer-producer." By comparison, *Variety* said, the first half hour under Brooks's stewardship, in early October, was "snappy and clean."

The series became complicated for Brooks, however, after two episodes spotlighting the English actress and comedienne Kay

Kendall, who was making her TV debut in the United States. Kendall had just starred in the MGM musical *Les Girls*. Her episodes were excellent, with Howard Morris and Kendall lighting up the small screen with ebullient song medleys. (Singing tended to overshadow comedy on *The Polly Bergen Show*.) Backstage, though, Brooks fawned over the tall, leggy, brunette actress, embarrassing some onlookers. He had done much the same kind of over-the-top flirting with the bosomy Italian screen star Gina Lollobrigida during her guest stint on *Caesar's Hour*.

The stars' husbands—Rex Harrison in the case of Kendall—were never far away when the shows were produced. With Brooks, an incessant flirter, it was not always clear if he intended the flirting to lead anywhere or if the flirting reached any fruition. Brooks told some people he had had a fling with Kendall, later even taunting his wife with the boast of "a sexual relationship," according to Mrs. Brooks's claim in later court records.

One group of people Brooks usually courted with extra charm were wealthy or famous personalities, famous women especially; celebrities got a pass from him on every level, even if they later turned out to be not nearly as much fun as their fame implied.

Not long after Kendall's last appearance on the series, Brooks's well-paid job ended abruptly. Lyricist Lee Adams was waiting outside his office for an assignment when Brooks came out with a long face and told him he had just been fired. *The Imogene Coca Show* had proved he was neither comfortable with nor adept at writing for women, and Bergen's show had affirmed that weakness. Actresses rarely played leads in Brooks's later big-screen comedies; they might get juicy parts, but the parts were usually secondary.

Bergen's series lasted only eighteen episodes before NBC terminated it. Yet Brooks had a survivor's ability to take something positive away from almost any bad experience, and he was able to stay on friendly terms with both Bergen and Fields. The latter would be a useful connection in the future when Fields broke away from MCA to form a new talent agency, Creative Management Associates (CMA), with his partner David Begelman.

Fortunately, Sid Caesar had other work waiting for Brooks. Initially Caesar had not budged in his negotiations with NBC, refusing, after the cancellation of *Caesar's Hour*, the network's proposal to further downsize his series into a half hour. ("There are only twenty-four minutes in a half-hour show," he noted, "and I have nothing to say in twenty-four minutes.") He had been off the air since the demise of *Caesar's Hour*.

In the end he caved in, however, taking a counteroffer from ABC for the new *Sid Caesar Invites You*, which boasted the same half-hour time constraint he previously had abjured. The ABC series was set to bow in January 1958. One attraction for Caesar of the ABC half hour was that it reunited him with Imogene Coca. Carl Reiner would also return to the lineup. More than ever the emphasis would fall on comedy. Once again Mel Tolkin was the chief writer of the series, along with Brooks, Neil Simon and his brother Danny, and Michael Stewart. (Larry Gelbart contributed only to the premiere.)

"Just so long as [Caesar and Coca] don't get egghead and do stuff that gets esoteric," one ABC vice president was quoted anonymously (and ominously) in *The New York Times Magazine* as saying, "I mean takeoffs on Japanese movies that nobody has even been to an art theatre in New York to see. They've got to give it that old common denominator—empathy."

After initially bright reviews, however, the show's familiarity bred contempt. The series began to falter in its 9:00 p.m. Sunday slot opposite *The General Electric Theater* and *The Dinah Shore Show*. The sponsor, Helena Rubinstein cosmetics, withdrew its support. The only vote of confidence came from BBC-TV in England, which offered Caesar a reported $140,000-plus to re-stage the series as a summer offering in London. The BBC rendition would also be a half hour, but the generous budget allowed Caesar to bring an entourage with him to London, including Brooks, Stewart, and head writer Tolkin.

Not long after word began to spread of the summer ahead in London, Brooks became a father for the second time, with Florence giving birth to their first son on December 13. The boy was named Nicholas or "Nicky" after Nikolai Gogol, an author they both revered.

His wife had made the private decision to escape from her marriage somehow after their second child was born. Her unhappiness at home, her husband's cold treatment of her, went unabated. He had an "ungovernable and vicious temper," according to later court documents. She suffered barrages of insults from her husband and "great humiliation, degradation, shame and embarrassment" before her friends and children.

Florence had been devastated by Brooks's affair with Eartha Kitt and by what had happened on the night of the *Shinbone Alley* premiere. Later she discovered a little black book of women's names belonging to Brooks that bore notations suggesting that her husband "has had sexual relations or openly associated with each of said women." When Florence was incapacitated or unwilling to go to bed with him, he upbraided her by boasting of the many beautiful actresses who had slept with him and were willing to do so again. He continued to go out most nights, often not coming home until dawn and refusing to account for his absences "except to state that he had been out having relations with other women."

Although some of her girlfriends knew about his womanizing, they tried to shield Florence. "It wasn't a good marriage," recalled Hope Holiday. "He cheated on her left, right, and center. I didn't tell her a lot of things that I knew because I didn't want to hurt her."

When the upcoming London trip was dangled in front of her, Florence temporized. Steffie was not yet two when Nicky was born; Florence had no profession or livelihood. Her father and grandparents were English. She yearned to go to London.

• • •

They knew, before the *Queen Elizabeth* sailed in late May, that future American sponsors were allergic to *Sid Caesar Invites You* and that ABC would take the series off the air indefinitely in the United States after its last broadcast. The news did not dampen their spirits, however.

Among the some 2,500 passengers on board the *Queen Elizabeth* were the Brookses, the Tolkins, Michael Stewart, and numerous mutual acquaintances including Leonard Bernstein's sister, Shirley; the documentary filmmaker Ofra Bikel (ex-wife of actor-folksinger Theodore Bikel); and Stella Adler.

Most of the friends and friends of friends enjoyed a carefree ten-day crossing. They played shuffleboard on deck and all kinds of memory and charades-type games to pass the time. At night they danced to the orchestra that held forth in the dining room.

By all accounts Brooks was the star of the crossing, always light and easy in his manner and making everyone laugh all the time, "almost to a fault," as Ofra Bikel recalled. There was no "off" button on that voyage. It took Bikel a few days to realize that the woman so often at Brooks's side was his wife; there were no telltale signs, including children, because Brooks had insisted on leaving two-and-a-half-year-old Steffie and six-month-old Nicky at home under the watch of his wife's mother, a nanny, and housekeepers. The wife, Florence, was not laughing much. "I was surprised to learn they were married," Bikel recalled. "They didn't act married. They didn't look married."

In London the couple moved into a hotel room while Brooks looked for a summer rental. Sid Caesar and Imogene Coca arrived separately by plane. Brooks spent his days huddled with the stars and working on the scripts with Tolkin and Stewart at the Shepherd's Bush production center, preparing for the first broadcast in July. Most of the pages would be spruced up from the half season of *Sid Caesar Invites You*. The main sketches as usual revolved around

Caesar and Coca; as with most Caesar shows, dancers and singers, including the Metropolitan Opera tenor William Lewis, were interwoven.

Brooks's wife had time to sightsee and to make a side trip to Italy, visiting a vacationing girlfriend. After returning to London for a few days, Florence began to worry about her children in New York and flew home, debating whether she would return to London.

While at home she took a phone call from the Italian vacationer, who had just returned to New York via London. Her girlfriend warned her that, one by one, Brooks was working his way through the chorus girls in Caesar's show. However, Brooks phoned a few days later and told her he had just leased a house in South Kensington. She should hurry back, he said. She did not want to return without their older child, and Brooks said okay, bring Steffie. They flew to London in time for the show's premiere.

After "unusually strident advance publicity," in the words of *The Times* of London, the BBC version of *Sid Caesar Invites You* proved "disappointing." Caesar and Coca were okay in their performances, but overall the program gave "no impression of the qualities which are said to have held American audiences in thrall." Something may have been lost in translation: *Variety*, reviewing the same premiere, said it gave a "favorable impression" with "solid yocks," even if overall it was "disjointed."

But Caesar's half-hour series, aired Tuesday nights at 8:00 p.m., competed against the top-rated *Emergency—Ward 10* on ITV, a commercial network, and it did no better in English ratings than it did with English critics (with the notable exception of a rave from *Punch*). Caesar had the drawback of being a virtual unknown in the United Kingdom, and besides his comic edge had begun "to blunt," in Mel Tolkin's words. Serial television had exhausted him and his talent, Brooks often told interviewers later. When Caesar and Coca appeared at a London benefit that summer, "The Night of a Thousand Stars," doing one of their surefire sketches from *Your*

*Show of Shows*, Sid emitted his nervous cough throughout the performance, which was "a theatrical disaster." The audience barely chuckled.

Caesar hoped that the BBC might offer him a fall series. Instead his second banana, Cliff Norton, who had been brought over to substitute for Carl Reiner, got those kinds of feelers. (Reiner had skipped London to finish his first novel, the quasiautobiographical *Enter Laughing*.) Caesar returned to the United States, tail between his legs, and quickly took the only deal ABC was willing to offer—for a string of "specials," not another weekly series.

In the end Caesar derived little professional or personal enjoyment from his BBC sojourn, according to Tolkin, while for Brooks and everyone else, that summer in London was virtually a holiday spree. A generally upbeat mood prevailed among the Americans.

Brooks circulated widely, forming lasting attachments in the city. One of the guests of "The Night of a Thousand Stars" was actor and comedian Peter Sellers, who was just then transitioning from *The Goon Show* on BBC Radio to attention-getting leads on television and in motion pictures. They talked about working together one day.

Brooks's house in South Kensington was large enough to accommodate non–Club Caesar friends whom the writer invited to join them in London: Ronny Graham and his wife came along with everyone's favorite add-on, the easygoing Speed Vogel, the New Yorker, Fire Islander, and passionate devotee of the arts, who toiled in his wife's textile business. Only a few people noticed any strain between the Brookses; the couple spent little time alone together and took excursions with shifting clusters of friends and the Club Caesar colony, sometimes including Coca, to Rome, Paris, and Madrid.

When not busy with the summer series, Brooks and Michael Stewart were toiling away on a "spec" TV series for Kay Thompson that Stewart had initiated in New York.* A droll, sophisticated

---

* "Spec" is an entertainment industry term for a script written "speculatively," without any advance payment, contract, or guarantees the material will be produced.

singer and actress on radio and in supper clubs, Thompson was also known for her lucrative sideline as the author of the Eloise series of children's books. Lately she had been working in Hollywood as a singer and songwriter, and earlier in 1957 she had made a splash with her third-billed role in Stanley Donen's *Funny Face*.

Brooks had adored Thompson since first seeing her act, which combined songs and comic monologues, at the Roxy after World War II; he followed her whenever she performed at niteries and had never forgotten her 1954 "wow" appearance on TV's *The Buick-Berle Show*, in which the comedienne, surrounded by male dancers, had sung "I Love a Violin."

A television series starring Thompson was the brainchild of the Brooklyn-born lawyer Theodore "Ted" Granik, a moderator of radio and TV shows, who hired first Stewart and then Tony Webster to draft a "pilot for Kay Thompson." Webster drifted away, and Brooks became Stewart's partner on the project. During off-hours in London, the Club Caesar duo completed a twenty-eight-page teleplay featuring Thompson as the editor of a fashion magazine, "juggling her business affairs in Manhattan with domestic duties in Westchester," according to her biographer, where her husband, two children, and a stuffy housekeeper constantly complain about her "gallivanting off to the city every day."

When Stewart's interest began to wane, the project was ceded to Brooks. Although they were jointly paid $2,000 for the "spec" pilot, Brooks eventually had advantages over Stewart in his payments, royalties, and profits if any network picked up the series. Sometimes Brooks got the better deal simply because he had tougher deal makers on his side. Often he gained an edge by pleading poverty, children, and career exigencies. Stewart didn't care; he was more interested in Broadway than in TV, and that summer the budding producer Edward Padula and the composing team of Charles Strouse and Lee Adams approached him to work on the musical that would become *Bye Bye Birdie*. Stewart dropped the Thompson series and left London in August before everyone else.

Accompanied by Speed Vogel, Mr. and Mrs. Brooks took one last jaunt to Cap d'Antibes on the Côte d'Azur at the end of August before returning to the United States at the end of the summer. In the Hotel du Cap, even as Florence was desperately trying to avoid lovemaking and scheming to get out of her marriage, their third child was conceived.


Not everyone thought Brooks was so funny when they first met him. Often people needed time to get used to his sense of humor and become accustomed to his manner.

Sometime in the fall of 1958, it must have been, the Brookses were invited to dinner at the home of actor Hal March, who was married to actress Candy Toxton. The Marches were squiring around a newcomer, Johnny Carson, a former comedian turned game show panelist and daytime television host, who had recently moved to New York from Hollywood.

The Brookses knew March, who now hosted *The $64,000 Question*, from *The Imogene Coca Show*, where he had played Coca's spouse in one of the incarnations of the doomed series. The dinner went okay except that Brooks, anxious to make an impression on the guest of honor, took over the occasion with his loud jokes and antics. Carson left feeling nonplussed. A few years would pass before Carson took over *The Tonight Show* and came around to thinking that Brooks was one of the funniest men alive.

Brooks tried just as hard—twice—to win over Jerry Lewis. The first time was in the fall of 1958, when he helped write a television special for the established entertainer. Not since his 1953 stint at Columbia Pictures had Brooks visited Hollywood, once the nation's flourishing film capital, nowadays looking more like a television capital. Moviegoers by the millions had defected to the small screen, and the major studios had cut back drastically on film production and were pouring their resources into the TV revolution.

Lewis was his idol of idols. Brooks loved Lewis's idiotic, childish humor, his spastic comedy, his mock-suave singing—all components of Brooks's own formative public persona. A writer besides, Lewis was the whole package in a way that Harry Ritz had never been. Many people in Brooks's circle—his wife, too—shared a professional background with Lewis, who had now split from his partner Dean Martin. Many of Brooks's writer friends—Norman Lear included—had worked for Lewis. Brooks knew it would be a trial by fire.

Yet he was dying for the opportunity. Mel Tolkin had written an earlier special for Lewis, who told Tolkin he could bring a collaborator along with him to Hollywood. Word got around. Tolkin's phone rang: one call was from Brooks, pleading for the job, another from Tony Webster. Both were qualified, but Big Mel thought it over and reached out to the more amicable Neil Simon. ("Best decision I ever made," Tolkin said later.)

Tolkin had passed on a second offer from Lewis, having had his fill of the notoriously crazed and difficult-to-please comedian during that first experience. So Brooks and fellow Club Caesar veteran Danny Simon got the nod for the fall 1958 premiere of *The Jerry Lewis Show*, which NBC was producing on the West Coast. A third known quantity, Harry Crane, a creator of *The Honeymooners*, would be joining them.

By the last week of September, Brooks was again ensconced in the Chateau Marmont, all expenses paid along with his largest salary to date. Lewis's TV special would follow the usual variety format with singing and dancing interludes, but the writers focused on the comedy, including the main sketch, on which Brooks made his greatest contribution. The sketch involved a sad sack against whom even foul weather conspires; he is forced into a movie theater, where he finds true love in the form of a sad sackess.

Brooks didn't bite his tongue when Lewis, at one of the very first story conferences for the special, told his well-paid pencil pushers that no matter how great a script they might write, it wouldn't make the grade for him. "Boys," Lewis announced, "I don't want to *do* the script. I want to get out there, and I want something magic to happen."

"Get Mandrake!" Brooks quipped. "Don't hire us."

"I—want—magic," Lewis repeated solemnly. "I want every word, every gesture, every sound to be spontaneous and exciting as it was in the Commedia dell'Arte."

The writers looked at one another, dumbstruck.

Lewis behaved like a teenager on espresso, running around the room, waving his arms, jumping onto his desk to shout, taking their ideas, if he accepted them as feasible, and performing them with bizarre exaggerations in order to turn *their* ideas into *his* ideas. Brooks, too, was known to jump onto desks, shout, perform, and fold other writers' suggestions into his own. But he couldn't out-shout Lewis, and deference inhibited him.

The story conferences were more cacophonous than those of Club Caesar; they got to be too much, and at one point Brooks vowed aloud, "I'll never work for you again, Jerry!"

Miraculously, the script came together for the October 18, 1958, broadcast, and although it was probably in the wording of his deal, Brooks was billed ahead of Simon and Crane on-screen. Lewis was pleased with the result. He told Brooks that his movies had become so successful, Paramount was thinking of letting him direct one. First he would have to direct another TV special, as a kind of try-out. He and Brooks really must work together again, Lewis said. Brooks reminded him of his vow. "Forget that," Lewis said.

In no hurry to return to New York, his wife, and his family, Brooks lingered on the West Coast, skipping Sid Caesar's first

ABC-TV special in early November. Larry Gelbart and Woody Allen, the latter joining Caesar's staff for the first time, penned the show.

Brooks felt the tug of Hollywood, its doors swinging open wide as the film studios, foundering, grabbed onto television ideas. He networked with Hillard Elkins, a Brooklynite once with the William Morris Agency, who'd represented the Kay Thompson project and brought Michael Stewart together with his clients Charles Strouse and Lee Adams for *Bye Bye Birdie*. Elkins, whom everyone called "Hilly," had offices in both New York and Hollywood, and he represented major small-screen personalities such as Perry Como and Patti Page. A self-important type who would go on to become a top Broadway producer, Elkins was a man people loved to hate, and Brooks was wary when Elkins tried to get him under personal contract. While jumping around agencies in the late 1950s, however, Brooks did succumb briefly to Elkins before having second thoughts.

Another displaced East Coaster with whom Brooks reestablished contact was Marvin Schwartz, whom he knew through the music publicist Wally Robinson. Schwartz had been an advance man for the promoter Norman Granz at Jazz of the Philharmonic jam sessions in New York, but now he was a partner in Lewin, Kaufman & Schwartz, a high-powered show business public relations firm in Hollywood. Schwartz dreamed of becoming a movie producer one day. The publicist was more of a bohemian kindred spirit, and together Brooks and Schwartz made the scene at clubs and recording sessions.

One of Jerry Lewis's friends was the drummer Bill Richmond, a backup musician in Lewis's early stage act, who, Lewis thought, was as bright and funny as anyone he knew. Richmond had been booked for the prestigious Capitol recording sessions with Frank Sinatra produced by Nelson Riddle, and he invited Brooks along to watch and observe Sinatra up close and hone the Ol' Blue Eyes imitation that was already in his repertoire. (His Sinatra imitation, first performed in the Catskills, later became a talk show staple of his and was incorporated into *High Anxiety*.) Brooks self-promoted his "huge ego," Richmond recalled, touring the recording studio during breaks, shaking the hands of musicians with the refrain "Hi, I'm Mel Brooks! I wrote the Sid Caesar show!"

When Florence's father passed away a few days before Thanksgiving, Brooks flew back to New York for the funeral. He took her an autographed photo of Lewis, who sentimentally had chosen one of him and Dean Martin together, reminding Florence that he had known her back when she was a dancer in their act, fondly inscribing it "What gams!"

# CHAPTER 6

# 1957

## The Genius Awakes

ABC broadcast Sid Caesar's first special of the new season on a Sunday night in October. After the ABC show, the comedian rejoined NBC and presided over several more specials for his old network over the course of the 1958–59 season. Although Brooks walked in and out throwing off sparks, he did not receive credit until the last special in May 1959. Officially, this was the first collaboration between Brooks and Woody Allen, Caesar's latest astute hire. Only twenty-three, an introverted personality, Allen had been forewarned that Brooks might "eat you alive," in Allen's words, "he's so difficult to get along with and so high-pressure." Girding himself for "a really unpleasant experience," Allen instead met the Nice Mel, "as nice, amusing, intelligent as could be—he was so nice to me."

That one-hour Sunday-night special returned to familiar Caesar terrain: "At the Movies." Art Carney and Audrey Meadows from *The Honeymooners* were the guest stars, as they had been for other Caesar specials during the season, along with the dance team Bambi Lynn and Rod Alexander evoking memories of *Your Show of Shows*. The highlights included a drive-in movies skit, a spoof cavalcade of musicals, and another of Caesar's bravura silent picture send-ups with the star as a Rudolph Valentino type, Meadows his preening costar, and Carney their exasperated director. Caesar's refurbishing of old material alienated some critics, even *Variety* complaining about the "spotty scripting."

The familiarity was comforting to other reviewers, however, and the ratings for the specials were solid. After his rocky previous year with *Sid Caesar Invites You*, Caesar had regained his footing. Switching once more to CBS, he got the budget and go-ahead for another year. Brooks accepted a contract second only to Mel Tolkin's, and he, Tolkin, and Sydney Zelinka would write a half-dozen more Caesar specials for 1959–1960.

The Kay Thompson pilot script, meanwhile, was being hawked to the networks. Brooks was optimistic about its chances. Besides chief writer, he had an option in his contract for directing episodes if the series was developed, and for producing the series.

As his ambitions broadened, Brooks switched his representation from the William Morris Agency to Ashley-Steiner, a hard-charging literary and show business venture that had been founded by Ted Ashley, who had started out in show business as an office boy at William Morris. Ashley-Steiner rivaled the Morris agency as a packager of television programming, but the newer, smaller venture also swaggered in the film business and made a specialty, on its client list, of top comics and comedy writers.

More important, Brooks signed with Greenbaum, Wolff & Ernst, an established New York law office, which represented authors and publishers and had been embroiled in landmark civil liberties and censorship battles over the decades—its lawyers had defended the US publication of James Joyce's *Ulysses* in 1933, for example. Brooks befriended a rising figure in the firm, a recent Yale Law School graduate named Alan U. [Uriel] Schwartz, who was building his career on literary and entertainment clients.

Those moves were intended to wean Brooks from his dependence on Caesar. Others in Club Caesar were making similar adjustments, although Brooks lagged behind most of his confreres. Though Caesar's salary, and the salaries of his writing staff, continued to rise, there were increasingly fewer specials and Caesar's heyday was past. The pay for his specials could not compare with the prospective rewards of successful Broadway playwrights, the writer-creators of TV series, the scenarists of major motion pictures.

Brooks's 1959–60 contract with Caesar alleviated his immediate financial concerns, however, and he collaborated with Tolkin on TV sketches for Perry Como and Ginger Rogers ("one of the best hunks of material I've had," Rogers praised their comedy skits). While waiting for Jerry Lewis's next offer to come through or for something to happen with the Kay Thompson pilot, Brooks also found time to jot down notes for an original plot that he thought he might stretch out into a novel or a Broadway play.

Florence Brooks's pregnancy had been progressing toward her May due date when, one night in the spring, very late, her husband woke her up to brandish the first few pages of "An Olde English Novel," which he'd dashed off in pencil on a yellow legal pad. His idea was premised on two English producers who contrive to produce intentionally awful stage plays—veddy English producers, almost precious types. There was not yet any mention of Hitler. He was very excited about his story, his wife told friends.

By now the Brookses had moved house yet again to a larger apartment for his growing family on East 72nd Street. Although the couple still attended the odd get-together at Stella Adler's or important dinner parties where the other guests were married couples, Florence felt like an increasingly peripheral add-on to Brooks's hectic life. The moment was long past when they had gone to foreign films or visited museums together. Nor, these days, did they discuss their favorite novels. Brooks rarely sat down to eat with his family, and the couple never dined out alone at restaurants—he still professed to have a hang-up about that.

Her pregnancy and two young children filled her life. She lunched occasionally with girlfriends, despite Brooks glaring at them when they dropped by. Her husband arrived home late most nights, stayed up late, slept late, and then raced off most mornings.

Early some mornings these days the phone would ring and

Florence would reach for it to hear, without any hello, the voice of Moss Hart: "Is the genius awake yet?" The genius would shake off any of his usual sleepiness or grumpiness to talk with the legendary Hart or, more often the case, listen at length to Hart's show business gossip.

The Joe Fields dinner party with Broadway luminaries had not proved to be an unadulterated success for the 2000 Year Old Man, since the old-fashioned Billy Rose and stuffy Alan Jay Lerner had not known what to make of the breezy straight man Carl Reiner and the madcap Brooks. On another night the comedy went over better at Kitty Carlyle and Moss Hart's place; that couple found the 2000 Year Old Man charming and amusing. A former Hollywood ingenue, once in Marx Brothers films, Mrs. Hart nowadays appeared on TV game shows, while her husband boasted a long, garlanded career of hit collaborations with George S. Kaufman dating from the early 1930s and more recently as the director of *My Fair Lady*, which was in the middle of its record six-year run.

Twenty years older than Brooks, Jewish, and born in New York, albeit with English parentage, Hart had been raised in humble circumstances, partly in Brooklyn. An Anglophile, Hart affected English airs that to many signaled his closeted homosexuality. Smitten by Brooks at the dinner party, Hart embraced the younger writer as a cause, touting him to friends, even asking Brooks, unnecessarily, for tips on his memoir in progress. To be adopted by Hart, a reigning king of Broadway, genuinely touched Brooks.

On May 24, 1959, Florence gave birth to the couple's third child, named Edward Anthony, or "Eddie," in honor of her father, who had passed away late the previous year. The summer of 1959 became a veritable blur to Mrs. Brooks, now a mother with a newborn and two other children under the age of four. Perhaps the summer was also a blur to Brooks, who strove with Mel Tolkin and two London writers to craft an NBC summer replacement series starring the British comedian Dave King. All their combined Anglophilia was not enough to avert the notorious failed experiment; the British humor of *The Dave King Show* did not travel well with either American censors or American audiences.

Increasingly, Florence Brooks felt she had no choice but to abandon her marriage. It was not just Brooks's womanizing: Later, both Lucille Kallen and Imogene Coca told her that Brooks had frequently arrived at work on Mondays holding up fingers to the men in the room, indicating how many times he had gotten laid over the weekend. Another summer Fire Islander, Edward Dunay, a swashbuckling ladies' man, told Florence he had run into the comedy writer on the subway on one occasion and Brooks had boasted that he was en route to a Harlem brothel; cheating on one's wife was the sacred duty of a husband, he told Dunay with a grin. With Brooks, it was never clear how much of his boasting was empty or whether the supposed womanizing suited his image of a manly man, like making cutthroat business deals or smoking the cigars that powerful men waved around to celebrate such deals.

More than because her husband was a cheat, Florence felt persistently heartsick owing to the coldness that emanated from him whenever other people weren't around laughing at his jokes, the belittlement and insults she endured when they were alone.

In the fall Brooks wrote a little for Victor Borge, but mainly he busied himself on Sid Caesar's specials for CBS. The first was "Holiday on Wheels" in October, followed by "Marriage: Handle with Care" in December, both of them written by Tolkin, Brooks, and Sydney Zelinka, credited in that order. Zelinka, the least mentioned of Club Caesar—if he ever happened to be mentioned at all—was an old-timer who had been among the Emmy winners for *The Phil Silvers Show* that had repeatedly beat out the Club Caesar writers and whose long career had begun with the Marx Brothers in vaudeville.

"Holiday on Wheels" featured guest star Tony Randall in a series of linked sketches about a pioneer carmaker's family—their rise and fall—with Caesar as the patriarch, Randall as the spoiled scion. Randall remembered it as a "brilliant show," among "the funniest things I ever did on television." The sketches involving Caesar's and his interplay were "all Mel Brooks," Randall recalled; and Brooks directed the first reading, delivering precise imitations of how both he and Caesar should essay their roles. Later during rehearsals, Randall said, he had "lost the flavor" of one "wonderful speech" he had to master in the sketch, so he had gone back to Brooks, asking for the line reading again. Brooks repeated his previous performance to a tee, delighting and guiding Randall.

The publishing event of the fall was Moss Hart's autobiography *Act One*, which reviewers lauded and which shot up the best-seller lists. Brooks was sent an advance inscribed copy, but he struggled to convey his admiration for the book in an unusual three-page letter he wrote to Hart. Also unusual for him, he typed the letter, because now he did type—laboriously—on rare occasions. When he typed, his usual sense of humor was muted and his language grew formal with earnest clichés ("from the bottom of my heart").

Brooks pecked the letter out late one night at East 72nd, jokingly relating how he had decided to devote himself to *Act One* rather than surrender to his wife's ("curlers et al") tempting invitation to watch a very good British submarine picture on *The Late Show*. (A die-hard fan of submarine pictures, Brooks channeled that incident into the semiautobiographical "Marriage Is a Dirty Rotten Fraud" script he later wrote.)

Initially fearing that his famous friend might have written a slick or dull memoir, Brooks explained, he had instantly been won over by Hart's life story, which was so magnificently told. Hart, who admitted to being a little peeved that Brooks had not read his book and reacted sooner, responded with an invitation to a gala party in his honor in October. He hoped that Brooks and Carl Reiner might perform their 2000 Year Old Man sketch.

The October 23 event was timed to celebrate Hart's fifty-fifth birthday (the next day) and the publication of *Act One*, which had been officially issued by Random House in September. Reiner was busy in Hollywood as a new writer for *The Dinah Shore Show*, so Brooks persuaded Mel Tolkin to stand in. Together they crafted a skit in the 2000 Year Old Man mold, this time with the ancient Jew, Brooks, as Hart's supposed psychoanalyst.

In between the final emendations for Caesar's maiden fall special, Tolkin rehearsed with Brooks, scribbling questions for the 2000 Year Old Shrink on both sides of an envelope. Little Mel would ad-lib "much of the answers" with "the freedom to come up with new material during the performance," Tolkin recalled. The two Mels practiced in front of José Ferrer, a frequent Caesar guest over the years and this season, too. Not only a consummate actor, Ferrer had a keen sense of comedy. He, too, had been invited to the Hart party. "Only what [Ferrer] approved of remained," Tolkin said.

It was the show business occasion of the year, and it was held at Mamma Leone's, a popular Italian restaurant in the theater district. The crowd of some two hundred people was "fairly eye-catching," in the words of Kenneth Tynan, who cast his mind back to the party years later in his *New Yorker* profile of Brooks. The gathering included emcee Phil Silvers, Bennett Cerf (the head of Random House), Truman Capote, Marlene Dietrich, Claudette Colbert, Alec Guinness, John Gielgud, Ethel Merman, Rosalind Russell, Simone Signoret and her husband, Yves Montand, and composers, songwriters, and the leading lights of acclaimed Broadway musicals, including Arthur Schwartz, Howard Dietz, Betty Comden, and Adolph Green. Looking around the celebrity-filled room Tynan noticed Brooks and Tolkin "as among the few [faces] not instantly recognizable."

Star performers lampooned the guest of honor, and among the singing and dancing highlights was a parody of "The Rain in Spain" from *My Fair Lady* featuring a youthful Hart being schooled in his posh English accent for future Broadway endeavors by writer Edward Chodorov (played by Melvyn Douglas) and producer Dore Schary (Ralph Bellamy). Finally the least recognizable faces were introduced, with Brooks whispering last-minute changes to their script as the pair approached the microphone. Brooks told Tolkin that "he was not going to play the shrink Jewish," as they'd planned. "And he would cut all homosexual or transvestite references." Those were "deep, surgical cuts" in their rehearsed skit, and Big Mel's natural nervousness multiplied. But after Brooks bit off his reply to Tolkin's first question—where had Herr Doctor obtained his medical credentials?—answer: "The Vienna School of Good Luck"—the duo were warmed by a roar of laughter from the crowd, and Brooks instantly reverted to Jewish affectations.

**Tolkin:** Tell me, Doctor, what was Mr. Hart's problem? Inferiority complex, sibling rivalry, Oedipus complex?
**Brooks:** Oedipus complex? What's that?
**Tolkin:** The instinctive desire inherent in every man to possess his own mother.
**Brooks** (after a long pause): That's the dirtiest thing I ever heard. Who thought up such filth?
**Tolkin:** Well, it's a myth, dramatized by the Greek playwright Sophocles.
**Brooks:** A Greek, maybe, but not our people. With my people, you don't even do it to your wife, let alone your mother. Of course, if you take your mother out for dinner and a movie, then maybe in the taxi you grab a kiss. But the other—feh . . . !

The least rich and famous among them convulsed the room, their performance ending with a standing ovation. A grateful Hart told

Brooks it was the funniest fourteen minutes he could remember. Alec Guinness shook his hand, saying he was a very, very funny man, and then froze as Brooks replied with a straight face, "You're not so bad yourself!"

Florence Brooks, also attending the party, did not find her husband very funny at all anymore. She would never miss his brand of mocking humor that in private too often made a merciless target of her. She *would* miss, she told friends later, all those times in years past when Brooks had illuminated books and movies for her and when the couple had had long, thoughtful, searching conversations about life's mysteries.

Soon after the Moss Hart celebration, just before their sixth wedding anniversary, Florence asked her husband to leave. His reaction was total astonishment. She said she needed some time and space. He stared at her uncomprehendingly. He couldn't simply leave his three children, he declared. He could see his children and be with them all he wanted, she replied. She begged him tearfully: *Please. Leave.* It's only temporary, she insisted, not even knowing if that was true. She felt on the verge of a breakdown.

Her tearful pleading went on for days. Brooks took long walks with his friend Speed Vogel, who had separated from his wife and was morphing from a businessman into a metal-sculpting artist. Vogel resided on Central Park West but also maintained a West 28th Street studio. Vogel listened "patiently and sympathetically" to his friend, while "staying carefully noncommittal. I was extremely fond of Florence." Vogel finally told Brooks that if your spouse asks you to leave more than once, it's probably time to leave.

So Brooks moved in with Vogel, staying sometimes at Central Park West, other times at Vogel's studio. "He was the worst" roommate, Vogel recalled, an insomniac with a "brushstroke of paranoia." Lacking a proper wardrobe, Brooks would borrow Vogel's expensive clothing, right down to his underwear. He'd jump up to answer the phone when it rang (he was big on answering phones) and, disappointed when people asked for Vogel, would hang up with an insult or wisecrack. He'd stay out late and then fall asleep in front of the TV set and be dozing there in the morning when Vogel got up.

One morning Vogel awoke to find graffiti splashed all over the white walls of his studio: "You snore, you son-of-a-bitch! Yes, that's what you do! All night! Snore! Snore! Snore! You fuck!" Some nights, because he was seeing a woman who would later become his second wife, Vogel didn't return home until the next day at noon, with Brooks waiting balefully. "You've eaten your breakfast—I didn't! You've eaten, and I'm starving!" Vogel would begin warily, "There's the fridge, there's the orange juice, there are the eggs, make yourself something" before shrugging and just fixing breakfast for Brooks.

Soon enough "I was treating him like a wife," Vogel recalled. Neil Simon heard about the strange bedfellows–type situation, "and I think that's where *The Odd Couple* came from," Vogel said later. (After *The Odd Couple* became a huge success, Brooks sometimes jokingly referred to the playwright as "Neil Swine-Man," a rare jibe at his Caesar colleague.)

Whenever Brooks felt pain, he felt the twinges first in his pocketbook. Shortly after leaving his East 72nd Street home, he proclaimed emergency budget measures. The rent had just been raised on their ten-room apartment, so Florence and the three children would have to move, he said; he couldn't afford to underwrite the comfortable lifestyle to which his family had become accustomed, especially if he had to endure hardships on his own. On the day after Thanksgiving, Florence and the children were obliged to move from East 72nd to a less expensive six-room place on East 63rd Street, reinforcing Brooks's physical dislocation from his family while he simultaneously made gestures of rapprochement.

The separation was passive-aggressive. Brooks fired the maid and cleaning woman and tried to lower the salary of Frances Barmore, the family nurse and nanny, hoping that she would quit. Florence was entirely dependent on Brooks; she had no professional income, nor "a single dollar of assets of my own," according to her court records. Her bills were sent to Brooks now and disappeared as though into a bottomless hole.

Brooks told his wife he had job prospects in Hollywood and would be moving there posthaste. Vogel phoned Florence, pleading: he'd help the couple patch things up; he'd do anything to get Brooks out of his life and back home. "Are you crazy?" Florence demanded. "Where did you get such a dopey idea? If you can't stand him anymore, throw him out!"

In truth, Florence was miserable: conflicted about having forced the separation yet glad to be free of her husband—his neuroses and his temper. Regardless, for weeks after leaving, Brooks would show up at East 3rd Street late at night and hang around for hours, eventually falling asleep in the living room in front of the TV or on her bed in the bedroom. She'd have to wake him up and send him off into the dark, all the while torn.

Michael Stewart took the unhappy Florence under his wing and invited her along on the train to Philadelphia for the tryout of *Bye Bye Birdie* in March. Stewart had written the book for the musical, which told the tale of an Elvis-type rock-and-roll star drafted into the army. Stewart sat Brooks's estranged wife next to *Birdie*'s composer, Charles Strouse, whom she had never met before, even though Strouse—whom everyone called "Buddy"—had started his career as a rehearsal pianist for *Your Show of Shows*. In his early thirties, slightly bald and pudgy, Strouse was another Jewish New Yorker, who had been educated under Aaron Copland and Nadia Boulanger at the Eastman School of Music in Rochester, New York.

Everyone in Club Caesar was excited about *Birdie*, which was going to be the great breakthrough for Stewart, his first Broadway musical. Brooks knew Stewart, Strouse, and all the principals, including the three stars: onetime radio deejay Dick Van Dyke, portraying the rock star's agent and songwriter; former stand-up comedian Dick Gautier, playing Birdie; and Chita Rivera, who had been Eartha Kitt's stand-in for *Shinbone Alley*, as the agent's secretary and sweetheart. Backstage, the man who had nurtured *Birdie* into existence was another mutual acquaintance, Edward Padula, who had kicked around behind the scenes on Broadway for years, first directing the Lerner and Loewe musical *The Day Before Spring*, later as a stage manager. (A "perfect producer," Lee Adams said of him, with "taste, guts, imagination and thoughtfulness.") Director Gower Champion had danced with his wife, Marge, on *Admiral Broadway Revue*.

Florence hit it off instantly with Buddy Strouse, who was everything Brooks was not: sweet, soft-spoken, self-deprecating. They embarked on a romance. "She was smart, beautiful, understanding, and had a great sense of humor," said Strouse, contacted for this book, "but then again, she would have had to have all these qualities to have lived with Mel." When her affair with Strouse, who had treated her graciously, ended, Florence realized that she would never go back to Brooks. In May, she began dating the stockbroker Edward Dunay, whom everyone knew from Fire Island. Later in 1960, she filed for divorce and asked for temporary alimony from Brooks, citing physical and verbal abuse and degradation and adulterous relationships "of which [Brooks] openly bragged."

At first Brooks told other people that the couple had separated because Florence had gone momentarily crazy, insisting that in the long run they would work things out. Motherhood, he'd say, shaking his head. The pressures. She just needs some alone time.

After rooming with Speed Vogel for a few months, Brooks moved into a fourth-floor walk-up on Perry Street in the West Village. Living in Vogel's studio had reignited his love affair with the Village; his impending divorce ruined the Upper East Side for him.

Brooks never learned of Florence's affair with Strouse. After Florence's lawyer filed divorce papers, Brooks grew terse on the subject of his first marriage. People learned not to ask about Florence, not then or in later years in interviews. Although personally devastated, he pretended their breakup had been just one of those things.

The collapse of his marriage, a relationship that had lasted for almost ten years, was one reason why it was nearly impossible for Brooks ever to write semiautobiographical comedies as Neil Swine-Man did. Brooks had to present his divorce as mutual rather than cast any blame on himself. He preferred to think of himself as Nice Mel.

Professionally, Brooks did put on a happy face. Very soon after Florence cast him out, he got the offer he had been waiting for from Jerry Lewis and returned to Hollywood.

Circumstantially, at this troubled time in his life, a personal and professional crossroads, the American public got its first introduction to Mel Brooks—not merely by name.

Sid Caesar's television specials led to Brooks's striking up what would become a long and profitable relationship with the producer David Susskind, whose company was associated with Caesar through its contractual relationship with Art Carney. Susskind was a deep-thinking producer who believed Brooks to be, in person as well as in his writing, one of the most amusing men on the planet. Among the many projects the prolific Susskind had going, which included highly commercial television and motion picture properties, the producer hosted a talk show on public television in New York, broadcast by Channel 13 and WNTA locally and distributed nationally to educational TV outlets. The show, *Open End*, convened panels to mull over cultural and political issues.

In mid-February 1960, Susskind put Brooks on television for the first time since his fleeting appearance on *Texaco Star Theater* ten years earlier, as part of a roundtable that included Mel Tolkin, Larry Gelbart, Sheldon Keller, Jack Douglas (a writer for Bob Hope and Red Skelton), and Charles Andrews (an occasional Caesar writer who also produced shows for Arthur Godfrey). The topic was "the truth behind your favorite comedians, comedy programs, and comedy writing," in Susskind's words. Noticed favorably by many broadcast critics, the low-key, high-prestige affair evidenced Brooks's gift of gab and presaged his future as one of TV's ubiquitous talk-show guests.

Thoughtfully, and with unusual candor, the congregated television writers rated and analyzed various famous small- and big-screen comedians, chewing over the differences in their styles of comedy—comparing, for example, Jack Benny to Bob Hope.

The panel also discussed critics, and not for the last time in his career Brooks took potshots at certain TV and Broadway tastemakers, i.e., those who had negatively critiqued his work, naming names. More compulsively than most public personalities, he held grudges and called critics out throughout his career. Jack Gould, the small-screen critic for the *New York Times*, was "dreadfully unfair," he said; ditto for Ben Gross, the New York *Daily News* columnist. "I wrote a show called *Accent on Love* for Pontiac with Ginger Rogers . . . and Ben Gross dismissed it with vitriol . . . 'I don't like you, Ben Gross.'"

For the first time Brooks publicly defined himself as a "dangerous" comedy writer, the modern equivalent of the "atomic comedian" he had tried to be in the army. He was outspoken, bemoaning the decline in sophisticated comedy (i.e., the Caesar shows) in favor of the bland family sitcoms that had swept prime time. "Low key plus inoffensiveness equals mass acceptance," he sniffed. That complaint would recur as a motif in his interviews. Again, he pointed fingers, mocking shows with laugh tracks such as the popular *The Loretta Young Show* ("Nobody can get hurt watching the show") or *The Donna Reed Show* ("I wouldn't say there are a lot of laughs in that show").

Interesting differences surfaced among the Caesar writers. Discussing how writers were valued and credited by the comedians they wrote for, Brooks admitted that "It bugs me" when writers were not mentioned in interviews or were insufficiently praised by critics. The milder-mannered Gelbart jumped in: "Well, I don't eat my heart out."

Not for the last time Brooks disparaged Bob Hope, describing the older comedian as "never really dangerous . . . Hope is America's pet, America's puppy." Gelbart, who had written for Hope early in his career, rose in defense, saying that Hope was a "joy" to work for.

"But," Brooks interjected, "does Hope *translate* anything of the things you wanted to say?"

Hope was a gentleman, Gelbart replied, and when he had worked for Hope he had not been concerned about messages, he had been happy just to write second lieutenant jokes.

"I don't mean '*message*,'" Brooks pressed Gelbart. "But the joy of creating something, you know, and having the comic *translate* that experience."

"I was not looking for a vicarious experience through the comic," Gelbart replied evenly.

The panel pondered the topic of Jerry Lewis, for whom most of them had written at one time or another. Brooks was surprisingly blunt, considering that he had a fresh contract with Lewis in his pocket. He said that Lewis was fun to work for yet "I find it impossible to write for him, in a big wide open sense." He told anecdotes about the previous TV special he had written with Danny Simon and Harry Crane, and how Lewis, in a meeting with Paramount executives and the writers, had jumped up onto a desk, then jumped around on top of the desk, then jumped off the desk. "He is a great jumper," Brooks finished, and that, he added, was what Lewis really wanted as his epitaph: "Jerry, you're the best jumper!"

"The horror of it, this is my own opinion," Brooks finished oddly, "is he is essentially one of the most brilliant comedic talents to have ever come upon the horizon."

• • •

By the time the *Open End* program was widely broadcast in August 1960, Brooks had already been residing in Hollywood for two months, working for that same "most brilliant comedic" talent: Jerry Lewis. Brooks arrived in late June with a ten-week guarantee and his best salary yet. Ashley-Steiner, in conjunction with Greenbaum, Wolff & Ernst, finalized the contract, with Brooks looking over their shoulders and learning.

Lewis was a beacon in the Hollywood firmament amid overall slumping attendance and declining motion picture production. Since Brooks had last seen the comedian, Lewis had made his debut feature as writer, director, producer, and star. Paramount had just released the result, *The Bellboy*, to solid reviews and box office. Studio publicity for Lewis's new project described "The Girl's Boy" as based on "an original unpublished story idea" by the comedian about a lovelorn schlub dwelling in a house of gorgeous gals.

This was the first time Brooks started on page one of a blank script for either Broadway or Hollywood. His contract stipulated that he would be paid $3,500 weekly for ten weeks in addition to first-class round-trip air travel from New York, an open-ended residential lease at the Montecito Apartments on Franklin Avenue, and generous per diems and expenses.

Brooks thought he would be working closely alone with the comedian, but it did not take long—only two weeks—for Lewis to decide he wanted a third sounding board in script conferences. The comedian hired his friend, big-band drummer Bill Richmond, to join them, starting after the July Fourth weekend. A novice who had never worked as a professional writer, Richmond was promised $500 weekly with no guarantees after week one.

The surprise of Richmond's hiring was softened by the disparity in their résumés and salary differences that automatically made Brooks the senior partner. In his free time the transitioning drummer studied the format and mechanics of screenplays in the

Paramount library. Brooks was already friendly with Richmond, and most of the time the two worked amiably together sans Lewis, who restricted himself to weekly conferences.

The weekly summits took place in the inner sanctum of Jerry Lewis Productions on the Paramount lot, which was filled from floor to ceiling with photographs of Lewis, plaques, certificates and gold records, innumerable electronic devices and gadgets, stacks of Kool cigarettes, and piles of sharpened pencils. The comedian was a bad listener with a short attention span, and he wielded a heavy gavel, interrupting the writers to deliver long rants and then rushing off busily. He recorded the conferences and had the tapes transcribed, so he wouldn't forget anything he had said that was brilliant or might be useful.

Sid Caesar often laughed when Brooks topped his jokes. Lewis took that strength away from Brooks. Lewis didn't like to be topped. At the very first script conference with his new writing team, he complained ruefully that Brooks and Richmond had tried to *alter* and *improve* every great idea in the script that he had already thought of.

It was one thing to have crafted short TV sketches for Lewis, as Brooks had done the previous year, and quite another, he quickly realized, to develop a feature-length screenplay revolving around Lewis's peculiar comic persona. The task was oppressive, even if Lewis's persona was not far from Brooks's own; the two shared a mutual enthusiasm for rubber faces, oinks and grunts, infantilism and tastelessness.

Lewis was as changeable as he was controlling in the script conferences. He was "balky," as Shawn Levy wrote in *King of Comedy: The Life and Art of Jerry Lewis*. When the star was absent, which was most of the time, the writers were obliged to try out their scenes on associate producer Ernest D. Glucksman and others on the Paramount lot. Lewis was irked when they reported back any outsider reaction. Folks thought *his* stuff was funny, too, Lewis chided them, "and we're never gonna know until I photograph it."

If Lewis cottoned to any of their proposals, he swiftly appropriated them as his own, even as the ideas were being voiced; he used the writers more as gagmen and took their ideas as springboards for his "long free-association screeds," according to Levy, "about what character names were funny or what sorts of wacky poems the main character (who, he'd decided, should be a serious writer) should compose."

Brooks could not shout louder, jump up higher on desks, or make crazier wisecracks; that was territory already carved out by Lewis. Very soon, Brooks didn't see the value of working too hard on any idea or scene before they got Lewis to sign off on it. "Mel would say, 'Let's run it by Jerry and see if he likes it,'" Richmond remembered. "So we'd call Jerry, and Jerry would say, 'I can't talk right now, but let me get back to you.' Now, if anybody had a bigger ego than Jerry Lewis, it was Mel Brooks. Jerry did this to Mel about four times, so finally Mel literally just said, 'Fuck this.'"

Brooks reverted to old habits, arriving late and lounging around, making phone calls to stockbrokers, griping to his agent, hobnobbing around the studio. Actress Hope Holiday, a longtime friend of his estranged wife, Florence, now lived in Hollywood; earlier in 1959 she had appeared memorably in the Christmas Eve sequence with Jack Lemmon in Billy Wilder's *The Apartment*. (Later, she'd play "Lolita" in Wilder's *Irma La Douce*.) She spotted Brooks touring Paramount on a golf cart. Never overly friendly before, now he was suddenly Nice Mel, striving to say hello and arrange an interview with Lewis for a part in the new film. "I thought he was being so sweet and so nice to me, but maybe it was because I had made an impression in *The Apartment*," said Holiday.

Brooks took increasingly long lunches, pondering the future with music and movies publicist Marvin Schwartz. Carl Reiner lived in Hollywood nowadays, still writing for Dinah Shore, and with so many other projects in the works he needed a sandwich board to list them. As always, Reiner, Brooks's best friend, lent a sympathetic ear.

When Lewis took a vacation in late August, Brooks bailed east to New York, the first of several breaks he stole from Hollywood. He walked the sands alone on Fire Island.

By now Richmond had gained the upper hand in the writing team, in part because Richmond was always on-site, loose and accustomed to Lewis's erratic behavior from club days, and better at "reading" the comedian and scratching his endless itch; better at rolling with the punches. The novice writer got a pay raise and a contract extension.

By late September, Lewis had noticed Brooks's absences, which occasionally stretched past weekends, and he'd begun sending curt memos to the writer to "polish" scenes already stamped for inclusion in the script. Famous for verbally topping people, Brooks now became a polish-and-finish writer, not his forte and not what he enjoyed.

By the end of the first week of October, Lewis had decided to dismiss Brooks. It would have been an awkward negotiation, except that Brooks was ready to leave. His pay was docked for the two weeks in August that Lewis had been on vacation and Brooks had gone AWOL and for two days in early October when Brooks again had traveled to New York and tarried, discussing his availability with agent Hillard Elkins, producer Edward Padula, composer Charles Strouse, and lyricist Lee Adams, who wanted him to write their successor to *Bye Bye Birdie*. Brooks had been wangling for just such an opportunity.

*Variety* had taken to calling Strouse and Adams "the *Birdie* boys" as shorthand for the magic touch they had showed with their first hit musical. Michael Stewart had declined to toil on the follow-up. (Stewart had already committed to a musical called *Carnival!*, which also involved Gower Champion, *Birdie*'s director.) The new *Birdie* boys' musical was going to be based on a 1950 comic novel by Robert Lewis Taylor called *Professor Fodorski*, which concerned a European professor who applies his brainpower to the football team of a southern Baptist college. The *Birdie* team (minus Champion and Stewart) envisioned another hit musical, another top-selling cast recording, national touring companies, and the proverbial big sale to Hollywood. Brooks, Stewart's friend and fellow Club Caesarite, was his natural heir apparent. Brooks "had never really written a stage story before," as the show's eventual director, Joshua Logan, recalled, but the *Birdie* team "was willing to take a chance on him because he was so brilliant with dialogue."

This prospect eased the severance talks between Paramount and Brooks's West Coast talent representative, Fred Engel of Ashley-Steiner. Brooks was freed up for *Professor Fodorski* without reward or penalty. Mutually it was agreed that he had "made no contribution whatsoever to the script" of *The Ladies Man*, as the Jerry Lewis vehicle was ultimately titled when released in June 1961. Lewis wanted sole credit on the screenplay with mention of "Special Material by Bill Richmond," but the Writers Guild, which had the authority to determine credits, refused to accept that language, which was atypical; instead the credit on the screen became "written by Jerry Lewis and Bill Richmond," and it stayed that way for seven more Jerry Lewis features.

The failure to harmonize with Lewis, on top of the collapse of his marriage, added to the sense of crisis in Brooks's life. Yet he did salvage one happy memento from his unhappy experience with Lewis. The comic had complained incessantly about the handling of the black '59 Jaguar, with red leather interiors, that he owned. Brooks thought it was the most beautiful car in the world. "He had paid $10,000–$12,000 a year before for it," Brooks recalled. Lewis told Brooks, "You want it? Give me five grand and it's yours." Lewis took the five grand out of the final salary payment he owed Brooks.

Almost accidentally, then, something else happened in Hollywood in late 1960 that involved Carl Reiner and that salvaged Brooks's stay in the film capital, refreshed his momentum, and in some ways became, in his career, the tail that wagged the dog.

• • •

Faster than most of the other fated-to-be-famous people associated with *Your Show of Shows* and *Caesar's Hour*, Carl Reiner had proved himself as a writer and as a paragon of hard work and accomplishment away from Sid Caesar. Remarkably, if only because it was done with such speed and seeming modesty, by 1960 he had written an acclaimed novel, a play, and several television scripts, including a pilot for a series starring himself that would soon evolve into *The Dick Van Dyke Show*. Reiner also had a handful of screenplays in development, including one with collaborator Larry Gelbart that would eventually be produced as a Doris Day comedy. Meanwhile he acted in films and TV specials and had launched his lifelong penchant for appearing on game shows.

Curiously, Reiner would never collaborate with Brooks as a writer, then or later, no matter how many setbacks buffeted Brooks, no matter how much money such a pairing might have brought. Brooks never wrote a single episode of *The Dick Van Dyke Show*, for example. "He's never done domestic comedy," Reiner explained in one interview.

With one exception: the 2000 Year Old Man was as much a writing partnership as a performing one, and by the end of 1960 the duo had been running the act, in private among friends, for nearly a decade. They had practiced, tape-recorded, and honed the routine for many small groups on Fire Island and in Manhattan. Its seeming spontaneity, if only partly genuine, was impossible to separate from its appeal. The act was a quirky cat-and-mouse game, with Reiner the cat trying to trap Brooks the mouse. "If I said, 'Here now is the world-renowned sculptor Sir Jacob Epstone,'" Reiner remembered, "he would, without skipping a beat, create a whole new person, complete with voice, attitude, and an extraordinary knowledge of the subject's profession."

Brooks's New York booster Joe Fields was ensconced in his Beverly Hills mansion in the fall of 1960, and hearing that both Brooks and Reiner were in town, he threw a party to show off the 2000 Year

Old Man. Among the big-name guests were actor Edward G. Robinson, who told them, "I would like to play this guy on Broadway"; comedian George Burns, who advised the pair to put their act onto an album before he stole it; and the versatile talk-show host Steve Allen, who offered to underwrite a recording session at World Pacific in Los Angeles, a label known for its cool jazz, where Allen had contacts.

Not long after the party, Allen booked Reiner and Brooks into the World Pacific studio on Santa Monica Boulevard. Although he was still reeling from the Jerry Lewis fiasco and his marital imbroglio, Brooks was never down in the dumps before an audience, which in that instance included "a hundred or so family members and friends," in Reiner's words, who had been corralled for their live reaction. The duo recorded for two hours, then trimmed the length down to forty-seven minutes for a November release. The atmosphere on *2000 Years with Carl Reiner & Mel Brooks* would be partylike, with Reiner chuckling along with the crowd as Brooks vamped on the Stone Age and Jesus.

**Reiner:** Could you give us the secret of your longevity?
**Brooks:** The major thing is that I never even touch fried food. I don't eat it, I wouldn't look at it, and I don't touch it. And never run for a bus, there will always be another, even if you're late from work. I never run for a bus . . . I just stroll, jaunty, jolly.
**Reiner:** What was the means of transportation then?
**Brooks:** Fear. Mostly fear.
**Reiner:** Fear transported you?
**Brooks:** An animal would growl, you'd go two miles in a minute. Fear would be the main propulsion.
**Reiner:** What language did you speak then?
**Brooks:** They spoke rock. Basic rock.
**Reiner:** That was before Hebrew.
**Brooks:** Two hundred years before Hebrew was the rock talk.

**Reiner:** Can you give us an example of that?
**Brooks:** Hey, don't throw that rock at me! Hey, what are you doing with that rock there?

Curiously, the 2000 Year Old Man and his time travels ("I'm gonna wash up," he remembers telling girlfriend Joan of Arc, "you save France!") were confined to about eleven minutes, or roughly one-fourth of the LP. The rest of that first recording was filled out by Reiner interviewing some of the other personas spun by Brooks's imagination, which included a pop singer named Fabiola who was not far from the Three Haircuts. But the eleven minutes of the 2000 Year Old Man was what really resonated.

Stand-up humor was in the early throes of a "dangerous" revolution. Mort Sahl and Shelley Berman were among the pioneers of a new, cool, candid, political, and philosophical style of comedy that grew to encompass the first recordings of Lenny Bruce, Elaine May and Mike Nichols, and soon Dick Gregory. *2000 Years with Carl Reiner & Mel Brooks* fit into the trend partly because the 2000 Year Old Man, the daft eyewitness to the turning pages of history, was—like many (not all) of the dangerous comedy avatars—as proudly Jewish as his creators. Jewishness had lurked in the closet and had in fact been unmentionable on Caesar's shows, for example, ever since Hitler and the Holocaust. That was one reason why it took the 2000 Year Old Man so long to go public. "Would WASP America get him?" Reiner recalled worrying. "Would Christians find the old Jew funny? Do 'our people' still consider the Yiddish accent to be non grata?"

Reiner was billed first on the LP in deference to his higher public profile. Brooks was a virtual unknown outside the entertainment industry. He had performed fleetingly on the *Texaco Star Theater* in 1951 but had never appeared on a single Sid Caesar program, except once, sort of: the time he had volunteered to voice a cat off camera during a sketch. He had come down with a bad case of stage fright.

"In the dress rehearsal my mouth turned to cotton," he said, "and I couldn't do the cat sound." Apologizing to everyone, he redeemed himself during the live broadcast with his off-stage meows.

Later Brooks often said in interviews that Caesar had been such a perfect vehicle for his comedy that he had not thought to nurture his own talent as an entertainer during the 1950s. In truth, he hadn't been ready to perform in public. Privately, everyone knew that Brooks was always "on," and for ten years the 2000 Year Old Man had nurtured the "on" button.

The first LP liberated something at Brooks's core: not only the Jewishness that was manifest in private but also his offbeat improvisational genius. The recording took off among laugh lovers, amid the explosion of new-breed spoken-word comedy sweeping across America. Some critics were unkind: "not very funny," declared *Billboard*; "only intermittently funny," said the *New York Times*. (Years later Brooks could quote those negative reviews.) Yet sales boomed. The 2000 Year Old Man became hip and popular.

Suddenly Reiner and Brooks found themselves invited to happening nightclubs such as the hungry i in San Francisco; interview requests came from all manner of daytime and late-night talk shows (including Brooks's first sit-down with Mike Wallace and return invitations from David Susskind); the 2000 Year Old Man was performed on *The Ed Sullivan Show*; FM radio gave the LP incessant exposure; and a spate of other comedians, including Vaughn Meader, who was making a second LP spoofing the Kennedy First Family, and a wild stand-up named Dick Shawn, asked Brooks to write fresh material for them. Faster than you could say "sequel," plans for a second 2000 Year Old Man recording with Reiner and Brooks were placed on the agenda for the spring of the following year by Capitol Records, which bought out the surging World Pacific catalogue.

Those and other positive repercussions from the first comedy album loomed ahead as Brooks returned to New York in late

December. He plunged into meetings with producer Edward Padula, composer Charles Strouse, and lyricist Lee Adams for *Professor Fodorski*, or *"All American"*, as their planned Broadway musical was now retitled.

Late in 1960, a judge approved a temporary divorce arrangement between Brooks and his estranged wife that allotted alimony of $400 weekly to Florence and their three children. When Brooks dodged his payments, early in 1961, her lawyers went to court.

The open hearings afforded a rare public glimpse behind the closed doors of Brooks's private life. His wife accused him of numerous extramarital flings, itemizing those suspected by her or claimed by him. He was a serial womanizer who had even recently consorted "with many women of various repute while in Hollywood," *Variety* reported.

Florence also alleged that Brooks, on several occasions, had struck her "over the face and body." The family's longtime nurse and nanny, Frances Barmore, filed an affidavit supporting her accusations, saying she had once witnessed "the defendant [Brooks] threaten to beat the plaintiff," while conceding that "I personally did not witness the assault." Nanny Barmore confirmed Brooks's constant berating of his wife and his customary use of foul language even in front of the children. Barmore said she had tried to be friendly with the head of the household on numerous occasions, greeting him the first thing each day with "Good morning!," to which he would invariably reply, "Good morning, my ass!"

While smarting from seeing his dirty laundry aired in the press, the normally talkative Brooks was tight-lipped in his sworn affidavit, dismissing "completely" his wife's "charges of adultery." Yet he declined to specifically rebut those charges. His brief denial rejected claims of "other misconduct," i.e., physical abuse, saying "there are no factual allegations to support them nor could there be since they are not true." His wife had been "guilty of serious misconduct" of her own, Brooks stated, but, gentleman that he was, he would refrain from "interposing such affirmative defensives and counter-claims."

Filings in the case attested that Brooks had earned $87,000 in 1960, with $41,000 of the total coming from television and $46,000 from his Hollywood spree with Jerry Lewis. After court actions forced Brooks to reveal that substantial income, Florence's lawyers demanded that the $400 weekly alimony, already in arrears, be upped to $1,000.

Brooks, in his court statements, argued that 1960 had been an extremely unusual year for him, and in actuality his prospective earnings had "dramatically dropped." It would be fairer, and he might be able to keep up with his payments, if his weekly alimony were reduced to $200, he said. The $87,000 did not take into account his stepped-up coast-to-coast travel, with costs often borne by him, he claimed; nor his agent, lawyer, and accountancy fees, or state and federal taxes; the total did not reflect the one-fourth of his income allotted to business expenses, including show tickets and "home entertainment," as well as entertainment "outside the home" for "professional associates."

Maybe his earnings had peaked in 1960, but the upcoming year looked dismal. So far he had been paid only $6,000 as an advance against royalties for many months of future work on *"All American"* ("I consider work on this musical crucial to my future for it offers me a real chance for a new kind of writing career") and $1,800 for rewriting Sid Caesar's scenes sans credit for a forthcoming film, probably *It's A Mad, Mad, Mad, Mad World.*

Yes, the 2,000 Year Old Man was selling "very well," Brooks admitted, but he had already been paid and spent his share of the $6,250 advance. His 2000 Year Old Man paycheck did not reflect the many business expenses he had had to absorb in order to participate in the recording. And he did not foresee significant royalties in 1961. (Years later, in interviews, he would boast that the first LP had "sold maybe one million copies.")

Yes, it was true that Brooks had a side deal with Capitol to produce four new recordings with favorite comedians. The first, *Here's Milt Kamen!*, had showcased an underrated comic who had substituted for Sid Caesar on *Caesar's Hour*. Brooks introduced Kamen on the recording, and Groucho Marx, now a fan of Brooks (he had seen the 2000 Year Old Man act in Hollywood), penned the liner notes. Brooks had also received $6,250 for the Kamen recording but, he said, he had had to pay Kamen his fee out of the advance. The sales were modest, and Capitol had tabled the other three recordings.

Having "no further offers for work as a writer," Brooks informed the court, and "no commitments for my services as a performer," he had been forced to liquidate his stocks and bonds, including a Wellington Fund of $11,000, using some of the money to prop up his career while doling out the rest to his estranged wife and three children.

Adding up all the circumstances, he told the court, if things went okay he might earn as much as $39,000 in 1961. But if things went badly, which seemed more likely, he said, he would gross something more in the neighborhood of $14,000.

Alden Schwimmer, the head of the Writers Department of Ashley-Steiner, weighed in with an affidavit analyzing the stasis of Brooks's career and supporting his client's claim that his prospects in the broadcast arena were "problematical." "We have offered his services, without success, to numerous people," Schwimmer said. "Indeed, we have been so concerned about his future . . , we have voluntarily released him from his commitment to pay commissions on moneys earned as a performer, recording artist, or writer, or playwright." That unusual waiver allowed Brooks to liaise with other agents; Ashley-Steiner represented him exclusively only for television or motion picture writing.

All Florence's lawyers knew about the state of Brooks's finances came from his voluntary affidavits and the personal tax returns covering the years of their marriage. Her lawyers fought to obtain access to all his contracts, especially those with ongoing payment clauses; any nonpaper agreements that might be off the books (as frequently happened when one comedian wrote for another); all stock holdings; his accountant's records; checkbook stubs; and so on. But Brooks's lawyers battled back fiercely, successfully blocking all subpoenaing of documents and keeping Brooks from having to make any formal depositions.

Florence had asked for more alimony than she could ever hope to obtain because she believed she would never get whatever amount the court ordered. She said her ex-husband had treated his family in a "niggardly fashion," making payments reluctantly and irregularly, letting her bank account fall as low as three dollars "time and again." Brooks derived "some enjoyment" from plunging her into dire circumstances and constant pleading, she said. Perpetually chasing after the money had put her on the constant verge of collapse.

Brooks still saw his children almost daily when he was in New York, stopping by the family apartment and often hanging around for hours until inevitably Florence asked him if he wanted to stay for supper. Then he'd sit a little off to the side of the family table, looking woebegone as he spooned from his plate. Though he bought the children lavish toys and took them on outings, he never took them home with him overnight to where he now lived in the West Village, however, not then nor later in time.

His woebegone look underscored his ceaseless entreaties to Florence to give their marriage one more try. Brooks was apologetic, saying he still loved her and the couple could still reunite. The sad face dovetailed with the explanations he made, over and over, in court and in person to Florence, about how "the new trend in viewing" had "cut into the market for humorous material," making his finances fragile; he expected to earn so much less money in the future, he said, that he couldn't possibly pay sizable alimony.

However sincere he may have been about wanting to repair his broken marriage, one of the first things Brooks did upon returning from Hollywood in late 1960, in consultation with his lawyer Alan U. Schwartz, was to form a private corporation called Crossbow Productions, Inc. That filing made him an employee of his own company, with all future professional activities, including stage, television, motion picture, and recording endeavors, wholly owned or licensed under the aegis of Crossbow. Crossbow could bank Brooks's earnings and pay his income out of the earnings while setting the bulk aside to invest in future company projects. The chairman of the board of Crossbow was of course Brooks himself, while his lawyer and accountant were the only other named directors.

Apart from that being standard operating procedure for rich people wishing to limit taxes on fluctuating income, Crossbow was useful for the shell game with Florence, who had sacrificed her dancing career for motherhood and now despairingly sought the best possible divorce terms for herself and her three young children. Brooks never mentioned Crossbow in his affidavits, nor was it referred to in court records.

Personally as well as professionally, Brooks was nothing if not agile and resilient; moss did not grow under his feet. Curiously, even while in the midst of ugly alimony disputes in the New York courts and pleading privately with Florence to give their marriage a second chance, he also began to court the actress who'd become his next wife.

A vivacious brunette from the Bronx, whose real name was Anna Marie Louisa Italiano, Anne Bancroft had started out in Hollywood in the early 1950s playing insignificant roles. Returning to her native New York, the actress had enrolled at Herbert Berghof (or HB) Studio before gravitating to the Actors Studio, where she studied under Lee Strasberg. She then embarked on a more auspicious stage career, winning two Tonys, the first for playing opposite Henry Fonda in William Gibson's two-character *Two for the Seesaw* in 1958, followed by her portrayal of Anne Sullivan, the tutor of the deaf-blind Helen Keller (played by Patty Duke), in Gibson's *The Miracle Worker*. *The Miracle Worker* had been selling tickets for a year and a half by early 1961 and would soon become an acclaimed Hollywood picture, with Bancroft Oscar nominated for Best Actress.

The thirty-year-old was Catholic, five years younger than Brooks, and at least three inches taller. No actress in New York show business was more instantly recognizable, successful, respected. Bancroft, too, had endured a bad first marriage; she was wary of men and intimidated them. Famously in New York, she was single and available.

There are many versions of how and when Brooks first got together with Bancroft, but there are William Morris agents who believed it was an "agency package," because the writer and the actress, both known to be available on the relationship market, were introduced by talent representatives who conspired for the two to meet and shake hands as they walked down agency corridors from opposite directions in late 1960.

Just as curiously, Charles Strouse, who had enjoyed a secret romance with the first Mrs. Mel Brooks one year earlier, believed he had played Cupid. Strouse had a day job in the late 1950s playing piano for musical theater lectures at the Actors Studio, where Bancroft practiced her singing with him. Strouse and Brooks were talking over the *"All American"* script one day when Bancroft stopped by to say hello, and after she departed, Brooks, tongue-tied in her presence, pleaded with Strouse for another try at catching her attention.

On February 5, 1961, Strouse took Brooks to a run-through for *The Perry Como Show* at NBC, where Bancroft was guest-starring. The actress was onstage in a shimmering white dress singing "Married I

Can Always Get" from Gordon Jenkins's *Manhattan Tower* suite. "She was gorgeous!" Brooks recalled. "My tongue was hanging out!" When Bancroft finished her number, Brooks stood and applauded wildly, then strode up to the stage, stuck his hand out, and said, "Hey, Anne Bancroft, I'm Mel Brooks!" Then he followed her to the William Morris Agency, where she performed a one-woman takeoff of *The Miracle Worker* for him, bringing him to his knees in laughter. The next day it was his turn, playing his 2000 Year Old Man LP for her at Bancroft's West 11th Street brownstone. That night, Bancroft told him, she was heading to the Village Vanguard, a jazz club in Greenwich Village, and Brooks connived to materialize at the Vanguard, too. Brooks started "following me around," Bancroft often said in later interviews, finding out beforehand where the actress was going to be and then showing up and accidentally running into her as though their relationship were kismet.

Both told versions of the Perry Como show anecdote over the years, with their own emendations. (According to one Brooks interview, right away Bancroft said she owned his LP, adding "You're a genius!") Suffice it to say that they began seeing a lot of each other: the taller, younger, pretty Catholic actress and the short, Jewish, homely comedy writer.

Years later, actor Frank Langella, who knew them both but was especially friendly with Bancroft, described personal qualities in the actress not far removed from Brooks's own. Bancroft possessed a "galloping narcissism" that would ultimately hinder her career, he wrote in his memoir. Although very funny in private, he added, the actress could be very angry, nobody angrier. Fiercely private, she was also chary of the press.

The new couple would not see very much of each other in the next few months. Bancroft was en route to Hollywood for work on the screen adaptation of *The Miracle Worker*.

The Recording Academy, an organization of music business professionals similar to the Motion Picture Academy of Arts and Sciences, nominated the first 2000 Year Old Man LP for a Grammy for Best Comedy Performance (Spoken Word) in March. *2000 Years with Carl Reiner & Mel Brooks* had to compete, in its category, against Shelley Berman (*The Edge of Shelley Berman*), Mike Nichols and Elaine May (*An Evening with Nichols and May*), Bob Newhart (*The Button-Down Mind Strikes Back!*), and Jonathan Winters (*The Wonderful World of Jonathan Winters*). When Newhart won, the 2000 Year Old Man began a drought of losing Grammy nominations that finally ended for the duo in 1998 with a Best Spoken Comedy Album prize for their fifth LP, *The 2000 Year Old Man in the Year 2000*.

No matter; the first LP was still selling well, and in April they recorded *2000 and One Years with Carl Reiner & Mel Brooks*. Again the audience, this time at weekend midnight sessions at Capitol Records's studio in New York, was friends and family.

For most of early 1961, Brooks was busy on *"All American"*. In the spring he met daily with Charles Strouse, Lee Adams, and Edward Padula. *Bye Bye Birdie* had evolved from Padula's original idea, and Gower Champion had been of tremendous assistance, guiding Michael Stewart through revisions of the libretto. The reconfigured *Birdie* team began slowly, acclimating themselves to the new project and one another. Sometimes Brooks seemed needlessly digressive or combative. "He's like a boxer who can't stop sparring, even when he's eating," recalled Strouse, who dubbed Brooks "The Screaming Samurai."

The months passed with gradually achieved consensus and progress. But the team needed Brooks to get a draft done, down on paper, by the end of the summer. So the writer holed up on Fire Island, taking introspective walks on the beach. "[Brooks] does his best work in longhand," Padula told the press, "or dictating to anyone handy."

The "anyone handy" was someone in particular, though: Alfa-Betty

Olsen. Although female and not Jewish, a fetching blonde who could pass for Miss Norway, Olsen fit the other prerequisites for a Brooks collaborator, having been born in a Norwegian pocket neighborhood of Brooklyn, where she had grown up, everyone else around her speaking Norwegian, with a pronounced Brooklyn accent. Olsen had started premedical studies at the University of Iowa before being corrupted by artistic and show business ambitions. After college she had moved back to New York, where she lived on West 15th Street with an aspiring actress named Candace Hilligoss. Olsen worked by day at an advertising agency and at night as a bonded babysitter. In the summer of 1960, she and her roommate attended a Fire Island party hosted by Charles Kasher, a hair care entrepreneur who pioneered the infomercial. Kasher, whom they knew from Manhattan, aspired to be a producer, and on weekends his house filled up with artists and show business friends.

At one Kasher party the roommates met Brooks, hitting it off right away. Their friendship transitioned to the Village, where Brooks and the young women lived in close proximity; because Brooks stayed up late, really late, he'd sometimes wind up his evenings over at their place. One Friday night Brooks said to Olsen, "You can type and I can't, and I have to have something ready on Monday. You have to help me." That something was Act One of *"All American"*. Brooks talked, Olsen typed, making choices and decisions, and "maybe [I] added a few things because I can't keep my mouth shut."

To write a Broadway musical had been Brooks's lifelong quest, and this was his first big chance. With his background in short sketches and his spotty record with longer scripts, however, it helped to have a solid story foundation to begin with: a novel (by a onetime Pulitzer Prize winner) with a lead character explicitly Eastern European and implicitly Jewish. He (and Olsen) started with a prose treatment of the book, carving out scenes for transfer into the musical, leaving holes for songs, building up the romantic subplot between a football player and a coed, developing a theme of "having the professor first attracted and then repelled by super-ficial success, go back to teaching," in Brooks's words.

Olsen accompanied Brooks to meetings with Strouse, Adams, and Padula. Brooks wrote a treatment, breaking the play into scenes, before completing a full script by summer's end. "Well, Mel didn't actually write, he just talked," Strouse said later. "He had a secretary [Olsen] who would transcribe what he said. Michael Stewart told me that on *Your Show of Shows*, none of the writers actually wrote, they simply copied down what Mel said."

All the while Brooks made frequent 2000 Year Old Man pro-motional appearances on radio and television. He also scripted a funny solo for Art Carney's guest stint on singer Connie Francis's ABC-TV special in September. He'd acquired a reputation for speed and availability and would squeeze in small paying jobs throughout the protracted work-up of *"All American"*, sometimes with his amanuensis, Alfa-Betty Olsen, at his side.

*"All American"* awaited the imprimatur of its director, Joshua Logan, who would not formally join the project until September, super-vising the final script and casting.

All along the team had pinned high hopes on Logan, who had shaken Edward Padula's hand on the triumphant opening night of *Bye Bye Birdie* and told the producer he wanted to stage the *Birdie* boys' next musical. The *"All American"* team met with the director in the first half of 1961, but he had previously committed to shooting a movie, *Fanny*, in Paris and Marseilles, over the summer. The delay was itself an augury: *Fanny* was the screen version of the last Broad-way play Logan had directed, in 1956, before going over to Holly-wood and film. And *Fanny* had run 888 performances.

The *"All American"* team hoped that Logan would bring a master's touch to the still evolving libretto, as Gower Champion had done so well for *Birdie*. To that end, in the fall they launched a series of meetings with Logan at his Japanese-style country home in Stamford, Connecticut, and his posh apartment in the River House in Manhattan.

Logan began by picking apart Brooks's draft, saying it needed "much more of a story" and "some new material." A tall, commanding presence, the stage and screen director was even taller standing up as he addressed the short folk of the team, who gazed up at him as he loftily expounded on the joys of a Broadway hit and the horrors of a flop.

Charles Strouse and Lee Adams impressed Logan ("cultivated and enthusiastic and comparatively contained"), but the third writer on the team, a "bustling original" named Brooks, who was often accompanied by a blond secretary, threw him. (Not that Logan had anything against secretaries; he had two—a personal one and a show business one.)

One of the hottest points of debate was who should play Fodorski, the European professor who must assimilate to American ways. All along Brooks and the *Birdie* boys had favored Zero Mostel, whom Logan now vetoed because he "could not visualize him as a romantic lead," Strouse recalled. Brooks proposed the Metropolitan Opera tenor Jan Peerce, whom Logan also rejected. Another candidate was an adept English actor named Ron Moody, who had just rocketed to fame as Fagin in the London musical *Oliver!* But when columnists were tipped off to Moody's chances, Logan angrily nixed Moody, too.

One day Brooks, who thought of himself as something of a casting whiz, stood and paced as he delivered a long "peroration," as Logan recalled, insisting that their lead did not have to be a funnyman with a funny-looking nose and face. Instead they might opt for "a romantic leading man," someone in the Charles Boyer mold. On and on Brooks perorated, until finally he halted dramatically with a long pause, before adding "two very emphatic words," as Logan recalled. "Or not!" the writer proclaimed, sitting down.

"Gray-haired, smooth Ed Padula was a permissive referee" for Brooks's constant extemporizing, Logan recalled. "I did listen to his rather off-center remarks with great interest because there was obviously a huge brain behind that rather Easter Island face," he wrote later. "It got so we began roaring with laughter any time Mel Brooks opened his mouth. It was no way to get a full afternoon's work done, but it was fun."

One of Brooks's repeated interjections was "Guess what? I'm going to marry Anne Bancroft!" The others took that revelation with a grain of salt. Brooks also spoke enthusiastically about his next musical. "An Olde English Novel" had moved on from his initial late-night brainstorm about London producers who cheat investors by producing an overcapitalized play that was guaranteed to flop. The idea had metamorphosed into a stage musical, not a novel. Brooks credited that progression to "my friend Moishe, who lived in my building"—perhaps another ghost collaborator—who had read scenes, entirely in dialogue without description or narrative, and told Brooks it made more sense as a play.

More important, inspired by the vogue for Jewish comedy that encompassed the 2000 Year Old Man, Brooks had taken the major step of bringing Hitler into the story as the subject of the producers' intended flop musical, thereby personalizing the comedy with one of his own obsessions. The Hitler innovation, as much as the basic story,* had antecedents and may have been indebted to Lenny Bruce, whose "Adolf Hitler and the MCA," from *The Sick Humor of Lenny*

---

* The idea of rapscallion producers who scheme to stage a hugely profitable flop musical was hardly original with Brooks. For one, Moss Hart and Irving Berlin's *Face the Music*, a 1932 Broadway musical, had featured a nincompoop producing Broadway failures in order to launder corrupt money. The film of Leonard Sillman's *New Faces of 1937*, which had starred Milton Berle, also centered on a crooked producer staging duds. Andrew Sarris, the film critic of the *Village Voice*, added another progenitor to the mix in his 1969 review of *The Producers*: "An old Reed Hadley *Racket Squad* sequence on television some years ago [1951–1953] had almost the identical plot."

*Bruce*, had been released in 1959. Or perhaps it was borrowed from an old summer stock friend. "Comedian-impressionist Will Jordan has sometimes claimed that the idea of a Nazi musical was part of his nightclub act in the early 1950s," Steve Allen wrote in *Funny People*. "And indeed, I recall that it was."

Brooks prided himself on titles, and he tried his new one out on the group: "Springtime for Hitler." In later interviews he would explain the title as being derived from a 1934 movie, a comedy called *Springtime for Henry*, which he had seen as a boy. "I'm not joking," Brooks told the *"All American"* team. "That's exactly what I'm writing. A play about Hitler's young and idyllic love life." He said he had spoken to Peter Sellers about maybe playing one of the leads. Padula liked Brooks's snappy title enough that at Christmastime the producer informed the press that he would produce "Springtime for Hitler" after *"All American".* "The setting is contemporary England," the producer told the *New York Times*, and Hitler would not be an actual character in the play; *Carry On*'s Kenneth Williams, "England's new comic discovery," was under consideration for the lead.

It's unlikely that there was a completed manuscript for Padula to read, however, and as with Brooks's boast about Anne Bancroft, "Springtime for Hitler" still had years to incubate.


December was dampened by the death of Moss Hart from a sudden heart attack at age fifty-seven. Brooks was in the final throes of his protracted divorce negotiations with Florence, which had been slowed and hampered by his constant pleas of poverty because of the declining television variety show market as well as his stubborn efforts to win his wife back.

Speaking to *Playboy* more than a decade later, Brooks painted himself as a *mensch* in the divorce proceedings. "Like a *schmuck*, I said, 'Take everything. I don't need a penny. All I need are my Tolstoy and my skate key. Give me these and I can live.'"

In fact, he adamantly fought every nickel and dime of the ultimate settlement. His lawyers gave his alienated wife a choice of alimony (a potentially higher sum earmarked for her while putting the tax burden for that sum on her) or child support (a tax-free set-aside). Wanting the whole thing over and done with, Florence agreed to a $300-monthly child support plan, per child. Skeptical, however, that $900 monthly was all that Brooks could afford, her lawyers managed to wangle a clause in the agreement promising Florence "a sum equal to one-third of her husband's net income in excess of $44,000 per year for the next 18 years, 1962 through 1980." Two thousand five hundred dollars of the excess of $44,000 was to be deposited monthly into her bank account. Brooks's accountant took her aside, telling her, not unkindly, that she would never see that money.

In mid-January 1962, the ex–Mrs. Brooks flew to Juárez for a quickie Mexican divorce. One month later, she married the Wall Street stockbroker Edward Dunay.

# CHAPTER 7

# 1962

## The Warm and Fuzzy Mel

With Ray Bolger in the role of Professor Fodorski, the European intellectual who learns to love football in the Deep South, *"All American"* opened at the Winter Garden on March 19, 1962, and lasted through May. Brooks shared 8.5 percent of the gross with composer Charles Strouse and lyricist Lee Adams. In the last weeks the principals' salaries were reduced, however, and the profit participants waived points to stretch out the run. (The show had six profitable weeks and "four losing stanzas," in the words of *Variety*.)

Gross revenue there was, but in the end no real profits. "$479,521 Deficit on 'All American'" *Variety* headlined several months later. The accompanying article autopsied the financial catastrophe: The production costs had been too high. The cast recording had never taken off in sales, although the score yielded one pop standard, "Once Upon a Time," later recorded by dozens of artists from Frank Sinatra to Bob Dylan. (Half of the show's production budget had come in the form of a loan against royalties from Columbia Records.) Despite the exertions of Hillard Elkins, there was no lucrative Hollywood sale.

Blame there was to go around. Ray Bolger had been director Josh Logan's choice. The seasoned director had insisted upon Bolger, even though Strouse had thought the Scarecrow from *The Wizard of Oz* might be badly miscast as a European Jewish professor with a Slavic accent. (Bolger was a Roman Catholic from Massachusetts.)

Moreover, Bolger had been absent from Broadway for a decade. ("Why is Ray speaking Japanese?" Brooks whispered to Strouse when Bolger debuted his accent for them.) Bolger never really settled into the role. He was also full of himself and made impossible demands.

The chemistry had never been right between Logan and the musical, the *"All American"* team came to believe. "Logan is a crazy lady," Brooks complained to friends, alluding to the bouts of manic depression Logan had confessed to on talk shows. The Philadelphia previews attracted a slew of negative notices, and Logan behaved in "childlike" fashion as tensions rose, Strouse recalled, "in turn forceful, angry, and thoughtful."

Brooks and the *Birdie* boys had wrestled with eleventh-hour changes in Philadelphia before the Broadway opening. Tensions ran so high that they had nearly come to blows; at one point Brooks grabbed Strouse by the collar, raised a fist, and threatened, "If you don't take that fucking song out of the show, I'm going to kill you!" "Not wishing to descend to his level," Strouse recalled, "I replied coolly, 'Yeah—you and who else?'" The fighting-mad Brooks backed off. But he also wrote like a street fighter who "keeps swinging wildly and wildly and wildly, and when he connects he knocks you out," Strouse said later. There were knockout moments in his script but no fulfilling arc in the story line. "Mel Brooks had delusions of grandeur," Logan remembered, "but he was so funny and so willing to turn anything into a comic situation that he was irresistible to work with. The trouble is, he would never sit down to write a playable second act . . . finally, in a moment of desperation, I called everybody together, and we all more or less dictated the act, using Mel's general idea. We were happy with it but Mel never liked it. I had a simple solution. I told him to write another one, but he never got around to it."

The Broadway reviews targeted Brooks and his responsibility for weaknesses in the book. The actors "seem better than their material," wrote Richard L. Coe in the *Washington Post*. "The Mel Brooks libretto," according to *Newsweek*, "bites off much that it should eschew." Brooks's script was merely "serviceable," complained *Variety*, with "flagrantly contrived and preposterous" plot twists. The script was "diffuse and heavy-handed," Howard Taubman wrote in the *New York Times*. "I'm not sure whether it means to be sentimental, satirical, or simply rowdy, and it ends by being dreary."

The reception was not entirely adverse: there were enough admirers of *"All American"* to nominate the musical for two Tonys in 1962: Directing (Logan) and Lead Actor (Bolger). Yet the team's dream of another *Birdie*-size hit was crushed. That particular brass ring would elude Brooks for decades. "We wanted to salute America and its opportunities," the librettist told interviewers. But his book had never jelled.

Chastened by two high-profile professional failures—with Jerry Lewis and with *"All American"*—Brooks would shift direction over the next few years. In television and film scripts, talk-show appearances and advertising jobs, he'd try accenting the Nice Mel, the warm and fuzzy side of his personality. The 2000 Year Old Man had showed the way to please a crowd. He'd endeavor to be as commercial as it was possible for him to be.

Despite *"All American"*, 1962 proved to be one of his busiest years thus far as a writer. Brooks chased after numerous diverse projects, shifting from one to the next like a decathlon athlete rushing from track to field. Perhaps the overlapping events affected his score.

Most of the jobs he stacked up were, not unlike *"All American"*, work for hire for producers whose options on story properties gave them ownership and control. In his mind Brooks always needed the jobs, the money, and the prominence of his name in credits. But it was also true that he usually needed other people's stories as starting points.

Having his own television series was one of Brooks's most lusted after goals, right up there with creating a hit stage musical. Even as he appeared on Mike Wallace's and David Susskind's interview programs railing about the trend of insipid situation comedies that had supplanted the artistry of Sid Caesar on network television ("If a maid ever took over my house like Hazel [in the 1961–65 show of the same name starring Shirley Booth], I'd set her hair on fire"), he tried hard to cash in on that booming market.

By late spring 1962, Brooks had formed a partnership with the producer Stanley Chase. Jewish, another child of Brooklyn, Chase had graduated from a different high school than Brooks had, though in the same class of 1944. The producer hung around with the group of show business lefties that included Stanley Prager, Jack Gilford, and Zero Mostel. (Chase would later produce the 1975 telefilm *Fear on Trial* about a seminal blacklisting incident.) Chase had produced noteworthy plays in the 1950s, including the long-running revival of Bertolt Brecht and Kurt Weill's *The Three-penny Opera*, which had been an off-Broadway fixture from 1955 to 1961. These days Chase worked in television, where he packaged programming for syndication or outright network sale.

Simultaneous with the closing of *"All American"* in May 1962, another musical, *A Funny Thing Happened on the Way to the Forum*—with music by Stephen Sondheim and a book cowritten by Larry Gelbart—opened on Broadway. The toga farce wowed critics and audiences and revived the future for Zero Mostel, who starred (along with Gilford) and reaped a Tony for playing an exuberant Roman slave who connives his way to freedom.

One of the first projects Brooks worked on with Chase was intended to showcase their mutual friend, once blacklisted, now reborn. "The Zero Mostel Show" posited Mostel as a "super-janitor" of Greenwich Village apartments, a soulful building manager who dabbles in painting and music while neglecting tenants' leaky sinks and defective lights. Brooks's script for a pilot (credited to him alone) was precious to a fault, its sincerity and playfulness light-years from his later brand. A string of writers contributed revisions over time, but no network could be coaxed into underwriting a filmed pilot.

The mercurial Mostel was never fully on board, eventually deciding that "The Zero Mostel Show" was "creatively worthless," in the words of his biographer Jared Brown. A veritable cottage industry had sprung up around the flamboyant big man, cashing in on his newfound cachet. Mostel had offers for months ahead; plus he was going to re-create his Broadway triumph in the film version of *Forum*. Still, Brooks never gave up on Mostel, and time and again in the 1960s he built trust by doing little writing jobs for the actor.

Equally precious was Brooks and Chase's next project: an adaptation of *The New Yorker* cartoonist William Steig's 1953 book *Dreams of Glory and Other Drawings*. It had long been Chase's ambition to adapt the whimsical book into a film or TV series, and he and producing partner Richard Brill optioned the story rights from Steig in 1961.

*Dreams of Glory* focused on a boy who lives a Walter Mitty–like existence. The boy has daydreams in which he becomes a sports hero, a fearless detective, and the first boy on the moon, achieving fame for his feats. Steig did not give the boy an age or name; probably Brooks came up with the moniker of Danny Baker, as his penchant for character names took a Gentile turn in this warm-and-fuzzy period. Brooks made Danny a twelve-year-old Brooklynite, the same age as he was during the few years he had lived in Brighton Beach. Danny also lived near the ocean in Brooks's story line, but the boy was not Jewish; he belonged to the WASP-y all-American Bakers—the kind of family unit that was a 1960s sitcom staple. Partly because of the boy-and-family setup, *Inside Danny Baker*, as the project was titled, had network potential above "The Zero Mostel Show."

Brooks got down to work on *Inside Danny Baker* after the July Fourth weekend, by which time his lawyer Alan U. Schwartz had ironed out a contract with advantageous clauses. Hillard Elkins was also involved in the packaging of the sitcom (his *Birdie* boys Charles Strouse and Lee Adams were writing the theme song). The Ashley-Steiner Agency still represented Brooks, but his changing agents over the years had been increasingly subordinated to the constant presence of "my Jewish lawyer," as Brooks liked to introduce Schwartz. Schwartz oversaw his contracts, but Brooks oversaw his lawyer, and they met regularly to discuss business at the Greenbaum, Wolff & Ernst offices on Madison Avenue.

Brooks was his father's son, with an abiding interest in legalities, and by now he could school Schwartz on the nuances of show business deals, with clauses that were almost as creative as comedy in his hands. Brooks asked for and got $7,500 for the pilot script for *Inside Danny Baker,* with an additional $400 royalty and $500 for consulting on each episode—paid to Crossbow Productions for "tax reasons," in his words. Brooks insisted upon 40 percent of the net profits stemming from the series (with 60 percent flowing to Chase and Brill); along with standard expenses he also got language reimbursing his attorney fees and protecting his rights to non-Steig characters or material.

After the deal was signed, Brooks worked closely with Chase over the summer. *Inside Danny Baker* picked up momentum in August, when Talent Associates, David Susskind's company, took the project over from the Frederick W. Ziv Company. Ziv was a prolific syndicator, but Talent Associates preferred to gamble on a network slot. Before too long, however, Brooks found himself tempted by another irresistible project dangled before him, and, as was his established pattern, he began to divide his time and attention.

Regardless of his recent Broadway misfire, Brooks found himself in sudden demand as a "script doctor" for other stage musicals with book problems, the producers hoping for some of the knockout punches (or "impish moments," as John Chapman of the New York *Daily News* had described the highlights of *"All American"*) he was capable of delivering.

In the early fall of 1962, one such Broadway-bound enterprise, called *Nowhere to Go but Up*, was going nowhere but down in its Philadelphia previews. Originally called "Izzy and Moe," the James Lipton–Sol Berkowitz musical recounted the misadventures of two comically bumbling federal agents during the Prohibition era. Estimable talents were involved in the show: the choreographer was Michael Bennett, the future mastermind of *A Chorus Line*; the director was Sidney Lumet, respected for his film and television work; the seasoned producer was Kermit Bloomgarden. The large cast featured Tom Bosley, Martin Balsam, and Dorothy Loudon in her Broadway debut.

The Philadelphia critics and the producer, too, saw defects in the libretto by Lipton (the future host of cable television's *Inside the Actors Studio*). By mid-October, after receiving $3,500 as his two-week minimum salary along with first-class per diems, with the guaranteed credit of "Additional Material by Mel Brooks" and assurances of 1.5 percent of the weekly gross of all future incarnations of the show (those royalties drawn from Lipton's contractual share), Brooks began to shuttle between meetings and deadlines on *Inside Danny Baker* for TV and *Nowhere to Go but Up* for Broadway.

Brooks was expected to inject laughs into feeble scenes and bulk up the proverbially weak third act. According to Bloomgarden, writing to investors afterward, Brooks hit his marks, proving to be "a very fine comedy writer" who had "helped the show enormously but apparently not enough." Lumet foresaw the looming disaster and quit the musical a week before its Broadway opening in the second week of November. Brooks took over the final rehearsals, but any eleventh-hour contribution he may have made to the musical—writing or directing—was not reflected in the playbill, which omitted his name. Lucky for him, Brooks also went unmentioned in the "very bad" reviews, in Bloomgarden's words, that shuttered the musical after only one week of performances. Speaking for the consensus, Howard Taubman in the *New York Times* pilloried *Nowhere to Go but Up* as "a dull-witted comic strip" and cited the laugh line "No man is a Coney Island"—vintage Brooks—as among its "higher flights of sententiousness."

*Nowhere to Go but Up* was Brooks's third Broadway letdown in a row, counting *Shinbone Alley*, each of them ushered to their death by a negative *New York Times* review. But he got something besides money for his pains. Bloomgarden agreed to read some pages of "Springtime for Hitler," and he told Brooks: It's not a play, Mel, it's a film.

The final revised teleplay of *Inside Danny Baker* was stamped November 16, 1962, the same week *Nowhere to Go but Up* opened and closed. Adapting William Steig's children's book into a television show had been Stanley Chase's pipe dream, and the earliest publicity said the series was based "on an idea created by Stanley Chase." Even with Brooks on board, the producer expected to see "Conceived by Stanley Chase" on the screen, standing alone, its size and typeface equaling the final wording of Brooks's credit. The size and sequence of the names were of supreme importance to Brooks, however, and he understood how they could lead to long-term rewards and distinctions. He insisted upon his own screen card as creator and a separate credit as cowriter of each episode.

Brooks's lawyer was adamant about those demands, and the arguments wore Chase down. He was not fixated on a future as a writer. If Brooks was happy, that was the important thing. Chase did not appreciate being totally eclipsed, however, and he wholly disposed of his interest in the series, selling his share of future profits back to his partner Richard Brill. Brooks ended up with sole credit on the pilot script; Chase was left with "Created by Mel Brooks and Stanley Chase"—Brooks first—in the closing scroll.

The script Brooks wrote saw Danny Baker and a friend creating a work of modern art, which they dub "Harry," by splashing paint all over the family Ping-Pong table. The boys trade "Harry" for a skiff to pursue their dreams of boating. Danny's dentist-father scolds him for ruining the Ping-Pong table. Danny daydreams about starving himself for art, dying as he paints his last masterpiece, as his father begs forgiveness.

All along, Brooks's name was key to the appeal of *Inside Danny Baker* for David Susskind, who belonged to Brooks's fan club. Talent Associates staff producer Robert Alan Aurthur supervised the filming of the pilot, with Roger Mobley as Danny and Arthur Hiller behind the camera, in late November. Brooks was not involved, although he urged the producer to use the borough locations that lent authenticity to the trial episode.

Aurthur, a veteran scenarist of live television, applied the final touches to Brooks's script, including casting Whitey Ford as the "guest star in a uniform" who appears in Danny's dying daydream, springing from a crowd to ask for the boy's autograph. "Somebody else's idea," Brooks, not a Yankees fan foremost, admitted in one interview. "A great idea—I would have said [New York Giants star] Mel Ott."

Brooks did not leave *Danny Baker* behind entirely. Susskind had learned to value Brooks's salesmanship, too, and Talent Associates called upon his expertise in that capacity one week before Christmas. The writer was filmed for a spot that Talent Associates could show to ABC-TV executive Daniel Melnick, who was considering the series for a prime-time slot. Brooks posed at a desk with his dread enemy—the typewriter—smoking a pipe and spieling in the manner of a writer floating his ideas into the camera.

"What can I tell you?" Brooks asked, warming up on the first take. "I'm a high-priced writer. I write it. How bad can it be? Will you buy it? Buy it already! Son of a bitch!"

Chuckling to himself, Brooks broke off, staring at the lens. "All right," he addressed the cameraman, "that's the first one. Now we'll try a new approach. Do you want to keep rolling, or do you want to make with sticks [the slate] again to make it legal? . . ."

Voice: "We'll keep rolling."

It took another half-dozen takes before they ended up with the version that worked best: "I'm Mel Brooks . . . and I don't write half-hour situation comedies . . . I write for Sid Caesar, and if you could remember, we did the *Show of Shows* and it ran for ten years.

"So when I write for television it runs ten years."

In fact, Brooks was still closely attached to Sid Caesar, even in superbusy 1962. For the first time in three years, Caesar was back on ABC-TV in the fall, starring in a series of half-hour specials on Sunday nights; sponsored by Dutch Masters cigars, the series was called *As Caesar Sees It*. The episodes were hit or miss ("Sid Caesar's return was not triumphant," *Variety* ho-hummed), and part of the problem was the sketches, which included town clocks gone haywire, man-on-the-street interviews, and silent-movie spoofs of the sort Caesar had done for ages. More than one critic found the specials stale.

There was no Imogene Coca, Carl Reiner, or Howard Morris. Part of the hook was all the fresh faces from off-Broadway clubs and theaters. The Club Caesar members from *Your Show of Shows* and *Caesar's Hour* were truant, too—except for Brooks, who not only contributed to the half-dozen episodes scattered over the 1962–63 season but now rose, in Mel Tolkin's absence, to head writer. He supervised *As Caesar Sees It* scripts at the same time as he prepared *Inside Danny Baker* and doctored *Nowhere to Go but Up*.

Although critics hurled brickbats at *As Caesar Sees It*, the star still displayed his old pizzazz, and *As Caesar Sees It* was invited back for the 1963–64 season, when it would be telecast on Tuesday nights, alternating with another variety series starring the comedienne-singer

Edie Adams. The successor version was renamed *The Sid Caesar Show*. As reported in the *New York Times*, when Greg Garrison, who had worked on *Your Show of Shows*, was installed as producer for the fall, he forced Brooks's departure. The veteran humorist Goodman Ace, who had written for Milton Berle, took over as head writer, reinforced by a new staff that included the battle-scarred Club Caesar members Tony Webster and Selma Diamond. Garrison promised "a new look" for *The Sid Caesar Show*.

The new look paid off briefly ("The comedy is more deft [and] the routines more inspired," *Variety* reported), but the show lasted only thirteen episodes before being axed.

Of all the Club Caesar writers, Brooks had the hardest time weaning himself from Caesar. Records indicate that he earned $71,000 in 1956, working almost exclusively for Caesar, while making just a few hundred dollars in freelance work. In 1957, it was $45,000 coming his way from Caesar out of Brooks's $60,000 total income. In 1958, he drew $36,000 from work for Caesar, out of $55,000. In 1959, it was $41,000 out of $49,000.

Caesar rang the dinner bell for Brooks. But although Caesar continued to hike Brooks's salary every year, there was increasingly less work. Only two Caesar specials were broadcast in the 1960 fiscal year, with Brooks earning just $15,000. That was the first year that other specials and the Jerry Lewis gig represented the bulk of his income.

Some of the other Club Caesar writers were already ringing Big Ben. They had taken bigger chances with their careers after the last club-written Caesar specials of the late 1950s. Foremost among them, Neil Simon, Larry Gelbart, and Carl Reiner mingled their comedy projects with the romance and sentiment Brooks had trouble mustering.

Simon's first Broadway play was *Come Blow Your Horn*, which opened in 1961 and was on its way to becoming a vehicle for Frank Sinatra in Hollywood. Simon also wrote the libretto for *Little Me*, which opened in the fall of 1962 and starred Caesar himself, even as the comedian continued to appear in his TV specials. At the 1963 Tony Awards, *Little Me* vied for Best Musical against *A Funny Thing Happened on the Way to the Forum*. The latter won the coveted top prize, and cowriter Larry Gelbart (who shared the libretto credit with Burt Shevelove), was also doing well independently of Caesar. He had written several telefilms and two features: the Doris Day comedy *The Thrill of It All* with Carl Reiner as his collaborator and *The Notorious Landlady* with Blake Edwards.

Reiner, while continuing to act in films and on television, was just about to have his first novel, *Enter Laughing*, adapted for Broadway (by Joseph Stein, another Club Caesar veteran). Where Reiner was really riding high was in prime time, where the multitalent had begun to collect multiple Emmys for *The Dick Van Dyke Show*, the hit weekly series that Reiner created, wrote, and acted in, which was lodged in Nielsen's top ten.

Nineteen sixty-two was an abortive year on paper for Brooks, with one marked exception.

His career was profoundly affected by one television appearance on Monday, October 1, at 11:15 p.m. EST. More important than *Inside Danny Baker, Nowhere to Go but Up*, and all the year's Sid Caesar specials was the premiere of *The Tonight Show Starring Johnny Carson*. Along with Rudy Vallee, Joan Crawford, and Tony Bennett, all better known to audiences than he, Brooks was a guest on NBC's new late-night talk show.

The kinescope of the first broadcast of *The Tonight Show* (as it became known) has been lost, and it might have been hard for a novice to stand out in that crowd. *Variety* felt that Brooks "talked a lot without making too much headway," and Jack Gould in the *New York Times* opined, "Mel Brooks went his strained way." In Hollywood, where Brooks was still a relative nonentity and the broadcast was delayed one day from the East Coast, his presence went unmentioned in the *Los Angeles Times*. Within a few years, however, that same newspaper would recommend *The Tonight Show* broadcasts repeatedly in its pages, if only because Brooks was a scheduled guest. He was "funny without uttering a word" and guaranteed to "brighten" the late-night show, the paper attested.

Carson competed with Carl Reiner for always seeing Brooks in a sympathetic light and laughing hardest at his jokes. The same age as Brooks, taller and dapper, thoroughly Gentile with midwestern roots, Carson had built a liking and mutual respect for Brooks since their first acquaintance. When Carson enjoyed the guests on his show, the night was always doubly enjoyable. He would watch Brooks "like a pup watching you for a cookie," Brooks recalled once. "Sometimes if I was really good, he'd lose it."

After the premiere, Brooks became one of Carson's recurrent guests (several of his many stints over the ensuing decades are featured on *The Incredible Mel Brooks* box set, and others can be found on YouTube). Brooks honed his salesmanship and the image-conscious side of his persona on *The Tonight Show*, telling warm, humorous anecdotes about his career and delivering favorite comedy bits such as (more than once) impersonating an Indian ichthyologist or imitating Frank Sinatra (recurrently) coolly smoking an imaginary cigarette while crooning "America the Beautiful" (". . . above the Tutti-Frutti plain . . ."). Early on—not on the maiden show—Brooks launched a decades-long running gag with Carson's "straight man," Ed McMahon: after mistakenly sipping from McMahon's coffee mug, he'd spit the liquid out, staring at McMahon in horror with his expression hinting at booze. "Gentiles! They'll drink anything!" he'd exclaim.

Carson's show catapulted Brooks into the first echelon of talk- and game-show guests in the 1960s, appearances that helped solidify his skills as a comedian and boost his recognition with the public. He had earlier attracted bookings for the 2000 Year Old Man with Carl Reiner, but in the wake of the first *Tonight Show* he increasingly materialized without his straight-man friend. Whether aired in the afternoon or late at night (it was never too late at night for Brooks), he began showing up on (a partial list) *The Jack Paar Show, The Ed Sullivan Show, The Mike Douglas Show, The Steve Allen Show, The Irv Kupcinet Show, The Les Crane Show, The All-Star Comedy Hour, The Arlene Francis Show, The Danny Thomas Show, The Andy Williams Show,* and *Jeopardy!*

He appeared often on *Hollywood Palace* from 1964 to 1967, recurrently on *The Celebrity Game* (a comedy quiz show hosted by Reiner) in 1964–1965, and several times on *The Face Is Familiar*, a summer replacement in 1966. Though certain variety shows and serious talk shows offered wider "exposure," in Brooks's parlance, others paid onetime sums ranging from $250 for *The Jack Paar Show* to $3,750 for *The Ed Sullivan Show*.

Nineteen sixty-two was also a hectic year personally for Brooks. Despite their ongoing relationship, he was still hedging his bets with Anne Bancroft, or so it seemed to some friends.

Brooks stayed attentive to his ex-wife and family, often stopping by to see Florence Baum Brooks Dunay (as she was now known) and their three young children—Steffi, Nicky, and Eddie—at the Dunays' apartment on Second Avenue near 61st Street. He tried to stop by when Florence's current husband, Edward Dunay, was not home. Brooks and Dunay had a patent dislike for each other, aggravated by the fact that Brooks's child support payments were chronically overdue or skipped entirely; he would miss payments, claiming "The check is in the mail." (In today's vernacular he might be called a "deadbeat dad.") The many tense standoffs between Brooks and the tall, handsome stockbroker, who was now a stand-in father to Brooks's children, often ended with the shorter man slinking away.

When alone with his ex-wife, Brooks sometimes wondered aloud forlornly if it was too late to resuscitate their marriage. He gave up forever when Florence became pregnant in the fall of 1962, delivering her fourth child, Peter Dunay, in April 1963.

To the outside world, it appeared that Brooks was crazy in love with Bancroft. The couple took long walks together and were spotted at clubs and cafés. Many nights the two stayed "home"— Bancroft's Greenwich Village brownstone—playing board games such as "Careers" with friends like actor Jerry Orbach and his wife, actress Marta Curro.

Bancroft was treading water in her career, taking Actors Studio classes and appearing on TV game shows, as she searched for a worthwhile Broadway vehicle that might compare to *The Miracle Worker*. The actress had spent months in 1961 reprising her signature role as Anne Sullivan, the teacher of the deaf-blind Helen Keller, in the screen version of *The Miracle Worker*, which arrived in New York in late May 1962, around the same time weak reviews and ticket sales were killing *"All American".* Bancroft had better luck with the critics, who praised her overwhelmingly; as Anne Sullivan, Bosley Crowther wrote in the *New York Times*, Bancroft brought Helen Keller's mentor to life, revealing "a wondrous woman with great humor and compassion as well as athletic skill." She was propelled to a dark-horse Oscar nomination for Best Actress.

On April 8, 1963, Brooks sat with Bancroft in her brownstone, watching the televised Academy Awards. Tears streamed down Bancroft's face as her name was read out for Best Actress, surprisingly winning over the year's strong competition, which included two aging Hollywood thoroughbreds, Bette Davis for her performance in *What Ever Happened to Baby Jane?* and Katharine Hepburn for *Long Day's Journey into Night*.

The Brooks-Bancroft romance had been firmly cemented in the press by then, even if the actress's New York celebrity at that point easily overshadowed Brooks's. (The *New York Journal-American* reported her Oscar-night companion as "boyfriend . . . Mel Blanc"—the voice actor for numerous cartoon characters including Bugs Bunny and Porky Pig.) When interviewers asked about marriage, both shrugged. "When two people have both had bad marriages, they're inclined to move slowly," Bancroft told a columnist. "Look, I've got love. That's enough, isn't it? What else would you want out of life?"

Behind the scenes some skeptics believed that Brooks deliberately moved in slow motion while Bancroft kept her eyes on the prize and nursed the relationship along. She was known to haunt *"All American"* run-throughs, lingering in the theater, with Brooks sometimes having to dodge out a side door rather than leave arm in arm with her.

But Bancroft was not really the clinging type, and she accepted Brooks's quirks and peccadilloes. Those included his night-owl roaming around the West Village, which suited Brooks better as home turf than the Upper East Side, where it was harder to know what fancy apartment might provide him with a temporary haven. "Mel used to come by my apartment," recalled agent, producer, and former Upper East Side neighbor Freddie Fields. "'Hey, just dropped by to say hello.' Six hours later, 'Hey, listen, I gotta go.'"

While Bancroft got her beauty sleep, Brooks roamed sleeplessly. And during those late-night rounds in the 1960s, his girlfriend was not always mentioned when Brooks flirted with the women he met or knew. Some were never sure of his intentions.

On his rounds he might ring ladies' doorbells "just to say hello." A young, pretty talent agent who also lived in the Village—she had met Brooks when she worked for David Begelman at ICA—recalled that it was normal for Brooks to show up unannounced after midnight. He'd ask to use her bathroom. "I was not the only one," she remembered. "It was an invitation of sorts. I showed him to the guest bathroom, I trust he took care of his business, and then I showed him to the door . . . all in good spirits, with lots of laughter. The invitation, if it was one, went begging."

Another person whose doorbell rang amid Brooks's late-night rounds was the documentary filmmaker Ofra Bikel. Bikel had known Brooks since 1958, when both had been passengers on the ship's crossing to London for Sid Caesar's summer program. "[Brooks] was very flirty, always," Bikel recalled. "The things he would tell you in a flirty way. There was nothing terrible about it, although of course there was unfunny stuff." Bikel had kept in touch with Brooks, sometimes asking him for tickets to this or that show. He'd drop by her apartment, too, just to use the bathroom or say hello. Brooks was usually flirty when he stopped by, Bikel said. She thought it likely that he was hinting at a tryst. But he wasn't her type, she gave no signals, and Brooks went away again.

Brooks waited for four years after meeting Anne Bancroft before marrying the actress, he explained in subsequent interviews, because he had been living hand to mouth, having plunged from "$5,000 a show" writing for Sid Caesar to averaging "$85 a week" and scrounging over the "next five years." He liked to say he did so many talk shows partly for the $300-plus fee he earned, for instance, for each *Tonight Show*. That half-truth fed a running gag in his talk-show or documentary-film turns, where he often interrupted the stream of questioning with "Hey, how much am I getting paid for this?!"

By comparison Bancroft earned a reported $150,000 annually during the run of *The Miracle Worker*—years encompassing the play and film. Bancroft amassed savings, investments, and ownership of the Federal-style four-story town house she lived in at 260 West 11th Street. Brooks liked to say she was his "patroness," paying the rent (then and later after marriage) and for some meals in the 1960s. Light and easy success was part of her charm.

The exaggerations of $5,000 and $85 were vital for Brooks to dramatize his artistic struggle, although actually, except for summer vacations, he worked regularly and steadily and was in the first half of the 1960s often paid handsomely. His fees were typically chan-neled into Crossbow Productions, the money flowing back to him according to a regulated plan that enabled him to pay lower taxes and justified his grudging payment of child support. There were always per diems and travel allotments. And Brooks had a continuing stream of revenue from his 2000 Year Old Man sideline with Carl Reiner; their third LP, *Carl Reiner & Mel Brooks at the Cannes Film Festival*, came out in early 1963.

He also gambled repeatedly on stage and TV properties that belonged to the producers who hired him. He took such work for hire because the jobs promised pots of gold. But both *"All American"* and *Nowhere to Go but Up* ended badly, and *Inside Danny Baker* did not run for even one year on television, much less the ten Brooks had predicted. Despite the best efforts of Talent Associates, the William Steig series was a no-go by the end of 1962, turned down by all the networks.

Not all of his hyperactivity was mercenary, however. In mid-1962, Brooks took a referral from Carl Reiner, who had narrated a short by the animator Ernest Pintoff called *The Violinist*, which was Oscar-nominated in 1959. Pintoff, a New Yorker they all knew from artist and show business circles, was planning "a spoof of the pseudo–art film" that might serve as a lead-in to the main attractions in art houses and other movie theaters. Pintoff needed a script, and Brooks hatched an idea for one as he sat in a movie house one day watching an experimental short by National Film Board of Canada animator Norman McLaren. The McLaren short was being shown before the feature, and Brooks overheard "an old immigrant man, mumbling to himself" a few rows back. "He was very unhappy," Brooks recalled, "because he was waiting for a story line and he wasn't getting one."

Brooks reimagined the 2000 Year Old Man as a grumpy old moviegoer watching "a fake Norman McLaren short," in his words, critiquing the weird and incomprehensible cartoon in a mangled dialect. "Don't let me see the images in advance, just give me a mike and let them assault me," Brooks told Pintoff. Then, just like the spots he had winged to sell the *Inside Danny Baker* pilot—whose script also mocked modern art incidentally—"I said, 'Roll 'em again,' and I tried some different things and we picked out the best."

**Brooks:** What is it, a squiggle? It's a fence. It's a little fence. Nope, it's moving. It's a cockaroach. I'm looking at a cockaroach. I came to see a hot French picture with a little nakedness, what am I looking at here . . . ? This is cute, this is cute, this is nice . . . Vat da hell is this?

One of the best investments of quick time and low money Brooks ever made was that one-off collaboration with Pintoff. *The Critic* was ready for its New York premiere by late May 1963, opening at the Sutton Theater on the Upper East Side ahead of a new British comedy starring Peter Sellers. United Artists acquired the animated short for national distribution, licensing it to US theaters. Not only did American audiences universally enjoy the cartoon (its four-minute brevity was a selling point), but actual critics also adored *The Critic*. ("Brooks' harsh comments and strange noises are truly hilarious," wrote *Box Office*. "The short itself is worth the price of admission," said *Back Stage*.) Indeed, *The Critic* proved to be so pop-ular that it was booked for months ahead, through Christmas in chains across the United States, billed in advertisements as an "Ex-tra Added Hilarious Short Short."

Brooks's contract made *The Critic* a Crossbow-Pintoff coproduc-tion: technically the animated short was the first Mel Brooks film. When the annual Academy Awards show rolled around in April 1964, Anne Bancroft was on the dais in Hollywood for the first time, presenting the Best Actor award to Sidney Poitier. Earlier in the ceremony, however, Shirley MacLaine handed the Oscar for Best Short Subject (Cartoon), to Pintoff, whose brief speech thanked "my collaborator, the wonderful and talented Mel Brooks."

So far, post-Caesar, *The Critic* was Brooks's most auspicious call-ing card.

• • •

Anne Bancroft returned to the stage in late March 1963 as the star, billed above the title, of a new production of Bertolt Brecht's *Mother Courage and Her Children*. It was the actress's first Broadway appearance since *The Miracle Worker* two years before.

A supporting role—albeit he was "terribly miscast," in his words, as the distinctly unamusing chaplain—was being played by a twenty-nine-year-old former Milwaukeean named Gene Wilder. Brooks may not have made much headway on "Springtime for Hitler," but the actor whose frizzy hair formed a halo around his beagle face captured his imagination. One night backstage during the three-month run of *Mother Courage*, Brooks buttonholed Wilder. "Anne Bancroft's boyfriend," as Wilder knew him, told the actor he was writing a script with a great comedy part in it for him. That took Wilder aback; he had been classically trained at HB Studio, where Bancroft herself had studied. Wilder did not yet think of himself as any kind of comedic performer.

After *Mother Courage* closed, Brooks and Bancroft invited Wilder to Fire Island for a weekend in late June. Bancroft had developed her own relationship with the summer colony and in early 1963 had purchased, for $28,000, an early house designed by the modernist architect Richard Meier. The big rectangular two-bedroom wood structure, constructed of precut cedar and Douglas fir panels, was situated at the ocean tip of East Walk in Lonelyville on the western coast of the island. It stood on stilts and faced the water. In time Bancroft and Brooks, who spent as much time as possible together in Lonelyville in the summers, added a second floor, shingled siding, and guest rooms.

"There are no autos and few phones on Fire Island," Bancroft told the press. "If I stayed home [West 11th] I couldn't get any rest. I'll do nothing for an entire month. Fire Island has the best beach I've ever seen. It is a narrow island with the bay [Great South Bay] on one side and the [Atlantic] ocean on the other. From our house you can see both."

Brooks met Wilder on the dock where the ferry passengers disembarked, and the two men went fishing off the surf together for about an hour. "After dinner," the actor recalled, "Mel asked Anne and me to sit down, and then he began reading the first three scenes of 'Springtime for Hitler,' almost verbatim as they eventually appeared on-screen."

By mid-1963, the extraordinary success of *The Critic* had triggered Brooks's first forays into another remunerative sideline—and occasional short form of comedy—movie trailers.

Again Carl Reiner trailblazed for Brooks. Reiner had worked to Americanize an Italian picture called *Arrivano i titani*, a tongue-in-cheek sword-and-sandals picture directed by Duccio Tessari. With Reiner's redubbed dialogue, *Arrivano i titani* was transformed into *My Son, the Hero* for release in the US market in the fall of 1963. United Artists, whose distribution arm also handled *The Critic*, wanted a funny teaser for the Tessari picture. Brooks took over from Reiner, extemporizing his verbiage over a highlights reel. The resulting two-minute trailer was so riotously funny that it overshadowed what it was intended to advertise. (Describing the on-screen hero dressed in loin-wear, Brooks narrates: "Look, he is wearing his sun-suit . . . it's one of 27 sun-suits that he keeps in his closet . . . I wanted a girl, my wife wanted a boy, I think we both got lucky!") "Audiences will be better entertained by the trailers than by the picture itself," *Variety* predicted.

*My Son, the Hero* led to similar chores for the Seven Arts production company, whose features were also distributed by United Artists. Late in 1963, Brooks created a series of offbeat radio and television spots touting the new "all-talkie" comedy *Sunday in New York* starring Jane Fonda and Rod Taylor. The spots imagined an interview with the grizzled director of *Sunday in New York*, played by Lou Jacobi, who reminisces about his box-office triumphs (their titles demonstrating Brooks's knack for such toss-offs: "Hello, Cincinnati, Hello," "The Sheriff of Warsaw," "The Thing That Ate Boston"). Again the spots were so outside the box that they alienated part of the target audience. "Key exhibitors around the country are refusing to support [the spots] via coop advertising budgets," *Variety* reported, deeming the plugs "too New Yorkish."

By then, however, Brooks had a toe firmly in the waters of New York advertising.

Many of his bachelor nights in Manhattan were spent with a new bunch of friends, rounded up by Speed Vogel, who dined together on Chinese takeout in Vogel's loft in Chelsea or at Chinatown restaurants. As Benjy Stone (Mark Linn-Baker) says in *My Favorite Year*, "Jews know two things—suffering and where to find great Chinese food."

Mostly Brooklynites and Fire Islanders, the men formed what they dubbed "The Gourmet Club." Besides Vogel and Brooks the group included novelists George Mandel, a pioneering Beat writer; Joseph Heller, whose *Catch-22* made him a literary star in 1961; and Mario Puzo, whose best-selling *The Godfather* was a few years down the road. Often joining them were the Club Caesar alumnus Joseph Stein, whose *Fiddler on the Roof* starring Zero Mostel would take Broadway by storm in 1964; diamond dealer Julius Green; artist and illustrator Ngoot Lee; and Broadway and ballet composer Hershy Kay.

"About once a week, sometimes more," the Gourmet Club assembled for wide-ranging banter over a gluttonous feast, wrote Heller and Vogel in *No Laughing Matter*.

Heller was a special thorn in Brooks's side, frowning whenever he mentioned his work-for-hire assignments. "Don't you really want to *write?*" the author challenged him. "Don't you want to use your narrative skills? Don't you want to say something about the arc of humanity? You're too good to just end up putting jokes on the screen!"

A few select personages were intermittent or honorary members. Carl Reiner boasted a lifetime pass to the club after he stopped by one time, waved away a menu, and summoned the chef to the table, telling him just to serve the dishes he was proudest of.

Among the strict rules: "No women." One night Anne Bancroft, who discovered a note Brooks had scribbled with the night's designated restaurant address, violated the rule by dropping by unannounced. "It was as if a blanket had descended on the gathering," the actress told Kenneth Tynan. "Dead silence. Faces falling." The group treated her with elaborate courtesy for as long as she stayed. She never went again.

Brooks often ended up at his lawyer Alan U. Schwartz's offices on Madison Avenue for lunch, just "to talk about the future," i.e., Brooks's future. He'd bring his regular cream cheese and walnut sandwich and cup of tea from the Chock Full o'Nuts coffee shop.

Schwartz had an illustrious list of writers for clients, including Joseph Heller and playwrights Anthony Shaffer and Tom Stoppard. "Mel is as intelligent as any of them," the attorney explained once. "He must have a fantastic I.Q. But sometimes if he's with playwrights or novelists, he feels he has to prove he's a serious literary person. When he met Shaffer, for instance, he kept saying things like 'pari passu' and 'ipso facto.'"

In rare interviews over the years Schwartz echoed Brooks's recurrent talking points about that hard-luck period in the mid-1960s. "He had no money—zero," in Schwartz's words. "Our firm carried him for a long time; he couldn't pay his bills." Schwartz viewed his estimable client as a former "street kid" with a chip on his shoulder, the attorney explained to *Saturday Review* in 1983, a "'little Jew' mentality about the way the big WASP world feels about him." Brooks had "a very realistic view of the way the world behaves," he said. "My impression was that he felt rejected, but expected that.

"He'd sit there and talk about the future," Brooks's lawyer recollected. "Included in the future was a very serious idea he had for the great comic stage play called 'Springtime for Hitler,' which would show through comedy what the Nazis were really like."

Still, no matter how much he talked about it, Brooks had not yet dug deep into "Springtime for Hitler," and besides advertisements and *The Critic* in 1963 he raked in easier money penning jokes and vignettes for Andy Williams, *The Revlon Revue*, *The U.S. Steel Hour*, other comedians' recordings, and Johnny Carson's Timex specials.

In late 1963 or early 1964, however, he embarked on a new project that was different from anything he had ever tried before; he decided to write an original full-length script on "spec," without any advance contract from a producer. Even more unusual, the on-spec script amounted to a thinly veiled autobiographical story about Brooks's own first marriage; it was a romantic comedy intended to entice the commitment of a mainstream star such as Rock Hudson, one of Marvin Schwartz's former clients.

Along with Anne Bancroft came many new friends and potential collaborators, including a bright bulb named Martin Charnin, who had worked with the actress on television shows. Not quite thirty, tall, gangly, long-haired, and always dressed to the fashionable hilt, a Mutt to Brooks's half-pint Jeff, the Bronx-born Charnin had played Big Deal, one of the Jets gang in the original cast of *West Side Story*, reprising the role for more than a thousand performances; and he had understudied Dick Van Dyke in the short-lived Broadway revue *The Girls Against the Boys*. Now a songwriter for Broadway musicals and television, Charnin socialized with Bancroft and Brooks, who were his Greenwich Village neighbors. Often at their dinner parties, Charnin recalled, the guests would play board games or marathon sessions of Charades that would descend into madness à la the "sed-a-give!" guessing game in *Young Frankenstein*. "I'd always beat [Brooks]," Charnin remembered. "And he couldn't stand it. He couldn't tolerate defeat."

One night Brooks asked Charnin if he cared to collaborate on a script with him. At first it was just a title that was dancing inside Brooks's head—a one-liner he tossed out: "Marriage Is a Dirty Rotten Fraud." "Mel always talked about writing or doing something," Charnin recalled. "I don't think I have ever spent more than five minutes with Mel that were not spent in him being on or performing in some way or other."

They started talking over scenes, meeting at Charnin's place—never at Bancroft's. Very soon it became obvious to Charnin that this was a semiautobiographical story revolving around Brooks's failed marriage to Florence Baum. The autobiographical aspect was merely implicit, however; Brooks never acknowledged it directly. "He wasn't necessarily forthcoming in terms of making the comparison as we were working," Charnin recalled. (*Playboy* got no further, asking him in 1975 if the script was based on "personal experiences." Brooks replied sardonically, "No, it's based on a very important conversation I overheard while waiting for a bus at the Dixie Hotel Terminal.")

Why did Brooks even need a collaborator, especially on a script that was semiautobiographical? "Mel likes to bounce things off people," explained Charnin. "In all of the material that he's done, he's always needed a collaborator who listens and maybe types better than he did. . . . All of his scripts are dual credits. I doubt strenuously that he ever sat down and just did something himself without the Tommy Meehan or Ronny Graham or whoever happened to be the person of flavor on that particular project."

That said, Brooks was the "driver" of the project. "I contributed a lot," Charnin said. "I edited a lot of what was ultimately written. I came up with a lot of structural ideas, but basically the entire thing was really a 'Mel project.' I don't even think my credit on the front page of the screenplay is a full credit. If memory serves, it says *with*

Martin Charnin. . . . Mel was not in any way, shape, or form above taking all the credit when he could. But point in fact, a lot of the stuff that ended up on the page was from Mel."

"Marriage Is a Dirty Rotten Fraud" evolved over a span of months into a sweet-natured romantic farce that might be suitable for Rock Hudson and Doris Day. It also had a major role tailored for a real-life media celebrity: the broadcaster Walter Cronkite.

The plot revolved around the deteriorating marriage of Larry, the Brooks character, and Pat, the Florence Baum character (with the "Larry" from Gelbart and the "Pat" from Mrs. Gelbart). A fashion model and fitness buff, Pat hogs the couple's marital bed, leaving Larry desperately horny and crouched miserably to the side. The Mrs. fills their medicine cabinet with jars of nail polish and their closets with expensive clothing.

Larry is an evening news anchor who suffers from insomnia, so he watches a lot of late-night submarine movies. His unhappy marriage is turning him into an angry man, which affects his on-camera performance. (His boss, Walter Cronkite, tells Larry he makes the news sound too much as though he's reading a will.) Larry's dentist friend Lou tells him he has ruined his love for Pat by marrying her; the only thing men and women need each other for is sex, which goes rotten in a marriage. Their sex isn't rotten, it's nonexistent, Larry says. He wonders if maybe he ought to rape his wife. The answer, Lou advises, is cheating.

Friends' attempts to counsel the marriage fail calamitously. Larry and Pat separate, and Pat obtains a quickie divorce in Mexico. Larry goes haywire during a broadcast, and high alimony forces him into sleeping on park benches and at his office.

In order to reduce his alimony Larry advertises Pat's availability to eligible bachelors, whose names he has itemized in a little black book. Hoping to score caviar at a big charity dinner, Larry runs into Pat, who has had too much to drink and strips on the charity catwalk just to prove she's a sexpot. The crowd goes wild. Larry, furious, carries her offstage, yelling "No wife of mine is going to make a spectacle of herself!"

Pat goes to London. Larry wangles an assignment from Cronkite and follows her, disguising himself as a wealthy Englishman with an eye patch and false beard. In disguise Larry woos and marries Pat, thus ending his onerous alimony, after which he plans to fake his death on board the *Queen Elizabeth*, which is ferrying the newlyweds back to America.

However, his disguise hasn't really fooled Pat, who is touched by his efforts and begins to fall in love with him anew. Pacing the deck, feeling guilty, Larry is debating whether to confess everything when he is suddenly blown overboard and goes missing. The crestfallen Pat thinks Larry has abandoned her because he got what he wanted: no alimony.

Until, back in her New York apartment with friends consoling her, the doorbell rings. It's Larry, who has been picked up floating in New York Harbor. They fall into each other's arms: HAPPY ENDING, the script reads. "It's like the ending of a movie."

Was it fun writing "Marriage Is a Dirty Rotten Fraud" with the madcap Brooks? "No," explained Charnin, "not fun. It was fun to be with Mel, it was not fun to write with Mel. It was fun to be in stitches seventy-five percent of the time because he was ad-libbing jokes and one-liners and ideas, and he would surprise you with a choice phrase or word at a given moment. But you didn't come away with any sense of having had a good time.

"Comedians are in their own way insufferable, because they cannot stop being comedians. They cannot stop consistently making jokes, telling jokes, making everything funny. And to calm them down is quite a task."

All along it was possible that "Marriage Is a Dirty Rotten Fraud" might become a stage play rather than a movie—that was up to Brooks. Finding a producer? That was also up to Brooks.

• • •

In early 1964, Brooks circled back to David Susskind with another impressive appearance on *Open End*—this time discussing components of humor on a panel that included comedians Bill Cosby and Nipsey Russell. A short time later the producer Daniel Melnick phoned him from Talent Associates, where he was now ensconced as Susskind's partner.

Although no network had picked up *Inside Danny Baker*, Brooks's unsold pilot was warmly regarded inside Susskind's company, and Melnick had another series he was packaging on behalf of Talent Associates for ABC-TV, for which the network had put up some development money. Melnick needed a comedy writer who could bring it home.

In fact, "the concept, lead character and format" of what became *Get Smart* "were exposed to several writers," according to Talent Associates executive Kirk Honeystein, "before Mel or Buck [Henry] ever became involved." The early candidates declined.

Brooks was more amenable because he was more available. Melnick first met with the writer at Talent Associates' Madison Avenue offices in late March and pitched Brooks his idea for a "super-spy satire series" parodying the spy/secret agent genre. "What are the two biggest movies in the world today?" Melnick mused aloud. "James Bond and Inspector Clouseau [the bumbling French sleuth of *The Pink Panther*]. Get my point?" Indeed, Talent Associates' first publicity likened its lead character to "a bumbling international spy, in the fashion of the Peter Sellers role in *Pink Panther*." Similar spy/secret agent television shows and movies—not all of them comedic—were enjoying a boom because of America's preoccupation with the Soviet menace during the Cold War.

Brooks said he always worked best with a collaborator. Fine: Melnick had expected that. Brooks said he would seek out a compatible cowriter and pay him or her through his Crossbow company, thereby making the collaborator his employee and answerable to Brooks, the senior writer. Again Melnick said fine.

A few weeks went by, however, with Brooks unable to fill the slot. He tried to recruit Lucille Kallen, whose novel *Outside There, Somewhere*, a prefeminist comedy revolving around a downtrodden housewife who finds new life as a television producer, had just been published. Anne Bancroft was encouraged to read *Outside There, Somewhere*, and Kallen was likewise encouraged to think of adapting her fiction into a Broadway play that would star Bancroft as the housewife turned TV producer. It was real enough for the *New York Times* to announce a stage production on the horizon for 1965. Kallen trekked from the Hudson River town where she lived to meet Bancroft for the first time.

At the Bancroft residence on West 11th Street, where Brooks was also living, Kallen greeted the writer, whom she had seen only infrequently and glancingly since *The Imogene Coca Show* ten years earlier. Bancroft, whom Kallen admired, was warm and welcoming, while Brooks, who said he was under the weather, acted somewhat lordly and above it all. Kallen remembered afterward that it was "sort of as though a younger brother of mine married the Queen of England," she told William Holtzman.

Kallen declined to contribute to the superspy spoof, and the Broadway adaptation of *Outside There, Somewhere* never eventuated. Soon Melnick got nervous about time passing; he called Brooks in and said they had to get going. The producer showed Brooks a list of writers acceptable to Talent Associates with Buck Henry's name on the list.

Brooks said yes to Henry, whom he knew only in passing. A Jewish New Yorker, Buck Henry was born Buck Henry Zuckerman in 1930. Short and bespectacled, Henry may have lagged behind Brooks in his career, but his reputation as a laconic wit was growing. He had attended Dartmouth College, where he had worked on the humor magazine, and after graduation he had crafted an elaborate hoax, for several years pretending to be president of a nonexistent Society for Indecency to Naked Animals, appearing as a guest on national television programs such as *Today*. More recently he had written for Steve Allen and *That Was the Week That Was*, a news satire derived from a successful BBC model. His first motion picture, *The Troublemaker*, scripted with its director, the improvisational troupe leader Theodore J. Flicker, was just about to be released.

Although the idea for the series had originated in-house, Talent Associates agreed to a credit of "Created by Mel Brooks" in its April 13, 1964, deal memo. Buck Henry's credit would be determined later, but the company saw Brooks as the more experienced and reputable writer. The first publicity for the series mentioned only Brooks, identifying him, in fact, as the planned "writer-producer" of the series. His bargaining position was strengthened when, even as the deal memo was being crafted, *The Critic* won its Oscar.

The deal memo hedged on making Brooks a producer of the series, instead offering him a generous consultancy. But his tentative terms, overseen by Alan U. Schwartz, gave him other edges, including escalations for residuals (up to $2,000 per episode in the third year), network reruns (from 50 percent of initial residuals down to 25 percent by the sixth and subsequent reruns), and syndication earnings ($250 per run around the world). Moreover, Brooks was guaranteed up to 25 percent participation in any postnetwork profits. While Brooks agreed to a $7,500 salary for developing the pilot, Henry, less famous and saddled with less effective representation, received $3,500 along with diminished royalties ($300 per episode over the run) and reduced postnetwork payments.

Susskind's company had brought Henry into the equation, so the second writer went under contract to Talent Associates instead of Crossbow Productions. The exact credits and terms—the split of future monies—would be nailed into place somewhere down the road, according to the deal memo.

• • •

The contractual fine points were fluid when, in mid-April, Brooks and Henry launched daily meetings at Talent Associates' offices. The two writers were given an office with chairs, desks, and typewriters. Melnick intermittently joined their work sessions, supplying the overview and company prerequisites: for example, the series with the working title of "Super Spy" ought to feature a beautiful girl agent, à la the James Bond girls.

Another person sometimes joining the sessions, though rarely mentioned in accounts, was Brooks's friend Alfa-Betty Olsen. Olsen was now an assistant to the Broadway producer Arthur Cantor. Brooks asked her if she would help with the new series's pilot script, manning the typewriter again. "Yes I could," Olsen recalled. "I would love to. I left Arthur."

Talent Associates boasted a pool table on its premises, and at first Brooks and Henry spent a lot of time playing pool and kibitzing. Susskind liked to join the pool games. "We were completely intimidated when he came into the room, and he was a crappy pool player and he beat us every time," recalled Henry. "I could have beaten him, but he was the boss," insisted Brooks. Actor Peter Falk, who was involved in various company projects, also popped in now and then and was included in the pool games.

"[The script] took us a long time to write," remembered Henry, "because we're both lazy and it's way more fun to talk about it than actually putting it down on paper."

Olsen was their typist as the work began in earnest in late April. Soon they had about a dozen pages. They couldn't decide on a name for the superspy, called "Bond" in the first synopsis, but they sketched in a "girl spy" who used knitting needles and a ball of wool to send telegraphic messages. They also proposed a "bumbling spy dog."

Melnick asked for a big tease opening that, each week, would proclaim the show's comic sensibility. Often a contrarian for contrarian's sake, Brooks argued against "the big joke opening" at one late April meeting. He preferred a more rarefied approach, according to production notes: "You can't do one laugh after another. Get more tension. Feels a level of reality must be retained like [*Dr.*] *Strangelove* [Stanley Kubrick's 1964 film starring Peter Sellers]. It should look like an adventure series, i.e., real bomber pilot as in *Strangelove*."

Everyone else opposed the Kubrick-type reality approach, and the series would ultimately offer no pretense of reality, with big teases the standard opening. The concept continued to evolve after Melnick, Brooks, and Henry took a trip to Boston to refresh their creativity. Many names were proposed for the super-spy—including Lance, Dagger, and Bounty Hunter—before Brooks came up with "Smart," first Raymond Smart, later amended to Maxwell Smart. Maxwell, Brooks explained in later interviews, was derived from Max, his father's name, the same as Max Bialystock in *The Producers*. The title was Brooks's; Melnick hated it at first because he thought it suggested a game show.

Which of the writers conceived of some of the famous running gags of *Get Smart*? Brooks and Henry hotly debated their provenance over the years. Brooks the cat lover believed he had conceived of the dopey spy-dog, Fang. Henry, informing Brooks in a rare joint interview years later that "I've got a much better memory than you," insisted that he devised the cone of silence while Brooks had dreamed up the shoe phone. (In his interview for the earlier *Get Smart* box set, Brooks had glibly taken credit for both.)

Topping each other with glee, the writers finished the first draft in May. The key characters were in place: the bumbling Secret Agent 86, aka Maxwell Smart; his beautiful sidekick, Agent 99; and the infinitely perturbable chief of CONTROL, the ultrasecret government agency that battles the evil personified by archrival KAOS. *Get Smart*'s pilot script also introduced the supervillain that would arrive to dominate each individual episode: Brooks named the first one Mr. Big and suggested he be played by a midget.

A daily presence at Talent Associates for weeks leading into the summer, Brooks also brainstormed an idea for his own TV series, which he hoped would follow in the successful wake of *Get Smart*. As usual he had a cowriter, paid by Crossbow: Art Baer, a veteran who had scripted for Victor Borge, Perry Como, and *Car 54, Where Are You?*

For this Brooks-only project, a family-friendly sitcom called "Triplets" that was more like *Inside Danny Baker* than *Get Smart*, Brooks imagined a comedy series revolving around high-earning young-married professionals who are overwhelmed by their new baby triplets. The couple hires a middle-aged dragon lady as their nanny ("think Hazel or Thelma Ritter," Brooks said), who assumes dictatorial command of the household.

The synopsis of "Triplets" promised "every familiar element to make it successful" and "good basic HUMAN comedy," in Brooks's words. "For beneath the surface and behind the façade, and when the moment of truth brings it out into the open, there is genuine love and real sentiment in all of the relationships" among the characters.

David Susskind was high on Brooks, who seemed to have an endless store of clever ideas. The "Triplets" deal memo was easy to write because Baer was an employee of Brooks's. Brooks was guaranteed a "Created by Mel Brooks" credit with regular consulting fees and escalating royalties for reruns and syndication. Talent Associates agreed to pay Brooks a little seed money to develop a pilot.

But if Talent Associates was cautiously optimistic about "Triplets," about *Get Smart*, whose pilot script was ready by September, it was supremely confident.


Four years had passed since Brooks and Anne Bancroft had met cute at a rehearsal for *The Perry Como Show*. Their friends often said they were magical together, always gabbing up a storm, laughing, enjoying the same kinds of foods and fun, the same pastimes mostly. Bancroft did not pester him about marriage. "Mel is so wonderful," the actress told *American Weekly* in 1962. "Most people, if you pinch them, they come out with a conventional 'ouch.' But he never says anything ordinary, he's so alive to the fun of life."

It helped that Bancroft had a separate career, acting on Broadway and in motion pictures. *Mother Courage* ran for only two months, but it was a taxing experience and preoccupied her for the first half of 1963. *The Pumpkin Eater* took up the second half. A stylish domestic drama directed by Jack Clayton, *The Pumpkin Eater* was shot in London, keeping Bancroft busy abroad for almost five months. It was an excellent role—as a dutiful mother discovering her husband's love affairs—and when *The Pumpkin Eater* was screened at the Cannes Film Festival the next year, Bancroft shared the prize for Best Actress with Barbara Barrie from *One Potato, Two Potato*. After *The Pumpkin Eater* was released in the United States in 1964, Bancroft got a second Oscar nomination for Best Actress.

Brooks visited Bancroft several times during the filming of *The Pumpkin Eater*. They adopted the lifelong habit of traveling to each other's film sets, especially when the location was London, their mutual favorite city in the world outside of New York.

In London in September 1963, the actress told the press she expected to marry "Mel Brooks, an American writer, this autumn," *The Guardian* reported. But another year soon passed; Bancroft was patient, however, and like an angler she had deeply set the hook.

Paradoxically it was true of the impetuous Brooks that certain notions took a long time to germinate with him, and the ones that took the longest often worked out best in practice. He was the ultimate improviser who was also known to have rehearsed some of his trademark lines or to have repeated them ad infinitum until they were warmly expected of him. He was the maximum controlled personality who also behaved off the cuff.

In mid-1964, Brooks was not yet quite a household name in the

United States. As a writer or performer he could not claim to enjoy the same level of recognition accorded to three other more successful Club Caesar alumni: Carl Reiner, Neil Simon, and Larry Gelbart. But suddenly he had especially promising irons in the fire, and he might strike it big with any one of them: *Get Smart*, "The Triplets," or "Marriage Is a Dirty Rotten Fraud."

His first marriage, memorialized in "Marriage Is a Dirty Rotten Fraud," had transpired after years of courtship. His second marriage was equally impromptu after long waiting.

As usual, in the summer of 1964, Brooks and Bancroft were spending as much time as possible at Bancroft's house on Fire Island, "repairing to separate rooms for family visits," according to biographer William Holtzman. Both made forays into the city for business purposes, however, with Brooks, Buck Henry, and Alfa-Betty Olsen meeting to polish the *Get Smart* pilot script at Talent Associates. Around lunchtime on August 5, the phone rang in their office. Anne Bancroft was calling. The trio of writers hurried down to the street, a cab pulled up, and Brooks jumped in. Henry and Olsen stood on Madison Avenue, waving as the cab bearing Brooks and Bancroft sped off.

A short time later the couple materialized in the deputy city clerk's office at City Hall and filled out the marriage license form as "Mel Brooks" and "Anne Italiano." Brooks grabbed a passerby, recruiting him as their witness. The spontaneity of it was such that they didn't bring wedding rings. Bancroft deployed her bendable silver earrings, which Brooks twisted into a ring for each of them. After signing the forms, Brooks returned to work at Talent Associates and Bancroft went home to prepare a spaghetti supper.

Although friends and family promptly learned about the marriage, the press was kept in the dark for almost a week. The *New York Times* reported the marriage on August 11 with the headline "Comedian Weds Anne Bancroft"—suggesting how Brooks's public identity had shifted. No longer "just a comedy writer," he was now a "comedian."

Both sets of parents were pleased. Kitty Kaminsky didn't care that the vows were secular or that Bancroft was Catholic. "When somebody becomes a star," Brooks explained later, "they're no longer, you know, Jewish or not Jewish. A star is a big thing, you know, six points is better, but a star! . . . my wife was a star. My mother was very happy."

Bancroft went almost straight from their brief honeymoon on Fire Island to Hollywood for rehearsals and Seattle for the filming of *The Slender Thread*, acting opposite Sidney Poitier. Her new husband visited her in both Hollywood and Seattle.

# CHAPTER 8

# 1965

## Springtime for Mel

ABC-TV surprised Talent Associates, in late October 1964, by passing on the *Get Smart* series. Remarkably, network executives felt that the bumbling US secret agent made the proposed series appear too un-American. Brooks, on one of his by now frequent trips to Hollywood, ran into Grant Tinker, NBC-TV's West Coast head of programming. Tinker, who already boasted spy/secret agent success with *I Spy* and *The Man from U.N.C.L.E.* on NBC, was eager to capitalize on ABC's stupidity. He wanted *Get Smart*, but he also wanted Don Adams, who was under contract to the network for *The Bill Dana Show*. Adams had a running part in the series as a bonehead detective not unlike the bonehead Maxwell Smart.

*Get Smart*'s lead had been crafted with the comedic actor Tom Poston in mind. Brooks knew Poston dating back to *Shinbone Alley*, when he had been Eddie Bracken's understudy. But Adams, whom everyone liked from stand-up and variety shows, was fine with Brooks and Talent Associates. Famous for his catchphrases, Adams would bring a few of his own to *Get Smart*, including the stalling-for-time "Would you believe . . . ?"

Barbara Feldon, a brainy brunette model whose acting résumé was modest, was Daniel Melnick's pick for Agent 99; and Edward Platt, the Chief, was a familiar face with a lengthy career that included a role as Cary Grant's lawyer in Alfred Hitchcock's *North by Northwest*.

Brooks had envisioned the pint-sized English actor Michael Dunn as Mr. Big—months before *Ship of Fools* would be released with Dunn's Oscar-caliber performance. On the commentary tracks for the *Get Smart* box set, Brooks also took credit for "that blonde," the British actress Janine Gray from *The Pumpkin Eater*, who portrayed the she-villain in the first episode. ("I hired that girl personally," he said, "because she was so talented.") Brooks also pushed to hire his friend Howard Morris, whose early TV-directing stints had included several episodes of *The Bill Dana Show*, to steer the pilot.

The pilot was shot at NBC Studios in Los Angeles in the second week of January 1965, with the standard schedule of one rehearsal day and five camera days. Brooks and Anne Bancroft flew to Hollywood for the occasion. Still being paid as a consultant for the series, Brooks had been involved in all the major casting and production discussions.

Curiously, the pilot was photographed in black and white, after which the series would switch to a brightly colored palette. Director Jay Sandrich, also from *The Bill Dana Show*, and writer-producer Leonard Stern were brought in by Melnick to manage the series, with Sandrich staying for the first season and Stern for the entire five-year run.

While in Hollywood, Brooks always rendezvoused with Carl Reiner, who had established a beachhead there and whose West Coast presence acted like a powerful magnet on the other Club Caesar writers. Brooks also met with Marvin Schwartz. The onetime press agent had made good on his ambition of forming a motion picture company with the veteran writer-director Philip Dunne. Blackhill, their new production entity, promptly optioned "Marriage Is a Dirty Rotten Fraud," to be filmed probably in late 1965 or early '66.

Both Mr. and Mrs. Brooks lingered for weeks in Hollywood after Bancroft accepted a role in John Ford's *7 Women*, replacing Patricia Neal on a moment's notice without seeing the script. (Neal, who had played Helen Keller's mother onstage in *The Miracle Worker*, had suffered several strokes.) Ford and Bancroft—Catholics both—got along splendidly. Shot mainly at MGM, *7 Women* was destined to be Ford's last feature.

Then, the way things worked in those days, NBC took the *Get Smart* pilot under advisement, mandating a few changes (including the switch to color) and shopping the show around to potential advertisers. It would be months before the series got on the air.

During those months, the bulk of 1964, Brooks sought short-term jobs that paid well for minimal amounts of time and effort. Doctoring Broadway plays had begun to taper off, and one of his last such fix-it jobs was for a musical called *Kelly*, which told the tale of Steve Brodie—called Hop Kelly in the show—who had become a celebrity at the turn of the century by jumping off the Brooklyn Bridge. Joseph E. Levine and Talent Associates were the producing partners for *Kelly*; it was the first Broadway musical for both Levine and David Susskind. *Kelly* had a score by Mark "Moose" Charlap (famous for his *Peter Pan* songs) and a book by the comic Eddie Lawrence (whose "The Old Philosopher" was a one-hit wonder in 1956). The earliest previews had been unfavorable.

The producers blamed the music and the book, and they had all but given up on Charlap and Lawrence. In late January, as *Kelly* continued to flounder in out-of-town tryouts, Susskind and Talent Associates partner Daniel Melnick thought of Brooks and Leonard Stern. Flown to Boston to watch and critique the musical, the *Get Smart* team arrived straight from the West Coast and high-level meetings with NBC in Hollywood.

A small group assembled in a Ritz Hotel suite for the postmortem late one night after Brooks and Stern had sat through a preview performance. The worried faces in the room included Susskind, Melnick, and the show's choreographer-director, Herbert Ross.

A *Saturday Evening Post* reporter, Lewis H. Lapham, was embedded with the production, and Lapham preserved a portrait of Brooks in action in this kind of emergency situation. Brooks ("a small energetic man with thinning hair") did most of the funny talking, Lapham noted, while Stern ("taller and heavier . . . wearing a goatee and elaborate gold cuff links in his silk shirt") listened, chewed gum, and spoke solemnly.

The talking/performing writer was typically blunt, his vernacular colorful. "You've got a Chink's chance [of saving the show]," Brooks told the producers. "As cloying, as horrible, and as saccharine as some of the scenes are, the audience seems to forgive." He advised them to give up on the prominent actress Ella Logan from *Finian's Rainbow*, who was unhappily cast as Hop Kelly's mother. "I didn't believe a mother's tears wouldn't work but it doesn't. She softens the show. She's out there selling torn-rubber raincoats."

"She is just dreadful," director Ross conceded.

"It'll be a pleasure to fire her," Melnick added.

"What we are up against, fellas," Brooks pursued, "is grievous errors in the structure of the book; too many extraneous characters sing extraneous songs. Moose and Eddie wrote some marvelous stuff, but they only brought you to the five-yard line. No touchdown."

"The end of Act One," Stern interjected, "I don't know where is the commitment."

"The first three numbers in Act Two," Brooks said, "are the worst, seventy-five miles an hour into a stone wall. Death. Three losers back to back."

"That song," Stern added, "that awful song . . . what's the name of it?"

" 'Home Again,' " said Ross.

"Well, it's terrible," Stern continued. "What should be an enchanting lyrical moment is a pedantic horror."

Everyone agreed wholeheartedly with the criticisms, according to *The Saturday Evening Post*. Ross sank into his chair, staring at Brooks through steepled fingers. "You have a very incisive mind, Mel,"

Melnick declared after the initial tensions in the room dissipated. The producer had begun to feel hopeful. "It's fabulous, Mel, fabulous . . ."

Susskind asked plaintively if there was anything at all worth saving in the musical. Then as later in his career, Brooks counted on performers to give a boost to lame material. He said that the young unknown playing Kelly, a Canadian named Don Francks, was "the best thing" the show had going. "Go all the way with the kid," Brooks exhorted the producer. "The love for the kid is the tickets. More love, more tickets."

Stern thought they should cut three or four of the worst songs, except that then *Kelly* would run too short. Brooks snorted. "So what? Light the blaze under Don Francks. A few happy moments for the tired businessman watching some girls jump around on stage, and everybody goes home at ten o'clock. They'll be glad to get the first cabs."

Susskind wondered aloud if Hop Kelly's leap from the Brooklyn Bridge, which climaxed Act Two, was ineffective because it was so obviously done with wires. "Leave it in," Brooks responded. "The hippies know he's on wires, but the Hadassah don't."

The talking wound down. By 2:00 a.m., the group was on its eleventh pot of coffee. The producers decided to commission tunes from new songwriters to replace the lackluster ones. Brooks and Stern were asked to write "two scenes" and "several comedy routines" that might bolster the sagging libretto. The confab lasted until dawn; then Susskind, Melnick, and Ross departed. Brooks and Stern lingered behind, charged with their task. Stern paced while Brooks stretched out on the sofa, smoking a cigarette.

"Isn't it fantastic?" Brooks asked Melnick as the producer wearily said his good-byes. "You see things in the last six days that you should have seen a year ago . . . fantastic. It's the same with all shows in trouble. The same sad tune but different lyrics."

All this went down regardless of Dramatists Guild of America rules barring major script surgery without the consent or involvement of Charlap and Lawrence. The two creators of *Kelly* sent an angry "cease and desist" letter to the producers, followed by a lawsuit.

*Kelly* finally made it to Broadway, closing after just one performance on February 6, 1965—an infamous flop that dwarfed that of *"All American"*. The investors (principally producers Susskind and Levine with their investment boosted by another LP advance from Columbia Records) lost $650,000. Talent Associates paid a substantial out-of-court settlement to Charlap and Lawrence, who felt that Brooks and Stern had trampled on the rights of fellow writers; years later, according to Lawrence, Brooks tacitly agreed, privately telling him he felt bad about the role he'd played in their highhanded exclusion.

Emergency writing had been Brooks's bread and butter for the first half of the 1960s. He was hardly to blame for the *Kelly* fiasco, but Broadway increasingly seemed a dead end for him. The last known example of his stage doctoring was notes he submitted on the comedy *The Best Laid Plans* for the persistent producer Hillard Elkins in 1965.

Meanwhile, with the success of Brooks's movie trailers one year earlier, advertising jobs for hire began to fill the gaps of time and money that were always an issue for Brooks.

The young whizzes of the Young & Rubicam advertising agency were among the fans of the 2000 Year Old Man, and the ad agency also had paid attention to Brooks's eccentric movie trailers. In mid-1965, the agency hired Brooks to incarnate "the 2500 Year Old Brewmaster" for Ballantine beer. Young & Rubicam recruited Dick Cavett to interview the brewmaster for a series of spots as "a Carl Reiner stand-in," in Cavett's words. A onetime stand-up comedian from Nebraska, Cavett knew Brooks from the days when he had been a talent coordinator and writer for *The Tonight Show*. Brooks had assessed Cavett early in their acquaintance as "spectacularly Gentile," which had become a running joke between them. Now they'd capitalize on their chemistry for Ballantine beer.

"There was not a word of script" for their sixty-second radio advertisements, Cavett recalled. Cavett impersonated a young eager beaver carrying his hand mike into an ancient cave, peppering the venerable one with queries about the client's product. "The ad agency guy directing our sessions urged, 'Just hit Mel with anything that comes to mind, the way Carl does. He's best when he doesn't know what's coming.'"

**Cavett:** Sir, I don't think you've actually tasted the beer we're selling. Do so now.
**Brooks:** All right, Fluffy. (Sipping sound: voop! voop!)
**Cavett:** How would you put it, sir?
**Brooks:** My tongue just threw a party for my mouth!

Their first taping session ran three hours, with Cavett, the ad agency director, and the recording engineer holding their sides in laughter. Later that year the outtakes were featured on a WNEW radio program called "The Making of a Commercial," and *Variety* said that Brooks's "ad-lib fallout had a span from brilliantly witty to embarrassingly inane." But they used only the brilliantly witty stuff in the commercials, and no less an authority than the *New York Times* described the Ballantine spots as "outstanding." Young & Rubicam attracted rare fan mail for its brewmaster spots. Unfortunately, the beer itself was "not equally adored," Cavett remembered; sales did not mushroom, and the sponsor declined to bankroll any future advertisements starring the 2500 Year Old Brewmaster. However, Cavett said, he and Brooks did enjoy a brief "storm of royalty checks."

Their friendship and repartee would stretch into the future. After Cavett became a successful talk-show host in the late 1960s, Brooks became one of his most willing interview victims. The professional talkers and listeners, button-down men such as David Susskind, Johnny Carson, and Cavett, embraced their opposite in the unpredictable Brooks.

Acclaim for the beer commercials opened up similar doors for Brooks in the late 1960s and early '70s. He began touting Circus Nuts, Bic pens, Fritos, and Teacher's Scotch, among other products. Some of his sales pitches are included in *The Incredible Mel Brooks* box set. In 1968, he even took home a Clio Award, the industry's top prize for excellence in radio and television advertising, for his U.S. Tobacco spots. The obscure Clio was usually slighted when his rare EGOT achievement—i.e., winning an Emmy, Grammy, Oscar, and Tony—was later mentioned.

With Lever soap and R. J. Reynolds Tobacco on board as sponsors, *Get Smart* finally saw its premiere on September 18, 1965, slotted at 8:30 p.m. EST on Saturday nights. Certain high-minded television critics, Jack Gould of the *New York Times* for instance, were not sure the series was a keeper, saying the pilot's humor was overdone and characters such as Mr. Big, played by a dwarf, evidenced (one of the first times the charge was leveled at Brooks) "an undercurrent of tastelessness." *Variety*, by contrast, saw Saturday evenings as "kid night at the tube." NBC had shrewdly positioned *Get Smart* as an alternative to the geriatric programming on ABC and the more sophisticated shows on CBS. The "broad and unadulterated hokum," *Variety* said, was poised "to show its heels to the pack."

Inside the business, the *Get Smart* series had only fans and admirers. The show drew four major nominations in the annual Emmy Awards competition in 1966, including an Outstanding Writing Achievement in Comedy nod to Brooks and Buck Henry for their "Mr. Big" pilot (they lost to a Sam Denoff–Bill Persky segment of *The Dick Van Dyke Show*). *Get Smart* was also nominated for Outstanding

Comedy Series (again losing to *The Dick Van Dyke Show*). Don Adams went up for Outstanding Continued Performance by an Actor in a Leading Role in a Comedy Series (although he lost to Dick Van Dyke, Adams would go on to win three acting Emmys for the series in the years ahead). And there was a nomination for Outstanding Directorial Achievement in Comedy—not the "Mr. Big" episode but a different one—with regular *Get Smart* director Paul Bogart losing to William Asher for a *Bewitched* installment.

Just as important, *Get Smart* ended the year at number twelve in the Nielsens—NBC's highest-rated show after *Bonanza* at number one. The superspy comedy would stay on the air for five years in prime time.

For Brooks, over the years, the series generated considerable first-run and syndication earnings, along with eventual video percentages—not only for the series but for the many spin-off versions: the first film rendition, *The Nude Bomb*, starring Adams, in 1980; the made-for-TV *Get Smart, Again!*, reuniting Adams and Barbara Feldon in 1989; the short-lived *Get Smart, Again!* television series in 1995; the rebooted 2008 film variation starring Steve Carell and Anne Hathaway; a made-for-DVD throwaway revolving around the secondary characters; plus numerous insignia products. "I got a [royalty] check today for $50,000!" for *Get Smart*, Brooks boasted to an interviewer in 1993.

Though in time the superspy spoof became a cash cow, the financial impact on Brooks was not instantaneous. Actually, he suffered a drop in expected income from the series before its premiere. After the pilot episode was made, clauses in his contract kicked in that had to be concretized, including the one in which, throughout the first season, he was supposed to function as a consultant, "read all scripts and make suggestions." He was supposed to earn an extra $1,500 per ten episodes as a credited story consultant.

In every possible way the initial deal memos had privileged Brooks over Buck Henry, starting with the informally agreed upon

"Created by Mel Brooks." Henry's agent had gone ballistic when he discovered that language, and Talent Associates' executives had grown sympathetic to the likelihood that Henry had been screwed. Eight months passed between the filming of the pilot and the NBC premiere, by which time everyone (except Brooks) saw Henry as an equal partner in the creation. Daniel Melnick and Leonard Stern wanted Henry's goodwill and steady hand; they wanted him as their script consultant. Melnick signed Henry to a story editor contract covering the first two years of *Get Smart*, which also called upon him to write multiple episodes of the series.

Though Henry's revised contract compensated him as story editor, his salary actually fell below Brooks's projected consultancy payments. Henry would receive $1,250 per show for his daily duties on *Get Smart*, while Brooks was due to earn an extra $1,500 per episode for doing—what both Talent Associates and Henry suspected, according to internal memoranda—as little as possible and farming out any real script troubles.

Using Brooks's consultancy as a wedge, Talent Associates went back into the deal memo on the eve of *Get Smart*'s premiere, revisiting the terms pledged to Brooks and Henry, "the two creative genii," as executive Kirk Honeystein phrased it felicitously. Based on the reality of what had transpired behind the scenes in the partnership, the company proposed new language: "Created by Mel Brooks and Buck Henry." Brooks dug in his heels, insisting his name take precedence, but Honeystein pointed out to Alan U. Schwartz that the solo "created by" credit had been tentative in April 1964 and its temporary nature "was exposed to you and to Mel very frankly. . . . I thought [that] had been agreed to." Honeystein reminded Schwartz that Talent Associates had consented to "created by" but that the company had actually conceived the show and controlled the creative rights. "For historical reference," he noted, "neither Mel nor Buck are really the creators here."

The dispute had simmered over the summer, with Schwartz

threatening litigation. Talent Associates stood its ground, believing it had the better chance of gaining a victory in any lawsuit. Brooks backed down in stages, asking for extra money and a consultancy credit on the first eight shows in the first season, then four, finally none. He was "irked" by the demotion, according to Talent Associates memos, and voiced threats to wash his hands of the whole series, "rendering no more consultancy services of any kind." A company executive privately wrote to Melnick, "Do we need his touch?"

The answer was no. Brooks was obliged to share the "created by" credit that would appear after the tease opener of each episode; his consultancy position was dropped; and as a final slight his 25 percent profit slice was reduced to 15 percent.

"Created by Mel Brooks *with* [author's emphasis] Buck Henry" became the compromise language for the originating credit. The *with* instead of *and* might have been arcane for audiences, but inside the business the distinction ranked Henry's contribution as secondary both creatively and financially. Henry's agent fought against *with* but was outlawyered by Schwartz. Brooks got his name on a line *above* Henry's and in bigger type. Henry was given a sop: "Written by Mel Brooks and Buck Henry," with Brooks's name still positioned above Henry's, was on the end credits for the pilot episode—only.

Henry had cause to grumble in later years when Brooks gave interviews explicitly or implicitly taking credit for this or that idea for the series, but the underlying cause of friction between them was Brooks's preferential contract, which gave him the upper hand in the originating credits and in future royalties and spin-off income for decades to come.

Down the years, the two creative genii sniped at each other behind the scenes. Sometimes they even sniped in public. Brooks was irate when Kenneth Tynan told him that Henry had bet that Brooks's name would appear an egomaniacal five times on the credits of *High Anxiety*, his 1978 Hitchcock parody. "Tell him from me he's wrong.

The correct number is six [lyricist, composer, actor, writer, director, producer]," Brooks snapped.

Asked by Tynan about the feud behind *Get Smart*, Brooks attacked Henry by way of defending himself. "I had a reputation for being a crazy Jew animal, whereas Buck thought of himself as an intellectual. Well, I was an intellectual too," he explained. "What Buck couldn't bear was the idea of this wacko Jew being billed over him. The truth is that he read magazines but he's not an intellectual, he's a pedant."

Over the summer, in advance of the premiere, Buck Henry and Leonard Stern gave Brooks the two *Get Smart* episode assignments mandated in his contract. Brooks wrote number ten, "Our Man in Leotards," with Caesar Club member Gary Belkin, and number fifteen, "Survival of the Fattest," with Ronny Pearlman. The scripts paid $3,500 each, with Brooks in charge of the split. Brooks received boosted royalties for airings of the two episodes, which were not among the best of the first season. And they were the last episodes of the hit series that he'd write.

Talent Associates desired his name for publicity, however, and Brooks gave many interviews promoting *Get Smart*, even its supposed social commentary, while disparaging other television series. "It's a show in which you can comment, too. I don't mean we're in the broken-wing business. We're not social workers, but we can do some comment such as you can't inject in, say, *My Three Sons*." And "It'll never be *Petticoat Junction*. I never want to do that. If I ever did I'd go out and put a bullet in my foot—wing myself."

Brooks acted above the fray with David Susskind. He was no longer "irked." He didn't care to alienate Talent Associates because he pinned such hopes on "Triplets," which was going to be *his* TV series, emblazoned with his name only as creator. With its family-friendly premise—a crusty nanny raising triplets for a professional couple—hopes for "Triplets" peaked in the fall of 1965, benefiting from the *Get Smart* hoopla.

Brooks's contract for the projected series, by now retitled "The Triplets and I," was easier to craft than the pilot script, however. Over the summer Brooks supervised Art Baer and his writing partner, Ben Joelson, but Baer and Joelson struggled with the tone of the comedy before Brooks gave up on them and sought Club Caesar reinforcements.

Again he tried wooing Lucille Kallen, who was busy with her novel writing and did not want to work on the project with Brooks as her boss. Then he turned to Big Mel—Mel Tolkin—who was available for the rewrite. Tolkin did what he could and moved on.

Domestic situations were never Brooks's forte, and like other times when he made stabs at family-friendly sitcoms, "Triplets" never came alive on the page. The project slipped off Talent Associates' radar after the initial *Get Smart* excitement died down.

Even so, Brooks and Susskind remained on good terms. Susskind had insulated himself from the contract wrangling; Melnick had handled that, and for Susskind it was the usual mud wrestling over a deal. He still found Brooks one of the funniest guys alive.


Similarly benefiting from the excitement surrounding the blastoff of *Get Smart*, "Marriage Is a Dirty Rotten Fraud," Brooks's script fashioned for a Rock Hudson–type star, saw a spike in its chances of becoming his first feature-length film.

Brooks traveled to Hollywood in the fall of 1965, trying to bolster the momentum. Briefly he worked out of the offices of Blackhill Productions (the Marvin Schwartz–Philip Dunne company) at Universal Studios in Universal City, located in the San Fernando Valley. Carl Reiner had nearby offices on the lot, as did Cary Grant, which led to a favorite Brooks anecdote, told on *The Tonight Show* more than once (including during Johnny Carson's final week in 1992). One version is included on *The Incredible Mel Brooks* box set.

Grant was an enormous fan of the 2000 Year Old Man and cadged free copies of the LPs from Reiner, claiming at one point to be taking them over to England for the royal family. Brooks was excited one Monday to glimpse Hollywood's debonair leading man spring out of a car on the Universal lot—in the retelling, sometimes it was a Rolls-Royce, other times a Porsche. The living, breathing icon looked as though he had stepped out of a screwball comedy, wearing a flower in his lapel (make that a boutonniere in Brooks's favorite color: yellow). Brooks shook the star's hand and was invited to lunch in the studio commissary, where they held the sort of conversation only Brooks could conjure up. (" 'What is your favorite car?' . . . I said Buick, he said Rolls-Royce.") Relishing his company, Grant phoned Brooks every day for a week, arranging more lunches. But Brooks found less and less to talk about ("he was a real *schnorrer*"), until on Friday, Grant called the office, Brooks answered and said no, Brooks wasn't there anymore.

Such anecdotes that built into laughs stretched like Pinocchio's nose in Brooks's hands: the specifics of what Grant had ordered for lunch ("just a hard-boiled egg") versus what Brooks himself ordered ("a tuna fish sandwich on whole wheat bread with tomato") were as writerly as they were changeable. Other parties that might have been present—in this case, probably Carl Reiner—were left out of the anecdotes altogether. Brooks's anecdotes were like oral short stories or comic sketches that he polished to a gloss over the years. "Who can tell when the manic Mr. Brooks is remembering and when he's improvising?" as Walter Goodman wrote some years later in the *New York Times.*

The Cary Grant encounter was the highlight of the whole "Marriage Is a Dirty Rotten Fraud" saga, however. Rock Hudson had agreed to be penciled in, but as it happened, Blackhill Productions got only one motion picture off the ground—*Blindfold* starring Hudson—before senior partner Philip Dunne, whose career harked back to the early 1930s, quit the business and Marvin Schwartz soldiered on alone as producer of the more sure thing, *The War Wagon*, starring top-ten box-office attraction John Wayne.

Schwartz was genuinely quirky. He left Hollywood several years later to travel around the world with a backpack, becoming a follower of Buddha. Brooks never lost his fondness for Schwartz, and Schwartz family members are convinced that "The Schwartz be with you!" is a tribute to their friendship. Although another Schwartz was Brooks's longtime lawyer, of course (Alan U. Schwartz would appear in cameos in several Mel Brooks films including *Spaceballs*), for Brooks two reasons for something were even better than one.

In any event, Brooks did not abandon "Marriage Is a Dirty Rotten Fraud" overnight. Nine years later, in 1975, a journalist visiting Brooks at 20th Century–Fox for the Directors Guild magazine reported that storyboards for the semiautobiographical romantic comedy lined one office wall. Brooks was still musing about filming his pet script.

It was a script that would have needed at least one more vigorous rewrite. Martin Charnin had nothing more to do with "Marriage Is a Dirty Rotten Fraud" after its first draft, other than hearing occasional mention of the project in the press. But Charnin recalled of the script, "It was long. Excessive. It needed a lot of pruning and caring. It needed to be focused more."

Although Brooks had personalized the story and characters, he also pulled his punches so that the script was neither particularly intimate nor confessional. Nor was it "dangerous" comedy. Striving for commercial appeal, he had tried instead for the Nice Mel, lending his most autobiographical script what was ultimately a conventional quality. By the end of 1966—much less 1975—"Marriage Is a Dirty Rotten Fraud" was a dead bunny.

• • •

Returning from Hollywood, Anne Bancroft accepted one of the leads in a new Broadway play, *The Devils*, which the Royal Shakespeare Company had originated in London. Based on Aldous Huxley's nonfiction-based novel about the demonic possession of a convent in seventeenth-century France, *The Devils* would open in November and last for sixty-three performances.

While Bancroft was busy and "Marriage Is a Dirty Rotten Fraud" slowly ran aground, Brooks had plenty of time on his hands. "Marriage Is a Dirty Rotten Fraud" was a pretty square comedy, considering that the sixties were in full flower. Nowadays, in public and private, he might throw around, even write words such as *hippie, dig it,* and *groovy,* but he also used *Chink* and *fag* on occasion and was no more engaged in the sixties—the antiwar and civil rights protests, the demonstrations and riots, the psychedelic rock and roll and recreational drug taking, the lifestyle revolution—than most people's grandmothers were.

Charles Strouse had been a participant in the Selma-to-Montgomery March for civil rights in 1965. Carl Reiner hosted anti–Vietnam War fund-raisers. Norman Lear went on to found the progressive advocacy organization People for the American Way. But the solipsistic Brooks steered clear of political commitments or contributions.

The notion that he can be spotted in Robert Downey, Sr.'s, *Putney Swope,* a satire that brought black power to Madison Avenue, seems plausible—because couldn't the 2000 Year Old Man turn up anywhere? Yet it is an urban myth sustained by the Internet; another Mel Brooks, an actor by that name, appeared in that ultrahip independent film.

Brooks could be said to wear a patchwork of influences, most dating back to his boyhood in the 1930s. He passed through the tumultuous sixties more like an accidental tourist, shrewd about seeing the sights and grabbing souvenirs. Traveling always in the same small circles—music, comedy clubs, theater, ad agencies, radio, television, and film—now and then, however, he incongruously intersected with the extremes of the decade.

Shortly after its opening in December 1965, Brooks became the most unlikely regular of Max's Kansas City at the corner of East 17th Street and Park Avenue. At Max's, which quickly became one of New York's trendiest restaurants and nightclubs, Brooks hung out at a round table of off-Broadway performers, writers, and artists, many of whom lived in the East or West Village. Among the group were Michael Elias and his writing partner Frank Shaw;* there were also the self-deprecating blonde Alfa-Betty Olsen and her boyfriend, David Patch, a director passionate about Henrik Ibsen; Kenneth H. Brown, a former marine who had written *The Brig* for the Living Theatre; and actors Rip Torn and Geraldine Page. In Max's more exclusive back room you'd be apt to find the poet Patti Smith, the artist Andy Warhol, and the acid-rock Lou Reed and Velvet Underground.

*Your Show of Shows* was already a faint memory to younger people, television was uncool, and Brooks was just another guy at the table, albeit famous for being the 2000 Year Old Man, but that was old-man Jewish comedy, already passé to sixties rebels. Brooks could listen as well as he talked if he felt like it, however, and he could never resist performing. He churned out bits for the Max's group, ad nauseam. Max's stayed open until very late, but at closing time, Brooks, who hated to walk home alone or pay for a taxi, would often jump into someone else's cab to share the ride.

His generous gestures—buying champagne for everyone at the table when someone's play opened—were fondly remembered. If someone rubbed him the wrong way, however, he'd erupt with a brusqueness and foul language that were equally memorable.

---

* One day in the future, Michael Elias would collaborate with Steve Martin on *The Jerk*, and Carl Reiner would direct the film; together Elias and Frank Shaw would write *The Frisco Kid* for Gene Wilder.

He was insulting even to the owner of Max's, Mickey Ruskin, who one night passed by the table, pulled up a chair, and snapped his fingers at a waitress. "Coffee!" Brooks stared at him stonily. "Who invited you to join us?" Ruskin was flustered. "Ha, Mel." Brooks rejoined, "No, I'm serious. You think just because you own the place you can sit down with the famous interesting people? You want to sit with us, pick up the check."

Ruskin left.

Perhaps Max's was where Brooks crossed paths for the first time with the quintessential sixties littérateur Terry Southern; or maybe David Begelman, Southern's agent, introduced them; or perhaps it was Alan U. Schwartz, who also represented the author of *Candy* and scenarist of *Dr. Strangelove* and other Peter Sellers pictures Brooks adored. Around the time of Max's opening, Brooks courted Southern, with his sixties cachet, to be his ghost partner for another spec script—probably intended as a film—called "The Last Man," which would take Brooks's wellspring of jokes about homosexuals into the realm of wild satire.

Brooks's story, which appears to have been typed up by Southern from their talks, devised, for the first time, a starring role for him—playing a character named "Mel"—who also narrates with a "voice characterization" (according to the synopsis) à la *The Critic*.

The story began with "Mel" convinced by John Rechy's novel *City of Night*, a *Life* magazine spread on "Homosexuals in America," and growing statistics from newspapers that "faggots" were everywhere, "8½" in his building alone, "not including the Super."

Believing that one out of every five men in America is a "faggot," which meant at least one of his own best friends is thus inclined, "Mel" jumps on a city bus to explore the new world of homosexuality blossoming all around him. He warily eyes tall, crew-cut Madison Avenue types. He goes shopping, making purchases that include an appropriate athletic supporter. (Saleslady: "What size?" Mel: "LARGE!") He balks when a "charming" male salesman tries to measure his inside crotch, however. And he likes it less when a psychiatrist tells him to lie down on the couch. ("Another Dirty Doctor!")

A "tall, well-dressed, well-built Negro man" winks at "Mel," and his voice-over mocks prejudices: "He's not a colored fellow . . . he's a FAG!" When another handsome man begins to follow "Mel," his paranoia grows until in an elevator the man whips out a gun and steals his money, his watch, his tiepin, everything. ("Thank god he was a mugger! I was afraid he was a fag!") His self-exploration ends when he attempts to make nice with a genuine "fag," who rejects his advances, leaving "Mel" to wonder "how come he is not attractive to 'them' and determined to take steps to alter the situation."

The six-page synopsis suggests that those vignettes were plotted out in an open-ended manner. Brooks had several dozen "other ideas" ready to flesh out the story line.

Although "The Last Man" was hardly a topical satire of gay liberation, neither was it as sweet and earnest as other Brooks script efforts in the 1960s. Its "faggot" and "colored man" language were already outdated, however, and its humor was corny. Perhaps Southern's Beat sensibility could have juiced it up the way Richard Pryor later elevated *Blazing Saddles*. But Southern and "The Last Man" did not progress beyond the synopsis.


The interviews he gave attest that Brooks still nursed lofty literary ambitions. "I like what I do—getting ideas and writing about them," he told one journalist in the 1960s, "and one day I'd like to be better at it. I'd like to write more screenplays, or a Broadway play, or a book, which—hopefully—would note people's tears and joys, and say something about the human condition. I'd like to grow up and be Sean O'Brooks."

But he still badly needed collaborators, and the collaborator who helped him achieve his breakthrough, his most important collaborator, was not Terry Southern, his show business friend Martin Charnin, or witty Buck Henry.

It was Alfa-Betty Olsen.

Turning dejectedly away from "Triplets," "Marriage Is a Dirty Rotten Fraud," and "The Last Man," Brooks finally set his sights on a project that had been on his back burner for almost eight years. As always, he needed the pretense of a typist's assistance. When, in mid-1966, he finally got serious about writing "Springtime for Hitler," he returned to the amanuensis who had helped with *"All American"* and *Get Smart*, a woman as clever and funny as she was Miss Norway–pretty. Olsen had moved on and was working as an assistant to Lore Noto, another Brooklynite, the producer of *The Fantasticks*, which was in the midst of becoming the longest-running off-Broadway musical in history. Noto was busy developing a musical based on Marjorie Kinnan Rawlings's novel *The Yearling*.

Olsen was so pretty that some people thought Brooks was having some kind of romance with her, despite the fact Olsen had a steady boyfriend whom she married in 1967. What she and Brooks did have was a mutual admiration society, a kinship in which he always laughed at her kooky humor and she always laughed at his antics and jokes. When they brainstormed scenes, with Olsen typing, Olsen had an editor's instinct for what should stay and what should go. Adding her two cents' worth to lines and scenes as they evolved (Kenneth Tynan described her as "an inventive secretary"), Olsen also had the great virtue, certainly in Brooks's eyes, of modesty and lack of concern about rewards.

Brooks had originally conceived of his story as a novel; then it had grown into a possible stage musical; now, as the stage musical became a film, the script became a musical within a film about two producers planning to mount "Springtime for Hitler," a surefire flop that they pitch as "A Gay Romp with Adolf and Eva at Berchtesgaden." Brooks and Olsen worked at Noto's theater district office, trading space for answering his phone and taking messages; other times they convened at the midtown apartment of producer Stanley Chase, who got his return favor by driving Brooks's '59 Jaguar around on the West Coast.

Over time Brooks had given names to the two producers: Max Bialystock was a middle-aged fop of a hustler whose surname derived from a large city in Poland and, in the words of Merriam-Webster, "a flat breakfast roll that has a depressed center and is usually covered with onion flakes," beloved by Jews. Leopold Bloom was his newly engaged, febrile young accountant, whose name came from the protagonist of James Joyce's *Ulysses*. ("I don't know what it meant to James Joyce," Brooks later informed *The New Yorker*, "but to me Leo Bloom always meant a vulnerable Jew with curly hair.")[*]

Brooks consciously crafted the two main characters as representatives of his divided self: the Nice Mel (Bloom) and the Rude Crude Mel (Bialystock). "Max and Leo are me, the ego and id of my personality," he explained later. "Bialystock—tough, scheming, full of ideas, bluster, ambition, wounded pride. And Leo, this magical child."

Bialystock was the more obvious Mel: all "flash and noise," as the treatment described him, "not an ordinary man—he is a FORCE... extravagantly alive." The impresario of forgettable Broadway shows, Bialystock finagles seed money from the sex-starved old ladies he seduces in his Times Square office. His new accountant, Bloom, is a shy number cruncher who figures out that a huge flop, which has been overly invested in by, say, 25,000 percent, could escape an Internal Revenue Service audit and make more in profits than a long-running hit. The odd bedfellows decide to stage the biggest

---

[*] Brooks would also have seen *Ulysses in Nighttown*, an off-Broadway sensation in 1958, for which Zero Mostel had won an Obie Award for his performance as another vision of Leopold Bloom—one who could hardly be described as "a vulnerable Jew with curly hair."

turnoff ever, "Springtime for Hitler," an ode to you-know-who, whose script has been submitted by a Nazi enthusiast. When critics and audiences greet the musical as a genius spoof, "Springtime" becomes a runaway success, and the crooked duo go to jail.

The dumb blond goddess that is their secretary was a patent burlesque of Olsen. Brooks mused about playing the Nazi-admiring playwright, another wacky supporting character, though he never wavered in his determination to direct the film himself.

For once Brooks did little else for months, turning down most other small jobs and offers, appearing on only a few game shows such as *The Face Is Familiar* and *Eye Guess* in 1966. Over the first half of the year, he and Olsen drew up a 150-page outline, which became a 400-page first-draft screenplay, then finally a 122-page shooting script. They spent most of the late summer on Fire Island at the Lonelyville house. "They worked in their bathing suits on the deck, with a portable electric typewriter set up on a small table among the folding chairs," according to *Vanity Fair*'s authoritative account.

Olsen listened and typed up the immortal maxims oozing from Brooks's mouth: "When you've got it, flaunt it!," "Money is honey!," and "He who hesitates is poor!"

Nobody who glimpsed the two working together, nobody who knew Olsen, thought the typist was "just a typist." Olsen was imaginative in her own right. "Not being able to keep my mouth shut again," she recalled, "I put a few things into it."

Olsen was never less than "thrilled," however, "in seventh heaven to be working with Mel," she said later. "After all, he had written for Sid Caesar." She felt Brooks's yearning for solo greatness. "You could feel him reaching for the brass ring. Writing *The Producers* was Mel creating himself; he wanted to declare himself on the world."

Brooks verbally pitched the daring comedy around New York offices and met with interest from the theatrical agent Barry Levinson, who was working closely with Sidney Glazier to line up properties for independent production.* An executive of the Eleanor Roosevelt Foundation for Cancer Research, Glazier had made a documentary about the former first lady that won an Academy Award in 1965, and now he wanted to produce feature films. Brooks knew Glazier in passing from Fire Island. They arranged to meet at a coffee shop. As usual Brooks was full of jokes, "some of which weren't too funny, and I was a little uncomfortable," as Glazier recalled. Then Brooks started reading highlights from the script. Glazier nearly choked on his coffee with laughter.

From Philadelphia, the son of Russian-Jewish immigrants, Glazier had been thrust into an Orthodox orphanage as a boy before rising up in the world with a knack for charming money out of well-heeled connections. To produce motion pictures, he had partnered with an investment company called United Marion, or U-M Productions, registered in New York and Florida, run by Louis Wolfson, a Wall Street financier and self-made millionaire with a passion for breeding thoroughbreds. Glazier took Brooks "to a horse-racing stable, whose big horse was Affirmed [the American Triple Crown winner of 1978], and I acted out all the parts for Louie and the Horse." From Wolfson, Glazier wangled $400,000, or about half of the estimated required budget of "Springtime for Hitler." He needed to secure the other half from a Hollywood partner.

Looking for the remaining $400,000, Glazier and Brooks visited the major studios and talked up the script. All of them passed. Brooks told an anecdote about Lew Wasserman, the top man at Universal, who was averse to Hitler as the centerpiece of a comedy. Wasserman said that Universal might agree to coproduce the proposed film if the title was changed to "Springtime for Mussolini."

Brooks needed more of a risk taker, someone like Joseph E. Levine, David Susskind's producing partner on the ill-fated

---

* This is not the same Barry Levinson who later worked with Brooks, first as a writer on *Silent Movie*.

*Kelly.* Levine had started out in the picture business as a distributor hawking schlock like *Godzilla* and *Hercules* but also arty foreign-language films such as Federico Fellini's *8½.* Levine was open to *The Producers,* and he invited Brooks, Olsen, and Glazier to the midtown offices of AVCO Embassy Pictures, which he headed and which had moved aggressively into film production. Levine's inner sanctum was reached through a hallway paved and decorated to evoke the West End neighborhood of Boston, where he had grown up in slums, another child of Russian-Jewish immigrants. Upon their arrival, the short, heavyset Levine, the very likeness of a rich and powerful producer (his press releases described him as "a colossus towering above the lesser moguls of filmdom"), immediately endeared himself to the visitors by showing them his favorite trick of making a silver dollar stick to his forehead.

Brooks spieled the story, performing some of his favorite scenes from the script. Levine loved it. The producer only had two issues. First, the title: Levine raised funds for Jewish charities and causes, and it would embarrass him to be associated with a movie called "Springtime for Hitler." On the spot the title was changed to *The Producers.*

Next: Who should direct such a problematic thing?

"Joe," Brooks told him, "I've got the pictures in my head. I know what the scenes should look like."

"You really think you can direct, kiddo?" Levine asked him.

Brooks said he would direct a little something to prove his mettle, a short subject or advertisement, something to show Levine beyond any shadow of a doubt that he knew how to make a comedy funny. Levine was a gambler. Okay, the producer nodded. They had a deal. Levine agreed to put up the rest of the total budget—not to exceed $941,000.

The producer kept a bowl of apples on his desk. He told Brooks, "Mel, my job is to get the money for you to make the movie. Your job is to make the movie. My job is then to steal the money from you. And your job is to find out how I do it. Here, have an apple!"

If he didn't know it already, Brooks would learn something about taking an apple from a producer. The casting and planning, the budgeting and scheduling could begin.

In the seven years since *The Miracle Worker* had opened on Broadway, Anne Bancroft had been deliberative in her career, appearing in a couple of plays and four movies (including the *Miracle Worker* film) and as a guest star with limited exposure on television shows.

In June 1966, the actress inaugurated a summer tradition of spending several weeks at the Berkshire Theatre Festival in Stockbridge, Massachusetts, this year starring as Sabina in Thornton Wilder's *The Skin of Our Teeth*, directed by Arthur Penn, who had guided *The Miracle Worker* to fruition on stage and screen. Among the ensemble was an actor who stood out for his talent, his towering height, and his dark, handsome looks. Bancroft touted Frank Langella to her husband, introducing him to Brooks when he visited.

"After performances, we'd gather almost every night around a table on a sun porch at the home of playwright William Gibson and his wife, a renowned psychiatrist," Langella wrote in his memoir. The gatherings, which included actress Kim Stanley, stage director Harold Clurman, and the Penns, "were about as full of consistently riotous laughter as any I have ever known. Led by Mel, they were stupendous evenings of improvised insanity. I can still see Mel standing before us, singing 'You're My Everything' to his imaginary penis, which grew larger and larger as he first took it in one hand, then both, flung it over his shoulder, wrapped it around his neck, tripped on it, and slowly began to roll it back in as if it were a garden hose on a storage wheel. Annie's hopeless, helpless laughter made it funnier, and up she'd get, put on the music and dance."

At the end of the summer, as always, Bancroft and Brooks

contrived to spend time together on Fire Island. No matter how absorbed Brooks was in the final revisions of the script and preproduction planning for *The Producers*, even if he was on the West Coast and had to fly back to New York, he tried to spend the weekends with his wife.

In early 1967, Mike Nichols approached the actress with a script adapted from a Charles Webb novel by Calder Willingham and none other than Buck Henry, offering Bancroft the plum part of Mrs. Robinson, the sexy seductress in *The Graduate*. Suddenly she was as excited about a new project as Brooks was about *The Producers*.

Before heading to Hollywood, though, Bancroft made her first television special, a two-person musical called *I'm Getting Married*, which aired on ABC's *Stage 67*. Dick Shawn costarred as her lover boy. When Bancroft shifted to the West Coast, she rented a Beverly Hills house with Frank Langella, her friend from the Berkshire Theatre Festival, along with Langella's girlfriend. The actor was preparing for his role in the Los Angeles premiere of *The Devils*, which had been Bancroft's showcase on Broadway. Director Nichols scheduled the first read-throughs for *The Graduate* in late March.

Amid final planning for *The Producers* Brooks took frequent plane trips to Hollywood in the spring. Besides visiting his wife, who was preparing for *The Graduate*, he had committed to a one-shot revival of *Your Show of Shows* that CBS was going to air in April. Sid Caesar had made a television pilot for a CBS series that had failed to make the grade, and the *Your Show of Shows* reunion special was his consolation prize. Inside the TV business the once almighty Caesar was now obsolete. It would be his and Club Caesar's last hurrah.

Imogene Coca, Carl Reiner, and Howard Morris were reunited with the star for the one-hour program, democratically titled "The Sid Caesar, Imogene Coca, Carl Reiner, Howard Morris Special." The special also brought back the Billy Williams Quartet, conductor Charles Sanford and his orchestra, choreographer James Starbuck, and director Bill Hobin from the original *Your*

*Show of Shows.* Oddly, for the first time on a Caesar show, the script was alphabetically credited: first Brooks, followed by Sam Denoff, Bill Persky, Carl Reiner (billed twice as a writer and star), and Mel Tolkin. Even more curiously, a separate title card credited the lengthy "Gallipacci" segment in the special, which was a reprise of the *Pagliacci* takeoff from *Caesar's Hour,* to (in nonalphabetical order this time) Tolkin, Larry Gelbart, Billy Wilder's longtime writing partner I.A.L. Diamond, Brooks, Sheldon Keller, and Michael Stewart. The original sketch had been elongated to fifteen minutes.

That was ten writers for one sketch. Two of the show's four main sketches were recycled from past Caesar shows with added music and jabber. In addition to "Gallipacci," The Three Haircuts were resurrected as sixties hippie rockers. One brand-new skit saw Caesar and Coca trapped in a marriage more poisonous than the Hickenloopers', and the other, an idea of Brooks's, found sailors Morris, Reiner, and Caesar submerged in a submarine and getting on one another's nerves. (Juggling revisions of the film script he was carrying around with ideas for Caesar's special, Brooks overlapped some jokes: Coca was nicknamed "Hitler" in the household skit, and Carl Reiner got a comforting blue blankie in the submersible, similar to the one clutched by Leo Bloom in *The Producers.*)

Noticing the repetition of previous bits and the broad and silly humor that belied the sophisticated comedy of Caesar's vaunted past, *Variety* panned the special mercilessly. CBS publicity had promised updates of "classic" *Your Show of Shows* material, *Variety* said, but "the years, the times and the updated manners have taken their toll on television's spectacular warhorses" and "there wasn't a classic apple in the entire orchard." The four stars, it said, had "tried hard for laughs," but the writing lacked ingenuity and zest.

Caesar still symbolized the gold standard for TV writers, however, and at the Emmy Awards ceremonies in June, Club Caesar finally won the high honor that had been denied it in the 1950s.

The Academy of Television Arts and Sciences voted the show the Outstanding Variety Special and gave the Outstanding Writing Achievement in Variety award to Brooks, Denoff, Persky, Reiner, and Tolkin. (Tolkin, designated to accept the award, pointedly thanked all past Club Caesar writers by name, mentioning the absent Lucille Kallen and Neil Simon.) The Writers Guild also honored the program for Best Writing in a Variety (Non-Episodic) Show. These were Brooks's first Emmy and first WGA awards.

While in Hollywood, communing with his wife and helping to write Caesar's TV special, Brooks also spared time for a performance of the 2000 Year Old Man for a *Colgate Comedy Hour* revival produced by *Rowan & Martin's Laugh-In's* George Schlatter. He and Carl Reiner appeared on the Colgate special in May, just before Brooks headed back east to begin shooting *The Producers*. Again the reviews were surprisingly sour; the duo were only "so-so," *Variety* wrote, not just compared to other guests—Rowan and Martin, Bob Newhart, Shelly Berman, and Dick Shawn—"more because of [Brooks's] tentative manner as a performer (he's a crack writer to be sure) than the quality of the dialogue." On the verge of a great leap forward, Brooks had still not hit his stride as a public personality.

Brooks and Alfa-Betty Olsen had finished the shooting script of *The Producers* by the end of 1966. As they had agreed, Olsen stayed on as casting director, although there was never any question as to who would play Max Bialystock. It was always Zero, or "Z," as his closest friends called him. Brooks had been chasing Mostel for more than a decade, first writing sketches for the flamboyant big man in the failed off-Broadway musical revue *Once Over Lightly* in 1955, later trying in vain to craft leads for Mostel that had never come to pass in the ill-destined *"All American"* and never-produced "The Zero Mostel Show." Brooks also wrote at least one skit for Mostel's one-man "Festival of the Performing Arts" TV special in 1964, a satire of an actor undergoing deep, Stanislavskian preparations for a role; he suffers horrific stage fright as the curtain is about to rise before finally stepping out onstage and taking a custard pie in the face. Mostel loved the tailor-made skit, which he reprised on his "Zero Hour" special on ABC-TV in May 1967.

Even though Brooks had done everything possible to win Mostel over (he even bought one of his paintings), they were never soul mates. Mostel was another Moby Dick—like Peter Sellers—whom he chased ceaselessly. But he harpooned Mostel in the end.

At that juncture of his career, Mostel had his pick of top Broadway roles. But the big man with outsized talent had not appeared in any motion picture since the rollout of the blacklist in the early 1950s; he was wary of the medium and put off by Bialystock. "What is this?" he bellowed. "A Jewish producer going to bed with old women on the brink of the grave? I can't play such a part. I'm a Jewish person!" Brooks got Mostel's wife, Kate, involved. She read the script and convinced the diffident Mostel that he was the very embodiment of the seedy, greedy Bialystock and that *The Producers* was worth his while.

Early on, Brooks had tried hard to land Peter Sellers. He couldn't convince the comedic actor, whom he revered, to play Leo Bloom. One day in the mid-1960s, he spent most of one afternoon at Bloomingdale's shopping with Sellers, whispering into the actor's ear about the role of a lifetime that was awaiting him. Leo Bloom also was dangled in front of a young unknown, Dustin Hoffman, a Greenwich Village neighbor of the Brookses, who read the script and said he was more tempted by the part of the Nazi-loving playwright Franz Liebkind. ("But of course that was impossible," Alfa-Betty Olsen recalled. "Nobody wanted him to be the German.") As Brooks was in the throes of casting, however, Hoffman was offered the part of the college graduate seduced by mother (Anne Bancroft) and daughter (Katharine Ross) in *The Graduate*, and suddenly he was on his way to Hollywood with Brooks's wife. Thus it was that

Brooks knocked on the dressing room of another relative newcomer, Gene Wilder, backstage after the final performance of *Luv* in January 1967. "You didn't think I forgot, did you?" Wilder broke down in grateful tears.

Brooks had promised Mostel that he could approve the selection of the actor playing Bloom to his Bialystock. Wilder therefore had to audition for Z. Having a dread of auditions, he felt himself draining away as, in lockstep with Brooks and Sidney Glazier, he climbed apprehensively up the stairs to Mostel's apartment. However, the big man reached out to shake his fellow actor's hand, pulled him tight with his arms around his waist, gave him a wet kiss on the lips, "and all my fears dissolved," Wilder recalled.

Another one of Brooks's hired-gun dalliances paid dividends now: Young & Rubicam trusted him, so much so that in early 1967 the agency let him try his directing hand with a couple of advertisements for Frito-Lay corn chips. Wilder gamely accompanied Brooks to a New Jersey location, where they filmed two television spots, one with Wilder as an aviator, which is inexplicably missing from *The Incredible Mel Brooks* box set. But the other commercial is there, full of verve: a *meshuganah* debate in a public park among teeter-totterers and bandshell musicians over what tastes best when eaten alongside Fritos. A young boy in the Danny Baker mold settles the argument. Producer Joseph E. Levine watched the two Frito-Lay sales spots, smiling and chuckling, and felt reassured that Brooks knew where to point the camera.

With Olsen at his side, Brooks's casting was never more variegated. The veteran Estelle Winwood, in her mideighties, campaigned for the part of the "Hold Me, Touch Me" dowager who is memorably wrestled to the couch by Bialystock in the opening title sequence. Another British-born player, Christopher Hewett, familiar to theatergoers as Zoltan Karpathy (and Rex Harrison's understudy) in *My Fair Lady*, became Roger De Bris, the director of stinkers who is drag-dressed for the annual choreographers' ball when the producers first meet him. (His flamboyant character's name is a double pun: *debris*, or garbage, and *bris*, which is Yiddish for the Jewish ceremony of circumcision.) The Sudanese-born Greek actor Andréas Voutsinas, whom Bancroft knew from the Actors Studio, became De Bris's black-clad, curly-bearded, swishy adjutant, just as cutely named Carmen Ghia. Brooks told him, "I want you to look like Rasputin and behave like Marilyn Monroe."

Kenneth Mars, who had appeared on *Get Smart* and as "a sort of gay psychiatrist" in *The Best Laid Plans* ("Mel loved that character," Mars recalled), arrived to audition for Roger De Bris but asked to read for the Nazi-loving playwright instead. Mel said no; he was still toying with playing Franz Liebkind himself. Mars read for Liebkind several times before Olsen convinced Brooks that Mars would be terrific in the part. From demanding pigeon droppings on his Nazi helmet to wild interpolations in his lines, Mars *became* Liebkind during the filming to the point that, Gene Wilder later said, "I didn't know if the character Kenneth Mars was playing was crazy or if Kenneth Mars was crazy."

Then there was the all-around entertainer and comedian Dick Shawn. Shawn had made an initial splash in the Max Liebman TV specials that followed *Your Show of Shows*. He had performed a wild Elvis impersonation in his act and was penciled in as the original Conrad Birdie before complications arose. Lately Shawn had appeared in the big-screen *It's a Mad, Mad, Mad, Mad World* and replaced Zero Mostel on Broadway as the lead of *A Funny Thing Happened on the Way to the Forum*. Brooks had written jokes for Shawn in the past, and Anne Bancroft heartily endorsed the screwball comedian from their two-person musical *I'm Getting Married*. Shawn got the part of the wiggy Lorenzo St. DuBois (aka L.S.D.), whom the producers cast as Hitler because he is so repellant.

Lore Noto told Alfa-Betty Olsen about a shapely former dancer with the Manhattan Rockets whom he had noticed in Academy of Dramatic Arts classes. She had never acted professionally before and wasn't quite twenty years of age, but Judi Lee Sauls looked the part of Ulla, the Swedish blond bombshell, Bialystock and Bloom's receptionist. Told the director was searching for an innocent but sexy type, Sauls wore clothes to the audition that had belonged to her grandmother: a long boxy yellow suit that fell below her knees with matching gloves. "Now, take off the jacket and pull in the blouse so we can see what is underneath all that," Brooks instructed her. Then Brooks put on a recording of Mitch Ryder and the Detroit Wheels' "Sock It to Me, Baby!"

"I danced like crazy," recalled Sauls, who later, for the film, adopted the stage name Lee Meredith. "They really liked it. I had to come back to read again and on my last audition I wore a tight Chinese dress with slits up the side. I think [Brooks] chose me because I was a challenge in a way because it was like making somebody over."

Among the joys of *The Producers* are all the New York eccentrics and personalities seen for the first, or only, time on the screen. The list included the nightclub comedienne Renée Taylor, who was in the cast of *Luv* when Brooks saw the show starring Gene Wilder; she portrays Eva Braun. The acting coach William Hickey, well known in theater circles, plays a drunk in the barroom intermission scene. The producer Lore Noto is among the packed audience looking aghast at the goose-stepping musical.

Many Brooks acquaintances were grabbed for wee parts, including Michael Elias and his writing partner Frank Shaw from the Max's Kansas City crowd. Elias's bit was left on the cutting room floor, although Brooks called him first to apologize. Shaw was pivotal as the guy in a gold tux in the bar between acts who is loving the Hitler musical "so far." People were grabbed wherever Brooks spotted them. Gretchen Kanne was a friend of Olsen's, living in the same building in a back room apartment. One day Kanne knocked on Olsen's door just as she and Brooks were ending a day of work on the script. Kanne asked for the phone number of a radiator repairman.

Minutes later, Brooks knocked on Kanne's door with a strange object in his hand, introducing himself as the repairman; he spent five minutes entertaining her and a visiting friend by walking around the place, banging on things, and diagnosing the radiator noises he himself made out of the side of his mouth. Brooks remembered the young, striking actress and through Olsen asked if she wanted to join the crowd in the barroom scene. "I say something like 'Best show on Broadway!'" Kanne, who later became a university theater professor, remembered.

Brooks made equally shrewd choices behind the camera. Although Joseph Coffey had spent years as an operator, he had just shot *Up the Down Staircase*, his first feature as cinematographer. The production designer, Charles Rosen, was new to motion pictures. (Brooks told him to use a lot of yellow, which the director regarded as a "funny color" and which did help to give the film an uncommon look.) Brooks needed a patient and resourceful assistant director, and he found one in Michael Hertzberg, whose list of credits included the film version of *Act One* and *The World of Henry Orient* starring Peter Sellers.

The editor, Ralph Rosenblum, had experience working on several Sidney Lumet dramas but recently he had cut the screen version of *A Thousand Clowns*, which had been a giant hit as a stage comedy; he had also supervised the editing of *Inside Danny Baker*.

The film's choreographer and composer were permanent acquisitions. Brooks tried to engage Ronald Field, the choreographer of *Nowhere to Go but Up*, before Field was diverted to *Cabaret*. Martin Charnin recommended his friend Alan Johnson, who had started out as a dancer in the chorus with Charnin, understudying one of the Sharks in the original Broadway production of *West Side Story* in 1957. Johnson was toiling in television, trying to make the transition to choreographer. "Mel threw out every crazy idea he could think of" for the big "Springtime for Hitler" number, according to Johnson, including an overhead shot of black-uniformed Nazi dancers forming a swirling swastika. "Oh my God," Johnson exclaimed, "are we allowed to show this? . . . can we show this anywhere?"

Johnson would learn that Brooks's "theory of filmmaking" included giving the audience a *zetz* (Yiddish for smacking an individual upside the head) with a musical number three-quarters of the way through the story. Johnson's staging of "Springtime for Hitler," in which the effete male dancers made reference to his own open homosexuality, couldn't have been more in sync with Brooks's sense of humor, and the number became the bravura template for the best song-and-dance *zetz*es of future Brooks comedies.

Composer John Morris and Brooks went way back. Born in New Jersey in 1926, the son of British parents, the composer was Juilliard trained and had started out as an accompanist for performers such as Judy Garland. A self-described "complete eclectic" in his knowledge and influences, Morris had arranged the music for dances and sketches on *Your Show of Shows, Shinbone Alley*, and *"All American"*. He had even arranged the dance music for the hit that was everybody's lucky charm, *Bye Bye Birdie*. *A Time for Singing*, a musical based on the novel *How Green Was My Valley*, with Morris's score—his co-lyrics and co-libretto, too—had just closed on Broadway after forty-one performances.

Brooks did not pretend to know how to choreograph a dance, although he knew what he wanted and liked in dance routines. Yet, taking his cue from the Caesar years, when all the writers had dabbled in music and lyrics, he did fancy himself a songwriter.

Technically, Brooks could not write music. He worked with a pencil and pad, writing down snatches of lyrics. Then he sang variations of the melodies into a whirring tape recorder. In the end he'd bring in Morris, "soft spoken, gentle, very bright and incredibly gifted," in Brooks's words, who worked closely with him first on *The Producers* and then on most of the screen comedies Brooks would create in the years ahead. Morris picked out the notes as Brooks hummed his ideas and adjusted the lyrics.

It was Morris who gave the "Springtime for Hitler" anthem its surge and lift, its buoyancy. "He suggested that the first eight notes be the theme," Brooks recalled. "He showed me what he could do with just eight or ten notes and I got very excited. I said, 'Have you ever scored a motion picture before?' He said no. 'Well, I never have directed one. If I get to direct this, would you be the composer? The only thing I insist on is having the numbers that I write in the movie.' He said, 'Sure! I think I can do it.'"

As happened with most of Brooks's scripts, there were other silent helpers behind the "Words and Music by Mel Brooks" credit. For example, "Look out, here comes the Master Race!" in the "Springtime for Hitler" song was Alfa-Betty Olsen's line, she said.

One of the best musical numbers in *The Producers* owed little to either Morris or Brooks: Dick Shawn's Hitler audition. The songwriter Norman Blagman ran into Shawn in the theater district one day, and Shawn told him he needed an offbeat tune for his character to sing in the movie he was doing. Blagman wrote regularly for *Mad* magazine but had also contributed dance tunes to Shawn's celebrated Las Vegas act, called "The Cockamamie." Shawn brought Blagman together with lyricist Herbert Hartig for a sixties peace-and-love ode called "Love Power," which Brooks approved. Shawn and Blagman went into a studio with an orchestra and recorded the song. Later, Shawn, in turtleneck, striped pants, hip boots, a soup can amulet, and a sparkly earring, lip-synched it for the camera, behind him a trio of foxy hippies faking it on instruments. His absolute weirdness and extraordinary oomph would make it one of the film's cherished highlights.

# CHAPTER 9

# 1967

## Auteur, Auteur!

Brooks had made it past the age of his father at the time of Max Kaminsky's death. But he was a late bloomer as a filmmaker, just shy of forty-one when he called action on the first take of *The Producers* on May 22, 1967. He'd spent almost a decade thinking about the script, years writing drafts, months planning the production. To be successful now, he would have to achieve, over eight weeks of photography and more in postproduction, a balance in his personality between the man who could be rigid, controlling, and combative, especially in private, and the comic who was loose, antic, and funny in public.

His idiosyncratic work habits and methodology were deeply ingrained. With so much riding on his shoulders, in fact, Brooks did not actually call "Action!" on the first take of his first film as director. Instead he nervously shouted, "Cut!" Assistant director Michael Hertzberg took him aside, not for the last time. "No, wait a minute—" Hertzberg advised sotto voce, "first you say 'Action' and when you're done you say 'Cut.'" Brooks was tentative out of the gate, Hertzberg recalled. "It was that rudimentary. We all just stood around waiting for him to say something." And perhaps for that reason Brooks began his custom of saying "Go!" instead of "Action!"

The production team had moved into the Hy Brown Studios on West 26th Street. The initial meeting of Bialystock and Bloom, which forms the extended opening sequence of *The Producers*, was the first to be photographed. Brooks said later that he had absorbed the barest concept of camera coverage or inserts for editing purposes and so was initially uncertain about how to frame his shots. He blocked Mostel and Wilder, but mostly for close-ups. "When the cameraman Joe Coffey gave Mel a lot of crap, because Coffey didn't understand the comedy, I was able to interpret," Hertzberg recalled. When early rushes showed the actors "standing on stumps . . . cut off at the ankles," in Hertzberg's words, Coffey exploded. "You can't do that! It's not cinematic!" Brooks agreed to do some reshooting, but "that was the end of our romance," in the cameraman's words.

He fared little better under his editor's scrutiny. "By the end of the first morning on the set, Mel was already becoming jittery," Ralph Rosenblum recalled. "Did he know that in the movies you could shoot only about five minutes of usable film in a day? . . . Brooks couldn't stand the waiting, and his impatience quickly extended to the cast."

The jittery novice provoked "a head-on conflict with the mountainous Mostel," Rosenblum said. "The first time the star couldn't perform with just the inflection Brooks wanted, the entire project seemed to be slipping from the director's grasp. After several faulty takes, he started to shout, 'Goddamn it, why can't you. . . .' But Mostel turned his head like a roving artillery gun and barked, 'One more tone like that, and I'm leaving.'"

Their on-the-set relationship was aggravated by the fact that Brooks did not criticize actors gently or sensitively. Indeed, he could behave like a "tyrant," even Dom DeLuise admitted later. He'd speak rudely or harshly. No shrinking violet, Mostel would roar back.

Not a mingler, Mostel camped out in his trailer between takes, nursing a bad leg from a 1960 bus accident that had never stopped aching, along with other lifelong grievances. "Is that fat pig ready yet?" Rosenbaum recalled Brooks sputtering. Mostel retorted, "The director? What director? There's no director here!"

Gene Wilder was treated differently. Wilder had just returned from Hollywood and his screen debut in *Bonnie and Clyde*, where he had milked his first laughs from his overwrought persona, playing an undertaker abducted by the notorious bank robbers who is taken along on the lam. *The Producers* was just his second picture, and he was still nervous; one of his strengths as a comedic actor was his manifest nervousness. He was susceptible to Brooks. He was Anne Bancroft's friend. Brooks didn't berate him.

But Wilder confided to Bancroft that Brooks worried him. She was among the very few visitors to the closed set, along with Carl Reiner, Joseph Stein, and playwright Arthur Miller, whose son was an assistant on the set. Bancroft reassured Wilder, "Just go with him!"

One late afternoon during the first week of photography, Wilder finished a demanding rehearsal for the introductory scene between Bialystock and Bloom, in which Bloom freaks out over Bialystock's lack of scruples, breaks down into hysterics, and demands the comforting blue blankie Bialystock has snatched from him. Wilder was weary and relieved after the long rehearsal was over and thought they would shoot the scene the next day. Brooks said no, he wanted to shoot right away, while the ideas were fresh. Wilder tried not to panic, just go with the flow, as Bancroft had advised. He thought back to his long-ago fencing classes at Bristol Old Vic, where his teacher had taught him to grab a handful of raw sugar if he ever needed a surge of energy in a scene. Wilder asked Brooks for Hershey's bars, someone ran to get them, and the actor gobbled two of the candy bars, gulping water with them.

**Bialystock:** What's the matter with you?
**Bloom:** I'm hysterical! I'm having hysterics! I'm hysterical! (Bialystock throws a glass of water on Bloom.) I'm wet! I'm wet! I'm hysterical and I'm wet! (Bialystock slaps Bloom.) I'm in pain! I'm in pain, and I'm wet! . . . and I'm still hysterical!

Brooks got his electric performance in one perfect take.

Joseph E. Levine wasn't sure. When the producer saw the first dailies, he was thrown by Wilder's unstrung persona and offered Brooks $25,000 extra for the budget if he would replace the peculiar performer. "Mel calmed him down and talked him out of having me fired," Wilder recalled, adding "I was only getting ten thousand dollars."

The trust between Wilder and Brooks grew, superseding the long-term yet iffier relationship between Mostel and Brooks. Wilder was ready to take any dare; his audacity as an actor impressed everyone. And, seeing Wilder blossom as a foil for his own bluster and extravagance, Mostel's survival instinct flared and he stepped up his energy.

Still, brusque and snarling in action, Brooks bred tension on the set, and it was inevitable that an outsider would witness it. A few weeks into the schedule a *New York Times* feature writer visited the set. Brooks was busy guiding the scene where Bialystock and Bloom pour flattery on the cross dresser Roger De Bris, recruiting him to stage their sure-flop Nazi musical. Knowing firsthand the power of the *Times* to destroy—its reviewers had savaged *Shinbone Alley* and *"All American"* and, more than once, his television scripts—Brooks reserved a special animus for the newspaper of record; hence the scene in *The Producers* where Bialystock attempts to bribe a *Times* critic to ensure the scribe's enmity.

Making clear his disdain for "lying interviews," in his words, after the shot was done Brooks rushed to a cot and sprawled facedown, ignoring the *Times'* emissary.

Earlier in her visit, the *Times* writer, Joan Barthel, had observed Brooks hurling "vivid invective" at his staff, flinging "sarcasm" at a still photographer, and blasting his cameraman. Producer Sidney Glazier told Barthel he had tripled his cigarette intake and added, "Pray for me." Now she approached the director warily. "What do you want to know, honey?" Brooks asked her with a distinctly unpleasant edge. "Want me to tell you the truth? Want me to give you the real dirt? Want me to tell you what's in my heart?"

Barthel said yes and then reported verbatim what happened next: " 'What would I tell you, really?' he snapped, with what has to be called a sneer. 'That this movie is the worst movie I've ever seen?' It sounded considerably more colorful than it looks, because he threw in some adjectives, or maybe some adverbs—based on four-letter words." The nearby producer, overhearing, "looked stunned."

Barthel asked nicely if Brooks had encountered any directing problems.

"No problems at all," he replied. "I know everything and that's my problem."

The press agent, nearby, "looked faint," Barthel wrote.

The other side of the coin was that most actors were accustomed to strange and autocratic directors. Brooks's craziness charged the atmosphere, ramped up the excitement on the set. "[Brooks] keeps you on edge," Dick Shawn told the press. "Mel has great craziness, which is the greatest praise I can have for anybody," Mostel agreed tactfully.

Some nights, when Brooks and friends wearily repaired to Max's Kansas City after a hard day of filming, "even Mostel, with his bad leg," reported *Vanity Fair*, "would make it to Max's, where he would greet the drag queens with a sloppy kiss on the lips."


Over time Brooks had proved himself a creator who was also, often enough to color his reputation, a wrecker; and there were the same two sides to this production: the ugliness and fractiousness that transpired behind the scenes and epitomized the wrecker, and the creative surges and locomotive drive that amped up the power and spontaneity of scenes.

More than once, budget limitations and scenes that had been deliberately left open-ended in his script allowed the tightly wound director to fly by the seat of his pants. Impromptu decisions resulted in some of the fondly remembered highlights of the film.

For example, the handshake that clinches the partnership between Bialystock and Bloom was originally supposed to be a "Top of the world!" climax atop the Parachute Jump in Coney Island, built for the 1939 World's Fair. Just as the two, belted into a canvas seat, reached the top of the ride, Bloom would shout James Cagney's immortal last line from *White Heat* and the pair would plunge sharply before their parachute opened, with their slow descent making a visual pun. But the Parachute Jump had not been operative for several years, and too much money was needed to get it up and running.

This issue dovetailed with another financial problem. The Hitler audition scene had originally been written for actors lined up onstage, in Hitler mustaches, singing a sequence of lyrics from "I Could Have Danced All Night" from *My Fair Lady*—a nod to Brooks's friend Moss Hart, the original director of the Broadway stage production. But the film's low budget, it turned out, could not afford the steep rights to the famous song.

As Brooks shot interiors on West 26th Street, Alfa-Betty Olsen journeyed to the Lincoln Center library to hunt for a public domain show tune that might be substituted. As Olsen passed the Lincoln Center fountain, its waters changed height, as they were timed to do intermittently, soaring high above her and giving her the idea for a location that could stand in for the Parachute Jump. After learning that the waters could shoot as high as forty feet, Brooks embraced the notion. The handshake scene had its "Top of the world!" moment.

In the end the Hitler auditions had to make do without Lerner and Loewe. Actors were rounded up, many straight from the choruses of Broadway musicals ("the tenor from *The Most Happy Fella* came in with a guy from *Fiddler on the Roof*," recalled Olsen). A man who liked winging it, Brooks gave each actor instructions for his or her vignette, while also encouraging free-form tomfoolery. The Hitler audition sequence turned out wonderfully, as did another scene left blank in the script—the intermission in the tavern near the theater, where Bialystock and Bloom gloomily observe the well-heeled throng as they jostle for drinks and gaily extol the merits of the "Springtime for Hitler" musical. After coaching from Brooks, all the action and dialogue was improvised. No other Mel Brooks comedy would have crowd scenes that pulsed with such immediacy.

From Dick Shawn's "Love Power" to Kenneth Mars's weird emendations, the actors were encouraged to add their own bits and touches. Mostel remained "heaven and hell" to deal with throughout the production, in Brooks's words. And no—Mostel would tell people forever after whenever they told him how much they loved *The Producers*—it was *his* film, *not* Mel Brooks's. Incorrigibly, many times he brought production to a standstill with his complaints, yet somehow under Brooks's handling he made Max Bialystock indelible. It remains one of Mostel's few consequential lead roles in films.

"Mel thinks of himself as a star maker," says Kenneth Mars half sarcastically in the documentary "The Making of *The Producers*," included as a DVD "extra." Because of course people like Mars—or Mostel or Dick Shawn—considered themselves to be known quantities. But star making did apply in the case of Gene Wilder, who was a New York secret before Brooks took a chance on him as Leo Bloom, and whose screen debut in *Bonnie and Clyde* was yet to be released as the shooting of *The Producers* wound down.

"With Gene I was simple and kind and nice and gentle," Brooks explained. "With Zero, I'd scream at him, 'You're a genius!'" By the time of the courtroom sequence—after "Springtime for Hitler" has become a hit and Bloom and Bialystock have been arrested—Wilder had become emboldened to the point where he found fault with Brooks's most carefully scripted dialogue. The actor asked permission to rewrite Bloom's final plea to the judge, touchingly explaining his friendship with Bialystock ("No one ever called me Leo before . . ."). The warmth of Wilder's last-minute rewrite made the speech stand out, and it rounded out Bloom with shadings the other characters lacked.

The pressures and tensions, the long days inevitably followed by sleepless nights, and the whole "on-time" nature of picture making transformed the director into a pale, shuffling zombie by the end— the last day of filming—which was Saturday, July 15.

After hours spent coordinating the lighting with the height of the waters of the Lincoln Center fountain, Brooks and Mostel faced off heatedly on the final day and Mostel threatened to walk off the set. Sidney Glazier was summoned to pacify the two men. Brooks canned the last shot around 5:30 a.m. Bloom pranced around the fountain, shouting joyfully "By God, I'll do it!" Bialystock, sur-rounded by geysering water, chorused, "He'll do it! He'll do it!" For some, that would be the iconic image of *The Producers*. "It's the 'I want everything I've ever seen in the movies!' scene," *Vanity Fair* observed, "the *cri de coeur* straight from Mel Brooks through his alter ego Leo Bloom."

Anne Bancroft finished her work on *The Graduate* in Hollywood in time for a summer visit to her husband's set, then August on Fire Island, then rehearsals for a revival of Lillian Hellman's *The Little Foxes*, in which she'd portray Regina, the Tallulah Bankhead part from the original stage production, which Bette Davis re-created in the film. Her director for *The Little Foxes* was Mike Nichols, who had also directed *The Graduate*.

As Bancroft began *Little Foxes* rehearsals, in cutting rooms at Eighth Avenue and 54th, conveniently near the Carnegie Deli, Brooks launched the assembly of *The Producers*. Regardless of all his experience in television and on Broadway, he couldn't pretend to any expertise in camerawork or editing. That gave him all the more rea-son to assert his dominance, fiercely clashing with cameramen and editors early in his directing career.

*The Producers'* cinematographer and editor both got to know the "two Mels," in Ralph Rosenblum's words. One was the Mel who "did five minutes of ad-lib routines in the morning for the grips and electricians until fifteen people had put their coffees down for fear of spilling them." That was the same Mel who would jump out of the car in the middle of a traffic jam on the way to a location shoot, run over to a stranger's car, knock on the window, point to himself and say, "Mel Brooks. The 2000 Year Old Man. Recognize me?" This Mel also took Chock Full o'Nuts orders with pencil and paper and then bumped his way up to the front of the queue, "as the crew watched in hysteria" telling everyone he was Mel Brooks, "famous comedian, Hollywood director."

"Then there was the other Mel," wrote Rosenblum in his memoir, "the Mel who seemed to feel he was being ganged up on by the pros, who felt exposed and isolated, who with barely a transition would become angry and tyrannical, whose neck would stretch and tighten and eyes bulge until . . . you were sure he would attack you."

Rosenblum said that there was also a "before" and "after" Mel. Before filming, the novice filmmaker behaved in a flattering and deferential fashion to the key technical artists, whose help he dearly needed. "Those of us who were meeting him for the first time found him a very funny, very eager man," Rosenblum recalled. "He spoke at length about the contribution I had made to *A Thousand Clowns*, and he said he wanted a relationship with me similar to the one I had had with [Herb] Gardner [the original playwright of the film directed by Fred Coe]. He touched just the right note when he suggested a collaboration of equals, and like Joe Coffey, I was immediately impressed."

Later, watching Brooks on the set—and early on at dailies, where they reviewed the latest footage every morning—Rosenblum and producer Sidney Glazier learned "to refrain from mentioning any flaws" they happened to notice. "There were certain things you just couldn't say to him," Glazier remembered. "Mike Hertzberg said more to him than anybody, because Mike worked for him. Mike was his boy, his assistant, and more often than not Mel would listen to him. But everybody else was a threat. Everybody else was the enemy. There was always a moment when you felt he would kill you. His face would turn white, his jaw would come out—and it was not so much a question of physical fear; how could you fear him? He was a little guy. But he terrified me, because I always felt he was going to do something that would blow the picture."

Quickly finding Brooks's tirades during the filming tiresome ("but none of them had involved me, so I was still relatively balanced"), Rosenblum asked permission to vacate the set and spend two weeks assembling a rough cut of the first twenty minutes. "Since this was a very primitive film in which everything depended on the words and acting, the editing was very basic and uncomplicated. Choices were few; in most cases the scene was funniest with full shots of both characters, and I think almost any editor would have cut it the same way. Indeed, when the movie was finished, 90 percent of the first two reels remained just as I'd put them together in the initial assembly."

Rosenblum screened the twenty-minute rough cut for Brooks and Glazier at Movielab. "In addition to revealing the inherent shortcomings of the picture," Rosenblum recalled, not unsympathetically, "the first rough cut lacks the refinements—the sound editing, the opticals, the finishing touches—that do so much to make a movie come alive. . . . for the beginning director, watching this first assembly is even more painful, because he can't allow for the enormous difference that the refinements will make—he's never had the experience of dragging a first cut into a dazzling finished film."

After viewing the assemblage, however, Brooks stomped to the front of the room and "with hideous intensity" pointed a finger at the editor. "*You just listen to me*," he growled. "I don't want you to touch this fuckin' film again! You understand? I just finished with Coffey this afternoon—I told him I don't need his help, and I don't need your help either! I'll do it all by myself. Don't you touch this film—you hear—don't *touch* it, until I finish shooting!" Shaken, Rosenblum said nothing. Glazier, on the drive home, apologized abjectly for Brooks. Though angry and resentful, the editor didn't quit.

Every morning during the editing, Rosenblum waited past ten o'clock for Brooks, who'd arrive late with coffee and crullers for the editor and his team of assistants, elaborately serving them with sugar, napkins, and stirrers. "Mornings were slow because Mel had a hard time waking up," Rosenblum said. "He'd free associate, improvise little skits, tell jokes, do word games and generally carry on" as he fueled up with coffee.

Then "he'd become manic," said Rosenblum, "fly around the room with his arms waving and eyes bulging, suddenly become a little old man again, a vendor on Orchard Street, a weaseling schemer, a pontificating rabbi, a sleazy seducer, or Super-Jew with J on his pajamas. He would carry on this way for about an hour, and as far as I could tell, he had no memory whatever of the tongue-lashing he'd given me two months earlier. . . .

"Once he paused in the middle of one of his routines and looked intensely at the ashtray sitting beside him on an end table. I was at my desk, drinking my coffee and expecting another funny line. Suddenly Mel's hand tightened around the ashtray, his face got very tense, and he looked up and screamed, 'Next time it's going to be *my* ashtray, goddamn it! It's going to be *my* desk, *my* telephone, *my* couch, *my* Movieola, *my* equipment, *my* supplies! Next time you're going to be in *my* office GODDAMN IT!' Then his face relaxed, he glanced casually about the room, and went back to drinking his coffee and thinking up jokes."

By eleven o'clock Brooks would have psyched himself up to look at footage but "he could not find the proper distance" and spent hours griping about how Coffey had "screwed him here by taking too damn long," in Rosenblum's words, "or how Zero never did get that line right," and so on. ("Those goddamned sons of bitches," Rosenblum quoted Brooks as saying after they'd watched the scene with Mostel, Wilder, and Kenneth Mars on the rooftop of Franz Liebkind's tenement. "They ruined it. That fat pig! He had to play it *his* way. If I ever get ahold of him I'll kick his head in!") The mornings were generally wasted with little real work getting done, Rosenblum said. Brooks perked up at lunch, schmoozing with other writers at the Carnegie Deli, flirting with waitresses, "bursting with playfulness, competitiveness, aggression, and a lusty satisfaction at being recognized by one and all"—albeit it helped to have his name proclaimed loudly at every opportunity.

Fully alert after lunch, "awake enough to realize he had some very boring hours and weeks of work ahead," in Rosenblum's words, and "awake enough to remember and resent his dependence on me," the fun and games ceased. Arguments about deleting "superfluous" glances, lines, or entire scenes became "angry, raucous, combative," in Rosenblum's words, with Brooks taking any such suggestions as "a direct attack," digging in his heels while aggressively blaming others. "Although his belligerence was rarely aimed directly at me," Rosenblum said, "I felt sullied by it and withdrew into a tighter, colder, more severe professional stance that could only have increased his resentment."

Brooks's "clutching and resistance" dragged out what should have been a simple eight-week task, Rosenblum wrote. With glazed eyes Brooks watched and rewatched the footage of "Springtime for Hitler," until he finally decided that what bothered him was one singer's solo line. He dubbed in his own voice "Don't be stupid, be a smarty! Come and join the Nazi Party!"—the only glimpse of Brooks the performer in his first screen comedy.

"No matter what portion of the film had to come out—and ultimately everything that needed to came out—he was neither appreciative nor cooperative," recalled Rosenblum. The close-ups seemed piled on top of each other; the editing team badly needed inserts for transition purposes. When, one day, the editor found "a piece of visual humor" to solve a transition problem, Brooks was appeased only for a moment before realizing whose solution it was. "Who wants a joke by a fuckin' editor?" he sniped.

"He always seemed ready to explode," Rosenblum wrote in his memoir. "Once he erupted by throwing every object within reach across my two rooms—grease pencils, film cannisters, tape dispensers, the ashtray that would one day be his ashtray." The editor's assistants cowered behind draperies.

"Only once did I shout back at Mel and reprimand him," Rosenblum wrote. "Mel calmed right down, looked a little contrite, and then went back to whatever he was doing, as if nothing had happened. I realized then that while shouting matches left me debilitated for hours or days, to Mel they were an accepted everyday phenomenon. He could demean, insult, or threaten you one moment—or suffer the same sort of treatment himself—and return to business as usual the next." But Rosenblum did not have the same thick hide and felt "violated by his rancor and moodiness until the last day of cutting."

Rosenblum's last day was not the last of editing, however. Brooks still wanted to rework a "few scenes" and "the main titles," recalled sound editor Alan Heim. Rosenblum suggested Heim could handle it and left. Heim agreed, although "I really didn't want to be in the room" with Brooks, "a very high-energy guy. He *tummels* a lot."

One of the scenes over which Brooks and Rosenblum had sparred, with Brooks insisting on his editing ideas, took place in Liebkind's apartment, with Liebkind comparing Hitler to Churchill as painters and imitating the latter with a V closely framing his face. (Kenneth Mars improvised some of Liebkind's best lines in the scene: "Churchill . . . and his rotten paintings. The Fuhrer. Here was a painter! He could paint an entire apartment in von afternoon—two coats"!) When Heim looked at the "trims and outs," he discovered this amusing bit and other "close-ups which were very, very funny" but which had not been used—an "enormous number of them." Rejigging the scene, he found that "within six or eight frames of my marks, there was a splice where the film had been reconstituted; it was clear that Ralph Rosenblum had already cut the scene this way and Mel hated it." With emendations, Heim restored the earlier editing. Brooks—if he noticed the similarity to Rosenblum's version, he didn't mention it—accepted Heim's cut.

On weekends, especially when in the company of his wife, Brooks was more relaxed. Frank Langella and his girlfriend lived in a $70 monthly flat at 61st and Third Avenue. The couples were in constant touch: "daily phone calls, long late-night visits to each other's homes, takeout, endless games of Scrabble, cards, Charades, and trips away to exotic beach locations. They willingly climbed the four flights to our modest rabbit warren of an apartment, and we made an equal number of visits to their luxurious Village town house."

By December, *The Producers* was ready for its East Coast previews, including Washington, DC, and Philadelphia. Brooks, who toured with the preview print, was already proficient at interviews. *Washington Post* critic Richard L. Coe loved the twisted comedy ("I roared like drains in April!"), but the first Philadelphia showing was a bust, occasioning anecdotes from Brooks down the years reinforcing his underdog credentials.

The Lane Theatre in Philadelphia, an eclectic, Art Moderne–style house on North Broad Street and 67th Avenue, had been the local first-run venue for the film version of *A Funny Thing Happened on the Way to the Forum* starring Zero Mostel. Brooks and a New York contingent went to Philadelphia for the midweek sneak preview of *The Producers*, following *Helga*, a German sex education film featuring actual scenes of childbirth.

"Mel did a local radio talk show and a local television talk show," remembered Alfa-Betty Olsen. "He was a great guest, funny and smart. He sparkled . . .

"[On the TV show] he sang 'Springtime for Hitler,' the song from the big production sequence in the movie and, hands on hips, imitated the long-limbed showgirls dressed as pretzels and beer steins who descended a staircase in the number. Mel invited the talk show host to the premiere. He said wild horses couldn't keep him away."

The small audience for *Helga* dotted the cavernous Lane Theatre. "There was a bag lady sitting in the second row just sleeping and maybe three or four people scattered around," according to Brooks. Present for *The Producers* were Olsen, Sidney Glazier, Joseph E. Levine, and AVCO Embassy staff members, and Florence and Edward Dunay and Brooks's children Steffi, Nicky, and Eddie, who had driven down from New York.

The laughter was as sparse as the crowd. According to Glazier, Levine wore a stone face throughout the preview and swore at them afterward. (Levine was there mainly "to see how much money they would spend on advertising," Brooks recalled.) Olsen didn't mention Levine's reaction in a reminiscence she wrote for a Writers Guild event, but she did say the local talk-show host rushed past them after the preview without saying a word. "He cut us dead," Olsen said. "The worst night of my life," Brooks often recalled. Disheartened, he and Olsen took the train back to New York.

Curiously, when the film officially premiered at the Lane on the weekend—advertised with Mostel's name above the title in huge type (dwarfing the director's) and a squib from the New York *Daily News* ("a wild and wacky comedy")—*The Producers* enjoyed a three-week run.*

A better time was had by all at the midnight preview convened

---

* Officially, somehow (it may have been producer Joseph E. Levine's maneuvering), *The Producers* would compete for Academy Awards as a 1968 film even though it had this initial 1967 run.

at the Cinema 57 Rendezvous near Carnegie Hall on West 57th Street in Manhattan. Hundreds of people came, "including scores of Mel's show-business friends and Joseph E. Levine with his entourage from Embassy Pictures," as editor Ralph Rosenblum recalled. "For fifteen minutes [before the screening] Mel stood in front of the crowded room and performed. The audience was in a state of utter comic delight before the film ever began."

After the show congratulators swarmed Brooks in the lobby. "My distaste for him was still strong," Rosenblum recalled, and the editor tried to slip past the director without being noticed. Brooks shook loose from his admirers, rushed over, threw his arm around Rosenblum, and led him outside and strolled him down the street toward Sixth Avenue. "Thanks for making it professional," Brooks whispered. It was the last time Rosenblum, who went on to edit several films for Woody Allen, including *Annie Hall,* ever saw him.

In the first week of December 1967, *Variety* jumped the gun with the first trade paper review of *The Producers,* which its correspondent had caught at the Washington, DC, preview. "Brooks has turned a funny idea into a slapstick film," the *Variety* critic enthused. Despite having some manifest flaws—a weak third act and climax—the movie was fast-paced and entertaining with a "hilarious" Third Reich production number and marvelous performances that were "unmatched in the scenes featuring [Zero] Mostel and [Gene] Wilder alone together, and several episodes with other actors are truly rare."

Still, Joseph E. Levine did not rush the film into theaters. The producer was focused on the Christmas release of *The Graduate,* with Oscar winner Anne Bancroft in the cast and Oscar nominee Mike Nichols as director, whereas *The Producers* lacked any name with marquee value outside New York City ("lack of a big name may hamper b.o. prospects," *Variety* had warned). Levine didn't care to see two of his pictures vie against each other in the marketplace; not only would that pit husband (*The Producers*) against wife (*The Graduate*), but, worse, it would be Levine versus Levine. He scheduled *The Producers* for national release in March—a slow release with targeted advertising, counting on critics and word of mouth to boost the film. That meant his two pictures would fall into different calendar years and not compete against each other for Oscars.

In Los Angeles, meanwhile, writer Paul Mazursky and Peter Sellers were busy filming *I Love You, Alice B. Toklas!* Typically, after a day of work, Mazursky and Sellers got together with friends, drank some wine, and gobbled marijuana brownies while watching prints of movies not yet in general release. One night Mazursky, a friend of Brooks's, offered *The Producers*. Sellers, who had eluded playing Leo Bloom, loved what he saw. Repaying Brooks for years of solicitous attention, Sellers took out full-page advertisements in the trade papers proclaiming the "true genius" of Brooks "in weaving together tragedy-comedy, comedy-tragedy, pity, fear, hysteria, schizophrenic-inspired madness and a largess of lunacy of sheer magic." Levine now had Sellers's encomium for his publicity file along with *Variety*'s and other glowing early notices.

Brooks had to be patient, which was not his forte. He joined AVCO Embassy meetings to map the release strategy, soaking up sales and distribution tips for the future; but, more important, he went back to work with Alfa-Betty Olsen on their next comedy, which they had announced in the spring before filming even started on *The Producers*.

The follow-up to *The Producers* was going to be a labor of love: an adaptation of the satirical Russian novel penned by authors Ilya Ilf and Evgeny Petrov entitled *Diamonds to Sit On*—more popularly, *The Twelve Chairs*. Either Brooks had heard the story "as a child" (according to one version of events) or stumbled into a Brooklyn library one day and chanced upon the novel on a shelf ("at age fifteen"), or Mel Tolkin had first handed it to him. However it began, filming *The Twelve Chairs* had been an idée fixe since the 1950s.

The famous comic novel had been turned into a motion picture multiple times before under various titles and in different languages, twice in fact in Hollywood. Set in 1927, one year before the book's publication, its story involved jewels worth fifty thousand rubles whose hiding place is secreted in one of twelve dining chairs that have been dispersed across the Soviet Union as former private property of the ruling class. Three scoundrels learn of the chairs from a dying dowager and frantically compete to find the hidden gems: the unscrupulous Father Fyodor; a young, handsome conniver named Ostap Bender; and an elderly aristocrat, ruined by the revolution, named Vorobyaninov.

In the first months of 1968, Brooks and Olsen carved out a working draft that stayed faithful to the novel's plot and structure. While eliminating much of the Soviet-era context and detail, which had enriched the satire of the original fiction, Brooks and Olsen narrowed their script on the three rivals and their hectic search, which crisscrosses the Soviet Union with vignettes in Moscow, the Crimea, Siberia, and other far corners. The trio's self-destructive greed made the story a thematic companion piece to *The Producers*.

Again Olsen did not expect to share credit on the screenplay; the Brooks-Olsen partnership was still wonderful, and they harked back to "our old procedure," as the writer's helper recalled. "Mel talked. I typed. And sometimes I talked too."

Their main departure from the novel was a rosier ending. Brooks didn't like unhappy endings; he believed audiences didn't like them, either. The conclusion of *The Producers*, with Bialystock and Bloom languishing in jail (the scene that triggers the closing number, "We're Prisoners of Love"), was the last somewhat downbeat ending he'd write.

In the novel (and film) Vorobyaninov and Bender form a fractious alliance to find the jewels before Father Fyodor does. Vorobyaninov goes insane and kills Bender after they learn that the jewels have long since been cashed in to underwrite a worker's chess club.

In the happier ending of the Brooks-Olsen script, the rogues part comically.

Their script also magnified the supporting role of Tikon, the aristocrat's former servant, stretching out his drunk scene. Brooks thought he might play that character.

By February 1968, Brooks had enough pages to show actor Ron Moody and to announce Moody's casting as Vorobyaninov. That same month, the 1967 Academy Award nominations were disclosed, with Anne Bancroft receiving her third Oscar nomination as Best Actress, for her iconic performance as Mrs. Robinson in *The Graduate*.

The *Twelve Chairs* production was organized as an AVCO Embassy release, but this time with Joseph E. Levine's investment and involvement limited. Yugoslavia had become a haven for international coproduction, and William Berns, an executive in Sidney Glazier's company, who had worked in the country for Yugoslav national television, had contacts in the Communist regime. The authoritarian nation could furnish any picturesque scenery a filmmaker desired: beaches, forests, Ottoman architecture, Roman coliseums. Yugoslavia could stand in for the Soviet Union. President Josip Broz Tito was a cinephile friendly to filmmaking, and American productions could save wads of money on studio facilities and equipment, behind-the-camera personnel, lodging and food, supporting players, and any number of extras. After *The Producers*, Glazier's company had filmed *The Gamblers*—also based on Russian source material, a Nikolai Gogol play—largely in Dubrovnik.

Yet Brooks also sought to restrict Sidney Glazier's input. He wanted Michael Hertzberg, i.e., "Mel's boy," as his staff producer, while he himself would function as the real producer of his second film in order to boost his control, ownership, and earnings. Through Crossbow Productions he now partnered directly with Louis Wolfson's new entity, Universal Marion Corporation (UMC). UMC agreed to bankroll *The Twelve Chairs*, which would cost about half the nearly $1 million budget of *The Producers*, with the funds coming almost entirely from UMC. Brooks had clashed with Glazier during *The Producers*, once angrily banishing him from the set, and now with an executive producer credit Glazier would have a circumscribed role distanced from the script and the filming.

On March 18, 1968, four months after its initial sneak previews, *The Producers* opened to the public at a single Manhattan theater usually a haven to foreign-language films: the Paris Fine Arts Theatre on 58th Street near Fifth Avenue. The Upper East Side art house booking positioned Brooks's first film as sophisticated comedy—i.e., too sophisticated for big commercial houses. Joseph E. Levine wanted blurbs from important New York critics before rolling the film out nationally. That was a time-honored strategy in the trade.

More than a handful of critics did acclaim the film, with Gene Shalit in *Look* magazine supplying (as was his penchant) the perfect squib: "No one will be seated in the last 88 minutes of *The Producers*, they'll all be rolling around on the floor." There was also farsighted appreciation from *Cue* ("one of the funniest films around") and major national periodicals such as *Time* ("uproariously funny") and *Mademoiselle* ("a riot") that would satisfy Levine's advertising plans and travel well outside New York City.

But many New York critics who laughed also winced and groaned, and their mixed notices augured a stubborn pattern in Brooks's film directing career. Some reviewers complained about the preponderance and inelegance of Brooks's close-ups, which was the visual equivalent of his in-your-face rude and crude humor. There was lively debate about the exuberant performance of Zero Mostel. The script petered out after "Springtime for Hitler," some critics said, without much in the way of catharsis.

There were caveats even amid the most enthusiastic partisans, with Wanda Hale in the New York *Daily News*, which gave the picture four stars, nonetheless delivering this backhand: "Anyone, from whose head came this fantasy with profound undertones, can be forgiven for occasional looseness in direction." *Newsweek* said it was "a high-class low comedy." The dean of auteurism, the school of criticism that touted directors as the true authors of films, was Andrew Sarris at the *Village Voice*. "Except for two or three expert sequences, the direction of Mel Brooks is thoroughly vile and inept," he wrote.

The queen bee of film critics was the antiauteurist Pauline Kael. Writing in *The New Yorker*, Kael saw *The Producers* as "amateurishly crude," dependent on "the kind of show business Jewish humor that used to be considered too specialized for movies." After excoriating the camerawork and "gag-writing," Kael confessed to laughing often enough. "For satire of the theatre as good as Brooks' gags at their best," she wrote, "one can endure even the rank incompetence and stupidity of most of *The Producers*."

The most hurtful words came from Brooks's longtime bête noire, the *New York Times*. Mostel grotesquely overacted "under the direction of Mel Brooks," though Wilder was "wonderful," *Times* critic Renata Adler wrote. The film's editing was often "crude and incredibly amateurish." The "Springtime for Hitler" number was "the funniest part of this fantastically uneven movie." The whole thing was "a violently mixed bag. Some of it is shoddy and gross and cruel; the rest is funny in an entirely unexpected way. . . . *The Producers* leaves one alternately picking up one's coat to leave and sitting back to laugh."

At home, Brooks later said, he wept in the arms of Anne Bancroft after reading Adler's decidedly mixed review, and years later he often quoted the *Times* piece to interviewers—spelling the critic's name for the uninitiated ("A.D.L.E.R.")—while exaggerating her grievances. "She said my leading man [Zero Mostel] was gross, my humor pedestrian, and that as a director I lacked pace"—none of which she had actually written.

His loathing of the critics who picked at his inadequacies had been festering for more than a decade; now it was cemented by the equivocal New York reviews for his maiden film as writer-director. Although he could also boast many favorable notices and bouquets, his cup was usually half empty, it seemed, where critics were concerned, with some of their jibes always echoing inside his head.

New Yorkers, however, took their critics skeptically and Paris Fine Arts ticket sales amounted to "one of the biggest opening week totals" in its history—a "socko" $34,562, according to *Variety*. A house record was also set in Los Angeles in early April at the small (379-seat) Granada Theatre on Sunset Boulevard. While cautioning that the comedy was "not for everybody," the *Los Angeles Times* praised *The Producers* as "outrageously funny." Brooks flew to LA to tout the film on *The Steve Allen Show*.

He planned to tour widely, giving interviews to promote *The Producers* when it went national in midsummer, but first he stole time in New York with Anne Bancroft before she departed for Stockbridge to appear as William Shakespeare's wife, Anne Hathaway, opposite Frank Langella in *A Cry of Players*, the new William Gibson drama. In the fall they'd take the play to the Vivian Beaumont Theater in Lincoln Center.

Levine had organized a "rather sporadic national opening schedule" for *The Producers*, according to *Variety*, and by late June the release was in slow progress. Disappointing single-theater bookings in Detroit and Pittsburgh were followed by premieres in Toronto, Baltimore, Minneapolis, and Chicago, where Brooks arranged a special campaign in the hub of the heartland. His friend Walter Robinson had moved back to his native Chicago and spearheaded the local promotion with tie-ins and ticket contests. The extra effort resulted in "the strongest U.S. showing the film has made to date," said *Variety*.

Levine backed the film with publicity and advertising. But the unveiling was drawn out and scattershot, partly because Levine had to scrounge for screen availability at independent theaters unaffiliated with the major chains in city centers. In the long run, that accrued to *The Producers'* cachet; in the short term, it drove Brooks crazy.

Never showing on enough screens at the same time, *The Producers* couldn't crack *Variety's* monthly "50 Top Ten–Grossing Films." Brooks had "net points" in his contract if the film made a profit, but, as he often told interviewers, up front he had been paid only his $35,000 writing-directing salary for *The Producers*—"one year of work." He was convinced that Levine and the system had snookered him. "It's impossible for a profit participant to make any money on a movie unless it's a gigantic hit," he explained later, "because overhead and interest are always being charged to the film." He'd wait years for his net points; all the decision making, accounting, and oversight rested with Levine.

Brooks did little grumping in public in the summer of 1968. But he griped privately to friends and his wife. The critical brickbats and modest box office accruing to his first screen comedy weighed heavily on him. He managed to get at least one silver lining in his contract: the clause that gave him future rights to *The Producers* as a stage property. Levine, still scarred by *Kelly*, had no interest in another Broadway musical.

By the fall, Brooks and Alfa-Betty Olsen had completed the shooting script for *The Twelve Chairs*. Once again, Olsen would continue on as casting director. Brooks made trips to Hollywood and London, interviewing actors and overseeing the preproduction.

Brooks never ceased to lust after Peter Sellers, this time for the part of Father Fyodor, the rapacious priest seeking the chair with the hidden jewels. But Anne Bancroft urged her husband to consider a loony actor she had been enjoying on television, most recently on his eponymous variety show, which had replaced Dean Martin's over the summer of 1968. Brooks met Dom DeLuise for the first time in his suite at the Beverly Wilshire Hotel—a distinct upgrade from the Chateau Marmont, where he'd stayed in the 1950s.

The thirty-six-year-old DeLuise was from Brooklyn, Catholic and Italian, as roly-poly and jolly as Ron Moody was spindly and ascetic. Although he had trained as a serious actor and occasionally performed in dramas with distinction, he had made his mark playing lovable birdbrains in New York revues, on Broadway, and in a couple of motion pictures. Brooks met with DeLuise at the end of a long day spent interviewing actors. DeLuise nervously devoured sweets laid out on the table. Soon the two found themselves talking easily and laughing; after four hours Brooks shook DeLuise's hand and said they were friends for life. DeLuise gasped at the low salary Brooks offered for months of work in Yugoslavia, but he took the part, and indeed they did become friends for life.

Although Alfa-Betty Olsen lobbied hard for Alan Arkin as Ostap Bender, Frank Langella hovered in the wings; he had Anne Bancroft's fervent endorsement. The thirty-year-old all-purpose actor was gorgeous, a sentiment echoed in the film by the shorter Tikon, who looks the strapping Bender up and down with awe. (Playing intimate scenes with Bancroft in *A Cry of Players*, Langella recalled that the actress had "resolutely never looked into my eyes, rather focused deeply on the second button down of my shirt." Langella refrained from asking her why until after the show had closed: "Oh, that's about where Mel comes up to on you.") Langella would be second billed and also be paid a "ridiculously low" sum, the actor recalled, but Brooks reassured him that the role would make him a star. (Langella didn't mention that he was already established onstage and as a star of his first film, *Diary of a Mad Housewife*, made and released before *The Twelve Chairs*.)

Andréas Voutsinas, the only holdover from *The Producers*, was cast as the stage manager and producer of a theatrical troupe that travels with several of the coveted dining chairs among its stock scenery.

Although his scenes were less dazzling than Carmen Ghia's, he did have one of Brooks's trademark quips: "I hate people I don't like."

Lesser-known supporting players, mostly British or Irish, were cast in England before the filming. Yugoslav professionals and amateurs were rounded up on location.

Alan Heim, who had inherited the final editing of *The Producers* from Ralph Rosenblum, would carry on in that capacity; Brooks's first cameraman Joseph Coffey yielded to a young Yugoslav, Djordje Nikolic, whose background was in documentaries.

John Morris, who had been vital to *The Producers*, returned to compose the score and cowrite the film's main theme with Brooks. Morris admittedly borrowed phrases from Johannes Brahms's Hungarian Dance no. 4 in F-sharp Minor for the melody of "Hope for the Best, Expect the Worst"—whose fatalistic title and lyrics were otherwise quintessential Brooks: "Hope for the best/Expect the worst/You could be Tolstoy/Or Fannie Hurst . . ."

Joseph E. Levine invested heavily in trade paper advertisements encouraging Academy Award voters to consider *The Producers*, with full-page displays targeting Brooks's "incomparable original screenplay" and Best Actor in a Supporting Role candidate Gene Wilder. The preproduction of *The Twelve Chairs* halted on February 24, 1969, when the 1968 nominations were unveiled. Both Brooks and Wilder drew nominations, and as frosting on the cake Ron Moody, the future star of *Twelve Chairs*, was in the running for Best Actor for portraying Fagin in the film version of *Oliver!*

Earlier in the month the Writers Guild of America, whose award categories were titled differently, had nominated *The Producers* as Best Written Comedy.

Brooks traveled alone to Hollywood for the April 10 Oscar ceremony, which had to be delayed two days following the assassination of Martin Luther King, Jr. Thinking her husband's chances were slim—Brooks was up against *Faces* (John Cassavetes), *2001: A Space Odyssey* (Arthur C. Clarke and Stanley Kubrick), *The Battle of Algiers* (Franco Solinas and Gillo Pontecorvo), and *Hot Millions* (Ira Wallach and Peter Ustinov)—Anne Bancroft stayed behind. Brooks had already lost at the Writers Guild, where in late March Neil Simon won the comedy prize for the film script of his Broadway hit *The Odd Couple.*

At the Oscars the Best Writing (Story and Screenplay Written Directly for the Screen) presenters were Frank Sinatra and Don Rickles, who traded barbs as they read out the list of nominees. It may have helped that *The Producers* was the only out-and-out comedy among the contenders, and Brooks certainly acted surprised when his name was announced. He raced to the podium to accept the trophy for the script he had worked on for so long, the most personal film he'd ever write. "I didn't trust myself in case I won so I wrote a couple of things here," the tuxedo-clad writer told the crowd. "I want to thank the Academy of Arts, Sciences and Money for this wonderful award." To loud laughter, he mimed searching his pockets for his nonexistent prepared speech. "Well, I'll just say what's in my heart. Ba-bump. Ba-bump. Ba-bump . . ."

"But seriously," he continued, "I'd like to thank Sidney Glazier, the producer of *The Producers*, for producing *The Producers*. Joseph E. Levine and his wife Rosalie, for distributing the film. I'd also like to thank Zero Mostel. I'd also like to thank Gene Wilder. I'd also like to thank Gene Wilder. I'd also like to thank Gene Wilder . . ." Levine, in the audience, beamed with pride; he had promoted *The Producers* as a sophisticated niche comedy, and his long-range strategy had paid off with one of the industry's highest honors for Brooks.

Not for Gene Wilder, who lost in his category to Jack Albertson in *The Subject Was Roses*. Although Brooks had thanked Wilder three times in his speech, he didn't so much as whisper the name of Alfa-Betty Olsen. Although happy for Brooks, the woman who had worked closely with him on *"All American"*, *Get Smart*, *The Producers*, and

*The Twelve Chairs* felt slighted. Brooks genuinely liked Olsen besides genuinely needing her; he belatedly took space in *Variety* and *The Hollywood Reporter*, expressing "My heartfelt thanks to Alfa-Betty Olsen for both her creative contribution to the script and brilliant casting. Mel Brooks." But that was small potatoes compared to praise on national television; and the "heartfelt" emotion didn't translate into official credit or monetary compensation. Olsen felt hurt and broke off contact with Brooks for years to come. Besides being such a valuable collaborator (by any WGA standard, she would have been entitled to a writing credit), her casting acumen—along with pillow talk from Anne Bancroft—enriched the ensembles of the first two Mel Brooks comedies.

Brooks spent the first weeks of the summer in London, finalizing the casting, overseeing the production design, and presiding over initial read-throughs for *The Twelve Chairs*. He hired as his assistant a young American living in London with a background in Yugoslavian film. She knew enough Serbian to get by and had previously worked for the Avala Film company, which was going to be Brooks's headquarters in Belgrade.

Wherever Brooks went in life, he took Brooklyn with him, and so, when he met with actress Rachel Kempson, now Lady Redgrave, in his Claridge's suite, for example, he put his feet up on the table facing her and asked nonchalantly, "Whaddaya got?"

For a while he pretended to vet actors for the role of Tikon, making an elaborate charade of finding fault with each candidate. Soon it became clear to everyone that Brooks himself wanted to play the part, and he did, liberally spritzing his scenes in a manner not unlike the 2000 Year Old Man. When Ostap Bender asks Tikon what goes on at the Home for the Aged, for example, Tikon replies, "The old ladies, they tippy-toe in. They have a bowl of porridge and then they—" This line, as one critic subsequently noted, is followed by "an abrupt, nasty Bronx cheer that, in Mr. Brooks' elastic vocabulary, may be either an insult or a euphemism—for death and lesser failures."

Before departing for Yugoslavia, Brooks gathered the production team together. He gave them a pep talk, saying that now they were all ambassadorial representatives of America and should behave responsibly as guests who were privileged to work in a foreign nation. But he forgot his own advice when encountering his first snafu at the Zagreb airport. The team's plane connection was unexpectedly delayed. Brooks stormed down the airport corridors, waving his arms and shouting "So, what is all this SHIT?"

Avala Film, situated in Belgrade's Filmski Grad studio complex, boasted reasonably up-to-date soundstages with the standard lofty ceilings and slate walls. In a smoky café across the street from Avala Film sat drably dressed denizens, drinking plum brandy and strong Turkish coffee from tiny cups. Portraits of Vladimir Lenin and Tito decorated the café walls.

Though the interiors would be shot at Avala Film, Brooks and his cast and crew also traveled to beautiful Dubrovnik on the Adriatic coast, the lakes region of Subotica, and the stone city of Novi Sad, all of which substituted for parts of the Soviet Union. For the first time Brooks used multiple cameras during the filming, which translated into fewer close-ups—the prevalence of which had given an extra charge to *The Producers*. The natural scenery of the locations lent a pictorial beauty to the photography, even if Brooks himself took some of the credit over the Yugoslav cameraman Djordje Nikolic, later telling one journalist, "I shot a lot of it myself on my belly in the fields of Yugoslavia. One incredible shot was the ghost train where I used an Arri[flex] with a long lens."

No other Mel Brooks film would be photographed outside the United States. On location the cast and crew were often housed in small red-roofed houses owned by local citizens, while Brooks typically stayed in luxury hotels where the water and electricity did not

always function. The locations were spectacular but also more demanding and stressful than the interiors; the sun could be blinding
during the beach scenes, with the night shoots long and exhausting. Spells of drenching rain caused unforeseen delays and wreaked
havoc with the schedule.

Brooks was forced into making constant adjustments. He moderated his on-set behavior after *The Producers*, but only gradually,
not all at once. In Yugoslavia, he still did not radiate happiness
or confidence. After Frank Langella and Dom DeLuise performed
their first scene between Ostap Bender and Father Fyodor, the actors
thought they had done well—they had been word perfect, following the script. Brooks exploded, "Garbage! Why are you giving me
garbage!" "He could be difficult," DeLuise recalled years later. "He
could scare you." Langella and DeLuise conferred, and for the next
few takes they overlapped the dialogue and tossed in their own bits.
Then Brooks was pleased.

He'd ask for repeated takes, sometimes giving his own line readings that kept changing inflection. One time, DeLuise said, he had
a single word of dialogue—"Maybe"—that Brooks shot more than
a dozen times. Finally DeLuise was heard to murmur plaintively, "I
don't really care about this anymore . . . ," breaking everyone up—
including Brooks.

The director suffered black moods, especially if the day's log was
rained out and he had to cool his heels, sulking inside his trailer.
The foreign members of the crew (some British, many Yugoslav) and
the stringencies of totalitarian society hampered their pace. Brooks
seemed especially rude to the Yugoslav crew and to the native secondary actors. He bellowed repeatedly at a young clapper boy who
didn't always get his task right.

Brooks lived and breathed the film; his mood darkened if his ox-
ygen was threatened. He liked to joke, "It's only a film," invariably
followed by "It's my WHOLE LIFE!" And it was his whole life: he
did not take exercise during filming, he drank bottomless mugs of

coffee, and he let his guard down only at night, when everyone gathered family style at a local restaurant and he entertained effusively from the head of the table.

On *The Twelve Chairs*, there were no enormous egos for him to wrestle with, no looming Zero Mostel monster. He was respectful to Ron Moody and helpful to Langella, who never laughed so hard as when Brooks and DeLuise teamed up for shtick one time at a Belgrade restaurant, marching into the kitchen, stealing the non-English-speaking chef's toque, loudly stirring pots, banging spoons, and twirling rolling pins, shouting "Slavic" gibberish until the chef, kitchen staff, and other restaurant guests dissolved in tears and laughter. Brooks and DeLuise would be each other's best audience for decades to come.

"We were a very tight, happy family," Langella, for one, recalled. "That's an overused phrase, but it's true. I was twenty-some-odd years old, waking up every morning in the presence of Mel and Dom, two of the truly funniest men on Earth."

Juggling work on a television project back in the United States, Anne Bancroft made several trips to Yugoslavia, delighting people with her cheerful enthusiasm and her invariable support for her husband. "She was a great and loving pal," Frank Langella remembered, "warming my feet in the dressing room when I'd come in from the cold, watching dailies, giving great notes to Dom DeLuise and me and generally keeping everybody's spirits up."

Spending time apart was one secret of the success of the Brooks-Bancroft marriage. Although they laughed a lot when they were together, they also frequently grated on each other. "I'm a moody person," Bancroft told the press. "I'm hard to live with and so is Mel hard to live with. But my husband is one of the funniest men who ever lived. Sometimes I laugh at him until the tears roll out of my eyes." The Brookses were "as well mated as any couple I've ever seen," Carl Reiner said, "quick to anger, quick to forgive." If Brooks went too far, with his wife or anyone else, the actress could silence her husband with a glance, but she also knew when to back away and give him center stage if he was on his high horse.

With her multiple Tony and Oscar recognitions, Bancroft was arguably the actress of the decade in the 1960s. Although she did not win the Academy Award for her role in *The Graduate*, still she was at the peak of her reputation when Brooks started his directing career. "What would Anne Bancroft the movie star do in her film career over the next five years [after *The Graduate*]? The answer was surprising," wrote her biographer Douglass K. Daniel, "almost nothing." Nor, for nearly a decade, would she star again on Broadway.

Stage and screen scripts came her way, but she was nearing forty; the parts were less attractive, perhaps, and she was picky. Over time she'd get "a reputation for turning down acting offers," according to Daniel. One reason: the demanding roles took a toll on her physically and emotionally. "After each role," she told the press, "I always take a rest, six months to a year." Slowing down also helped the balance in her marriage.

Bancroft continued her summer appearances at the Berkshire Theatre Festival in Massachusetts, but for the wider public she preferred television and its lighter responsibilities, including the TV special she was working on between her trips to Yugoslavia.

"Annie: The Women in the Life of a Man" was the brainchild of Martin Charnin, their Greenwich Village neighbor and Brooks's onetime collaborator on "Marriage Is a Dirty Rotten Fraud." Charnin produced the one-hour show, shot in the fall of 1969 and aired on CBS in February 1970. The format, which amounted to a one-woman show, allowed Bancroft to declaim poetic monologues, sing ("acceptably in a throaty voice" according to *Variety*), dance ("looking at ease"), and perform light comedy in disparate sketches, including one boasting "additional material" by her husband.

Hailed as clever and entertaining, "truly a tour de force," in the words of *New York Times* critic Jack Gould, the Bancroft special drew on the talents of past and future members of Club Brooks, which had emerged to gradually supersede Club Caesar: Dick Shawn (playing Bancroft's groom, as he'd done in *I'm Getting Married*), baritone Robert Merrill (who similarly guested on *Your Show of Shows*), and David Susskind (playing himself) made appearances. Alan Johnson choreographed the show. The auspicious writing credits included Peter Bellwood, Thomas Meehan, Herb Sargent, Judith Viorst, and Gary Belkin, with four "additional" ones listed (Brooks, Reginald Rose, Jacqueline Susann, and William Gibson, playwright of *Two for the Seesaw* and *The Miracle Worker*).

The acclaimed highlights of the special included Bancroft as a graying mother listening to Tommy Smothers soulfully croon the antiwar song "Maman" from the short-lived 1967 musical *Mata Hari* (lyrics by Martin Charnin); and a comedy skit, which has gained a second life on YouTube today, with Bancroft confiding a recurring nightmare to her psychiatrist. She relates her difficulty hosting a dinner party for the Peruvian soprano Yma Sumac and introducing the singer with a funny first name to the other guests that rhyme: Ava (Gardner), Ida (Lupino), Mia (Farrow), Uta (Hagen), Oona (O'Neill).

Still more the writer, Brooks did not appear on camera in the Bancroft special. The couple was wary of mingling their careers. The columnist Earl Wilson asked Brooks, during the publicity campaign for *The Twelve Chairs*, if he'd ever make a film starring his wife. "My wife is my best friend," he replied flatly, "and I want to keep it that way."

"Annie: The Women in the Life of a Man" went on to win two Emmys: one for Outstanding Variety or Musical Program and one for the main writers (not Brooks).

• • •

Alan Heim launched the editing of *The Twelve Chairs* at Avala Film in Belgrade, putting together a half-hour cut of early footage and screening the scenes for a handful of people that included Brooks, the visiting Anne Bancroft, and producer Michael Hertzberg. "I felt pretty good about the cut," Heim recollected, although he also understood that such first cuts are usually "really horrendous." Bancroft got up to leave immediately after the viewing; "she sort of backed out of the room," Heim said. Brooks stood up and began by complimenting himself: "It's remarkable how close you are to my original concept . . ."

"From there to what seemed like forty-five minutes later," Heim recalled, "it was pure excoriation. He just lit into me about touching his material and daring to change what he had in mind." They patched things up, and "we eventually ended up working well together." Certain editing touches—the speeded-up, Keystone Cops–type comedy at intervals—became Brooks trademarks. But Heim, who would have a long, respected career, winning an Oscar for *All That Jazz* in 1980, never edited another film for the director.

The rest of the editing and postproduction took place in New York, occupying the first half of 1970. The manic Brooks slowed to a crawl when editing. "I can never let a picture go," he explained. "I could work on *Twelve Chairs* for the rest of my life. I spent a year of my life making that picture, I thought it was going to be my masterpiece!"

He issued a public warning to future editors applying for work on future Mel Brooks films. "What you want in the end is a fraternal relationship where you are the absolute boss," he explained to *Action!*, the Directors Guild magazine, coinciding with the release of *The Twelve Chairs*. "I am schizoid about editors. I love them and I hate them. . . . A lot of editors like to go home at six o'clock. If you meet one like that, fire him."

By June, Brooks had finished the post-production gloss, and he and Bancroft embarked on a London vacation, which was becoming an annual tradition. Brooks could conduct business—planning the European release of *The Twelve Chairs*—while the couple enjoyed the shopping, restaurants, museums, theater scene, and private clubs for celebrities like Tramp. And no summer was complete without August on Fire Island.

Revving up for the fall, Brooks devised an accelerated release schedule for *The Twelve Chairs* that would put the film into more and bigger theaters faster than *The Producers*. He'd key the publicity and advertising in foreign capitals to the novel, which was better known in Europe. In September, he shuttled between Los Angeles and New York, organizing the publicity and distribution, and made trips to London accompanied by Sidney Glazier.

In the third week of October, Brooks hosted a sneak preview for European exhibitors and distributors in London. Glazier, Michael Hertzberg, and Alan U. Schwartz flew in for the occasion. "Elite show biz turnout was copiously wined and dined and supped before and after the show," reported *Variety*, which predicted, however, "doubtful mass appeal" for Brooks's second comedy film.

One week later, *The Twelve Chairs* saw its bicoastal US premiere at two theaters picked for their size and prestige: the Loew's Tower East on the Upper East Side in Manhattan and Loew's Beverly Theatre in Beverly Hills. Brooks gave countless print and broadcast interviews. He talked about his deep-seated connection to the story ("I'm a Russian Jew, and finally, I could bathe in everything Russian that's in me") and the strides he believed he had made as a filmmaker ("I may have moved ahead cinematically. . . . The shots are more beautiful, and the whole ambience, look and texture . . .").

By now the press looked forward to talking to Brooks. If his boasting didn't always endear him to reviewers, he made those journalists who were not critics laugh.

Yet the critics once again proved hard to please. Brooks's second film as writer-director was well made, likable, picturesque. The three leads romped. But the serious, literary side of the novel, which Brooks touted in interviews, was disarmed by too much silliness. (One could argue that silly comedy was as personal for Brooks as the Russian setting was.) Some critics did applaud the film, to be sure, and some were overly negative; but many—already it was a set pattern with Brooks—mixed pros and cons in the same notice.

Again the *New York Times* delivered the bitterest pill. Like Renata Adler before him, while commending the three stars—Ron Moody, Frank Langella, and Dom DeLuise—Vincent Canby assessed *The Twelve Chairs* as "a comedy for Brooks-watchers somewhat more indulgent than I." Canby was conflicted by "a sense of humor [that] is expressed almost entirely in varying degrees of rudeness and cruelty," and a split personality in the filmmaker, who "wants to be lovable and to stomp on your foot at the same time."

The "praise" from Charles Champlin in the *Los Angeles Times* and Gary Arnold in the *Washington Post* was just as equivocal. Champlin wrote that "despite some nicely farcical and stylized moments," the comedy ended up "thin and disappointing." Arnold thought that "the movie certainly looks better than *The Producers*" and the performances were mostly good. "This new comedy is much more consistent and fluid than Brooks' first film. . . . You don't gyrate as wildly between inspired and rather mediocre bits."

One consolation: the majority of reviewers praised Brooks's own performance. His scenes buoyed the film. "As able as the three leading actors are," Canby wrote in the *Times*, "it is Mr. Brooks who, though he appears only briefly in the film, dominates it from the beginning." Otherwise diffident about *The Twelve Chairs*, Pauline Kael agreed. "When Brooks is on-screen, he brings a fervid enthusiasm to his own nonsense," she wrote in *The New Yorker*. "When he isn't around, there's no comic tension."

The early turnout in New York and Beverly Hills was impressive, regardless of the critics. *The Twelve Chairs* was ushered into a peak number of seventy-two theaters and briefly rose to number two at the

US box office in late January. Europe also responded well initially, with the London revenue boosted by Ron Moody, a national treasure because of *Oliver!* US ticket sales fell off abruptly in February, however, with *The Twelve Chairs* slipping into sub-run. And in Europe, strong bookings beyond the United Kingdom were scarce.

It is hard to say what went down worse with Brooks: the critical caveats or the humble earnings. He had touted *The Twelve Chairs* as a major advance in his filmmaking—his "great statement about man's relationship to man," as his lawyer Alan U. Schwartz later explained to Kenneth Tynan, "and how revolutions fail to work because of human frailty. Mel wanted to be serious and literary." Critics by and large rejected the film as being serious and literary, and worse, the masses did not flock to his comedy.

After the bicoastal premiere, after the bulk of the interviews and promotion, Brooks and Anne Bancroft traveled to Miami Beach to visit his mother. From Florida they flew to an island in the Caribbean, where they could relax and follow the fate of *The Twelve Chairs* from afar. Brooks fished, walked the sands, and brooded over the rejection—a film that was almost as personal for him, as steeped in his genes, as *The Producers*; it was a favorite novel he'd been carrying around and thumbing for years.

There was not much he could do about the critics. He had complained about them in the past, and he would be vociferous about them in the future. If critics continued to snipe at his films, he would have to bypass them, go over their heads to the people.

*Variety* had said that *The Twelve Chairs* lacked "mass appeal," and *Variety* appeared to be right. The trouble, Brooks decided, explaining later, was that he had been making films that were *too* personal. *The Producers* had been "a private story with universal features," he realized, and *The Twelve Chairs* had been similar, "though the human aspects were once again universal."

Because it was such a private story, *The Producers* had attracted only a cult audience and *The Twelve Chairs* an "even smaller one," he continued. "It didn't make a lot of money, ever," he said of *The Producers*. "I mean, it played in the big cities, but would people in Kansas understand about raising 1,000 percent to put on a Broadway show?"

He had made his first two movies trying too hard to please critics—and Jewish intellectuals. "If you were a Jewish intellectual," he said, "whose parents had emigrated from Russia you could like my pictures, but there were hardly any of those in Amarillo, Texas, where you gotta play in one of their three or four theaters or else you're outa luck. You gotta get into one of the John Wayne houses or you ain't ever gonna break out."

Forget the carping critics and elite Jewish intellectuals; Brooks would have to make his name as big as John Wayne's in order to conquer "John Wayne country." In the future, he vowed, he'd make only mass-appeal comedies, films that could be counted on to fill the biggest theaters in the heartland or, for that matter, anywhere else in the world.

# CHAPTER 10

# 1971

## Blazing Mel

Along with *The Twelve Chairs*, many other dark, freewheeling, often scatological comedies exploded on the scene in the early 1970s, including Robert Altman's *M\*A\*S\*H*, Hal Ashby's *Harold and Maude*, Paul Mazursky's *Alex in Wonderland*, and the first films directed by Club Caesar writers Carl Reiner (*Where's Poppa?*) and Woody Allen (*Bananas*). Although certain of these young Turks—Brooks, Reiner, and Altman—were over forty, the American nouvelle vague was young in spirit and reflected the late-sixties zeitgeist.

*The Twelve Chairs* got lost in the jumble. In later interviews Brooks often cited his second film as his most neglected work. It stayed a favorite among some of his fans, though, especially those who felt he deserted them later with less literary, less serious comedy.*

At least *The Twelve Chairs* got respect from the Writers Guild, which nominated the script for best adapted comedy of the year. (Brooks's script lost to Ring Lardner's for *M\*A\*S\*H*.)

But after *The Twelve Chairs*, what? In the months following the

---

\* Not all Brooks fans were *Twelve Chairs* fans, however. Kenneth Tynan, in his otherwise admiring profile of the comedian in *The New Yorker*, said that *Chairs* "as a whole never comes to life, its jokes seem shod with lead, and one watches glumly as, like the wounded snake in Pope's poem, it drags its slow length along." Tynan preferred the jokey Hollywood adaptation of the Russian novel called *It's in the Bag* (1945). "Though rampantly disloyal to the original," he wrote, "it has many more laughs than the Brooks version."

release of *The Twelve Chairs*, Brooks floated several projects. "Have You Heard, Bronsky Is Dying?" which James Robert Parish described as a story about "a New York City garment industry businessman who hoped to build a pyramid to himself in the suburbs," had a lead character supposedly tailored for Zero Mostel, but it sounds more like one of those snappy titles that rolled off Brooks's tongue than a script with many actual pages.

An eighteenth-century comedy of manners might seem equally unlikely, but Brooks invested time and energy into developing a screen version of Oliver Goldsmith's *She Stoops to Conquer*. He had recently seen an off-Broadway production of the time-honored farce, whose tangled plot involves an affluent countrywoman posing as a serving maid to woo a wealthy Londoner, and felt that he could easily modernize the text. He mused about Albert Finney playing the role of Tony Lumpkin, who instigates the practical joke that triggers the plot, and met with Finney in New York. Finney was a fan of the 2000 Year Old Man ("He thought I was God," recalled Brooks), but the actor declined.

Not only did Brooks need a bankable star, he needed new financial partners. Louis Wolfson, who'd sunk money into *The Producers* and *The Twelve Chairs*, had been convicted of stock manipulation, perjury, and obstruction of justice in 1968, and after exhausting his legal appeals he had spent nine months in prison. Emerging from jail in 1970, he dissolved Universal-Marion, the parent company of UMC Pictures, the spin-off that had been created for Sidney Glazier to produce movies with Brooks and other filmmakers.

UMC re-formed as Sidney Glazier Productions. Glazier announced Brooks's forthcoming adaptation of *She Stoops to Conquer* with a $1.5 million budget and Gene Wilder as its possible star instead of Albert Finney. Still, Glazier had to find money somewhere. He and Brooks spoke to Bud Austin, a former executive of Filmways, a film and television production company with a successful game-show division (Brooks had appeared on its *Hollywood Squares*). Austin now headed up his own Austin Productions and he was seeking film properties. He liked Brooks and said he was interested in the project.

Brooks and Michael Hertzberg took a jaunt to Europe to meet with people and scout location sites. But *She Stoops to Conquer* was too big a lift for Austin Productions, especially given the fact that Brooks never completed a script with his take on the eighteenth-century play.

Flailing, Brooks tried to cash in on a television project that was baldly imitative of *Get Smart*. Together with Gary Belkin (with Brooks listed first in the "created by" and "written by" credits), he conceived of a hapless "world-renowned Master Detective" summoned from Italy by a secret international police agency to stymie the planned assassination of the "Shah of Tyrhan." He and Belkin wrote a pilot for the proposed "Inspector Benjamino" series, registering it as a Crossbow Production. But their script was tepid, the vogue for Clouseau-type spoofery had waned, and there were no buyers.

These and other air castles occupied Brooks for more than a year after *The Twelve Chairs*, before his financial insecurity and need for constant activity compelled him back toward television. A late-1970 appearance on *The David Susskind Show*, where he joined a panel that included comedian David Steinberg, actor George Segal, and author Dan Greenburg, mulling over the topic of "How to Be a Jewish Son," returned Brooks to the fold of Talent Associates even as *Get Smart*, whose royalty checks had kept him afloat for five years, ended its prime-time run and went into profitable syndication.

Talent Associates began to tease out possible new Brooks projects. The first of them was "The People on the Third Floor," a proposed two-hour NBC special that would star "the writing" more than the actors. Six or seven vignettes would be "tied together by a single premise," according to Leonard Stern's story summary, depicting the third-floor tenants of a large apartment building who gather together for a house party. Their pitch called for reality-based comedy à la *The Odd Couple*, with Brooks, Buck Henry, Joseph Stein, Max Schulman, and Peter Stone among the proposed writers of intermeshing stories. Martin Charnin was attached to the prospectus as the show's producer.

The second was a situation comedy called "Annie," built around the married comedians Jerry Stiller and Anne Meara. Renée Taylor (Eva Braun from *The Producers*) and Joseph Bologna (her actor-writer husband) wrote the pilot episode for the series, which was shot under Charnin's direction in early 1971. Brooks gave input and was executive producer, but ABC, which underwrote the pilot, declined to air the series.

The third was *The Comedians*, a one-hour syndicated program with Carl Reiner hosting a mock talk-show panel of comedians riffing on timeless topics. Although "The People on the Third Floor" did not survive beyond the publicity stage, *The Comedians* snagged a sponsor, Canada Dry, and several episodes were staged and shot in late 1971. The premiere, mulling over the subject of "Money," featured Brooks, Tony Randall, Peggy Cass, Ron Carey, and Don Adams, while the second episode, "Love and Children," featured Brooks, Marty Brill, Pat Carroll, Jack Cassidy, and Phil Silvers.

The guest comedians sat around on folding chairs on a threadbare soundstage set, betraying the show's "telltale on-the-cheap" investment, according to *Variety*. Reiner and Brooks traded "'2,000-year-old man' type of repartee," *Variety* noted, while the panel as a whole kicked around deep questions—"some answers being straight from real life, others lifted from comedy routines." The series was offered on a barter basis to TV stations across the United States, with the Canada Dry commercials ready-made and paying for the first half hour of each episode; the balance of advertising fell to local outlets.

Indicative of his higher name recognition—and his more likable persona—Reiner was on the in-house shortlist of possible hosts acceptable to both Talent Associates and Canada Dry; Brooks was not.

They also shared a pay disparity: Reiner would receive $2,500 per episode, while Brooks earned $1,000. Otherwise Brooks's contract was optimal, specifying a most-favored-nation clause for reruns (meaning that he'd be among the first paid), first-class airfare between New York and Los Angeles, another $2,000 for "general expenses plus [all] transportation to and from airport and reimbursement for rented automobile in California, plus additional expenses in the amount of $500."

Anne Bancroft had just accepted her first screen role since her Oscar-nominated performance in *The Graduate*. The actress would play Winston Churchill's mother in *Young Winston*, a historical epic set during the British prime minister's youth and his years as a Boer War correspondent. Director Richard Attenborough supervised the filming in London, which lasted through the summer of 1971. Brooks paid several long visits to his favorite European city, where he planned to shoot *She Stoops to Conquer* if that came to pass.

In August, the couple sojourned on the French Riviera before returning to the United States. Shortly thereafter, the actress learned she was pregnant, with her baby due in the spring.

By then Brooks had been running on a career treadmill for a year. The demand for future episodes of *The Comedians* had plunged after its heavily promoted premiere in dozens of markets late in 1971; by early 1972, the syndicated series had been abandoned.

No matter how much he talked about *She Stoops to Conquer*—with Gene Wilder as Tony Lumpkin—producers weren't buying it. Brooks needed another story, a more commercial one, and as always he needed the right collaborator for the script. More than two years had gone by since he had called the last take on *The Twelve Chairs* by the time, in early April, he flew to Mexico for another television paycheck, an appearance on the one-hour Timex-sponsored "Aquacade in Acapulco," hosted by Tony Randall, with

Ed McMahon, Jerry Stiller, and Anne Meara among the guest stars who congregated around the pool at a lavish Mexican resort. It was one among hundreds of television specials produced by Joseph Cates, who had served as coproducer of "Annie: The Women in the Life of a Man," and directed by Walter C. Miller, who also had been behind the camera for Bancroft's 1970 special. "Aquacade" sprinkled comedy sketches in between water sports and games: champion divers, famous swimmers, synchronized swim teams, and cliff-divers.

Brooks had a moment in the special where he impersonated an ex-Nazi hiding out as an Argentinian archaeologist. McMahon is interviewing him at poolside. According to *Variety*, Brooks "looked like he was winging it" on camera. But he did have a script: Gary Belkin from Club Caesar had written the special along with an up-and-comer named Norman Steinberg. Brooks hung out after hours with Steinberg, bonding with the younger writer. Steinberg was the missing link. A promising project had dropped into his lap, Brooks told him. Would he read the script and let Brooks know what he thought?

One month after the broadcast of "Aquacade," on May 22, 1972, Bancroft gave birth in New York City to a boy whom the proud mother and father named Maximilian Michael Brooks. His first name paid tribute to Brooks's own father; his middle name to Bancroft's. The couple had nearly given up trying to have a child, and Bancroft's pregnancy was difficult, the birth cesarean. She had suffered "strange labor pains at seven months," she told talk-show host Charlie Rose years later, "and we all thought I was going to lose that baby. So I went to bed for three months, and I didn't lose it."

The new mother was almost forty-one years of age. Brooks was nearing forty-six and now the father of four, including his three children from his first marriage. Baby Max was baptized Catholic, with Bancroft promising to bar mitzvah the boy in due time.

Baby Melb'n (photographed in 1927) started getting laughs in the cradle.

Melvin Kaminsky, senior class, from the 1944 Eastern District High School yearbook.

Melvin with older brothers in arms (left to right) Bernard, Leonard, and Irving.

Brooks began as sidekick and stooge to Sid Caesar, the "*Apollo of the Mountains,*" but from the beginning there was also genuine rapport and friendship.

Persistence got Brooks into the writers' room of *Your Show of Shows*. He is seen here huddling with (from left) Sid Caesar and the original writing team of Mel Tolkin and Lucille Kallen.

Sid Caesar and Imogene Coca were the nonpareil stars of *Your Show of Shows*.

The world's greatest second and third bananas, Carl Reiner (right) and Howard Morris, became lifelong Brooks friends.

Club Caesar circa 1956: (front row from left) Gary Belkin, Sheldon Keller at the typewriter, Michael Stewart, and Brooks; (back row) Neil Simon, Mel Tolkin, and Larry Gelbart. *(Photofest)*

An early 1950s photograph of Brooks and Florence Baum when they were still a stealth couple.

The seemingly happy young marrieds on the beach at Fire Island with baby Stefanie, their firstborn.

Relatives visiting the couple on Fire Island included Kitty Kaminsky (with glasses), standing close to her granddaughter, baby Stefanie, held in the arms of Florence Baum's mother. Florence Baum's father stands in the background.

Eartha Kitt played the sultry cat Mehitabel in *Shinbone Alley*, and had a backstage fling with Brooks.

A later iteration of Club Caesar with Brooks in full jumping-on-the-desk mode and (left to right) Woody Allen, Mel Tolkin, and Sid Caesar, writing the 1958–59 television specials.

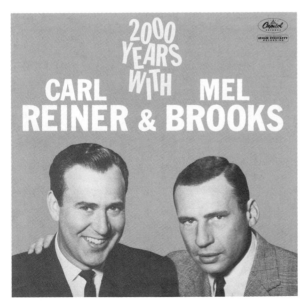

The first *2000 Year Old Man* LP took off in hip popularity and became the tail that wagged the dog in Brooks's career.

The brain trust behind the ill-fated *"All American"*: (left to right) lyricist Lee Adams, composer Charles Strouse, director Josh Logan, and Brooks, the musical's librettist. (Photo by Friedman-Abeles@New York Public Library for the Performing Arts)

With Anne Bancroft and Cary Grant, a fan of the 2000 Year Old Man, at the 1962 Hollywood premiere of *The Miracle Worker. (Photofest)*

*Get Smart* secret agents Don Adams and Barbara Feldon.

The first-time director shows Zero Mostel how to make love to "Hold Me, Touch Me" (actress Estelle Winwood).

Brooks and Alfa-Betty Olsen, his frequent amanuensis in the 1960s, at work on *The Producers* script on Fire Island in the summer of 1966.
(Courtesy of Alfa-Betty Olsen)

Brooks gleefully displays his own dance moves for the cameras while staging "Springtime for Hitler."

Playing a small role in *The Twelve Chairs*, his first screen acting, Brooks held his own—and some say stole—scenes from stars Ron Moody (left) and Frank Langella.

Brooks wanted Richard Pryor to play Sheriff Bart in *Blazing Saddles* but the studio said no. Cleavon Little proved sly and witty in the role.

Gene Wilder was an eleventh-hour substitution as Jim, aka the Waco Kid, but on- and off-screen he found an instant chemistry with Cleavon Little.

Madeline Kahn, as Lili Von Shtupp, performed "I'm Tired," and cemented her immortality among fans of Mel Brooks films.

The television special *Annie & the Hoods* aired in November 1974, testing the waters for future husband-wife teamings with a skit that featured Bancroft married to the philandering Brooks and serenading him with "Guess Who I Saw Today."

When not out and about, Brooks and Anne Bancroft were happy homebodies in Hollywood. Making music was a shared enthusiasm. The cigarette smoke dates this photograph to the early 1970s, before healthier California habits took over. (© Don Ornitz/Globe Photos/ ZUMApress.com)

*Young Frankenstein* was Brooks's most controlled direction, but there was plenty of improvisation and laughs on the set, as is illustrated by this still showing Teri Garr, Gene Wilder, Peter Boyle, Marty Feldman, and the director breaking up.

The cast of the short-lived television series *When Things Were Rotten*: (left to right) Dick Van Patten as Friar Tuck; Richard Dimitri as Bertram/Renaldo; Dick Gautier, playing Robin Hood; Bernie Kopell as Alan-a-Dale; and David Sabin as Little John.

The Three Silly Musketeers of *Silent Movie*: Dom DeLuise, Marty Feldman, and Brooks.

Brooks's star rose as Sid Caesar's waned, but Brooks stayed faithful and gave his mentor a pivotal role as the chief of Big Picture Studios in *Silent Movie*.

Often wearing outlandish costumes, Brooks made countless personal appearances to promote his films. Here he is with Mike Douglas (center) onstage at the Las Vegas Hilton for *The Mike Douglas Show*, which was cohosted by Brooks friend and *Silent Movie* cameo-star Burt Reynolds (at left). Pop singer Engelbert Humperdinck is at far right.

Out to dinner with wife Anne Bancroft and the Master of Suspense while planning *High Anxiety*, Brooks's satire of Hitchcock thrillers.

The *High Anxiety* troupe: (from left) Howard Morris, Harvey Korman, Cloris Leachman, Brooks, Madeline Kahn, and Ron Carey.

John Hurt starred as the Elephant Man, one of the first Brooksfilms productions—the "serious" side of Brooks's filmmaking that was meant to help Anne Bancroft launch her directing career with *Fatso*. *Fatso* tanked but *The Elephant Man* became a phenomenon, surprisingly successful commercially and nominated for eight Academy Awards.

"The Inquisition/Let's begin/The Inquisition/Look out, sin!/We have a mission to convert the Jews . . ."

Film critic and *Shadowland* author Bill Arnold, among the writers who challenged the king of Hollywood comedy for poaching their ideas—and the only one who actually got Brooks into court.

Brooks's and Anne Bancroft's Polish-language duet of "Sweet Georgia Brown"—the highlight of *To Be or Not to Be*.

*Solarbabies*, a science fantasy parable for teenagers, promised the "stars of tomorrow" with cast members (left to right) Peter DeLuise, Jami Gertz, Lukas Haas, Jason Patric, Claude Brooks, and James Le Gross. Directed by Alan Johnson, it had Brooksfilms's biggest budget and proved a box-office stinker.

*Spaceballs* showed Brooks still had his comedy mojo. The casting was refreshed for the *Star Wars* generation with goyish leads and younger comedians like John Candy as Barf the Dog.

Brooks added to the fun by playing two parts: numbskull President Skroob and (as seen here with Bill Pullman) the sawed-off, wisdom-spouting Yogurt the Magnificent.

*The Nutt House*, with Harvey Korman and Cloris Leachman, was Brooks's last failed stab at a TV series in 1992.

Another "Re-Do," *Life Stinks*, Brooks's reimagining of Preston Sturges's *Sullivan's Travels*, did not attract his usual fans. Brooks always defended the film as one of his finest and said his fantasy dance with Lesley Anne Warren ("gorgeously staged by me") was a favorite moment from all his films.

A joke publicity shot of Brooks with young admirer and *Robin Hood: Men in Tights* screenwriter J. D. Shapiro. (The joke was that the price Brooks paid for Shapiro's script constituted highway robbery.) Later, their collaboration would sour.

Brooks as Rabbi Tuckman marrying Maid Marian (Amy Yasbeck) and Cary Elwes (Robin Hood) in *Robin Hood: Men in Tights*. Mark Blankfield (right) played Blinkin.

*Dracula: Dead and Loving It* in 1995 was arguably the weakest Mel Brooks comedy—and destined to be the last with Brooks behind the camera. Here the director guides Lysette Anthony and Leslie Nielsen through one of their scenes.

Brooks launched his fantastical third act with the stage musical of *The Producers*. He is seen here in a publicity pose for the film version of the musical with original Broadway stars Nathan Lane and Matthew Broderick. Stage and screen director Susan Stroman peeks out from behind. (© Andrea Renault/Globe Photos/ZUMAPress.com)

Brooks and Anne Bancroft at Radio City Music Hall for the 2001 Tony Awards. The actress died in 2005 after a marriage that had lasted four decades. (Andrea Renault/Globe Photos from ZumaPress)

Brooks, son Max, and lifelong friend Carl Reiner at 2010 Hollywood Walk of Fame ceremonies. (© Clinton Wallace/ Globe Photos/ZUMApress.com)

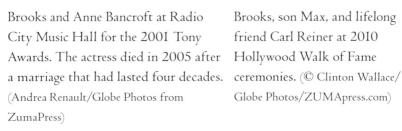

•  •  •

At the time of *The Comedians* and "Aquacade in Acapulco," Brooks's agent was David Begelman, the vice chairman of Creative Management Associates (CMA) under its chief executive officer, Freddie Fields. CMA, by late 1972, was in talks to merge with International Famous Agency (IFA), formerly Ashley-Steiner before the agency had become Ashley-Famous. The merger would give birth to the mega-agency International Creative Management (ICM).

Within months of the merger, the new management of Columbia Pictures appointed Begelman to head up its film production division in Hollywood. Ted Ashley, another former agent, who had represented Brooks when Ashley led Ashley-Steiner, was already installed at Warner Bros., dating from mid-1969, as its chief of film production.

The growing power nexus between onetime New York talent agents and the Hollywood studios would profoundly shape Brooks's career. Brooks did not care to make another East Coast independent picture and have to scrounge for his production costs and bookings. He also didn't want to affiliate with another Joseph E. Levine–type producer. Working for a major Hollywood studio would guarantee his production budget, a higher investment in publicity and advertising for his films, and ready access to many more theaters around the world: ergo, a bigger audience with commensurate grosses and profits.

By early 1972, he admitted in later interviews, his air castles had evaporated. He was practically skipping meals and missing auto payments. ("I've used up all my money, and I'm living on Anne's money, but she's pregnant, and soon she won't be able to work, and so we're going to be homeless.") One day, while walking on a New York street, searching intently for quarters on the sidewalk, as he liked to say, he literally bumped into his agent. His stomach rumbling, he jumped at Begelman's invitation to lunch.

Over lunch, Begelman told Brooks about a property called "Tex

X"—as in Malcolm X—a Wild West comedy about a hip, militant black sheriff who is hired to uphold the law in a prejudiced frontier town. Warner Bros. had taken an option on "Tex X," which had originally taken the form of a ninety-three-page novella, employing its author, a former film publicist named Andrew Bergman, to develop a viable script. At one point, Alan Arkin was set to direct the Bergman screenplay that resulted, with James Earl Jones as "Tex X." Then everyone involved, the studio included, balked. Judy Feiffer, a Warner's story editor acquainted with Brooks—she was the wife of *Village Voice* cartoonist Jules Feiffer—thought Begelman should offer "Tex X" to Brooks. "The idea is crazy but not crazy enough," Begelman told Brooks. "You could give it the real craziness."

Brooks made a show of reluctance, often claiming, in such instances, "You know me . . . I don't write anything I don't initiate." Besides handing him the unique story idea he sorely lacked, Begelman arranged the deal with Ted Ashley and Warner Bros. Brooks never forgot it was Begelman who had kept the faith with him at that low point of his career and opened a magic portal to the future; later in the 1970s Brooks would submit an effusive deposition as to Begelman's good character when the agent turned producer, still at the helm of Columbia, was disgraced by charges of forgery and embezzlement.

After his meeting with Begelman, Brooks put in a courtesy call to Bergman, whose PhD in film studies from the University of Wisconsin–Madison had led to a dissertation that was published as *We're in the Money: Depression America and Its Films.* Back in his late-sixties college days, feeding off the black militancy of the period, Bergman had imagined a Western that would begin with the image of an H. Rap Brown or Stokely Carmichael–type sheriff, black and proud, wearing "his finest Sixties threads" as he trots on his horse down the Main Street of all-white Rock Ridge, Kansas, in 1874. Working as a film publicist for United Artists as his day job, Bergman had written the "Tex X" novella.

The first meeting between Brooks and Bergman happened "over the phone," the "Tex X" author recalled. "I was a huge fan of his, and he was very warm and of course utterly hilarious." Brooks asked Bergman if he'd work with him on a new version of the script, and Bergman said yes; agents and lawyers went to work on the contracts. Brooks went off to Acapulco for ten days, where he looked forward to re-connecting with Norman Steinberg.

Brooks knew Steinberg from earlier in time. Brooklyn born, Steinberg had been beavering away as an entertainment lawyer in the late 1960s, handling copyright and music rights for a legal firm in a high-rise near the Chock Full o'Nuts that Brooks frequented for late-morning coffee and doughnuts when, one day, he spotted him. The lawyer revered the 2000 Year Old Man recordings and dreamed of writing comedy himself.

Steinberg dared to approach Brooks, saying "I want to be a writer." Brooks put his hands on the lawyer's shoulders, looked deeply into his eyes, and said, "Leave me alone." Steinberg had persisted over the next few weeks, becoming something of a pest. Brooks finally handed him Leonard Stern's name and telephone number on a scrap of paper.

In short order Steinberg wrote a *Get Smart* script on spec. Stern called him to say that if the series was picked up for another season, he'd option the script. Unfortunately for Steinberg, *Get Smart* was canceled in early 1970, but he had already quit lawyering forever. He picked up an agent at William Morris, quickly won a Grammy writing for comedian David Frye's album *I Am the President*, and found regular work on a CBS summer show called *Comedy Tonight* with Robert Klein, Peter Boyle, and Madeline Kahn among the cast. *Comedy Tonight* led to *The Flip Wilson Show* and a writing staff–shared Emmy.

Reuniting with his comedy idol in Acapulco, dining out nightly with Brooks, collaborating with him on his fugitive-Nazi sketch "was just the greatest thrill of my life," Steinberg recalled. The writer performed a cameo in the Brooks/McMahon vignette as a bellhop interrupting the Q and A with Brooks's Argentinian archaeologist. A package has arrived that is addressed to the ex-Nazi. Brooks harrumphs, "Hold that package for me over there by the pool!" Bellhop Steinberg walks away, and an explosion is heard with gold buttons flying into the frame. "Oh," Brooks says sadly, "that was such a beautiful uniform." A beautiful human being was inside that uniform, McMahon scolds him. Brooks nods. "Yeah. That, too."

Steinberg was flattered when Brooks gave him "Tex X" to read and said that if Steinberg thought the script was up his alley, they might work on it together with the originating author, Andrew Bergman, back in New York. Brooks might have said something like "We are going to need other writers, too"—the more the merrier—and Steinberg said he had a New York friend named Alan Uger, a former dentist, with whom he'd crafted comedy sketches for Alan King and Robert Klein. Uger held a day job with the New York City Department of Health, but he could take a leave of absence. A former lawyer and dentist for writing partners? Brooks was amused. He said fine to Uger also.

Shortly after Anne Bancroft gave birth to their son, Brooks, Bergman, Steinberg, and Uger began their daily rendezvous in the sixth-floor conference room of the Warner Bros. building at 666 Fifth Avenue. Huge table, no windows, blank walls. From the outset Brooks urged the writers to go for no-holds-barred comedy. He had loved Westerns since boyhood; now he wanted to skewer the genre as never before. He had hit a wall with critics and audiences on *The Producers* and *The Twelve Chairs*. He felt he had nothing to lose. "Write from the gut," he urged them. "Write from the heart. Write the craziest shit."

But they did not get very far—it was still early days—before Brooks looked around the room and made an observation that would raise the stakes on the project immeasurably. "I see four white guys here," Brooks said. "Four Jews. We need a person of color."

Who might that be? Brooks reached out to the political activist–comedian Dick Gregory, but Gregory said no. Then Brooks thought of Richard Pryor, a comedian even more incendiary and controversial. Or else Norman Steinberg thought of Pryor. Even though in multiple interviews Brooks insisted that Pryor's name had rolled off his tongue ("one of my best friends . . . since I was, like, twenty-two years old, and we really loved each other"), Steinberg was just as adamant that he knew Pryor from Flip Wilson's TV series. "When Mel tells the story, he says he called him, but in point of fact, I called him," Steinberg said.

At the time Pryor had acted in only a few films, and *Lady Sings the Blues*, with his breakthrough appearance, had not yet been released. Nor was Pryor well known as a writer, though he had done scripts for television, including for Norman Lear and *Sanford and Son*. Pryor was known principally for his dangerous stand-up comedy; as a writer he'd be an equally dangerous proposition and a gamble. "Richie was not in demand and had a bit of a checkered reputation," recalled Bergman, "but we knew there had to be a black voice in the room or the project was doomed to some level of toothlessness."

In his autobiography Pryor said he read "Tex X" and asked Brooks, "So this is a comedy?" Yes, affirmed Brooks. "Then why don't we make it one?" challenged Pryor.

Brooks asked him about the word "nigger," which was sprinkled throughout "Tex X."

"Well, Mel, *you* can't say it," Pryor said. "But the bad guys can say it. They *would* say it!"

Hiring Pryor was a risk. Everyone knew Brooks had made the right decision when, on the legendary first day he joined the story conferences, Pryor "sort of ambled in about noon," in Steinberg's words, Courvoisier in hand. As Brooks brought Pryor up to date on their progress, Pryor whipped out a little container, took a snort, and then offered the white powder around. There were no takers among the four white Jewish guys, nondruggies all.

"Brother Mel?" Pryor offered Brooks a toot.

"Never before lunch," declared Brooks without missing a beat.

When, two years later, a journalist from *Film Comment* asked Brooks "How was *Blazing Saddles* written?" Brooks began his reply curiously with "I didn't have time to write it myself…" That was why, he explained, he needed the team of Andrew Bergman, Norman Steinberg, Alan Uger, and Richard Pryor. Perhaps Brooks meant he didn't have all the time he would have preferred, the years it had taken for *The Producers* to develop, for example; he couldn't write it alone, and having five writers would multiply the speed. Even so, the task took about a year.

Through the first half of 1972, first in the Warner's building and then at CMA offices, the writers met to hash out the scenes. In later interviews Brooks consciously invoked a comparison with Club Caesar, saying he had tried to recapture that group dynamic with the *Blazing Saddles* team of writers. He was loud and combative and often obstreperous during the script arguments, but he also fostered "a great free-swinging atmosphere," Steinberg explained. "It was sort of a game of telephone, in which someone would say something and then it would be a sort of creative free-for-all of additions and subtractions and endless transmogrifications, if that's a word."

By July 26, they had a date-stamped first draft with the new title of "Black Bart," which renamed the black-and-proud sheriff formerly known as "Tex X." Most of the other characters' names flowed from Brooks's mouth, including Governor Le Pétomane (the role Brooks had designated for himself), which was derived from the stage name of a celebrated French flatulist, whose Moulin Rouge act consisted of farting out cannon fire, musical notes, and animal noises (*pétomane* translates roughly as "fartomaniac").

As in Club Caesar days, it was tricky after the fact to separate out any individual's contribution to certain scenes subjected to "endless transmogrifications" by the writers. But one thing most participants agree on: despite (or because of) the cocaine and Courvoisier, the July 26 draft was suffused with Pryor's race consciousness and audacity.

First and foremost, the black comedian unleashed the word "nigger," which had been pervasive in the novella, just as it was pervasive in the black culture of the 1960s and '70s, flavoring black militant speeches, blaxploitation films, and Pryor's own stand-up routine, among other things. Did Pryor write the craziest shit? Brooks later insisted that Pryor had actually been more drawn to writing for the Jewish or kookiest white characters, such as Mongo ("Mongo only pawn in the game of life"). True or not, Pryor cast a long shadow over the script sessions. If Brooks did not think something was funny, it didn't go into the script, but if Pryor didn't think something was funny, its chances were equally slim.

At work, Pryor was "amazing, he was astounding," recalled Steinberg. Pryor's instinct for constantly pushing the boundaries of outrageousness was like an accelerant poured on fire. "I do think Richie saved us from the PC dilemma," agreed Bergman.

At least one friend of Pryor's, actor and writer Paul Mooney, believed the comedian had dreamed up "the most memorable scene in the movie, where the cowboys sit around the fire, cutting farts." Pryor was "king shit in that group," said Mooney, who wrote for Pryor's stand-up and television specials, in his book *Black Is the New White*.

Brooks often claimed the campfire farting scene as his own inspiration, but no one else could say the same with certainty. "I don't remember how the campfire scene turned into a farting scene," recalled Bergman, "but it just did. We all free-associated, and so 'campfire' evolved into 'eating' and then 'eating beans,' and then the vision of a bunch of guys in chaps farting their insides out was inevitability. There were lines and concepts besides the central notion I know that I came up with originally, but everyone's ideas were shaped by everyone else, which is why the script had so much formal unity."

Steinberg took on an unofficial responsibility: he was Pryor's "designated gatekeeper," hanging out with the comedian after hours in order to temper his debauchery. This much is incontrovertible: Pryor didn't last long. One day the comedian simply went AWOL. He had clocked in for "about a month of steady work," said Steinberg. Some of Pryor's more whimsical stuff (an extended "Candygram for Mongo!" animated sequence) was ultimately excised, but the King Shit had left his imprint.

How long Alan Uger stuck around after the July 26 draft is another question that later disturbed the group consensus. In interviews, Bergman and Steinberg said that Brooks's in-your-face argumentation and nit-picking of the comedy wore on Uger, and the former dentist abandoned the script before his time was up. With a few exceptions—Buck Henry was one—Brooks was careful about what he said publicly about his collaborators, but he recalled Uger fondly. "He was at the typewriter and we were all just pitching."

"Rashomon is having a picnic," Uger said when asked about accounts that minimized his participation. His contract had extended only through the first draft, after which he returned to the Department of Health, he said. He contributed his share and was fully credited on-screen according to contract. In fact, he said, he had enjoyed the "amazing experience" of working with Brooks, "a comic genius and an uncommonly decent man." Uger would go on to write for and produce the hit television series *Family Ties*, winning an Emmy, a Writers Guild Award, and a Humanitas Prize.

"I assure you that my writing credit would not be there [on *Blazing*

*Saddles*] if Mel thought I was unworthy," Uger noted for this book. And "incidentally, I can't type," Uger added. "Never learned to. If I were at the typewriter, we'd still be there."

Of course, there was *someone* at the typewriter—Brooks himself, never. In New York, for the July 26 draft, that person was a hired secretary, one of the unsung heroines in the motion picture business who are omnipresent, getting something down on paper as the writers sometimes shouted over one another. In California, another girl Friday did the job; she wore a Western costume because she was an actress with a stenographic sideline hoping for a part. No one remembers either of those women's names. They go uncredited.

The July 26 draft was definitely overstuffed (as many as 412 pages, according to some reports, or 156, per other estimates). Among other things, the lengthy first draft included a Catskills-type comedian who opens for Lili Von Shtupp and a long, rap-style "street poem" Richard Pryor had written for Black Bart to intone as he edges closer to the gallows.

Brooks seemed to be in no hurry. And he could be doubly loyal to his worst ideas if they met opposition, his obstinacy a way of testing people or a means of sparking internal debate.

For example, he concocted a cowpoke named Bogey, just so, it seemed, he could perform the "paranoid 'strawberries' bit from *The Caine Mutiny*" for the group, as Andrew Bergman recalled. ("Mel did a very nice Bogart, with the wet lips and the crazy eyes.") Bogey was penciled into the draft despite people's qualms, later to be removed.

Brooks evinced a peculiar fondness for characters with physical deformities and devised a midget character named Ash Tray, whose ashtray hat also honored Brooks's love of cigar jokes. The midget slavishly served the villain, who initially was going to be called "John Carradine" because he would be played by the real-life John

Carradine, the lantern-jawed veteran of many Westerns. (Carradine's innumerable screen credits would be listed on his office door.) When Carradine called "Ash Tray!," the midget would pop up from beneath a table and offer himself as a receptacle for cigar ashes. "I hated the character and Andy hated the character, but Mel was adamant," said Steinberg.

"The trick with Mel," said Steinberg, "is to not fold, to stand up for what you believe in, and if you don't believe [something's] funny, say that—and he respects that."

The dumb behemoth Mongo emerged in the July 26 draft, as did the saloon chanteuse Lili Von Shtupp, modeled after the character of Frenchy, played by Marlene Dietrich in *Destry Rides Again*. In the July 26 draft, however, the chanteuse was called Lili Von Dyke, evoking the star of *Bye Bye Birdie* and a certain TV series created by Carl Reiner. The eventual "Shtupp" means "fuck" in German slang; the script (like most Brooks scripts) was sprinkled with faux German such as Lili's aphrodisiacal sausage, the *schnitzengruben*.

In a definitive article on the *Blazing Saddles* script, published in *Written By*, the Writers Guild journal, Greg Beal listed the elements that had survived from Bergman's novella into the July 26 draft and later persisted into the film: Black Bart's arrival in Rock Ridge, triggering the first use of the N-word; the white deputy who becomes Black Bart's best friend (later to evolve into the Waco Kid, played by Gene Wilder); Black Bart adopting a patois to save himself; the plot thread of the railroad route "necessitating the destruction of Rock Ridge"; Black Bart's romance with a sexy white woman; the tollbooth that slows the bad guys; "the hitting of a little old lady." The basic structure of the film-to-be was in place in the July 26 draft with one major exception: "the grand finale from the Warner Bros. lot free-for-all and the Grauman's Chinese shoot-out," wrote Beal.

Still, there were rewriting and polishing ahead and fewer writers left to do the job.

• • •

Brooks and his family took a summer break on Fire Island, and he also made several trips to Hollywood to confer with Warner Bros. executives. On the West Coast he reunited with Carl Reiner for a private performance of the now 2013 Year Old Man in Warner's Burbank recording complex. Two hundred friends and family lounged on huge sofas, dined on cracked crab and chili from Chasen's, and savored the act. *2000 and Thirteen* would go on sale late in 1973 as a Christmas package, along with a reissue of the early recordings, recently taken over from Capitol by Warner Bros. Records.

There was "talk that the pair had given in to their fears and disappeared while ostensibly preparing backstage," according to *New York Times* reportage. Brooks "hasn't been very easy to live with this week," admitted the wife of the 2013 Year Old Man, Anne Bancroft. Brooks was "chain-smoking and initially rusty," according to the *Times'* account, but Reiner warmed up his friend onstage, and the laughs began to flow.*

The best dancer in all of history, the 2013 Year Old Man revealed, was the American president Abraham Lincoln. "He used to lock the door and jump and twirl in graceful arabesques," he said. "But he never went on the stage because of his warts."

The 2013 Year Old Man just happened to be passing through LA for his bicentennial physical, he explained. Everything had checked out fine, which was good because he feared dying and meeting Jesus, having once paid him "only four bucks for a cabinet."

Bancroft had an ulterior motive for sitting in the audience. In Hollywood the actress met with director Melvin Frank about her forthcoming part opposite Jack Lemmon in the screen adaptation

---

* Brooks's old tablemate from Max's Kansas City, Michael Elias, now Carl Reiner's writing partner on *The New Dick Van Dyke Show*, helped Reiner think up the new questions for the 2013 Year Old Man.

of Neil Simon's *The Prisoner of Second Avenue*, her first film role since *Young Winston* and motherhood. Also a Warner Bros. production, *Prisoner* would be shot in the fall, partly at the studio, partly in New York City. Other celebrities dotting the appreciative crowd included *Miracle Worker* director Arthur Penn, journalist Nora Ephron, and longtime Brooks friend Norman Lear, now the producer of the hit television comedy series *All in the Family*, which had Reiner's son Rob in the cast.

In the fall, Brooks and his writers—minus Richard Pryor and Alan Uger—reconvened. Andrew Bergman and Norman Steinberg's selective memory may be owed to the fact that they persevered for months beyond the July 26 draft, forging a Three Musketeers–type kinship with Brooks. Often the three writers dined together in Chinatown after work sessions on the follow-up drafts, taking long discursive walks home through the Village, where they all resided (Brooks on West 12th Street, Steinberg in the East Village, Bergman in Gramercy Park). The trio argued about scenes and discussed writing and films and life.

The peculiar gestation of the script and the rare mix of the collaborators would give it a singular flavor in Brooks's oeuvre. For one thing, although there were often allusions to real-life people and topics within a Mel Brooks comedy, in *Blazing Saddles* those references were more crammed and variegated: apart from the many Johnsons (Dr. Samuel Johnson, Olsen and Johnson, Van Johnson, and an early Howard Johnson's that advertises only one flavor of ice cream), there were allusions to Jesse Owens, Mae West, *The Treasure of the Sierra Madre* ("Badges! We don't need no stinking badges!"), Cecil B. DeMille, ABC's *Wide World of Sports*, Gabby Hayes, *Dr. Kildare*, Guccis, Charles Laughton in *The Hunchback of Notre Dame*, Warner Bros. cartoons, and even, improbably for a Western,

Adolf Hitler in the big finale ("They lose me right after the bunker scene").

Before Christmas, the Three Musketeers had completed the final draft. The villain was no longer "John Carradine." Sometime in mid-1972, they had all attended a screening of *Everything You Always Wanted to Know About Sex*, Woody Allen's new film, discovering that Allen had beaten Brooks to Carradine. The veteran actor appeared in one distinctly unfunny segment of the anthology comedy along with—shades of Ash Tray—a strange deformed servant. In addition, Brooks had spotted Carradine in the Warner's commissary one day and decided the actor did not radiate good health. For weeks Bergman and Steinberg had begged Brooks to drop Ash Tray. Now he did ("Fuck it, he's gone!"), and "John Carradine" became "Hedley Lamarr." ("Big upgrade there," Bergman said.) The name was Brooks's twist on Hedy Lamarr, which later prompted a nuisance lawsuit from the Golden Age screen siren, who was still alive and didn't think it was funny.

The grand culmination, the melee that spills over onto a Warner Bros. soundstage and then segues to Grauman's Chinese Theatre, also emerged in the final draft: that was Brooks's inspiration, all agree. It was what *The Producers* and *The Twelve Chairs* had lacked—a finish to beat all finishes. "The notion of opening the movie up at the end was Mel's, and his instinct was dead-on," recalled Bergman. "He didn't want any kind of traditional ending to this picture. It was a brilliant idea. The details of the ending we all worked on, but the concept was pure Mel."

Brooks and Norman Steinberg, who were closest in age, became the closest thing to soul mates. Besides showering people with medical advice and career tips, Brooks had another specialty: counseling his male friends on their relationships with women. He showed up on

Steinberg's doorstep one Sunday night amid his usual nocturnal rounds in the Village. Brooks and Steinberg's wife launched into an argument about a Stanley Kubrick film, and Steinberg's wife stormed off angrily. Brooks and Steinberg stayed up late talking.

Steinberg and his wife had just spent hours in a car bickering all the way home from a weekend getaway in New England. The gulf in their marriage was widening.

"Look," Brooks told him, "I'm going to save you about twelve years of therapy. She is manic-depressive. You have to get out of the marriage. You can't win this."

Whatever else transpired between them in the years to come, Steinberg never forgot that Brooks had given him a leg up early in his career, hired him for *Blazing Saddles*, and also given him sound marital advice. Soon after that talk, Steinberg divorced his wife. "[Brooks] did save me twelve years of therapy, and maybe more," he said.

New fatherhood, marriage, and divorce were very much on Brooks's mind when he wrote *Blazing Saddles*, true-life concerns of the sort that never intruded on his comedy—one reason people found his films such a respite from their own pressing problems.

Even as *Blazing Saddles* took shape in writers' meetings, Brooks's ex-wife, Florence Baum Brooks Dunay, was pressing for a divorce from her second husband, the stockbroker Edward Dunay. Dunay had verbally and physically abused Florence to the point where she had called the police on him several times. Dunay had abandoned his family's East 62nd Street apartment and no longer contributed to the rent or other household expenses. The couple were battling over custody of their ten-year-old son.

Brooks's three children from his marriage to Florence still lived with their mother, as they always had. Stefanie, Nicky, and Eddie were teenagers now, and they had educational, medical, and everyday expenses. Florence was lagging far behind on her rent and had mounting debt; many times she felt desperate for cash, including for Brooks's monthly payments, which came erratically. Florence phoned Brooks, pleading for him and Anne Bancroft to take his three children for a spell and help her get back on her feet. "My wife is an artist, not a nanny!" he yelled, and slammed down the phone.

Besides evading child support payments over the years, Brooks never once remitted the one-third percentage of his net income over $44,000 annually, which had been promised to the first Mrs. Brooks as part of their 1962 divorce settlement. The word "net" had pretty much scuttled that clause, which nonetheless still hung ominously over Brooks.

Acting on the advice of a lawyer, Florence began pursuing a remedy that would kill two birds with one stone: she offered to sell the one-third-above-$44,000 clause back to her husband for a onetime financial settlement. In return she would drop all future claims against him. As he always did, Brooks, through his attorney Alan U. Schwartz, emphasized his failures and hardships, and how his earnings were modest. His career had hit such a low, low point. *The Producers* and *The Twelve Chairs* had achieved only *succès d'estime*—or, as Carl Reiner liked to say, success without the steam.

The talks between Florence's lawyer and Schwartz were just beginning as Brooks moved to Hollywood to shoot *Blazing Saddles*. She was cut off from show business, and she and her lawyer had no access to his contracts, no inkling of the gusher he was about to strike.


Hollywood had been transformed from the mighty kingdom Brooks had first visited twenty years earlier. "Suits," with New York agents David Begelman and John Calley among the first wave, had replaced the founding-father moguls as huge corporations began to take over the major studios at the end of the 1960s. Warner Bros. was one of the last studios to sell off in 1969, with the last surviving brother, Jack L. Warner, handing his studio over to Kinney National, a conglomerate that was the parent company of funeral home, parking lot, cleaning service, comic book, and music businesses—and Ashley-Famous.

The transition between the old guard and the new guardians was a period of tremendous ferment and experimentation in American filmmaking. Traditional genres, especially the Western and the musical, were either dead or dying and ripe for parody.

"Hollywood is really two Newarks," Brooks had cracked in the 1960s. But all along it had been part of his plan to abandon New York after the "Black Bart" script was completed. He was going to shoot his first major studio picture in Hollywood on Warner Bros. soundstages and the back lot. The move west, once unthinkable and wrenching for a man with Brooklyn pulsing in his blood, was made easier by the dead ends he had encountered on Broadway, the setbacks in television, and the limitations, chiefly economic, he had encountered while making *The Producers* and *The Twelve Chairs*.

Virtually the entire Club Caesar, with the exception of Lucille Kallen, had gone before him. Most of the old gang was already ensconced in the bosom of the film and television industry. Carl Reiner and the others welcomed him with open arms.

Brooks made trips back and forth to Hollywood throughout 1972, planning for the production at Warner Bros. During one of his meetings at the studio, after showing the latest draft of the screenplay to the head of the studio, John Calley, Brooks asked Calley if he might be going too far with the Western comedy—pointing out the scene in the third-act free-for-all, where a gang of westerners beat up an old lady. What the onetime Ashley-Famous agent said to him bolstered his confidence. Brooks repeated Calley's advice in many interviews: "Mel, if you're going to go up to the bell, ring it!"

By the end of the year, Brooks, Anne Bancroft, and six-month-old Max had relocated to Los Angeles. First the family leased a place on Rising Glen Road above Sunset Strip. Soon, however, Brooks signed papers and slapped a down payment on a high-ceilinged ranch house on Foothill Road in Beverly Hills proper, with a U-shaped swimming pool, a garden, and a citrus orchard that covered half an acre. Lew Wasserman, another former agent now running a studio—Universal—was one close neighbor.

Sue Mengers, a superagent at International Creative Management, whom Brooks had first met at Freddie Fields's Creative Management Associates, hosted one of the first extravagant Hollywood parties the couple attended. Van Cliburn played the piano as guests snacked on beluga caviar. "So I figured this was the place to be," Brooks recalled.

At first Brooks told Stefanie, Nicky, and Eddie that he really hadn't moved to Hollywood. The change of address was merely temporary. It would be especially important for the next two years, while his lawyer was busy whittling down the onetime payoff that would rescue Brooks from future financial obligations to his first wife and family, that Florence and the children be misled.

The Brookses were stealthy about the move to Hollywood inside the screen colony itself. But *Variety* tracked the "drift of film personages," paying special attention to East Coast celebrities who changed their address. "Even such 'committed' New Yorkers as Mel Brooks and Anne Bancroft have swallowed their 'tinseltown' sneers (a New York habit) and joined the migration," the trade paper reported early in 1974.

Meanwhile, casting for "Black Bart" progressed. Keeping with his notion of dotting the cast with Western old-timers, Brooks signed Slim Pickens, who had been seen to hilarious effect in *Dr. Strangelove*, as Hedley Lamarr's henchman, Taggart. He gave Mongo to the muscled ex–football player Alex Karras, who had not yet appeared in movies. (Karras would make the mentally challenged enforcer lovable as well as fearsome.) The capable character actors included John Hillerman, David Huddleston, Liam Dunn (who'd crossed paths with Brooks in his youth), and Dom DeLuise's wife, actress Carol Arthur, all playing unrelated townsfolk bearing the last name of Johnson. DeLuise himself accepted a small part that he made unforgettable as the poufy director wielding a megaphone, exhorting a Busby Berkeley–type chorus in the lavish musical of the grand finale. (His character's name, Buddy Bizarre, is listed only in the credits.)

Anne Bancroft had a hand in Madeline Kahn's casting. "Don't miss this one! She's the best!" she told Brooks, having met Kahn on her television specials and followed her in the Broadway musical *Two by Two*. A triple-threat actress, singer, and comedienne with a kewpie-doll face and mocking voice, Kahn had stolen scenes in Peter Bogdanovich's *What's Up, Doc?* and *Paper Moon*; for the latter picture, released in early 1973, she garnered an Academy Award nomination for Best Actress in a Supporting Role.

Brooks asked Kahn to audition for Lili Von Shtupp. The actress prepared the Brecht-Weill spoof "Das Chicago Song," which she had sung in another Broadway show Brooks would have seen, Leonard Sillman's *New Faces of 1968*. Brooks took Kahn aback when he said he needed a good look at her legs. "What, are you crazy?" Kahn sputtered. "I thought I was auditioning for a part in your movie. I didn't think you wanted to screw me on your desk." Brooks hastily explained that he wanted Kahn to straddle a chair in her net stockings in a classic Marlene Dietrich pose that he planned for her character to strike in the film. He was happily married, Brooks assured her, and not in the habit of casting on the couch. Having put him on the defensive and drawn a permanent line in their relationship, Kahn did as she was asked and displayed her wares. Brooks nodded approvingly. They talked for two hours. Then, and on numerous future occasions, Brooks invited Kahn home to dinner, "so she could see how much I loved Anne, and there was no straying from that love," in his words.

"My audition for Mel for *Blazing Saddles* was . . . intense," the actress later reflected. "I felt like I was at the Mayo Clinic. For a funny man, he's very serious."

The hallowed name Randolph Scott was evoked in the script, and Brooks had a notion that another icon from the Golden Age, Dan Dailey, might play Black Bart's white deputy, his friend and ally, the Waco Kid. Brooks tried hard to lure Dailey, better known for hoofing in musicals than for shoot-'em-ups, into the part, and until just before the March start date *Variety* still listed Dailey in the cast. However, Dailey had "an attack of qualms," in Kenneth Tynan's phrase, so Brooks showed the script to Johnny Carson, "and we had a couple of days of fantasizing about that before Johnny told Mel he really couldn't do it," Andrew Bergman recalled. Brooks finally glommed onto Gig Young—an actor better known for drama but capable of comedy and a recent Oscar winner for his role in a picture with hints of a Western in its title: *They Shoot Horses, Don't They?* The Waco Kid in the story was an alcoholic, and Young knew that addiction personally.

When, late in the script writing, "John Carradine" became "Hedley Lamarr," Brooks riffled through candidate after candidate without settling. Finally, hat in hand, he approached Carl Reiner to play the scenery-chewing villain. Reiner demurred; he was busy with *The New Dick Van Dyke Show*. Once again Bancroft rode to the rescue, asking Brooks, "Why don't you use that guy from *The Carol Burnett Show*?" That was Harvey Korman—Carol Burnett's Carl Reiner—who was as freewheeling a second banana as Reiner and who before then had bestowed his talent almost exclusively on television.

Korman, who knew the 2000 Year Old Man routines by heart, revered Brooks, and he went nervously for an interview with the director. Brooks got up, script in hand, and pranced around the office, acting Hedley Lamarr and belting out the film's songs. Korman felt intimidated. "I'll never be able to keep up with this man," he told his agent afterward. "Don't worry," said his agent. "He needs you as much as you need him."

By his third film, Brooks's casting philosophy had evolved away from trained, serious actors, famous stars, or personalities who might be either too high maintenance or too expensive. He began to speak of his preferred troupe as "self-starters," often musical performers or stand-up comics who brought their own craziness to his scripts. "I don't look for actors as much as I look for comics," he liked to say. Korman and DeLuise, Kahn as well, embodied the self-starter quality. But who was going to play Black Bart?

One reason why it is hard to believe that Richard Pryor focused on the white and Jewish characters when laboring on the script is that during the writing of scenes Pryor performed Black Bart's vignettes with relish. "It was glorious," Brooks recalled. All along, Pryor as Black Bart had been the unspoken wish of the team of writers, including the black comedian, who believed he had been penciled in and was a lock for the role.

But the studio knew about Pryor's drug habits and rejected him, Brooks always insisted. "I asked [Warner Bros.] on bended knee to let Richie do it," he said. The studio officials told Brooks that Pryor might vanish (as happened during the script writing) and he wasn't a big enough box-office name besides. Steinberg talked it over with Pryor after he got the bad news. "Don't blame Mel," Steinberg said. "He wanted you." Pryor was dubious. "The truth," Steinberg always said, "is Mel really fought for him."

Pryor wavered about who to blame. "It's a thorn in my heart," he told *Ebony* in 1976, not long after the film's release. Yet by the time of his 1995 memoir he had softened. "Before we even finished writing it Mel was talking about me starring as the black sheriff," he wrote. "I think people at the studio more powerful than Mel didn't want me."

His successor certainly did not have much of a box-office name. In his early thirties, the Oklahoma-born Cleavon Little had been trained at Juilliard and the American Academy of Dramatic Arts. In

1970, Brooks had seen him in his Tony Award–winning role as the eponymous traveling preacher of *Purlie*, an all-black musical about the Jim Crow era. Little had acted on television shows and in a few interesting movies such as *Cotton Comes to Harlem* and *Vanishing Point*. Maybe Anne Bancroft—who merited an "assistant casting director" credit for Brooks's early films—reminded Brooks of him.

Pryor was more like Brooks: his dangerous comedy could be abrasive. Little's screen test evinced a sly, likable personality. Little was "handsome as all get-out," and he paused like a Broadway actor when delivering his lines, giving "a measured reading" rather than rushing the words, Brooks said later. Little would make for a different sort of Black Bart, enigmatic and winning. Announced in late December, Little was one of the accidents of fate that turned out serendipitously for Brooks's third screen comedy.

There was no suspense about the casting of two of the characters: Governor Le Pétomane had been crafted as Brooks's showcase so the writer-director could play the film's silliest character with a flat paddle, a rubber ball, and a busty babe as props. Brooks also gave himself a cameo as an Indian chief, aiming this bit at intellectuals and Jews, with reference to the *schvartze* (the Yiddish N-word) and the lost tribes of Israel. Many jokes in the script were funnier for being lost on the majority of the audience.

The photography was set to begin in March. Andrew Bergman and Norman Steinberg had been in Hollywood for weeks, reworking and polishing scenes. Michael Hertzberg was back as Brooks's producer. The cameraman was the veteran Joseph F. Biroc, whose long career, harking back to *It's a Wonderful Life*, included the screen version of *Bye Bye Birdie*. Still looking for a compatible editor, Brooks hired two: one for the comedy, Danford B. Greene, who had been Oscar nominated for Robert Altman's free-form *M\*A\*S\*H*, and one for the Western, John C. Howard, who had coedited *Butch Cassidy and the Sundance Kid*. John Morris and Alan Johnson returned for music and choreography.

However, on the opening day of photography, Thursday, March 8, 1973, Gig Young suffered a breakdown during his first scene, the one where the Waco Kid wakes up hanging upside down in a jail cell. (The sheriff asks, "Are we awake?" and the Waco Kid, taken aback by seeing a black lawman, asks, "Are we black?") A notoriously heavy drinker who had gone on the wagon for the filming, Young began "spewing" green vomit, according to Brooks, and was rushed away in an ambulance. His agent-manager assured Brooks that Young was a recovered alcoholic. "Well, he ain't quite recovered," Brooks replied.

Young was done. Casting Gene Wilder as the Waco Kid was just another lucky break.

Since his Oscar nomination for *The Producers*, Wilder had been active: he had given a signature performance in *Willy Wonka and the Chocolate Factory*; starred in *Start the Revolution Without Me*, directed by Norman Lear's partner Bud Yorkin; and filmed the Eugène Ionesco play *Rhinoceros* with Zero Mostel. He had also appeared in the "What Is Sodomy?" segment of Woody Allen's *Everything You Always Wanted to Know About Sex*, playing a doctor in love with a sheep. As the ambulance bearing Gig Young sped away toward the hospital, Wilder was getting ready to depart for London, where he was playing the Fox in Stanley Donen's film of Antoine de Saint-Exupéry's *The Little Prince*.

Oddly, just a few months earlier, after the dream of John Carradine had died, Brooks had visited the actor he had publicly thanked three times at the Oscars for his importance to *The Producers* and offered him the role of Hedley Lamarr in "Black Bart." "I'm all wrong for that part," Wilder demurred. "How about Jim, the Waco Kid?"

"No, no," Brooks replied, "that's Anne's favorite part, too. No, I need an older guy—someone who could look like an over-the-hill alcoholic. I'm trying to get Dan Dailey."

"Mel, there are so many wonderful comics who would be much funnier than I could ever be playing Hedley Lamarr," Wilder told Brooks, refusing the role.

Now, though, Brooks was desperate. He made a phone call from a booth outside a Warner Bros. soundstage, reaching Wilder back east and pleading with the actor to take the first plane to Hollywood and take over the role of the Waco Kid. Wilder called Stanley Donen, and the director agreed to arrange all of his London scenes to be shot at the end of *Little Prince*'s schedule. Wilder promptly left for Los Angeles and over the weekend was fitted for a costume and gun belt and picked out the horse he'd ride in the film.

A few days after answering the call from Brooks, as Wilder wrote in *Kiss Me like a Stranger*, "I was looking at Cleavon Little, who appeared to be upside down, since I was hanging upside down in a jail cell." Little asked, "Are we awake?" and Wilder spoke the Waco Kid's first lines, "We are not sure—are we black?" with a bemused, quizzical intonation that confirmed he was a godsend, the ingratiating character the film needed. It's hard to imagine *Blazing Saddles* without him. The casting switch made Waco Jim and Black Bart contemporaries in age and helped forge their conspiratorial brotherhood.

"Go bananas!" Brooks reportedly urged all the principals, encouraging them to take liberties with the script. A few years later, Brooks told *Film Comment* that he had filmed the *Blazing Saddles* screenplay "word for word," but as Greg Beal noted in his in-depth examination, "dozens and dozens of lines in the movie don't appear in the shooting script." The enhancements to what was already an exceptional screenplay came fast and furious; Harvey Korman's scenes especially—some shared with the bubbling Brooks—were enriched with "wonderful asides and additions," in Norman Steinberg's words.

The campfire farting scene had been minimally described in the February 17, 1973, shooting script:

```
Five of Taggart's henchmen are seated around the
campfire.

No one talks. They are busy, noisily scraping the
last of their beans off tin plates. The only SOUND
WE HEAR is a vulgar symphony of eating, grunting,
belching and farting. Taggart steps out of his tent
and approaches the campfire.

                    TAGGART
        Got word there's a new sheriff in town.
        Who wants to kill him?
```

Now it was maximally staged. Even traditionalists such as Slim Pickens (Taggart) and Burton Gilliam (Lyle) got into the act, adding little improvements as the scene was filmed, starting when Taggart steps from the tent and sniffs the aroma of farts.

```
                    TAGGART

(As he waves his hat)


                    Goddam!


                     LYLE


        How about some more beans, Mr. Taggart?


                    TAGGART
        I'd say you've had enough.
```

Of course Brooks staged the scene without any actual fart sounds, just the up-and-down of cowboy butts. "Lift, turn, cross your legs!" exhorted the director. "Do the normal gestures you would do to let a fart escape." He'd add the right fart noises later.

Madeline Kahn, in a black bustier and with a peroxide rinse, blew onlookers away when she performed Lili Von Shtupp's big number, "I'm Tired," which again referenced Marlene Dietrich in *Destry Rides Again*, in which Dietrich sings a German-accented "See What the Boys in the Back Room Will Have." Brooks instructed the actress to "harmonize the way Dietrich would," but Kahn toyed with the phrasing (the suspended "Ah" in the middle of the song that she vocalized "in a key that was just a little wrong," in Brooks's words) and with the staging, too, at one point reaching to grab the set to keep from toppling over.

"Her most important contribution, however," according to Kahn's biographer William V. Madison, "was to point out that the song had only verses and a chorus. Brooks went home and, in one night, wrote the words and music to the introduction that begins, 'Here I stand, the goddess of desire.' . . . [even] though it meant re-staging the number."

Some of the actors' inflections were nonverbal—for example, the moment in "I'm Tired" that "always makes me laugh and cry," in Brooks's words. As the number ends, the cowboys shoot up the saloon, and the chorus of Prussian soldiers bears Kahn/Von Shtupp off the stage in their arms, Kahn "looks around as if to say, 'Oh, the hell with it all.'"

Though it was not quite a full-fledged musical, the score for the Western comedy would boast several of Brooks's standout compositions. Arranger and composer John Morris shared credit with Brooks on the title theme, but Brooks got ghost assistance on the lyrics of some of the other songs also. "Look, we wrote the songs, too," said Norman Steinberg in an interview for this book, "and he's the only one who gets credit for that . . . but still, who cares? It's not just his, it's ours . . . a true collaboration."

For the title theme, Brooks had the witty notion of recruiting Frankie Laine, who had crooned on many Western soundtracks (his voice would be instantly familiar to *Rawhide* fans). Laine's caterwauling, with whip cracks punctuating the stanzas, immortalized the tune.

The other musical highs included a chain gang of railroad workers, responding to the redneck foreman's exhortation for "a good ole nigger work song," delivering Cole Porter's "I Get a Kick Out of You" in silky harmony; and Count Basie and his orchestra materializing in the desert for the Vernon Duke–Yip Harburg evergreen "April in Paris," frosting on the cake and a personal touch from Brooks, a longtime fan of the maestro.

The third-act melee would break actual as well as invisible walls: the free-for-all spills onto a studio set where the top-hat-and-tails chorus of all-male dancers is being guided through their fancy footwork for a vintage Warner's musical. The handsome boys are singing the Brooks ditty "The French Mistake," which is defined by the urban dictionary as "when an otherwise straight male is persuaded to, or on a whim in the heat of the moment, engages in a homosexual act of which he later regrets and is ashamed."

Throw out your hands/Stick out your tush
Hands on your hips/Give 'em a push
You'll be surprised/You're doing the French Mistake
Voilà!

Alan Johnson's staging rivaled that of "Springtime for Hitler." "Piss on you, I'm working for Mel Brooks!" Hedley Lamarr's henchman Taggart snarls when Buddy Bizarre (Dom DeLuise) strenuously objects to the cowboy invasion. Pandemonium ensues with hilarious cutaways. The film within a film shifts to Grauman's Chinese Theatre, where the action soars to self-reflexive heights as Black Bart and the Waco Kid share popcorn while enjoying the climax on the screen. Never again would a Mel Brooks film feel so liberated. "*Blazing Saddles* is Dixieland jazz," Brooks reflected later, "where everybody gets up, has a riot or a solo, and there's a fierce harmonic blend of joy and freedom."

The title had remained "Black Bart" throughout the filming. Warner Bros. did not pinch pennies. The studio furnished Brooks's largest budget to date: $2.3 million.

# CHAPTER 11

# 1974

## Tops in Taps

Warner Bros. also had no idea of the lightning about to strike, however, or the studio would not have fumbled the next Mel Brooks film. Just days before he answered the phone call offering him the part of the Waco Kid, Gene Wilder had completed "the first draft" of the script for that project: *Young Frankenstein*.

One day in mid-1972, while on vacation in Westhampton after finishing his role in *Everything You Always Wanted to Know About Sex*, Wilder had sat down with a legal pad and written those two words—"Young Frankenstein"—at the top of a page. He contacted Brooks in New York, where the "Black Bart" writers were hard at work, saying he had dashed off the synopsis for a comedy about the great-grandson of Baron Beaufort von Frankenstein, a young scientist who scoffs at the Frankenstein legend until he inherits the Transylvania estate. "Cute," said Brooks, "that's cute. Keep at it." Nothing more.

Wilder's agent, Mike Medavoy, had encouraged the actor to try his hand at screenwriting, and now he urged Wilder to imagine parts in the embryonic project for Marty Feldman and Peter Boyle, because they were Medavoy's clients, too.

A Jewish Londoner, Feldman was an eccentric comedian with protruding, misaligned eyes, who had been introduced to US audiences in the 1972 summer replacement TV series *The Marty Feldman Comedy Machine*, produced in England by Larry Gelbart. Wilder conceived of Feldman as Igor, the hunchbacked assistant to Dr. Frankenstein, which was similar to a character in the classic 1931 *Frankenstein* film, based on Mary Shelley's novel and starring Boris Karloff. Boyle was a New York actor who was perhaps best known as the pathological hard hat in *Joe*, a surprise low-budget hit in 1970. Boyle was just hulking enough for Wilder to envision him as the Monster.

Besides a brief synopsis, Wilder wrote an introductory scene, which takes place at Transylvania Station, "where Igor and Frederick [Dr. Frankenstein] meet for the first time, almost verbatim the way it was later filmed," with "the *EE*gor and the *AYE*gor and the *Fran*kenstein and the *Fron*kensteen." He sent the synopsis and scene to Medavoy, who phoned him a couple of days later. Knowing of Wilder's relationship with Brooks, Medavoy said he was going to pitch the comedy with Brooks directing. "You're chasing the wrong rainbow," Wilder said, "because he won't direct anything that he didn't write."

A few days later Brooks phoned Wilder, asking "What are you getting me into?"

"Nothing you don't want to get into."

"I don't know, I don't know—I'm telling you I don't know."

Soon after, Medavoy phoned to say that Brooks had climbed on board. He had been seeking a long-term contract with Warner Bros. before the release of his Western comedy, but the deal Brooks wanted was "an expensive one," as studio officials later told *Variety*, and Warner's declined. Brooks then took *Young Frankenstein* to David Begelman at Columbia.

Medavoy explained that the Columbia deal was contingent on Wilder and Brooks working together on the screenplay. Wilder would write the first draft and "send Mel every twenty pages," in Wilder's words, and Brooks would give him feedback. If either *The Producers* or *The Twelve Chairs* "had been a commercial success," wrote Wilder, "I don't believe Mel would have said yes to *Young Frankenstein*. Lucky me! Lucky Mel!"

One day amid West Coast preparations for "Black Bart," Brooks visited New York and called to order their "one working session on 'Young Frank,' as he [Brooks] always called it," Wilder recalled. That was the day Brooks tried to convince Wilder to play Hedley Lamarr. "We spent forty-five minutes making coffee and discussing the merits of different brands while we ate little *rugelachs*," according to Wilder. "This was a ritual with Mel before anything serious could be discussed. (He preferred Kentucky Blue Mountain coffee, and I preferred Columbian White Star.) When coffee matters were finished, we went into my study and talked for about an hour about *Frankenstein*."

Brooks did most of the talking. Wilder scribbled notes. "Mel is like a shotgun with fifty pellets going, it just spurts out," Wilder recalled. Some pellets hit the target, such as Brooks's admonition to ground the Dr. Frankenstein character (earmarked for Wilder) in "scientific things, about the medulla oblongata, and the gray cells," according to the actor. Brooks urged Wilder to seek out a copy of *Gray's Anatomy*. "You've got to study it," explained Brooks, "so that when you give the lecture you'll know what you're talking about. Find out all that stuff . . . make it sound good, make it sound scientific."

Other pellets went astray. Brooks had one idea he hated to relinquish: when the monster woke for the first time, hands trembling, fingers twitching, eyes fluttering open, chains falling away, his first words should be a famous Cary Grant phrase. That idea gave Brooks the opportunity to perform his Cary Grant imitation for Wilder, which was "not exactly Cary Grant, but like Cary Grant talking about Judy Garland at the Palace," in Wilder's words. *Judy, Judy, Judy!* "I didn't say anything," according to the actor. "I just didn't write. I had my hand moving a little bit but I didn't write that down."

They traded victories. Wilder won one crucial, early disagreement, insisting that he wasn't going to write any part into the film for Brooks himself to play. Brooks as an actor was always riffing;

he wasn't acting. He always winked at the audience, Wilder said, breaking the fourth wall. *Young Frankenstein* should be performed with a straight face; no winking. Brooks could concentrate on the directing, as he'd done with *The Producers*, destined to be the only other Mel Brooks film without Brooks himself on-screen.

After that single meeting, Brooks went off to Hollywood to shoot "Black Bart." Wilder got down to brass tacks and launched into the first draft. "In black & white" was stipulated from the first on the title page as part of Wilder's intended homage to director James Whale's *Frankenstein* films, which had been photographed in black and white. Apart from the original, made in 1931, Wilder soaked up 1935's *Bride of Frankenstein* ("the most helpful") and *Son of Frankenstein*, directed by Rowland V. Lee, not Whale.

In January in Los Angeles, where Wilder was shooting *Rhinoceros* at Twentieth Century–Fox, the actor showed the first fifty-eight pages to Brooks, who was preoccupied with "Black Bart." Brooks said only, "Okay. Now let's talk about what happens next."

"I assumed he liked the pages but I wasn't sure," the actor recalled. They spent an hour mulling over the second half of the script, "what could happen, how it could happen," said Wilder. "Enough that I felt there was a track, that I could start to find my way."

Wilder headed back east and developed the second half of the script. Making a little time during the filming of "Black Bart," he continued working on the draft. And then, after he was done with his role as the Waco Kid, Wilder quickly departed California for London to meet up with director Stanley Donen and shoot his scenes for *The Little Prince*.

The trade papers did not learn about *Young Frankenstein* until September. Brooks was announced as directing the screen comedy "from a Gene Wilder script," with Wilder as Dr. Frankenstein, Peter Boyle as "the monster," and Marty Feldman as Igor.

Surprise: it was now a 20th Century–Fox production. Over the summer, Columbia also had let *Young Frankenstein* slip away, ordering a budget of $1.75 million, which fell short of the $2.2 million ceiling Brooks wanted. He managed to find trims in the budget, but the last straw was when Columbia balked at the black-and-white photography.

Another development: "Mel's boy," producer Michael Hertzberg, who had worked on *The Producers*, *The Twelve Chairs*, and *Blazing Saddles*, had demanded greater creative input and profit participation. That wasn't going to happen. So Hertzberg left Brooks to nurture his own projects; the trades also announced Hertzberg's new company in September.

Hertzberg's departure opened the door to another Brooklynite, Michael Gruskoff, who had first crossed paths with Brooks at Charles Kasher's house parties in the late 1950s. Gruskoff had been a mail room clerk at the William Morris Agency before becoming a top agent at Creative Management Associates with a reputation for handling temperamental clients. He was instrumental behind the scenes of Dennis Hopper's ill-fated *The Last Movie* and had produced Douglas Trumbull's science fiction thriller *Silent Running*. Mike Medavoy brought the two old acquaintances together. "You *pisher* you!" Brooks greeted Gruskoff, recognizing him instantly from Fire Island. "Where's your bathing suit?"

Gruskoff sent the *Young Frankenstein* script over to Gordon Stulberg and Alan Ladd, Jr., the president and vice president of 20th Century–Fox. They were the new leadership at 20th Century–Fox, and Stulberg and Ladd were anxious to build up the studio roster. The son of the famed actor Alan Ladd, "Laddie," as everyone called him, had started out as a talent representative with Creative Management Associates in Hollywood before moving to London and putting in a stint with the Lew Grade Organization. Longtime friends, Laddie and Gruskoff had worked together closely on projects in Hollywood and London.

Accompanied by Gruskoff, Brooks made an in-person pitch, doing most of the talking, his usual supersales job. Between Brooks and Laddie it was love at first sight. Laddie's Golden Age connection was as important to Brooks as his European business outlook was. Laddie loved *The Producers* and thought that "Gene and Mel were brilliant together." He was not keen on the planned retro look, but Peter Bogdanovich's *The Last Picture Show*—a Columbia picture, ironically—had demonstrated that black-and-white cinematography was no hindrance at the box office. 20th Century–Fox agreed to buy *Young Frankenstein* from Columbia and provide Brooks with a budget of $2.8 million. Ladd's considerable mystique in the Hollywood of the 1970s was greatly owed to the fact that, after stealing Brooks from Columbia, he signed the writer-director to a multi-picture contract (three films over the next five years with first pick of all of Brooks's "original concepts"). The contract gave the funnyman a decade-long haven at 20th Century–Fox.

There was interesting fine print in the contract between Brooks and Wilder. On "Black Bart," Brooks had no choice but to forfeit the story rights to the originating author, Andrew Bergman. There was nothing he could do about Warner Bros.'s attempt, in 1975, to turn *Blazing Saddles* into a television series; the studio produced a pilot episode, written by Michael Elias and Frank Shaw, with Bergman credited for the story. The pilot garnered a damning review in *Variety*, and the series idea died. Brooks had no say about any of it and didn't get a penny. He hated that.

Even though Wilder had conceived of *Young Frankenstein*, in most ways he would be Brooks's junior partner in the contract. As the film's star and cowriter, he received the equivalent of Brooks's $100,000 writing-directing fee. But as a first-time scenarist, compared to Brooks—an Emmy and Oscar winner—he was obliged to share the story credit. But Wilder's name would be listed *before* Brooks's in both the story and the script credits, the first and last time that would happen on a Mel Brooks film.

Wilder's star salary was secondary to his long-term writer's share of profit percentages. However, the apportioned writing credits did not translate into equally divided revenue, nor into equal control over the story property unto perpetuity. All the contractees belonged to a joint venture, with Crossbow Productions the principal entity in a limited partnership with companies formed by Gruskoff (officiating the joint venture) and Wilder (Jouer Limited). The joint venture managed the financing and distribution deal with 20th Century–Fox, which paid out 20 percent of all net profits according to this formula: joint venture, 14.28 percent; Jouer Limited, 28.57 percent; Crossbow Productions, 57.15 percent.

Among the proprietary advantages that accrued to Crossbow in the overall arrangement was one unusual clause that Alan U. Schwartz extracted for the future. That clause took note of the rights of original authorship, as the Writers Guild defined the term. Those rights did not apply strictly to *Young Frankenstein*, as they had to *Blazing Saddles*, because the script was manifestly an adaptation of a previously existing novel and several earlier films. "Notwithstanding that you are not entitled to separation of rights, as that term is defined in the WGA Minimum Basic Agreement of 1970," the 20th Century–Fox contract stated, Brooks and Wilder—with Brooks the controlling partner under the aegis of Crossbow—would retain the "dramatic live stage rights" for *Young Frankenstein*.

Over the summer of 1973, Brooks began the assembly of what, around the studio, was still being called "Black Bart," a temporary title that did not satisfy anyone. Not until later in time did he experience a brainstorm one morning in the shower. He first tried out *Blazing Saddles*—another fart allusion—on Anne Bancroft, then told John Calley, who exclaimed, "That's a great fucking title! I'm sending out a press release immediately." Later Brooks added an equally mirthsome subtitle: "Never Give a Saga an Even Break."

Taking over Warner's postproduction facilities, the filmmaker worked closely with editors Danford B. Greene and John C. Howard. Brooks was his usual obsessive-compulsive self during editing, moving around a few frames here, a few there, insisting "I know where the laughs are!" Often it was true, and the scene got funnier. Other times, after days of shuffling a few frames around, they'd end up back where they'd started.

In the long months between the end of shooting and the release of the film, Howard was the editor with the patience of Job. A big, jolly man attuned to Brooks's sense of humor, Howard was willing to try cuts, music, and sound effects with endless permutations. His iron butt would make him Brooks's editor for the foreseeable future.

Especially with music and sound effects, the editing gave Brooks a way to top off scenes the way, as a writer, he topped off comedy sketches with his zingers. The campfire farting scene received the full Brooks spritzing. "The sound editors got their friends together and then put soap under their armpits," the director explained in one interview. "Wet soap. And they slapped at it and made air pockets and did the noises that way. I came in to do some with my voice, a few high ones that they couldn't do under their arms. Y'know, *bvrrrrvt*. But nobody put an actual fart on the soundtrack."

After a summer break, as the editing of *Blazing Saddles* progressed, Gene Wilder returned to Hollywood to work on the rewrite of *Young Frankenstein*. "Think you're pretty good, huh?" Brooks greeted the actor after Wilder had checked in to the Hotel Bel-Air in West Los Angeles. "Well, I got news for you, Jew boy—now the work begins!"

Brooks spent most days in the editing room in Burbank, while Wilder holed up writing at the Hotel Bel-Air. Brooks rendezvoused with the actor in the evenings, beginning their meetings with a "coffee ritual," according to Wilder—"Earl Grey Tea and digestive English wheat biscuits," according to Brooks, which better facilitated "an Old English feeling"—before the filmmaker delivered his notes on Wilder's latest pages.

Even in tête-à-têtes Brooks's customary mode was shouting. Wilder, in his memoir, renders some of Brooks's criticisms in caps: "YOU DON'T HAVE A VILLAIN! You understand what I'm saying? WE'VE GOT TO HAVE A VILLAIN! Otherwise there's no story tension." One time, during a fierce argument about something or other, Brooks *really* yelled at him. "I can't even remember what it was about," Wilder said, but Brooks stormed out and ten minutes later phoned Wilder from his house: "WHO WAS THAT MADMAN IN YOUR HOUSE? I COULD HEAR THE YELLING ALL THE WAY OVER HERE. YOU SHOULD NEVER LET CRAZY PEOPLE INTO YOUR HOUSE—DON'T YOU KNOW THAT? THEY COULD BE DANGEROUS."

"That was Mel's way of apologizing," Wilder explained.

The script evolved into a series of well-knit blackouts. The sequencing of the blackouts builds the story. You can almost spot Brooks's toppers, which are sprinkled into the lead-ins or -outs of scenes, and his throwaways about penises or breast size. (Brooks always insisted, however, that Wilder had come up with Dr. Frankenstein's "What knockers!" followed by Inga's "Thank you, Doctor!") The Monster's *schwanzstucker*, a riff that became the film's punch line, could only be Brooks's. Ditto the Blind Hermit's reaching for the top of the Monster's head: "You must have been the tallest one in your class!"

One prolonged argument was prompted by Wilder's brainstorm for the scene in which Dr. Frankenstein and the Monster sing and dance to Irving Berlin's "Puttin' on the Ritz," a scene that couldn't help but evoke one of Brooks's boyhood favorites, the Ritz Brothers vamping "The Horror Boys from Hollywood" with Al as the dancing Boris Karloff. "I said to myself, now Mel's going to smile," Wilder recalled thinking, because everyone knew Brooks loved iconic songs, which at the slightest cue he belted out to audiences of one. Brooks went into his contrarian mode, however, exploding "Are you crazy? It's frivolous! It's self-indulgent! You can't just suddenly burst into Irving Berlin . . ."

First Wilder "argued softly," leaving Brooks unmoved; then he started "arguing vehemently," until finally "my face started to turn from red to blue." Almost half an hour passed with Brooks standing firm in his opposition. As Wilder began to sag in defeat, Brooks suddenly switched. "Okay—it's in!" Wilder was stunned. "How can you argue with me for twenty-five minutes and then just casually say, 'Okay—it's in!'"

"Because I wasn't sure—do you understand?" Brooks replied. "I wanted to see how hard you'd fight for it. If you gave up right away, I'd know it was wrong."

Brooks unleashed his spray of pellets: big, small, good, bad. Sometimes Wilder wrote the ideas down, sometimes he let his pen glide over the page. Still, Brooks had never had a better typist or amanuensis. "I had to tone Mel down," Wilder summarized, "and he had to keep me from being too subtle." Several drafts were stacked up over the next six months, with a few of the film's unforgettable moments not in any of them.

"The only time we actually sat down and wrote together," Wilder credibly claimed, "was on the creation scenes: 'From this stinking bit of slime! . . .'"

They finalized the scenes with the luxury of knowing the actors who were going to play many of the roles, not only Wilder, Peter Boyle, and Marty Feldman but also Madeline Kahn. While filming "Black Bart," Wilder had been bowled over by Kahn; he talked with Brooks about the actress playing Inga, Dr. Frankenstein's sexy assistant. But after Kahn read a draft, she said she'd rather play the ingenue, Elizabeth, Dr. Frankenstein's coy fiancée—done! Wilder also knew Teri Garr, a perky former dancer who had been glimpsed in Elvis movies and who had just finished a small picture for Francis Ford Coppola called *The Conversation*. And just like that, Garr became Inga.

Early on, the third important female role—more than in any other Brooks film—was set aside for Cloris Leachman. She'd play Frau Blücher, "a really frightening woman," in Wilder's words, a Mrs. Danvers–type keeper of the household à la *Rebecca*. Leachman had won an Oscar for Best Actress in a Supporting Role in *The Last Picture Show* and twice been Emmy nominated for her recurring role on *The Mary Tyler Moore Show*.

Another alumnus of *The Conversation* and a top box-office name of the era, Gene Hackman, heard about the project while playing tennis with Gene Wilder and wanted to get in on the fun. Hackman volunteered to play the lonely Blind Hermit, yearning to befriend the Monster: free of charge—four days of shooting for about four minutes of running time. Kenneth Mars, Franz Liebkind from *The Producers*, returned for good luck as the comical villain, Inspector Kemp—one of the roles Brooks had thought he might play until Gene Wilder said no—a policeman straight out of *Son of Frankenstein*, which had had Lionel Atwill similarly dressed and coping with a false arm torn off by the monster.

Brooks had worked with a different cameraman for each of his previous three films. Now he met with a New Yorker with credits dating from the late 1940s. Gerald Hirschfeld was thrown when Brooks scolded him about "errors" in pictures he'd lensed, such as *Diary of a Mad Housewife*. Didn't Hirschfeld think the white tub in the bathroom was too bright? Didn't the gels shimmer too much? "At first, I took him seriously and was more than a little upset," the cameraman recalled, "until I realized he was doing his 'thing' and pulling my leg, because there was no tub and the bedroom was an interior set that didn't require window gels. So I pulled his leg, and said, 'One more derogatory remark about my work, and I'll leave.' We understood each other and laughed."

Brooks learned that Kenneth Strickfaden, who helped create the special effects for *Frankenstein* in 1931, had kept parts of the laboratory set from the classic horror film in his Santa Monica garage. Dale Hennesy, a production designer and art director whose previous credits included *Dirty Harry* and *Sleeper*, retrieved the parts and reproduced the laboratory, adding it to his atmospheric production design. Dorothy Jeakins created costumes faithful to James Whale's oeuvre, and Alan Johnson stopped by for "Puttin' on the Ritz." There were no new songs for John Morris to orchestrate, but he did compose the background score, "one of his masterpieces," according to Brooks, who asked for a full, rich score, nothing "tinny scary." So Morris "went way back into Transylvania folk music and came up with this incredible gypsy song" that became the picture's main theme.

Putting the postproduction finishing touches on *Blazing Saddles* while cowriting and preparing *Young Frankenstein*, Brooks was never more on top of his game. If the Western comedy was anarchic, the Frankenstein spoof became his most controlled work. 20th Century–Fox approved the *Young Frankenstein* script, and the first day of photography was slated for February 11, 1974. That was the Monday following the weekend opening of *Blazing Saddles* in New York, Los Angeles, Seattle, and Vancouver.


One piece of footage Brooks always regretted leaving on the *Blazing Saddles* cutting room floor was the penis joke in the scene between Lili Von Shtupp and Black Bart in her dressing room, where she puts the moves on the sheriff. Von Shtupp blows out the candles and asks in her German-accented lisp, "Tell me, *Schatzi*, is it twue what they say about the way your people are gifted?" The studio did not want to provoke censors with the sheriff's punch line—"I hate to disappoint you, ma'am, but you're sucking on my arm"—so the director snipped it out. However, what Lili said next was preserved—"It's twue! It's twue!" rising in pleasure—which pretty much said the same thing just as well.

Even so, *Blazing Saddles* became the first Brooks film to receive an R rating.

Warner Bros. president Ted Ashley is said to have freaked out at one of the early screenings for executives. Ashley steered Brooks and production head John Calley into an office and, in "a litany of anger," in Brooks's words, ticked off all the stuff that had to go: the N-word, the farting, the horse getting punched, yada yada yada. Brooks solicitously jotted down notes; then, after Ashley stormed out, he balled them up and shot the paper into a wastebasket. Calley, "the only one who laughed" during the screening, muttered, "Good filing." Brooks convened a separate screening for studio employees, got roars of laughter and instant buzz around the lot, and *Blazing Saddles* was set for release.

*Blazing Saddles* shot out of the gate like Secretariat, running "hot" (*Variety*'s phrase) at showcases on both coasts, the Sutton on 57th Street and Third Avenue in Manhattan and the AVCO Center Cinema in the Westwood/UCLA neighborhood of Los Angeles. With robust ticket sales, the release was quickly expanded to ninety theaters across the United States—which in those days, when theaters were cavernous, constituted a wide release—and by mid-April, Brooks's film had risen to the top of the box-office chart: number one.

*Blazing Saddles* was the comedy of the year for audiences and the debate of the year for many critics who didn't think so, although many wrote guiltily of their enjoyment.

"There are grand bits and pieces," wrote Judith Crist in *New York* magazine in one such review, "but there are ungrand bits and pieces." Brooks's new comedy, Charles Champlin wrote in the *Los Angeles Times*, was "often as blithely tasteless as a stage night at the Friar's Club and almost continuously funny." Even *Variety* carped. "If comedies are measured solely by the number of yocks they generate from audiences, then Mel Brooks' *Blazing Saddles* must be counted a success," wrote the trade paper's critic, "Beau," who added "Brooks is such a funny man, however, that it seems a shame he still doesn't know how to harness his stable of gags into something more than an updated Abbott & Costello farce."

One reason the critics hedged was that Woody Allen's futuristic *Sleeper* had opened in December 1973 and the pundits had begun to compare Brooks with Allen, both Jewish New Yorkers, both graduates of the Sid Caesar college of comedy. *Sleeper* belonged with Jacques Tati's *Playtime* as pictures that "stay with you after you've seen them," Vincent Canby wrote in the *New York Times*, while *Blazing Saddles* was more like Chinese takeout, "every Western you've ever seen turned upside down and inside out, braced with a lot of low burlesque, which is fine. In retrospect, however, one remembers along with the good gags the film's desperate, bone-crushing efforts to be funny." Judith Crist agreed with Canby. "Odious" comparisons between *Saddles* and the better *Sleeper* only served to underscore that "with each one of his feature films, Woody Allen has become more and more his own man, perfecting his skills as a triple-threat writer, director, and star."

Some critics sided with Brooks. America's dean of auteurist criticism, Andrew Sarris, in the *Village Voice*, said he had experienced a "mini-auteurist epiphany of sorts vis-à-vis the movies of Mel Brooks and Woody Allen" and preferred *Blazing Saddles* to *Sleeper*. Confessing that "I had written off Brooks as a film director after *The Producers* and I hadn't even bothered to see *The Twelve Chairs* when it came out," Sarris said he had come around to viewing Brooks's pursuit of mass audiences as a canny survival strategy. "What Allen lacks is the reckless abandon and careless rapture of Brooks," Sarris wrote. "Indeed, Brooks reminds me in his most serious moments of artists like Renoir and Sternberg. But, alas, in his most comical moments he reminds me of the Ritz Brothers."

• • •

As the reviews and receipts rolled in, Brooks was preoccupied with the first scenes of *Young Frankenstein* at 20th Century–Fox. Most of the photography took place on studio soundstages, with excursions to the University of Southern California, where Brooks shot the medical school sequence, and to the back lot of MGM for that studio's standing sets.

At the end of the first week, Brooks and Wilder asked cameraman Gerald Hirschfeld to stay and chat after dailies. They were not happy with the look of the film.

"What are you talking about?" Hirschfeld demanded. "You showed me *Frankenstein* and *Bride of Frankenstein*, and that's the look I'm giving you."

"Oh, that's not what we want," Brooks responded. "We want to *satirize* that look."

Hirschfeld pointed out that nobody had said as much, and Wilder piped up, "Mel, he's right. We never told him that." Hirschfeld said he would make some adjustments.

At the next viewing of dailies, they told the cameraman, "Oh, this is more like it!" and then, as time went on, "Oh, this is even better!" Halfway through the picture, Brooks drew Hirschfeld aside at lunch and said, "Gerry, I'm glad I didn't fire you four weeks ago." And Hirschfeld thought to himself, "Mel, you're lucky I didn't quit."

Apart from that little misunderstanding, the filming of *Young Frankenstein* was, by all accounts, "the happiest I'd ever been on a film," as Wilder wrote in his memoir. "It was like taking a small breath of heaven each day." There had been little rehearsal time for *Blazing Saddles*, but *Young Frankenstein* was more of an actor's showcase, and Brooks set aside three weeks before shooting for read-throughs and staging. More than usual on a Mel Brooks film, the script was protected by the lead actor. Although Wilder often insisted, "we never improvised dialogue on the set," Brooks said, "Gene did what I call 'aftermath' ad-libbing," supplying what he called "prop-wash" to follow through on jokes: lines such as "You son of a bitch, you ruined me!" or "Momma, I want my momma!"

One joy of the film is Wilder's intensely focused performance, as harebrained as it is charismatic, in the lead role he'd crafted for himself. The actor "could be Krakatoa," Brooks explained. "He could be the greatest volcano ever . . . or he could be sweet and mellow and very moving." The director developed a code for calibrating Wilder's performance during the filming. Brooks would say, "Too orange!" if Wilder went too big, too volcanic in a scene, or "More purple!" if he wanted the sweetness and mellowness.

The camera kept rolling after the director called "Cut!" to catch interpolations by the cast. And Brooks was likely to print several takes of the same shot, giving him options later in the editing room. "The one [take] that's perfect, that I love," the filmmaker explained, "and then I do one slightly over the top, just in case it's needed in the picture puzzle of the film—later, when you think, I need a little more energy here. Gene played everything vibrantly. The only direction I'd ever have for him is, I'd say, 'Softer.' "

The others in the ensemble matched Wilder in their high spirits and comic inventiveness. As Dr. Frankenstein's assistant, Inga, Teri Garr "played her sexuality fully and naively, innocently," Brooks recalled, and added "little things that were wonderful." Her line in the script was "You mustn't. No, you mustn't!" But Garr would say, "No, you mozzn't!" with "a wonderful German feeling," in Brooks's words. Garr's chemistry with Wilder was boosted by the fact that the costars were amorously involved off the set.

Madeline Kahn added her usual daffy nuances, asking for musical changes the night before the crucial scene was shot in which the Monster (Peter Boyle) rapes Elizabeth, her character. The script called for Kahn to burst into Irving Berlin's "Cheek to Cheek"—a bookend to "Puttin' on the Ritz." She thought that "Ah! Sweet Mystery of Life!" from Victor Herbert's operetta

*Naughty Marietta*, with its "Oh . . . oh! . . ." (as the Monster lowers him-self upon her) seguing into the song's ecstatic opening phrase, would be funnier.

A naturally reserved person, Kahn flinched at the oft-crude vernacular in Brooks's scripts (and in the similar language fre-quently echoed on his sets). But the actress never came off as sensually in other people's movies, perhaps because on the screen Brooks saw her as "a dirty uncle" might, in Kahn's words. "Off-screen," wrote Kahn's biographer William V. Madison, "Brooks made her feel appreciated and protected. Yet his movies threw her into Transylvanian rapes and Roman orgies."

The outtakes (later shared on the DVD and in documentaries) show the troupe breaking up repeatedly over each other's asides and mistakes. Brooks proffered his own "aftermath" suggestions—toppers by any other name—with Marty Feldman particularly susceptible to the whispering provocateur. In one instance that led to Igor/Feldman growling and chewing on a fox-fur stole slung around Elizabeth/Kahn's neck, after their characters first meet, with bits of the fur getting stuck in his mouth. Feldman's other notable add-on came from either Brooks (according to him) or Feldman himself (per his biographer Robert Ross). In rehearsals for the Transylvania Station scene, where Igor greets Dr. Frankenstein/Wilder, leading him off the train platform to-ward a hay wagon, Feldman threw in a "silly ad-lib," as the actor recalled, telling Wilder to "Walk this way!" as Feldman hobbled along. It was an "old Yiddish joke," in Feldman's words, but the crew laughed their heads off and so did Brooks. He told Feldman to keep the phrase in for the filming.

Wilder, finding it a "cheesy joke," later asked Brooks where "Walk this way!" had come from. "Man walks into a drugstore," he replied, "and says to the pharmacist, 'I got terrible hemorrhoids—have you got some talcum powder?' Pharmacist says, 'Yes, sir—walk this way.' Man says, 'If I could walk that way, I wouldn't need the talcum powder.' "*

If Brooks laughed, it was funny. The director was never as relaxed, staging *Young Frankenstein* and not having to worry about his own performance on camera. Gone, at least for now, were the shouter and insulter from *The Producers*. "Mel never loses his temper," Garr told the columnist Earl Wilson. Most days Brooks collegially ate lunch with the cast and crew, rather than disappearing into his trailer to stare at the script, as had previously been his wont. Numerous times, in interviews, Brooks said that *Young Frankenstein* was the best-directed picture of his career. Wilder thought the reason was simple.

"Mel could see what's wonderful" when he directed *Young Frankenstein*, Wilder explained in an interview. "The difference between Mel when he's not acting in it, and just directing, as opposed to when he is acting and directing, is the difference between a great director and a good director. Because if he doesn't have to worry about 'how's my make-up, how's my hair, how's my nose, how's my lighting,' just 'what do I see in front of me? How can I make these actors better?'—that's when all these things happen."

John C. Howard from *Blazing Saddles* was in position for the editing of this and the next three Mel Brooks comedies, patiently awaiting final decisions from Brooks. By now Brooks had a clear editing philosophy: he didn't like to be preempted by an editor's assembly, as had happened on *The Producers* and *The Twelve Chairs*. First he wanted to look at all the takes and outtakes, "every frame" that had been shot, laboriously piecing together the scenes, snipping frames out here and there, fine-tuning the laughs.

If Brooks did not appear in the picture, well, he could create

---

* It helped the line's durability when later, after seeing *Young Frankenstein*, the rock group Aerosmith wrote and recorded "Walk This Way," which became one of the band's signature hits.

cameos for himself at the postproduction stage. For *Young Frankenstein*, he voiced werewolf sounds for one particular scene and the deceased Baron Frankenstein for another. Kenneth Mars had a wacky moment in which he plays a darts game with Gene Wilder, cheating to intimidate him. When his turn comes, Wilder sprays darts outside the frame. That permitted one of Brooks's favorite impressions. "One goes through the window," Brooks explained, "and you hear, 'Yeow!' a cat sound, like he hit a cat? That's me! That's my guest appearance."

"After *Young Frankenstein* was in the can," a *Playboy* writer later reported admiringly, Brooks "edited the picture frame by frame at least twelve times, and in the last week of production spent several hours in a recording room, gleefully snorting, grunting, snarling, groaning, sighing and guffawing to fill tiny gaps in the talk track."

Taking a break from editing *Young Frankenstein*, Brooks made a rarer guest appearance acting alongside his wife. Since the birth of their son Anne Bancroft had made only one film, the screen version of Neil Simon's *The Prisoner of Second Avenue*, which had been shot around the same time as *Blazing Saddles*. Now Martin Charnin coaxed the actress into another television special, again written by a small army of writers led by Gary Belkin and Thomas Meehan, with Charnin also in on the writing and directing the show.

Airing on November 27, 1974, "Annie and the Hoods" encompassed all the "hoods" in a woman's life: bachelorhood, motherhood, unlikelihood, and so on. Bancroft sang, danced, and portrayed a dozen characters in sketches with costars Jack Benny, Alan Alda, Tony Curtis, Lily Tomlin, Polly Bergen, Gene Wilder, and Carl Reiner. "Other Womanhood" was a mirror-of-reality sketch that found Anne married to a philandering spouse played by none other than her real-life hubby. In the sketch Bancroft sarcastically serenaded Brooks with "Guess Who I Saw Today?," first made popular in *New Faces of 1952*.

They had been married for ten years, but it was the first time the couple had performed together publicly. Bancroft had vowed in private that she would never work with Brooks, Charnin said, and her husband was equally reluctant. "I made her cave," recalled Charnin. "I said, 'I really want to do a sketch with you and Mel,' and she agreed." Brooks did very little, simply gazed at his wife as she sang, "because the sketch was created around his noninvolvement," according to Charnin. "It was being done for Anne."

The experiment was a pleasant surprise, however. "They didn't criticize one another [behind the scenes] or chew one another out or kill each other," recalled Charnin.

Yet the television special did not repeat the success of the first Bancroft/Charnin collaboration, "Annie: The Women in the Life of a Man," four years earlier. *Variety* found the new special a dull "embarrassment." No Emmy nominations came as before.

Promoting "Annie and the Hoods," Bancroft gave numerous interviews with journalists, who frequently asked her when people were going to see her in a film directed by her husband. "Mel, as you know, does those way-out comedies like *Blazing Saddles*," was her standard response, "and they don't usually have big parts in them for women. But if he ever came up with something he wanted me to do, I'd jump at the chance."

Brooks had *Young Frankenstein* all ready for a mid-December opening in ten American cities, but the bookings quickly multiplied and the film rocketed to number three at the box office by the first week of March. It hovered in the top ten throughout the first half of 1975.

Brooks campaigned vigorously for his new screen comedy, which he'd been too busy to do for *Blazing Saddles*, giving umpteen interviews to New York media, culminating in the February 17, 1975, cover of *Newsweek* and his first full-length Q and A in the February 1975 *Playboy*, a hallowed honor in the men's magazine with nudie photographs, usually reserved for the likes of Fidel Castro or Norman Mailer.

Unlike the way they had reacted disparately to *Blazing Saddles*, the critics united on the subject of the PG-rated and more blithe comedy of *Young Frankenstein*. "Those who hated *Blazing Saddles* because it was coarse and tasteless," Charles Champlin wrote in the *Los Angeles Times*, "will be able to join hands with those who loved *Blazing Saddles* because it was coarse etc. to walk down the aisles loving *Young Frankenstein* together." *Variety* compiled the New York reviews: eight favorable, three unfavorable, none mixed.

*Young Frankenstein* stands apart from other Brooks films in many ways. The cast members were not stand-up comedians; they were actors in career ascendancy giving ebullient performances. The design elements are first-rate. Brooks's direction is restrained.

The comedy is sprinkled with risqué moments. (Brooks proved impervious to the women's movement with his Monster/Elizabeth rape scene, and feminists picketed one Boston theater, objecting to the "use of rape as a source of humor.") But most reviewers celebrated the film's relative discretion, its dialing down of crude humor. Gene Wilder's hand in the script, his constant presence on-screen, lent the film a singular charm.

Even the *New York Times* was won over, with Vincent Canby declaring *Young Frankenstein* to be Brooks's "funniest, most cohesive comedy to date," adding, equivocally, "Some of the gags don't work, but fewer than in any previous Brooks film." Roger Ebert in the *Chicago Sun-Times* was effusive, hailing the work as Brooks's "most disciplined and visually inventive film (it also happens to be very funny) . . . it shows artistic growth."

Still, there were a few prominent skeptics, including Gary Arnold in the *Washington Post*, who was left "untickled" by the horror-film spoof. Arnold trotted out more comparisons to Woody Allen, appraising *Sleeper* as "the work of someone who has mastered a considerable amount of technique" while *Young Frankenstein* "reveals a director whose visual imagination and technical resources remain pretty elementary."

Yet Brooks, in his interviews, had fewer naysayers to grumble about. Instead he pontificated about the underlying deep themes of his comedy. "We dealt with bigotry in *Saddles*," Brooks said in one interview, "and with neo-Fascism in *Producers*. Underneath the comedy in *Frankenstein*, the doctor is undertaking the quest to defeat death—to challenge God." *Young Frankenstein* was treating the subject of "womb envy," according to Brooks, and "the monster is what people who are afraid of intelligence think intelligence would look like if it were a person." Behind the comedy of all his pictures, Brooks insisted, was serious commentary about society or human nature, racism or greed.

Modesty did not become him. "I think in ten years," he told *Film Comment*, "*Blazing Saddles* will be recognized as the funniest film ever made." In response to a *New York Times* query about his favorite recent films, he said, "Both mine. I go back and watch my films." Asked by the BBC's *Desert Island Discs* to name his favorite music, he listed Beethoven's Fifth Symphony, Chopin's Prelude in E Minor, Bach's Brandenburg Concerto no. 3, Frank Sinatra's "In the Wee Small Hours of the Morning," Helen Forrest and Dick Haymes's "Just My Luck to Love in Vain"—and "Springtime for Hitler."

He did give good interviews. "The funniest man in the world," as Harry Stein* proclaimed him to be in *New Times*, could be more compelling and entertaining in person than his films. Yet even the flattering *Newsweek* profile noticed that Brooks's personality seemed a constant balancing act. "Beneath the cheerful informality bubbles a volcanic energy that fuels his comic genius," the newsweekly noted,

---

* Incidentally, Harry Stein was the son of the former *Your Show of Shows* writer and *Fiddler on the Roof* playwright Joseph Stein, a longtime Brooks friend.

"and occasionally launches him on extended transports of anger, especially at a negative or tepid review of his work."

After the New York publicity push, Brooks headed to London, where the comedy filmmaker introduced *Young Frankenstein* at the National Film Theatre (its premiere timed for an NFT retrospective of his first three pictures), then Paris, where "besides top reviews," in *Variety*'s words, "Brooks' appearance, interviews, and TV stints also helped swell press coverage." (The Paris reviews and box office prompted distributors to dig out and release *The Twelve Chairs*, which had never been shown in France.) Duplicating the sizzle of *Blazing Saddles* abroad, *Young Frankenstein* established Brooks as the "top foreign comic force" in Europe, in *Variety*'s words, especially in London, Paris, and Rome.

Brooks could reasonably have anticipated any number of year-end awards. Since both had come out in 1974, *Blazing Saddles* and *Young Frankenstein* ended up competing against each other for Oscars (and other year-end recognitions), and that may have divided potential voters and hurt both films. *Blazing Saddles* earned three Academy Award nominations: Best Song ("Blazing Saddles" with Brooks's lyrics and John Morris's music), Best Editing (Danford B. Greene and John C. Howard), and Best Actress in a Supporting Role (Madeline Kahn). In all three categories, however, it fell short of winning.

The membership of the Writers Guild voted the *Blazing Saddles* screenplay—credited, in nonalphabetical order, to Brooks, Norman Steinberg, Andrew Bergman, Richard Pryor, and Alan Uger—the year's Best Comedy Written Directly for the Screen.

Curiously, *Young Frankenstein* fared even less well in the postseason awards derby. The Writers Guild nominated it for Best Comedy Adapted from Another Medium, but it lost in that category to *The Apprenticeship of Duddy Kravitz*. The film's sound (Richard Portman and Gene S. Cantamessa) and the Wilder/Brooks script (again for adaptation) were Oscar nominated; both lost, the script to *The God-father, Part II.*

As the Oscar-winning writer of *The Producers* could attest, however, in Hollywood money spoke louder than any prizes. In 1975, Brooks was, in his own parlance, tops in taps; the filmmaker boasted two extraordinary hits, and the stream of revenue for *Blazing Saddles* and *Young Frankenstein* marked a seismic shift in his status and power.

When *Young Frankenstein* was released in late December, *Blazing Saddles* was still showing in certain US and European cities (in Denmark, the Western spoof played continuously for three years). *Blazing Saddles* would be rereleased widely several times in the years ahead before topping out at a reported $100 million in gross earnings, a figure that doesn't include revenue from video, DVD, TV airings, and licensed insignia products.

*Young Frankenstein* would rank as the fourth-highest-grossing film of 1975, behind *Blazing Saddles* (number one), *The Towering Inferno* (number two), and *The Trial of Billy Jack* (number three). It grossed nearly $90 million worldwide before also being rereleased several times.

Only his accountant knew the extent of Brooks's earnings. Brooks was paid something in the neighborhood of $50,000 for his captaincy of the *Blazing Saddles* script and another $50,000 for acting in and directing the film. The other writers earned far less both up front and down the road. Richard Pryor's salary has never been made public, but the comedian cannot have been paid much more than Norman Steinberg, who earned a mere $21,000. ("Guess what? I'd do it again for the same money," said Steinberg.) According to Steinberg, the originator, Andrew Bergman, was given five net points in his contract, and Brooks had anywhere from fifteen to eighteen. "Each point was worth about $1 million," Steinberg said. He'd hoped that Brooks might throw him a thank-you point, but no way.

Brooks's net points and ancillary rights clauses made him, for the first time, a truly wealthy man. But his first wife and three children didn't get any thank-you points, either.

Brooks arrived in New York for interviews to promote the opening of *Young Frankenstein* already certain of reaping a financial bonanza in 1974. And while he was in New York, the man of the hour signed the agreement that would free him from all future financial claims from Florence Baum Brooks Dunay.

Florence's lawyers had wrestled all year with Brooks's lawyers without making much headway. Brooks badly wanted to buy back the clause that promised his ex-wife one-third of his net income above $44,000 until 1980, and his lawyers were shrewder than hers in concealing his fortune-to-be. She was ultimately offered and accepted a total settlement of $325,000. The first check for $125,000 arrived on Christmas Eve. After paying back debts, taxes, and payments to her lawyer and accountant, she was left with $95,000.

It was another shrewd deal for the filmmaker of *Blazing Saddles* and *Young Frankenstein* and one of the worst in history for the first Mrs. Mel Brooks.

# CHAPTER 12

# 1975

## Club Brooks

By mid-1975, his *annus mirabilis*, Brooks was ensconced in a big corner office on the third floor of the 20th Century–Fox executive building, which he stocked with a black lacquer piano, a large portrait of Leo Tolstoy, and a blow-up label of a 1929 Château Latour. Over time he'd decorate the space with posters of his films and a table of awards.

"I was king of movies for that year," Brooks rightly boasted.

"To have those two movies in a year," producer Michael Gruskoff echoed, "as he says, he wasn't Mel Brooks, he was MEL BROOKS."

"I can walk into any studio—any one in town—and just say my name and the president will fly out from behind his desk," Brooks informed Kenneth Tynan.

Moving to Hollywood was one of the best things he'd ever done. "I like it here in California," he'd told interviewers wryly soon after the move, "but it isn't like my home. New York is my home. I don't *like* it [New York]. But like your family, you don't like them but they're your family . . ." Success eased the relocation, however, and now the formerly die-hard Brooklynite took to California like a religious convert, making West Coast lifestyle adjustments that once upon a time might have seemed unthinkable.

Weaning himself from cigarettes, Brooks switched to Trident and Raisinets. (It would take him a few years to succeed in quitting smoking, however.) He and Anne Bancroft launched a daily regimen of jogging. They even took up tennis, often playing doubles with other show business couples at the home of Club Caesar friends Larry and Pat Gelbart. Every bit the achiever, Gelbart was busy writing and producing the hit comedy series *M\*A\*S\*H*. The Gelbarts would lay on extra masseuses. "Tennis, sauna, massage, then tennis, sauna, massage" is how one guest described the Gelbart soirees.

Playing tennis had long been a way of doing business in Hollywood while enjoying the sunshine. The Club Caesar crowd, with their spouses and children, formed a circuit of their own, which was sprinkled with other people on the A-list—film and television writers, directors, producers, agents, attorneys, studio executives, performers, and comedians.

The Brookses exhibited their tennis expertise at public events, including Carl Reiner's annual benefits held at the La Costa Resort Hotel & Spa in Carlsbad, where Hollywood players were matched up with professionals for the tournaments. Tennis was one way for Brooks, not then or ever a big donator of actual money, to support charitable causes.

Reiner was Monsieur Hulot on the tennis court: light on his feet, never throwing a tantrum, making everyone else feel good and invariably mocking himself. Brooks was pretty much the opposite. "Mel wants to be the best," Gene Wilder explained to the *Los Angeles Times*, "but he hasn't taken lessons. Mel watches tennis on TV. He then thinks God should come down and kiss him and he'll be able to play as well as he visualizes. He sees perfect tennis in his mind's eye. If he screams and yells, there's a reason. He figures it's good to do that and then it's *done*. We just duck when rackets get thrown."

Brooks and Bancroft were sometimes a hard "get" for the big Hollywood parties outside the realm of Club Caesar. But they were hardly "homebodies," as Brooks liked to describe them. The couple usually made the opening nights at the Mark Taper Forum, and they regularly appeared at major museum events. Brooks alone or accompanied by his wife could be counted on to show up at most industry occasions: Writers Guild, Academy Awards, American Film Institute, and Golden Globe fêtes.

The couple was often spotted at Beverly Hills watering holes with the Reiners, huddled over pasta at La Famiglia or ribs at Tony Roma's. They frequently dined out alone as well, that bugaboo of Brooks's having long since been laid to rest by Bancroft.

Although they shuttled to New York at the drop of a hat, it was not long before they sold their Village town house and took an expensive co-op on East 89th Street for extended stays in Manhattan. They still spent quality summer time on Fire Island, but with his newly minted wealth Brooks bought other non–New York houses, including a condo on Fisher Island, a barrier island for millionaires off south Florida, reachable only by water, where he could stay when visiting Kitty, his mother, who had retired to Miami.

He also quietly purchased a Malibu beach cottage that dated back to 1927 and had once belonged to the Golden Age movie director Mervyn LeRoy. The Malibu retreat boasted five bedrooms, six bathrooms, and 3,400 square feet. Their nearest neighbors were Jack Lemmon and the producer Aaron Spelling. On weekends, in the perpetual summer of Los Angeles, the famous couple could forget the wild Atlantic coast as they woke up in the upstairs master bedroom overlooking the tranquil blue Pacific.

At 8:00 a.m., Bancroft would throw a bathing suit into Brooks's face, waking him up. "We'd rush to the ocean," Brooks said of those idyllic days. "I'd say, 'Is it cold?' She'd say, 'No, it's fine.' It was freezing, but she loved it. Afterward, we'd put on records and dance."

Hollywood was his home for now and would be for the foreseeable future. In his early interviews after the move, Brooks had a tendency to grump about Los Angeles. The East Coast newspapers and museums were better, he said. "I miss the one millimeter of rudeness," he told the *New York Times*. There was no more walking around the Village after midnight, if the fears of mugging were less. Plus: "A New York bagel really tests your teeth."

Curiously, Los Angeles also grumbled about Brooks early in their coexistence. Though *Los Angeles Times* critic Charles Champlin was generally complimentary to his films, one columnist, Burt Prelutsky, who held a day job as a comedy writer for movies and TV, launched a tradition in the *Times'* pages of dissent on the subject of Brooks.

In a piece entitled "Creating a Monster," Prelutsky protested both Brooks's ego and his success. *Young Frankenstein* was "just O.K.," he wrote, "which made it fifty times funnier than *Blazing Saddles*," but neither film was on a par with Chaplin, Keaton, or, he said (perhaps knowing it was one of Brooks's favorites), the Italian comedy *Big Deal on Madonna Street*. Brooks's "pompous quotes" glorified his accomplishments, Prelutsky wrote, but *Frankenstein* was padded and "boring for long stretches." Brooks's new hometown paper frequently published letters to the editor that agreed with Prelutsky.

Brooks's self-praise, in interviews and advertising, aggravated the hostility that certain critics and members of the cognoscenti felt toward his rowdy sense of humor. The grand old humorist S. J. Perelman, a Hollywood pro who had written for the Marx Brothers, was quoted in a new book reviewed in the *New York Times*, saying only that "Mel Brooks is good when he is doing the 2000 Year Old Man" and nothing more. Buck Henry, Brooks's bête noire, weighed in acidly: "Hollywood writers take themselves too seriously. It is the only place where someone like Mel Brooks could be called a genius."

The Canadian Mordecai Richler, another specialist in Jewish humor, echoed Henry's barb. Richler had scripted the film version of his novel *The Apprenticeship of Duddy Kravitz* (with Lionel Chetwynd), which had beat *Young Frankenstein* at the Writers Guild for the year's Best Comedy Adaptation. Richler, in a *New York Times* essay covering new books about Woody Allen, approvingly quoted "somebody [who] told me on a recent visit . . . 'All you need to know about Hollywood is that Mel Brooks is considered a genius.'"

• • •

Time and again Anne Bancroft was asked when she might appear in a Mel Brooks film.

"There are very few big women in his scripts, you've noticed?" was Anne Bancroft's stock reply to journalists. "He writes to men, male relationships."

Now in her midforties, the actress was of an age where important parts in Hollywood pictures were growing scarce. Although Bancroft was billed as the female lead of *The Hindenburg*, a big-budget recreation of the airship disaster of 1937, her role as a countess fleeing Nazi Germany was secondary to the special effects and did not tax her abilities. Shot at Universal, just north of the Hollywood Hills, in the fall of 1974, while Brooks was editing *Young Frankenstein* at 20th Century–Fox, *The Hindenburg* did not go to theaters until late 1975. It did reasonably well at the box office but critics saw it as a dud.

The fate of Bancroft's recent films—*Young Winston*, *The Prisoner of Second Avenue*, *The Hindenburg*—stood in contrast to her husband's *annus mirabilis*. Pondering changes in her career, she reunited with an old friend she knew from having grown up in the Bronx, David Lunney, who worked at the American Film Institute (AFI). The AFI was headquartered in the Greystone Mansion on the Doheny estate, near the Brookses' Foothill Road residence. Bancroft and Lunney had acted in high school plays together; once he had even kissed her onstage. Lunney began to stop by regularly.

Lunney talked up the AFI's new Directing Workshop for Women, which had been inaugurated in 1974 with a small group of Hollywood women who wanted to learn the technology and techniques of filmmaking. The prominent graduates of the first class included producer Julia Phillips and actresses Lee Grant and Ellen Burstyn. Lunney piqued Bancroft's interest in joining the second women's workshop, set to start in 1975.

The two were poring over the application one day when Brooks arrived home. He acted surprised by the news. "He said, 'Well, what would she do?'" Lunney recalled. "She said, 'It's a women's directing workshop, it's an application for it, I'm going to direct a film,' and he said, 'Oh, you don't want to do that.' And she said, 'What? You can't stand having two directors in the same house?'" It was "a flash of temper—and a joke."

Bancroft signed up for the 1975 workshop, which included fellow actresses Dyan Cannon and Kathleen Freeman and future *Children of a Lesser God* director Randa Haines. For two years Bancroft immersed herself in the assignment of crafting two short films. One was a quasiautobiographical vignette about the role food plays in an Italian American family dominated by a binge eater. Dom DeLuise agreed to portray the binge eater, and Carl Reiner's wife, Estelle, also would perform a small role. Brooks lent his staff to her short films shot on low budgets, largely within the confines of the Greystone Mansion.

Bancroft's genius husband had not yet settled on the subject of his next—fifth—screen comedy. He mentioned "Marriage Is a Dirty Rotten Fraud" to interviewers, but subliminally, if not on a conscious level, as he explained later, the runaway success of the Western send-up and the Frankenstein spoof had sparked a eureka moment for him.

"Ergo," he explained later, "satire pays the rent."

Spoofing genres—something he had largely avoided with his first two pictures, *The Producers* and *The Twelve Chairs*—was in his DNA. Satire of genres had been a staple source of comedy on Sid Caesar's shows all those years ago. The past was the future.

But what should the next spoof be? He dithered. He dallied.

He found another outlet for his acting in voice jobs à la *The Critic* or the Ballantine beer commercials. Playing the 2000 Year Old Man for an animated television special in 1975 was old hat. But somewhat paradoxically, considering his stance as a dangerous comedian, he also began to become a fixture of G-rated fare. He gurgled as a puppet baby on Marlo Thomas's "Free to Be . . . You and Me" special in 1974, played the Blond-Haired Cartoon Man on *The Electric Company* from 1971 to 1977, and had one of the best parts among the all-star cast as a mad German scientist—in this case, it was his voice *and* body—trying to lobotomize Kermit the Frog in *The Muppet Movie* in 1979.

Children's television helped forge a connection to the television series lampooning Robin Hood that Brooks tried to launch into prime time in the first half of 1975. The idea for a series about the Robin Hood legend originated outside of Brooks's fiefdom with John Boni, who had credits on Alan King specials and *The Electric Company*, and Norman Stiles, a regular writer for *Sesame Street*. Boni and Stiles pitched a pilot script to Norman Steinberg, who had accepted a day job after *Blazing Saddles* and was now developing programming for the TV division of Paramount Pictures.

The Boni/Stiles pilot script was wacky but not wacky enough, Steinberg thought. Knowing that Brooks had grown up as a fanat- ical fan of Robin Hood pictures, he walked the idea into Brooks's office at 20th Century–Fox. Brooks said wow—great—let's do it. Together over the next few months they revised and planned the pilot. "We actually sat down and wrote it in his office at Fox," Steinberg recalled. ABC-TV picked up the series for the fall of 1975.

The network, however, tempered the wackiness. Prince John, for example, was going to be depicted as a "flaming faggot," in Brooks's words, until ABC raised a red flag. The title, *When Things Were Rotten*, was Brooks's formulation, and he was also deeply engaged in the casting, starting with the actor signed to portray Robin Hood, Dick Gautier, who had been the original Conrad Birdie on Broadway— not to mention, just as famously, Hymie the Robot on *Get Smart*. Brooks recruited "the *Birdie* boys"—his old friends from *"All Ameri- can"*, Charles Strouse and Lee Adams—to pen the theme song.

From the weekly ensemble (his tennis-playing friend Dick Van Patten was cast as the abbot) to the episode writers (Thomas Meehan), directors (first-timer Marty Feldman), and single-episode guest stars (Sid Caesar), *When Things Were Rotten* became a mingling of past Brooks friends and associates and a tryout for future Club Brooks card holders.

With Brooks's name emblazoned on its advertising and publicity, *When Things Were Rotten* easily became one of the season's most highly anticipated shows. Many critics found it frenetic with its excruciating wordplay ("Does a willow weep? Does a Forrest Tucker?"), however, while often, at the same time, very funny. Brooks's usual percentage of jokes hit the bull's-eye in the pilot. "The comic bits are not uniformly successful," John J. O'Connor wrote in the *New York Times*. "Only about one in six is on target. But as they are being flung at the audience every fifteen seconds the final total is still impressive. . . .

"Much will depend on the extent of Brooks' participation."

Yet Brooks did not participate much beyond the template. His agreement with Steinberg guaranteed that he would be listed first in the "created by" credits. Steinberg had to forfeit his credit, because the Writers Guild had a rarely breached rule that limited television script names to only three. So it was just Brooks, Boni, and Stiles, with Steinberg as the producer.

Brooks's top billing made it all the more galling when Paramount killed the series after just thirteen episodes. The ratings had been solid. The cast, many of them personally picked by Brooks, was first rate, and the scripts were finding a rhythm; the show had a demented flavor, like a Brooks comedy, yet with its own peculiar spice. Barry Diller, the chairman and CEO of Paramount, personally pulled the plug one day, summoning Steinberg's boss, Bud Austin, the head of the studio's TV division, and telling him he didn't want to produce any more episodes. Diller said he detested silly humor and preferred more sophisticated comedy such as *Barney Miller*, another Paramount series.

Steinberg was as flabbergasted as he was crushed. As for Brooks, he was furious when, in October, the producer relayed the news to him in his 20th Century–Fox office. "They canceled the show! What, they're telling me I'm not funny! Get the fuck out of here!"

Throughout the film industry people wondered: What would Brooks do to top *Young Frankenstein*? By October, he had made several bold decisions, the most important of which he had been gradually preparing himself for ever since the first 2000 Year Old Man recording: not only would he write and direct his next comedy; he'd star in it.

Brooks's post–*Young Frankenstein* thinking had revolved around Gene Wilder—or, more accurately, the lack of Gene Wilder. After his glowing reviews and Best Screenplay Oscar nomination for *Young Frankenstein*, Wilder had signed a three-picture pact with 20th Century–Fox and in short order had notched his first film as a triple hyphenate: writer-director-star. *The Adventures of Sherlock Holmes' Smarter Brother* borrowed Madeline Kahn, Marty Feldman, and Dom DeLuise from Brooks's stable and producer Michael Gruskoff, too.

Though Wilder's films as writer-director would never match the artistic and commercial double whammy of *Young Frankenstein*, his vehicles did perform reliably at the box office in the 1970s, many becoming substantial hits. Often enough his costars were veterans of Brooks's films, and he would have an especially fruitful chemistry on-screen with one actor who never quite made it into a Brooks picture: Richard Pryor.

Wilder was not the world's most easygoing or most likable personality. (His costar and onetime girlfriend Teri Garr described him succinctly in one interview: "He was a jerk.") Neither, manifestly, was Brooks. They had had creative differences on both *The Producers* and *Young Frankenstein*. It didn't help their professional relationship that Wilder had had to surrender control and percentages to Crossbow Productions in his *Frankenstein* contract, nor that studio advertising and publicity had elevated Brooks's name over his.

The Writers Guild formally complained, pointing out that Wilder's name had been omitted from the end credits (which listed Brooks only as director and producer). "Guild beefed that the writing credit must appear whenever the 'directed by' credit appears," *Variety* reported. The Guild objected to *Young Frankenstein* advertisements and press books that privileged Brooks while sometimes forgetting Wilder. An eighty-foot-high billboard on the Playboy Building on Sunset Boulevard touted "A Mel Brooks Film," for example. An arbitrator fined the studio ten thousand dollars, the bulk of that sum going directly to Wilder.

"I can't find other people to be vehicles of my passion," Brooks began telling interviewers, because his preferred star "Gene Wilder is making his own films" now.

Tellingly, despite incentives and a friendship that endured, Wilder—a leading man like no other in three Mel Brooks films— never worked with him again in any capacity.


Shortly after taking over *Young Frankenstein* from Columbia Pictures and soon after approving Brooks's multipicture contract with 20th Century–Fox, Gordon Stulberg was forced out of the studio leadership. It became the privilege of Dennis Stanfill, the new president and chairman of the 20th Century–Fox board, to announce the fifth Mel Brooks film, a spoof of silent-picture making, to the National Association of Theatre Owners (NATO) convention in New Orleans in the first week of October 1975. The exhibitors cheered.

Curiously, though he'd been spoofing silent pictures since the 1950s, the film was not Brooks's idea to begin with, as had also been true of his hits *Blazing Saddles* and *Young Frankenstein*.

One day in mid-1975, as publicity told the story, Ron Clark

phoned Brooks with a pitch. A Canadian and graduate of McGill University, Clark was a successful television writer who regularly took time off from well-paid Hollywood jobs to write stage plays, often with a collaborator, Sam Bobrick. Their comedy *Norman, Is That You?*, about a father who discovers that his son is gay, had been produced on Broadway in 1970. Clark wrote for TV performers that Brooks followed (Steve Allen, Danny Kaye, Tim Conway, Marlo Thomas, Paul Lynde), and he had won Emmy and Writers Guild awards while on the Smothers Brothers' staff. He also mingled socially with Brooks and Bancroft at dinner parties and tennis matches.

While shaving one morning, Clark had the sudden inspiration of a washed-up movie director in contemporary Hollywood, desperately plotting his comeback by making the first silent picture in decades. The film itself would be entirely silent except for music, sound effects, and a single declarative word of dialogue, which was Clark's idea from the get-go, to be uttered by Marcel Marceau when the famous French mime declines a role in the proposed silent picture.

Everyone knew that Brooks was looking for a vehicle for himself as the star of a Mel Brooks comedy. Brooks could play the washed-up director, Clark felt. Although Brooks immediately told Clark, "I don't need ideas, I've got plenty of ideas already," the two agreed to meet for lunch, where Brooks quickly decided on *Silent Movie* as his follow-up to *Young Frankenstein*. The project seemed doubly daring: no one had made a soundless film in Hollywood since the early 1930s, and Brooks was primarily a verbal comic.

Right away, after lunch, Clark phoned his friends Barry Levinson and Rudy DeLuca as they logged hours at their jobs on *The Carol Burnett Show*. Levinson and DeLuca had won an Emmy in 1974 as part of Carol Burnett's staff (which included Gary Belkin) along with a Writers Guild award for the comedienne's television series in 1975. The two also shared writing credits on Tim Conway's TV series and *Marty Feldman's Comedy Machine*. Levinson and DeLuca had started out with an improvisational troupe in Los Angeles in the early 1960s (another member of the troupe was actor Craig T. Nelson) and had a knack for the kind of physical comedy that would have to carry *Silent Movie*. Moreover, DeLuca co-owned, with Sammy Shore, the Comedy Store on Sunset Boulevard.

*Marty Feldman's Comedy Machine* rang the right bells because already Brooks and Clark had brainstormed Feldman and Dom DeLuise as sidekicks to the lead character, whom Brooks had named faster than you could say "Mel Funn." Funn and the two other zany men would march through scenes in antic lockstep à la the Ritz Brothers. Brooks had never met Levinson or DeLuca. "Will I like them?" he asked. "You'll love them," said Clark. The new Club Brooks was at work on the script by midsummer.

Ron Clark's story had Funn, Dom Bell (DeLuise), and Marty Eggs (Feldman) struggling to launch a silent picture in modern-day Hollywood. Funn has convinced the head of Big Picture Studios that a novelty silent movie with marquee names could save the slumping studio. Lurking in the background is a soulless New York conglomerate called Engulf & Devour—a name echoing Gulf & Western, the parent company of Paramount, which was among the film's stinging Hollywood in-jokes. Engulf & Devour schemes to ruin Funn's plans in order to take over Big Picture Studios at a bargain price.

The writing team met informally most mornings for coffee and bagels at a Hollywood deli before migrating to Brooks's suite of offices at 20th Century–Fox in Century City. No writer was the designated typist; in fact, there was not always a typist in the room with them, sometimes just a tape recorder rolling with the secretary coming in later as a transcriber.

There were other differences between the ad hoc group that had written *Blazing Saddles* and the team that was now shaping *Silent Movie*. For one thing, there was no raging iconoclast in the room, no truly dangerous comedian like Richard Pryor. That dovetailed with another decision Brooks made that would have long-term repercussions in his career.

Even though *Blazing Saddles* was, dollar for dollar, his outstanding success, his new film would take pains to be PG rated. The industry was veering from the R-rated content maverick filmmakers briefly made commercial in the early 1970s. The R rating was retreating to art houses and by now was anathema to the major studios and big exhibitors.

The one-upmanship and argument that had swirled around every scene of *Blazing Saddles* was also conspicuously missing from the new Club Brooks. The group sought "consensus," in Levinson's words. Their work sessions were surprisingly amicable and friction free. The three writers formed "a great working relationship" with Brooks, according to Levinson. "You'd say something, somebody would laugh, if you said it and somebody didn't laugh, then it didn't hold up. It was no more and no less than that."

Another clear difference was that most of the scenes revolved around Mel Funn—a character name that translated into the Nice Mel. Brooks usually pranced around, performing his part in the work sessions, as it was being crafted to please him. Although it was adventurous for Brooks, who was a physical comedian mainly from the neck up, to be making a silent movie, the writers constantly moderated the challenge by aiming for his comfort zone. "You're writing towards who's going to be in it," Levinson recalled, "so it's going to shift in some ways, subtly perhaps, and maybe without even thinking about it you're writing for Mel Brooks. You're going to make those adjustments."

Just as it would have been done for a Sid Caesar show, the script created slots for celebrities in the stars who are being courted by Mel Funn to appear in the silent film-within-the-film. Their names would be good for publicity and advertising and take some of the pressure off first-time star Brooks. The only suspense surrounding the script, as it gradually coalesced during the second half of 1976, was who those celebrities might be.

Brooks approached Steve McQueen, but the serious-minded actor rejected any comedy role, and the good-humored Paul Newman took over his car-racing scenes. James Caan and Liza Minnelli proved to be amenable. So did Burt Reynolds, who had bonded with Brooks and Bancroft over their shared friendship with Dom DeLuise. When Marcel Marceau gave an opportune performance at UCLA, Clark went backstage to meet with the French mime and coax him into his first and only screen appearance. (Marceau would speak only one word—"Non!"—rejecting an appearance in Mel Funn's silent picture.)

"It was amazing to see Mel talk people like James Caan into being in [Silent Movie]," Marty Feldman recalled. "Caan was in preparation for his next film and needed to be in good shape. Mel convinced him to move his mobile workout trailer onto our set—he would pay for it—and told him he could take advantage of our nutritious catering." Caan "bought" Brooks's sales pitch, Feldman said, "and was in the film before he knew it."

Anne Bancroft was a natural thought, although no one recalls who first proposed the writer-director-star's wife. (Bancroft, in one interview, said she read the script and recommended herself as the diva drawn into a wild flamenco by Brooks, DeLuise, and Feldman.) Her television tryout with Brooks earlier in the decade had paved the way.

In interviews Brooks propounded his theory of casting as it had now become fixed: "self-starters who don't have to have every nuance of behavior explained." In effect: no Zero Mostel or Gene Wilder, who might take thespianism too seriously. With Brooks more established and their lives centered on Hollywood, Bancroft was also less involved in making whispered suggestions of actors with Broadway or stage credentials. More and more Brooks turned to seasoned comics who could be counted on to tweak their roles.

The exception to that rule on the *Silent Movie* roster was Bernadette Peters, a noted Broadway actress and singer who had not yet broken out in Hollywood. Madeline Kahn reportedly declined the role of the sexpot who seduces Mel Funn on assignment from Engulf & Devour, only to fall in love with the washed-up director; she didn't find the character as substantial as the ones she'd played in *Blazing Saddles* and *Young Frankenstein*. Peters was arguably better qualified for the dream dance, one of the nougats of the film, with Brooks reimagining himself as his boyhood idol Fred Astaire.

The chief self-starter was the man who had long before mastered silent-picture spoofery: Sid Caesar. He accepted the fourth-billed role, which had been tailored for him all along, as the "Current Studio Chief" of Big Pictures Studio. The Club Caesar writers stayed close to Caesar, who lived in Beverly Hills nowadays, rooting for their mentor and helping him out as they followed his seesaw fortunes. Most of Caesar's contemporary appearances were in theater and telefilms. If younger audiences knew the former king of TV comedy at all—as Brooks learned to his dismay when mentioning Caesar in later publicity interviews—it was from his ensemble role in *Airport 1975*. His part in *Silent Movie* was "almost the first since the high old days of television," *Los Angeles Times* critic Charles Champlin would write, "which allows something like full display of his gifts as a clown."

The rest of the cast was filled with stand-ups and comedic personalities, including Ron Carey (the first of several roles he'd play in Brooks's films), Henny Youngman, Charlie Callas, Fritz Feld, and Harry Ritz, the youngest Ritz brother, in his seventies, whom Brooks lured out of retirement. The other familiar faces included Lee Meredith, Ulla from *The Producers*, performing a nurse bit ("Mel gave me no direction at all," she recalled. "He explained the scene and I don't know what possessed me but I started hitting Marty Feldman over the head with my purse and Mel loved it"), and Liam Dunn, the director's boyhood acquaintance, appearing in his third and last Brooks comedy (Dunn died shortly after the filming).

After failing in his attempt to launch his own company, Michael Hertzberg returned to the fold as Brooks's producer. Also back were John C. Howard as the editor (with Stanford C. Allen, his first assistant on *Young Frankenstein*, sharing the credit); John Morris would pick a few oldies for the soundtrack and also write the score; Alan Johnson would choreograph the dance moves. The easygoing New Yorker Paul Lohmann, who had distinguished himself on Robert Altman's *Nashville*, became the cameraman for this and the next Mel Brooks film, the first cameraman to work on consecutive Brooks pictures.

When filming started in the first week of 1976, Barry Levinson and Rudy DeLuca stuck around the set to consult on the script and staging. The writers on the set—Brooks's writers gathered around him as he directed, just as Sid Caesar's writers had gathered around Caesar—became one of the filmmaker's publicity points over the next decade. The writers helped critique the video playbacks (another shift in Brooks's directing regimen, a method that had begun to spread in Hollywood after Jerry Lewis introduced the practice). And as onetime improv comics, Levinson and DeLuca also played cameos.

The filming, achieved mostly on 20th Century–Fox soundstages and studio acreage, ran a crisp ten weeks on a $4.4 million budget. Even Brooks's editing was unusually quick, as the continuity relied heavily on sound effects, music, intertitles, and sight gags. (Some of the film's funnier sight gags—the "Our Toilets Are Nicer than Most People's Homes" placard in the men's room of Engulf & Devour—were akin to verbal one-liners.)

*Silent Movie* was in the can in time for a June 1976 release.

Brooks could do no wrong with summer audiences in the 1970s, and this was his silliest, most carefree movie yet: the PG-rated Nice Mel, without any rudeness, crudeness, or subversion. Whereas *Blazing Saddles* had alluded to hard truths and *Young Frankenstein* was made twice as funny by the slightest familiarity with Mary Shelley or James Whale, *Silent Movie* was a spoof of silent-picture making that offered pure escapism to American moviegoers weary of chaos, division, and the Vietnam War.

The critics were on the same wavelength. They liked *Silent Movie* almost as much as the ticket holders did, praising the sunny, heartfelt comedy. Their majority opinion belied Brooks's stubborn canard that critics never admired him. What he really meant was that they did not admire him *enough* as a comic and film-maker, or without adding qualms.

*Variety* totted up the New York notices, counting only three critics who had offered no clear opinion and twelve who had been favor-able: Vincent Canby, *New York Times*; Jay Cocks, *Time*; Kathleen Carroll, *Daily News*; Joseph Gelmis, *Newsday*; Howard Kissel, *Women's Wear Daily*; Stewart Klein, WNEW-TV; Jack Kroll, *Newsweek*; Frank Rich, *New York Post*; Gene Shalit, NBC-TV; Walter Spencer, WOR; Frances Taylor, Newhouse; William Wolf, *Cue*.

Not all the favorable reviews were out-and-out raves, though. Vincent Canby, for one, saw *Silent Movie* as "a virtually uninterrupted series of smiles" but qualified his kudos. *Silent Movie* did not rival the "lunatic highs" of *Blazing Saddles* or *Young Frankenstein*, he wrote. It "is not the greatest movie Mr. Brooks has made," partly because his character, Mel Funn, embodied the "polite, sweet, and vulnerable qualities one associates with some of the old silent film comedians and that fit Mr. Brooks less well than a nun's habit."

Doling out interviews to tout the release in New York ("*Silent Movie* is the funniest picture I ever made, the best picture I ever made"), Brooks was neither polite nor sweet on the subject of Canby. "Why should Canby—why should he appreciate my humor? I'm too Rabelaisian for his sensibilities," he snapped, speaking to the

*Village Voice.* "Canby's review refers back to the great *Blazing Saddles*, and it's bullshit. Canby forgot he hated *Blazing Saddles*," Brooks pointed out—even though "hate" was too strong a word for Canby's problems with *Saddles*, which in any case he had never called "great."

Roger Ebert, in the heartland where Brooks had worked so hard to make inroads, proclaimed, "Brooks has taken a considerable stylistic risk and pulled it off triumphantly." Ebert loved the "great scenes" that were sure to become "classics": the arcade-video Pong game in the intensive care unit, the fly in the soup, the horse and merry-go-round, the Coke machine battle. He had laughed "a lot," Ebert confessed in the *Chicago Sun-Times*. Even so, on the "Brooks Laff-O-Meter," Ebert added, *Young Frankenstein* had made him laugh more, *Blazing Saddles* about as much, and *The Producers* most of all.

Gary Arnold in the *Washington Post* was a skunk in the woodpile for *Silent Movie* as he was for other Mel Brooks comedies down the years. Arnold's review singled out the "stretches of dead air and arid clowning" in *Silent Movie* and the scenes in which the actors were okay but the directing floundered. ("The commissary scene falls flat partly because we can't distinguish one falling-down comic from another but also because the camera remains rooted in place at an unhelpful middle distance.") "If one strung them together, the good gags and spontaneous laughs in *Silent Movie* probably wouldn't amount to more than one hundred and twenty seconds," Arnold complained.

However, it was a strong comedy in a weak summer for funny movies (Woody Allen, who was spending extra time on the next year's *Annie Hall*, had nothing in release), and Americans swarmed to the new Brooks film. By August it was number one at the box office.

Yet quite apart from Ebert's Laff-O-Meter—a complaint about diminishing returns echoed by other critics—there were distinct warning signs. The film stalled at $36 million in US grosses, a dramatic drop-off from *Blazing Saddles* ($119 million after reissues) and *Young Frankenstein* ($86 million domestically). After Europe was added to the total, those grosses might have doubled, however, because Brooks oversaw heavy promotion in England, France, Germany, and Italy and overseas his profile continued to rise.

Regardless, *Silent Movie* was the bonanza of the summer for 20th Century–Fox, and the Writers Guild wound up nominating the Club Brooks script as Best Comedy Written Directly for the Screen in 1976. (It lost to Bill Lancaster's script for *The Bad News Bears*.)

After periods of hard work, twice yearly in the late 1970s and early '80s, Brooks and Anne Bancroft stole long weekends with an elite group of friends: Norman Lear and his wife, Frances, Carl and Estelle Reiner, Larry and Pat Gelbart, Dom DeLuise and Carol Arthur.

Lear began organizing the getaways after learning from a friend, Cliff Perlman, the owner of Caesars Palace in Las Vegas, that the casino and resort maintained two five-bedroom villas as "freebies for their high rollers," in Lear's words. Both villas, one located in La Costa, California, and the other in Palm Springs, were fully staffed, and Perlman offered free use of the villas to Lear, who made up a guest list of compatible couples for a trial weekend. "We all loved the mix," Lear said, "had the time of our lives, and spent two weekends a year together for a number of years thereafter."

The famous and funny friends dubbed themselves "Yenem Veldt," which they translated as "The Other World." "In the history of fun," Lear recalled, "no group ever had more." The Other World began their Saturday mornings in pajamas, laughing at DeLuise slicing fruit—"you cannot believe how funny Dom DeLuise was slicing fruit"—and then they laughed so "continuously that we often stayed in our bedclothes all weekend."

This was a straight crowd that still liked to play the Dictionary Game or Pass the Orange. For added entertainment, Brooks offered his impersonation of Fred Astaire, and Bancroft, Pat Gelbart, and Estelle Reiner transformed themselves into a singing trio called the Mother Sisters. DeLuise's wife, Carol, imitated Imogene Coca so accurately that they all wept with laughter. Lear threw in his specialty of pratfalls. Larry Gelbart offered running commentary. Carl Reiner emceed, praising all of the performers to the skies.

As merry a bunch as ever was found under the same vacation roof, each tried to outdo the others with their comic skills. "But Mel was clearly the most hilarious, north, south, east, and west," Lear recalled. "I thought he was just as funny as anyone I ever met," he continued, "just naturally. Maybe he qualified [as] the clown [of the group], [although] that's a word I use very, very seldom. We get a few of those every century—clowns. He qualified for the clown because it was very difficult for him to not be funny."

Among friends Brooks was sometimes funniest when he was angriest. Every year, because Lear made the vacation arrangements, he and his wife took the largest bedroom or the one with the best view. "It always pissed [Brooks] off," Lear recalled. Brooks would complain all weekend. Decades later he was still complaining. "I said to Mel [recently], 'You were always mad,'" Lear said in an interview. "He said, 'I'm still angry.' I was laughing [as we talked about it]. 'What can I do? It pissed me off,' he said."

By the time *Silent Movie* had petered out in theaters at year's end, Brooks, Ron Clark, Rudy DeLuca, and Barry Levinson had another script on the griddle: a comedy spoofing the cinematic masterpieces of director Alfred Hitchcock. It was another idea Brooks might have pitched to himself in the mirror, but it came up among the group during the *Silent Movie* script-writing sessions. None of the writers or Brooks took the story credit.

The idea gave Brooks the excuse to ring the doorbell of Hitchcock, another boyhood idol. The Master of Suspense was in his seventy-seventh year and had just finished his fifty-third and last feature as director, *Family Plot*, which was released in the spring of 1976. Hitchcock's age, fragility, and steadily declining health are one reason why it is difficult to credit Brooks's anecdote—spun with variations—of the time he and Hitchcock dined at Chasen's in Beverly Hills, Hitchcock devouring a full-course meal, pausing after dessert before lighting his cigar, then asking the waiter to serve the whole repast again.

Yet Hitchcock was flattered and cooperative. At a series of meetings at Hitchcock's office in Universal, and at Chasen's, the auteur of auteurs, who had often mingled humor with terror in his films, listened to Brooks's ideas for scenes and gave his feedback. Brooks's version of their friendship emphasized their mutual greatness.

"Luckily for me he liked me," Brooks said. "He had seen *The Producers* and had liked it, he really liked it. So he warmed up to me and allowed me to pump him for information for hours. I had expected a man with a really dry English sensibility and I found a warm human being instead. He kissed my hand and he said, 'You're the new master.'"

When Club Brooks again convened, with Hitchcock spoofery on the agenda, Brooks wielded the gavel. Assistant director Jonathan Sanger, who was new to Crossbow Productions, watched. "Far from anarchic," he recalled, "it was highly collaborative, four writers sitting in a room and pacing and tossing out ideas, jokes, situations."

The regimen had become formulized: the scene ideas, key dialogue exchanges, and approved jokes (verbal or visual) were typed on cards and pinned on a corkboard wall in Brooks's office, according to Sanger. "As the wall became filled, some cards got amended, some rearranged, and some just got cut. I saw that there were no 'bad' ideas. It was important for each writer to feel safe enough to express anything that came to mind."

Gradually the story emerged: a mash-up of *Spellbound*, *North by Northwest*, *Psycho*, *The Birds*, and, first and foremost, *Vertigo*. In *Silent Movie*, Brooks had kidded his way through most of his scenes with Marty Feldman and Dom DeLuise. Now he was going to portray the lead character of the film, the troubled psychotherapist Dr. Richard H. Thorndyke—the H. for Harpo and the surname a twist on Cary Grant's in *North by Northwest*. Dr. Thorndyke must overpower enemies real and imagined, including his acrophobia. He must overcome an angry bellboy who attacks him with a newspaper in the shower, fight off swarms of birds and their droppings, and defeat a murder attempt in a phone booth.

It was a "kid's fantasy," in Brooks's words, to play the straight role usually reserved for Cary Grant or Jimmy Stewart in classic Hitchcock pictures, the prototypical wronged man trapped in a nightmarish situation. If Brooks was not as tall or handsome, as English or *goyish* as Hitchcock's leads, at least, as had been true of Mel Funn in *Silent Movie*, he'd be playing another version of Nice Mel: dapper, warm, and likable, even heroic. Playing it as romantic as possible, too, Brooks would even get to woo an enigmatic Hitchcock blonde and sing a Frank Sinatra–type song in a nightclub.

This was Brooks's first starring part. "In the past he would have written that, been working on that, putting that together for Gene Wilder [as] the pseudo–leading man," Barry Levinson reflected. "Mel is a falling-down-funny personality, a comedian type. But in a sense, when you're going into *High Anxiety*, it's pushing the boundaries of what you're calling a real character performance. That's why Gene would come to mind if you were thinking, who could be funny and sort of a leading man? With all those attributes."

The writers wrote the character to Brooks's requisites, and he performed his pages "step by step" as the script progressed, Levinson recalled. "You're talking out loud in a room. 'What is this moment?' You talk it. He begins to talk it. You hear it and say, 'Well, that's funny, he can do that . . . that doesn't hold up so well.' You begin to hear it [working]. You're almost unconsciously rewriting as you're writing, to fit [him]."

Pinpointing parts for Brooks's informal stock company, the script team also tailored characters for Harvey Korman and Cloris Leachman, who were set to portray a psychiatrist and his nurse embroiled in an S-and-M relationship; Madeline Kahn, aping the Hitchcock blonde; and Dick Van Patten from *When Things Were Rotten*—the murder victim of heavy-metal rock. Hitchcock's faithful matte artist Albert Whitlock would play an in-joke small role. And scenarists Levinson and Rudy DeLuca could write their own bits—Levinson as the newspaper-wielding bellboy, DeLuca the phone booth attacker.

Having rebooted Sid Caesar in *Silent Movie*, Brooks now brought back another pal from *Your Show of Shows* days, Howard Morris, to play Dr. Thorndyke's analytical mentor, a character with the punning name of Professor Lilloman. As with Caesar, it was the first time Brooks had acted with or directed Morris in one of his films.

Paul Lohmann was again the cameraman, John C. Howard was the editor, and John Morris composed the score and helped with the music for the Frank Sinatra–style title song, "High Anxiety," which Brooks serenades Kahn with in the nightclub scene.

Hitchcock had located several of his most famous pictures in northern California, and *High Anxiety* was likewise shot, in the spring of 1977, with some San Francisco landmarks in the background. A few scenes were photographed at the San Francisco and Los Angeles airports and at Loyola Marymount University in Los Angeles, where a university edifice became the Institute for the Very, Very Nervous. The interiors were done at 20th Century–Fox.

Levinson and DeLuca were a constant presence, monitoring the script and video playbacks. Although Brooks had been faithful to *Young Frankenstein*'s script when restricted to directing, all the post–*Young Frankenstein* scripts were less sacrosanct. "Mel's technique is to be thoroughly prepared with his script and to have a precise idea of what he wants to put on that screen," Harvey Korman explained. "The problem is that when he does a scene, the crew laughs and he loves it. So he does the scene again, and the crew laughs again. But by the third or fourth take, the crew isn't laughing anymore, and Mel panics and looks for new stuff to make them laugh again. As a result, he's constantly improvising."

*High Anxiety* occupied Brooks for much of 1977. By the summer he was immersed in postproduction. Often geography separated him from his wife, Anne Bancroft.

During the first half of 1977, the actress juggled the part of the district attorney in a rape-revenge film entitled *Lipstick* with a stint as Mary Magdalene in a *Jesus of Nazareth* television miniseries directed by Franco Zeffirelli. The latter called for her to be in Tunisia and Morocco when not on the *Lipstick* set in Los Angeles. "I had all the jet lag to contend with," Bancroft told journalists. "At times it was gruesome. I would catch a cold in L.A., recover, fly to North Africa and catch a cold, recover and fly back."

In the second half of the year, although plagued with illness, Bancroft was just as busy. She agreed to make her first Broadway appearance in nearly eight years in *Golda*, William Gibson's new drama about the life of Israeli prime minister Golda Meir. After its mid-November opening, *Golda* had a three-month run before the actress came down with acute bronchitis, shuttering the play and sending her back home in early 1978.

By that time the sixth film to be written and directed by Mel Brooks, with numero uno also billed as the star, the composer and lyricist of the title song, as well as the producer of the screen comedy, was in theaters. There was a late-1977 premiere for publicity, reviews, and awards consideration. Brooks broke with traditional film industry release patterns by holding simultaneous Christmas Day openings at immense Westwood and Hollywood theaters and at the Sutton on East 57th Street in Manhattan. *Variety* reported that he had rejected substantial offers for some outdoor theater bookings to follow, looking instead for 800- to -1,000 seat "hard-tops for a communal intimacy not possible in drive-ins."

Brooks's arrangement with 20th Century–Fox called for the studio to add forty venues across the United States on February 1, another forty houses two weeks later, then seventy-five more by March 1. That was a record number of theaters for a comedy in that era of huge movie theaters.

Although the reviews were uneven, the initial crowds again filled the theaters. While noting the obvious as well as "in" references to Hitchcock's oeuvre—one scene had been shot from under a glass table, another with the camera gliding toward a window and crash-ing through—many critics weren't sure how cinematic or funny the parody was.

"A low-intensity, absent-minded pastiche," Gary Arnold averred in the *Washington Post*. "A manic, hit-or-miss roller-coaster ride," America's leading feminist film critic, Molly Haskell, opined in *New York*, "best described as a compilation film in which famous bits and pieces and visual conceits from the ten most familiar Hitchcock films have been shuffled, crossbred, rewritten and staged with Jewish punch lines."

The picture's PG rating reflected how quaint the crudity—and rating system—had become. The film included a storm of bird feces, Nurse Diesel's (Cloris Leachman) torpedo breasts, and Dr. Thorndyke's "pee-pee envy" and "caca-doody" speech to a packed hall of psychologists; not only did *High Anxiety* plunge on the Laff-O-Meter, according to many reviewers, the "low points," in Molly Haskell's words, could be blamed on stale locker room humor—"tired jokes, old jokes, and gratuitous obscenities that make one long for the euphemisms and ingenious circumlocutions necessi-tated in the bad old days by the Production Code."

Many film critics focused on Brooks the star, who was playing it straight but also trying for a little sex appeal as Dr. Thorndyke. "Well-tailored in imitation of Cary Grant, I suppose, as the proto-typical Hitchcock hero, he is having sport with a romantic type, but it is kidding on the square" wrote Charles Champlin in the *Los Angeles Times*. While adopting a "pale cast of sincerity," Brooks had forsaken his strong suit as "king of the leer."

"What *High Anxiety* lacks," Haskell echoed in *New York*, "is the compelling charismatic figure of the comedian himself. As a per-former, Brooks is ambiguous, neither entirely comical nor quite seri-ous. Close your eyes and you hear the rich baritone voice of a leading man; open them and you see—what? A character out of Malamud or Bellow. But behind the elusiveness of the actor is the whirring and scheming mind of the emcee."

Nevertheless, Brooks galvanized publicity by campaigning tire-lessly on behalf of his sixth film ("my consummate height in artistry at this point"). Besides visiting as many US cities as possible for the opening and giving interviews in those places, he stopped in Sweden (a burgeoning market for his films), Madrid, Rome, London, and Paris, where he met with French feature writers and German jour-nalists who were flown in to meet him.

In most interviews Brooks spoke of his friendship with Hitchcock and told anecdotes about his own experience under analysis in the 1950s. He preferred the audience's verdict to quibbling critics, he said in interviews, and he dropped into theaters to sit anonymously and bask in people's laughter. Nonetheless, the brickbats from "crickets," as he had taken to calling critics, stung. "They chirp and make noise but they should be ignored," he said.

Especially the big-city crickets. "You know," Brooks explained, "it hands me a laugh when the critics come out with their Ten Best lists at the end of the year. The New York critics more than the oth-ers. Jesus! There are always six films no one has ever heard of. It has so little relationship to moviegoing taste in the rest of the country."

Even so, he admitted, he longed for one "good review" from

Pauline Kael in *The New Yorker*. (Kael had written, in her *High Anxiety* notice, that "Mel Brooks grabs us by the lapels and screams into our faces, 'Laugh! It's funny!' The open secret of his comedy is that his material isn't necessarily funny—it's being grabbed by the lapels that makes us laugh.") Regardless, flattery from Kael, he told one interviewer, "wouldn't matter to the movie any more than a good review from my brother Bernie, who's just as tough a critic."

Tickets sold, and *High Anxiety* rose to number six at the box office, staying in the top fifty for the first half of 1978. Throughout the United States, however, the film proved to be "a nonperformer in the second quarter" of its release, in *Variety*'s words, tapping out at $31 million gross. Again, overseas revenue boosted the numbers, but the aggregate fell below that of *Silent Movie*, which itself ranked below *Young Frankenstein* and *Blazing Saddles*.

The faint air of disappointment surrounding *High Anxiety* was reinforced by its disappointing awards season. Brooks had hoped that his title song might be Oscar nominated, but no. Both the Academy of Motion Picture Arts and Sciences and the Writers Guild passed over the script. Brooks was devastated. "He was as low as I've ever known him," Anne Bancroft told Kenneth Tynan. A page had turned: *Silent Movie* was the last Brooks script to be nominated for an award by the membership of either organization.

What made things worse was that 1977 was the year of Woody Allen's *Annie Hall*, the kind of semiautobiographical comedy that had once been Brooks's ambition to make. The romantic comedy collected four Oscars, including for Best Actress (Diane Keaton) Best Writing (Screenplay Written Directly for the Screen)—a collaboration between Allen and Marshall Brickman—Best Picture, and Best Directing. (The film was nominated in five categories, with its only loss Allen's nomination as Best Actor.) Although Allen, Brooks's obvious Club Caesar rival for king of comedy in the 1970s, rarely enjoyed box-office hits, *Annie Hall* ultimately surpassed *High Anxiety* in worldwide ticket sales, too.

• • •

Perhaps the dip in figures was only momentary. Fans and exhibitors were still fervent. Theater owners ranked Brooks among the top ten box-office attractions in the annual Quigley polls of 1976 (number five) and 1977 (number seven). The National Association of Theatre Owners named him Director of the Year in 1977. Brooks was proud of those achievements, which rebuked the "crickets" and reinforced his idea of himself as a populist artist.

One unabashed fan of *High Anxiety* was Alfred Hitchcock. The master of the suspense métier sent Brooks a case of Château Haut-Brion 1961, timed to arrive shortly after the Oscar and Guild nominations were announced, with no nominations for Brooks. Brooks and Anne Bancroft were conspicuous mourners at Hitchcock's funeral one sunny day in May 1980.

After keeping an intense promotional schedule for *High Anxiety*, Brooks and Bancroft embarked on a three-week Caribbean idyll in February 1978, stopping in Miami, as Brooks frequently did to visit "my little Jewish mother." In the Caribbean the couple swam, took long walks, and socialized with Alan and Arlene Alda. Alone, Brooks surf fished, wearing a plantation hat, one day on the beach bumping into playwright Arthur Miller.

The couple recharged their batteries. Behind the scenes, there was going to be a changing of the guard among the Club Brooks writers. Brooks had to reverse the downward trends and recapture the magic of *Blazing Saddles* and *Young Frankenstein*.

The project Brooks talked about most often was "Bombs Away," which he described to interviewers as a parody of World War II movies reuniting the three sillies of *Silent Movie*—himself, Dom DeLuise, and Marty Feldman—as aviators bumbling into heroism. But that travesty of Brooks's own wartime adventures was never more than talk and never got down to a script; with declining box office it seemed at once too personal and ambitious as well as— like *Silent Movie*—more of the silly and Nice Mel.

Another way to look at it: Was Brooks going to make his next comedy for the "smarties," as he liked to call them—critics, sophisticates, and intellectuals—or would he make another "potato salad picture" for the great unwashed? He defined the potato salad picture in interviews. "You're in the deli and there's this guy with a little piece of potato salad stuck in the corner of his mouth," he explained, "and he's talking about your picture to his cronies. He's saying, all the time with the potato salad hanging, 'You gotta see this Mel Brooks pitcha, you'll laugh so hard you'll *pish* yourself.'"

During the making of *Silent Movie* and *High Anxiety*, which he helped write, Barry Levinson confided his professional ambitions to Brooks. Levinson had a trove of anecdotes about the adventures he and a bunch of friends had shared in their hometown of Baltimore, when they were in their early teens, which he thought might be strung together into an autobiographical script akin to Federico Fellini's *I Vitelloni*. Brooks loved *I Vitelloni*, one of his favorite "smarties," one of the Neorealist films that had inspired him in the 1950s. He encouraged Levinson to pursue his dreams. Levinson was the first member of Club Brooks to say he wouldn't be back after *High Anxiety*.

Soon enough, in 1982, Levinson wrote and directed *Diner*, an *I Vitelloni*–type memory film based on his solo script, which was Oscar nominated. He went on to craft several pictures about growing up in Baltimore while also directing "smarties" such as *Good Morning, Vietnam* and *Rain Man* from other people's scripts. He became one of the premier "hyphenates" (film industry slang for a "writer-director") of his generation, widely admired inside the industry and by critics.

Over the course of time, Levinson and Andrew Bergman stood alone in the category of scenarists who had graduated from Club Brooks to become "hyphenates" with, eventually, their own independent body of work and reputations beyond Brooks's.

Levinson's onetime improvisational partner Rudy DeLuca also decamped after *High Anxiety*. He would write a number of telefilms with occasional big-screen credits, independent of Brooks, over the next decade. He also tried the "hyphenate" route in 1985, directing *Transylvania 6–5000*, which was a thin comedy, Brooks-like in ways, trading on the public appetite for horror comedies spurred by *Young Frankenstein*.

Ron Clark never strayed far from Brooks's circle. He and his wife spent holidays with Brooks and Bancroft; the couples took vacations together and often stopped in Paris, where Clark's plays were staged on occasion. Yet Clark's screenwriting tapered off, and he would disappear entirely from the credits of Mel Brooks films for the next decade.

Clark worked quietly behind the scenes on at least one project before he faded away, however. Brooks told interviewers while on his *High Anxiety* publicity tour that he had been thinking a lot about Preston Sturges, a pioneering "hyphenate" of the 1940s whose witty comedies were the quintessential "smarties," beloved by critics and fans alike. Brooks loved *Sullivan's Travels*, a 1941 picture written and directed by Sturges, that starred Joel McCrea as a successful Hollywood director of escapist farces whose desire to finally do something worthwhile as a filmmaker—make a socially meaningful message drama for a change—leads him to adopt the guise of a bum and go on the road to experience hardships. Remaking classic films was yet another way of feeding off his boyhood enthusiasms, and after *High Anxiety* Brooks talked with Clark about concocting a story that might serve as his "personal version of *Sullivan's Travels*," according to the *Washington Post*, "in part because he liked its picaresque format."

Another god of Golden Age comedy was Ernst Lubitsch, and Brooks considered remaking Lubitsch, too. Partly that came about because of the sequence featuring Brooks and Bancroft, mugging and dancing up a storm, that was among the consensus highlights of *Silent Movie*. The positive reception of that scene revived the temptation to turn some future Mel Brooks film into a joint starring vehicle for husband and wife.

David Lunney, the high school friend of Bancroft who worked

at the American Film Institute and socialized with the Brookses, was also a passionate movie buff. With a partner, William Allyn, Lunney had snapped up the remake rights to several golden oldies, including *Old Acquaintance,* a popular 1943 women's drama starring Bette Davis and Miriam Hopkins, and *To Be or Not to Be,* from 1942, a Lubitsch classic. The latter starred Jack Benny as the egocentric leader of a thespian troupe in Poland who, after the Nazi invasion and takeover, turns gutsy against Hitler. Carole Lombard played the egocentric's wife, the troupe's lead actress, who is just as brave as she is flirty.

Lunney thought *To Be or Not to Be* would be perfect for Brooks and Bancroft. The actress related to the concept instantly, but Brooks was skeptical. Lunney arranged a screening of the Lubitsch film at the AFI, and afterward Brooks and Bancroft emerged gung-ho.

Lunney wanted to hire a topflight screenwriter who would re-imagine the original story by Melchior Lengyel and the scenario by Edwin Justus Mayer, close collaborators with Lubitsch on many pictures. The outside scenarist was okay with Brooks, at least at first, it seemed, because he himself was wary of tackling the Lubitsch remake head-on. The producers therefore approached Robert Towne, an Oscar winner for *Chinatown* in 1975, who was then one of the most famous names in the profession. Towne was intrigued, but Brooks ultimately felt more comfortable with a newly established playwright, James Kirkwood, Jr., who had won both a Tony and a Pulitzer Prize the year before for writing the book of the hit musical *A Chorus Line* on Broadway.

After signing a "pay or play" deal with 20th Century–Fox in 1975 that included the participation of Brooks and Bancroft, Lunney and Allyn commissioned a first-draft script from Kirkwood. However, studio officials were not enthusiastic about the prospect of Brooks switching from his strong suit of audience-friendly spoofs with bad-taste humor to a sophisticated comedy with a hallowed pedigree. And Brooks himself developed cold feet about committing to any script written by a reputable writer outside his usual club, which would have a vastly different tone than his own work and yet have to be honored.

After Kirkwood's script was delivered, it was shelved. Among those who urged Brooks to write his next comedy alone without collaborators were his wife and Alan U. Schwartz. Brooks's attorney was rarely quoted on the subject of his client, yet he had strong views. "I'd like to see him doing his own stuff," Schwartz told Kenneth Tynan. "Give us pure, vintage Brooks, not Brooks riding on the backs of a lot of other people. There's a strange legal phrase that expresses what I mean. Suppose I'm working as a driver for a guy named Al. If I run someone over in the course of my duties, Al is responsible. But if I take the car to the beach and run someone over, that is called in law a 'frolic and detour,' and I'm responsible. I think Mel should go in for more frolics and detours."

A man who bubbled over with ideas and jokes, Brooks had trouble deciding on an original story of his own that he could flesh out into a film. He needed to have confidence in the story and ample time for the writing. Four years would go by before his next comedy.

While vacationing in the Caribbean, however, Anne Bancroft had arrived at an important decision, which effectively slowed down the momentum on Brooks's seventh film as writer-director, regardless of the subject. She had just reached another pinnacle in her career, playing an aging prima ballerina locked in a lifelong rivalry with Shirley MacLaine in *The Turning Point*, which was released around the same time as *High Anxiety*. Her performance earned her her fourth Oscar nomination as Best Actress in a Leading Role.

Bancroft decided that she no longer wanted to be "just an actress." She wanted to write and direct and hoped to turn one of her AFI projects, *Fatso*, the short film about a binge eater in an Italian American family, into a feature. Joining the uptick of women in

Hollywood who were directing first pictures, who included comedienne Joan Rivers and actress Joan Darling, Bancroft also planned to
act a key role in the film. She'd portray the older sister and business
partner of Dom DeLuise, who agreed to repeat the character he'd
played in the AFI short, the titular fatso trying to lose weight to
woo a girl.

Going into his supersalesman mode, Brooks pitched *Fatso* with
his wife at 20th Century–Fox, securing a $3 million budget for
the film. His sales pitch: *Fatso* was going to be a smartie *about* potato
salad. His own staff would serve as a kind of insurance policy for
Bancroft's directing debut: Brooks's assistant Stuart Cornfeld, who
had produced her AFI short, would now produce her debut feature;
Jonathan Sanger, the assistant director on *High Anxiety*, would be the
associate producer and production manager of *Fatso*.

Brooks put his reputation on the line, but not his name, which
he did not want to overshadow Bancroft's. In more ways than one,
Bancroft's decision to direct altered Brooks's own career path. It
would take his wife a year to write the script and prepare the picture, and that was the year Brooks spent developing other properties
to be produced under a new company umbrella. The trade papers
did not announce *Fatso* as a Crossbow Production until early 1979.
Soon after, *Fatso* was folded into Brooksfilms Limited, a new entity
for California filings and another name change—corporate—for
Brooks, a rebranding that allowed him to produce other films without writing, directing, or starring.

If the publicity is to be believed, Bancroft wrote the script alone
and "hasn't asked me for one bit of advice on how to shoot a scene
so far," as Brooks told one columnist.

Yet according to *Fatso* cinematographer Brianne Murphy, when
Bancroft started the production in April 1979, shooting the exteri-
ors in New York, Brooks kept his hand in. Only he and Bancroft,
unusually so, were admitted to dailies. Although it was normal for
most cinematographers to view the footage, Murphy was barred. "I

guess he told her what he liked," said Murphy. "Word had gotten around that he was very controlling."

The famous husband's visits to the set were also out of the ordinary. "Around four or five in the afternoon, Mel would come to pick [Bancroft] up," Murphy said. "We never knew when he'd arrive and it seemed to be at his convenience rather than hers because whenever he did appear, she'd start wanting to complete a shot." One day Brooks showed up, "not introduced to anyone and not saying hello to anyone. . . . Mel goes over to the video assist to look at it and in the middle of the shot, he says, 'Cut, cut, that's no good, that won't work, cut it.'" The camera operator, Bob Lamar, a big man, took his eye from the camera, looked down at Mel, and asked, "Who the fuck is that little guy?"

"All hell broke loose," said Murphy. "Very upset, Anne picked up her stuff and left. It was a wrap. Everybody was proud of Bob for saying what he'd said, telling Mel off for cutting her cut. That's unheard-of behavior. No one ever says 'Cut' except the director."

The next day, Murphy recalled, a scene was lit and ready to be photographed but Bancroft would not leave her dressing room. After "an hour or so" Murphy knocked on her door. The first-time director told Murphy that she had wept all night. "This is just terrible, what happened yesterday," Bancroft said, "and I hate to tell you this, but Mel says you have to fire Bob, the operator." Brooks said the operator was "potentially dangerous," Bancroft reported. Murphy dug in her heels, insisting that her operator, whom she had worked with for years, was "as potentially dangerous as I was," and moreover he had bravely protected Bancroft's rights as a director by objecting to Brooks calling cut.

Bancroft agreed to come out in half an hour, but after two hours of inactivity Murphy returned to her dressing room. Bancroft had spoken to her husband again, with Brooks still insisting that the operator be fired. The director and camerawoman talked it through again, Murphy refusing to fire her operator, who instead, she said, "should get a medal." Not much filming was done that day. "It was a stand-off," Murphy recalled. Bancroft went home, she and Brooks had a battle of the wills all night, the next day the issue was dropped, and "we all got back to work," Murphy said. Regardless, Bancroft felt defeated.

# CHAPTER 13

# 1980

## Uneasy Lies the Head

Although the original impetus behind the formation of Brooksfilms was *Fatso*, the new production entity gave the head man something to do with his extra energy, and soon there was a second project, a third, a fourth . . . although the second, *The Elephant Man*, would loom above them all.

Born in Brooklyn in 1944, Jonathan Sanger first came to Brooks recommended by Barry Levinson, after serving as production manager on difficult locations including William Friedkin's *The Brink's Job*, which had been shot in Boston. Sometime during the filming of *High Anxiety*, Sanger's babysitter pleaded with him to read a spec screenplay that had been written by her boyfriend, Christopher De Vore, and his collaborator, Eric Bergren. Their script told the true story of a severely deformed man, suffering from a rare disease known as neurofibromatosis, who lived in London in the late nineteenth century. Named Joseph Merrick, the man was dubbed "The Elephant Man" and publicly exhibited as a freak. The De Vore–Bergren script moved Sanger to tears.

The writers had obtained a low-cost option of anthropologist Ashley Montagu's nonfiction book *The Elephant Man: A Study in Human Dignity*, which was based on a memoir by Dr. Frederick Treves, who'd treated Merrick in London Hospital in his last years. They had ignored—according to them—a successful English stage play treating the same story, which was about to open on Broadway with a title identical to Montagu's book and their script. (The playwright would later sue Brooksfilms over the title.)

Sanger, who aspired to produce films, paid for an option on the De Vore–Bergren script out of his own pocket and one day left it in the outer office with Brooks's secretary, whom he knew from *The Brink's Job*, asking for her opinion. Brooks prowled his offices like a jungle cat. Not the smallest thing happened without his awareness. Brooks picked up the script, read it over a weekend, and called Sanger in.

"I had assumed," Sanger wrote later, that Brooks had only wanted to make "his own broad comedies. I knew that many people had tried to get him to produce and direct their comedies, and that this was the quickest way to court rejection. Trying to trade jokes with Mel was a popular pastime with people who came to meet him for the first time. It was rarely a successful gambit. The man's mind was agile and his responses often funny, but trying to compete with him was foolish and not destined to win his respect.

"Unlike other comic writers, actors or comedians I had met— Woody Allen, Steve Martin, Nathan Lane—who were mostly dour and introverted when out of the spotlight, Mel was always 'on.' If you met him on the street he'd do a ten-minute improv with you. When I had lunch with him at the commissary at Fox, he would go to each table in the Executive Dining Room and have something clever to say to everyone, while I waited to order lunch. Yet he once told me that he dreaded going on *The Tonight Show* with Johnny Carson. 'Why?' I asked. 'Because I always have to follow that introduction: "And here is the funniest man in the world." Too much responsibility."

Right away Brooks spoke about mounting *The Elephant Man* as a Brooksfilms production. 20th Century–Fox would never go for it. "The triumvirate of Alan Ladd Jr., Jay Kanter, and Gareth Wigan had recently left Fox," Sanger recalled. "Dennis Stanfill, a 'suit' and not a creative type, was running things now." Brooks saw Dustin

Hoffman playing the Elephant Man. Sanger argued that they needed "a great actor, but one with not so well-known a face," hiding under tons of makeup. Brooks nodded. But then they would need "the best actor in the world" to play Dr. Treves, the deformed man's physician, he said.

They concurred on "a couple of basics." The picture ought to be shot in London on "as small a budget as we could manage," in Sanger's words. Brooks would sign off on the director and lead players, and he'd guide De Vore and Bergren on script revisions.

Now they had to iron out a contract. Brooks arranged a meeting with Alan U. Schwartz, advising Sanger, "Bring your people if you like." Not having a lawyer and unable to obtain one on short notice, Sanger went alone to a Beverly Hills Hotel room to meet with Brooks and Schwartz, "a distinguished looking man, tall, slim, Armani-suited with a blue striped Turnbull and Asser shirt and red tie, and with a great head of white hair." Sanger was acquainted with him since the lawyer had played a bit as a psychiatrist in *High Anxiety*. "As usual," Sanger recalled, Brooks "got right down to business."

Brooks offered him $100,000 to produce *The Elephant Man* and "a deferment of another $50,000 after the film breaks even." Considering that Sanger was currently earning $2,500 weekly as a production manager, he was overjoyed. "We'll split the profits, two-thirds to Brooksfilms and one-third to you," Brooks continued evenly. "We will give percentage points away proportionately but you'll have a hard floor of twenty-five percent of the net." Schwartz said little, limiting himself to smiling and nodding.

Sanger felt that the terms were "very fair." ("A hard floor," he explained later in his memoir, "meant that no matter how many percentage points we had to give away to writers or actors, I would never be reduced to less than twenty-five percent.") Brooks said there would also be icing on the profits cake. "Look kid," the namesake of Brooksfilms said. "We are going to own this film. We're not giving it to the studios. They'll distribute it, but that's it." Sanger left the hotel room, excited as never before, paperwork to follow.

Within days Sanger had a lawyer who phoned him with the bad news relayed from Schwartz: Brooks had changed his mind. The fees were okay, but the split was too generous. Now Sanger was being offered just 10 percent on the back end. "I was both angry and hurt," Sanger recalled, "angry that Mel could be so quick to change, hurt that he didn't even see fit to talk with me and let me know himself. It was chicken shit."

Yet he knew that Brooks was "a tough man with a buck." Michael Hertzberg had left his employ forever after he had been shut out of creative involvement or participation points in *Silent Movie*. And Club Brooks had gone "on strike," refusing "to come to the set for several days" during the filming of *High Anxiety*, "until their back deals had been sorted out."

Tossing and turning all night, Sanger didn't care to feel "victimized" and couldn't decide if he should accept the reduced offer. If he accepted, his wife advised him, "you need to forget this even happened . . . it will eat at you and ruin the experience." The next day he phoned his lawyer, "told him to close the deal," and "never mentioned it again."

Sanger went on to produce *The Elephant Man*; *Frances*, the Frances Farmer biopic; and *The Doctor and the Devils*, another English gothic, for Brooksfilms. And later, after twenty years of working independently of Brooks, Sanger returned to Brooksfilms to share the producing credit with Brooks on the musical film of *The Producers* in 2005.

Brooks earned his extra points with his financial as well as creative acumen.

At the suggestion of Stuart Cornfeld, who was the first-time producer of *Fatso* for Brooksfilms, Jonathan Sanger met with David Lynch, the director of the cult film *Eraserhead*, a surrealist oddity Lynch had made as an American Film Institute student. *Eraserhead* was set in an apocalyptic landscape and revolved around a mutant baby, which was perhaps not far removed from a deformed Elephant Man in nineteenth-century London.

Sanger personally liked Lynch, who looked and acted surprisingly normal. Swallowing hard, the budding producer screened *Eraserhead* for Brooks. "It's an adolescent's nightmare of responsibility," Brooks summarized after watching the film with Sanger. "I like it!" Brooks met Lynch, liking him personally just as much as Sanger did, later often referring to him as Jimmy Stewart from Venus. ("Mel took to David right away and loved that he had a strong and solid hand-shake," Sanger recalled.) Brooks approved him as director.

Lynch wanted to shoot *The Elephant Man*, like *Eraserhead*, in black and white. "You guys know I love black and white," Brooks reassured the director and producer. "We shot *Young Frankenstein* in black and white and it was my best photographed film."

However, the black-and-white photography had to be approved by Fred Silverman, the president of NBC. Brooks had the shrewd idea of financing *The Elephant Man* through a television "prebuy" on later broadcast airings, and to that end he made an appointment with Silverman, now the head of the network where Brooks was best known and had started out in the business. Brooks walked in carrying a life-size bust of the Elephant Man, planting it on Silverman's desk. Silverman was sold, and he wasn't fazed by their insistence on shooting the picture in arty black and white. "All movies are in color today," Silverman explained. "Doing it in black and white will make it special."

NBC offered Brooksfilms $4 million for the picture, and Alan U. Schwartz then "concluded a deal with one of his foreign clients, EMI films, to sell the foreign rights to the film with an additional guarantee of $1.2 million," in Sanger's words, "which we could dis-count at a bank and get more cash [as] needed to make the film." The only hitch: Silverman wanted to have "a Mel Brooks comedy special" in NBC's future. "Mel agreed in principle to do a special, but with fees and timing to be negotiated later."

With Brooksfilms wholly owning *The Elephant Man*, 20th Century–Fox, under Dennis Stanfill, was unlikely to be interested in even distributing the film. So Brooks took the now fully bankrolled project to Paramount and Universal, two studios where he knew the executives would fly out from behind their desks to greet him; the higher-ups were akin to the button-down talk-show men, happy to have their dull days enlivened by Brooks. He aimed to pit Paramount and Universal against each other in the bidding for "a strong domestic distribution deal," Sanger said, keeping the foreign rights separate. "He was determined to split the rights between domestic and foreign because he did not want the film [to] be cross-collateralized between territories. This was often how it worked on films where studios owned all rights. A film might make money in one territory, say the U.S., but lose money in another territory. The studio could then write off the loss against the gain and the filmmakers might get nothing. Mel wanted none of that."

Brooks prided himself on his "strong relationships" with Barry Diller and Michael Eisner, the first in command and his lieutenant at Paramount. He sent the script ahead and booked a powwow on the top floor of the executive building on the Paramount lot. Accompanying him and letting Brooks do most of the talking, Sanger observed Brooks at the top of his form, playing poker with a stone face, "no hat in hand," as though he were holding an unseen card. "Mike, remember," Brooks told Eisner, "we're only interested in a domestic distribution deal. We're not selling the picture."

The Paramount honchos were clearly intrigued by *The Elephant Man*, but they had one off-putting suggestion. Pauline Kael of *The New Yorker* had taken a leave of absence from her film-review column and was now employed by the studio, reading scripts and inputting on projects. She was a fan of *Eraserhead*. Could she meet with David Lynch?

Brooks didn't blink during the meeting, but in the car returning to 20th Century–Fox, Sanger asked him what he thought of the request that Lynch meet Kael. "Oh, I don't know," said Brooks. "We'll put that meeting off. I don't really think we need to have David meet with a 'cricket.'"

Off the two went, on another day, to Universal. In the end both studios submitted "reasonable" distribution offers, albeit both were inclined toward a "not very high print and advertising investment." All monies would go to Brooksfilms out of "their percentage of the gross from the box office after the exhibitors take their cut," in Sanger's words. Paramount wanted to keep fifteen percent of the gross until the film reached $20 million, then twenty percent from $20 million to $25 million, and twenty-five percent after $25 million for as long as the film had revenue. The balance of the gross would go to Brooksfilms. Universal countered with twenty-five percent until the film grossed $20 million, twenty percent from $20 million to $25 million, and fifteen percent after $25 million.

Talking it over with Brooks and Alan U. Schwartz ("our point man on these deals and he did about as well as he could"), comparing the two offers, Sanger believed it was a no-brainer: "If the film was a big hit, we'd make more money with Universal," he thought.

Brooks surprised them with his brainier decision: "Let's go with Paramount."

"Why?" asked Sanger.

"Because they'll chase the money."

Observing his bewilderment, Brooks explained. "Look," Brooks said, "at Universal, they make less the longer the movie runs so they have no incentive to chase the grosses, while Paramount is giving us a bigger taste earlier and then will push for higher grosses because they stand to make more in the long run. I like that way of thinking."

Paramount acquired the distribution of *The Elephant Man*. Pauline Kael, the "cricket," never met with Lynch. And Brooks had only pretended enthusiasm for doing a television special for NBC. Still, in a clever way, that trade-off "was a safety valve for [Fred] Silverman, if the movie failed," according to Sanger. "As it turned out, Silverman left NBC before the movie was delivered to the network and Mel never did have to do the comedy special."

David Lynch wanted to join in the script conferences with Brooks, Christopher De Vore, and Eric Bergren. "David and the boys," as Brooks called them, congregated in his office along with Sanger, shortly after the producer's first trip to London to begin hiring personnel and plan the filming. "Chris was the brooding soul of the work," said Sanger. "Eric kept the spine in place and David brought a new, visual spark to the writing."

What role did Brooks play? Sanger hoped he'd "allow us the same freedom that took place in the comedy writers' room" when Club Brooks had written *High Anxiety*.

More than once that writers' room had reminded Sanger of a James Agee essay entitled "Comedy's Greatest Era." "In that piece," the producer reflected, "Agee described the working methods of Mack Sennett's writers. They would often bring in a 'wild man' whose job it was to come up with crazy situations for the others to take off from. He acted as the group's subconscious mind. In Mel's comedies, each writer might take a turn as the wild man, but Mel himself tended to allow the irrational to surface the most."

Brooks introduced the very first script conference with "a simple analysis of the heart of the story," Sanger recalled. "This is Pinocchio,"

Brooks told the assemblage. "It's about a lost boy—Merrick. Treves is Geppetto. He loves him and wants him back."

Brooks said he wanted the scenarists to go to work writing fearlessly and return to his office once a week, reading aloud their pages for his feedback and group discussion.

For several weeks, that MO worked relatively smoothly. "David and the boys would come to Mel's office and we would read the new pages out loud," Sanger recalled. "Mel would listen and make a few comments and we'd be good for another week."

But sometimes "Mel would make comments that none of us agreed with," Sanger wrote, and they'd go back to their respective offices at 20th Century–Fox and scratch their heads.

"What are we going to do?" the others would ask Sanger. "We can't follow all those suggestions. Some are just crazy." Sanger would say, "Listen, I've seen this before. He's just tossing out all kinds of ideas. Many are good, some are not. If we challenge him he'll defend each idea with his life. Let's just hear what he has to say and come back here afterward. We'll act on the ideas we really like and just forget the other ones.

"I bet you he never mentions them again."

The casting moved ahead simultaneously. John Hurt as the Elephant Man and Anthony Hopkins as Dr. Treves met with Brooks's quick approval. ("Mel felt that Hopkins was one of the best actors in the world," explained Sanger. "It didn't hurt that Mel's wife, Anne Bancroft, adored working with Hopkins in *Young Winston* a few years earlier.")

Calling Sanger and Lynch in one day, Brooks "seemed uncomfortable. But in his inimitable style he jumped right in," Sanger recalled. Brooks always used his wife's full name when referring to her in professional situations. "Anne Bancroft" had read the script, Brooks said, and the four-time Oscar nominee was interested in the part of Dame Madge Kendal, a famous English actress of the era who had befriended Joseph Merrick. "This is neither a request nor a suggestion, just information," he said. "It's entirely your choice."

Lynch, who admired Bancroft, and Sanger, who as production manager had just finished working with her on the filming of *Fatso*, were delighted. "It was really a great coup for us to get her," said Sanger. "She was a great actress and a valuable name and someone I knew."

Although the reviews were generous to Dom DeLuise, critics were unduly cruel to the uneven *Fatso* as a whole. Anne Bancroft's first directorial effort, which was completed before *The Elephant Man* and became the maiden Brooksfilms release in February 1980, was weighed down by "not particularly funny material to begin with," Roger Ebert wrote in the *Chicago Sun-Times*, in addition to Bancroft's "ambiguous" approach to potentially comic scenes and poor camera choices. "Sentimental" and "unfocused," Janet Maslin agreed in the *New York Times*. "Bumbling" and "sluggish," *Variety* pronounced. Stanley Kauffmann in *The New Republic* asked, "What in the world persuaded financiers to back this picture?"

*Fatso* did not have a national distribution deal, and the film had only a limited release in US theaters before sinking like a stone. Bancroft's directing debut cured the actress of her ambition to direct. Later in the decade, she told *Films and Filming* that she had loathed the experience and would prefer to forget the onetime experiment. More than once Brooks told interviewers he was proud of *Fatso*, "a beautiful film" and underrated.

*The Elephant Man* held its premiere in October in New York City, and the vast majority of critics who saw it there and everywhere else were roused to superlatives. Considering that it was a black-and-white period drama set in London, revolving around a hideously deformed man who wears a cloth sack over his head, the film became an unexpected "giant hit," in Brooks's words. Its US grosses alone amounted to $26 million, but the film did well internationally and eventually returned $70 million, according to estimates. And unlike *Fatso*, *The Elephant Man* would have a future life in television, cable, and video. Even John Morris's score sold extremely well for a nonpop soundtrack.

Brooks, in interviews both then and later, was coy about his contribution, often saying "I very skillfully hid my name when I created Brooksfilms," other times pointedly mentioning his uncredited contribution to the script and other aspects of the production.

Actually, there were *three* Brooksfilms titles in 1980. The surreptitious third was a lampoon of movie trailers called *Loose Shoes*, aka *Coming Attractions*, which was directed by Ira Miller, a former Second City improv comic from Chicago turned bit actor in Hollywood. Miller appears in an eye blink in many Mel Brooks comedies, including *Blazing Saddles*, *When Things Are Rotten*, *High Anxiety*, *History of the World, Part I*, *Spaceballs*, *Life Stinks*, *Robin Hood: Men in Tights*, and *Dracula: Dead and Loving It*.

*Loose Shoes* was a mélange of comedy sketches, musical performances, and satirical film clips with a cast that included Buddy Hackett, Avery Schreiber, Kinky Friedman, and Van Dyke Parks. Brooks may have contributed to the skits, which feature, among other setups, men farting in submarines; and he and another Club Caesarite were referenced in the trailers, which proclaimed, "Here's a movie that makes Mel Brooks' humor seem sophisticated, Woody Allen's statuesque!" With graphic nudity, which Brooks avoided in his own films (tits, one critic wrote of his fare, were "oft-mentioned, never seen"), and the snappy theme song "Black Pussy, Loose Shoes, and a Warm Place to Shit," *Loose Shoes* made *Blazing Saddles* seem like a Sunday sermon.

R rated, *Loose Shoes* proved negligible both as comedy and at the box office. It is noteworthy primarily in retrospect as the first big-screen appearance by a rising *Saturday Night Live* comedian named Bill Murray. Most Brooks fans have never heard of it.

One vehicle for Bancroft to direct, one respectable drama (co-starring Bancroft), and one unruly mishmash: that was pretty much the way future Brooksfilms productions would divide. Not all of them were Elephant Men. Joseph Merrick's story became a true sensation in 1980, going on to earn eight Academy Award nominations, including Best Picture, Best Actor in a Leading Role, Best Directing, Best Writing (Screenplay Based on Material from Another Medium), Best Art Direction, Best Costume Design, Best Film Editing, and Best Music (Original Score). The Directors Guild nominated Lynch for Outstanding Directorial Achievement in Motion Pictures, and the Writers Guild nominated the screenplay for Best Drama Adapted from Another Medium (the script was ultimately credited to De Vore, Bergren, and Lynch).

Although *The Elephant Man* lost in all of those disparate races, including in every Oscar category in which it was nominated, even so, Brooks had gambled and won.

His propensity for ceaseless multitasking and diversifying continued to pay surprising dividends. The once undisciplined writer, who had bristled under Max Liebman's sovereignty, now waved his scepter over the vast undertakings of others. The bad-taste comedian had successfully transformed himself into the good-taste producer of serious, if not to say—perhaps to underline the point—often exceedingly solemn dramas.


Using the success of *The Elephant Man* and high expectations for his next comedy as leverage, Brooks tore up his current deal with 20th Century–Fox and, in effect, delivered an ultimatum to the new management: improve his terms, or he would walk.

Shortly after signing his initial 20th Century–Fox contract, Brooks had jettisoned his talent agency, Creative Management Associates, over dissatisfaction with the escalations and perks in his 20th Century–Fox deal, which had seemed generous before the release of *Young Frankenstein* and the two ensuing comedies he made for the studio—all increasingly remunerative to Brooks, despite their gradually declining box office overall. His abrupt severance of CMA led to an agency lawsuit against him for unpaid percentages—a protracted case quietly settled, as was most Brooks litigation, out of court.

Brooks switched to a personal manager, Howard Rothberg, who had followed David Begelman as his agent at CMA. Rothberg had launched himself as a personal manager with a client list of familiar names: Larry Gelbart, Dom DeLuise, and Sid Caesar, as well as Brooks and Anne Bancroft. Alan U. Schwartz, however, handled Brooks's renegotiation with an eye to unique clauses that raised Hollywood eyebrows.

Key to the revised contract was the Belgian-born Emile Buyse, who had resigned as president of 20th Century–Fox International, where he had overseen the foreign marketing and promotion for *Young Frankenstein*, *Silent Movie*, and *High Anxiety*. Moving to Los Angeles, the defector joined Brooksfilms to handle non-US territories exclusively.

People debated whether Brooks or Woody Allen was the king of American comedy, but Brooks was the undisputed king of Hollywood comedy, as far as 20th Century–Fox was concerned. The new studio officials, worried that they might lose him, would take clauses in the agreement for his next film. Brooks agreed to accept only a "nominal fee" for his multiple functions as writer, composer, director, producer, and star—a concession that amounted to "a considerable investment in the negative cost" and a kind of personal "completion guarantee," according to press accounts. In return, 20th Century–Fox would supply the $10 million–plus budget and reap all the US exhibition profits only. Wary of net theatrical profit points in the United States, Brooks conceded this revenue to the studio. But non-US markets had added $7 million to $10 million gross to each of his previous comedies, so he asked for and received all the foreign monies, including television and home entertainment licensing. He also went after small pockets of earnings previously ceded to the studios, such as airplane play on foreign flights, until then counted as domestic revenue. Another example: from RCA Brooks extracted a six-figure basic minimum on video rentals, that sum to rise in accordance with theatrical earnings. In those early days of video, the market was almost entirely rentals, and in addition to the minimum guarantee, a hefty slice of every rental, running to $75 each in that era, would flow directly to Brooksfilms.

In order to cinch the deal, Brooks acted out the script in progress for executives, selling it as a shift away from the Nice Mel of *Silent Movie* and *High Anxiety* back to the bad-taste excesses that had made *Blazing Saddles* his biggest moneymaker. As with *Blazing Saddles*, he promised an R rating. He was calling the new film *History of the World, Part I.*

The deal looked reasonable on paper. Brooks's reduced up-front fees would lower the above-the-line costs and risk. 20th Century–Fox counted on *History* proving a tremendous hit in the United States with profits to spare.

The eighties dawned with Brooks scribbling away on *History of the World, Part I.* He would be credited as the sole writer for the third and last time in his career. Some friends and associates cannot believe that he wrote the script entirely alone; he always needed sounding boards and people who wrote down and edited what he said. "I heard he had some help on that one," said one Club Brooks writer, who asked to remain anonymous.

The help may have come from his collaborator on the film's only original song: his old friend Ronny Graham, who cowrote the

408 | FUNNY MAN

deliberately extravagant, intentionally tasteless (part of the overall R-rated strategy) "The Inquisition."* With its lyrics mocking the Christian persecution of Jews in the fifteenth century and nuns peeling off their habits and swimming synchronously, "The Inquisition" was patently reminiscent of "Springtime for Hitler."

Much of the script was similarly derivative of the past: spoofs trotted out previously on Sid Caesar shows or voiced by the 2000 Year Old Man. This time Brooks's targets were blockbusters and biblical epics. The story line wove through historical epochs, visiting the dawn of time, the Stone Age, the Roman Empire, the Last Supper, fifteenth-century Spain under the Catholic monarchs, and the French Revolution.

The through line, "the natural glue," in his words, was Brooks himself playing five key roles: Moses (delivering Ten Commandments after he drops five of the fifteen stone tablets); Comicus, a Borscht Belt–style stand-up philosopher; the Grand Inquisitor Torquemada; bawdy King Louis XIV of France; and his look-alike Jacques, a *pissoir* boy.

The ensemble also referenced his greatest hits: Sid Caesar returned as head caveman (in size and quality his role a demotion from the studio chief in *Silent Movie*); Howard Morris was the official spokesman for the Roman Empire (a similar downgrade from his meatier part in *High Anxiety*); Dom DeLuise played the gluttonous Nero with Madeline Kahn as his gum-chewing Empress Nympho; Harvey Korman was the Count de Monet and Cloris Leachman was Madame Defarge, reunited in the French Revolution segment.

Brooks trumpeted his discovery of Mary-Margaret Humes, whose face on a billboard had caught his fancy and whom he cast

---

* Another song, not cowritten with Ronny Graham and not on the film's soundtrack, Brooks's single "It's Good to Be the King," was recorded later and released to promote *History of the World, Part I*. It rose to number 67 on the *Billboard* charts.

in her screen debut as the vestal virgin Miriam, nominally the film's ingenue; but her role shrank during the filming and editing.

There were many small parts and gigantic crowd scenes. Sticking to his self-starter philosophy, Brooks cast a veritable Roman legion of stand-ups in fleeting roles, including Sammy Shore, Shecky Greene, Charlie Callas, Henny Youngman, Jackie Mason, and Jack Carter. Recent as well as long-standing members of Club Brooks, writers as well as lawyers, alumni of previous Mel Brooks comedies, and old friends such as actress Bea Arthur, stepped up for cameos. The voice of God speaking to Moses was, uncredited, Carl Reiner. The bigger-than-life maker of *Citizen Kane*, Orson Welles, known for his stentorian voice-overs, was employed to lend pearly tones to the narration.

The part of Josephus, the Roman slave who tags along after Brooks in the loose-knit plot, was crafted for Richard Pryor, and the inarguably dangerous comedian who helped write *Blazing Saddles* was announced for the role. But after freebasing cocaine for days, Pryor drenched himself with rum and set himself on fire on June 9, 1980, right before principal photography was due to begin. He was rushed to the hospital, beginning a long recovery mixed with deterioration. And Brooks had to come up with a quick substitute.

Madeline Kahn suggested her friend Gregory Hines, then best known for tap-dancing in the Broadway musical *Eubie!* Hines did not hesitate; he got on a plane to Hollywood, and then did his best to make people forget the legendary name of Richard Pryor.

Everything had to be more—bigger and louder—including the budget, which swelled to $11 million, the highest price tag yet for a Mel Brooks comedy. And that was not due to the stratospheric salaries of so many self-starters. Even though bona fide stars had appeared in Brooks's films for scale and the fun of it, the most ac-claimed of the self-starters, including Harvey Korman, grouched that Brooks refused to pay their going rate.

The above-the-line costs went principally to the sixteen weeks of filming, Brooks's longest schedule yet, the costumes and grandiose sets in London (where scenes were shot) and on the 20th Century–Fox lot, and the lavish "The Inquisition" staged by Alan Johnson.

The photography took most of the summer, after which came the shuffling of the footage, whose challenges included the melding and continuity of disparate story lines. In the fall Brooks worked closely with his patient editor, John C. Howard, moving scenes around with sometimes just a few frames added or subtracted for comic timing. *History* was fated to be Howard's last editing assignment for Brooks, however, as the big, good-humored man, who lived with heart problems, passed away before Brooks's next feature.

With corporate optimism, 20th Century–Fox launched *History* into hundreds of theaters in the summer of 1981. At first, as usual, the audiences were decidedly enthusiastic. The jokes stampeded across the screen, and if one historical episode happened to flag, the next one quickly made up for it. The familiar faces were comforting, and the biggest names had moments to shine. There was always gold among the dross in a Mel Brooks comedy.

For many reviewers, however, *History* crossed a line. The familiarity of the jokes and sketches bred contempt. They were bothered when Brooks's script brazenly recycled "Walk this way!" And Robert Altman had already done the Last Supper in *M*A*S*H*. Dom DeLuise burped and farted as the cowboys had in *Blazing Saddles*. And the writer, director, and star, falling back on his adolescent sense of humor, piled on the vomit, masturbation, shit, piss, "faggot," and mammary jokes. He boasted in interviews of being "at the height of my vulgarity." He got his R rating and was proud of it—"I put an enormous R on this picture," he said—the only R in his career besides *Blazing Saddles*.

But many critics in major American cities trashed the film. Janet Maslin in the *New York Times* said *History of the World, Part I* was too often crude, sour, or "crashingly unfunny," its jokes "so tired that the cheerful outrageousness of Mr. Brooks' earlier films has become waxen." Gary Arnold in the *Washington Post* concurred: "The lapses in taste go beyond the pale and it becomes hard to recall a more offensive Mel Brooks movie." Writing in the *Chicago Sun-Times*, Roger Ebert thought that *History* was "a rambling, undisciplined, sometimes embarrassing failure." Sheila Benson, in Brooks's hometown *Los Angeles Times*, described his latest offering as a sorry "self-indulgence" relying on "in joke and old joke and no joke and mostly gone off to bathroom humor."*

The film claimed some surprising defenders, though, including Vincent Canby of the *New York Times*, who wrote separately to dispute Maslin, championing Brooks's "spirit" and "vision" in his piece entitled "In Defense of Bad Jokes." Though not everything Brooks's former bête noire said could have pleased the comedian (*History* "is essentially a sketch film, which may be the best format for a filmmaker whose attention span is sometimes too limited to sustain easily an entire movie on a single subject," Canby wrote), the critic admitted that he had come around to applauding the funny filmmaker. "I'm no longer as concerned as I was earlier about whether or not he finds the end-laugh," he explained. "The pursuit and the madly irreverent mind behind it are worth the price of admission [for *History*], which is something I didn't fully appreciate when I first saw 'Blazing Saddles.' Now I'm prepared to take the Brooks films at their own face value and not at the value that we—that is, most critics—would impose on him."

However, word of mouth was another medium of criticism, and the audience dropped by 35 percent after the opening weekend. By September, *History* had bottomed out in the United States, with Aljean Harmetz, the Hollywood correspondent for the *New York Times*, reporting it as "a considerable disappointment" to 20th Century–Fox. The final US grosses, tallying somewhere in the vicinity of $24 million, continued the downward trending of Brooks's comedies, especially in light of *History*'s steep $11 million budget.

Once again, however, just as Brooks had foreseen, Europe—where Emile Buyse supervised the film's promotion and distribution under the auspices of Columbia Pictures—proved the salvation. Brooks touted *History* on television shows in London, Stockholm, Copenhagen, Amsterdam, Rome, and Paris. He spent a full week in France, where the director is "more important than the stars," in Buyse's words, giving interviews. The foreign exhibitors' rentals and box-office grosses ultimately surpassed the US total.

Ancillary earnings improved on the overall US revenue, but still *History* "didn't live up to Brooks' usual commercial standards" in the homeland, reported the *Washington Post*. The foreign profits went straight to Brooksfilms, however, with Brooks later telling Gene Siskel of the *Chicago Tribune* that his aggregate earnings for a picture that was "generally perceived to be a failure" had been around $18 million. "Mr. Brooks made more money from *History* than any other film," the *New York Times* reported.

The Hollywood studio that had made a one-sided deal for *History* felt a distinct letdown that was not purely financial. Ironically, according to the *Washington Post*'s account, "Insiders say lots of 20th Century–Fox executives—definitely including the studio's new owner, Marvin Davis—weren't very pleased with the movie's low-brow comedy."


"It's good to be the king!" the egoistic King Louis XIV (Brooks) proclaims in *History of the World, Part I*. Repeated several times for emphasis in the film, that phrase—more so later than noticed at the time—became one of the iconic lines associated with Brooks.

Though he publicly saluted himself as the king of Hollywood comedy from the 1970s on ("I am the funniest man America has ever produced," he declared in one interview*), the public bluster was not always congruent with the private Brooks.

The public experienced the antic and funny, warm and fuzzy Mel on talk shows; they saw the Nice Mel. His public ire was reserved for "crickets" and the Hollywood awards organizations that overlooked him, but mainly that anger flashed in print interviews. As time went on, the press was less eager to compare him to Woody Allen, since their differences as filmmakers and comedians was increasingly manifest. But in the 1980s, interviewers began to mention younger comics, often Jewish, who had grown up in awe of Brooks and were now making their own comedies that raked in millions of dollars.

Often Brooks gave double-edged kudos to the new generation. "I enjoyed *Airplane!,*" he said. "I laughed my sides out. But it didn't *dare* much." On other occasions, he might slag Jim Abrahams and the Zucker brothers—David and Jerry—the *Airplane!* filmmakers. "I don't think they have the other side of it. I think they rush to the joke without an overview or structure. They're not from the school I grew up in. I grew up under the boardwalk in Brooklyn. Our mandate was to learn what this whole world was about, who was in it, and why it happened. And we were well read."

Not all the younger avatars saw him as a guiding light. Michael Palin, one of the Monty Python's Flying Circus comedy troupe that became a worldwide phenomenon in the late 1960s and early 1970s, encountered Brooks at 20th Century–Fox around the time

---

* It may be true, as Brooks wrote in his follow-up Letter to the Editor, that he had been misquoted and actually said, "Sid Caesar is the funniest man America has ever produced." However, he added in his letter, "I am probably the sixteenth funniest." And he had been rehearsing his sobriquet as far back as the October 4, 1965, issue of *Newsweek*, in which he was quoted as saying "People say I'm the funniest man alive. Why, three people have told me that already."

of *History of the World, Part I*. "Chunky, rack-like, barrel chest, with a firm, no-nonsense light paunch," Palin described the moment, "he grabs my hand a lot—shakes it probably five or six times."

Brooks then took Palin further aback. "I forgive you guys everything," he told Palin. ". . . I want you to know . . . you're so good, I forgive you for all those ideas you used."

("Is he joking?" Palin thought.)

"Spanish Inquisition?" Brooks inquired knowingly, referencing the celebrated Monty Python sketch that had been commandeered for the water ballet in *History*.

"Not sure what's going on," Palin scribbled in bafflement in his journal. Later, Christopher Guest—actor, musician, and soon to be writer-director of *This Is Spinal Tap* and other comedy "mockumentaries"—"tells me that Brooks has an almost pathological inability to accept competition—it's all a reduction of his own world."

Palin politely did not inform Brooks that he had recently seen *History* at its gala Los Angeles opening. "The film is dreadful," he wrote in his journal, "it's like a huge, expensive, grotesquely-inflated stand-up act. A night club act with elephantiasis."

One difference between Woody Allen and Mel Brooks comedies was that Allen invited audiences into his semiautobiographical fictions, in which his lead characters often behaved as variants of himself. Brooks's films had little or nothing to do with his private self.

High gates and sturdy walls insulated Mr. and Mrs. Brooks on Foothill Road and in Malibu. Other Hollywood personalities invited journalists into their homes for soul-baring talks. Never Brooks, nor Bancroft. They lived on the other side of a Maginot Line of privacy. "Only close friends are invited to visit the Brookses' house," observed Brad Darrach in *Playboy* in 1975. (All of *Playboy*'s tape-recorded sessions were arranged at Brooks's 20th Century–Fox offices.) "Nothing about my wife, nothing about my kids, and nothing about money," Brooks warned, opening another interview appointment ten years later—rules he himself occasionally waived, especially if the topic was money.

Earlier in the mid-1970s, Brooks had been in line for a major honor; his face would decorate the cover of *Time*, coinciding with the release of *Silent Movie*. However, he had to open his doors and life to the magazine. "Reporters followed me around night and day for weeks," Brooks complained to Kenneth Tynan. "They tortured my mother and my children all the time looking for negative things about me. Everyone I ever knew was called and cross-examined." Then, "a couple of weeks before the cover was due, I was told I'd been dumped and replaced by Nadia Comaneci," the Romanian gymnast who had become the star of the 1976 Summer Olympics. Brooks had to settle for the cover of *Newsweek*. Never again would he go through such humiliation, the comedian vowed. He admitted to temptation, if another *Time* cover was guaranteed. But the peak moment had passed.

The people who knew Brooks best were those who saw him most often on those occasions at which the press and public were not welcome: his wife and son, of course, but also the Club Caesar fellowship, which continued to thrive in Hollywood, gathering for events usually linked to a personal or professional milestone in Sid Caesar's odyssey.

Often Caesar hosted big parties at his house. The couples were always there: the Carls, the Mels, the Larrys, the Docs, as Mel Tolkin ticked them off on one occasion in a letter to Lucille Kallen, along with Sid's brother, Dave, and a sprinkling of name comics such as Jack Carter, Jan Murray, Buddy Hackett. Caesar's gatherings were "warm, fun, easy," said Tolkin, the host "flitting about, very much up, talkative and quite incoherent."

Early in the 1980s, Tolkin, who enjoyed bumping into Brooks in Caesar's aerie, took the measure of his old friend at one of the parties. Outside the limelight, Brooks looked pale, worn out, more vulnerable than he'd ever seen him, Tolkin wrote to Kallen. Bancroft looked worse: like a yenta with her stove on the fritz, Tolkin reported uncharitably.

Tolkin didn't know that after *Fatso* Bancroft had been diagnosed with breast cancer. "She kept her illness secret to the point that it was not reported in the press or shared with all her friends," wrote her biographer Douglass K. Daniel. The press was never informed. Narrating, in 1998, the documentary *Living with Cancer: A Message of Hope*, the actress did not disclose her own battle with the disease, even to producer-director Fred Silverman.*

Rumors about Brooks's private life swirled on the picket lines during the three-month Writers Guild strike of 1981, which tried to carve out improved compensation for scenarists in the fresh markets of cable television and home video. Brooks had first crossed similar picket lines during the 1973 strike, which coincided with the filming of *Blazing Saddles*.

As, over time, the Writers Guild ignored his scripts for awards, Brooks increasingly identified himself as a director as much as a writer. He earned generous residuals denied to mere writers through his writer-director hyphenation. His directing, he increasingly hinted in interviews, also deserved industry prizes. At a Guild meeting, Brooks argued, "I crossed the picket line to *direct*, not write." The well-known sitcom writer Bob Weiskopf cried out, "You call that directing?!" The room erupted in laughter, Brooks, too.

The big-name hyphenates were resented for crossing picket lines. Brooks was among eighteen Guild members who were fined $250 for not participating in the 1981 strike.

One rumor about Brooks, heard on the 1981 picket lines, concerned his paranoia about his son Max. Age nine by the time *History*

---

* This Fred Silverman is not to be confused with the former NBC-TV president with the same name.

*of the World, Part I* was released, Max had been diagnosed with dyslexia. His mother went into overdrive to alleviate the disorder, reading classic books to the boy while also introducing him to audiobooks. Bancroft did most of the daily parenting. Although she often said she had sacrificed her career to raise their son, she also worked steadily after his birth; and family friend Frank Langella noted the "huge phalanx" of assistants and nannies who were attached to the Brooks household, including an African American woman who superintended Max's well-being.

Later in life, Max gave interviews emphasizing that the "old-fashioned existence" he had led in Hollywood while growing up had been due to his "overprotective" parents. "My mum was not just overprotective," Max told the *Times* of London in one interview, "she was also a brilliant actress. So she would act out what might happen to me, and because she was raised in the Thirties the bad guy was like some bad gangster. 'Hey kid, come here.'"

Brooks, in his midforties when Max was born, was no laid-back father. His own humble upbringing prompted him to yell at his son one day "because I opened a new box of cereal without finishing the old one. Boy was he mad, I had to go back and eat the dust." Brooks put his foot down a couple of years later when Max asked to camp out in their backyard. "He said, 'What if I wake up tomorrow and you're dead?'" Max recalled. "We had just had the Night Stalker, the guy who used to go around killing people in LA."

The picket-line rumors revolved around a similar fear of Brooks's. The comedy filmmaker imagined the possibility that his young son might be kidnapped by thugs and held for a million-dollar ransom demanded from his celebrity mother and father.

That was why, everyone whispered, Brooks and Bancroft were building such a big, new fortified residence in Santa Monica close to Pacific Palisades. The immense white, four-story stucco structure overlooking the nearby Riviera Country Club golf course had a slanted copper roof and indoor pool. The building was going to be set back forty-four feet from the street and rise thirty-five feet over other residences on La Mesa Drive; it would occupy nearly twelve thousand square feet, easily making it "the largest house in the city," according to Santa Monica planning director Jim Lunsford. The Brookses wanted a six-foot fence around the house and estate (only three-and-a-half-foot fences were normally permitted). Neighbors were fighting the size and style of the design.

Beyond the paranoia, another parental issue influenced the house construction. Max would enter seventh grade in the fall of 1983, and the Brookses planned to enroll him in the Crossroads School for Arts & Sciences, a college preparatory academy with a focus on writing. Their new home was closer to that prep school, which was in Santa Monica.

At Sid Caesar's parties the old friends did not ask directly about such gossip. The norm there was chitchat, jokes, catching up. Wounded warriors of show business, all of them, they were sympathetic to Brooks for all his peccadilloes. Yet Brooks must have known, even if his former colleagues did not say it aloud in his presence, that few among them wholeheartedly loved his post–*Young Frankenstein* films, especially when Sid Caesar himself was in the cast. "Associates and fans from the days of *Your Show of Shows* and *Caesar's Hour*," wrote biographer Will Holtzman, "were genuinely appalled at the irony of seeing Sid Caesar play second banana to Mel, in a silent picture [*Silent Movie*] no less."

Caesar himself could be touchy when questioned about Brooks's fame and success. He told one interviewer he was "a little jealous." Another, pressing him for his reaction to being directed by his one-time protégé, got "It was okay. It didn't make any difference."

Club Caesar's scorn for the Mel Brooks comedies was buried in letters. Imogene Coca, for example, wrote to Lucille Kallen asking if she had seen *History*. Brooks was such "a bad actor," she complained, and the film "such an extravagance of bad taste. . . .

"I thought Sid's episode was the only good thing in it."

Lightning flashes of genius amid a downpour of dreck, Mel Tolkin agreed, corresponding with Kallen. Additionally, it bothered Tolkin that so many of the jokes targeted Jews, or involved sex or toilet jokes. "[Longtime TV writer] Jay Burton [who had bit parts in *High Anxiety* and *History*] had an excellent suggestion for Mel after seeing the movie previewed," Tolkin reported to Kallen. "'Cut two quarts of pee.'"

In 1981, Hollywood's king of comedy was busy fighting public and private affronts, attrition at the box office, crosswinds from his guilds, a creative as well as physical torpor, and a cumulative pile of lawsuits with allegations that did not flatter him.

Before the release of *History of the World, Part I*, Anne Bancroft had accepted a guest role in the Italian Broadcasting Corporation's (RAI) television miniseries *Marco Polo*, from the producers of *Jesus of Nazareth*. Partly the reason was that her pages of the telefilm were going to be shot in Venice, Italy. Bancroft played the explorer's dying mother in the star-studded production. Max accompanied his mother to Venice and watched her enact her death scene. The head of the family came over for sightseeing and beach time. This was the family vacation when, according to accounts, their boy hid out in a beach shack for one day and scribbled his first short story, the quality of which impressed his father.

In the fall of 1981, Bancroft began rehearsals in New York for her first Broadway play since *Golda*, costarring with Max von Sydow in a two-character drama that revealed the angst of a world-class violinist (Bancroft) who is suffering from multiple sclerosis and who experiences revelations in her sessions with a psychiatrist (von Sydow). *Duet for One* was not well received by critics, however, and its run was the shortest Bancroft had ever had on Broadway; it was fated to be her last Broadway appearance.

Still, *Duet* gave the Brookses an excuse to spend some time at their

New York apartment and Fire Island getaway. Brooks never skipped a Bancroft play, never missed the opportunity to visit one of her film sets. His visits—when she was acting, not directing—were always quiet and respectful; he went out of his way to defer to her.

Brooks could surprise people with behavior that seemed the opposite of his reputation: sudden sensitivity or gestures of extravagant generosity. Medical or romantic problems particularly sparked his empathy. Despite his dread of hospitals, nowadays when in New York he regularly stopped by the bed of his Gourmet Club friend, the author Joseph Heller, who had been diagnosed with the debilitating Guillain-Barré syndrome in 1981. One day, similarly but less publicized, Brooks stopped a bit player passing by on the 20th Century–Fox lot, whom he recognized only because every time he spotted the actor he was wearing the same inexpensive, nondescript suit. "Are you fricking insane?" Brooks demanded. "You're here every fricking day with the same fricking clothes on!" The actor, with whom Brooks struck up a friendly relationship, developed obsessive-compulsive disorder (OCD) and suicidal impulses, and Brooks took phone calls from him for twenty years, cheering him up and coaxing him out of despair.

In the mid-1960s, Howard Morris was down on his luck, and one day, strapped for transportation, he borrowed Brooks's black Jaguar, the one left over from Brooks's stint writing for Jerry Lewis, which had always stayed in California. When Morris brought the car back, Brooks said, "That's okay," and handed him the keys with the ownership papers signed over to him.

An acquaintance might comment on the nice new bomber jacket Brooks was wearing, and he might whip off the jacket and hand it over with his compliments.

Even as he lorded it over some people in their contracts, he went out of his way to find work for other people so they would qualify for standard long-term benefits. One day in the *Los Angeles Times*, which kept up a lively pro-and-con debate about Brooks in the letters to the editor, a performer thanked Brooks for having given him a small role in *Spaceballs* "to meet the minimum yearly required earnings for medical insurance coverage for my family." Brooks knew the actor, Ted Sorel, because their children both attended Crossroads. "When I mentioned this thoughtfulness to one of Brooks' associates on the movie, he remarked that I was one of many remembered with similar favors."

At the same time, privately, Brooks's anger and his resentments never quite disappeared, and he could instantly revert to the Rude Crude Mel with cruel quips or verbal assaults on people that burst out of the blue with him and impaired friendships.

Burt Reynolds was one frequent dinner guest at the Brooks/Bancroft abode. He and Brooks were both top-ten box-office stars in the 1970s, and Brooks would phone his friend and begin the conversation with "Hello, Six. This is Five speaking." Reynolds's shower scene in *Silent Movie*, where he was groped by Brooks, Dom DeLuise, and Marty Feldman, was arguably the funniest of the celebrity cameos. Reynolds usually enjoyed Brooks's company, but he recognized his "nasty sense of humor that's hysterical if you're not the brunt of it. I think he considered himself a tough guy. I don't know where he got that idea."

At dinner they often talked about the difficulty of finding worthy projects for Bancroft. One night Brooks suggested that Reynolds, in those days at the height of his box-office prowess, make his wife the costar of a Burt Reynolds film. Reynolds said that was a great idea. "Yeah," Brooks went on, "you'll bring them into the theater, and she'll keep them there." That cut Reynolds "to the quick," the actor recalled, "and I didn't talk to Mel for a long time afterward. We got to be friends again, but it was never the same."

Martin Charnin suffered a worse ordeal, arriving one night at a Chinese restaurant in London where Brooks and other old acquaintances were holding a dinner reservation. Charnin had not seen Brooks in several years, not since Brooks had skyrocketed to fame and fortune as the king of Hollywood comedy. Charnin had been busy developing the musical *Annie*, based on the *Little Orphan Annie* comic strip, which was his brainchild. He'd recruited Charles Strouse for the music, written all the lyrics himself, and directed the show on Broadway, where *Annie* had a six-year run. *Annie's* afterlife—in community theaters and around the globe—would rival that of *Bye Bye Birdie*. Charnin was in London to open *Annie* in the West End. Brooks and the dinner guests had seen the show.

The night started out cordially, but then Brooks veered into a merciless critique of *Annie*, mocking the show and Charnin's success on Broadway, a success that had been denied to him on *"All American"* with both the *Birdie* boys, a field—the stage musical—that Brooks had abandoned for an autobiographical film script, "Marriage Is a Dirty Rotten Fraud," with Charnin as his writing partner. As was often true, Brooks's tirade was disguised with humor, and the dinner guests laughed nervously as he belittled Charnin.

Everyone was laughing except for Charnin, who, hurt and furious, departed vowing never again to speak to Brooks. Charnin thought the evening might not have gone down the same way if Mrs. Brooks had been present. Bancroft might have silenced her husband with a look. But Brooks would be Brooks when Bancroft wasn't around. The actress never reached out to Charnin, and their long professional relationship was over.

One outlet for the Rude Crude Mel was litigation, of which there was a surprising amount after he hit the jackpot with *Blazing Saddles* and *Young Frankenstein*. Though court cases are commonplace in Hollywood, not every celebrity spurred or attracted as many lawsuits. Brooks almost seemed to relish the court actions as another arena in which he could test his gladiatorial skills. And a surprising number of the court cases, moreover, revolved around story origination and rights, issues long entangled in his reputation.

The dispute over the authorship of *Silent Movie* was not reported in the press until one year after the Mel Brooks comedy was released. The complainant, Nathan Cohen, had made documentaries for ABC in the 1960s, then in 1968 directed an admired independent feature called *The Song and the Silence*, depicting a small Jewish family in Poland torn apart by the Holocaust. In the early 1970s, Cohen hatched a story idea with writer Marion Zola, who had another script, a big-band love story, under development by Michael Hertzberg for his company. The two wrote a treatment for a modern silent film set in New York; they called it "Jack and the Lean Talk," as in "Jack and the Beanstalk."

Zola, more the writer, had an agent, who submitted the thirty-three-page treatment to Hertzberg at his New York offices in early 1974. Though the treatment was offered to Hertzberg for development, their submission letter made it clear that they were also thinking of Brooks, for whom Hertzberg had produced *The Producers*, *The Twelve Chairs*, and *Blazing Saddles*. Their story, they said, might have possibilities as a Brooks comedy.

The Zola/Cohen treatment recounted the rags-to-riches tale of a young, idealistic New Yorker who becomes a country-and-western sensation. Their romantic comedy shared little enough with Brooks's eventual *Silent Movie* except for its "major aspect," in Zola's words: "Lean Talk" was proposed as a silent picture, with silent-era title cards.

Hertzberg's office rejected the treatment as "too revolutionary" for two unknown writers, Cohen's agent reported. Until an interview with Brooks in the February 1975 *Newsweek*, mentioning his new project, they had no inkling of *Silent Movie*. "Lean Talk" was worthless now: Hollywood was surely not going to make two silent pictures.

What made the *Silent Movie* allegations even more provocative, however, was the time Zola spent on the West Coast in May 1975, developing her big-band script with Hertzberg. The producer also had offices at 20th Century–Fox, near Brooks's, and one day he took her to meet Brooks. They interrupted a *Silent Movie* script conference with the Club Brooks writers in Brooks's office. Brooks tried to impress or intimidate her, Zola couldn't decide which it was. She warily mentioned that she had written a silent-film script, too. Brooks said that it should have been a comedy. "It *was* a comedy, Mr. Brooks," Zola replied. "Yeah," he returned, "but honey, we're the best comedy writers in the business."

Brooks took Zola over to the bulletin board "to show me the index cards on which he was working," she said in her subsequent deposition. "He stopped work for several minutes to tell me about the process." Elaborating on the process, Brooks "explained a joke that they were building. I suggested a punch line, and he said, 'Great. I'm going to use that.'" When a lawyer asked if it had been used in the film, she replied, "I don't recall."

A month or so later, Brooks announced that Hertzberg had been signed to produce *Silent Movie*. They hadn't worked together since *Blazing Saddles*. Zola and Cohen were "dumbfounded." The writers discussed filing a lawsuit against Brooks and Hertzberg, but decided to hold off until seeing *Silent Movie* one year later in the summer of 1976.

They had been cheated, they decided, after seeing the film. Besides the "major aspect," they noticed a few gags shared by their treatment and *Silent Movie*, including Marcel Marceau's single spoken word of dialogue, which echoed a moment toward the end of "Lean Talk," when sound is also heard for the first and only time on the soundtrack: applause.

The "Lean Talk" writers decided that Cohen should take the lead on the lawsuit so Zola could pursue her other writing projects. It took him a while to organize a lawyer on the West Coast and file in court in April 1977, alleging plagiarism and breach of confidence. That was over three years since the inception of "Lean Talk" and the submission of their treatment to Hertzberg. The long interval plus the typical court delays allowed Brooks's lawyers to concentrate their defense on two grounds: that a contemporary silent film was a public domain concept too broad to be plagiarized and that the statute of limitations had run out on any breach of trust inherent in their spec script submission.

When Brooks was deposed, he insisted that his knowledge of "Lean Talk" was vague, stemming from the lawsuit itself, and he adamantly denied any piracy or knowledge of piracy, saying that *Silent Movie* had been entirely Ron Clark's brainchild. He said he had never solicited "creative advice" from Hertzberg. The producer had been paid his salary of $100,000, Brooks said, for organizing and supervising a production crew. "He can stick his two cents in every once in a while" creatively, "but it's not required and it's not paid for," he explained. "He could never just tell me something was funny or unfunny."

Brooks, in his depositions for that case and others, cracked jokes to entertain the lawyers in the room, to the point where, one day, Cohen's lawyer asked him to cut it out and take the interrogatory seriously. Likewise, more than once he had to be reminded not to make funny faces or gestures in response to queries but to use words for the record.

The case dragged on until late 1981, when the court ordered a "mandatory settlement conference," which is something judges do when they feel both sides have an equivalence of facts and legal basis. It is not rare for aggrieved parties to receive financial compensation to end protracted litigation, especially in Hollywood, and often production company contracts carry insurance clauses to absorb such costs, which need not concern the filmmaker unnecessarily. Nor is money always tendered without cause. Cohen and Zola received undisclosed sums to end the suit, so it never went to open court.

• • •

Joseph Merrick's story was arguably in the public domain, too: Merrick had died in 1890, and Dr. Frederick Treves's book about the Elephant Man, which popularized the tale, was originally published in 1923. In any event, copyright law was generally liberal on the fact- or history-based life stories of famous people now deceased, as opposed to fictional versions of their lives, a distinction that would bear on future lawsuits involving Brooks.

There was, however, the prominent play with the same title as the Brooksfilms production. Written by Bernard Pomerance, *The Elephant Man* debuted in London at the Hampstead Theatre in 1977 before shifting in repertory to the National Theatre, then in 1978 to off-Broadway and finally to Broadway, where the play initiated a long run and won a Tony.

According to his memoir, Brooksfilms producer Jonathan Sanger did not learn of the stage version, surprisingly, until Brooks's secretary phoned him in October 1978 to tell him that *The Elephant Man* had arrived from London, with "ecstatic" reviews for its off-Broadway production. The Brooksfilms version of Joseph Merrick's story was already well under way, Sanger wrote later, based on the script that his babysitter had handed to him, written by her boyfriend and a partner, based on the anthropologist Ashley Montagu's 1971 book. Montagu's book, however, drew its account almost wholesale from Dr. Treves's.

"We still had the option on Ashley Montagu's book," Sanger said, "but of course I knew that gave us no legal position." Soon afterward, Sanger met with Brooks, who was "quite pragmatic," Sanger wrote. "He had no intention of abandoning the project."

"Look," Brooks said, "they don't own the Elephant Man. Just their version of it. And the transition from their play to a movie will not be easy. It's a stylized play. Let's just stay on the track we're on. This isn't the first time there's been a competing project."

Their working title was the same as Pomerance's. Brooks liked batting titles around, and for a while they considered other "mostly ludicrous" titles, until Brooks called in a specialist, Bert Fields, "the renowned entertainment lawyer," Sanger wrote, "a friend of Mel's," to parse the issues. Although a title could not be copyrighted, the renowned lawyer explained, the playwright could invoke the question of "secondary meaning," i.e., "a developed association in the public's mind," according to the Merriam-Webster Law Dictionary, to stop another confusing use of the same title. However, "secondary meaning" was difficult to prove in a courtroom, and Fields was confident that he could build "a tidy case around the title issue with plays and other works that were unable to make the precedent."

Sure enough, ten months later, after winning the Tony Award for Best Play that year, Pomerance and his producers filed suit against Brooks's production company, arguing that their "valuable property rights" would be diluted by the film called *The Elephant Man*, then in preproduction in London. The suit did "not object to Brooks' production of the film," *Variety* reported, "only to his use of their title." Brooks and the soon-to-be-renamed Brooksfilms countersued for damage to his reputation, claiming a right to the title.

At their first legal conference, Brooks reminded Sanger "that it would be best, regardless of our curiosity, for all of us, the writers, [director] David [Lynch], me and our office staff, to avoid seeing the play." While taking pains to point out big differences between Pomerance's play and the eventual Brooksfilms production, Sanger admitted in his memoir that he himself rushed to New York to see the play "early in its run," shortly after getting the call from Brooks's secretary. He "never mentioned" that to Brooks.

Whether the two scenarists, Christopher De Vore and Eric Bergren, saw Pomerance's play in London or New York, or whether Brooks himself saw it, is unknown; Brooks attended nearly every important play on his frequent visits to London, and that went double for New York, especially plays that won Tonys. Whether they saw the Pomerance play remains unclear because the court records are sealed and a nondisclosure clause accompanied the eventual settlement as it often does. Brooks was allowed to capitalize on a hit play with a film of the same title. Pomerance declined to comment for this book.*

Another court case involving Brooks, story origination, and a public domain defense was the lawsuit surrounding *Frances*. The life story of actress Frances Farmer, whose meteoric Hollywood career was marred by abuse and tragedy, *Frances* was another example of a superserious Brooksfilms production, the one that immediately followed *The Elephant Man*, released in 1982. Starring Jessica Lange, who was Oscar nominated for her lead performance, the production also involved producer Jonathan Sanger and scenarists Christopher De Vore and Eric Bergren, who had help on the script from Nicholas Kazan.

One of the people who filed suit against *Frances* had met with the comedian in New York, back in early 1978, when Brooks was giving interviews to promote *High Anxiety*. William Arnold was the film critic for the *Seattle Post-Intelligencer*, the morning daily of the largest city in the state of Washington, dubbed "Movietown USA" for its avid film-going population. Arnold was also the author of the forthcoming book *Shadowland*, a biography of Farmer, a native of Seattle, which was due to be published by McGraw-Hill in mid-1978. His searching biography integrated scrutiny of the facts of the actress's memoir with his own reportage and research into her shadowy life, deploying himself in the narrative as a character who falls in love with Farmer as he digs for the truth.

Accompanied by Susan Stanley, a reviewer for the *Oregon Journal*, a Portland daily, Arnold met Brooks at the Manhattan offices of 20th Century–Fox. "The three of us talked for more than two hours," Arnold recalled. "It went way beyond an interview to be this

---

* Playwright Bernard Pomerance died in August 2017.

profound and very personal conversation about the meaning of life." They also discussed Arnold's book about Frances Farmer. Brooks was "quite interested," Arnold said. "At the end of this love fest, we were all misty-eyed, and Mel actually kissed each of us on the cheek. I got his autograph, addressed to my infant daughter, the only time I've ever asked for one. I thought he was one of the grandest human beings I had ever met."

Arnold already had partners for a prospective screen adaptation. The actress Tippi Hedren's husband, producer Noel Marshall, had optioned the book under the auspices of Marie Yates, an aspiring producer acting as Arnold's Hollywood literary agent, who had read an early version of the manuscript. As part of the deal, Yates also contracted with Marshall to coproduce the Frances Farmer biopic based on Arnold's book. While Marshall was preoccupied with producing another film, Yates assisted Arnold's writing of the first-draft script. That script, credited to him alone, was dated March 1979.

Marshall and Yates experienced a falling-out, however, and Arnold felt torn between the two people. Yates phoned not long after Arnold's New York meeting with Brooks. She said she had another producer on tap, "one much more prominent than Noel Marshall, who would finance me in a lawsuit to wrest the rights away from Noel so I can sell them to him," according to Arnold. The much more prominent producer was Brooks.

Yates asked Arnold to come to Hollywood for a parley with Brooks. Arnold thought, without yet deciding against Marshall, "Gee, it would sure be great to see my pal Mel again." He flew to Los Angeles, meeting first with Yates, her husband, and their lawyer, undergoing "a lengthy briefing on the legal basis by which Mel Brooks' team of attorneys would get the film rights back to me." He, Yates, and the lawyer then drove to 20th Century–Fox and proceeded to the administration building, climbing the stairs to Brooks's third-floor office. Brooks was busy in an adjoining conference room, "through which I could occasionally make out the name of Frances Farmer in muffled conversation. After more than an hour had passed, the door finally opened and we were ushered in."

Brooks was "not noticeably" happy to see his old pal. "As we shook hands, he couldn't have been any colder," said Arnold. "He didn't even smile. When I alluded to our earlier happy meeting in New York, he said he didn't remember it." The group all sat down at a long conference table, Brooks at one end, Arnold at the other, between them Yates, her lawyer, three attorneys representing Brooks, and other members of his staff. "The air was solemn, with little cheerful small talk or the usual social niceties."

Brooks launched into a monologue saying he had decided to make a movie about Frances Farmer's life and thought *Shadowland* would be "the best source for it." He was prepared to finance a lawsuit against Marshall, who in his view had in various ways defaulted on his obligations. Brooks's attorneys had advised him that they could get a quick judgment.

"Then the monologue got weird," Arnold recalled. Brooks said he understood from Yates that Arnold wanted to contribute to the script and be part of "the movie team." That was not going to happen, declared Brooks. He wanted this project for "his boys," who were the writers of the *Elephant Man* script, Christopher De Vore and Eric Bergren. Arnold would have "no input into the script, and my only connection to the movie would be an invitation to its premiere. Then he went on to tell me that I was 'nothing' in his eyes and that he was an important filmmaker and how I should be happy that he was willing to have anything to do with me. He went on with this theme for some time. I mean an eerily long time. It turned into a rant, with me the object of his anger. He kept [saying] that he loathed journalists and didn't like having anything to do with them."

Arnold felt stunned; he didn't utter a word, thinking the whole situation was unreal. Yates and her lawyer squirmed in their seats. "The gallery of yes-men were punctuating Mel's pronouncements with wise nods and every so often seconding his comments with a 'That's right, Mel!'" similar to the scene with the studio mogul and his troop of flunkies knocking one another down to light the mogul's cigar in *Silent Movie*.

Brooks ended his monologue on a dire note, recalled Arnold, declaring "in so many words that if I didn't go along with him, he could go ahead and make the movie anyway because it was about a public domain figure and he didn't really need to buy the book."

Brooks exited. One of his retinue, realizing that Arnold was livid, apologized: "Mel's bark is worse than his bite." Arnold's side repaired to a cocktail lounge to lick their wounds. Yates was in tears. Her lawyer told Arnold he had heard Brooks was the kind of guy who liked to "brutally humiliate an employee in public and then buy him a new car."

The dazed Arnold told Yates he was not interested in any partnership with Brooks. ("I didn't want to be in the same hemisphere with him," Arnold recalled.) The despondent Yates tried to talk Arnold into accepting Brooks's offer anyway. Arnold said no. Months passed. Zoetrope and Francis Ford Coppola evinced an interest in *Shadowland*. Then one day, at the end of October 1980, Arnold read in *Variety* that Brooksfilms was going to produce a biopic on Frances Farmer with Jonathan Sanger sharing the "production duties" with an expert on the sad life story of the actress: Yates, Arnold's agent, was the said expert.

Arnold was shocked, although not devastated. "I didn't think Marie could get away with it," he said. "I also didn't think Mel Brooks could get away with it. . . . He wanted to make *Shadowland*, as he said to me face to face and in front of witnesses. My unique and very personal take on the subject. To the point of hiring a woman whose only qualification for the job of his coproducer was her fiduciary relationship to me."

Sanger flew to Seattle for another stab at diplomacy in the living room of Arnold's house on Queen Anne Hill. "The thinking was, probably, that away from Brooks and Marshall, the two of us would hit it off and become pals and come to terms." That did not happen. "It was like my second Brooks meeting all over," with Sanger repeating Brooks's cold admonitions. Prepared to be conciliatory, Arnold felt doubly insulted.

Arnold joined Marshall in filing a suit against Brooks and Brooksfilms. The discovery process obliged Brooksfilms to show script drafts to the plaintiffs as the case progressed. "It became apparent," said Arnold, "they were barely even trying to disguise the fact that they were doing a film version of *Shadowland*. The same structure and arc . . . essentially the same progression of scenes. It used surmised dialogue from the book or the screenplay I had done, much of it word for word. It was totally the same vision."

One difference was a character expressly crafted for the film, inspired by a real-life private eye cited in Arnold's book. Sam Shepard portrays the character in the film who became the stand-in for Arnold, who is the narrator of the events in the book.

Brooksfilms sold the project to Universal. Much of *Frances* was subsequently shot on location in Seattle, adding to Arnold's public humiliation. He was offered settlements but steadfastly refused them. Thus the *Shadowland* lawsuit became the rare Brooks legal case to actually wind up in a Los Angeles courtroom in February 1983.

A law firm represented the author pro bono, so convinced was the firm that the facts were on their side and the potential payoff was great. The plaintiffs could prove Yates's prior contractual relationship with Marshall and Arnold; they had witnesses to Brooks praising *Shadowland* as the best story source and "also the ace in the hole of the screenplay adaptation I had written and Yates had read," in Arnold's words, "which had more than the five points of similarity needed in a plagiarism suit: indeed, whole scenes."

Though Arnold believed his legal team did their utmost and

were like the "good guys" in a John Grisham thriller, they made one unwise decision, which was a late addition to their brief: they decided to characterize Shadowland as a "nonfiction novel"—that is, a nonfiction work of New Journalism with fictional elements. Categorizing it as a novel would strengthen their argument for copyright protection, they believed.

The case was heard not by a jury but by a judge, Malcolm M. Lucas, a staunch conservative, later the chief justice of the California Supreme Court. Brooks's flotilla of lawyers fixated on the "novelistic" definition, hammering away at the question of whether "nonobjective journalism or history written with the techniques and freedom of the novel deserve any of the copyright protection of fiction," in Arnold's words.

Brooks was the star witness of the proceedings. "My heart sank when he took the stand because I could tell the judge was excited to see him there," recalled Arnold. Although Brooks had been "nasty and defensive" earlier in the case, when deposed, his "whole manner changed [on the stand], and he was very deferential." Through one entire day of testimony the king of Hollywood comedy was "incredibly humble and endearing. I was even liking him again. He made a very favorable impression on the judge."

Still and all, the plaintiffs' lawyers thought they were bound to win the case on the merits. One month later, however, Judge Lucas ruled against them, dismissing the collusion charges and scolding Marshall and Arnold's legal team "for the gall of arguing that a book that was widely regarded as nonfiction deserved the protection of fiction," in Arnold's words. "The tactic was even more of a misfire than I feared. It made the judge furious at us."

Arnold's pro bono legal team decided they could no longer pursue his case on a contingency basis. Brooks's lawyers offered to forgive their side of the court costs if there was no appeal; if Arnold and Marshall lost, they might have to bear all the costs. The case was over.

Yates, paid $100,000 and low net points on a film that probably never turned a profit, was credited as "coproducer" and never had any credit on another Hollywood picture. Sanger, in his memoir *Making the Elephant Man*, states without elaboration that he "brought" *Frances* to Brooks as a project. He doesn't mention Arnold or the lawsuit.

# CHAPTER 14

# 1983

---

## Why So Angry?

Brooks could supervise Brooksfilms productions with his left hand ("I spend about 30 per cent of my time on Brooksfilms," he told an interviewer) while making Mel Brooks comedies with his right. The Brooksfilms projects were more of a hobby, while the filmography of his comedies was going to be etched on his gravestone, like John Carradine's credits on the door to his office in the scene from *Blazing Saddles* that was never shot.

Brooks was the decider in chief. Only he could say yes to producing any particular film under the company banner. He oversaw the subjects and scripts, the major casting, the choice of director, and, almost always, he got involved in the editing and scoring of the Brooksfilms productions. He was capable of inserting himself into the production process at any stage, and then, although not always, he was capable of shrewd decision making.

The Brooksfilms non-comedies were touted as the bleak antitheses of Brooks's comedies. An adaptation of Toni Morrison's *Tar Baby* to star Howard Rollins; a film of the Pulitzer Prize–winning playwright Marsha Norman's novel *The Fortune Teller*; an adaptation of John Fante's Depression-era *Ask the Dust*; a partnership with the Dutch filmmaker Paul Verhoeven to chronicle the life of "Jesus the Man," based on the research "of the New Testament scholars who vote on the authenticity of sayings attributed to Christ"; a collaboration with the South African playwright Athol Fugard on "an epic film about apartheid"—those were among the wishful Brooksfilms projects announced, explored, never actualized.

Occasionally Brooks himself considered directing a serious, dramatic Brooksfilms project, and he almost did just that in the case of the same folktale that had inspired the farcical television series *When Things Were Rotten*. Quietly, in the early 1980s, he commissioned an earnest film, mixed with a little humor—not much—about Robin Hood.

He did not pay for many screenplays without filming them, but in this instance he hired Clive Exton to script an account of Robin and his band of merry men and their exploits in Sherwood Forest. Unlike most first-time writers associated with Brooksfilms, Exton boasted BBC credits and top-notch big-screen dramas, including a version of Emlyn Williams's psychological thriller *Night Must Fall* with Albert Finney and *10 Rillington Place* about the British serial killer John Christie. In 1982, Exton was paid handsomely for a foundational draft called "Robin Hood." Brooks planned to add in some comedy later (Marty Feldman and Spike Milligan were rumored to be joining the cast).

There was no part in Exton's script for Brooks to play, however; he was going to stay behind the camera—the first time since *Young Frankenstein*. Furthermore, Brooks was intending to direct the Robin Hood drama/comedy in England, which had always been a dream of his: to direct an English picture entirely on English soil.

20th Century–Fox was not interested, however, largely because Brooks, continuing the trend of his contract negotiations, wanted a bigger cut for himself of certain foreign markets, beginning with England itself. So in Mel-on-a-mission style he took the idea across town to Columbia Pictures. But Columbia also harbored doubts about a "Robin Hood" drama with Brooks directing—without his comedic presence on the screen—so for the first time Brooks sought public sector financing to ameliorate the budget. The Wall Street firm of D. H. Blair & Co. was recruited to raise the $8 million that was considered necessary. Columbia would control the world rights, but Brooks would get the percentages 20th Century–Fox had balked at conceding. Be that as it may, the deal remained too daring for both Columbia and Wall Street, and the serious "Robin Hood" was shelved after months of effort. Brooks could have fought harder, he could have done the film cheaper without his preferred financial guarantees, but he didn't care to take the risks, and, as was true for much of his career, he'd get paid better for an easier path with his characteristic comedy.

During this busy time of producing, which coincided with his court performance in the *Frances* lawsuit, Brooks probably worked hardest on the script for another Brooksfilms production that was going to be directed by someone else. Yet it was the rare Brooksfilms production that was also a comedy and, curiously, the most autobiographical film he'd ever make, the type of which he'd attempted only once before with "Marriage Is a Dirty Rotten Fraud."

*My Favorite Year* began in 1979 when Dennis Palumbo, a writer of television sitcoms, pitched a script to Michael Gruskoff about Wyatt Earp going to New York at the turn of the century in order to promote his memoir. The story revolved around the relationship between Earp and a young publicist designated to keep the lawman sober. Gruskoff thought the idea was doomed by its period setting, and he encouraged Palumbo to develop a similar yarn about a wayward movie star who must be babysat by a young comedy writer during his guest appearance on a *Your Show of Shows*–type variety series. Absent from Brooks's circle since *Young Frankenstein*, during which time he had produced other motion pictures, including *Rafferty and the Gold Dust Twins* and *Lucky Lady*, Gruskoff molded the idea for Brooks, seeing it as a chapter torn from the comedian's life.

Brooks huddled with Palumbo, trying to inject his concepts into the script drafts. The fading movie star became Errol Flynn, and the working title became "In like Flynn." But Palumbo and Brooks never enjoyed any chemistry. Palumbo resisted Brooks's pet notions, and his drafts disappointed the boss; partly, according to Brooksfilms sources, because Palumbo hailed from Pittsburgh and the pivotal Brooks character, a junior writer who is assigned to manage the hard-living movie star, came from the Bronx in Palumbo's drafts. Palumbo stubbornly refused to make the kid from Brooklyn. Palumbo was too Pittsburgh, Brooks didn't care for the Bronx, and Palumbo didn't know Brooklyn.

Brooks ended up phoning Norman Steinberg, another member of Club Brooks, who had been out of the loop since *When Things Were Rotten* had gone off the air in 1975. Steinberg had turned down several writing jobs from Brooks in the intervening years, feeling ill suited to the projects on offer. But he had batted two for two with Brooks as part of the *Blazing Saddles* writing team and as producer of the Robin Hood television comedy series; the friends felt they were good-luck charms for each other. Also, Steinberg's writing evinced the warmth and sweetness that "In like Flynn" needed.

Brooks pitched the story excitedly in his salesman mode ("Mel Brooks meets Errol Flynn on *Your Show of Shows!*"), pointing out the inadequacies of Palumbo's drafts and the long road ahead. A fan of *Your Show of Shows*, Steinberg was instantly hooked.

"Norman," finished Brooks, "I need you very badly, but I can't pay you enough."

"Can't or won't?" asked Steinberg, knowing his man.

A long pause followed before Brooks replied, "One of those two."

Steinberg, who never cared enough about the money, said yes: "I'll do it for whatever you want to pay me." But the writer had a couple of nonfinancial stipulations: he did not want to forgo his writing credit this time; nor did he want to share the credit with a long scroll of other people. And he especially did not want to share the writing credit with Brooks, whose name had automatically come to overshadow everyone else's.

Steinberg could not do anything about Palumbo, who was guaranteed his "original story" credit and, because Palumbo had written several drafts, a cocredit on the screenplay. But Steinberg wanted to see his name first in the script credits, before Palumbo's, just the two of them with no one else's name on the screen. Not even Brooks's.

Swallowing hard, Brooks said yes.

The other proviso was, if anything, even harder for him to accept.

"I'm not going to write you into the story as the young comedy writer," Steinberg told Brooks.

"Why?" Brooks demanded.

"Because you're too abrasive. I'm going to write myself."

Another long pause. "Okay," Brooks said with a sigh, "go ahead."

Steinberg quietly put in a few years of work, consulting with Brooks and writing multiple drafts. The Brooks character became Benjy Stone, who has changed his name from the too-obviously-Jewish Benjamin Steinberg (as in Norman Steinberg) to join the American melting pot. Stone narrates the story, reminiscing about his favorite year: 1954. That was the year the youngest writer on a hit network show known as "Comedy Cavalcade" was called upon to superintend an aging, hell-raising movie star. Steinberg also changed the star: no longer the real-life Errol Flynn, now the fictional Alan Swann.

The Sid Caesar character was also sculpted into Stan "King" Kaiser, who reigns dictatorially over "Comedy Cavalcade." Other good parts were fashioned for an ingenue in the form of K. C. Downing, the chief assistant to the Max Liebman stand-in, and Belle Carroca, to be played by an older actress, the overbearingly Jewish (despite her own exotic name change) mother of Benjy Stone. There was also a beleaguered writers' room with a tower-of-Jell-O head writer, a Lucille Kallen type, and a Neil Simon–like whisperer.

In the story line Stone haplessly woos Downing; and he accompanies Swann to Brooklyn's Ocean Parkway—which echoed Brooks's own past, near where he had once lived—for a boisterous dinner with Stone's mother surrounded by starstruck relatives and neighbors.

Steinberg wrote the screenplay "totally alone," he said, but Brooks made himself constantly available for input and *Your Show of Shows* reminiscences. "I had Mel's editorial help," Steinberg remembered, "and he's a great editor, and a great, great story confrere. We worked together a lot, I saw him a lot during that time, and I loved being with him."

The script had glints of Brooks: nods to Buicks, Chinese food, and Al Jolson. (Benjy Stone admires the same comedy pantheon as Brooks: the Marx Brothers "except for Zeppo," the Ritz Brothers, and Laurel and Hardy; however, Steinberg added one for the laugh: Woody Woodpecker.) Yet the script was also as different as night and day from other Mel Brooks comedies. There was chronological continuity. Characters breathed humanity and had emotional arcs. The humor was farcical, but the only F-word was "humping."

Brooks took the package to MGM, where his onetime agent David Begelman, rebounding from his embezzlement scandal at Columbia Pictures, was now ensconced as president and CEO. The script was ready for location work in New York in October 1981, with Brooks okaying actor Richard Benjamin—best known as a droll comedic presence in such films as *Goodbye, Columbus, Diary of a Mad Housewife*, and *Portnoy's Complaint*—as the first-time director. Benjamin could rely on cameraman Gerald Hirschfeld, who'd shot *Goodbye, Columbus, Diary of a Mad Housewife*, and *Young Frankenstein* for Brooks.

After trying for Albert Finney, once more in vain, Brooks snared another of the consummate English actors he worshipped, Peter O'Toole of *Lawrence of Arabia*, to play Swann. (O'Toole richly deserved his subsequent Oscar nomination.) Actor-writer Joseph Bologna, whose wife, Renée Taylor, had played Eva Braun in *The Producers* and who had appeared in a failed sitcom pilot with Taylor produced by Brooks in 1971, made King Kaiser almost as watchable as Sid

Caesar. The eventual screen credits said that the film was "introducing" Mark Linn-Baker as Stone, because his debut in Woody Allen's *Manhattan* had been left mostly on the cutting room floor. A Yale School of Drama MFA graduate, Linn-Baker had the required puppy face and boyish likability.*

Jessica Harper would be fetching as K. C. Downing, and Lainie Kazan put all of her pizzazz into Jewish mother Belle Carroca. Bill Macy was the pompous head writer, Anne De Salvo and (the whisperer) Basil Hoffman were his colleagues. Other solid parts went to veteran Cameron Mitchell as a labor racketeer objecting to King Kaiser's merciless impersonation of him on television; lyricist Adolph Green as the Max Liebman–ish Leo Silver; and Club Caesar member Selma Diamond as a wisecracking wardrobe mistress.

As was customary on Brooksfilms productions, the namesake stayed out of the way during the filming. He was usually more active in pre- and postproduction. Producer Stuart Cornfeld told a story about the time they had shown a first cut of *The Elephant Man* to Paramount executives. Soon after, Brooks had gotten a call from studio officials with their comments, which began with not liking the beginning or the ending—"too oblique." Brooks replied slowly, his voice rising in volume. "We showed you the cut," he said, "because we are involved in a business deal and we wanted to bring you up to date on the progress of the product we're working on. Don't misconstrue that as soliciting the input of raging primitives!" Then he slammed down the phone. "Mel at his best," Cornfeld recalled.

Brooksfilms productions were modestly budgeted on principle, and director Richard Benjamin recalled how Mel went commando one day when he had discovered that the film needed more money to accommodate the schedule. Benjamin asked Brooks to make an

---

* A few years later on Broadway, Linn-Baker would play another Club Caesar writer, the Mel Tolkin character, in *Laughter on the 23rd Floor*, Neil Simon's re-creation of *Your Show of Shows*.

appointment with David Begelman in his MGM office. "No, no, we can't go into an office," Brooks told Benjamin. "You go into an office, you don't get anything. They take phone calls, they don't pay attention, they [have to] go to another meeting." Brooks said they would ambush Begelman in the hallway at lunchtime, not before lunch, when he'd be hungry, but after "a nice big lunch, we get on him on the way back." Benjamin said okay. ("I hadn't heard about this in film school or anywhere else," Benjamin noted.)

They go to MGM, wait in the corridor. Begelman comes down the hall, Brooks grabs him. "Hi ya, David, how ya doing?" Brooks cracks three or four jokes as they all walk together toward Begelman's office, with Begelman laughing at the jokes, moving all the time. "Then Mel says to him, just before we hit his office doorway, 'David, do you got any cash on you?' He said, 'Why?' Mel said, 'The kid'—that was me—'the kid here needs $300,000 to finish the picture.' 'Really?' he asks." Begelman turns to George Justin, the production manager, who is with them in the hallway. "Is that true?" Justin nods. Begelman says, "Alright, give them the money," and he's still laughing, and then suddenly "he's laughing not quite as much, and he has a look on his face like what happened here?—and he's in his office." Brooks asks, "Do you need anything else?" Benjamin says, "Uh-uh, not now." "And he's gone . . . like Lamont Cranston, the Shadow. . . . He was there and then he was not there. It's the Mel school of how to make movies."

Like most of the Brooksfilms productions, *My Favorite Year* was not expected to be a big moneymaker, and boffo it was not. Yet none, with the exception of *The Elephant Man*, collected better reviews. Gary Arnold, who had excoriated most of Mel Brooks's comedies in the *Washington Post*, acclaimed the film as exuberant and "superlative." Although she lamented its sentimental streak (referring to the subplot of Swann's estrangement from his young daughter, raised in Connecticut by his divorced wife), Janet Maslin in the *New York Times* described *My Favorite Year* as "occasionally inspired, always snappy, and never less than amusing." Sheila Benson hailed the comedy as "effervescent" in the *Los Angeles Times*, while Pauline Kael in *The New Yorker* said the film bubbled with invention and authentic performances, especially that of the "simply astounding" O'Toole.

One informal group of Brooks skeptics was pleasantly surprised. Club Caesar members noted how the film about *Your Show of Shows* departed from the reality: Benjy Stone softened Brooks and turned him into a heroic figure, Mel Tolkin complained to Lucille Kallen. Brooks never babysat a drunk, Tolkin pointed out in a letter to Kallen; indeed, his constant clowning, Tolkin thought, might have enabled Caesar's alcoholism. And the backstage scenes portraying the writing and producing of the TV show were silly. Still, even Tolkin confessed that he found *My Favorite Year* "in some way, sort of sweet."

Other compatriots of Sid Caesar, in Hollywood and on the East Coast, in letters, and at social events, said they thought Brooks had done well—this kind of thing he never did.

Brooks could be justly proud. In a reflective interview three decades later, he commented on the three major works by different Club Caesar writers that had attempted to reimagine the special alchemy of *Your Show of Shows*. The first show to touch on the experience was Carl Reiner's hit television series *The Dick Van Dyke Show*; the only movie was *My Favorite Year*; then there was Neil Simon's *Laughter on the 23rd Floor*, which came along on Broadway in 1993 with a character, Ira Stone, closely modeled after Brooks, whom Simon's script describes as "all energy with a touch of madness."

"Which one came the closest to getting it right?" the interviewer asked.

"None of us," Brooks quickly replied. "We're all near misses. No one could get the exact feelings, the rhythms. You can only approximate."

Brooks went on. "The funniest writers' room I thought was on *The Dick Van Dyke Show*, but they were very honest. They didn't try to exactly approximate the composition of the [*Your Show of Shows*] room."

Neil Simon "did the best job in terms of getting the real stuff" about what went on in the writers' room in *Laughter on the 23rd Floor*, Brooks said.

"I think we were the best at [getting the characterization of] Sid Caesar" and the guest stars such as Alan Swann/Errol Flynn in *My Favorite Year*, Brooks concluded.

He spoiled it only a little by claiming too much credit for himself, as was his wont, in later interviews. On the Club Caesar reunion panel in front of a Writers Guild audience, he said, "I gave [Norman Steinberg] chapter and verse of everything we did." And "My mother put on her wedding dress to make *kugel* and *latkes* for Sid Caesar."

Brooks insisted, moreover, that he himself had escorted Errol Flynn around New York back in the day, prepping the aging star for his appearance on *Your Show of Shows*. "I was locked in the Waldorf Towers with Errol Flynn and two red-headed Cuban sisters," he insisted. "For three days, I was trying to get them out of there, and he was trying to get me drunk. It was the craziest weekend of my life. I was twenty years old."

Everyone in Club Caesar knew that to be dubious, and legions of Flynn fans have tried in vain to fact-check Brooks's boast. "The truth of the matter," said Norman Steinberg with a sigh, "is Errol Flynn was never on *Your Show of Shows*. It was Basil Rathbone on *Your Show of Shows*. Once the film was made, as far as Mel is concerned, the story becomes Mel and Errol Flynn have gone to the Waldorf with two Cuban girls—okay, fine. I don't want to refute those things. I don't want to say it's bullshit."

Despite its R rating, *History of the World, Part I* continued the downward slide of box-office receipts and reviews for the three 20th

Century–Fox comedies of Brooks's that followed *Young Frankenstein*. Under pressure to reverse the trend and innovate, Brooks revived the idea of a remake of an Ernst Lubitsch gem, *To Be or Not to Be*, with his wife, Anne Bancroft, as costar.

Seven years had gone by since 1975, when the remake had been initiated and abandoned after James Kirkwood, Jr., had written a draft of the script. The original producer, Bancroft's high school friend David Lunney, had quit the American Film Institute and moved to Portland, Oregon, where he was running the Oregon Repertory Theatre.

20th Century–Fox would have been happier about its revenue from Brooks's comedies if not for deepening inflation, the escalating budgets of his vehicles, and his steep contract sweeteners. By hosting Brooks on its lot, the studio was also helping to support the "serious" Brooksfilms productions, but the most prestigious ones were being parceled out to other studios. Wouldn't remaking a vintage sophisticated comedy anointed by the Lubitsch touch, with Brooks costarring with his wife, an Oscar-winning actress, be one way of wedding the superserious Brooksfilms productions with the wacky Mel Brooks comedies?

By early 1982, Brooks and 20th Century–Fox had agreed on parameters, and the "Re-Do of Ernst Lubitsch" was announced in the trades. The "Re-Do" would stick to the time frame and setting of the original: Poland before and during the Nazi invasion and occupation, from August 1939 to September 1941. While the original film had been photographed in black and white, the "Re-Do" would be made in color. "Brooks will essay the role that Jack Benny originated as a hammy matinee idol with a penchant for playing Hamlet," *Variety* reported. Bancroft would portray his wife, the lead actress of his troupe, who flirts with a handsome Polish officer in the audience. "After the invasion, the stock company upsets German officers and Gestapo with various impersonations, including one of Hitler."

The most eye-opening detail about the "Re-Do," which was promised in time for Christmas 1983, was that Brooks would neither write nor direct. Ronny Graham and Thomas Meehan were going to team up as the scenarists, and Brooks's longtime choreographer Alan Johnson would sit in the director's chair. 20th Century–Fox would bankroll and distribute the film worldwide, although the announcement said little more about the financial details, suggesting that Brooks had backed away from demanding additional foreign or ancillary market shares.

Brooks did not want Robert Towne or James Kirkwood. He needed "his boys," a new Club Brooks. His longtime friend Ronny Graham had spent a decade in a professional Siberia of his own devising after his first career triumphs. The multifaceted performer had notoriously served months in jail in 1967–1968 for nonpayment of alimony. The hard years had taken a toll on his looks; now he was best described as "a handsome gargoyle," in Brooks's words. ("Often inept in life," Brooks later eulogized his friend, "but always ept in art.") Graham had rebounded as a writer for TV's *M*A*S*H*, and he would bring to the job the old camaraderie, a musical knack, and a lunacy to match the boss's.

As for Thomas Meehan, he had haunted the periphery of Club Brooks for years, while working often with Martin Charnin in television and on Broadway. A native of Ossining, New York, the rare Catholic among Brooks's pool of Jewish writers, Meehan had graduated from Hamilton College and done a stint in the army, afterward taking an editorial job at *The New Yorker*. There he had written short pieces, including "Yma Dream" in 1962, which later became Bancroft's funniest monologue in "Annie: The Women in the Life of a Man." In 1977, he had won a Tony for writing the book for *Annie*. Meehan was a meticulous writer, mild-mannered to a fault, with a sweet temperament that rivaled Graham's.

Both Graham and Meehan were Brooks contemporaries; like him, they could have seen *To Be or Not to Be* in its first release. Neither had scripted a film before. They faced a daunting task: the 1942 comedy, with its original story by Melchior Lengyel and script by Edwin Justus Mayer, was admired as one of Lubitsch's best and bravest. It mingled, during World War II, anti-Nazi fervor, tight-rope suspense, and sparkling humor.

According to Meehan, Brooks regarded the Lubitsch classic as "slightly dated." The writers spent the first few days debating a modernized title, which Brooks favored, but they ultimately couldn't agree on a viable alternative. *To Be or Not to Be* would be less applicable to the remake because Brooks wanted to substitute a vaudeville-style troupe for the dramatic repertory company in the Lubitsch version, in order to have musical numbers and openings for his "off-the-wall zaniness," in Meehan's words. In the "Re-Do," Brooks's character, Frederick Bronski ("world famous in Poland"), would perform only "highlights from Shakespeare" as a break from the vaudeville material or, as things would transpire in the new script, as a forced substitution for Nazi-censored fare.

One significant departure was how Hitler himself would be depicted in the remake. In Lubitsch's *To Be or Not to Be*, the real Hitler is glimpsed twice from behind: once entering the theater for the climactic play within the film and once in his box. Meanwhile, a faux Hitler prepares himself; one of the lesser repertory players has courageously volunteered to imitate the Führer to facilitate the troupe's flight to England. That player—Greenberg in the original, Lupinsky in the "Re-Do"—is clearly Jewish in Lubitsch's comedy, although his ethnicity is never stated; his role playing bars his own escape. His Hitler masquerade is among the original film's nail-biting moments.

But Brooks was "obsessed with ridiculing Hitler throughout his career," Meehan wrote later, and he wanted his character, Bronski, to impersonate Hitler—first in the silly song-and-dance number "Naughty Nazis," which comes early in the film and helps set the broader tone of the "Re-Do." Later, because audiences already know that Bronski likes to imitate Hitler, the number has the effect of dulling the plot turn of Bronski/Brooks substituting for the lesser player and posing as the real Hitler at the height of danger.

Another major change was the prominent gay character created as a symbol, in the remake, for the many homosexual victims of Nazi oppression. (Unlike the original, the film made explicit mention of Jewish victims, some of whom are hidden in the theater basement until the final escape.) Critics had singled out the many, often tin-eared, "fag" jokes that had cropped up in Club Brooks comedies following *Young Frankenstein*. In *High Anxiety*, for instance, the dapper Dr. Thorndyke (Brooks) attracts same-sex attention instantly upon his arrival at the Los Angeles International Airport after the opening credits. Thorndyke is lured into the men's room by a handsome stranger who promptly exposes himself, asking plaintively, "You find me attractive?" This, in the world of Mel Brooks, demonstrated, not very humorously, how "fags" expressed their crushes.*

Perhaps because first-time director Alan Johnson was openly homosexual, the Graham/Meehan script introduced a swishy backstage dresser named Sasha, whose job it is to faithfully attend Anna Bronski (Anne Bancroft's character) and facilitate her love affairs. (The character was a matronly type in the original Lubitsch comedy.) When Sasha comes under Nazi scrutiny, he is forced to wear a humiliating and self-incriminating pink triangle—the equivalent of the yellow star forced on Jews. The character suggested amends for earlier Brooks comedies with debatable "fag" humor while illuminating the neglected plight of gay people under the Third Reich.

How extensively the script renovations departed from the Lengyel/Mayer original became another one of those murky writing controversies that has clung to Brooks throughout his career. Meehan later

---

* This presumption of Brooks's appeal to homosexuals was perhaps a leftover from his "Last Man" script fling with Terry Southern.

insisted that although the screenplay adhered to "Mayer's scene-by-scene construction of the movie's intricate plot," their new version used "at most perhaps only a total of five pages of dialogue from the earlier script." Not everyone saw it that way.

Vincent Canby, for example, praised the Brooks version as an "exuberant delight" in his review in the *New York Times*, yet he expressed dismay that so much of the screenplay had been "lifted directly" from the Lubitsch film, while Mayer, Lengyel, and even Lubitsch himself were mentioned only in small type in the end credits, their names trailing after those of the last of the cast. In publicity and interviews, Brooks stubbornly insisted that his *To Be or Not to Be* was not really a "Re-Do" any more than when the male star of any generation (i.e., him) took on *Hamlet*. "That's true," returned Canby, "but when each great star of a succeeding generation does Hamlet, *Hamlet* doesn't have a new author."

Incidentally, David Lunney was not involved in development of the Meehan/Graham script; nor did he or his partner, William Allyn, have anything to do with the remake they had set into motion. One day Brooks himself phoned Lunney in Oregon to discuss the awkward fact that he and Allyn were still the producers of record. The producing partners had given legal notice to Brooks that hiring his own team of writers and moving ahead without their involvement violated the contract they had with him dating back to 1975, whereby the parties had agreed to jointly produce a new version of *To Be or Not to Be*, sharing the creative decisions and financial rewards with guaranteed producer credits.

Lunney no longer had any interest in Hollywood and no longer cared about producing films, but he and Allyn were owed fees as part of their pay-or-play contract, meaning that their money was guaranteed if *To Be or Not to Be* proceeded without them through no fault of their own. Brooks phoned repeatedly. "Mel kept trying to convince me to take far less money than we were contractually owed," Lunney recalled. "He was trying to schmooze me down. I said a firm no." The partners were forced to file suit for their money, and Brooks countersued; then he phoned some more, always keeping a friendly tone with his wife's ex–high school friend, still trying to schmooze him down. "I said, 'Mel, why don't you just pay it? It's costing us lawyers. It's costing you money to do this.'"

Business was business, Brooks always replied. Lawyers eventually settled the case out of court, with Lunney and his partner receiving their original promised sums without diminution. A slice of the money did go to their lawyers, as Lunney had predicted. Eventually he saw the remake in a Portland theater, with his negotiated credit trailing after Mayer, Lengyel, and Lubitsch's: "Production Suggested by William Allyn and David Lunney."

Brooks took no writing credit but supervised Ronny Graham and Thomas Meehan. The screenplay and the actors were ready for action by the end of January 1983.

As with *My Favorite Year*, it was a script that called more for trained players than for self-starting comedians. Brooks rounded up a capable ensemble: his movie-star friend from Sid Caesar days, José Ferrer, was engaged to play the duplicitous Professor Siletski; Charles Durning was cast as the irrepressible heavy Colonel Erhardt ("So they call me Concentration Camp Erhardt!"); James Haake, who had a career sideline as a female impersonator, signed on for Sasha, the swishy backstage dresser; and the clean-cut Tim Matheson got the role of the amorous aviator Lieutenant Andrei Sobinski. (Among Sobinski's physical attributes, Anna Bronski muses, is that he's *tall*—unlike her husband.)

In Club Brooks tradition, Ronny Graham would play the beleaguered stage manager named Sondheim ("Sondheim, send in the clowns!").* The camera would also linger lovingly on

---

* Graham had also acted a small part in *History of the World, Part I.*

eleven-year-old Max Brooks in a small part, playing one of the Jewish refugees hiding in the theater basement who must be rescued at the film's climax.

The production was shaped as a showcase for the Brooks family. The married stars were as famous in real-life America as the Bronskis were in the fictionalized Poland of 1939. The Brookses had never shared billing as equals. Their billing became a running joke in the film, carried through in the perfect touch of the traditional curtain call with all the key performers taking bows onstage at the end of the film. (Brooks had reportedly shot a similar curtain call for *Young Frankenstein* but cut it.) Bancroft, everyone realized by now, could perform comedy with abandon and sing and dance as though it were second nature. Her Polish-language duet with Brooks, "Sweet Georgia Brown"—which Bancroft had also danced to with Dom DeLuise in *Fatso*—was a delight.

Jack Benny had distinguished himself with his lead performance in the Lubitsch version. Benny had inhabited his part superbly, absorbing his own mild-mannered, ironic persona into the character of Josef Tura, as Bronski was called in the original film. Exasperated at every obstacle his character must overcome—the dalliances of his wife are almost as upsetting as the Nazis—Benny never lost sight of the underlying gravity.

Though many of Bronski's scenes replicated scenes from the original, others, such as the Brooks–Ronny Graham frolic with showgirls entitled "Ladies," were devised to showcase Brooks's zanier persona. Yet Brooks felt the pressure to measure up to Benny's greatness in the role, and Benny's ghost haunted Brooks as much as the ghost of Lubitsch did.

How much director Alan Johnson had to do with the script or the casting is conjecture. How much sway the first-time director had over the camera moves or Brooks's performance is hard to calculate. Brooks was omnipresent during filming, just as he had promised 20th Century–Fox. Adding to his stress, he was suffering from dental bridge problems and more than once interrupted takes to rush to a dentist in his Hitler costume.

"It was a very strange period for me," Johnson told Bancroft biographer Douglass K. Daniel in a rare interview about Brooks and *To Be or Not to Be*. "Because it was Mel's movie. I'd stage something, a little bit of a scene, and he'd see it and say, 'No, no. That's terrible. Go look at the original movie . . .' He was just hateful and a little crazed."

The dilemma for Brooks was that he wanted to stay true to the original Lubitsch film yet put his own stamp on the material. Second-guessing the staging was one symptom of that conflict. His acting insecurity led to demanding multiple takes of his own scenes.

Johnson found Bancroft "very supportive [of Brooks]. She was on the set all the time with him, even when she wasn't called. [Once] I was sitting next to her on the set. They were doing a take with Mel . . . they were setting [it] up and [someone] said, 'OK, take nineteen.' And she went, 'Jesus, nineteen! How come I get two and he gets nineteen?' And I said, 'Well, you know what you're doing.' But he hated to let go of what he did. He always felt he could do it better. And so there were endless counts of takes for him."

On- and off-camera, however, Brooks reverted to the rude, hyperbolic personality who when under extreme pressure found fault with other people, never with himself. He trained much of his ire on Lewis J. Stadlen, the Brooklyn-born, Sanford Meisner– and Stella Adler–trained character actor who was portraying Lupinsky, "the role of a Jewish spear-carrier," in Stadlen's words, a spear carrier who aspired to play Shylock. Lupinsky was supposed to recite Shylock's "Hath not a Jew eyes?" speech twice, according to the script, off the cuff and somewhat wistfully the first time, and then later in the film courageously, in front of German soldiers, risking his life to save the troupe. As Greenberg, Felix Bressart had made the speech truly memorable in the Lubitsch version.

The script for the remake used the word "Jew," which was

Shakespeare's language verbatim, whereas the original Lubitsch comedy, which had had to cope with that era's censorship and taboos, substituted the word "we," referring more broadly to human beings and the anti-Nazi resistance. Brooks wanted the word "Jew" emphasized, and he fixated on Stadlen's line readings. "Mel just put him through hell," Johnson recalled.

Before Stadlen's audition, Brooks had been among his major idols. ("I could repeat from memory most of his dialogue from his first film, *The Producers*, as well as his *2000* and *2001 Year Old Man* albums.") Flown to Hollywood, Stadlen was borne by limousine to the 20th Century–Fox lot and escorted into a large room, where he was seated facing Brooks with "a hundred other people crowded behind him." There is no mention of Alan Johnson in this anecdote, but "sitting at Mel's feet was the majestic Anne Bancroft."

Stadlen recalled, "Something about Mel has always reminded me of a street tough trying to escape the body of an elderly Jewish woman. It's like he's holding a knife to your throat and demanding that you eat chicken soup. After I'd auditioned every scene the character [Lupinsky] had in the film, Mel looked as if he'd eaten a bad clam. 'I can't make up my mind!' he barked." Brooks hastily added, "Listen, go back to where you came from, and I'll have to think about this, because I can't make up my mind."

Hoping to win his idol over and avoid another round-trip to the West Coast, Stadlen made a joke: "Listen, Mel, I think I'm uniquely qualified to play this part because even when I eat my eggs in the morning, I do it with a Holocaust sensibility."

That got a laugh from everybody in the room, except Brooks, who "glared back at me as if my very presence in the room was undermining his confidence in the Jewish people." Stadlen quickly followed up with a line from *The Producers*: "If you want me to play this part, all you have to do is ask me!" Again laughter from the room, but not from Brooks, who was still glaring; a silence ensued, then he yelled, "Wait a minute, that's my line! You just stole my line!"

"Yes," said Bancroft quietly.

("Begging him to see the humor in the situation," according to Stadlen.)

"*I can't make up my mind,*" Brooks reiterated. ("Sounding even more like a big-breasted Jewish woman hanging out a Brooklyn window," in Stadlen's words.) Brooks waved Stadlen away. Days later, however, he learned that the part of Lupinsky was his.

A few days before shooting began, however, the first read-through convened and the audition nightmare was repeated. When they got to the scene where Lupinsky delivers his first reading of Shylock's speech, perhaps Stadlen performed it too casually; Brooks interrupted the actor in midsentence, shouting at him in front of the assembled cast, "Now that is the *very opposite* way I want you to do that speech!" Stadlen and the others were embarrassed by the "totally disproportionate emotional outburst," Stadlen recalled. "I would come to understand that whenever Mel lacked confidence in a situation, he believed he was totally within his rights to punish the source of his doubt."

During the first break Ronny Graham came over and threw his arm around Stadlen. "I thought you did that speech wonderfully," Graham consoled the actor, leading him sympathetically down a hallway away from the room. "I wasn't aware that we were expected to deliver a finished product," Stadlen responded defensively. "You have to understand Mel," continued Graham as they walked. "He's a wonderful, warmhearted human being. He's just in the habit of saying whatever comes into his mind."

"*Why are you apologizing for me!*" screamed Brooks, suddenly close behind them. He had followed them into the hallway.

"I was just telling Lewis—" began Graham.

"Don't tell Lewis anything! Stop being the best boy! He doesn't understand how to do the speech!" Brooks snapped, pushing past the two into the men's room.

Rehearsal and filming went no better. "The conceit" of *To Be or Not to Be*, in Stadlen's words, was that Brooks was not directing, but in fact "Mel *was* directing the film and while we all had to pretend he wasn't, he absolutely demanded that we recognize that he was."

One of Stadlen's first scenes to be photographed was the one where he takes the stage to inform the audience of a sudden change in the night's program, announcing that Bronski's detested "Highlights from *Hamlet*" would be performed rather than their new play mocking the Nazis. Brooks was absent, and Stadlen performed several takes for Johnson: long shot, medium shot, close up—improving, he felt, with each take.

In the afternoon, Brooks arrived on the set in his Elizabethan Hamlet costume, wearing a blond wig. "He was agitated," Stadlen wrote, "because he was about to recreate one of the most memorable moments from the original film," the one that begins with Bronski reciting "To be or not to be . . ." (He is interrupted by a handsome young bomber pilot who stands up from his seat and leaves the theater, because the phrase is a prearranged signal to meet Bronski's wife backstage in her dressing room.) Stalling for time before his big scene, the star gathered the "entire cast and crew around a television monitor" to review the morning's footage. "Sitting in his director's chair in his blond wig and blue Shakespearean tights," Stadlen recalled, "he seemed to be gathering strength from the absurdity of his appearance, the class clown having merged with the school principal."

The first footage up was the long shot of Stadlen's curtain speech. "It wasn't very good," Stadlen noted. "My performance was self-conscious and over-gesticulated."

"What is that idiot *doing?*" roared Brooks, although Stadlen was standing only two feet away from him. "The man is an absolute moron!" Stadlen thought his second take was better ("I could see I was beginning to work things out") but Brooks did not concur ("The man is a complete *imbecile!*"). Mercifully, Stadlen's third take, his close-up, came up for review, and Brooks announced, "O.K., that's good!" suddenly pacified.

"It was an ugly moment," Stadlen recalled, "and as soon as Mel walked away, several colleagues came over to see if I was still breathing." He'd be all right, he reassured them. "But I wasn't all right," he confessed in his memoir. "No one had ever bullied or embarrassed me that way. I was not a confident enough actor to be berated at the beginning of what was certain to be a challenging eight-week process."

The next day Brooks tried to make nice with Stadlen during a filming break. ("It was my romantic notion that the night before, just before she dozed off, Anne Bancroft had whispered in her beloved's ear, 'You know Mel, for a great man you sure can be a terrible prick. You have to apologize to Lewis Stadlen.'") But Brooks offered only small talk, no apology.

Not long after, Brooks, not Alan Johnson, directed the scene in which Stadlen as Lupinsky initially performs his "Hath not a Jew eyes?" speech; it was the first time in the story, with Lupinsky's only audience a spear-carrying pal standing next to him in a stairwell. "He gave me two takes," Stadlen recalled. After the second, Brooks grumped, "Well, the first part's a piece of shit and the second part's all right. All right, print it!"

Brooks later cut the scene during editing, which not only reduced the importance of Stadlen's role but meant that "Hath not a Jew eyes?" is heard only once in the "Re-Do." The repetition of the speech, the second time under dangerous circumstances, was what had lent it special resonance in Lubitsch's film; it also gave a supporting player the chance to shine, adding texture and roundness to the original. Cutting the scene, despite having photographed it, continued the drift toward spotlighting Brooks.

After "a horrible first few days," Stadlen said, "I was hurt and disillusioned but I was also really pissed at Mel Brooks." Stadlen was not the only actor on whom Brooks took out his frustrations. One day, showing up on the set after root canal surgery, every bit the "Jewish man in pain," in Stadlen's words, Brooks interrupted a scene between Bancroft and Charles Durning that in everyone else's eyes was going fine, "berating their performances." Bancroft cut him off. "Let me get this straight," the actress said. "Mel Brooks is telling Anne Bancroft and Charles Durning how to act? Ha ha ha ha!" She loftily stormed off the set with Brooks plaintively dogging her heels.

Another day, decked out in his Nazi regalia as Hitler, Brooks materialized before supporting actor George Wyner, who was portraying Ratkowski, a character in Bronski's troupe who figures pivotally in the plot. Brooks told Wyner he wanted him to come to his house on Saturday morning to run through crucial lines in his scenes that simply were not making the grade. "Because you don't understand the speech!" Brooks explained to him, adding as an afterthought, "But you'll call up the union first so you don't get into any trouble!" The Screen Actors Guild strictly forbade unpaid weekend services.

Wyner had a philosophy about it that he imparted to Stadlen, an eyewitness to the incident. "When Mel Brooks asks you to do something," explained Wyner, "he wants you to shake your head yes and then go out and do it. He doesn't appreciate your weighing whether it's a good or bad idea." So Wyner went to Brooks's house on Saturday morning and rehearsed.

One day Brooks took Stadlen aside and said he was going to give him some useful tips. He asked Stadlen if he had ever heard of the acting coach Robert Lewis. Yes, Stadlen said warily. ("Mel figured New York had lost most of its intellectual wattage the day he decided to move to Los Angeles," Stadlen thought.) Brooks said he was going to send him to Lewis to bolster his understanding of the nuances of his Shylock speech. Perhaps Brooks kept singling him out because "as much as I admired Mel as a comic innovator (I was beyond referring to him as a genius), I thought he was a terrible actor."

Referring him to Lewis was "truly insulting" to Stadlen, who had already logged time with Sanford Meisner and Stella Adler and who, besides, was earning "a substantial weekly salary" for appearing in *To Be or Not to Be*. Stadlen thought he probably did need some acting advice, but he was not getting any real help from Brooks. He realized he might have interpreted his Lupinsky character, early in the filming, as too much of a victim, too cognizant of the Holocaust, rather than playing him as watchful and ready to do his utmost under dire circumstances. "Unfortunately," Stadlen wrote in his memoir, "Mel didn't have the acting vocabulary to say 'Stop playing a victim. Play him like a winner, and events will take care of themselves.' His approach was to tell me I didn't understand a great piece of literature because I wasn't a good enough actor."

Came the day when Brooks also summoned Stadlen to his home. Again Brooks wore his Hitler makeup, though his body was draped in a satin robe. Brooks told Stadlen he wanted to see him on Saturday to go over his Shylock lines. Be sure to alert the Guild, he added, so no rules would be broken. "I won't pretend that I wasn't a little afraid of Brooks," Stadlen recalled. "He exuded authority, and he had a very loud voice. But I had taken quite enough." The Guild would not pose any difficulty, Stadlen replied evenly, because Brooks would have to pay for any weekend work he was asked to do.

A long pause followed. "Mel looked at me with the insolence of someone who had never been told he wasn't everybody's favorite," Stadlen recalled. "He searched my face as if trying to determine what manner of man I was, to tell him an unpleasant truth."

Well, Brooks said, what are you doing on *Friday*? Brooks commanded the actor to see him during his Friday lunch break "because you don't understand the speech!"

Friday lunchtime came, and Stadlen went to Brooks's trailer—

with the star again draped in his satin robe, wearing a Hitler mustache, his hair combed over his forehead.

"Do you like it here in Los Angeles?" Brooks began.

"No, I don't," Stadlen replied.

"You don't like it here? Why not? You don't like the smell of azaleas?"

"I guess nothing good has ever happened to me here."

"That's too bad, because it's a very beautiful place," Brooks said ruefully.

("If Mel Brooks could be submissive, this was as close as he was ever going to get," recalled Stadlen.)

"I'm going to show you how to do the speech," Brooks said, "because from the very beginning you have never understood the meaning of that speech. Listen to the way I do it. *Hath* not a Jew eyes?" he singsonged. "*Hath* not a Jew hands? Did you see what I did there? The operative word of the first two sentences is *hath*. You have to stress the *hath*."

His eyes narrowed. "Wait a minute, I'm wrong," Brooks continued. "The operative word is *not*, not hath! Hath *not* a Jew eyes? Hath *not* a Jew hands?"

(Stadlen thought that sounded vaguely like the 2000 Year Old Man, albeit "in classical style.")

"Wait a minute. Goddam it! I'm wrong again. The operative word is *Jew*. Hath not a *Jew* eyes? Hath not a *Jew* hands?"

Spotting the warm pastrami sandwich that awaited his pleasure across the room, Brooks ended the tutorial abruptly. "Do you see the way the poetry rolls off my lips?"


By and large the "crickets" found much to enjoy about the *To Be or Not to Be* "Re-Do" when it was unveiled in theaters just before Christmas 1983. The cast glittered; together Brooks and Bancroft were a joy; and the trappings were top notch, the more affirmative reviewers agreed. Thomas Meehan penned a *New York Times* piece saying he had counted eleven "favorable" reviews out of fifteen in New York. One was by Vincent Canby of the *Times*, who probably became the first critic to describe Brooks as a "national treasure."

Brooks and Bancroft underwent publicity chores and endured the inevitable interrogations about their marriage. Appearing on the national morning show *Today*, where they were questioned by Gene Shalit—one of the most rhapsodic Brooks fans, who in his review declared that the Lubitsch remake should be ranked "eight trillion on the laugh meter"—the couple was less guarded than usual. "Marriage is a retail store," Brooks told Shalit. "Somebody has to watch the register, and somebody has to get the pretzels down for the kids. . . . Life is very hard. I think you need a partner that you love and who loves you to get through it successfully. And I think we were very lucky."

Shalit pressed, asking if after nearly twenty years of togetherness the old marrieds were content with each other. "I'm more than content," Bancroft answered. "I mean, when he comes home at night, when that key goes in the door, I mean, my heart's fluttering. I am so happy he's home, you know. I mean, it's like the party's going to start."

Again, however, the "favorables" included caveats such as the one voiced by Pauline Kael in *The New Yorker*, who found Brooks's *To Be or Not to Be* "benign but not really funny" and said that the lead actor seemed ill at ease and "never cuts loose." Andrew Sarris in the *Village Voice* said the remake was "guilty of undermining the original with mocking facetiousness" and complained about the "lumpy and leaden performances compared to the original." Outright pans came from a number of critics in major markets, including Kevin Thomas in the *Los Angeles Times* and Gary Arnold in the *Washington Post*. The latter agreed with Kael that whereas Jack Benny had been sly and elegant, Brooks blustered and foundered. "I've never seen Brooks at such a loss," Arnold wrote.

Kevin Thomas attempted to explain why the remake did not, like the original, convey any sense of urgency, despite a homosexual character wearing a pink triangle that tried for "a serious message." As written and directed, gay Sasha came off as a "stereotypic sissy," he wrote. Brooks himself set an unsubtle tone, overegging his performance. And except for a brief newsreel, the "Re-Do" offered little historicity. "We know far more than was known in 1942 of the full extent of the Nazi evil, especially in regard to the fate of the Jews," Thomas wrote thoughtfully. "In *The Producers* Brooks carried off his 'Springtime for Hitler' number. . . . Somehow an entire movie that depicts Nazis as the buffoons of fantasy, while we know full well that the peril of Brooks' largely Jewish acting company is all too real, isn't very funny but instead is merely crass. Ironically, for all its sparkle, the original actually took the Nazis far more seriously than this remake does."*

Brooks desperately yearned for the approval of critics while at the same time he resented their power and opinions—that is, their mixed or negative opinions. He had made this "smartie" just for them, and even if many critics accepted the remake kindly on its own terms, he'd never forget the slights. The worst insult the even-handed Kevin Thomas could muster was that Brooks's remake was "disappointing." A few years later, Brooks, interviewed by the same newspaper to promote his latest film, ate up the clock venting about Thomas's critique. "What I really want to know is this. What did Kevin Thomas think was so terrible about 'To Be or Not to Be'? Why that awful review? . . . Sometimes I feel like writing these

---

* The glibness of *To Be or Not to Be* was reinforced by Brooks's "Hitler Rap" single. The faux hip-hop song with some lyrics borrowed from "Springtime for Hitler" was included in the soundtrack album but was not heard (or seen) in the film; it was more of a spin-off that would add revenue that could be separately accounted for. Though the single had only "limited success" in the United States, according to Wikipedia, it charted high in the United Kingdom, Australia, and Sweden and reached number one in Norway.

critics a letter, saying 'Why so angry? What was there to hate so much?' I want to tell them, 'I meant no harm. I only wanted to entertain you.' "

After the United States publicity Brooks and Bancroft toured extensively overseas, cheerfully performing "Sweet Georgia Brown" for TV cameras and giving interviews in England, France, Italy, Sweden, and, for the first time, West Germany. The $13 million US gross barely covered the budget. The foreign take augmented the total but not enough to tally meaningful profits. *To Be or Not to Be* did not attract his usual fans, nor any enthusiasm from moviegoers in the American heartland, and the dismal box office did not bode well for his future at 20th Century–Fox.

Which of the married Bronskis in *To Be or Not to Be* is the faithful one? It is the husband, Frederick Bronski, played by Brooks. Asked whether the nuptial contract means devoting herself to one man only, Bronski's more lustful wife, Anna (Anne Bancroft) tells her bomber-pilot admirer (Tim Matheson), "I've always felt that true love should never stand in the way of a good time."

In real life was it the other way around? Had Brooks ended the trifling and womanizing that helped poison his first marriage? And was it Bancroft who was the stoic, steadfast partner, understanding and accepting the behavior of her errant husband?

Since Brooks persistently batted his eyes at women—secretaries at the studio, waitresses in coffee shops, ladies at the airport—it was just as hard as ever to know if he was, at any time, doing anything more than simply flirting. He had a reputation among Hollywood insiders for having a "zipper problem," in the words of one associate, who traveled with him. But was it a real "zipper problem" or just the whispering of detractors?

According to the author and film critic William Arnold, the

plaintiff in the *Frances* lawsuit, one court reporter who took depositions in the case was a cute young woman in her early twenties still living at home with her parents. She transcribed Brooks's sworn affidavit in the case. Smitten by her look of youthful innocence, Brooks made a play for her. Somehow he ascertained the woman's home address and appeared outside her house late one night, tossing pebbles at her window and pleading for her to come out. A light appeared in her parents' bedroom, however, and Brooks skedaddled. "I'm not sure how much of that story I believe," said Arnold, "but I swear to God it's what she told us."

A person who traveled with Brooks in the 1980s said he had been eyewitness to Brooks's "zipper problem." One day, as the two rode in a taxi together, Brooks took out a little black book of female contacts, similar to the type that had been mentioned in the Florence Baum divorce and that had figured in his screenplay "Marriage Is a Dirty Rotten Fraud." Brooks thumbed through the book and phoned a call girl, the eyewitness said.

If true—the source, though reputable, did not care to be identified because of Brooks's litigiousness—it was a rare transgression in the presence of another party. Brooks and Bancroft enjoyed the image of the perfect couple, the parents of a happy family, spouses who might bicker, might clash, but always ended up in each other's arms. In an industry that manufactured pleasant fakery, they seemed the romantic ideal.

"People don't write wonderful parts for women," Anne Bancroft complained astutely to the *New York Times* in 1984, "because women have not been given a chance to live wonderful lives that people want to write about, and because most writers are men."

Riding a wave of glowing reviews for her performance in *To Be or Not to Be*, Bancroft continued to evolve professionally, entering into what she jokingly referred to as her "old ladies" phase. Comedic parts came her way more often now, yet increasingly she played supporting roles, older, powerful women, in films that flaunted tasteful pedigrees: a terminally ill social activist who aspires to meet a legendary actress in the sentimental *Garbo Talks*, directed by Sidney Lumet in 1984; a mother superior in *Agnes of God* in 1985, for which she earned her fifth Oscar nomination; the filmed play *'night, Mother* with Sissy Spacek in 1986; *84 Charing Cross Road*, opposite Anthony Hopkins for the third time in her career in 1987; and first billed, though in a small role, as drag queen Harvey Fierstein's mother in *Torch Song Trilogy* in 1988.

Only *84 Charing Cross Road*, directed by the Englishman David Hugh Jones, was one of Brooksfilms' "smarties." The title refers to the mailing address of an antiquarian bookseller in London, whose twenty-year epistolary friendship with a New York writer, Helene Hanff, had inspired a memoir by Hanff and a subsequent Broadway adaptation. Bancroft always said the property had come to her attention when a Fire Island neighbor pressed the memoir on her at the beach; her husband optioned the screen rights as an anniversary present. Hopkins, who had also appeared in *Young Winston* and *The Elephant Man* opposite Bancroft, played the bookseller in the mostly two-character drama.

Her husband turned sixty in 1986 without having written, directed, or starred in a Mel Brooks comedy for three years following the anticlimax of *To Be or Not to Be*.

But Brooks was hardly lying low. Whether in New York or Los Angeles, he made grand entrances, sweeping into the 20th Century–Fox commissary or his favorite deli, shouting "Hiya from Mel Brooks!" to friends and strangers alike. He'd wave at tourist buses passing by on the 20th Century–Fox lot, or as he sat at a sidewalk café in Hollywood. "Hey, here I am, Mel Brooks! A genuine celebrity!" Even at funerals, if a fan dared to approach him, Brooks was likely to scold the person first before launching into rib-tickling patter. "He was consciously his own best publicity hound," explained Norman Lear. "He's Mel Brooks all the time. But I can't say that without saying he's funny. He delivers."

Keenly aware of the public interest in him, which he stoked, yet also self-conscious about basking in the limelight, Brooks was known to poke fun at himself among his long-standing circle. One time the Brookses were dining with the Lears and the Reiners on Rodeo Drive. When the group paid the bill and got up to leave, Brooks asked them, "Why don't you guys walk out in front of me? I don't want to be bothered by paparazzi or autograph seekers just now." The others formed a protective cocoon around him, moving outside, only to discover no paparazzi or fans waiting. Brooks looked around and cried out forlornly, "Hey, it's Mel Brooks! I'm Mel Brooks!! Where is everybody?" It broke everyone up, with Brooks laughing the hardest—at himself.

After *To Be or Not to Be* Brooks took numerous excursions to New York, especially when Bancroft was filming *Garbo Talks* in the city, but also visited Quebec, where Bancroft shot *Agnes of God*. Early every summer the couple went to London, where they shopped for antiques and Brooks bought his silk dressing gowns and custom-made shirts from Turnbull & Asser on Jermyn Street (Joseph Heller and Woody Allen were other American customers). From London there were always side trips to cities and other sites in Europe, sometimes purely for vacation, sometimes to shore up Brooksfilms outposts.

When home in Hollywood, he stayed conspicuous. He kept his 20th Century–Fox offices, ran Brooksfilms, prodded dramatic subjects into films that were usually taut and grim as opposed to light and comedic, and, as before, he often took chances with new or singular directors. This was a productive phase for Brooks the producer. In 1986 he fronted a low-key remake of the schlocky fifties horror film *The Fly*. The remake starred Jeff Goldblum and Geena Davis and was directed by the cult Canadian filmmaker

David Cronenberg; a *succès d'estime*, it solidified Cronenberg's grow-ing artistic reputation.

Three years later, in 1989, Brooksfilms sponsored a sequel, *The Fly II*, with Eric Stoltz and Daphne Zuniga, which was directed by first-timer Chris Walas, who had designed the creature effects and won an Oscar for his makeup for the remake of *The Fly*. If the follow-up was not as interesting, still *The Fly II* made moolah—especially overseas.

Less coherent and successful were *The Doctor and the Devils* in 1985 and *Solarbabies* in 1986. The former was the long-elusive adaptation of the only motion picture scenario written, in the 1940s, by the Welsh poet Dylan Thomas. Thomas's scenario told the tale of a real-life surgeon in nineteenth-century Edinburgh who paid two Irish immigrants to rob graves and kill people in order to obtain corpses for his anatomy classes. Freddie Francis, the cameraman who had photographed *The Elephant Man* so strikingly in black and white, mentioned the property to producer Jonathan Sanger, and Brooksfilms optioned the scenario. Brooks agreed to let Francis di-rect, with Sanger producing. (It was hardly Francis's first directing job; the Englishman with distinguished camera credits dating from the 1950s had also directed cult horror pictures.)

Over the years many efforts to convert Thomas's scenario into a film had defeated better men than Gunga Din (*Rebel Without a Cause* director Nicholas Ray was one of those who had labored fruitlessly on a screen version in the 1960s). Thomas's language, right down to the staging directions, was poetic but unfilmable. Brooks turned to a gold-medal name, Londoner Ronald Har-wood, to rework the Thomas scenario, "because he had just been nominated for an Oscar" for his script for *The Dresser* in 1983, according to Francis.

Francis envisioned the movie-to-be as "a straight gothic story about historical characters," in his words, "a reflection of the Victorian life, the poverty and crime that gripped Edinburgh as it did all cities in the nineteenth century." But the head of Brooksfilms, looking to build on the genre success of *The Fly* and *The Fly II*, saw *The Doctor and the Devils* as more of a highbrow horror flick about body snatchers. "I remember on one occasion that [Brooks] called me from Los Angeles," Francis recalled, "and I spent an hour trying to persuade him that it was a psychological story, not a horror story."

As was his wont, Brooks focused most of his preproduction time on the script, supervising Harwood. "Mel bullied Ron to do what he wanted, which was to turn it into an out-and-out horror script. The original screenplay by Thomas had been beautifully written but the rewrite was somewhat less so." (Harwood declined to comment for this book and in his authorized biography does not even mention the film or Brooks.)

Francis organized a superb ensemble, led by actors Timothy Dalton, Jonathan Pryce, and Stephen Rea, and during the shooting he also tried to amend and repair the Harwood script. "Day by day I was pushing more of the Dylan Thomas stuff back in," he said.

Francis filmed scenes that he hoped would enable audiences to understand how the two Irish immigrants, who were altogether unscrupulous and villainous, corrupted the surgeon's decent intentions and humanity. Brooks took control during the editing, however, and deleted ruminative scenes about science versus morality, and "in the end, a five-minute section that recounted the doctor's remorse was cut by Mel without my approval," Francis said. "It was that scene that gave the story credibility and a conclusion, but no matter how I fought to retain that scene, Mel was adamant that it be cut."

Sometimes the ultra-serious Brooksfilms films were just botches. Released in late 1985, *The Doctor and the Devils* might qualify as the worst of them ("unredeemed, dreary, boring, gloomy dreck," Roger Ebert wrote in the *Chicago Sun-Times*) if not for close competition, the next year, from *Solarbabies*, which was Brooks's gift to Alan Johnson after the duress of *To Be or Not to Be*. Far from being a musical,

*Solarbabies* was a futuristic parable set in a parched landscape inhabited by a bunch of young orphaned "Solarbabies," or skateball players (a hybrid of hockey/roller skating). Their water is rationed by a draconian regime. The skateballers discover a glowing ball named Bodhi that could lead to a water paradise.

Dreaming of a science fantasy franchise of the type that was suddenly the nirvana of Hollywood (all the major studios had at least one prototype in the hopper), Brooks broke his own rules, giving a green light to the production after 20th Century–Fox passed on any involvement without nailing down another studio as his financial partner.

The photography had been planned in Spain to exploit natural locations and save on below-the-line costs. Trying to get started before the rainy season, Brooks dispatched Johnson and his cast and crew to Madrid and rugged Almería. Elaborate sets were constructed to the specifications of Englishman Anthony Pratt, known for the otherworldly visual design of John Boorman films such as *Zardoz* and *Excalibur*. The cast was mostly youthful unknowns (including Dom DeLuise's son Peter), but sprinkled among them was a handful of veterans including Charles Durning. The project had a sensible minder in Irene Walzer, who had risen up the Brooksfilms ladder from publicist to producer.

What could go wrong? Location vagaries, logistical problems, and overruns quickly devoured the initial $5 million allowance, and there was a surge of panic and turmoil in Spain. Brooks flew to Spain for a lordly walk-through, assessing the crisis. He flew back, rattled, as he exaggerated in later interviews. He needed another $18 million or so to finish *Solarbabies.* "I'm getting a second mortgage on the house," he said in one interview. "I had two cars, I put them up. I mean, I'm practically ready to jump off a roof."

Almost straight from the airport he headed over to Culver City to see his old friend Alan Ladd, Jr. After running 20th Century–Fox during Brooks's glory decade at the studio in the 1970s, Laddie had fired up the Ladd Company and run it for several years, until that noble enterprise began to hemorrhage losses. Not long before Brooks's visit, Laddie had wound up as the first production head of the MGM half of the newly merged MGM/United Artists Entertainment Company. Although MGM/UA, under the ownership of the Las Vegas wheeler-dealer Kirk Kerkorian, was from the outset in a state of constant flux and anxiety, Laddie had a brief window of opportunity to do anything he wanted.

More than any other studio boss, Brooks liked and admired Laddie, a former agent with whom he could talk dollars and cents and who was also the son of a Golden Age movie star. Laddie was honest; he didn't say bullshit things. He was "a dry martini," in Brooks's words, more of a joke getter than joke teller but dryly humorous all the same.

According to insiders, Brooks wept actual tears as he pleaded with Laddie to pledge the necessary dough and guarantee the completion of *Solarbabies*, making MGM the senior partner on the fantasy film. That was the easy part of the conversation. Laddie was happy to announce the pickup a month later, the first authorization of the Ladd regime, as Brooks liked to boast. (Ladd's later MGM/UA go-aheads would include *Moonstruck* and *A Fish Called Wanda*.) MGM ended up taking a bath on *Solarbabies* when the misbegotten film was released to yawns and groans in late 1986. "A hilariously bad movie," wrote Paul Attanasio in the *Washington Post*. *Newsday's* Stephen Williams called it "garbage." Vincent Canby in the *New York Times* scoffed, "An embarrassment."

But the ledger loss didn't matter to the Brooks-Ladd friendship. As much as Brooks mocked "suits" in interviews, he meant the "new" suits of the successive regimes at 20th Century–Fox and other studios with whom he had to ingratiate himself. He had been compatible with the first generation of "suits," the post-1960s generation with whom he had come up as agents.

Laddie was the best of them all: soft spoken but hard hitting;

canny. Unlike Brooks, with whom he sometimes played tennis, Laddie could return any serve. Why, Ladd asked him, was the ultimate funnyman, Brooks, fooling around with a mirthless existentialist science fantasy epic, a "slumgullion," as one critic later described it, that was part *Road Warrior*, *E.T.*, *Rollerball*, and *Dune* mingled with profundities borrowed from Carlos Castaneda and Buddhism? Ladd knew the joys and perils of the fantasy genre as well as anyone in Hollywood. As the boss of 20th Century–Fox back in the day, he and his retinue had traipsed dutifully into the first preview of *Star Wars* in Westwood, not really expecting much, only to have their hair blown back by the whoosh of the opening credits and the roar of the packed crowd, the vast majority in their teens and twenties. The phenomenon of *Star Wars*, low-expectation genre filmmaking, had not been foreseen.

Brooks was restless at 20th Century–Fox, Laddie understood, and his future there was cloudy. Since *To Be or Not to Be*, Brooks had brought the studio into partnerships with Brooksfilms on a couple of his noncomedies, and a couple of the pictures had been profitable. Then along had come *The Doctor and the Devils*, a 20th Century–Fox coproduction. The studio had declined to gamble on *Solarbabies*. Brooks had outlived his time at 20th Century–Fox, and Laddie, attuned to the growing home entertainment bonanza, could make MGM/UA attractive to Brooks with the new pay television and video percentages.

What Brooks should be doing, instead of *Solarbabies*, Ladd felt, was a comedy *spoofing* pablum like *Solarbabies*—spoofing films like *Star Wars*. If Brooks tamed the comedy a little, even the kids and families who loved *Star Wars* would be teased into a Mel Brooks science fantasy spoof. Laddie volunteered to act the diplomat with *Star Wars* creator George Lucas, who owed him a favor or two and who kept tight reins on his franchise.

Or maybe Brooks met with Laddie with the idea already swirling in his mind, having been inspired by his teenage son, Max Brooks, who had a mania for the *Star Wars* series. Hadn't Brooks himself pointed the way with the mock trailer that ran at the end of *History of the World, Part I*, the coming-attraction teaser for "Jews in Space" that Janet Maslin in the *New York Times* said she thought was probably the funniest single thing in that film? Later Brooks would tell the press he had quietly been working on the *Spaceballs* script, under its original title, "The Planet Moron," for close to two years.

Either way, the trade-off benefited both men: take *Solarbabies*, and I'll give you *Spaceballs*. By midsummer, the contract had followed the handshake, and the script had made headway, with the *To Be or Not to Be* unit, writers Ronny Graham and Thomas Meehan, back collaborating with Brooks. The July 20, 1986, announcement in *Variety* mentioned *Star Wars* along with *Star Trek*, *Alien*, and *Planet of the Apes* as among the "futuristic films" to be lampooned by *Spaceballs*. (There would also be distinct allusions to *The Wizard of Oz*.) "Princess Druish . . . as in Jewish" (Brooks's words), the lead female character, would boast matching luggage and a nose job the Evil Empire threatens to reverse. His own roles were already sketched out: Brooks would portray "the pic's most evil character, President Skroob [an anagram of "Brooks"], and its most benign sage, Yogurt (a takeoff of Yoda from George Lucas's *The Empire Strikes Back*)."

The *Variety* announcement summarized the forthcoming Mel Brooks comedy as a parody of the "space adventure" genre to rival the Western satire of *Blazing Saddles*, only "less vulgar." The once self-styled dangerous comedian promised a PG-rated *Spaceballs*.

# CHAPTER 15

# 1986

## Frolics and Detours

That summer the Brookses moved into their spacious mansion and estate on La Mesa Drive in Santa Monica, where Bancroft swam daily in the indoor pool, relieving back pain that had persisted after a horse-riding mishap on the set of *The Last Hunt* in 1956, while devoting herself to the organic horticulture that increasingly preoccupied her free time after her cancer scare. A terraced garden was sculpted into their backyard. She and her husband took Pritikin training to eliminate fat and eat less animal protein and more fruits and vegetables and to lower their cholesterol levels. Together they took long walks and jogged.

Max commuted to the nearby Crossroads School. His parents volunteered for benefits and for the safety council that was formed after school incidents raised security concerns.

Brooks worked a short drive away at 20th Century–Fox, where he maintained offices for daily meetings on the *Spaceballs* script. Brooks, Ronny Graham, and Thomas Meehan—three men who had first voted in the Truman era—felt emancipated by their shared lack of respect and affection for the youth-oriented spaceship genre. *To Be or Not to Be*, the first coming together of this particular Club Brooks, had been more hallowed ground.

Their screenplay for *Spaceballs* would be positively effervescent, the scenes almost as chock full of intertextual and extratextual references, lowbrow and worldly, as *Blazing Saddles*: nods to Kentucky

Fried Chicken, Perrier, and Afro hair picks, among other things, and a feast of film industry jibes, from the gliding camera that smashes into Dark Helmet (a joke reworked from *High Anxiety*) to the vicissitudes of videotape. Surprisingly, however, their script offered no musical numbers for Alan Johnson. The choreographer was still embroiled in the headache postproduction of *Solarbabies*.

Some of Brooks's methods hadn't changed in the thirty years Ronny Graham had known him, over which time they had written diverse and sundry scripts together. Brooks has the "overview," Graham informed the *Los Angeles Times*. "Mel's very vehement. If he doesn't like a line you write, he'll shout and stomp and holler. He'll bellow, 'You're totally wrong. You don't know anything about comedy!' But here's what really happens. He'll fight ferociously against something Ezra [*Spaceballs* producer Ezra Swerdlow] or I suggest, but all the while he'll be rolling that idea around in his head. And if the idea has any merit at all, he won't necessarily admit it. But he'll find a way to use it in the scene."

Of course there was also, embedded in the script, a surfeit of penis jokes, bimbo ladies whose main job it was to flash cleavage, and no limit to the expletives, especially with an entire evil regiment carrying the last name of "Asshole." Graham defended the "healthy vulgarity" (in his words) of Brooks's comedy. "I have friends that love his work, and many who loathe it," he said. "But that's OK. As George Bernard Shaw once put it: 'Better half of them love you and half of them hate you than everyone think you're nice.'"

The casting would be refreshed, for the first time in a Mel Brooks comedy, with young, good-looking *goyish* leads—a twenty- and thirtysomething—playing the characters evoking Princess Leia and Han Solo from *Star Wars*. Daphne Zuniga, who'd co-starred in *The Fly II*, would make for an appealing Druish princess Vespa, whose royal father has promised her in marriage to the yawning Prince Valium—Brooks was still adroit with characters' names. (Zuniga would return for *Spaceballs: The Animated Series* in

2008.) And Bill Pullman, whose breakout role had been in 1986's *Ruthless People*, would serve as the feckless antihero Lone Starr, *Spaceball's* stand-in for Harrison Ford.

Rick Moranis and John Candy were Canadian, both graduates of the improvisational *Second City Television* (SCTV) series, marquee names of the younger generation of comedians already prospering in Hollywood. The pint-sized Moranis would have a field day as the glowering Dark Helmet, the Darth Vader of the saga, while the big, fat Candy was equally entertaining if heavily costumed as Barf, the Chewbacca takeoff, Lone Starr's faithful Mog—half man, half dog ("I'm my own best friend!").

Dom DeLuise led the names of yore, although he was squandered as the voice of the grotesque blob Pizza the Hutt. Joan Rivers, who voiced a C-3PO–type robot maid named Dot Matrix, was another example of Brooks's penchant for casting veteran stand-ups. John Hurt from *Alien* and *The Elephant Man*—he had also played Jesus in *History of the World, Part I*—provided the only celebrity sighting. (Seen at a diner, Hurt parodies his famous scene from *Alien* by undergoing a tummy ache that spews forth a singing-dancing minimonster.) Other old-school faces from other Mel Brooks comedies included George Wyner, who was rewarded with a large part as Dark Helmet's toady, Colonel Sandurz; Dick Van Patten as King Roland, the regal father of the spoiled Princess Vespa; and Ronny Graham as the marrying prelate whose scenes echoed *It Happened One Night*.

The eye-popping $22.7 million budget was twice that of *History of the World, Part I*, the last comedy Brooks had directed, but it afforded a production design as elaborate as *Young Frankenstein's*. The Englishman Terence Marsh, who had art directed for David Lean and Carol Reed and also designed the remake of *To Be or Not to Be*, created the spaceship mock-ups and interiors that were constructed on Stage 30, one of MGM's biggest soundstages. (The filming also visited desert locations near Yuma, Arizona.) Donfeld's witty costume designs might have made unusual demands on the budget, but the costs of everything, including special effects, were steadily rising in Hollywood.

Brooks launched twelve weeks of shooting in late October, with Nick McLean as his first-time (only-time) cameraman. The filmmaker had gotten some bug out of his system by eschewing the responsibility of directing *To Be or Not to Be*, or maybe he had been tempered by age and experience. Anecdotes about his explosions on the set were increasingly rare. Now, on his sets, he was the nonstop clown as well as ringmaster.

Brooks's preference for intense close-ups, as witnessed in *The Producers*, had long since given way to a more conventional visual approach—long shot, medium, close-up, two-shots, inserts. Yet *Spaceballs* also called for some genuine action sequences, rare in his previous comedies, and his camera work—the later editing, too—was fluid and agile.

The filming went smoothly, and the editing, with Brooks working alongside Conrad Buff, an editor who had done his best to save *Solarbabies*, stretched into early 1987. The "space adventure" genre wallowed in sound effects, and Brooks could revel in the computers clacking, radar beeping, alarms sounding, hyperjets whooshing, "ludicrous speed," and so on. There was no real hurry, as MGM was aiming for a summer 1987 release. There was time for nitpicking the length of scenes, moving a few frames around to fine-tune the comedy rhythms, adding in the models, the mattes, the animatronics and animated effects, and finally the score by old faithful John Morris, who simulated *Star Wars* and quoted from *Lawrence of Arabia*. According to the master plan of appealing to the youth audience, Morris also assembled the only playlist of pop-rock heard in a Mel Brooks comedy: Jon Bon Jovi, the Pointer Sisters, Van Halen, et al., and a title song by Brooks and others sung by the Spinners and produced by Madonna's former fiancé Jellybean.

• • •

The ninth Mel Brooks big-screen comedy was booked into the maximum number of theaters with the usual hoopla in late June. Brooks doled out interviews around the clock in the United States; he appeared on *Today*, joined Johnny Carson on *The Tonight Show*, and donned dress and wig to host *The Late Show* as "Joan Rivers," who was ailing.

If there was ever a Mel Brooks film that proved that reviewers were out of touch with his devotees and validated some of Brooks's griping about the "crickets," it was *Spaceballs*.

After a long, worrying hiatus, Brooks had gone back to the well and against expectations delivered his most boyish and buoyant film in years. Brooks the actor was essential to the fun as President Skroob, interrupted during coitus and at the urinal, a variation on Governor Le Pétomane, the boob he had played in *Blazing Saddles*. ("Skroob the People!" is his slogan.) He was even more inspired as the sawed-off, elfin-eared Yogurt, possessor of the power of the Schwartz and the wisdom of merchandising, "where the real money from the movie is made." Yogurt was not far from the 2000 Year Old Man, but Brooks had stepped back from starring, and *Spaceballs* benefited from more of an ensemble feeling.

The critics didn't really get it. The *Washington Post* thought the new Mel Brooks comedy was embarrassing and unfunny, "the worst" offering yet from the filmmaker. "Sometimes it's painfully juvenile," wrote Roger Ebert in the *Chicago Sun-Times*. Stanley Kauffmann in *The New Republic* said his opinion of *Spaceballs* echoed one of its oft-repeated lines: "Shit." In Brooks's backyard, the *Los Angeles Times* diagnosed the film as a lumbering burlesque, pointing to the less grandiose Woody Allen as the real paragon of Jewish comedy. *Variety* said that *Spaceballs* was unoriginal and burdened with a script "dismal on a story level," the whole production suggesting a home movie displaying a "colossal ego."

The gags about the motion picture industry were "extremely

funny," conceded Julie Salamon in the *Wall Street Journal*: the *Spaceballs* T-shirts and toilet paper; Dark Helmet popping the video into his VCR to catch up with the plot; the "Spaceballs II: The Search for More Money" sequel promised in the end credits. Salamon confessed to having laughed a lot during the film, but summarized *Spaceballs* as "icky adolescent humor."

Yet icky adolescent humor was also the argument in favor of *Spaceballs* that lured millions of people into theaters, much of the audience in the target age group, including many younger first-time Mel Brooks comedy attendees holding the hands of their parents because, in the end, *Spaceballs* did get its G rating despite all the leering and vulgarity.

The money poured in from overseas, too. (" '*Spaceballs*' A Comer in Paris," *Variety* headlined.) *Spaceballs* would ultimately gross more than $38 million, ranking the space adventure spoof in the middle of Brooks's top ten hits—behind *Blazing Saddles*, *Young Frankenstein*, *Silent Movie*, *High Anxiety*, and *History of the World, Part I*.

True, the grosses of those comedies declined in the chronological order of their release, and the $22.7 million budget of *Spaceballs* cut into the actual profits. But Brooks and Laddie counted on the new video and ancillary markets kicking in big, and they did; *Spaceballs's* posttheatrical life coincided with the historical peak of cable/video buying. In time the film would take in enough extra proceeds from rentals, sales, and television and cable airings to rank as Brooks's third highest moneymaker overall. "Do you know it's my greatest income?" the filmmaker told an interviewer in 1993. "These kids never stop renting this video." And ever after, wherever Brooks went, if he was dining out or shopping at a mall, people shouted, "Hey, Yogurt!" or "May the Schwartz be with you!"

Brooks and Alan Ladd, Jr., had done well together again. Although Laddie squirmed under Kirk Kerkorian and resigned from MGM/UA the next year, the studio boasted a winner on its summer books. And *Spaceballs* proved that Brooks still had his mojo.

• • •

A pistol to the end of her life, Kate "Kitty" Kaminsky died of heart failure on August 19, 1989. The ninety-three-year-old mother of Brooks had resided for twenty years in Hollywood, Florida, an East Coast city situated between Fort Lauderdale and Miami, in an apartment with a porch overlooking Biscayne Bay. Her sister Sadie, who had helped Kitty raise her boys, lived with Kitty, who had never remarried after her husband's death in 1929.

In her circle of mostly older retirees, Kitty was known for the best homemade gefilte fish, her devotion to the card game Kalooki (a variation on gin rummy), and her participation in a Zionist women's organization called Hadassah. Brooks had supported his mother financially for many years, and he helped his brothers out on occasion, too.

The Brookses flew in from Barcelona, where they were taking a post-*Spaceballs* vacation, and the clan of Brookmans and Kaminskys gathered for a memorial to the matriarch in Florida that would be followed by a funeral and burial on Long Island.

Brooks had not written any letters to his mother in years, Kitty had earlier told a reporter; he was always too busy. But her youngest son had stayed close, phoning her weekly, sending her flowers on Valentine's Day, taking her to *his* Hollywood and to Las Vegas, proudly introducing her to all the celebrities she wanted to meet. Their half-hour phone talks weren't rushed. "He talks a lot. That's his main thing. But he doesn't tell jokes."

The eldest Kaminsky brother, Irving Kaye, as he was now known, was in his early seventies. A former chemist, Irving was the brother living closest to the old neighborhood, and he ran a hospital supply company on Long Island, where he was also known as a keen amateur fencer. War hero Leonard Kaminsky had worked for years for the US Post Office and was living off his pension and savings in Tamarac, Florida, a short drive from his mother and Aunt Sadie. Bernard was itinerant professionally and moved around; for a while he had lived in Encino, California, running a bookstore, and later he'd reside in Las Vegas, where he met up most often with the brother closest to him in age.

Time and distance had separated the brothers, who had grown up sleeping in the same bed sprawled across one another. Kitty's death reunited them. "We all spent three or four days together," Leonard told the *Miami Herald*, "like we'd never done since we were kids."

Leonard would die the following year. Irving Kaye made it to almost ninety-one, passing away in 2007. Bernard went to his grave not long after attending, with his younger brother, the 2007 after-party in Las Vegas for the road show musical of *The Producers*.

Phobic about illnesses and hospitals, Brooks was a stalwart at funerals, weepy but also cheering people up with his jokes. He was conspicuous among the mourners at Marty Feldman's service, Buddy Rich's, Mel Tormé's, Artie Shaw's, and those of many other friends and luminaries whose career paths had crossed his own. But Kitty Kaminsky's death, and those of other family members to come, struck painfully close to home.

Brooks kept up a punishing travel schedule, but his geographic home was in Los Angeles, which increasingly was the home of his heart. New York City had become a "paranoid maze of apartment blocks," he told *The Independent* in England. Broadway and the Village—most of his old haunts—were gone or changed utterly. He had an abiding nostalgia for Brooklyn, but it was the Brooklyn of his boyhood, the warmth of the community. In Los Angeles he frequented favorite delis and restaurants and places where he counted on seeing familiar faces (many displaced New Yorkers with ties to his own past). Nowadays, he said, he found Los Angeles "a great deal more gemütlich."

Despite the tease in the ending credits of *Spaceballs*, a tease that was repeated for years in Brooks interviews, there would never be a "Spaceballs II: The Search for More Money." Instead, for the next few years after his surprise hit, Brooks returned to his longtime dream of creating a television series under his own name, one whose popularity would outdo that of *Get Smart*. He'd tried before with the ill-starred *When Things Were Rotten*.

As before, someone else came to him with the concept, and that person did much of the grunt work and supervised the episodes. In exchange for trading on Brooks's name, Alan Spencer shared the credit of cocreator and co—executive producer. (He and Brooks would also share writing credit on the pilot and second episode.) Spencer was a Whittier, California, native, an unabashed Brooks fan who had begun penning letters to the *Los Angeles Times* as a fifteen-year-old, saying "I consider Mel Brooks a genius." He had written in his high school yearbook of his dream to work with Brooks and later sneaked onto the set of *Young Frankenstein* and befriended Marty Feldman. In time he became the writer-creator of offbeat TV series such as *Sledge Hammer!* and *The Ghost Writer*.

With Spencer as his collaborator, Brooks concocted a *Fawlty Towers*—like sitcom that took place in the once fancy, now disreputable Nutt Hotel, presided over by a suave and contemptuous hotel manager who holds a buxom Prussian housekeeper in his thrall.

Together the partners drove to Burbank for an appointment at Walt Disney Studios, with Brooks doing "non-stop routines" in the car and most of the pitching to executives. "Talk a lot and make 'em laugh, then leave. You're on the air," Brooks coached Spencer. Disney's Touchstone division agreed to produce the half-hour series for NBC, Brooks's lucky old network. The sitcom boasted two stars with cachet from previous Brooks hits: Harvey Korman as the disdainful hotel manager and Cloris Leachman as the Prussian sexpot. Also in the mix was Ronny Graham in a recurring role as a hotel doorman.

With publicity trumpeting the Brooks name, *The Nutt House* was the most anticipated new series of the season approaching its September 1990 premiere. The show was slotted at 9:30 p.m. on

Wednesdays opposite *Doogie Howser* (ABC) and *Jake and the Fatman* (CBS). Some critics loved it. "Rude, crude and very, very broad," Andrew J. Edelstein exclaimed in *Newsday*. Many did not. "A major disappointment," reported *Variety*, marred by creaky "shtick" and "the absence of real lunatic humor."

Either way, the *Spaceballs* audience did not crowd around the TV set to watch *The Nutt House*. By late October the show rested in 46th place in the weekly Nielsens. Although ten episodes were produced, NBC yanked the ballyhooed series after just five airings. At least *When Things Were Rotten* had made it to thirteen.

Dead now forever was Brooks's dream of having his own hit TV series.


A harbinger of worse things to come was the announcement, in late 1989, of the first public offering of stock in Brooksfilms Inc. In an attempt to carve out greater profit participation and autonomy without personally investing any more of his money, Brooks proposed to divest one-third of his privately held company shares. He would retain the remaining shares and majority ownership of Brooksfilms. The stock offering was intended to raise $27.5 million for future Brooksfilms productions. The extra money would give him more leverage in his partnerships with the Hollywood studios. His Malibu neighbor, producer Aaron Spelling, had tried a similar gambit with some success five years before.

A high-profile investment banking firm, Oppenheimer & Co. in New York City, handled the Brooksfilms venture and suggested an unusual "road show," with Brooks himself giving in-person presentations to brokers in Seattle, Houston, Atlanta, Chicago, New York, Boston, Seattle, and Portland. To accompany Brooks on those trips, aiding and advising him, Oppenheimer recommended Mallory Factor, a public relations specialist who had performed similar duties for the Italian producer Dino De Laurentiis.

Factor flew out from New York to meet Brooks at his studio of-fices. Although Factor had an appointment, he was made to wait an hour and a half before Brooks finally made a grand entrance. Factor confronted Brooks with his rudeness, saying that he had been kept waiting too long and was heading back to New York straightaway. Brooks dropped the pretense, apologizing profusely. "He's a bully if you can be bullied," said Factor.

Together they went on the road, often accompanied by another Oppenheimer representative, Joel Reader, traveling intermittently for weeks in late 1989 and early '90. Brooks wore sober Wall Street suits into his meetings with brokers, but he also took his showbiz shtick. He'd open up his jacket to display a rack of watches he was selling or reel off joke after joke, until the potential investors began to stir uncomfortably.

When, sooner or later, Brooks switched to business talk, however, he could really talk the talk about options and leverages. He impressed everyone with the scope of his financial acumen. "Brooks is first and foremost a businessman," Oppenheimer executive Robert Manning informed *American Film* magazine. "He's a serious man who is also very funny. But life is not a joke to Mel Brooks. That's been borne out in the meetings."

He was a celebrity to the businessmen, and most thought he was the funniest man they had ever met, in a boardroom or anywhere else. After the boardroom meetings, at a restaurant with a hand-ful of the moneymen, he could be just as winning and funny (he'd bring out his old waiter routine, sauntering around the room with a napkin draped over his arm asking about "les vins"). Anywhere in public or with a third party present, he was gold.

After an investor or restaurant meeting, however, after he had performed for the businessmen, he and Factor would jump into a taxi, and Brooks would go blank, saying very little—just as Sid Caesar had used to do after a show. "In private," recalled Factor, "Mel turned off. No personality, deadpan, sullen. It wasn't rude. But without an audience, he just turned miserably blank, which no one who saw him publicly would believe."

It didn't help when Factor told Brooks that he sometimes ran on too long with the jokes and shtick and crowing about himself until investors' eyelids drooped. "Why the hell didn't you get me out of there?" Brooks would snap. "Mel, Christ, I tried," said Factor, "but I couldn't without actually tackling you and pulling you away."

Factor thought that Brooks was least happy when he was alone, or alone with just one other person. The comedian had massive insecurities and "needed an ego boost all the time." One time, trying to cheer him up, Factor mentioned a close relative who was a big fan of his work. Brooks perked up. "Let's phone her!" Factor dialed the relative, handed the phone to Brooks, and Brooks came alive. He rattled off jokes and snatches of songs, as though he were on a stage in a bright spotlight performing before a sold-out crowd.

Privately Brooks thought of himself as the Nice Mel. He referred to himself as a *mensch*. "I'm such a *mensch*," he'd say, "I'm so generous." "Mel, you're cheap!" one of the writers on the Club Caesar reunion panel called out once when Brooks went on and on about being such a big tipper in restaurants, "Some of us worked for you!" Brooks called on the testimony of Howard Morris, who was sitting in the audience. "Not very much," Morris humorously rebuked him. ("A good tipper," the ever-loyal Carl Reiner chimed in.)

As Brooks traveled around, "he tried to do *mensch*-type things at times when he was losing that impression," recalled Factor. One day, sharing a taxi, Factor had had enough of the *mensch* self-compliments, and he informed Brooks, "Mel, you're a lot of things, but you're not a *mensch*." First Brooks got upset. Then he turned blank, sullen.

The jokes went over better in the broker meetings than the investment package ultimately did. The $1.5 million unit offering was priced at $9 to $11 per unit, which entailed one share and also what is known as a warrant, or a fixed price with an expiration date, on a third of a second share. Brooks would keep 3 million shares of the

company, whose net worth was estimated, according to the prospectus, at $45 million. But details in the prospectus showed the stock
priced "at a side-splitting 65 times [the] earnings" of Brooksfilms,
according to an account in the business journal *Forbes*. Brooksfilms
had reported only $323,000 profit on revenues of $6.5 million
in fiscal 1989, reported *Forbes*, while the top man had collected
a $4 million company salary, with other fees and expenses—travel,
per diems, etc.—flowing from his myriad contracts.

"Taxes!" Brooks roared to *American Film* when asked about the
disparity. "Why the hell should I produce revenues and pay taxes on
them when I own the company? I took the money and paid it to Mel
Brooks to avoid double taxation. By going public, I'm taking a one
thousand percent drop in salary. How can I ask the public to invest
in a company that produces annual revenues of only $323,000. I
mean, that's ridiculous."

A number of experts regarded the Brooksfilms venture as "a
vanity offering," according to *American Film*, in effect a greedy
prospectus that would provide a kind of golden parachute for the
director verging on retirement age. The venture gave Brooks all
the control and compensation while limiting investors' rewards.
("I don't want a single rich man to call me on the phone to tell
me his niece had just graduated from drama school," Brooks told
*American Film*. "The public, the shareholder, won't do that.")

"Comedy is hot today but Brooks may be running out of gas,"
*Time* magazine reported on the venture. "Hollywood insiders say
dealmakers have been wary of Brooks."

After Oppenheimer dispersed a reported 40 percent of the offering, the stock sales slowed to a halt. Brooks was left with "egg on his
face," reported *Forbes*.

Brooks promptly sued Factor's New York–based public relations
firm, seeking $15 million in damages for its failure to perform in
a "professional, competent and workmanlike manner." Factor told

*Forbes* that the suit was Brooks's "desperate attempt" to evade paying rightful fees and expenses for his company's "road show," including limos and meals. "He wanted to scare me," said Factor. "He was pissed off that the thing never went on and he blamed everything in sight. The last thing he wanted to do was pay expenses."

Lawyers took up the dispute. Alan U. Schwartz, who had overseen the language of the failed prospectus, now oversaw the settlement. Brooks paid Factor in full. The next time Brooks saw Factor on a plane, he gave him a bear hug as though nothing had happened. "Classic Mel," Factor recalled. "Fundamentally I liked the guy. I still like the guy."

All of that transpired as Brooks and a new team of writers were crafting his first new big-screen comedy since *Spaceballs*, the first that was to have been undergirded by the rejected public offering, a story about a rich man who learns that money isn't everything.

Four years elapsed between *Spaceballs* and *Life Stinks*. Brooks worked on *The Nutt House*, but he also supervised the Brooksfilms productions that were not his starring vehicles and spared time for extracurricular professional activities, including a notable guest appearance on one episode in the last season of *The Tracey Ullman Show*, where he played a sleazy producer enticing A-list goddess Ullman into his B picture.

During that same time period, Alan Ladd, Jr., found himself back in charge of the former MGM studio. Laddie, who had quit MGM/UA in September 1988, resurfaced in February 1989 as head of a new entity, Pathé Communications, which was affiliated with the venerable French film firm of the same name. An Italian business shark named Giancarlo Parretti had taken over Pathé and signed a distribution deal with MGM/UA, then swiftly acquired

MGM/UA, forming a parent company, in 1991, renamed MGM-Pathé.*

When Ladd, Jr., returned to the former MGM lot, now the MGM-Pathé lot, Brooks moved his offices from 20th Century–Fox to Culver City, and Laddie, who had expeditiously approved *Spaceballs*, just as swiftly okayed Brooks's plans for an informal "Re-Do" of Preston Sturges's *Sullivan's Travels*. The title of the new film: *Life Stinks*.

Brooks had often spoken reverently of the celebrated Sturges picture from 1941, in which a successful Hollywood comedy director disguises himself as a hobo to experience hardships that would be grist for his first serious film. Brooks had flirted with the subject of homelessness before, notably in his semiautobiographical "Marriage Is a Dirty Rotten Fraud" script, in which the lead character, divorced and foundering financially, briefly becomes a down-and-outer rousted by police from sleeping on a Central Park bench.

Ron Clark's homeless comedy, revolving around a similar reversal of fortune, had sat on the shelf for a decade before Brooks, done with *The Nutt House*, dusted it off in 1989.

Oddly, Clark, a friend of the Brookses who had spent most of the ten-plus years after *High Anxiety* working in television and writing stage plays, did not involve himself further in the planned film. And *Spaceballs* had proved to be the last hurrah for Ronny Graham, who was undergoing health issues and whose acting and writing career had begun to peter out. Thomas Meehan had decided he was not a movie or Hollywood man and returned to New York to work on long-gestating Broadway musicals; for several years he wrote the annual Tony Award telecasts. A fresh Club Brooks was needed.

---

* Later, the banks that had financed the maneuvers ushering in Giancarlo Parretti overthrew him for bad management, and for a few years the itinerant Laddie reigned as chief executive officer of MGM-Pathé.

Rudy DeLuca was still in Hollywood, writing for movies and television. DeLuca was a friend of Brooks's who had played small parts in most of his screen comedies since helping to write *High Anxiety*. He was brought in early enough to share the story credit for *Life Stinks* with Brooks and Clark. DeLuca recruited Steve Haberman, a former storyboard artist with an almost encyclopedic knowledge of classic films, who'd worked on *Transylvania 6–5000*, DeLuca's 1985 film. Shazam!—the new writing team.

By the time *Life Stinks*—touted as a "serious" comedy about homelessness—was first cited in news items about Pathé's buyout of MGM/UA, their script was nearly done.

The lead was tailored for Brooks, playing Goddard Bolt, an arrogant tycoon who covets a large slum property. (Bolt keeps in his office a model of his dream phallic structure—"one of the film's funnier puns," *Village Voice* critic Georgia Brown wrote later—which he hopes to build on the property.) Bolt makes a bet with a rival scumbag developer that he can last thirty days of homelessness: the winner gets the slum property. But once he has adopted his homeless guise, Bolt finds himself adrift and beleaguered. He meets vagabonds who befriend him, including the beautiful Molly, a feisty bag lady. In the end, although Bolt wins the bet, his desperate adventures change him profoundly.

There was warmth and sweetness in the script along with coarse humor—scenes of drifters urinating on Bolt as he lives rough—that hedged on the supposed "seriousness."

Laddie thought the script was *too* serious, however, especially its original ending, which was messagey. Brooks agreed with the criticism: *Life Stinks* would have greater commercial potential if it finished joyfully, as most Brooks comedies did; only *The Producers* and *The Twelve Chairs* had had endings tinged with defeat. "He felt [*Life Stinks*' ending] was a little too negative," Brooks explained to *The Times* of London, "and he asked us to change it before we had finished shooting. . . . I was happy to take his advice."

The new Club Brooks could write with certain actors in mind. For one thing, DeLuca wrote the biggest part yet for himself as a skid rower who insists he was once richer than Bolt. Old Brooks crony Howard Morris was in the pipeline, too, as the grubby, dim-witted Sailor, whose death is the film's darkest note, albeit made humorous by the acting out of one of Brooks's oft-told anecdotes about cremated ashes scattered by the wind.

The scriptwriters may have hoped for Harvey Korman as the rival scumbag, but in the end the part was not very sizable, and instead Brooks snagged Jeffrey Tambor just as Tambor was getting noticed on television. Madeline Kahn's biographer said the actress, absent from Brooks comedies since *History of the World, Part I,* had taken as a "personal slight" the fact that the director offered her no "substantial" roles in subsequent films. It would be easy to picture Kahn as Molly, the touched and touchy bag lady, but that part ended up in the hands of the well-regarded actress-singer Lesley Anne Warren, who had begun her career as a ballerina. She could carry off the dreamlike dance, with Alan Johnson's choreography, that Molly and Bolt perform to the tune of Cole Porter's "Easy to Love."

Using a new cameraman, Steven Poster, Brooks called the first take on *Life Stinks* in early June 1990. Shooting fast, without fuss, Brooks finished the filming in time for a brief August vacation. Then the director worked for almost eight months with three editors on the cutting and with his composer in chief, John Morris, on the score.

The high expectations Brooks nursed for *Life Stinks* reflected his long-simmering ambition to craft a comedy that would be regarded, by both audiences and critics, as not simply a funny parody but a "smartie" that spoke to the human condition. Looking for an artistic liftoff, in May 1991, he took *Life Stinks* to the 44th International Cannes Film Festival, where his new comedy was screened out of competition as a "Surprise Film."

France was Brooks's biggest non-English-language market, and

Canal+, a French company, was Brooksfilms' partner for the European exploitation and percentages of the film. Anne Bancroft flew in with her husband for a week of promotion and celebration.

Among the appreciative capacity audience for the Cannes premiere was a film critic who had been slow to join his fan club, Vincent Canby of the *New York Times*. Canby hailed *Life Stinks* as "close to being vintage Mel Brooks . . . in a Frank Capra mode."

The admiring tone was echoed by a few other major reviewers when *Life Stinks* was released the next month in the United States, with Michael Wilmington of the *Los Angeles Times* praising the film as "risky" and likable, despite defects, and Roger Ebert in the *Chicago Sun-Times* calling it the most thoughtful and soft-hearted of Brooks's oeuvre.

"This is the first time I've been able to come out of the closet," Brooks told interviewers, "allowed to fuse the quiet, dark serious elements in me, and the happy-go-lucky silly comedy." His many opening-week interviews to publicize the film included another stint on *The Tonight Show* and a *Fresh Air* segment for National Public Radio.

A majority of the critics, however, found *Life Stinks* as insincere as the attempt to spread the wealth of Brooksfilms through a greedy public offering. The *Village Voice* described the implausible uplifting ending and the transformation of Brooks's character as "mushy Schmaltz." Desmond Ryan in the *Philadelphia Inquirer* described the comedy as "wretchedly off the mark." Hal Hinson in the *Washington Post* ranked it at "the bottom of the [Brooks] barrel" and said that, just like the title, the film stank. *Rolling Stone* said that "it's hard to judge what stinks worse—the tasteless jokes or the hypocritical piety."

Never had the "crickets," his lifelong nemeses, struck him a lower blow.

Whether or not they applauded *Life Stinks* usually depended on how convincing they found the lead actor—Brooks himself—appearing in practically every scene. Ebert saw the comic as "his own best asset. As an actor, he brings a certain heedless courage to his roles. His characters never seem to pause for thought; they're cocky, head-strong, confident." Hinson watched the same film and found Brooks "charmless" and unfunny.

Preston Sturges was in his early forties when he made *Sullivan's Travels*; his lead had been the tall, handsome Joel McCrea in his prime. Brooks was in his mid-sixties and looked his age. Always limited as an actor, he seemed daunted by his role, and though many critics singled out his MGM-style fantasy dance with Lesley Anne Warren as the highlight of *Life Stinks*, Brooks could sing but he was no Fred Astaire. This warmest, fuzziest Brooks made critics pine perversely for the Rude Crude Mel who had offended them in the past.

"I was crucified," Brooks often said later. But it wasn't just the critics.

Was it too late for him to have taken a thoughtful turn with a script and his audience? Yes: his usual aficionados gave wide berth to the "serious" comedy about homelessness. Despite its release to 850-plus theaters in late July, *Life Stinks* became "one of the quickest flops of 1991," according to the *Los Angeles Times*, accruing less than $4 million before sub-run and video.

Brooks took the gauntlet overseas, traveling widely for print, radio, and television interviews, promoting *Life Stinks* in England, France, Sweden, Denmark, Germany, Spain, and Italy, his best foreign markets. "There are three pillars that make a movie," he explained to *The Guardian*, "the script, the production, and the one that nobody realizes—the selling of the film." In Italy, *Life Stinks* stayed at "number one for six weeks," he claimed. "They were lining up like [for] a cinnamon bun around the block." Foreign moviegoers, along with ancillary bucks, helped the film, budgeted at $13 million, edge into the black. "Europeans got it," Brooks liked to aver, "but in America it may have hit too close to home, and audiences may not have wanted to deal with that."

American audiences still balk at *Life Stinks*, which ranks lowest among the Brooks comedies on imdb.com at this writing, with a 5.8 out of 10 approval rating and only 8,443 respondents who have rated it. That actually ties it with *Dracula: Dead and Loving It*, but the horror spoof counts more than four times as many people who bothered to vote.

The failure of *Life Stinks*, kindred to the failure of his other more formal remake, *To Be or Not to Be*, was devastating to Brooks's morale. There would be no more attempts at "serious" comedy. Defiantly, Brooks always spoke of *Life Stinks* in superlatives, listing the comedy about homelessness among his underrated works, the dance scene ("gorgeously staged by me") as one of five favorites in all the films he had written, directed, and starred in.


If *Life Stinks* was a "serious" comedy, it was facile seriousness, and partly what made it artificial was its detachment from any auto-biographical resonances of the type that deepened Woody Allen's best films. Apart from being a very wealthy man, Goddard Bolt was not a character who closely resembled Brooks himself. Bolt is a pure businessman; he has no relationship to the film industry or the arts. His relationship with other people, his personal backstory, is restricted to fleeting references to a prior failed marriage: "It didn't work out . . . she said I spent all my time making money."

Brooks and his wife, Anne Bancroft, in real life, were at no risk of homelessness, although the couple had recently become empty nesters. By the time of *Life Stinks*, Max had gone off, though not very far away, to Pitzer College, a liberal arts school belonging to the Claremont Colleges consortium, in the city of Claremont in eastern Los Angeles County. He would study history and spend a semester at the University of the Virgin Islands before taking graduate film studies at American University in Washington, DC.

If anything, Bancroft stepped up her profile in television and films. While she never again starred in another Broadway play after *Duet for One*, she did play the lead in a Manuel Puig drama staged closer to home in Los Angeles in 1989. Television frequently showed her to the best advantage: she had good parts in telecasts such as Neil Simon's *Broadway Bound* (for which she earned an Emmy nomination) and "Mrs. Cage" for *American Playhouse* (another Emmy nomination). She also played the title role in a broadcast of Paddy Chayefsky's "The Mother" for *Great Performances* and portrayed the centenarian in the telefilm *The Oldest Living Confederate Widow Tells All*.

In 1990, the actress even briefly starred in her own television series, called *Freddie and Max*, which revolved around a down-on-her-luck American diva in London who is collaborating on her autobiography with a harried personal assistant (Charlotte Coleman). *The Times* called the short-lived British sitcom "magnificently forgettable," but Bancroft was paid $175,000 for six episodes and spent extended quality time in London.

There was also steady work for her in motion pictures in the 1990s, even if she was increasingly relegated to brief roles. Among her credits were turns as a former dancing partner of Fred Astaire in Carl Reiner's *Bert Rigby, You're a Fool* in 1989; Nicolas Cage's dying mother in Andrew Bergman's *Honeymoon in Vegas* in 1992; and a gypsy fortune teller in *Love Potion No. 9*, also in 1992. Bancroft appeared in three films in 1993: *Point of No Return*, *Malice*, and *Mr. Jones*. She was among the ensemble in *How to Make an American Quilt* and portrayed the difficult matriarch in Jodie Foster's Thanksgiving-themed *Home for the Holidays*, both in 1995. Nineteen ninety-seven saw Bancroft in another film for Sidney Lumet, *Critical Care*, and as a flinty US senator in *G.I. Jane*. She was Mrs. Dinsmore in Alfonso Cuarón's modernized *Great Expectations* in 1998.

Aging actresses struggle for substantial roles in an industry that prizes youth and beauty, and Bancroft herself said she stopped going to dailies after *Point of No Return*. By the 1990s, she was already a two-time Tony winner, an Oscar winner for *The Miracle Worker*, and a five-time Academy Award nominee. She'd been nominated multiple times for a television Emmy, finally winning in 1999 for her supporting role as the once-raped mother who gives up her child for adoption in *Deep in My Heart*. Arguably one of the most honored actresses of her generation, perhaps Bancroft did play "decreasingly important parts" in motion pictures as time passed, as playwright William Gibson was quoted as saying after her death, and too often as "somebody's drunken mother-in-law." But that point of view is unnecessarily harsh. Even when the roles were fleeting, when the pictures lacked prestige or significance, Bancroft gave distinctive performances and the critics, so hard on her husband (in his opinion), often saved up their praise for her.

Funny no longer made as much money for Brooks, and "Exec was (more than ever) dreck"—the second half of Dave Caesar's pronouncement. The producing was as much hard work as the comedy. Brooks's meteoric filmmaking career was winding down, although Hollywood and the public—and probably Brooks himself—did not realize it yet.

   With US studio support increasingly problematic, Brooks forged a pact between Brooksfilms and Le Studio Canal+, a subsidiary of a French cable network, which agreed to put up 40 percent of the budgets of three to five inexpensive productions in return for percentages of their foreign exhibition, broadcast, and video monies. MGM-Pathé (it was one of Alan Ladd's last acts) was the partner for US rights and distribution. Out of that agreement emerged *The Vagrant*, the last official Brooksfilms production—that is, the last film the company made without Brooks writing, directing, or starring. The director in this case was special effects maestro Chris Walas, who had also directed *The Fly II*.

The Richard Jefferies script concerned a nebbishy business analyst (played by Bill Paxton) who tries to evict a creepy derelict (Marshall Bell) from a property he has acquired. Their psychological warfare escalates into grisly violence.

Roughly half of the Brooksfilms productions boasted a horror component, but *The Vagrant* was an offbeat horror-comedy. Brooks's hand in the script is suggested by the wacky names of characters (Mrs. Howler and Lieutenant Barfuss) and the manifest potty humor (penis and urination jokes aplenty). The only credit he took was executive producer.

Whether *The Vagrant* was "not remotely funny . . . gruesomely violent . . . [and] routine" at best (*Chicago Tribune*) or "the perfect mix of horror and comedy" (according to *Fangoria*, a genre fanzine) depended on taste—and catching up with the cheaply made quickie. It was shown in precious few US theaters. That had always been the plan: to send *The Vagrant* overseas and focus on the video market Brooks prided himself on maximizing.

Writers had a harder life than actors, Brooks constantly reminded his wife. Writers began the day with a blank page and had to face many blank pages before they finished a novel, a stage play, or a motion picture script. Surprisingly often in his career, what was written on that first blank page—the original story for a Mel Brooks comedy—came from elsewhere. Frequently as well, the story idea was supremely obvious as spoof material, could easily have come from him, and therefore struck an immediate chord with him.

*Robin Hood: Men in Tights* was déjà vu all over again. When Norman Steinberg read in *Variety*, in January 1993, that Robin Hood and his merry men were going to be the subject of the next Mel Brooks comedy, he instantly viewed the project as overlapping with *When Things Were Rotten*, the short-lived television series Steinberg and Brooks had developed in the mid-1970s. He and Brooks had brainstormed bits, scenes, and characters that had fallen by the wayside, some of it stripped out by the network—including Brooks's customary "fag" humor about the merry men prancing around in tights.

Steinberg, who had also cowritten *Blazing Saddles* and *My Favorite Year*, phoned his friend. "Mel," he asked good-naturedly, "when do you want me to sue you—now or after the film comes out?" Brooks was outraged: "How dare you? How dare you?!" They argued. The new project was bound to borrow stuff from *When Things Were Rotten*, Steinberg insisted. They mined the same comic territory and sensibility. The furious Brooks didn't budge. One Robin Hood comedy was not the same as another, he said.

Steinberg backed down and hung up. "I was just kidding about suing Mel," he reflected. "I would never sue Mel. I just wanted him to know that it was not right."

No doubt Robin Hood had been "one of my great childhood heroes," in Brooks's words. He'd done Sid Caesar skits about Robin Hood, and the 2000 Year Old Man was also acquainted with the outlaw (he had answered Carl Reiner's question "Did Robin Hood really steal from the rich and give to the poor?" with "No, he didn't—he stole from everybody and kept everything"). In the early 1980s, when *When Things Were Rotten* failed, Brooks had even paid for a serious script about Robin Hood and then shelved it.

Despite all that deep background, the idea for *Robin Hood: Men in Tights* was launched not on a blank page in Brooks's hands but in a Beverly Hills dentist's chair.

Dr. Evan Chandler, in his late forties, was a "dentist to the stars," with show business patients who included studio executive Sherry Lansing, actor Christian Slater, and actress Carrie Fisher. Fisher later wrote about Dr. Chandler in her memoir *Shockaholic*, confessing that she had undergone several nonemergency surgeries by Chandler in exchange for the morphine he supplied her; he had provided similar services for other celebrity patients, she wrote.

Dr. Chandler nursed ambitions of becoming a movie producer.

One day, he had a new patient, a young, aspiring actor-writer from New Jersey named J. David Shapiro. Dr. Chandler befriended Shapiro, took him to dinner, and told him about one of his patients, Emile Buyse, the head of foreign marketing for Brooksfilms. Dr. Chandler had an "in," he said, through Buyse, with Mel Brooks. All he needed was the right comedy script.

A huge fan of *Blazing Saddles* and *Young Frankenstein*, Shapiro proposed a comedy called "Robbin' the Hood," which would lampoon Errol Flynn, Kevin Costner, and all the many other Robin Hoods that had come before. (*Prince of Thieves* starring Costner was a humorless drama made two years before that critics loved to hate, but it had grossed almost $400 million worldwide.) Dr. Chandler gave Shapiro a little seed money to develop a script over a period of weeks. Shapiro tailored it for Brooks, writing in all the sorts of things he imagined Brooks would love, including a character for Brooks to play: the roving wine seller and cut-rate circumciser ("half off"), Rabbi Tuckman. Shapiro also wrote in a small part for himself: Will Scarlet O'Hara.

Dr. Chandler corrected the spelling and grammar and made minor suggestions for improvements. Shapiro's spec script went to Buyse, who knew of Brooks's fascination with Robin Hood and his constant need for story ideas. Brooks got the script on a weekend, and on Monday morning Buyse phoned Dr. Chandler to send Shapiro in.

Shapiro had written a perfect imitation of Brooks: the spec script had rap music and silly songs, as well as all the major characters of the eventual film, including Maid Marian with her chastity belt, and most of the minor ones including the "bizarre-looking, witchlike" Latrine and Rabbi Tuckman ("a cute little man with a beard"). Right away Brooks got along splendidly with Shapiro, who knew his films and laughed at all his jokes.

At first Brooks wanted to take the project to Paramount, where he thought he could get an optimum deal. When Paramount passed,

Brooks was taken aback and none too pleased since he thought his name—as guarantor of quality—should have been enough to get the backing. He then offered the project to MGM-Pathé and 20th Century–Fox, putting his name on the title page of the script, first before Shapiro's. That angered Shapiro, who confronted Brooks. "Look," Brooks explained defensively, "no one knows who you are. This will help get it set up. Once it is set up, I'll take my name off the script."

MGM-Pathé and 20th Century–Fox both made offers, but 20th Century–Fox proposed the more advantageous division of spoils, paving the way for Brooks to return to the studio of his heyday, when it had once been good to be king of the lot. 20th Century–Fox agreed to put up half of the estimated $20 million production budget in return for domestic rights, with the rest of the money coming from Sony in the United States and Gaumont in France, another Paris business partner that was eager to invest in a comedy by Brooks, now practically a French national hero. Columbia TriStar was pieced in to handle the foreign sales and distribution.

Joe Roth had taken over as the head of 20th Century–Fox, but he left the studio shortly after approving the Robin Hood comedy, and executive vice president Tom Jacobson became the in-house shepherd of the project. One thing nobody liked was Shapiro's title, "Robbin' the Hood," which Brooks thought implied a black Robin Hood and which was too close to the Black Bart of *Blazing Saddles*. Even so, for a while they batted around the idea of Eddie Murphy as Robin Hood. Brooks's working title was no better: "Robin Hood: The *True* Story."

One day, mulling over possible titles, Jacobson said he liked the lyric in a Shapiro ditty in the script that sang of manly men wearing panty hose. Remembering something Kevin Costner had once said in an interview—that Robin and his merry men had never worn tights—Shapiro suggested they change the lyric to "Men in Tights" and use that as the title. Jacobson guffawed. More important, Brooks didn't say, "That's funny"; he roared with laughter. Everyone knew that was big, coming from Brooks. They had their title.

Brooks and Shapiro launched into story conferences to hone the shooting script—just the two of them, the smallest Club Brooks since *Young Frankenstein*. What could be better than to collaborate with a living genius of comedy? Quickly, however, Shapiro discovered that Brooks was wedded to the kind of reminiscent humor he had popularized in previous films. At a time when Tracey Ullman, Garry Shandling, Jerry Seinfeld, and others were rewriting the boundaries of edgy modern comedy, Brooks was clinging to his traditional ideas and old favorite shtick. He gave Shapiro videos to watch of *When Things Were Rotten*. He was incorrigible about wanting to recycle familiar stuff: the camera would break a window during Maid Marian's toilette; Prince John would have a roving face mole, comparable to Marty Feldman's mobile hunched back in *Young Frankenstein*; the Sheriff of Rottingham would—Brooks insisted—tell his guards to "Walk this way!" If critics winced, fans lapped up the self-referencing humor.

Apart from a preoccupation with the character he was going to play, Rabbi Tuckman, Brooks made only a modest contribution to the characters and to a plot that was already established in the spec script. He did not alter the content or sequence of scenes; he mainly injected humor into the names of characters and places in the story, inserted his usual silly puns and wordplay, and mapped out the sight gags he'd toss in here and there.

Although he and Dr. Chandler did not meet until after the deal was signed, Brooks felt an instant aversion to the dentist, and Chandler sided with Shapiro whenever there was an argument. So did Tom Jacobson on occasion. There was little of the usual Club Brooks camaraderie. The boss could get his way only by shouting, and not always then.

Shapiro stubbornly resisted Brooks, defending his scenes, characters, and dialogue, many of them originally crafted to please the comedian. Brooks screamed and screamed at the novice, who feared he was going to be witness to Brooks having a heart attack. Brooks usually backed off when Shapiro stood his ground, however. He seemed constantly distracted by other obligations and impatient to launch the filming.

As much as 75 percent of the spec script remained intact, according to behind-the-scenes sources, and Shapiro wrote close to 25 percent of the new material. He also contributed heavily to the songs, on which, ultimately, only Brooks's name appeared.

The situation became more complicated when Dr. Chandler asked Shapiro if they might share the script credit. With Brooks as his enemy, the dentist was not feeling confident about his producer's credit. He wanted *some* credit. Shapiro felt grateful to Dr. Chandler and thought the dentist had been fair and good to him. Shapiro said yes.

Shapiro and Dr. Chandler had long since decided that Brooks had not contributed very much to the final form of the shooting script when, later in time, Brooksfilms submitted its proposed official accreditation to the Writers Guild, which was obligatory for the producer of any movie. According to Brooksfilms, Shapiro and Chandler ought to share the story credit (with an ampersand signaling their partnership), while only Brooks and Shapiro should be listed for the script—with Brooks's name appearing first.

Shapiro and Dr. Chandler maintained their alliance, filing for arbitration with the Guild, insisting that Brooks had claimed more credit than he deserved. That was a thorny issue because Brooks was a Guild VIP, admired by many writers and increasingly by the younger membership. Brooks muddied the waters by publicly repeating the fillip, a joke of Shapiro's, that Dr. Chandler's teenage son, Jordan, had contributed a few jokes to the script—which Jordan had, by hanging around during meetings at Chandler's home.

According to sources, a preliminary Guild committee, after comparing the original draft with the shooting script, sided with Shapiro and Dr. Chandler. The partners were awarded the shared story and script credit. But Brian Walton, the executive director of the Writers Guild, took Shapiro aside. "It would be best if you gave Brooks equal credit on the script," he cautioned Shapiro. Why? the young writer demanded. Because Brooks was threatening to bring in a big gun, the powerful entertainment lawyer Bert Fields, and sue the Guild if necessary. Walton was afraid of Fields and enamored of Brooks.

When the partners refused to budge, the issue was sent back to a special hearing for another review. Dr. Chandler's claim as a writer had taken Brooks by surprise, and Shapiro's explanation of Chandler's input was garbled. The ultimate ruling gave Shapiro and Chandler shared story and script credit and listed Shapiro first on the story because of his primacy. Yet the ruling also gave Brooks a script credit with first position, supposedly because of alphabetical order. (*Spaceballs*, by comparison, had listed, nonalphabetically, Brooks's name first, followed by Thomas Meehan's and Ronny Graham's.) Chandler was given the sop of associate producer, a credit that demeaned his ambitions.

The whole imbroglio especially irked Brooks because he had enjoyed Shapiro's company and gone out of his way to include the young writer in all phases of the production, right down to the major casting decisions. He recognized Shapiro as the "voice" of the project, and Shapiro made him laugh. But Shapiro did not return Brooks's affection. Writers were usually welcome on the sets of Brooks comedies, but this time the main writer was scarce. Shapiro walked off angrily after Brooks reneged on his promise to let him play Will Scarlet O'Hara, and he refused all invitations to the filming—renewed almost daily by phone calls from Brooks or members of his staff.[*]

---

[*] The bad blood between Brooks and Dr. Evan Chandler lingered. In the summer of 1993, Chandler made headlines when he accused the pop star Michael Jackson of molesting his son, Jordan, during his son's visits to Jackson's Neverland Ranch. That was the summer *Robin Hood: Men in Tights* was released, and Brooks's office told journalists that he would grant interviews about the new film only if the interviewers agreed "under no circumstances" to mention Chandler.

• • •

Because J. David Shapiro's deft script had come in over the transom, the filming was able to begin shortly after the project was unveiled in early 1993. Brooks cast as Robin Hood an actor whose handsome looks evoked Errol Flynn: the charming British Cary Elwes from Rob Reiner's *The Princess Bride*. "Unlike some other Robin Hoods," Elwes declares in the film, a dig at Kevin Costner, "I can speak with an English accent."

The other performers in the potpourri ensemble included Amy Yasbeck, briefly a member of the *Nutt House* cast and now sexy Maid Marian; the stage veteran and Tony winner Roger Rees as the tongue-twisted Sheriff of Rottingham; the neurotic comedian Richard Lewis as the neurotic Prince John; Dom DeLuise as Don Giovanni, sending up a cotton-mouthed Don Corleone; Patrick Stewart as King Richard doing the same with Sean Connery, another former Robin Hood (*Robin and Marian* in 1976); plus the veteran funnyman Avery Schreiber, the old reliable Dick Van Patten, the soul singer Isaac Hayes, and the up-and-comer Dave Chappelle.

Madeline Kahn's biographer reported that Brooks tried to inveigle her into playing the role of filthy Latrine, Prince John's cook and soothsayer, but Kahn demurred and the short part went instead to Tracey Ullman as payback for Brooks's guest appearance on her TV show.

Brooks had a new director of photography, Michael D. O'Shea, who would stick around for *Dracula: Dead and Loving It*, and a new editor, Stephen E. Rivkin. Missing for the first time, however, was his longtime confrere John Morris. Morris had grown weary of Brooks's sudden late-night appearances at his house for protracted discussions about music, and he had said nevermore. Brooks filled in, now and later for *Dracula*, with Hummie Mann, a Canadian-born composer for Emmy telecasts. With the help of one of those classic tunes that was expected in a Mel Brooks score (the Billy Rose–Irving Kahal "The Night Is Young and You're So Beautiful"), the music was sprightly and the song credits were shared except for the title tune, which was credited to Brooks alone.

Brooks never worked more efficiently to get his shots and angles and later his final cut, sound effects, and musical scoring. Announced in January and shot in the early months of 1993, *Robin Hood: Men in Tights* was ready for theaters by the end of July.

The heavy advance television advertising, with a clever 20th Century–Fox trailer that broke people up (an arrow mimicking Kevin Costner's supersolemn Robin Hood, missing and splitting a tree), heightened anticipation. The studio laid on a lavish media junket, flying a hundred journalists into Los Angeles from all around the nation—mainly interviewers, not reviewers—for a stay at the Four Seasons and a day with the stars and Brooks.

The comedian shamelessly insisted that, like *Life Stinks*, there was a socially conscious subtext to his new version of the Robin Hood legend. "I'm always questioning the current socio-economic values," Brooks told the press. "I'm always pointing the finger."

Only a small number of critics saw the latest Brooks comedy as *Variety* did, however, as heralding a return to form: "a primer of all the familiar and visual jokes in his bag of tricks . . . a paean to the obvious that is more delight than retread." Gene Siskel, cohost of the Siskel and Ebert program *Sneak Previews* on PBS, ranked the film among the worst comedies of the year. Rita Kempley in the *Washington Post* described *Robin Hood: Men in Tights* as "about as funny as a buttload of boils," its humor suffering from too many mentions of "pansies, fabalas and fruits" and other "broadsides derogatory to women and the one interest group you can readily afford to offend on film—blind folks."

The public did not agree. Audiences saw a breezy, unpretentious, entertaining burlesque of an old familiar story with the Mel Brooks stamp. In a movie summer that was starved for laughs, *Men in Tights* opened in 1,261 theaters with brisk ticket sales that sent it to fourth place at the box office, the best Brooks showing since *Spaceballs*. By

September, the *New York Times* could describe the film as "a modest success" with $26 million gross in the United States. In Europe, where the reviews were no kinder, *Men in Tights* did well enough to add another $9 or $10 million to the figures. Future television and cable showings and video buys would continue to grow the returns, although with its $20 million budget the actual profits would disappoint everyone—20th Century–Fox and Brooks included.

Back to the future Brooks went for the dubbing of a French picture—a job of work that harked back to similar assignments he had taken for the pocket money in the mid-1960s.

For much of 1994, he poured himself into writing and recording English-language dialogue for Jean-Marie Poire's comedy *Les Visiteurs*, which concerned a time-traveling knight and his squire. *Les Visiteurs* had been a smash hit in France in 1993, but Gaumont and Canal+, the producing companies, were convinced that enhanced jokey dubbing would boost the US prospects and equally convinced that Brooks was the man to make it funnier.

According to *Variety*, however, director Poire disliked Brooks's version, which did not test well with American audiences. "I wasn't happy at all," Poire said. "Instead of remaining a comedy, which involved a French knight [played by Jean Reno], the film had become a parody, with the knight's accent so French that it was almost impossible to understand."

"It was an experiment," Brooks told *Variety*. "I love the film and I'm very proud of the dubbing, but [research company] NRG tested it mostly on young people, and I don't think this film is for them; it's a great film for Francophiles, not 12- to 15-year olds."

Miramax put the US release on hold until the summer of 1996, when *Les Visiteurs* was kitted out with standard subtitles and sent to art theaters without a trace of Brooks's involvement. He was paid $500,000 for his time, however—not too shabby.

# CHAPTER 16

# 1995

## He Who Laughs Last

*Robin Hood: Men in Tights* would be the last Mel Brooks comedy for 20th Century–Fox.

In 1994, the filmmaker moved his operations back to the MGM lot at Culver City. Though, during his US publicity tour, he praised 20th Century–Fox for its handling of *Robin Hood: Men in Tights*, overseas he slagged the studio in interviews whose clippings 20th Century–Fox officials probably read. Perhaps his motormouth compelled him, but perhaps, too, the 20th Century–Fox bloom was already off the rose and he knew he was done at the studio of his glory years.

"*Demolition Man* [a 1993 20th Century–Fox action picture starring Sylvester Stallone, Wesley Snipes, and Sandra Bullock]," Brooks mused aloud in an interview with *The Independent* in London, "probably one of the greatest adventures in stupidity, one of the least important and dopiest films, right? You go to the commissary at Fox, and these schmendricks, these . . . assholes, they're all very proud because it's done $27 million the first weekend. Now I don't want to seem bitter, but I jumped up on the table and I said, 'This is shit. This is ridiculous.' I said, 'We have to run [Jean Renoir's] *Grand Illusion* and *Demolition Man* side by side, just once—once—once!—to see what a great movie is.'"

Another member of the Reiner family stepped into the breach: Carl's son Rob and his company, Castle Rock Entertainment, were riding high owing to such hits as *A Few Good Men* (directed by Reiner) and *In the Line of Fire* (starring Clint Eastwood). Castle Rock was partnered with Columbia Pictures and had offices on the shared Warner's-Columbia lot. Castle Rock made a deal with Brooksfilms to produce the next Brooks comedy, and Columbia, which had been involved in the foreign handling of *Robin Hood: Men in Tights*, invested in the production budget in exchange for US distribution and ancillary rights, with Gaumont joining for a European share.

The subject this time would be Dracula—another ancient legend like Robin Hood; a vampire comedy was an idea Brooks had bandied about for years. The notion of spoofing *Dracula*, Bram Stoker's 1897 horror masterpiece, which had inspired a classic horror film starring Bela Lugosi in 1931, had floated around for decades as a natural successor to *Young Frankenstein*. Brooks had sniffed at the likelihood in 1970s interviews, however, because the horror story was too similar to Mary Shelley's classic, he said, and because "*Dracula* is too fantastical and does not have the philosophical granite."

But Dracula lingered in Brooks's mind. For one thing, the story was in the public domain; for another, Francis Ford Coppola had recently guided a lurid adaptation of the novel, with the title *Bram Stoker's Dracula*, to stratospheric worldwide box office in 1992. Brooks's devoted friend and admirer, the Italian farceur Ezio Greggio, had been in and out of Hollywood around that time, making his first comedy in the United States, *The Silence of the Hams*, in which Brooks had made a spot appearance. Greggio's all-horror spoof had included Dracula.

Not to mention the only film directed by Rudy DeLuca: *Transylvania 6-5000* in 1985, a monster/vampire comedy with Jeff Goldblum, Ed Begley, Jr., and an actor Brooks had always liked, Joseph Bologna, as a mad scientist. DeLuca and Steve Haberman, the *Life Stinks* team, went back to work with Brooks on *Dracula: Dead and Loving It*.

The two were fated to be the last official roundup of Club Brooks.

DeLuca and Haberman channeled the boss's trademark humor into a PG-I3 script that affectionately drew from Bram Stoker and Dracula movies dating back to the German silent-era *Nosferatu*. In their story Count Dracula was a debonair klutz who enslaves a solicitor visiting Transylvania and then travels to London to prey on the bosomy daughter and ward of a mental asylum director. The daughter is engaged to Jonathan Harker (the main protagonist of Stoker's novel). A Mittel European vampire expert (not in the novel) must save the day from the night.

Nothing was inherently wrong with the cast: not Brooks himself, chewing up scenery, as the vampire expert Dr. Abraham Van Helsing; Peter MacNicol as the silly enslaved solicitor; Steven Weber, from TV's *Wings*, as Harker; Amy Yasbeck and Lysette Anthony as the beautifully endowed Mina and Lucy; and Harvey Korman enjoying his last fling in a Mel Brooks film as the asylum chief. There was also one last stagey cameo for Anne Bancroft as a soothsaying gypsy, named (what else?) Madame Ouspenskaya, after the florid Russian character actress who played a similar role in I941's *The Wolf Man*.

Although the trade papers reported that Brooks had offered Kelsey Grammar, the small-screen star of *Cheers*, $3 million to play Count Dracula, that news item was undoubtedly a feint. In the end the director went for the mock-suave Leslie Nielsen in a fluffy wig and speaking with a Bela Lugosi accent. Brooks told interviewers he had cast Nielsen, a former straight actor reborn as a droll, unflappable comedy lead in the 1980s, after watching *The Naked Gun 2½: The Smell of Fear*, a Zucker brothers film, on cable television one night. ("I was amazed at the comic skill of Leslie Nielsen," recalled Brooks. "I had no idea!") Nielsen did not get the $3 million supposedly dangled in front of Kelsey Grammar, but *Dracula: Dead and Loving It* inched over a $30 million budget anyway.

Since Columbia did not own soundstage facilities, *Dracula: Dead and Loving It* was shot at Culver Studios from late May through July

1995. The cast recalls Brooks doing the job in his now customary fashion—no hint of the bell tolling on his career as a filmmaker. He shot scenes efficiently and evoked laughter on the set with bombastic antics; Nielsen added to the fun with his battery-operated fart machine. The postproduction was also done faster than usual to get *Dracula: Dead and Loving It* in theaters by Christmas.

Never did a Mel Brooks comedy land with more of a thonk, which was pretty much the reaction from critics and moviegoers alike. "If anybody hears of any good reviews, which are very rare, tell me about them and I will read them," Brooks told *USA Today*. "But even in a good review, they're gonna say something that's gonna be shattering." Although *Dracula: Dead and Loving It* made its debut in tenth place in the holiday box-office charts, the word of mouth was unfavorable and the US grosses topped off at $10 million, which was not only an embarrassment but also a genuine loss on the books for Castle Rock and Columbia Pictures—though probably not for Brooksfilms, which counted on rights and percentages overseas, where Brooks's comedies still fared okay.

American critics were attuned to the revolution in comedy that was upending the paradigm: badder-taste comedies such as 1994's *Dumb and Dumber* (where the farting jokes became shitting jokes). "Crickets" saw the last Mel Brooks film as creaky, and sometimes their language was harsher than that. "Anemic," declared *Rolling Stone*. Tame and cheesy, agreed the *Los Angeles Times*. "Quick, drive a stake through its heart!" pleaded the *Village Voice*. "Dead on arrival," pronounced the *Washington Post*.

Other longtime Brooks enthusiasts, such as Roger Ebert in the *Chicago Sun-Times*, more ruefully submitted their thumbs-downs. The comedian's strategy of satirizing other movies, "prolonged at feature length," he reported, had been "exhausted," making one yearn for the days of *Blazing Saddles* or *Young Frankenstein*. "The movie's not very funny," Ebert said, the kind of review that hit Brooks doubly hard; it dimly assessed the present state of his creativity while helping to depress box-office hopes for *Dracula: Dead and Loving It* in America's heartland, the middle swath of the nation Brooks had stooped to conquer.

Perhaps the critics would have gone easier on Brooks if they had known they were helping to write his obituary in Hollywood. Never mind that audiences never warmed to the film, either. Brooks held the failure against the "crickets," as he always had. "Critics are like eunuchs at an orgy—" the comedian liked to say, "they just don't get it."

Brooks ran into Ebert not long after his negative review was published and barked at the Pulitzer Prize–winning journalist. "Listen, you, I made 21 movies. I'm very talented. I'll live in history. I have a body of work. You only have a body."

Later, responding to a query from a reader, Ebert confirmed the unpleasant incident. "I was saddened by my encounter with Mel," the film critic wrote, "because I have been a supporter of his work (when it deserved it) since 'The Producers.' . . . I was one of the few critics who liked 'Life Stinks.' I was surprised he didn't realize himself that 'Dracula: Dead and Loving It' just didn't work. Yes, Brooks has put together a body of work and yes, a lot of it has made me laugh, but I would not be doing him a favor if I did not tell the truth."

"It, I think, felt more like a *Mad Magazine* parody," actor Steven Weber said later of *Dracula: Dead and Loving It*. "Not bad in itself, but it wasn't enough of Mel in a way."

The critics' hectoring and the audiences' turning away didn't help, but in effect Brooks had gradually priced himself out of the business in Hollywood. He had played the domestic market against the foreign at a time when cheaper, more dangerous, younger-generation comedies were winning over American audiences. His rising budgets, his high salary and percentages, his slice of overseas and ancillary revenue made the financing of his productions a house of cards. By the 1990s, with the major studios preoccupied by mega-hits and sequels, Brooks had made himself an increasingly less attractive sell job.

Like Woody Allen or Robert Altman, Brooks could have worked with creative freedom at a lower salary, making less expensive pictures. He might have discovered, as Allen and Altman did, that stars would appear in his vehicles for the frisson of it. But the top guy would have made less money, and in his eyes, he would have devalued his brand.

Repeated attempts to obtain cofinancing for Mel Brooks comedies and Brooksfilms productions, focusing over time increasingly on French sources, had once seemed farsighted in industry circles, and in the short term the European monies added to the company coffers. But the French could not completely underwrite the making of a $30 million English-language comedy without taking the lion's share of the US income, and the only entities capable of handling wide US distribution were the major Hollywood studios, which had seen profits from Brooks's comedies steadily eroded by his contracts and declining grosses.

A few years later, Brooks reflected with rueful candor on the decisions he'd made in his career. He'd once aspired to be the American Molière, the modern Aristophanes. His comedy had been going to be based on "pathos and real life," as Sid Caesar's was. He was going to write scripts revolving around characters and the human condition. His "fantasy of success," Carl Reiner once said, "was to write the great Russian novel."

He'd eschewed the "crickets" and intellectuals and embraced John Wayne and Lawrence Welk country. He had spent too much time crafting deals, promoting his films, and selling himself. He'd gone broad for big numbers instead of digging deep.

Speaking to the *Los Angeles Times* in 1998, Brooks seemed unusually chastened, perhaps because he was being jointly interviewed with his old friend, novelist Joseph Heller, who'd managed to do what Brooks had not: juggle the literary and popular labels.

"I often tell myself, 'Mel, if you did nothing but be one of the writers on *The Sid Caesar Show*, nothing but that and *The Producers* and maybe The 2000 Year Old Man, that's enough,'" Brooks told the *Times* during their joint interview.

"Once you have a hit," he went on, "you're chained to capitalism. You're inextricably linked to supply and demand. I did *The Producers*, I was free. I did *The Twelve Chairs*, I was still free. I did *Blazing Saddles*, I was captured."

"You were a prisoner," Heller interjected.

"I was okay for a while," Brooks continued. "*Blazing Saddles*, great movie. *Young Frankenstein*, top of my game as a director-writer. After that, capitalism. Artists shouldn't work because they can sell; they should work because they're inspired."

The onetime king of Hollywood comedy issued no official proc-lamation, but *Dracula: Dead and Loving It* was the last of just twelve comedy features he'd made over thirty years.*

Turning seventy in 1996, Brooks had his share of low moments in private. He could have rested on his laurels. But he still had round-the-clock energy and stayed busier than an ant farm.

With filmmaking behind him, in 1997 he found time to record a fifth and final 2000 Year Old Man album with Carl Reiner, another reluctant retiree. Their time-honored colloquy was less improvised than it had been for the first LP in 1961; certain exchanges were written out for rehearsal, and some expletives were added by Brooks that had not been in the vernacular of his character back in the button-down era. The septuagenarian friends performed the update

---

* Thirteen—if you count *My Favorite Year.*

on television and appeared at events, and finally they won the elusive Grammy for *The 2000 Year Old Man in the Year 2000*—after failing to do so for their first three duologues.\* For almost two decades Brooks had been wary about acting in other people's films. Larry Gelbart had originally written *Oh, God!* with Woody Allen and Brooks in mind—Allen as the modern common man who is tapped for a mission by Brooks the almighty. Brooks had said yes, but after Allen declined to participate, he had reneged. Nothing could convince him, not as a favor to Gelbart nor to the director of the film, Carl Reiner.\*\*

Director Stuart Gordon boasted a cult following for the offbeat horror comedies he had concocted, such as *Re-Animator* and *From Beyond*. After Gordon developed a friendship with Brooks over their shared passion for the horror genre, Gordon asked Brooks to play a pivotal character in his adaptation of Ray Bradbury's play *The Wonderful Ice Cream Suit*. Gordon thought Brooks might portray the elderly haberdasher who sells fantastical wish-come-true suits to five amigos in the story. After Gordon outlined the character for him, Brooks demurred, joking "I don't play Jews." He recommended Sid Caesar instead.

Brooks shied away from roles outside his comfort zone. But his stint on *The Tracey Ullman Show* reignited his sideline of comedic cameos (he played a loan officer rejecting the ragamuffins posing as Amish in Penelope Spheeris's film *The Little Rascals*) and voice work (he played Mr. Toilet Man in *Look Who's Talking Too*). The acting cameos and voice work supplanted filmmaking and picked up momentum

---

\* Brooks had also been Grammy nominated unsuccessfully in two comedy categories for the *History of the World, Part I*: for the soundtrack album as a whole and for the music video of "The Inquisition."

\*\* The role of the deity ultimately landed in the hands of another comedian, George Burns, when *Oh, God!* was produced in 1977, with the folk-pop star John Denver as his message bearer.

over the years until the list of his voice and cameo roles on imdb.com grew as long as a tapeworm. Often, still, the formerly dangerous comedian performed his bits in animation and family fare.

In his zone Brooks could be positively electric. He proved that as the wild-man Uncle Phil—Paul Reiser's Uncle Phil—in several episodes of *Mad About You*. Reiser, a onetime stand-up and cocreator of the hit television series, concocted the recurring role for Brooks, whose 2000 Year Old Man he considered the "Rosetta Stone" of comedy. Reiser and costar Helen Hunt went on bended knee to persuade Brooks to appear on their program. ("He seemed to like that," Hunt said.) Uncle Phil was a part that hewed close to the real Brooks. Although acting had been his Achilles heel and previously he might have been unimaginable as a finalist in the category of Outstanding Guest Actor in a Comedy Series, Brooks took home three consecutive Emmys for playing Uncle Phil in 1997, 1998, and 1999.

Also in 1998 came one last unofficial Mel Brooks comedy, a stealth film without his name attached as writer, director, or producer— and a work still obscure to most of his fans.

*Screw Loose* was the dream project of Ezio Greggio, a comedian, actor, and director who was a household name in Italy and all but unknown in the United States. Discovered in 1983 among a group of innovative young zanies behind a weekly two-hour variety show broadcast on a Milan television channel, Greggio became a leading light of contemporary comedy in Italy. Tall and boyishly handsome, he was especially adept at physical humor; his stock in trade was Inspector Clouseau–type bumbling. His shows included the long-running news parody called *Striscia la Notizia* (literal translation: "The News Slither"), which he had starred in and cohosted since 1988.

Greggio had also starred in a series of comic feature films, usually writing the scripts and sometimes directing them. He revered

Brooks, who had appeared on *Striscia la Notizia* over the years, initially for Italian publicity purposes. Their bonds of friendship strengthened when Greggio spent several months in Hollywood in 1992 and 1993, directing his first made-in-America film, *The Silence of the Hams*, with Greggio as a Norman Bates–type motel owner, Dom DeLuise as a serial killer, and Brooks in a cameo. Later, Greggio could be glimpsed as a panicky coachman in *Dracula: Dead and Loving It*.

Brooks was preoccupied with *Life Stinks* during the making of *The Silence of the Hams*, and the Italian comedian got to know Rudy DeLuca and Steve Haberman. DeLuca and Haberman cooked up a script for Greggio to star in and direct, this time with a pivotal role for Brooks. Their story involved a dying Italian industrialist whose last wish is that his son, the oppressed heir to his fortune, find the American soldier who had saved his life during World War II. The son goes in search of the soldier, who, ever since the war, has been confined to an Italian mental asylum. And he's still crazy after all those years . . .

The appeal of *Screw Loose*, for Brooks, was spending two months in Europe over the summer of 1998. He spent part of every summer in Europe regardless, but this way he could escape Hollywood and star in someone else's movie without worrying about all the headaches. The story line found the inept industrialist's son (Greggio) chasing the fugitive mental patient (Brooks) across Italy and France, with picture-postcard locations that included Monte Carlo and Nice. Although her roles were steadily dwindling, Anne Bancroft was still working regularly in television and movies, and she came over to visit for a few weeks; otherwise the comedian was on his own. The filming was a carefree experience.

"Mel, as usual during the filming," Greggio said, "came up of course with new ideas, gags, lines." Only DeLuca and Haberman were credited for the script, which nonetheless bore the Brooks imprint: fart jokes and song snippets for him to sing.

"[The production] gave him an opportunity to reflect, [to] just be out of the normal life that he had and maybe to take a look at things from a distance," recalled Whitney R. Hunter, the producer of *Screw Loose*. "And he had fun. He had a blast."

"He knows how to make people laugh," agreed Greggio. "Even on the road, at a restaurant, on the phone, he is wonderfully funny."

Besides being the life of the party, Brooks used those carefree months, shooting a picture away from Hollywood and out of the limelight, to refocus his ambitions on the future. During breaks in the filming, he could be heard tinkering with new songs, singing snatches into a tape recorder. "He would bounce some of the lyrics off me," said Hunter. "That's what he was doing, writing the lyrics and songs to *The Producers*."

Building a film around Brooks's persona was a labor of love for Greggio, who said that his idol took them all to acting school during the production. However, *Screw Loose* did not become an instant classic. On-screen almost continually once the plot introduces his character, Brooks displays amazing energy in his performance, literally leaping and dashing through his scenes. But he is also unbridled to the point of being frenetic, and his comic touch is shrill.

"It's a cute film," insisted producer Hunter.

US film critics could not disagree. No reviews, unkind or otherwise, appeared in the *New York Times*, *Los Angeles Times*, or *Variety*. It wasn't easy for American audiences to catch, either, because *Screw Loose* was not shown in US theaters. One appeal of the project for Brooks was the all-foreign strategy. Emile Buyse put together a partnership with Columbia TriStar and French film companies that sent *Screw Loose* straight to video in the United States while maximizing the bookings in Europe and other parts of the world. Brooks took modest money up front in order to earn disproportionately on the back end. "No complaints about the deal," said Hunter. "They made money."

• • •

After *Dracula: Dead and Loving It*, the producer David Geffen had phoned Brooks one day and put a bug in his ear about a stage musical version of *The Producers*, reminding him that with "Springtime for Hitler" and "Prisoners of Love" he had a great start on the score. Geffen may not have known that the original script had been launched forty years earlier as a prospective novel or Broadway musical and that Brooks had kept the latter hope alive with separation of rights in his contract with the original producer, Joseph E. Levine.

At first Brooks thought he himself might play Max Bialystock ("a FORCE!") in the musical, but that idea evanesced because of his age and the rigors of stage performing. At first also, Brooks felt nervous about writing the needed additional songs, because every musical boasted a dozen or more numbers, which would require a lot of fresh material.

John Morris was out of the running to help. The arranger and composer of the original *Producers*, who had been vital to nine of Brooks's twelve screen comedies, was permanently estranged from him and now worked almost exclusively in television.

Brooks courted other music men, including Jerry Herman, the composer-lyricist of *Hello, Dolly!*, whom Brooks had known since his first Broadway musical, *Milk and Honey*, for which, in 1961, Don Appell had written the book. Brooks called on Herman in Beverly Hills. "'Springtime for Hitler' and 'Prisoners of Love' are such wonderful songs," Herman supposedly told him, "I'd have to be crazy to try to write something that could stand up to them in the same show." Privately, he fretted a little about being too closely identified with a show with a dancing Hitler and a chorus line of goose-stepping Nazis.

Both Ronny Graham, who had agreed to assist with the stage adaptation, and Anne Bancroft massaged Brooks, encouraging him to write the new songs on his own.

Back in Hollywood by the fall of 1998, Brooks forged ahead with drive and determination. He had to go forward without Graham, whose ill health forced him to drop out of the collaboration. In his stead Brooks lured Thomas Meehan back to Hollywood. Before teaming up with Graham on *To Be or Not to Be* and *Spaceballs*, Meehan had won a Tony for his book for *Annie*, and now he would attempt to do the same with *The Producers*, turning it into the Broadway show it was always meant to be. Meehan's credentials for the job included the fact that, like Graham, he was a clever man with lyrics and played piano well enough to accompany Brooks's lusty singing during writing sessions.

The two men went to work without fanfare in office space at MGM, where privileged friends and visitors were invited to hear scenes in the work in progress as they evolved, and the songs, too, as the project gradually consolidated over the next two years.

"At the end of a day with Mel," Meehan would say in later interviews, "I have to go back to the hotel, lay down, and put cold compresses on my head. I'm only half-joking. . . . Mel's a fountain of genius. Remarkable things no one would think of pop out of his head, one hundred ideas a day. Many are wonderful. Many aren't. And he wants you to tell him which ones."

Another time, Meehan explained, "My main job in collaborating with Mel is to say, 'That idea really stinks. You're Mel Brooks!' Mel knows where the laughs are . . . but also, oddly, he doesn't."

Brooks and Meehan would share the book credit. The changes from the film revolved mostly around the music: where to fit the songs in, what characters would sing them. A journeyman Broadway composer and arranger, Glen Kelly, was brought in to fill John Morris's shoes and help develop the songs with orchestration.

Early on, Brooks decided to drop "Love Power," and that led to dropping Lorenzo St. DuBois (L.S.D.), the character Dick Shawn had played in the original film. Shawn's wacky rendition was a highlight of the film, but Shawn had passed away in 1987 and, more to the point, Norman Blagman (lyrics) and Herbert Hartig (music) had composed the song. Hearing of the impending musical, Blagman wrote Brooks, offering "Love Power" inexpensively, but Brooks replied politely that he was going to write the entire score himself.

To make up for the loss of L.S.D. and "Love Power," Brooks and Meehan expanded the "fag" humor from the original film, just as they had opened up *To Be or Not to Be* to a gay character with a camp sensibility. Their script made room for a retinue of swishy assistants to the effeminate Roger De Bris, who became (in their stage script) not only the director but the Führer-star of "Springtime for Hitler." The Village People lineup of boys (and one rare lesbian) sang "Keep it Gay!," which would become a showstopper.

Other supporting characters from the film were handed ditties. Ulla, a small part immortalized by Lee Meredith, was enlarged into the third lead behind Max Bialystock and Leo Bloom. The sexy stenographer develops a crush on Bloom, which blossoms in the third act, and her "If You've Got It, Flaunt It" solo derived from a memorable line in the original film. More of Brooks's greatest hits were reprised with "Walk this way!" from *Young Frankenstein* and "It's good to be the king!" from *History of the World, Part I*.

The old-lady investors, a montage in the film, became a lavish old-lady tap dance with crutches and walkers. Thinly characterized before, Bloom got a "backstory" explaining his lifelong Broadway itch. A visit to his accounting office (never glimpsed in the film) provided the excuse for another chorus extravaganza. Bloom's coupling with Ulla also allowed for the show to escape briefly to Rio de Janeiro (with appropriate song), from which he'd return at the eleventh hour to vouch for Bialystock at his trial. That, and Bialystock's "Betrayed" solo in a holding cell, filled the film's void of a third act.

Over the course of two years, Brooks and Meehan worked the script out in Culver City sessions. In the end theirs was a faithful adaptation, with a number of scenes and substantial dialogue carried over virtually intact from the film. It took so long because Brooks never seemed to be in any particular hurry. Also, he "doesn't like to do Scene II until Scene I has been rewritten 85 times," Meehan said later. "Mel Brooks is a fountain of comedy and smarts," he explained another time, "but he's not necessarily good on structure. He doesn't really write; he talks. I would take notes, then go away and write."

Meehan took time off for other projects, then returned refreshed. Brooks made trips back east, setting up the financial end, the Broadway connections, the scheduling.

All that happened with scant notice in the press. Brooks and Meehan rarely met on Fridays, allowing for long weekends and flights as needed back and forth from New York. Fridays in Los Angeles were also organized around Brooks's regular lunch date with old 20th Century–Fox friends at Orso's, a restaurant in West Hollywood, close to Cedars-Sinai Medical Center. The lunch group included Alan Ladd, Jr.; Laddie's longtime lieutenant, Jay Kanter; former agent and producer Freddie Fields; producer Michael Gruskoff; and writer-director Paul Mazursky. The friends had known one another, in most instances, dating back to the late 1950s. At one moment in the 1970s, they had all occupied adjacent offices on the third floor of the main executive building at 20th Century–Fox.

Brooks always signed autographs for fans who drifted over to their table in Orso's courtyard, not recognizing the face of anyone else at the power lunch, unless the group had a famous guest, such as Peter O'Toole one day. Leaving the restaurant, Brooks might shout out his name to tourist buses as they passed. He made everyone laugh, especially Laddie.

Their careers were winding down. Mazursky, for example, celebrated as an auteur filmmaker in the 1970s, now eked out small parts as an actor; acting had been his first love. Brooks could not claim any genuine hit since early in the decade. He was done with directing films, although he never said "done." The others knew about the embryonic stage musical. Brooks talked about how *The Producers* would fulfill his dreams and rock Broadway. Nobody doubted it, least of all him. He had the confidence, the belief.

Most Saturdays Brooks visited Santa Anita Park, where he indulged in small bets on horses, his one vice. People at the racetrack recognized him, yelling "Say harrumph!"—one of the governor's lines from *Blazing Saddles*. "Harrumph!" he'd yell back.

By the year 2000, the Brooks family had effectively moved their household to New York.

Twenty-eight-year-old Max prepared for his first real writing job, from 2001 to 2003, as a staff writer for *Saturday Night Live*, television's long-established comedy series.

Anne Bancroft was a staunch New Yorker and happy to be back in the orbit of the Russian Tea Room, Elaine's, the Carnegie Deli, and the Four Seasons. Approaching seventy, she acted less frequently and appeared in only a handful of telefilms and independent features after 1999. Together she and her husband made openings and galas and sneaked off to their new weekend and summer sanctuary in Southhampton.

In the late 1990s, Brooks and his wife finally surrendered their beloved Lonelyville house on the now overcrowded Fire Island and purchased a beachfront home in the hamlet of Water Mill in Southampton, which is located east and north of Fire Island but still verging on the Atlantic. Over time the Hamptons had become the exclusive preserve of wealthy celebrities. The Brookses' $3 million, 2,000-square-foot cottage on Flying Point Road sat on seventy acres with sunrise and sunset views. Former supermodel Christie Brinkley was one neighbor. Their longtime friends Alan and Arlene Alda lived nearby.

Brooks enjoyed precious little downtime. Somehow, raising money for the stage version of *The Producers* proved easier than convincing a Hollywood studio to underwrite another one of his films, however, perhaps because the show's estimated $10.5 million budget, though steep for Broadway, was one-third the cost of *Dracula: Dead and Loving It.*

One of the early major investors was Robert F. X. Sillerman, a New York friend and Hamptons neighbor of Brooks's. Sillerman owned a string of radio and TV stations that he'd parlayed into a show business empire including SFX Broadcasting, later expanded and renamed SFX Entertainment (music rights, concerts, and all types of venues, including being the "owner of most of Chi's [Chicago's] theater district," according to *Variety*). Sillerman could boast deep pockets, especially after 2000, when the multibillion-dollar sale of SFX Entertainment to Clear Channel, the number two US radio broadcaster, was finalized.

The other bankrollers included the veteran Broadway producers Rocco Landesman and Rick Steiner; the Frankel-Baruch-Viertel-Routh Group of stage producer-investors; Bob and Harvey Weinstein, the brothers behind Miramax Films; and Brooks himself.

On one excursion to New York to plan the musical, Brooks had penciled in his director: the London-born Mike Ockrent, who was best known for *Crazy for You*, a variation on George and Ira Gershwin's 1930 musical, *Girl Crazy*, which had won the Tony for Best Musical in 1992. Brooks cast a spell over Ockrent and his wife, the choreographer Susan Stroman, who had collaborated with her husband on *Crazy for You* (also winning a Tony for Best Choreography), by bursting into their apartment for his appointment with them, tapping and twirling up and down their hallway, as he belted out "That Face!"—and timing his close with a plop onto their sofa, exclaiming grandly, "Hi, I'm Mel Brooks!"

After Ockrent died of leukemia in 1999, Brooks persuaded Stroman to assume the reins. He told Stroman that she might cry all night but he'd keep her laughing all day. A ponytailed blonde whom everyone called "Stro"—she had the look and pep of a cheerleader—Stroman had begun to direct as well as choreograph Broadway shows and in 2000 made her debut as a choreographer-director with two musicals: the critically acclaimed *Contact*, her co-conceived "dance play," which ran a thousand performances and won the Best Direction of a Musical Tony; and that year's heralded revival of *The Music Man*.

Nathan Lane's casting was cemented, early on, when the roly-poly actor said a serendipitous hello to Brooks, swimming up next to him in the swimming pool of the Hotel Ritz in Paris. They bonded easily. "Mel was a hero to me, growing up," Lane said later. Everyone knew Lane as the voice of the meerkat Timon in the Disney animated feature *The Lion King*, but he was also a growing force on Broadway. He had played the Sid Caesar role in *Laughter on the 23rd Floor* and then evoked Zero Mostel's bigness of personality in the lauded revival of *A Funny Thing Happened on the Way to the Forum*. Now, as the new Max Bialystock, he would again try to make people forget Mostel.

The veteran actor Matthew Broderick (also in the voice cast of *The Lion King*) was not quite Gene Wilder. But for almost twenty years he had balanced expert stage roles (winning a Tony for the lead originated by Robert Morse in the 1995 revival of *How to Succeed in Business Without Really Trying*) with pinpoint performances in motion pictures (including *Torch Song Trilogy*, with Anne Bancroft in the cast). In his early twenties he had played the teenage lead in the iconic *Ferris Bueller's Day Off*, and fifteen years later remained perpetually boyish.

Cady Huffman had been admired in three Broadway shows: as a replacement in the long-running *La Cage aux Folles*; as Dancer in Bob Fosse's final musical, *Big Deal*; and as Florenz Ziegfeld's favorite chorine in her Tony-nominated performance in *The Will Rogers Follies*. She became Ulla. The seasoned performers Brad Oscar and Gary Beach became Franz Liebkind and Roger De Bris, respectively. Roger Bart, who had just won a Tony as Snoopy in the revival of *You're A Good Man, Charlie Brown*, was cast as Carmen Ghia.

Partly to win over potential investors, the first read-through, led by Nathan Lane, with piano accompaniment but sans scenery, costumes, props, or lights, took place in April 2000 in studio space on West 54th Street in New York. The handpicked audience of friends and family included Anne Bancroft and Brooks's longtime lawyer, Alan U. Schwartz. The "producers and moneymen," recalled Thomas Meehan, "laughed all afternoon long."

Other players were slotted, a topflight backstage team was engaged, and in December Susan Stroman launched five weeks of intensive rehearsal at the New 42nd Street Studios, with Brooks omnipresent, pushing his notes but always funny and upbeat. By late January 2001, the cast and crew were in Chicago for the first out-of-town tryout.

Brooks deliberately kept advance publicity to a minimum in Chicago and (later) Pittsburgh, where the press corps scrounged for crumbs. "Local critics were kept away for three weeks [in Chicago]," wrote *Variety*, "little money was expended on marketing and stars Nathan Lane and Matthew Broderick did very limited media appearances."

One underlying issue for the show was how much vulgarity the self-proclaimed emperor of bad taste could insert into the dialogue and songs for stage audiences. Brooks wanted to attract the traditional Broadway crowd of playgoers, but he also wanted to lure the burgeoning new demographic—commuters from the New York and New Jersey suburbs, tour bus riders from the Midwest, tourists from overseas. How much vulgarity would be a turnoff?

There was one line in "The King of Broadway," Bialystock's introductory song, in which he asks, "Who do you have to fuck to get a break in this town?" In Chicago during the show's tryout, the line got huge laughs. "In Pittsburgh, however, it drew only a gasp," according to an authoritative account, "so Brooks and Meehan changed it temporarily to 'shtupp.'" Nathan Lane argued fiercely with Brooks, who told him, at a post-Pittsburgh run-through, "We can't say *fuck* in a musical!" "Wait a minute?" Lane reportedly rejoined. "Have we met? *You're Mel Brooks!*" "Fuck" went back in.

Since the era of *New Faces of 1952*, Chicago had superseded Philadelphia as the lead tryout town, and Chicago was where the drumbeat of success for *The Producers* began. The reviews were glowing, but equally auspicious were the grosses of $4 million accumulated in three and a half weeks, breaking records at the 2,300-seat Cadillac Palace Theatre. Among the portents: orchestra seats scalped for $1,000. Brooks knew he had rolled the dice on a winner, and one cold day, as he and Meehan headed for a run-through, the wind whistling around them, he exclaimed, "This is the happiest I've been since I was nine years old!"

Wildly received in Chicago and Pittsburgh, *The Producers* arrived at the St. James Theatre on West 44th Street for March previews and its April 19 opening with "theater pundits," according to *Variety*, "already talking about boffo box office and Tony Awards."

For once the pundits were right. Never before had there been such "a fantastical third act" (Brooks's words) in a life story: *The Producers* musical bulldozed all expectations. On the verge of turning seventy-five, by dint of willpower and persistence, Brooks had managed to transform his decades-old pet script and writing-directing debut—a story about the worst possible idea for a stage show—into a triumph that transcended the dreams of his youth.

Critics gushed with praise for Nathan Lane and Matthew Broderick, for the miracle of the staging, above all for Brooks's "genius" in reinventing his film; "genius" became his permanent honorific in the excitable press coverage. Hillel Italie, the longtime reviewer for the Associated Press, hailed the musical as "demented, deliriously funny." Amy Gamerman of the *Wall Street Journal* called it "rude, irrepressible, and riotously funny." The hard-to-please John Lahr of *The New Yorker* wrote that Brooks "has found the secret that Broadway feared it would never find again: not money . . . but joy."

Of course, with Brooks and "crickets" there would always be

camps and curmudgeons with their sour notes. Did the stage musical improve upon or water down the original film? Was "Springtime for Hitler" as outrageous as it once had been? Did the comedy slight the Holocaust, which is never mentioned in the film or stage musical?

Thane Rosenbaum in the *Los Angeles Times*: "The film had a much darker, smarter edge to it than the musical, which is actually funnier, camper and more gay than the original." Daniel Mendelsohn, in *The New York Review of Books*, said the musical was pablum that "risks absolutely nothing. . . . [Brooks] smoothly processed his movie, whose greatest virtue was its anarchic, grotesque energy, into a wholly safe evening."

Though Bialystock and Bloom might "bring tears of joy to any anti-Semite," Tom Teicholz wrote in *Jewish Journal*, when the road company later visited Los Angeles, Brooks's "exuberance in both being Jewish and making fun of Jews forgives a lot of slurs." The musical fed on nostalgia for an idealized past, Teicholz opined, the kinder, simpler past of popular culture in the 1960s, when the original film was made and Nazis could be treated comically in *The Producers* or on television's *Hogan's Heroes*. If the film had offended, Teicholz wrote, the musical had matured into "delightful inoffensiveness."

What about the "central-casting faggotry," in the words of *New Republic* literary editor Leon Wieseltier, which was the culmination of a longtime strain in Brooks's humor? Stephen Hunter, writing about the film version later in the *Los Angeles Times*, said, "Mel didn't get the memo. . . . It is no longer appropriate to make fun of the way certain highly feminized gay men walk or talk." Paris Barclay, in *The Advocate*, lamented the "over-the-top caricatures," writing "I couldn't help feeling we were being laughed at, made the butt of jokes by a straight laughmeister who knows that we are the final frontier when even jabs at Hitler aren't enough to proudly wear a badge of political incorrectness."

The overstuffed score for which Brooks alone was credited was his great personal accomplishment, but that, above all, seemed to divide the critics.* The dozen-plus songs that augmented "Springtime for Hitler" and "Prisoners of Love" found lovers and haters. "Brooks' lyrics are formulaic," conceded John Lahr in *The New Yorker,* "but when they abandon any attempt at articulacy and revel in Yiddish folderol they are sublime." Michael Feingold in the *Village Voice* agreed that the music was among the show's limitations, adding "No one would accuse Brooks of high lyrical wit or great melodic invention." Tom Shales in the *Washington Post* stated flatly, "The score stinks."

This was one time Brooks could afford to overlook the nitpickers. So could the public, if they were able to shell out the $100 top ticket announced one day after the opening. *The Producers* became the first Broadway show to list that price. Yet theatergoers voted with their pocketbooks, stampeding to the box office. The show's entire $11 million investment was recouped by Christmas, after advance tickets were sold. "These are the biggest numbers ever in the history of Broadway," Lahr reported. Nothing could stem the tide, not even the September 11 terrorist plane attacks that devastated the World Trade Center in the autumn. "Come [to New York] and spend money, go to a restaurant, a play," New York City mayor Rudy Giuliani was quoted in the press as saying. "You might actually have a better chance of getting tickets to 'The Producers' now."

Less than two months after the opening of the musical, on June 3,

---

* John Morris received no credit for any contribution to the stage musical's score, although at least two of its best known songs, on which he assisted, were carried over from the original film. "While Mr. Brooks said that he solicited Mr. Morris's opinions on some of the show's songs," the *New York Times* pointedly noted in Morris's obituary in 2018, his daughter, Bronwen Morris, with whom Morris had worked on his reminiscences, said she had been "unaware of her father communicating with Mr. Brooks about the musical."

2001, the 55th Annual Tony Awards were held at Radio City Music Hall. With Nathan Lane and Matthew Broderick as cohosts, the event was presaged as a love-in for Brooks. Musicals had fallen into a vulnerable state—one reason why *The Producers* had been greeted with such euphoria in the theatrical community—and Brooks's revamping of his 1967 film garnered fifteen nominations, a record. Its twelve Tonys, sweeping a weak field at the ceremony, also broke records, winning for the year's Best Musical, Best Performance by an Actor in a Leading Role in a Musical (Lane over Broderick), Best Performance by an Actor in a Featured Role in a Musical (Gary Beach as Roger De Bris), Best Performance by an Actress in a Featured Role in a Musical (Cady Huffman as Ulla), Best Book of a Musical (Brooks and Thomas Meehan), Best Original Score (Music and/or Lyrics) Written for the Theatre (Brooks), Best Scenic Design (Robin Wagner), Best Costume Design (William Ivey Long), Best Lighting Design (Peter Kaczorowski), Best Orchestrations (Doug Besterman), Best Choreography (Susan Stroman), and Best Direction of a Musical (Stroman).

"A familiar grinning face at the lectern," as *Newsday* put it, Brooks sprinted away from his seat in the audience next to Anne Bancroft three times during the ceremony, becoming, during the night of awards, one of fewer than a dozen people to have reached the EGOT milestone—winner of an Emmy, Grammy, Oscar, and Tony. "I'm going to have to do the hardest thing I've ever done in my life— act humble," Brooks said, accepting his first award of the evening for Best Book. "This is a phenomenon!" he exclaimed the second time onstage, hugging the Best Score prize. He promised the crowd he would return and he did so for Best Musical, "reportedly the win he most coveted," *Newsday* reported, this time remembering "to thank Hitler . . . for being such a funny guy on stage."

He dampened the afterglow somewhat in late October when he and the show's producers announced that they would raise the top ticket price for the musical to an all-time Broadway zenith of $480 for select seating. Brooks insisted that the unprecedented price tag was intended to undercut scalpers, who were reportedly getting $745 for seventeenth-row orchestra seats. "We may be in for some flak," he explained, but "there should be some legal way for there to be no scalping whatsoever [so] we wouldn't feel raped and robbed by strangers who take advantage." In that respect, however, Brooks was a trendsetter. Despite widespread grumbling, once established, the $100-plus floor and sky-high select seats for *The Producers* became de rigueur for future Broadway musicals.

# CHAPTER 17

# 2001

## Unstoppable

Even the musical's most rabid enthusiasts could not have predicted that *The Producers* would run for six years on Broadway. The "crickets" who had bedeviled Brooks's films seemed like ancient history. The hit stage musical with twelve Tonys opened the floodgates of career tributes and awards from national organizations.

Arguably the sweetest of them was the least widely reported. The board of the Writers Guild of America West voted to confer the Laurel Award for Screenwriting Achievement on the "exquisitely outrageous" Brooks at its March 2003 annual awards program. Brooks had been prominent in the Guild, intermittently holding minor offices since 1959, but the Laurel was the organization's highest honor, bestowed annually on only one individual or writing team for advancing the literature of motion pictures. The Laurel formed a roll call of the greatest scenarists in Hollywood history, among them Preston Sturges, Ben Hecht, Billy Wilder, Joseph L. Mankiewicz, John Huston, Blake Edwards (the previous year's winner), and several Club Caesar members. Larry Gelbart and Carl Reiner had preceded Brooks in winning the Paddy Chayefsky Laurel Award for Television Writing Achievement, as had Norman Lear. Neil Simon and Woody Allen had collected their screenwriting Laurels in 1979 and 1987, respectively.

When the Writers Guild membership was invited to vote on the "101 Funniest Screenplays" of all time in 2016, *Young Frankenstein* came

2001: Unstoppable | 529

in at number six, *Blazing Saddles* ranked number eight, and *The Producers* made twelfth on the list. *My Favorite Year* charted at number 87.

In their time Brooks's comedies had been nominated for six Writers Guild awards. But the last Brooks script up for any single-year Guild award had been *Silent Movie*, which had been nominated—and lost—in the comedy category in 1977. Comparisons between Brooks and Woody Allen, the rival Jewish gods of screen comedy in the 1970s—although to be fair there were other contenders, such as Paul Mazursky—had long since subsided. Allen had directed many more films; his thirteen script nominations and five wins stand today as the all-time Guild record.

The Brooks-Allen rivalry was not a figment of the journalistic imagination, although perhaps it was one-sided, according to Allen's producer Charles H. Joffe, who once said that Allen "feels no competition with Mel Brooks, who spends his time in anger about Woody."

Although typically they praised each other in print, Brooks could be oblique on the subject of his onetime Club Caesar colleague, even finding fault with his prolificacy. "I admire Woody Allen so much," Brooks told the *Rocky Mountain News* in an interview promoting *The Producers* musical. "He's given us so much, these masterpieces like *Annie Hall*, that I wonder what drives him to do the two movies a year that he does. Is it the 'gotta get it all done before I die' or is it that 'I don't want them to forget me'? I would say to him . . . 'Woody, let the field lie fallow for a year.'"

The next few years were given to managing the phenomenon that was *The Producers*. Brooks supervised the original cast recording, winning two Grammys in 2001, Best Musical Show Album and Best Long Form Music Video for *Recording the Producers: A Musical Romp with Mel Brooks*. He oversaw the American road companies and presided over the London opening in 2004, where Nathan Lane bailed

Brooks out, returning to his role as Max Bialystock after Richard Dreyfuss quit the cast at the eleventh hour before the West End premiere. London was followed by versions mounted around the globe, from Tokyo and Buenos Aires to Tel Aviv and Berlin (at the Admiralspalast theater, where Hitler had once had his own purpose-built box). Brooks was usually involved in the major casting and any local tweaking of the script. He traveled to major venues for openings and gave untold interviews. As the New York run began to taper off, he began planning a film version of the stage musical with Susan Stroman directing.

The non–New York versions did not always soar to the same heights as the Broadway template. "Productions in Toronto and Australia closed early, and even a version in Los Angeles starring Martin Short and Jason Alexander had trouble selling out," reported Adam Sternbergh in *New York* magazine. The stage musical was too "verbal, manic, Jewish, and very, very New York," he explained. Yet the profits accrued.

One spillover from *The Producers* was Brooks and Anne Bancroft's joint appearance on *Curb Your Enthusiasm*, the cable series starring the cringe comedian Larry David, in 2003. Amusingly, the couple played themselves, auditioning David to costar with David Schwimmer in a cast reshuffle of *The Producers*. The clever story line had them secretly counting on David to flop so they could finally close the long-running hit. Their performances revived the memory of *To Be or Not to Be* and made audiences long for more of the married couple together. It also advertised the show still playing on Broadway with constant cast changes.

The couple continued to travel together when possible, joining up for weekends in the Hamptons, at Malibu, or in foreign capitals. As ever, journalists asking questions about their marriage elicited effusion. "Every stray thought I get I have to tell her right away so she can get a kick out of it, or she can have some input," Brooks informed the *Boston Globe*, "and every thought she gets she tells me. We really have a terrific time together. We laugh together, we cry together. We're very lucky to have found each other."

A lingering bout of pneumonia, which interrupted and then shortened Bancroft's 2002 appearance in an off-Broadway production of Edward Albee's play *Occupant*, in which she played the sculptor Louise Nevelson, proved to be a tragic portent, however.

Late in 2003, Bancroft went to work in writer-director James L. Brooks's new comedy, *Spanglish*. The film starred Adam Sandler and Téa Leoni as an upscale husband and wife, with Bancroft as the alcoholic matriarch of their dysfunctional family, a role that promised to be her juiciest in years. After a few weeks of photography, however, the actress went to the doctor for a checkup, and the tests that were ordered revealed a tumor. She was replaced by Cloris Leachman and underwent what the trade papers reported as "minor surgery." The press did not learn about the tumor or know her cancer history.

Brooks and his wife retreated to the Hamptons for most of the summer of 2004, staying close to family and friends who lived in the New York area. The surgery had halted the cancer, the couple believed. Bancroft thought she might write a memoir, and with actor Alan Alda she attended a summer memoir-writing seminar at Stony Brook University presided over by Frank McCourt, who had won a Pulitzer Prize for *Angela's Ashes*, about growing up in Ireland. Around the same time, Harper Entertainment announced that it had acquired Brooks's proposed "anecdotal book" telling his own life story.

The previous year, their son, Max, had married a budding playwright, Michelle Kholos, whom he had met at American University, and in the fall of 2004 Max published *The Zombie Survival Guide: Complete Protection from the Living Dead*, his first book. "My dad was disappointed" in *Zombie*, Max joked in interviews. "He said I needed to cut it down and get to the jokes faster. I said there were no jokes. He was very unhappy, like I had left the family farm." That fall as well, Kholos learned she was pregnant.

Bancroft foresaw new career paths for herself. She laid plans to produce an off-Broadway play, an offbeat one-woman show called *Squeeze Box*, that depicted mentally ill women crowded into a homeless center. She and her husband had seen the show performed in Los Angeles by Ann Randolph, its playwright. Bancroft had worked with Randolph to sharpen the script, and Brooks arranged the necessary financing to bring the stage play to New York. Eventually Bancroft intended to produce a Brooksfilms screen version, following its off-Broadway run.

Brooks, meanwhile, was immersed in preparations for filming *The Producers*. The stage play had to be "cleaned up for heartland families," *New York* magazine reported. Brooks wrote a new opener, "There's Nothing Like a Show on Broadway," hoping to wangle an Oscar nomination (only "new" songs were eligible). That also took care of the edgy "Who do I have to fuck to get a break?" lyric from the stage musical's opening number (the "fuck" was shot for the film but cut). Journalists listed that and other differences between the play and eventual film, which was shaped for broader appeal. (The film would be "just a teeny bit less 'New York'—long Hollywood code for 'too Jewish,'" Sara Stewart wrote later in the *New York Post*.) In other ways, though, the film script, emendated and polished by Thomas Meehan, closely followed the stage play.

Susan Stroman was directing a movie for the first time. Nathan Lane and Matthew Broderick were reprising their famous roles, while Uma Thurman, who had a prominent Hollywood career, was brought on to fire up the box office, replacing Cady Huffman, the original Ulla onstage. Former *Saturday Night Live* comedian Will Ferrell, now a marquee name in movies, would add his younger-generation cachet to Franz Liebkind, which Brad Oscar had originated on Broadway. (Oscar was now playing Max Bialystock in the

West End production.) Most interiors would be shot at the new Steiner Studios, a vast complex within the Brooklyn Navy Yard, near Brooks's old stomping ground Williamsburg.

Even as the late-February 2005 start date of filming neared, however, Bancroft returned to doctors and was diagnosed with uterine cancer. She immediately began intensive chemotherapy. Losing her hair, the actress wore self-knitted caps, "marvelous inventions of texture and color," according to Alan Alda, and hid out in the Hamptons as much as possible. As filming began on *The Producers* musical, there were days when the usually fussy and bossy man in charge absented himself from the set. Meehan filled in, watching over the script and speaking quietly to Stroman if he felt the line readings were off. Brooks shuttled between the Hamptons and the Mount Sinai Medical Center in Manhattan, keeping the secret of his wife's critical illness. "He didn't want to get a lot of sympathy from people on the set," said Jonathan Sanger, who had returned to Brooksfilms to produce the musical version of *The Producers*, "so he didn't talk about it and nobody on the set really knew what he was going through. It was all about Annie."

One day Bancroft stopped by a shooting location, a Fifth Avenue town house, just as she had always visited other sets of Mel Brooks comedies. "She was really tired," Sanger recalled, "but it was great to have her there. Obviously, at that point, people knew that she had been ill. They didn't really know the extent of it." In fact, she was dying.

Her grandchild, Max and Michelle Kholos's baby, named Henry, was born in March, "in time for Anne to hold him," in the words of Bancroft biographer Douglass K. Daniel. For a few months, Max told an interviewer several years later, his days consisted of "waking up in the afternoon, seeing my mom in the hospital, taking Dad to dinner, bringing him back to see the baby, then taking him back to the hospital. I'd stay up all night writing and changing diapers and warming milk. This was my routine."

Bancroft succumbed on June 6, 2005. Seventy-three at the time of her death, the actress had been married to Brooks for forty-one years. Broadways lights were dimmed in her honor. The obituaries extolled "one of the most versatile and resourceful actors of her generation," in the words of *Newsday*. Private memorials were held on both coasts.

Carl Reiner hosted one gathering at the Academy of Motion Picture Arts and Sciences in Los Angeles. A hundred invited guests also convened at the St. James Theatre in New York, where *The Producers* still played nightly. Nathan Lane, Matthew Broderick, Patty Duke, Mike Nichols, and Alan Alda delivered testimonials. Arthur Penn, the director of *The Miracle Worker*, wept during his eulogy, and Paul Simon performed "Mrs. Robinson" from *The Graduate* on his acoustic guitar. "If any of you are grieving," the bereft Brooks told people at both events, "keep it to yourself. I don't want to hear it."

Bancroft was laid to rest in a cemetery in the small community of Valhalla within the town of Mount Pleasant in Westchester County, near the grave of her father. (Her mother outlived her.) A small sculpture of a bereaved kneeling angel topped her tombstone, which was inscribed "Anne Bancroft Brooks," with her birth and death dates, and "Cherished Actress, Beloved Wife, Mother, Grandmother, Sister and Daughter."

Returning to Manhattan after the funeral, Brooks upbraided the limo driver, "What the hell are you doing? We don't take tunnels!" Considering the time of day, the driver explained hesitantly, this route was fastest. "That doesn't matter!" Brooks shouted. "We don't take tunnels! We can't!" Max, in the limo, took his father's hand. Dad, he reminded Brooks gently, Mom was the one who disliked tunnels. "He'd been her shield against those dark, closed spaces, and he wasn't putting down his guard yet," Max recalled.

Many nights—long nights now—Brooks would knock on his

son's door. He would switch off his cell phone, help with the baby's bedtime bottle. He'd fall asleep on the sofa watching television until Max woke him up and insisted that he go to bed. Max was now "my father's keeper," he realized, writing about that period for *Men's Journal* two years later.

"What am I going to do?" Brooks repeatedly asked his son, "sad, anxious, sometimes angry," Max recalled. All Max knew to reply, he said, was "One hedgerow to the next, Dad," which was one of Bancroft's maxims, meaning one day at a time.

"My dad liked going to the same restaurant, so I took him every night," Max wrote. "Just a hole in the wall, one of the few in New York where he wouldn't be recognized. He also liked old war flicks, so I scoured Froogle and Amazon for all the black-and-white DVDs I could find. I could probably act out every scene in *Run Silent, Run Deep.*"

For a spell Brooks avoided longtime friends, especially couples who reminded him of his loss. He'd go to the racetrack with old cronies; that was different—it was about the horses. One day he ran into Dick Van Patten at Santa Anita, however, and Van Patten interrupted their conversation to phone his wife, arranging to meet her later at a restaurant. Nothing was said about it until the next day, when the two chanced to meet again, and Brooks upbraided him, "You know, Dick, you really hurt my feelings yesterday. That was very inconsiderate." Van Patten was stunned, asking what he had done to upset him. "You have a wife to go with to a restaurant," Brooks replied, "and I don't."

Bancroft's death revitalized Brooks's relationship with his children from his first marriage, too. Though at times they all had held small Brooksfilms jobs (without screen credit), Stefanie, Nicholas, and Eddie had struggled to establish themselves professionally.

Stefanie Brooks had married and moved to New Jersey, where she lived out of the public eye. Nicholas had worked as a story editor for Brooksfilms and other production companies for twenty years;

he aspired to be a filmmaker like his father. Eddie was in the music business and trying to launch an album that would pay tribute to his father (with U2, who drew the title of their seventh studio album, *Achtung Baby*, from *The Producers*, among the hoped-for pop-rock lineup of artists).*

Brooks's three children with Florence Baum were not particularly close to Max, their half sibling, when Bancroft was alive, because they had been treated like add-ons to the close Brooks-Bancroft family unit. Now the half siblings engaged with Max and conspired with one another to keep their father company. Around the same time, Brooks began to show up at the apartment of Florence's son from her second marriage to Ed Dunay, turn on the TV set at his place, too, curl up on the couch, and fall asleep.

Out in public Brooks upheld his comic profile. In August the *New York Post* reported a late-night sighting at the twenty-four-hour French Roast coffee shop in Greenwich Village. A woman sidled up to Brooks and offered condolences on his wife's passing. "I know how you feel," she said. "I just lost my mother." How old was your mother? Brooks asked politely. "Ninety-six," the woman replied. "Well," he said, "she was asking for it."

After a few months, Max began pleading with his father to go back to work. "I'd always been jealous of my father's passionate devotion to his career," he wrote. "My mother called it his mistress. I called it his favorite son. Of all the emotional barriers I'd overcome to help my dad, embracing my childhood archrival was the toughest."

Somewhat anticlimactically, Susan Stroman's film version of *The Producers* was released to theaters at the end of 2005. It was a point of pride for Brooks to see the stage musical filmed—"memorialized . . . fixed forever." Stroman infused the screen adaptation, especially the dance numbers, with cinematic energy. But if time had been kind to

---

* As of this writing, no such LP has been released.

*The Producers* on Broadway, which was fond of musicals set in a rose-ate past, the world of film had moved on. Mick LaSalle in the *San Francisco Chronicle* wrote that Nathan Lane and Matthew Broderick, "reputedly great on stage (I never saw them), are barely good on-screen." A. O. Scott in the *New York Times* said that the 134-minute movie "feels, in every sense, like a rip-off." (Brooks was soon quoted in the *New York Post* as going around saying that he was tempted to send Scott a letter: "Be sure to save this because, after you're gone, it'll be the only thing of yours people want to read.")

The film never returned its reported $45 million budget, four times the initial cost of the Broadway show. Nor did any Oscar or Writers Guild nominations come to pass.

By year's end, though, the old gleam had returned to Brooks's eye—"the passion," in Max Brooks's words. He made his first public appearance since his wife's death at the January 2006 Golden Globe Awards in Los Angeles (*The Producers* had received multiple nominations). Not long after that he summoned director Susan Stroman, writing partner Thomas Meehan, and musical arranger Glen Kelly, and they rolled up sleeves on the musical version of *Young Frankenstein*. At times Meehan had doubled as his "grief therapist." The past year had been "the worst year of [Brooks's] life," Meehan recalled.

Brooks's inner *mensch* awakened after the megasuccess of *The Producers* and the death of Anne Bancroft. Apart from signs of renewed devotion to his children, sources say Brooks gifted a sum of money to Alfa-Betty Olsen, his amanuensis on the original *Producers* film. He began to mention the overlooked Olsen's help on the script in interviews, though he stopped short of saying that she had been an actual collaborator. But the Brooks-Olsen friendship had survived its onetime breach and continued stronger than ever.

When Nathan Lane took leave from *The Producers* in 2003, the company needed a replacement for Bialystock and Brooks approved the casting of Lewis J. Stadlen, the actor he had tyrannized during the filming of *To Be or Not to Be*. Stadlen was eminently qualified for the role, but still there was a hint of an apology in Brooks's decision.

On camera Buck Henry looked a little trapped when his *Get Smart* cocreator behaved so deferentially to him the day they shot "extras" for the boxed set of the sixties television series, which included background interviews with Henry and Brooks.[*]

"I'm so embarrassed," Brooks explained as the credit "Created by Mel Brooks with Buck Henry" flashed by on a screen during their joint interview, "that my lawyer or agents stuck the word 'with' [in the contract] and I didn't see it—I never saw it in the contract—I knew it was you and me writing it—until I saw it on the screen. They were protecting me. They wanted to make me a big star. And I didn't apologize to you too profusely enough, but I did in the future—you've cost me—every time I'm interviewed, every program, I say, 'It's Buck Henry, he is the best. . . . I was so glad to tag along with him and get some credit.' You know that, every time I'm on, I always say that."

"I don't know that," Henry replied dryly, "because of course I never watch you . . .

"But here's the other half of that," Henry went on, "the other half of that is yes, of course I was furious and blamed you. But later on I figured out that Talent Associates made this deal with you without telling me, so the blame got shifted. Then for the audience's delectation, what happens one day . . ."

"The audience's delectation!" Brooks interrupted. "Okay, continue."

---

[*]  Although Henry himself had fanned the "heritage of bad blood," in Kenneth Tynan's phrase, he was also pained by the conflict between him and Brooks, saying that Tynan had exaggerated it. "In a terrific drunken moment," Henry told *American Film* magazine, "[Tynan] told me he was inventing a feud between Mel and me. . . . It was unconscionable. At the *New Yorker*, apparently, they told him his article was too friendly, too nice. So he got us into a wrangle, which shouldn't have been. It's always 'yesterday's news.'"

"For the audience's delectation, I was sitting in the office some-where—at Talent Associates—and you came by and said, 'I've got it! Here are the credits: Mel Brooks *or* Buck Henry,' and I thought, 'I can't really hold a grudge when he says stuff like that.'" Henry paused, staring into the camera with the slight shadow of a smile. "But I did anyway."

On April 22, 2007, the curtain finally rang down on *The Producers* after 2,502 performances and $300 million in tickets sold over the course of six years. The night began with a standing ovation for Brooks as he took his orchestra seat in the St. James Theatre. He gave the final curtain speech, with the audience calling out "We love you, Mel!"

Brooks was two months shy of his eighty-first birthday, and *Young Frankenstein* was revving up for fall tryouts and its November 8, 2007, opening at the Hilton Theatre.

Gene Wilder had shouted down the phone—something that wasn't "We love you, Mel!"—when informed of the planned stage musical based on the horror-film spoof that Wilder had originated and cowritten in 1976. For one thing, how could "Puttin' on the Ritz," the Irving Berlin evergreen sung by the Monster, the *only* song in the original *Young Frankenstein*, still be a "showstopper if you've got eighteen other songs in the show?" in Wilder's words. The long-time friends did not speak again for a week.

Wilder had recovered from a bout with non-Hodgkin's lymphoma and was married to his fourth wife and living in Stamford, Connecticut. Although he spent his days painting and writing—he told interviewers he had retired from acting—he did not involve himself in the *Young Frankenstein* musical. Yet as angry as he was initially, the actor was resigned to the show ultimately billed as "The New Mel Brooks Musical, *Young Frankenstein*." Brooks's cowriting and producing contract gave him overriding control.

"Mel was always driven by money," Wilder told *The Independent* in London. "Even after he started earning good money, he was still so driven by it." By the time the two spoke on the phone again, a week later, Wilder was ready to accede; he had come around to thinking "I had everything to win and nothing to lose. If it's a flop, they're not going to blame me." Brooks had sounded so happy and excited about the musical. "If I dampened that experience," said Wilder, "I'd feel terrible for the rest of my life."

Brooks went the extra mile, phoning Wilder as the songs were being constructed, singing them over the phone. Brooks and Anne Bancroft had often driven up to Stamford to see Wilder. The friendship between Brooks and Wilder endured. Roger Bart, Carmen Ghia from *The Producers* musical, was cast in Wilder's role, Dr. Frankenstein. The stage veteran Shuler Hensley would portray the Monster, which Peter Boyle had portrayed in the original film.

Robert F. X. Sillerman and Harvey Weinstein were principal investors in the new show, along with Brooks himself. But when, after tryouts and previews, the $18 million production opened in late 2007, many reviewers lambasted Brooks's second musical overhaul. One of the most consequential critics, Ben Brantley of the *New York Times*, complained of "a monster-size headache" and said he had "laughed exactly three times" at the tired jokes. "Despite its fidelity to the film's script, 'The New Mel Brooks Musical Young Frankenstein' (to use its sprawling official title) feels less like a sustained book musical than an overblown burlesque revue, right down to its giggly smuttiness."

The chink in Brooks's armor, his songwriting, came under special fire. "There are some enjoyable musical routines," conceded Brantley, but "my count is 2 out of nearly 20." The score was "nondescript," wrote Terry Teachout in the *Wall Street Journal*. Charles McNulty in the *Los Angeles Times* described some of the songs as "schlocky." So many of Brooks's tunes were "tinny," according to Peter Marks in the *Washington Post*, that "even some of the better material ends up feeling a bit shrill and hollow."

A number of critics sneaked in disapproving mention of the $450 select seating. Brooks would earn a quarter of the profits after investors were paid, according to rumors.

Feeling persecuted anew by reviewers, the mastermind of the musical flared up when appearing on a City University of New York panel with Susan Stroman and cast members, moderated by *New York Times* reporter Campbell Robertson. "Why don't you say anything nice about *Young Frankenstein*?" Brooks demanded of Robertson. "I'm not Ben Brantley!" Robertson replied, squirming. "Holy [expletive]!" Brooks responded, his mouth a bagel of astonishment, getting laughs from the audience before "the lovable egomaniac," according to an account in the *New York Post*, pressed his "relentless defense strategy," "wildly" overpraising his own musical and interjecting "self-adoring things like how an arrangement of one of his songs made him cry."

Brooks also singled out *Seattle Times* theater critic Misha Berson (Berson thought *Young Frankenstein* was "too close to the movie," Brooks complained. "What should it have been close to? *Gone With the Wind*?") and attacked a *New York Post* columnist ("a flimsy excuse for a journalist") while taking a broad swipe at all the New York drama reviewers. "I feel sorry for the critics. They've got to report the show and run alongside it. But with my show they can't run alongside because they're not that talented."

Brooks told the audience listening to the panel, "Look, critics want to support a green caterpillar inching towards the sun. They want to play God. But we're a butterfly!"

An enterprising *Newsday* reporter phoned Brooks at his Upper East Side pied-à-terre to ask about the $450 top ticket and the quarter share of profits said to be guaranteed in his contract. Brooks insisted that the $450 price tag had been the idea of entertainment mogul Robert F. X. Sillerman, who'd also been a backer of *The Producers*—which had been the first $450-ticket musical. Brooks stoutly defended the steep pricing. "A lot of people have the money, and want special seats, and they're rich . . . so why give it to the scalpers?"

As for his personal remuneration, Brooks appeared to confirm the scuttlebutt. "For writing half the book, all the score, being around to assist the actors, do I not deserve it?" he snapped at the *Newsday* reporter. "After four or five Broadway shows [in the 1950s and 1960s] where I worked for two or three years and didn't get a paycheck, am I not entitled to twenty-four percent of the show if it is a big hit? . . . My argument is: I supply. If the stuff is really memorable, then I deserve a fair share of the profits."

Bad notices notwithstanding, Brooks stuck with the production, tweaking it only in the way he edited his films, with small substitutions and deletions. "I was there last night," Brooks told one columnist, "and took out one exchange that didn't work. One pause was three seconds too long, so I shortened it. And there's a tap routine. I suddenly realized we had to raise the sound on the dancers' taps for the final eight bars."

At Tony time, however, *Young Frankenstein* garnered only three nominations, which was not many compared to the fifteen for *The Producers*. There was not one for Brooks personally, none won, and the audiences began to slack off. (The initial crowds had arrived "so keyed up to see their favorite bits—cheering the first glimpse of Frau Blücher, mouthing 'What hump?' with Igor," as Jeremy McCarter wrote in *New York*, "that if you don't share their ardor, you may feel you've wandered into a tribute act for the wrong band.") In June, according to press items, the stars, some of them earning $10,000 or more weekly before bonuses, were forced to accept 50 percent salary slashes in order to help keep the musical afloat until January 2009. Brooks and Stroman, "said to earn nearly six figures a week," reported the *New York Post*, took no such reductions.

By any measure, *Young Frankenstein* enjoyed a healthy run: one year of curtain calls, 485 performances. But the media sniping had left a familiar sour taste in Brooks's mouth. "It still smarts," he told the *Los Angeles Times* in 2012. "I don't feel welcome on Broadway." By then he was said to be at work on a *Blazing Saddles* musical, but "I'm torn between taking a new show like that to Broadway and being slaughtered."

Indefatigably, Brooks marched toward being a nonagenarian. The awards and recognitions continued to rain down upon the— operative phrase—"national treasure."

Brooks joined jazz pianist Dave Brubeck, actor Robert De Niro, rock-and-roller Bruce Springsteen, and opera singer Grace Bumbry for ceremonies feting their lifetime achievements in the arts at the 32nd Kennedy Center Honors gala in Washington, DC, in 2009. Carl Reiner introduced his 2000 Year Old friend, and Frank Langella opened a musical tribute with the *Twelve Chairs'* theme song. Other performers included actor Jack Black in green legwear offering a snippet from *Robin Hood: Men in Tights*, Harry Connick, Jr., crooning "High Anxiety," and Matthew Broderick with a medley from *The Producers*.

The occasion was also celebratory when the American Film Institute conferred its 41st Life Achievement Award on the comedian in June 2013. Inaugurated by an award to John Ford in 1973, the AFI Life Achievement Award had been bestowed on a list of Hollywood paragons that included such Brooks heroes as Alfred Hitchcock, Fred Astaire, and Billy Wilder. The Life Achievement Award had eluded Woody Allen, among other notable omissions over the decades, because recipients had to agree to appear at the staged and televised ceremony, which was an annual income booster for the organization.

Characteristically, Brooks saw the Life Achievement Award as partial reparation for past motion picture industry oversights. "I was never recognized as a movie director," the honoree told interviewers. "Never! They always talk about my being a great writer and comic and an important producer. But I've never been saluted as a filmmaker."

Brooks often arrived at such events with prepared shenanigans, as was true when, in 2014, he was invited to add his handprints, footprints, and autograph to the forecourt of the TCL Chinese Theatre on Hollywood Boulevard, a tradition dating back to the 1920s. Norman Lear and Carl Reiner stood with him, waving to the crowd and photographers, as Brooks flourished a prosthetic digit and left the first six-fingered handprint in the cement.

The United States Marine Band saluted the comedian with "Springtime for Hitler" as US president Barack Obama conferred the National Medal of Arts & Humanities on a select group of artists and professionals including Brooks in the East Room of the White House in 2016. Among the "impressive crew," in Obama's words, were Motown Records founder Berry Gordy, six-time Tony winner Audra McDonald, National Public Radio host Terry Gross, nonfiction author Ron Chernow, novelist Sandra Cisneros, poet Louise Glück, and chef José Andrés. When his name was called, Brooks stepped up to the stage, and as Obama placed the heavy medal around his neck, his knees sagged under its weight, sending the president and audience into hysterics. Later, Obama told Brooks that he loved *Blazing Saddles*, which he'd sneaked into as a kid, and Brooks told the press he'd use the medal "as something to put a hot cup on, so it doesn't burn the table."

He embarked on a series of shows staged for cable television and extended interview programs that reunited him with Dick Cavett and the BBC documentarian Alan Yentob (the 2012 show, called *Mel Brooks Strikes Back!*, was nominated for an Emmy). He retold favorite anecdotes, sang songs from his films, and just kibitzed. The appearances were usually timed with the release of products such as box sets, and often his lines were written or ghostwritten by Club Brooks longtimers Rudy DeLuca and Steve Haberman.

Once Johnny Carson's most frequent guest, Brooks found endless time for chitchat and reminiscences on *60 Minutes*–type news-magazine TV programs (Mike Wallace had been interviewing him intermittently for nearly half a century). These days he frequently showed up on late-night talk shows hosted by younger admirers. He logged time with Conan O'Brien, Tavis Smiley, Jimmy Kimmel, Queen Latifah, Bill Maher, James Corden, Jimmy Fallon, David Letterman, and more. Brooks continued his prolificacy with interviews—on the web and in print—and his face decorated many magazine covers, probably even more now, in the twilight of his career, than in the 1970s.

Usually he joked in interviews, but on occasion he could be soul searching. "I had the three thirds that make one whole," Brooks told the Jewish monthly *The Forward*. "One third is the neurotic need for attraction. That's the first third. The second third is God-given talent, the ability to sing on key, to move your legs well and dance well, to machine gun a joke with the right rhythm. The third is unstoppable diligence and work."

The same year as the AFI award, PBS's ambitious and respected *American Masters* series devoted an installment to Brooks's life and career. Rudy DeLuca and Steve Haberman built laughs into his staged entrance and exit. Beyond the timeworn anecdotes, however, Brooks was still reticent about discussing personal matters, and the interviews barely touched on Anne Bancroft. He'd wave away questions about the deceased actress, saying, "Too soon . . ." or "*Pas un mot.* That's French for 'not a word . . .'" while tearing up. He didn't want to include the "Sweet Georgia Brown" clip from *To Be or Not to Be* in the Alan Yentob television special because it was too "painful" for him to watch, he said. The producers convinced Brooks that "there will be hundreds of thousands of young people who don't know anything about our marriage, our relationship, they only know about the number, and they would appreciate it."

Although he still regularly shuttled between coasts, in 2010 he sold the Water Mill oceanfront cottage that had been his and Anne Bancroft's retreat in the Hamptons. The price was a reported $5.3 million. Hollywood was more home, and after living there for so long, he told interviewers, he knew more people in Los Angeles than in New York.

When home on the West Coast, he wore a groove between the offices he occupied in Culver City, his son Max's place in Venice, where he stopped nightly to see his grandson, and his Santa Monica house. Max "seems to have made peace with his father's career," the *Washington Post* reported. Since Bancroft's death, Brooks had "really made up for lost time" in fathering, Max told the *Post*, adding "in my Dad's day, as long as you didn't get drunk and smack the wife around—and brought home a check—you're father of the year."

Brooks himself reflected on past parental neglect. "It's not easy being a father," he told *AARP The Magazine* in 2015. "I wasn't a bad one, but I wasn't great either; I was too busy building my temple to me. Getting famous, writing and directing movies—they take up a lot of hours, and often I would come home late. I regret this very much."

Most days now his breakfast was one squeezed orange from his backyard, bran flakes and fruit, coffee with 2 percent milk. He jogged a little daily until he turned ninety.

Nowadays he celebrated his favorite holiday, Passover, which in boyhood had been hosted at his grandfather's house, at Ron Clark's. Occasionally actor–folk singer Theodore Bikel led that Seder; more frequently it was West Los Angeles rabbi Jerome Cutler, a former Catskills and Atlantic City comedian. On the second night of Passover, Brooks usually led a Club Caesar parade to the nursing home where Sid Caesar resided. "He can't feed himself," Brooks told *The Forward*, "and he goes from his bed to a wheelchair, but we try to have a Seder on the second night. He may not get it, but we try."

Caesar made it to ninety-one, dying in 2014 and hailed in obituaries as one of the early geniuses of television comedy. Ronny Graham had passed away in 1999, Howard Morris died in 2005, Mel Tolkin in 2007, and Larry Gelbart in 2009. Gene Wilder's death came in 2016, the year Brooks celebrated his ninetieth birthday. Jerry Lewis, whom Brooks had failed to satisfy as a collaborator, lived to ninety-one, dying in 2017. Brooks had idolized and arguably surpassed Lewis in his popularity and accomplishments.

Brooks reliably showed up at friends' funerals and offered tributes for press obituaries. When *Jewish Journal* asked him what the hardest thing to accept about aging was, he replied, "It's empty spaces. That used to be filled with the people you grew up with, the people you love, your family—they're all gone. That's the toughest."

Two show business friends who seemed to last forever were Norman Lear and Carl Reiner, both four years older than Brooks. Both men, like Brooks, remained active. Lear led his People for the American Way organization, continued to produce television shows, and published his autobiography in 2015. Reiner acted occasionally for TV and movies, performed voice work, and wrote a never-ending series of memoirs and novels.

Reiner had lost his wife, Estelle, in 2008, and almost daily, when home on the West Coast, Brooks visited Reiner's Beverly Hills house for dinner, where they were often joined by Lear. The conversation, always humorous, occasionally touched on mortality.

Alone together many nights, the 2000 Year Old cohorts ate from trays, bent to work on crossword puzzles, and watched TV shows on Reiner's sixty-inch set. They favored musicals or Ritz Brothers comedies. Sometimes they'd strike it rich with a Sonja Henie musical with Harry Ritz as a tea leaf–reading gypsy. They'd fall to the floor laughing, slipping into remembered routines. Much later they'd debate who had fallen asleep first. Jerry Seinfeld visited the lifelong friends for an episode of *Comedians in Cars Getting Coffee*. Later, in 2017, Brooks also appeared in a documentary about long-lived artists and celebrities, hosted by Reiner, called *If You're Not in the Obit, Eat Breakfast*.

Brooks's reactions to the younger comedians they saw nowadays on the tube could be oddly old-fashioned. "Mel sometimes doesn't like dirty jokes on television," Reiner explained to one interviewer. Once Brooks even took offense at a *Saturday Night Live* sketch that was heavy on fart jokes. Reiner admonished his friend. "I said, 'Mel, you started it!'"

Home alone on other nights, Brooks compulsively watched videos and television—old black-and-white movies, PBS, sitcoms, really anything. When he cast David Hasselhoff as Roger De Bris for a road company of *The Producers*, he told Hasselhoff he had seen him in the Adam Sandler film *Click* and on *America's Got Talent*, besides *Knight Rider* and *Baywatch*. He slipped in the occasional DVD of old Anne Bancroft movies, relishing her great performances in films he still loved to watch such as *The Miracle Worker*.

Like Reiner, Brooks still accepted small acting jobs, mostly voice work for TV series and family-friendly animated films. He involved himself in several books—a 2000 Year Old Man children's book with Carl Reiner and a couple of coffee-table tomes telling the screen-to-stage sagas of *The Producers* and *Young Frankenstein*. But his publicized autobiography never eventuated; he was not the let-your-hair-down type. And besides, there wasn't much money in books. His longtime literary agent, Ed Victor—who also represented Max Brooks's *The Zombie Survival Guide* to huge success—was taken aback one day when Brooks screamed at him for delivering a modest contract offer.

Though it was unclear how much progress was made on the *Blazing Saddles* musical, Brooks did phone Nathan Lane one day to ask the Max Bialystock of *The Producers* if he would be open to playing

Hedley Lamarr, the Harvey Korman role, in the stage version of *Blazing Saddles*. A *Blazing Saddles* musical was a big mountain to climb, however, and instead Brooks and Thomas Meehan fitfully worked on trims for the *Young Frankenstein* musical, which New York critics had excoriated as too long and dull. Finally there might be a London opening; the 2007 show had never crossed the Atlantic.

The film of *The Producers* musical became the last Brooksfilms production. Brooks insisted that the company was still active, though, and occasionally announced projects such as *Pizzaman*, a horror comedy by Rudy DeLuca and Steve Haberman that has not yet come to be.

One sign of the mellowed Brooks was his quiet involvement in the first independent film directed by Nicholas Brooks, his oldest son from his marriage to Florence Baum. Nicholas was almost sixty when he cowrote and directed *Sam*, starring Natalie Knepp and Sean Kleier with Stacy Keach and Morgan Fairchild in featured roles. The film was a comedy unlike any made by his father: a sweet, old-fashioned romance involving magical happenings and a gender switch. Produced on a shoestring, *Sam* did not compel the support of a major studio, however, and it became a DVD release in 2015. Though it was not an official Brooksfilms offering, Brooks was listed as executive producer.

Brooks owned stocks but not very many, the *New York Times* reported in 1997; the comedian preferred safe, tax-free California state bonds. Much of his savings, the *Times* said, was invested in his Manhattan apartment, his Fire Island residence, two Fisher Island, Florida, beachfront condominiums, Los Angeles and Malibu homes, and a Wilshire Boulevard office building. The real estate alone added up to "a market value of close to $20 million." The *Times* estimated that his net profits since *Blazing Saddles* "probably came to $5 million for each film" (whether that was for Brooks comedies and Brooksfilms productions, too, the article did not say). The newspaper also said that Brooks had earned "12 or 15 percent of the net profits" of *Blazing Saddles* alone; that megahit—plus "all the foreign rights" for *History of the World, Part I*—had added considerably to his total worth.

The *Times* published its piece before his two Broadway musicals appeared. *The Producers* dramatically enhanced Brooks's portfolio, while *Young Frankenstein* turned a profit both on Broadway and on the road. The Internet's best estimate—from www.therichest.com—that Brooks was worth $85 million by the age of ninety is probably on the conservative side.

You might think the rich man would spend his days dandling his grandchildren on his knee or basking in the sun reading Russian novels. You would be wrong. He still had things to prove: that the "crickets" had been wrong about the *Young Frankenstein* musical, for example.

Soon after turning eighty-eight Thomas Meehan died, in August 2017. Before his death, however, Brooks's meticulous cowriter had managed to revise the *Young Frankenstein* script for a London reboot. Brooks spent several weeks in Newcastle after Meehan's death testing the show on British audiences. It amounted to "a leaner, meaner *Young Frankenstein*, if you will," according to director Susan Stroman, who was back on board to steer the musical toward its West End premiere. The Broadway version had been "cumbersome," Brooks admitted, so Meehan and Brooks had crafted "a whole new opening." Brooks had added two new songs and changed some vernacular. ("I've kind of cockneyed it up a little bit.") The show's three-hour length on Broadway was reduced to two, and the elaborate New York staging was refreshed for the intimate Garrick Theatre in London. Stroman cast the British actor Hadley Fraser as Dr. Frankenstein ("Fronk-en-steen!") with Broadway's Shuler Hensley repeating his role of the Monster. As usual, Brooks sat in on all the rehearsals and gave notes. His outbursts of "You're ruining the show!," which in olden days might have rubbed people the wrong way, were now a regulated in-joke to alleviate rehearsal tensions.

The standing ovations for the leaner, meaner musical began in Newcastle. In London, Brooks moved into his favorite hotel away from home, the five-star Savoy, which by now was accustomed to highlighting his name in its advertising. He made the rounds of London talk shows, looking and sounding like a contented man ten years younger. He appeared on *The One Show*, seated next to the beaming movie star Russell Crowe, who boasted of seeing *Blazing Saddles* seven times while growing up in Sydney, Australia; Crowe endearingly segued into a hilarious imitation of Brooks with Jewish inflections, imitating the comedian extemporizing as he watches a rerun of *Gladiator*.

The October opening supplied a happy ending to the *Young Frankenstein* saga that had begun in 1974 with Gene Wilder's original idea for the spoof and a popularity that had made it one of Brooks's most enduring films. The comedian was the darling of the London paparazzi, which swooned over his stunning "date," nineteen-year-old Samantha "Sam" Brooks, the daughter of Eddie Brooks, who wore a gold choker above a strapless burgundy velvet gown with a thigh-high split and metallic heels. After the critics rapturously embraced the leaner, meaner show, the Brooklyn-born boy who used to scrounge pennies for egg creams took his granddaughter on a Prada shopping spree.

Though not unanimous (*Time Out* found the whole schmear "desperately old-fashioned"), four-star reviews emanated from *The Telegraph*, *The Evening Standard*, *The Times*, *The Independent*, and more. "An evening of gloriously impure fun," wrote Michael Billington in *The Guardian*. "It's every bit as good as, if not better than, its predecessor in that it piles on the gags even more relentlessly and wittily parodies musicals past and present."

One last time Brooks had prevailed. The interviews and reviews had the feeling of a valedictory, and the ninety-one-year-old certainly had little left to prove. But while you're in London, Graham Norton asked Brooks, are you also working on the next thing?

"Her name is Sheila, she's from Cincinnati, what a knockout," the American national treasure replied before teasing out an oft-mentioned possibility. "What am I really working on? I'm thinking, actually, there could be a musical in *Blazing Saddles*. There are so many songs in it. . . . I would just have to add another tune or two. I'm at the very early stages of pencil sketching some ideas and writing some tunes that might work."

The third act in the life story of Melvin Kaminsky, aka Mel Brooks, was fantastical indeed. His victory lap after *The Producers* musical was glorious, and in any film, much less one of his own, it would call for a montage of medals and trophies and dollar bills accompanied by cheers, laughter, and applause building with music to a magnificent din.

Perhaps the emblematic moment of this third act occurred in the year that Brooks turned ninety. He launched a national dog-and-pony tour of more than a dozen US cities that wound up, after months on the road, with a triumphant booking, in September 2016, at Radio City Music Hall in the metropolis of his birth. Every seat in the vast Radio City auditorium—Brooks proudly told friends exactly how many seats there were—was filled.

He showed *Blazing Saddles* to all the audiences, and afterward he performed a variation of the stand-up-comedian routine he had first auditioned in the Catskills before World War II and that, really, had never quite proved his forte. There are rumors that Brooks plans to do this tour again and again for years ahead, as long as he is able, next time showing *Young Frankenstein* and then *The Producers* and then perhaps *Spaceballs*.

Touring paid better than books. Creative Artists, now his agency, saw to it that he received a reported floor of $175,000 for most of the one-nighters, augmented by a share of each house. The format of the 2016 template was simple: after the screening Brooks took a chair onstage and answered questions from adoring fans. But he didn't stay seated; he jumped up, danced around, and sang, including the complete "name" song from seventy-five years before, his Catskills days, which as ever he ended, Al Jolson style, on bended knee: "I'm out of my mind . . . so please be kind—to Mel-vin Brooooks!"

People love people who make them laugh. Slowly, over the decades, Melvin Kaminsky had turned his invented identity into a brand name of laughter—a delicious taste, like Marcel Proust's madeleine, that sweetens life and forever after triggers a deluge of affection. When the laughter worked, it was warm, fuzzy, rude, and crude in a balanced recipe.

His material for the national tour might have been mostly re-used jokes ("The toughest thing about making movies is putting those holes in the celluloid"), and almost the entirety of it may have been scripted, right down to the questions from the audience. ("Do you wear boxers or briefs?" Brooks was asked at each stop, and his answer: "Depends!") Still, every night, the comedian gave his all, *schvitz*ing through his suit with each "performance," so breathless and drenched one might fear he was about to die.

But Brooks was having the time of his life, and at every stop the sell-out crowds of thrilled baby boomers shouted out, "We love you, Mel! We love you! Love you!"

# Sources and Acknowledgments

Every book is a journey with many helping hands, some of them invisible (as the source notes indicate, there were more invisible helpers than usual on this project). I am grateful for the extra work and income provided by *Cineaste*, *Film International*, the Fulbright Commission in the United Kingdom, and the Seamus Heaney Centre at Queen's University Belfast. While teaching on a Fulbright at QUB in early 2018, I finished the submission draft of *Funny Man*; and one fortuitous day I was privileged to enjoy a local "live read" of the *Spaceballs* script, reminding me how much I like that film.

Thank you to Cal Morgan, Jr., for his guidance and pointers in the past. Jonathan Jao offered judicious advice and strived to improve the book with his meticulous editing. I don't remember life without my longtime agent, Gloria Loomis, and her associate Julia Masnik, without whom I would be lost (and broke). My wife, Tina Daniell, and family have learned to live with constant mention and/or discussion of my work in progress, but perhaps it was easier for everyone this time as they are all more or less Mel Brooks fans.

### ADVICE AND ASSISTANCE

Thank you to John Baxter, Greg Beal, Sheila Benson, Ksenjia Bilbija, Jacob R. Billig, Michael Billington, David Bordwell, Alan Brostoff, Paul Buhle, Mark Burman, Lorenzo Codelli, Melissa Cohen, John Conway, Robert Crane, Gary Crowdus, Douglass K. Daniel, Wheeler Winston Dixon, Jim Drake, David Ehrenstein, Art Eisenson, Thomas Eurell, Scott Eyman, Chris Gage, Myron Gittel, Edward Guthmann, Ray Kelly, Vanda Krefft, Daniel Kremer, Roger Lewis, Vinny

LoBrutto, Moira Macdonald, Ken Mate, Tom Matthews, Joseph McBride, Anthony McKenna, Paul Nagle, Gabriella Oldham, Jaclyn Ostrowski, Eddy Portnoy, Burt Prelutsky, David Rensin, Jeremy Robson, Alan Rode, Henry Schipper, Nat Segaloff, Roxanne Sennett, Clancy Sigal, Nile Southern (Executor and Trustee, Terry Southern Literary Trust), Jeffrey Spivak, Nick Thomas, David Thomson, Janet Wainwright, Gwenda Young, and Francesco Zippel.

Thank you as well to Lisa Pearl Rosenbaum, formerly of the Jewish Television Network, for supplying a copy of *A Conversation with Robert Clary*; and the Research & Study Center in the UCLA Film & Television Center for screening "Later with Bob Costas."


CORRESPONDENCE AND INTERVIEWS

Many interviews were confidential. Although I have written other books about people alive at the time of my research—Robert Altman, Jack Nicholson, Clint Eastwood—I have never been faced with as many people who either did not reply to inquiries, expressly declined to cooperate with an interview, or spoke on the condition of anonymity. Probably in the majority of cases, but certainly for those who spoke off the record—I know because I heard the constant refrain—people feared Brooks's temper or litigiousness. While corroborating their interviews, I have protected their identities.

The list of people who went on the record, either for interviews or in correspondence (or email), includes Sanford C. Allen, William Arnold, Andrew Bergman, Ofra Bikel, Norman Blagman, Ken Brown, Carleton Carpenter, Martin Charnin, Charles Cohen, Nisan (Nathan) Cohen, Michael Elias, Mallory Factor, Raoul Felder, Bob Gill, Sandy Glass, Stuart Gordon, Ezio Greggio, Gilda Grossman, Valerie Hanlon, Hope Holiday, Lawrence Holofcener, Whitney R. Hunter, Gretchen Kanne, Nora Kaye, Norman Lear, Barry Levinson, David Lunney, Djordje Nikolic, Alfa-Betty Olsen, Stevie Phillips, Jay Plotkin,

Saria Kraft Richmond, Bob Schwartz, Norman Steinberg, Charles Strouse, and Alan Uger.

## ARCHIVES AND ORGANIZATIONS

Special Collections (including the Paramount Studio Collection), Margaret Herrick Library, Academy of Motion Picture Arts and Sciences (Los Angeles, CA); Peter Ward, Brentwood Public Library (Brentwood, NY); Mark Burman, British Broadcasting Corporation (BBC, UK); Colleen Bradley-Sanders, College Archivist, Brooklyn College of the City University of New York; Library & Archives, Brooklyn Historical Society (New York); Broward County Main Library (Fort Lauderdale, FL); Ellenville Public Library (Ellenville, NY); Brenda L. Burk, Special Collections & Archives (including the Charlie Spivak papers), Clemson University Libraries (Clemson, SC); Heidi Marshall, Archives & Special Collections (including material relating to Walter H. "Wally" Robinson), Columbia College (Chicago, IL); American Comedy Archives, Emerson College (Boston, MA); Mary Paige Lang-Clouse, Director, Ethel B. Crawford Public Library (Monticello, NY); Fallsburg Library (Fallsburg, NY); Bill Guiton, Reference Department, Fort Lee Public Library (Fort Lee, NJ); Freeman/Lozier Library (including the video interview with World War II veteran Stanley Kaplan), Bellevue University (Bellevue, NE); Regina G. Feeney, Librarian/Archivist, Freeport Memorial Library (Freeport, NY); Special Collections (including the Jared Brown papers), Ames Library, Illinois Wesleyan University (Bloomington, IL); Elisabet Paredes, Johnson Public Library (Hackensack, NJ); Patrick Kerwin, Manuscript Division (including the Theodore Granik papers), Library of Congress (Washington, DC); Robin Sampson, Archivist, Special Collections (including the Clive Exton papers), London College of Communication, University of the Arts London (UK); Middletown Township Public Library (Middletown, NJ); Milwaukee Public Library (Milwaukee, WI);

Monmouth County Archives (Manalapan, NJ); *The Monmouth Journal* (Red Bank, NJ); National Archives (College Park, MD); Alumni Relations, The New School (New York); Isaac Gewirtz, Curator, Berg Collection (including the Terry Southern papers), New York Public Library; Billy Rose Theatre Division (including the Joe Darion, Doris Frankel, Lucille Kallen, Max Liebman, Edward Padula, and Michael Stewart papers), New York Public Library; The Irma and Paul Milstein Division of United States History, Local History and Genealogy, New York Public Library; Division of Corporations, New York State Archives (Albany, NY).

Free Library of Philadelphia (Philadelphia, PA); Reference Desk, Palm Beach County Library (Palm Beach, FL); Office of Alumni Relations, Red Bank Catholic High School (Red Bank, NJ); Lisa Iannucci, Red Bank Public Library (Red Bank, NJ); Gina Garcia, Public Information Officer, Santa Cruz Public Libraries (Santa Cruz, CA); Special Collections (including the Eulalie Spence papers), Schomburg Center for Research in Black Culture (New York); Michele R. Combs, Special Collections (including the Mike Wallace papers), Syracuse University Libraries (Syracuse, NY); Carol Montana, *Sullivan County Democrat* (Callicoon, NY); Sullivan County Historical Society (Hurleyville, NY); W. S. Hoole Library, University of Alabama; Kristin Lipska, California Audiovisual Preservation Project (including the Mel Tolkin oral history by the Kitchen Sisters Davia Nelson and Nikki Silva), University of California, Berkeley (Berkeley, CA); Special Collections (including the Stanley Chase and Larry Gelbart papers), Charles E. Young Library, University of California at Los Angeles (Los Angeles, CA); Jacque Roethler, Special Collections (including the Gene Wilder papers), University of Iowa Libraries (Iowa City, IA); USC Archives of the Cinematic Arts (including the Hal Humphreys, Jerry Lewis, Hunt Stromberg, and Jerry Wald papers), University of Southern California (Los Angeles, CA); Kyle Hovious, Special Collections, Hodges Library, University of Tennessee (Knoxville, TN); Wisconsin Center for Film and Theater Research (including the Kermit Bloomgarden, Hillard Elkins, Moss Hart, Joseph Stein, David Susskind, and Nick Vanoff papers and National Broadcasting Corporation Records 1921–1976), University of Wisconsin (Madison, WI); Mary Laura Kludy, Archives and Records Management, Virginia Military Institute (Lexington, VA); Missy Brown, Agency Coordinator, Writers Guild of America West (Los Angeles, CA); Molly Beer, Communications Coordinator, Writers Guild of America East (New York); Hilary Swett, Archivist, Writers Guild Foundation (Los Angeles, CA); Beinecke Rare Book & Manuscript Library (including the Max Wilk papers), Yale University (New Haven, CT).

Special thanks to the following for graciously handling many queries and requests: Alla Roylance, Senior Librarian of the Brooklyn Collection, Brooklyn Public Library; and Edward "Ned" Comstock, USC Archives of the Cinematic Arts. Colin Sandell in nearby (to Milwaukee) Cedarburg supplied his expertise for documenting MB's role in World War II. Aaron Prah, a Preservation Technician of the National Archives at Riverside (Perris, CA) labored to dig out court case transcripts and documents. I relied upon the resourceful Mary Troath for research in London. From Serbia, Miroljub "Miki" Stojanovic generously volunteered sources and information relating to *The Twelve Chairs*. The voluminous archives— and helpful archivists—at the Wisconsin Center for Film and Theater Research kept me busy with trips to Madison. Marquette University in Milwaukee, my home academic institution, found rare items through the Interlibrary Loan Department, and the Reference Desk answered my frequent questions. (Nia Schudson, above all, went the distance on queries and requests.) Last but definitely not least, my son, Sky McGilligan, who was living in Brooklyn as I worked on this book, invaluably assisted me in tracking down material in New York libraries and courts.

## PHOTOGRAPHS

Andy Sharlein, Allied Digital Photo; Getty Images; Historic Images; Jerry Ohlinger's Movie Material Store; Movie Market; Adam Miszewski; New York Public Library; Djordje Nikolic; Alfa-Betty Olsen; Photofest; Norman Steinberg; and the author's collection.

## KEY TEXTS

Three earlier books were essential reading and rereading: *Seesaw: A Dual Biography of Anne Bancroft and Mel Brooks* by William Holtzman (Doubleday, 1979); *It's Good to Be the King: The Seriously Funny Life of Mel Brooks* by James Robert Parish (Wiley, 2007); and *Anne Bancroft: A Life* by Douglass K. Daniel (University Press of Kentucky, 2017). Many others were useful—I will spare the readers an overlong bibliography—but especially valuable and insightful was the unpublished "Where Did I Go Right?: My Days from the Czar to the Kings of Comedy" by Mel Tolkin, from the Writers Guild Foundation archives.

William Holtzman and I have in common the fact we both worked for the *Boston Globe* at different times long ago. I have known James Robert Parish since the 1970s, when he befriended me; I value all his books, and his biography of Brooks is one of his best. Douglass K. Daniel published his biography of Richard Brooks in the Wisconsin Film Studies series under my editorship at the University of Wisconsin Press, and his Bancroft biography under my Screen Classics series editorship at the University Press of Kentucky. When, ages ago now, Daniel told me that he was developing a biography of Bancroft, I urged him to include Brooks as a dual subject, à la William Holtzman. He demurred and strategically covered Brooks's life and career in his Bancroft book. When I took up the gauntlet of Brooks as a subject, I had *Anne Bancroft: A Life* as a constant reference, and also Daniel's goodwill, advice, and many favors as I progressed.

I am grateful to Daniel, moreover, for reading several drafts and pointing out inaccuracies and making helpful recommendations for changes. Sheila Benson and Michael Elias also read and commented constructively on the manuscript. Yet another tip of the Hatlo hat goes to my old friend Joseph McBride, an eminence in the field, who selflessly read draft after draft. McBride has been a diligent early reader of many of my books, identifying problems and making sharp criticisms. Other key people who must remain nameless read the drafts, too, and everyone tried to steer me in better directions. Any stubborn errors of fact or interpretation are regretfully my own.

# Chapter Notes

People identified by name in the text are quoted from their interviews with me, our (email or paper) correspondence, or—as chapter-listed below—from published sources.

Only key published sources are acknowledged. Mel Brooks (hereafter MB) often began interviews with a disclaimer: "I don't like doing interviews, you know—I never do 'em" (Jan. 22, 1974, *New Times*). But at the height of his fame he was likely to answer the office telephone himself and spend "twenty minutes explaining why he didn't want to be interviewed," as a *New York Times* journalist told Lucille Kallen in 1982, busily giving the interview that he wasn't giving. In fact, during his career MB gave interviews to literally thousands of newspaper and magazine outlets, book authors, and radio, television, and other media; he turns up, in a supporting role, in numberless other published works and Internet pieces. Though I have tried to collect and consult every source possible, my notes are confined to what has been incorporated and cited.

## CHAPTER 1: 1926: LITTLE WORLD

Trying to reconcile disparate accounts and reconstruct the Kaminsky/ Brookman genealogy, I looked at telephone directories, US and New York State Census records, World War I draft registration papers, New York State marriage and death records, probate filings, and New York Hebrew Orphan Asylum archives. I also drew on MB's interview touching on his family history, broadcast in March 1990 on *A Conversation with Robert Clary*, a short-lived series produced for the Jewish Television Network.

One of the early substantial profiles of Brooks is "Frolics and Detours of a Short Hebrew Man" by Kenneth Tynan in *The New Yorker* (Oct. 30, 1978), and one of the most extensive and searching interviews is Brad Darrach's Q and A for *Playboy* (Feb. 1975). Both these pieces are quoted from frequently in the text. In this chapter "the strange amalgam . . . ," Joseph Heller's "There's a side of Mel . . . ," "an avid talker and doer," and "the first sketch I ever wrote" are from the *New Yorker* profile. "A great softball pitcher," "the lady next door . . . ," "lively, peppy, sang well," "They were afraid . . . ," "as a boy, I could make . . . ," "swoon with ecstasy," "the best cook . . . ," young MB's sex life, "The class would laugh . . . ," and "undisputed champ . . ." are from the *Playboy* interview.

"My feet never touched . . ." is from "The Making of *The Producers*" by Sam Kashner, *Vanity Fair* (January 2004). "A little Jewish rhino" is from *Alan King: Inside the Comedy Mind: Mel Brooks*, broadcast on Comedy Central in 1991. "So short she could walk . . ." is from "Mel Brooks: Live in London" by Alice Jones, *The Independent* (UK) (March 22, 2015). "Absconded" is inscribed in New York Hebrew Orphan Asylum records. New York State Corporation Records confirm Max Kaminsky's involvement as an officer or investor in various businesses publicly listed in the *New York Times* and other East Coast newspapers.

Marc Eliot's *Song of Brooklyn: An Oral History of America's Favorite Borough* (Broadway Books, 2008) contains MB's reminiscences about his boyhood. "Close to the corner of Hooper . . . ," anecdotes about his youthful moviegoing, his brother's help with homework ("I got an A on the exam"), and the long walk across the Williamsburg Bridge to the Lower East Side ("there were a lot of Jews there") are from *Song of Brooklyn*.

Another excellent account of Brooks's early life is "Williamsburg Days," the interview with MB in *Brooklyn: A State of Mind*, edited by Michael W. Robbins (Workman, 2000). "And he'd often get into the picture . . . ," "He gave us money sometimes . . . ," "with dirty old, very thick cards," "We were really poor . . . ," "One big bed for us . . . ," "Without thinking I turned . . . ," "I could call the police . . . ," "Right near the sea . . . ," "bathing suit sashes," "enormous bags," "Roughly a year . . . ," and "I think my mother missed her mother . . ." are from *Brooklyn: A State of Mind*.

"He was very talented" is from the interview with Kitty Kaminsky in "Mel Brooks' Mom Is Alive and Well" by Eunice Martin, Women's News Service, *The Daily Times-News* (Burlington, NC) (March 15, 1978). "A hotbed of artistic intellectuality . . ." and "My very first impressions . . ." are from *The Director Within: Storytellers of Stage and Screen* by Rose Eichenbaum (Wesleyan, 2014). "A frankfurter, a root beer . . ." is from "Believing in Make Believe: An Interview with Mel Brooks" by Dan Lybarger, *The Keaton Chronicle* (Autumn 1997). Brooks talked about Chaplin and Keaton in "At the Movies" by Guy Flatley, the *New York Times* (Aug. 27, 1976). "Life was dirty . . ." is from "Mel Brooks: King of Clowns" by Maurice Zolotow, *Reader's Digest* (April 1978). "The sire of mugging" is from "Mel Brooks: They Laughed When I Stood Up" by Arnold Reisman, *Boston After Dark* (Jan. 12, 1971). "Tooth problems . . ." is Max Brooks from "I Am a National Treasure" by Scott Vogel, *Washington Post* (Dec. 6, 2009).

"I brought the house down . . ." is from "The History of Mel Brooks, from Jelly Jars to *Yahrzeit* Glasses" by Curt Schleier, *The Forward* (May 13, 2013). "I always got 'em at family parties . . ." and the vignettes of Uncle Joe and *Anything Goes* are from Brooks's bylined "Springtime for the Music Man in Me," *New York Times* (April 15, 2001). "That day infected me . . ." and "A musical not only transports you . . ." are from *Broadway: The American Musical* by Michael Kantor and Laurence Maslon (Bullfinch, 2004), based on Kantor's documentary film of the same title. "My all-time favorite composer" and "the tunes and lyrics to a whole bunch . . ." are from MB's bylined "Let Me Tell

You How I Made It in Movies," *The Sunday Times* (UK) (June 10, 2001). "On cold winter mornings . . ." is from "10 Questions" by Belinda Luscombe, *Time* (Dec. 3, 2012).

"Exuberant joy of living" is from "And Then He Got Smart" by Joanne Stang, *New York Times* (Jan. 30, 1966). "Dump neighborhood theater . . ." is from "King of Clowns." "How many beans . . ." and "The garbage trucks were big . . ." are from "What I've Learned: Mel Brooks" by Cal Fussman, *Esquire* (Dec. 17, 2007). "My Labor Party beginnings . . ." is from "The Entertainers: Max and Mel Brooks" by Taffy Brodesser-Anker, *Town & Country* (Aug. 5, 2014). "Lived on welfare checks" is from "Pell-Mel" by Roger D. Friedman, *The Daily News* (New York) (July 25, 1993).

*It Happened in the Catskills*, an oral history by Myrna Katz Frommer and Harvey Frommer (Harcourt, 1991), and Stephen Citron's *Jerry Herman: Poet of the Showtime* (Yale University Press, 2004) added to my portrait of Don Appell. Stefan Kanfer's *A Summer World: The Attempt to Build a Jewish Eden* (Farrar, Straus and Giroux, 1989), *The Catskills: Its History and How It Changed America* by Stephen M. Silverman and Raphael D. Silver (Knopf, 2015), and Peter Davis's 1986 documentary *The Rise and Fall of the Borscht Belt* helped illuminate the background and legacy of the Catskills.

"Go to the diving board . . ." is from "Up a Notch or Two from the Borscht Belt" by Norman Mark, *Los Angeles Times* (July 14, 1968). "Sid was the Apollo . . ." is from "And Then He Got Smart." *Uncle Harry* and the Joseph Dolphin anecdotes are from "Mel Brooks!" by Mel Brooks (as told to Eric Estrin), www.thewrap.com (July 21, 2009). "You hear about the people . . ." is from "A Man Who Makes Us Laugh" by Dick Schaap, *Parade* (Jan. 22, 1984). "Court jester" and "Pretty soon, I came to hate . . ." are from "Mel Brooks Is Finally Taken Seriously" by Charles Champlin, *Los Angeles Times* (Dec. 29, 1974). "Very influential on my work" is from *It's Good to Be the King*. "One of my favorite swing recordings" is from *Desert Island*

*Discs*, BBC radio (July 1, 1978). "Some punch lines should be . . ." is from "Quiet on the Set!" by Robert Weide, *DGA Quarterly* (Summer 2012).

"Charcoal-gray thick alpaca coat" is from *It's Good to Be the King*. "I was his sixteen-year-old assistant . . ." is from "The Producer" by Frances Hardy, *The Daily Mail* (UK) (Dec. 26, 2005). "Having the greatest influence . . ." is Joseph Papp quoted in *Free for All: Joe Papp, the Public and the Greatest Story Ever Told* by Kenneth Turan and Joseph Papp (Doubleday, 2010). "The class *shmendrick*" is Lester Persky from "Out of the Tax Shelters and Into the Trenches with Lester Persky" by Marie Brenner, *New West* (Jan. 31, 1977). Background on *Bright Boy* and producer Arthur J. Beckard is from *The Absolute Joy of Work: From Vermont to Hollywood, Broadway and Damn Near 'Round the World* by Carleton Carpenter (BearManor, 2016) and *David Merrick: The Abominable Showman* by Howard Kissel (Applause, 2000).

## CHAPTER 2: 1944: BIG WORLD

"Almost immediately . . ." is from " 'Fort' Gun Jammed, Boro Man Freezes Repairing It," *Brooklyn Daily Eagle* (Dec. 20, 1943). "I went for a little while . . . ," "For years I thought Roosevelt . . . ," "Only when it's dirty . . . ," and "A stork that dropped a baby . . ." are from the *Playboy* interview. "I knew what Hitler was doing . . ." is from Lisa Ades's 2018 documentary *GI Jews: Jewish Americans in World War II*. "The flowers of Virginia . . ." is from "Mel Brooks Sang for Mal Vincent" by Mal Vincent, *The Virginian-Pilot* (Norfolk, VA) (July 31, 2015). "A tough Jew from Brooklyn" is from "Mel Brooks: King of the Politically Incorrect" by Lynda Gorov, *Moment* (November– December 2010). "Somewhere in my head I said . . ." is from "Mel Brooks on Blazing New Comedic Trails in *Blazing Saddles*" by Adam Pockross, www.yahoo.com (May 7, 2014). "Near suicidal" is from "Mel Brooks Keeps Joking While Revisiting His Hits" by Steven

Zeitchik, *Los Angeles Times* (Dec. 9, 2012). "Brooklyn-in-the-West..." is from *"Young Frankenstein* Creator Knows the Score" by Lawson Taitte, *Dallas Morning News* (Jan. 2, 2011).

The Virginia Military Institute kindly furnished roster, curriculum, and group records from MB's stint at VMI. Also informative was "Mel Brooks: After VMI" by George Austin Adams, *The Virginian* (Fall 1986). 1104th Combat Engineering Group activities were described and tracked with the help of *Group History: 1104 Engineer Combat Group: 25 March 1943—9 May 1945* by Glenn E. Allred; *The Corps of Engineers: The War Against Germany* by Alfred M. Beck, Abe Bortz, Charles W. Lynch, Lida Mayo, and Ralph F. Weld, tothose-whoserved.org (1985), especially "Chapter 22: The Roer Crossing and the Remagen Bridgehead"; and "Army Engineers at the Battle of the Bulge" by Gustav J. Person, *Engineer* (September–December 2014). Brooks's discharge records were obtained from the US National Archives.

"I might be the first man..." is from *It's Good to Be the King.* "Fired on by a lot of kids . . ." is from Terry Gross's interview with MB on *Fresh Air* (National Public Radio) (Jan. 1, 2004). "That molten ball of hatred . . ." and "I had a wide audience . . ." are from "Mel Brooks: King of the Politically Incorrect." "Barracks character," "Every time Bob Hope came by . . . ," "chauffeuse," "certain rare cognacs," "There wasn't a nineteen-year-old . . . ," and "Nothing frightened me . . ." are from the *New Yorker* profile. The *Fort Dix Post* layout of MB's rubber faces is undated and flashes by on-screen in Robert Trachtenberg's 2013 *American Masters* documentary *Mel Brooks: Make a Noise.* "In the barracks there . . ." is Stanley Kaplan from his 2005 interview in the Freeman/Lozier Library, Bellevue University, Bellevue, NE.

The saga of the Red Bank Players is reconstructed from numerous *Red Bank Register* and *Asbury Park Evening Press* clippings, but also crucial was William Holtzman's account in *Seesaw*, which includes an interview with Wilbur Roach/Will Jordan. Brooks's signature song is excerpted in many MB interviews with slight variations dating from its first appearance in an Associated Press wire service feature in 1950. The version in this chapter is from ". . . And Please Love Melvin Brooks!" by Lisa Mitchell, *Saturday Evening Post* (May–June 1978). "I'm a better salesman . . ." is from "Brooks' Bookshop" by Marc Kristal, *Saturday Review* (August 1983). "Sort of groupie . . ." is from Sid Caesar's *Where Have I Been?: An Autobiography* (with Bill Davidson) (Crown, 1982).

Martha Schmoyer LoMonaco's *Every Week a Broadway Revue: The Tamiment Playhouse, 1921–1960* (Greenwood, 1992) was useful for context. "It looked like a family of birds" is from *Caesar's Writers*, the 1996 documentary capturing the Writers Guild–sponsored reunion of Caesar's writers. "A lovely little lady . . . ," "I always called [Coca] Immy . . . ," "He didn't know how right . . . ," "He would make catlike noises . . . ," and "the funniest, the most good-hearted . . ." are from *Caesar's Hours: My Life in Comedy, with Love and Laughter* (with Eddy W. Friedfeld) (Public Affairs, 2003). "Transferred in toto" is from Max Liebman's June 28, 1977, letter to Carl Reiner (CR), among Liebman's papers. "More tics than a flophouse mattress" is from Larry Gelbart's *Laughing Matters: On Writing M\*A\*S\*H, Tootsie, Oh, God!, and a Few Other Things* (Random House, 1998). Kenneth Tynan is always quoted from his bylined *New Yorker* profile of MB. "Out of her guts" is Mel Tolkin (MT) from a Feb. 17, 1989, letter to Lucille Kallen; unless otherwise noted, the Tolkin letters are among Kallen's papers. Steve Allen includes the "Bomba, The Jungle Boy" sketch in his MB profile in *Funny People* (Stein & Day, 1981). "I belonged to Sid . . ." is from *Caesar's Writers*. "I lost my father when I was only two . . ." is from "Hollywood Jew" by Danielle Berrin, *Jewish Journal* (Jan. 29, 2015).

CHAPTER 3: 1949: FUNNY IS MONEY

*Your Show of Shows* by Ted Sennett (Macmillan, 1977), the first book on the series, remains an essential source on Sid Caesar's acclaimed program. MB discusses his psychoanalysis in many interviews, but I particularly relied upon "On and off the Couch with Mel Brooks" by Dick Hobson, *Los Angeles* (December 1977); the chapter on MB in Dick Selzer's *The Star Treatment* (Bobbs-Merrill, 1977); and "Brooks Puts a Spin on 'Vertigo'" by Mel Gussow, *New York Times* (Dec. 23, 1977). Unless otherwise noted, Mel Tolkin (MT) is quoted from his unpublished memoir "Where Did I Go Right?"

"What we did, every night . . ." is from *Caesar's Writers*. "I was not entertained . . ." is from a typed, one-page, undated reminiscence of MB among Liebman's papers. "He always had a joke . . ." and "I always resented the fact . . ." are from Sunny Parich's 1998 interview with Lucille Kallen in the Television Academy Foundation oral history archives. "The Russian novelists . . ." is from the *Playboy* interview. "An ancient Jewish respect for literature" is Lucille Kallen from *Seesaw*. "The human condition" is from Mel Tolkin's Associated Press obituary (Nov. 28, 2007). "He was never Bob Hope . . ." is from MT's obituary in *Los Angeles Times* (Nov. 27, 2007). "We were too stupid . . ." is MT from "Forty Years Later, the Laughter's Still Loud" by William Grimes, *New York Times* (Aug. 18, 1996). "I was the king of Williamsburg" is from MB's commentary on *The Incredible Mel Brooks* box set. "Brooks was on the staff . . ." is from "An Interview with Bill Persky" by Kliph Nesteroff, classicshowbiz.blogspot (March 11, 2011). "Without a character . . ." is Larry Gelbart from *Laughing Matters*. "Humiliation of being held by his feet . . ." is from a June 6, 1991, letter from MT to Kallen. "Incoherent with fear" is from "Where Did I Go Right?" "I wanted credit . . ." is from "Mel Brooks Zaps the Movie Schmendricks" by Albert Goldman, *New York* (Aug. 12, 1968). "Part of the whole business . . ." is from "The Mad Mad Mel Brooks" by Paul Zimmerman, *Newsweek* (Feb. 17, 1975).

Earl Wild is always quoted from *A Walk on the Wild Side: A Memoir by Virtuoso Pianist Earl Wild* (Ivory Classics, 2011). "Mel coming in at one . . ." is CR from "Dialogue on Film: Carl Reiner," *American Film* (Dec. I, 1981). "He used to bare his teeth . . ." is MT from the *New Yorker* profile. The limerick anecdote and my version of the oft-told Scotch tape anecdote are from "Where Did I Go Right?" Marsha Mason is quoted from *Journey: A Personal Odyssey* (Simon & Schuster, 2000).

"He performs brilliantly . . ." and "a rule observed more in the breach . . ." are MT from his oral history with the Kitchen Sisters for the California Audiovisual Preservation Project. "You have to distinguish . . ." is Joseph Heller from the *New Yorker* profile. "I instantly knew Mel Brooks . . ." is CR from "Brooks and Reiner" by Claudia Dreifus, *Modern Maturity* (March 1999). "Recognized that performing talent . . ." is from Larry Wilde's probing interview with MB in *How the Great Comedy Writers Create Laughter* (Nelson-Hall, 1976). "What he secretly wanted . . ." is CR from the *New Yorker* profile. "For a good part of an hour" and the origins of the 2000 Year Old Man are from CR's *My Anecdotal Life* (St. Martin's Press, 2003); Reiner wrote about Brooks in several books, and I also drew from his later memoir *I Remember Me* (AuthorHouse, 2013). "Even if I remembered . . ." is from "Mel Brooks: The TV Worth Watching Interview, Take 2" by David Bianculli, www.tvworthwatching .com (Dec. 10, 2012). Lester Colodny is quoted from *A Funny Thing Happened: Life Behind the Scenes—Hollywood Hilarity and Manhattan Mayhem* (SciArt Media, 2010). "Berserk faggot row" is from the *New Yorker* profile. Herman Raucher is quoted from his novel *There Should Have Been Castles* (Delacorte, 1978); he declined an interview for this book. "Hebrew chipmunk" is from Alan Yentob's 1981 documentary *I Thought I Was Taller: A Short History of Mel Brooks* (BBC/Arena).

CHAPTER 4: 1952: DREAMS AND NIGHTMARES

"Envisioned his death" is Lucille Kallen from the "Great Caesar's Ghost!" special section in *Esquire* (May 1972). "A *tummler* . . ." is from the interview with Greg Garrison in the *Your Show of Shows* chapter of *Emmy Award Winning Nighttime Television Shows, 1948–2004* by Wesley Hyatt (McFarland, 2006). "Add two jokes . . ." is from MT's Jan. 1, 1990, letter to Kallen. "A very, very funny mind . . ." is MT from "Neil Simon's *Laughter on the 23rd Floor*: The Show Behind *Your Show of Shows*" by Alan Wallach, *Newsday* (Nov. 22, 1993). Bill Hayes is quoted from his joint autobiography (with Susan Seaforth Hayes) *Like Sands Through the Hourglass* (NAL, 2005). "The same background . . ." is from the *New Yorker* profile.

The Harry Cohn anecdote is constructed from versions Brooks told on *Open End* (Feb. 14, 1960) and *The Dick Cavett Show*, the latter where MB was joined by fellow filmmakers Robert Altman, Peter Bogdanovich, and Frank Capra (Jan. 21, 1972). "So were the girls" is from *Serious Jibber-Jabber with Conan O'Brien* (Oct. 21, 2013). "Crass . . ." is from Robert Alan Aurthur's "Hanging Out" column in *Esquire* (May 1972). Production records and memoranda from the USC Archives of the Cinematic Arts, particularly items in the Jerry Wald Collection, informed my account of MB's stint at Columbia Pictures.

My account of *The Vamp* is drawn partly from *The Ballad of John Latouche: An American Lyricist's Life and Work* by Howard Pollack (Oxford University Press, 2017). MB's stint on *The Red Buttons Show* is reconstructed from the version he told on *Open End* and Kliph Nesteroff's interview with him in "Red Buttons and the Acrimony of Hilarity," blog.wfmu.org (March 26, 2015). "He just takes everything . . ." is from Michael Rosen's 2000 interview with Max Wilk in the Television Academy Foundation oral history archives. I also consulted Sunny Parich's 1998 interview with Ernest Kinoy (another staff writer of *The Imogene Coca Show*) in the Television Academy Foundation oral history archives. "We were political people . . ." is from *Caesar's Writers*. Sono Osato is quoted from her memoir *Distant Dances* (Knopf, 1980). "Substituting energy and noise . . ." is from *Seesaw*.

CHAPTER 5: 1955: CLUB CAESAR

"We became our own fan club" is from "Maybe Forgetting a Detail, but Never a Punch Line" by Walter Goodman, *New York Times* (Aug. 19, 1996). "[Simon] would have to tell Carl Reiner . . ." is from "On and Off the Couch." "We nearly got to punching each other" is from "Mel Brooks," *People* (May 4, 1989). The leprechaun/Irish saloon anecdote is from "Where Did I Go Right?" "[Brooks] wasn't writing . . ." is from CR's bonus interview in "In the Beginning: The Caesar Years" on *The Incredible Mel Brooks* box set.

"Kind and warm and bright" and "psychological mess" are from the *Playboy* interview. "All I could say . . ." is from *It's Good to Be the King.* "Anxiety hysteria" and "multiple guilt on every level . . ." are from "Brooks Puts a Spin on 'Vertigo.'" "Was really responsible for the growth . . ." is from "And Then He Got Smart." "Accepting the mantle . . ." is from "On and Off the Couch." Stefan Kanfer wrote about Freud, Reik, and Jewish humor in *A Summer World.*

"We thought we were bringing . . ." is from "Blazing Mel" by Anne Marie Welsh, *San Diego Union-Tribune* (Dec. 29, 2002). "Concerned that my probing questions . . ." and "our number one benefactor" are from CR's *My Anecdotal Life.* "A sexual relationship" and all other characterizations of what transpired inside the Brooks/Baum marriage are from mutual acquaintances, court depositions, and divorce records. "There are only twenty-four minutes . . ." is Sid Caesar from *Seesaw.* "Just so long as [Caesar and Coca] . . ." is from "TV's Comics Went Thataway" by Gilbert Millstein, *The New York Times Magazine* (Feb. 2, 1958). The Kay Thompson project is reconstructed from Theodore "Ted" Granik's papers and *Kay Thompson: From Funny Face to "Eloise"* by Sam Irvin (Simon & Schuster, 2010).

CHAPTER 6: 1957: THE GENIUS AWAKES

"Eat you alive . . ." is from "A Conversation with the Real Woody Allen" by Ken Kelley, *Rolling Stone* (July 1976). "One of the best hunks . . ." is from "TV Keynote: Ginger Rogers Reaps Benefit of Work," *The Troy* [NY] *Record* (May 1, 1959). MB's typewritten letter to Moss Hart can be found among Hart's papers at the Wisconsin Center for Film and Theater Research. Tony Randall is quoted from Matt Roush's 1998 interview in the Television Academy Foundation oral history archives. Speed Vogel is quoted from *No Laughing Matter* by Joseph Heller and Vogel (Simon & Schuster, 2004); "Masterly Method in Brooks' Madness" by Joan Goodman, *The Times* (UK) (Oct. 6, 1981); and Vogel's bylined "The Gourmet Club" in *The Southampton Review* (Summer 2008). "Perfect producer . . ." is from Lee Adams's Aug. 16, 1961, letter to Hillard Elkins, in Elkins's papers. The *Open End* transcript, dated Feb. 14, 1960, is among Larry Gelbart's papers in Special Collections at UCLA. MB's failed collaboration with Jerry Lewis is reconstructed from production memoranda in the Lewis collection in the Cinematic Arts Library of USC. I also incorporated information from the Hunt Stromberg and Hal Humphreys papers at USC; items in Hillard Elkins's collection at the Wisconsin Center for Film and Theater Research; and clippings and documents from *The Ladies Man* file of the Paramount Studio Collection at the Margaret Herrick Library. Shawn Levy's *King of Comedy: The Life and Art of Jerry Lewis* (St. Martin's Press, 1996) was indispensable. I also drew from Justin Bozung's two-part interview with Bill Richmond on blog.tvstoreonline.com (May 5 and 7, 2015) and consulted "The Sidekick" by Tom Keller in *Written By* (April–May 2011). "Made no contribution whatsoever . . ." is from Associate Producer Ernest D. Glucksman's Feb. 15, 1961, memo to Paramount executive Eugene H. Frank in *The Ladies Man* files. "He had paid $10,000–$12,000 . . ." is from *Serious Jibber-Jabber with Conan O'Brien*. Bob

Schwartz supplied background information relating to his father, Marvin Schwartz.

The saga of *"All-American"* is pieced together from many newspaper, periodical, and other published sources. Important books covering the production include Charles Strouse's *Put On a Happy Face: A Broadway Memoir* (Union Square Press, 2008) and Josh Logan's *Movie Stars, Real People, and Me* (Delacorte, 1978). Unless otherwise noted, Strouse and Logan are always quoted from their memoirs. "He's never done domestic comedy" is CR from *Mel Brooks: Make a Noise*. "If I said, 'Here now is . . .'" and "Would WASP America . . ." are from *My Anecdotal Life*. "In the dress rehearsal . . ." is from MB's Feb. 14, 1960, appearance on *Open End*.

"She was gorgeous! . . ." is from "Mel Brooks 'Makes a Noise'" by Kam Williams, *Philadelphia Sun* (May 17, 2013). "Following me around" is Anne Bancroft (henceforth AB) from *Anne Bancroft: A Life*. Frank Langella is always quoted from *Dropped Names: Famous Men and Women as I Knew Them* (HarperCollins, 2012). "He's like a boxer . . ." is from Karen Herman's 2005 interview with Charles Strouse and Lee Adams in the Television Academy Foundation oral history archives. "[Brooks] does his best work . . ." is Edward Padula and "having the professor first . . ." is MB from "How to Succeed in Show Business by Really Trying" by Robert Wahls, *Daily News* (New York) (April 15, 1962). "My friend Moishe . . ." is from "Where Did He Go Right?" by Lisa Rosen, *Written By* (January 2016). Padula first announced "Springtime for Hitler" in the Dec. 17, 1961, *New York Times*.

CHAPTER 7: 1962: THE WARM AND FUZZY MEL

"Logan is a crazy lady" is from Stuart Ostrow's *Present at the Creation: Leaping at the Dark, and Going Against the Grain* (Hal Leonard, 2005). "Keeps swinging wildly . . ." is Charles Strouse from *Seesaw*. "We wanted to salute . . ." is from "How to Succeed in Show Business by Really Trying." "If a maid ever took over . . ." is from "Smart Money," *Time* (Oct. 15, 1965). Kermit Bloomgarden is quoted from his Nov. 15, 1962, letter to investors, in his collection. Stanley Chase's papers include scripts, memoranda, and production records for the unrealized "The Zero Mostel Show" and the *Inside Danny Baker* pilot and projected series. I also consulted Jared Brown's *Zero Mostel: A Biography* (Atheneum, 1989). "Somebody else's idea . . ." is from Jim Benson's interview with MB on tvtimemachine.com (YouTube) (undated). A transcript of the *Inside Danny Baker* promotional spot is in the David Susskind collection.

"Like a pup watching you . . ." is from MB's commentary on *The Incredible Mel Brooks* box set. "When two people have both . . ." is AB from Sidney Field's column in the *New York Mirror* (April 7, 1963). "Mel used to come by . . ." is from "Postcards from Hollywood: Things I Did and Things I Think I Did" by Freddie Fields and David Rensin, unpublished, and quoted with Rensin's permission. "He was very unhappy . . ." is from the *New Yorker* profile. "A fake Norman McLaren short" is from "Blazing Mel." "I said, 'Roll 'em again' . . ." is from MB's commentary on *The Critic* on *The Incredible Mel Brooks* box set. "There are no autos . . ." is AB from "The Craft of Bancroft" by Hedda Hopper, *Chicago Tribune* (Oct. 31, 1965). "After dinner . . ." is from Gene Wilder's *Kiss Me like a Stranger: My Search for Love and Art* (St. Martin's Press, 2005); unless otherwise noted, Wilder is always quoted from his memoir. I also drew on the insightful *Gene Wilder: Funny and Sad* by Brian Scott Mednick (BearManor, 2015).

The Gourmet Club is reconstructed from *No Laughing Matter*, the *New Yorker* profile, "The Gourmet Club" (Vogel), and "Eating with Their Mouths Open," *The New York Times Sunday Magazine* (Nov. 3, 1985). "To talk about the future" and "He had no money— zero . . ." are Alan U. Schwartz from "Brooks' Bookshop." "Mel is as intelligent . . ." is Schwartz from the *New Yorker* profile. Drafts of "Marriage Is a Dirty Rotten Fraud" and "The Last Man" are among Terry Southern's papers in the Berg Collection at the New York Public Library.

Unless otherwise noted, all production background, memoranda, and contracts relating to *Get Smart* and "Triplets" are cited from David Susskind's papers, which include Kirk Honeystein's and Daniel Melnick's Talent Associates files. I also drew from *David Susskind: A Televised Life* by Stephen Battaglio (St. Martin's Press, 2010) and consulted *The Get Smart Handbook* by Joey Green (Collier Macmillan, 1993) and *The Life and Times of Maxwell Smart* by Donna McCrohan (St. Martin's Press, 1988). "We were completely intimidated . . ." (Buck Henry), "I could have beaten him . . ." (MB), and "I've got a much better memory than you" (Henry) are from the *Get Smart* "extras" on *The Incredible Mel Brooks* box set. "[The script] took us a long time . . ." is from Jenni Matz's 2009 interview with Henry in the Television Academy Foundation oral history archives. "Mel is so wonderful . . ." is from AB's interview in *American Weekly* (Aug. 5, 1962). "Mel Brooks, an American writer . . ." is from Michael Wall's "Miss Italiano Thriving on Challenges," *The Guardian* (UK), reprinted in the *Washington Post* (Sept. 15, 1963). "When somebody becomes a star . . ." is from *It's Good to Be the King*.

## CHAPTER 8: 1965: SPRINGTIME FOR MEL

"I hired that girl . . ." is from MB's commentary on the *Get Smart: The Complete Series* box set (2008). Lewis H. Lapham's "Has Anybody Here Seen *Kelly*?" was published in the April 24, 1965, *Saturday Evening Post*. The "cease and desist" correspondence and papers relating to the Moose Charlap–Eddie Lawrence lawsuit are among David Susskind's papers. The making of the Ballantine Beer commercials was recalled by Dick Cavett in "The Great Melvino, or Our Mr. Brooks," *New York Times* (Sept. 9, 2011).

"I got a [royalty] check today . . ." is from "Pell-Mel." "Tell him from me . . ." and "I had a reputation . . ." are from the *New Yorker* profile. "It's a show in which you can comment . . ." is from a 1965 *New York Herald-Tribune* interview quoted in *Seesaw*. "It'll never be *Petticoat Junction* . . ." is from "Viewers 'Get Smarter' with Breakthrough in Hip Satire" by Don Page, *Los Angeles Times* (Jan. 28, 1966). The Cary Grant anecdote is reconstructed from several versions, including the one MB told on the February 13, 1975, broadcast of *The Tonight Show* and reprised on his final appearance on the program during Johnny Carson's last week (May 19, 1992). "Who can tell when the manic Mr. Brooks . . . " is from "Maybe Forgetting a Detail, but Never a Punchline" by Walter Goodman, *New York Times* (Aug. 19, 1996). Brooks showed storyboards of "Marriage Is a Dirty Rotten Fraud" to Digby Diehl for his profile in *Action* (January–February 1975).

"I like what I do . . ." is from "And Then He Got Smart." "I don't know what it meant . . ." is from the *New Yorker* profile. "Max and Leo are me, the ego and id . . . ," "They worked in their bathing suits . . . ," "to a horse-racing stable . . . ," "All my fears dissolved" (Gene Wilder), "Mel loved that character" (Kenneth Mars), and "I didn't know if the character . . ." (Wilder) are from "The Making of *The Producers*" by Sam Kashner, *Vanity Fair* (January 2004). "Some of which weren't too funny . . ." is Sidney Glazier from Ralph Rosenblum's *When the Shooting Stops, the Cutting Begins: An Editor's Story* (Viking Penguin, 1980). Lee Meredith is always quoted from Tom Lisanti's *Glamour Girls of Sixties Hollywood: Seventy-Five Profiles* (McFarland, 2017). Alan Johnson is quoted in this chapter from "Alan Johnson, 81, 'Springtime for Hitler' Choreographer, Dies" by Richard Sandoir, Johnson's obituary in the July 12, 2018, *New York Times*. MB's reflections on composer John Morris and his film music are from "Lost Issue: Mel Brooks Interview 1997" by Jeffrey K. Howard, *Film Score Monthly* (August 2001). I also drew on "John Morris Interview" by Howard, in the same issue.

**CHAPTER 9: 1967: AUTEUR, AUTEUR!**

Michael Hertzberg is quoted from "The Making of *The Producers*." Ralph Rosenblum is always quoted from his memoir *When the Shooting Stops . . . the Cutting Begins: An Editor's Story* (Viking Penguin, 1980). Dom DeLuise is quoted from his appearance in the Screen Actors Guild Foundation Conversations series in 2006, the transcript of which was provided to the author by Nat Segaloff. Joan Barthel visited the set of *The Producers* and wrote about the experience in "Brooks: To Lie and Sound Jolly?," *New York Times* (Sept. 3, 1967).

"[Brooks] keeps you on edge" is Dick Shawn from *Seesaw*. "Mel has great craziness . . ." is Zero Mostel from "Brooks: To Lie and Sound Jolly?" "Heaven and hell" is from "Mel Brooks and David Steinberg Trade Tales from Film and TV's Golden Years at the Wallis" by Jordan Riefe, *Hollywood Reporter* (Oct. 7, 2015). "With Gene I was simple . . ." is from "The Making of *The Producers*" "extra" in *The Producers* DVD. "There were certain things . . ." is Sidney Glazier from *When the Shooting Stops . . . the Cutting Begins*. Alan Heim is quoted from Vincent LoBrutto's *Selected Takes: Film Editors on Editing* (Praeger, 2000). Alfa-Betty Olsen recounted the Philadelphia preview of *The Producers* in "I Have Loved Every Job I Ever Had Even When There Was Heartbreak Involved," published in the WGA East's event program for the 59th Annual Writers Guild Awards (Feb. 11, 2007).

"She said my leading man . . ." is from "The Producer" by Frances Hardy, *Daily Mail* (UK) (Dec. 26, 2005). "It's impossible for a profit participant . . ." is from Jason E. Squire's *The Movie Business Book* (Simon & Schuster, 2004). "I shot a lot of it myself . . ." is from "Mel Brooks on *High Anxiety*" by Robert Rivlin, *Millimeter* (December 1977).

"I'm a moody person . . ." is from Hedda Hopper's column in the *Chicago Tribune* (Oct. 31, 1965). "My wife is my best friend . . ." is from the *Playboy* interview. "I can never let a picture go . . ." is from "Mel Brooks" by Jacoba Atlas, *Film Comment* (March–April 1975). "What you want in the end . . ." and "I may have moved ahead . . ." are from "Confessions of an Auteur" by Franklin Heller, *Action* (November–December 1971). "I'm a Russian Jew . . ." is from Maurice Yacowar, *Method in Madness: The Comic Art of Mel Brooks* (Book Sales, 1983). "A private story with universal features" is from "The Making of *The Producers*."

### CHAPTER 10: 1971: BLAZING MEL

"He thought I was God . . ." is from the *New Yorker* profile. All background relating to "The People on the Third Floor," "Annie," and *The Comedians* comes from the David Susskind papers. "Strange labor pains . . ." is from AB's appearance on *Charlie Rose* (April 25, 2000). "I've used up all money . . ." and "He was at the typewriter . . ." are from "Where Did He Go Right?"

Greg Beal's authoritative backstory of *Blazing Saddles*, "Backward in the Saddle Again," appeared in the April–May 2017 issue of *Written By*. "One of my best friends . . ," is from "Mel Brooks Didn't Try to Pants the President" by Erik Adams, film.avclub.com (Jan. 18, 2017). "When Mel tells the story . . . ," "about a month of steady work," and "I hated the character . . ." are Norman Steinberg (NS) from "Backward in the Saddle Again." "I didn't have time . . ." and "So much of the role . . ." are from the *Film Comment* interview. Paul Mooney is quoted from *Black Is the New White* (Simon Spotlight Entertainment, 2009). "Paranoid 'strawberries' bit . . . ," "Big upgrade there," and "and we had a couple of days . . ." are Andrew Bergman from "Backward in the Saddle Again."

"Hasn't been very easy . . ." (AB) and the performance anecdotes are from "Brooks, Reiner Revive 2,000-Year-Old Man, Now 2,013" by Judith Kinard, *New York Times* (Aug. 27, 1973). "Hollywood is really two Newarks" was attributed to MB by Abel Green, the editor of *Variety*, in his review of Oscar Levant's *The Unimportance of*

*Being Oscar* in *New York Times* (July 14, 1968). "So I figured this was the place to be" is from "The Entertainers: Max and Mel Brooks." The Brookses are reported to have "joined the migration" in "His Own WB Job Lost, Himself in NY for Now, Mike Mindlin Cites Exec Drift to Hollywood" by Richard Albarino, *Variety* (July 10, 1974).

"What, are you crazy? . . . ," "so she could see how much . . . ," and "harmonize the way Dietrich would . . ." are from William V. Madison's *Madeline Kahn: Being the Music, A Life* (University Press of Mississippi, 2015). "My audition for Mel . . ." is from "Woses Are Wed, Madeline's a Wow!: Madeline Kahn" by Robert Berkvist, *New York Times* (March 24, 1974). Harvey Korman's first meeting with MB is reported from Jennifer Howard's 2004 interview with Korman in the Television Academy Foundation oral history archives. "I don't look for actors . . ." is from *A Conversation with Robert Clary*. "I asked [Warner Bros.] on bended knee . . ." is from "Backward in the Saddle Again." "It's a thorn in my heart" is Richard Pryor from "Cabaret Comedy Champ Hits New Career High as Film Funnies Hero" by Martin Weston, *Ebony* (September 1976). Pryor is also quoted from his memoir *Pryor Convictions: And Other Life Sentences* (William Heinemann, 1995). "Handsome as all get out . . ." is from "Where Did He Go Right?" The tale of Gig Young's breakdown is from "Mel Brooks Reveals Stories Behind 'Blazing Saddles'" by Virginia Rohan, USA Today Network (Aug. 23, 2016). "*Blazing Saddles* is Dixieland jazz . . ." is from "Mel Gets the Last Laugh" by Lisa Bornstein, *Rocky Mountain News* (Jan. 3, 2004).

CHAPTER 11: 1974: TOPS IN TAPS

Unless otherwise noted, all Gene Wilder and MB quotes in this chapter are from "Writing and Acting in *Young Frankenstein*: A Talk with Gene Wilder" and "Writing and Directing *Young Frankenstein*: A Talk with Mel Brooks," both in the same issue of *Scenario* magazine (vol. 4, no. 1, 1998). "I assumed he liked the pages . . ." is from *Kiss Me like a Stranger.* "Gene and Mel were brilliant together" is Alan Ladd, Jr., from Mel Brook's *Young Frankenstein: A Mel Brooks Book: The Story of the Making of the Film* (Hachette UK, 2016). Gene Wilder's *Young Frankenstein* contract is among his papers in Special Collections at the University of Iowa Libraries.

"The sound editors . . ." is from "You've Got Mel" by Steve Daly, *Entertainment Weekly* (March 2000). "At first, I took him seriously . . ." is from "The Story Behind the Filming of *Young Frankenstein*" by Gerald Hirschfeld, *American Cinematographer* (July 1974). The anecdote about John Morris and *Young Frankenstein*'s musical score is from MB's interview in *Film Score Monthly.* "A litany of anger" is from "An Interview with Comedy Legend Mel Brooks" by Corey Stuice, *The Telegraph* (Alton, IL) (Jan. 6, 2013). "The only one who laughed . . ." is from the *Playboy* interview. The anecdote about the early dailies of *Young Frankenstein* is from David E. Williams's interview with Gerald Hirschfeld in *American Cinematographer* (April 2007). "Could be Krakatoa . . ." is from "Quiet on the Set." The "Walk this way!" anecdote is from *Marty Feldman: The Biography of a Comedy Legend* by Robert Ross (Titan Books, 2011) and *eyE Marty: The Newly Discovered Autobiography of a Comic Genius* by Feldman (Hachette, 2015). MB's explanation of "Walk this way!" is from *Kiss Me like a Stranger.* "Mel never loses his temper" is Teri Garr from Earl Wilson's Feb. 13, 1975, column in the *Los Angeles Herald-Examiner.*

"Every frame" is from "Quiet on the Set." "Mel, as you know, does . . ." is AB from Norma Lee Browning's column in the *Chicago Tribune* (Nov. 25, 1974). "Use of rape as a source of humor" is from "Pictures: Gal Pickets Hit Mel Brooks' Rape for Laffs Scene," *Variety* (Jan. 15, 1975). "We dealt with bigotry . . ." is from "Blazing Brooks," *Time* (Jan. 13, 1975). "Womb envy" and "the monster is what people . . ." is from "Comedy: The New King" by Hollis Alpert, *Saturday Review* (Nov. 2, 1974). "I think in ten years . . ." is from the *Film Comment* interview. "The funniest man in the world" is Harry

Stein from "Springtime for Mel Brooks," *New Times* (Jan. 22, 1974). *Newsweek* noted MB's constant balancing act in "The Mad Mad Mel Brooks."

## CHAPTER 12: 1975: CLUB BROOKS

"I was king of movies . . ." is from "Loud and Lively at 90" by Josh Rottenberg, *Los Angeles Times* (Oct. 13, 2016). "To have those two movies . . ." is Michael Gruskoff from *Mel Brooks: Make a Noise.* The Brookses on the tennis court are from items and features in the *Los Angeles Times,* including Joyce Haber's July 9, 1974, column and Paul Rosenfield's "The Rites of Hollywood: Only on Sunday" (Sept. 26, 1982), which includes the sidebar "[Gene] Wilder Rates the Players." "We'd rush to the ocean . . ." is from "Mel Brooks: What I Know Now" by Mel Brooks, *AARP The Magazine* (August–September 2015). "I miss the one millimeter . . ." is from "Funny Is Money" by Herbert Gold, *New York Times* (March 30, 1975). Burt Prelutsky's "Creating a Monster" appeared in the *Los Angeles Times* (March 2, 1975). "Mel Brooks is good . . ." is S. J. Perelman from David W. McCullough's *People, Books & Book People* (Harmony, 1981), which was noted in the book review by Herbert Mitgang in the *New York Times* (Aug. 15, 1981). "Hollywood writers take themselves . . ." is Buck Henry from *Seesaw.* Mordecai Richler is quoted from "On Being Funny," *New York Times* (June 1, 1975).

"There are very few big women . . ." is AB from "Annie" by Tom Burke, *TV Guide* (Nov. 23, 1974). "Ergo . . . satire pays the rent" is from "Mel Brooks Looks Back on Sid Caesar, *Blazing Saddles* and More" by Alan Sepinwall, uproxx.com (Dec. 10, 2012). "He was a jerk" is from Angela Bishop's video interview with Teri Garr for Network Ten's Studio 10, YouTube (May 24, 2017). "I can't find other people . . ." is from "Brooks Puts a Spin on 'Vertigo.'" "It was amazing to see Mel . . ." is Marty Feldman from *eyE Marty.* "Self-starters who don't have . . ." is from "Seven Revelations About

Mel Brooks" by Charles M. Young, *Rolling Stone* (Feb. 9, 1978). "Why should Canby . . ." is from "Mel Brooks: 'How Do You Like Me So Far?'" by Jane Shapiro, *The Village Voice* (July 19, 1976).

"Freebies for their high rollers" and other recollections of the Other World weekends are from Norman Lear's *Even This I Get to Experience* (Penguin, 2014), mingled with snippets from my interview with Lear. "Luckily for me . . ." is from "Mel Brooks on *High Anxiety*." Unless otherwise noted, Jonathan Sanger is always quoted from *Making* The Elephant Man: *A Memoir* (McFarland, 2016). "Mel's technique . . ." is Harvey Korman from "Funny on the Outside— but Inside, He's a Charming Cad" by Guy Flatley, *New York Times* (May 28, 1977). "I had all the jet lag . . ." is AB from *Anne Bancroft: A Life*. "Hardtops for a communal intimacy . . ." is from "Bid Drama: High Anxiety," *Variety* (Sept. 28, 1977). "My consummate height . . . ," "You know . . . ," and "wouldn't matter to the movie . . ." are from "The Other Side of Mel Brooks" by Gary Arnold, *Washington Post* (Feb. 5, 1978). "They chirp and make noise . . ." is MB from *Making* The Elephant Man.

"My little Jewish mother" is from "Notes on People" by Albin Krebs, *New York Times* (Sept. 21, 1977). MB talks about "smarties," "potato salad pictures," and his plans for his "personal version of *Sullivan's Travels* . . ." in "The Other Side of Mel Brooks." "Hasn't asked me . . ." is AB from Maggie Daly's column in the *Chicago Tribune* (March 15, 1979). Brianne Murphy is quoted from Mollie Gregory's *Women Who Run the Show: How a Brilliant and Creative New Generation of Women Stormed Hollywood* (St. Martin's Press, 2002).

CHAPTER 13: 1980: UNEASY LIES THE HEAD

"I very skillfully hid my name. . . ." is from "Mel Gets Last Laugh." "Nominal fee" and "a considerable investment. . . ." are from "Pictures: Brooks Man-for-Europe Is Buyse; Fox Finances, Brooks 'Defers'," *Variety* (Feb. 11, 1981). "The natural glue" and "I put an enormous

R . . ." are from "At the Movies" by Chris Chase, *New York Times* (July 10, 1981). "At the height of my vulgarity" is from *It's Good to Be the King.* "A considerable disappointment" is from "Hollywood Is Joyous over Record Grossing Summer" by Aljean Harmetz, *New York Times* (Sept. 9, 1981). "More important than the stars" is from "Dubbing, P.A. [personal appearance] Stints by Brooks Vital to History Paris B.O.," *Variety* (Feb. 10, 1982). "Didn't live up to Brooks' usual . . ." is from "You Wash Up, I'll Save France" by Steve Pond, *Washington Post* (Nov. 5, 1981). "Generally perceived to be a failure" is from "Mel Brooks Is Funnier Than Ever if He Does Say So Himself—and He Does" by Gene Siskel, *Chicago Tribune* (Feb. 27, 1983). "Mr. Brooks made more . . ." is from "Talking Money with Mel Brooks" by Geraldine Fabrikant, *New York Times* (Oct. 26, 1997).

"I am the funniest man . . ." is from "Playing Comedy Is No Laughing Matter" by Fred Ferreti, *New York Times* (Nov. 14, 1982). "I enjoyed *Airplane!* . . ." is from "At the Movies," July 10, 1981. "I don't think they have . . ." is from "Pell-Mel." Michael Palin is quoted from *Halfway to Hollywood: Diaries: 1980–1988* (Thomas Dunne Books, 2011). "Nothing about my wife . . ." is from "Mel Brooks: After VMI." "Warm, fun, easy" is from MT's Dec. 15, 1980, letter to Lucille Kallen. "Old-fashioned existence," "My mum was not just overprotective . . . ," and "because I opened a new box . . ." are Max Brooks from "Dad Was Too Afraid to Let Me Camp" by Helena de Bertodano, *The Times* (UK) (July 19, 2007). "The largest house in the city" is from "Mel Brooks' 'Immense' New House Upsets Neighbors" by Michelle Markel, *Los Angeles Times* (Aug. 21, 1983). "A little jealous" is Sid Caesar from *A Short History of Mel Brooks.* "It was okay . . ." is from Dan Pasternack's 1997 interview with Caesar in the Television Academy Foundation oral history archives. Imogene Coca's Sept. 15, 1982, letter to Lucille Kallen is among Kallen's papers. MT comments acerbically on *History of the World, Part I* in a June 15, 1981, letter to Kallen.

Brooks's friendship with the OCD-afflicted James Bailey is recounted in Bailey's *Man, Interrupted: Welcome to the Bizarre World of OCD, Where Once More Is Never Enough* (Random House, 2011). Ted Sorel's letter to the editor appeared in the *Los Angeles Times* (April 5, 1987). Burt Reynolds is quoted from *My Life* (Hoddard & Stoughton, 1994). The "Jack and the Lean Talk" lawsuit is recounted from clippings and court documents. *Variety* reported the *Elephant Man* litigation in its Aug. 15, 1979, edition. The *Frances* court case is reconstructed from court documents, newspaper items, and William Arnold's reminiscences in dialogue with Wallace Reid Boyd, published as *Shadowland Revisited: The Story of a Book and Its Aftermath* (Kindle, 2017).

### CHAPTER 14: 1983: WHY SO ANGRY?

"I spend about 30 per cent . . ." is from "On the Next Frontier, Mel Brooks Aims His Fazers at the Stars for a Space-Epic Parody" by Gene Siskel, *Chicago Tribune* (Jan. 11, 1987). "Jesus the Man" is from Martin Kasindorf's "From Hollywood" column in *Newsday* (Aug. 7, 1988). "An epic film about apartheid" is from "Brooks' Bookshop." Stuart Cornfeld is quoted from his "Dialogue on Film" in *American Film* (April 1, 1987). "I hadn't heard about this . . ." is Richard Benjamin from *Mel Brooks: Make a Noise*. MT commented on *My Favorite Year* in his Oct. 12, 1982, letter to Lucille Kallen. MB compares *The Dick Van Dyke Show*, *My Favorite Year*, and *Laughter on the 23rd Floor* in "Mel Brooks Looks Back on Sid Caesar, *Blazing Saddles* and More." "I was locked in the Waldorf Towers . . ." is from MB's *Film Score Monthly* interview.

"A handsome gargoyle" is from "The World According to Mel Brooks" by Mel Brooks, *New York Times* (June 7, 1981). "Often inept in life . . ." is from "It's a Classic Case of Chutzpah" by Richard Christiansen, *Chicago Tribune* (Feb. 11, 2001). Unless otherwise noted, Thomas Meehan is quoted in this chapter from his bylined

"How a Team of Filmmakers Worked with Mel Brooks on Making a New Version of the Classic Comedy, 'To Be or Not to Be'," *New York Times* (Jan. I, 1984). Alan Johnson discussed *To Be or Not to Be* with Douglass K. Daniel for *Anne Bancroft: A Life*; Daniel provided a transcript of Johnson's interview to the author. Lewis J. Stadlen is always quoted from his memoir *Acting Foolish* (BearManor, 2016).

Gene Shalit's interview with the Brookses originally aired on *The Today Show* on Dec. 16, 1983, and was excerpted in Eric Mink's *This Is Today: A Window on Our Times* (Andrews McMeel, 2003). "What I really want to know . . ." is from "Mel Brooks: Back on the Launch Pad" by Patrick Goldstein, *Los Angeles Times* (March 8, 1987).

"People don't write wonderful parts . . ." is AB from "Bancroft Portrays a Feisty Frump" by Leslie Bennetts, *New York Times* (Oct. 15, 1984). Freddie Francis is quoted from *Freddie Francis: The Straight Story from Moby Dick to Glory, A Memoir* (Scarecrow, 2013) and his interview in *An Autobiography of British Cinema* by Brian McFarlane (Methuen, 1997). "I'm getting a second mortgage . . ." is from "Mel Brooks Was Ready to Jump off a Roof over Sci-Fi Fiasco *Solarbabies*" by Clark Collis, EW.com (May 27, 2016). "A dry martini" is from "Secret Lunch Honors Ladd" by Bob Verini, *Variety* (Sept. 27, 2007).

## CHAPTER 15: 1986: FROLICS AND DETOURS

Ronny Graham is quoted from his interview in "Mel Brooks: Back on the Launch Pad." "Do you know . . ." is from "Pell-Mel." "He talks a lot . . ." is Kitty Kaminsky from "Mel Brooks' Mom Is Alive and Well." "We all spent three or four days . . ." is Leonard Kaminsky from the "Kate Kaminsky, Mother of Mel Brooks" obituary by Jean Marie Lutes, *Miami Herald* (Aug. 20, 1989). "A great deal more gemütlich" is writer Zoë Heller's characterization of what Brooks told her in "Sentimental Journey: Boy, Can Mel Talk" in *The Independent* (UK) (Dec. 19, 1993). "Non-stop routines . . ." is

Alan Spencer from *"Nutt House* Wobbly but Worth a Try" by Robert P. Laurence, *San Diego Union* (Sept. 20, 1989).

"Brooks is first . . ." is Robert Manning from "Pilluminations: Notes, Reflections, Fulminations, Ballyhoo & Hullabaloo" by Robert Wolfe, *American Film* (April I, 1990). MB is also quoted ("Taxes!") from this column. "Hollywood insiders say dealmakers . . ." is from "Public Offerings: Blazing Shares," *Time* (Dec. II, 1989). "Egg on his face" is from "Flack Attack" by Eric Schmuckler, *Forbes* (June 16, 1990).

"This is the first time . . ." and "one of the quickest flops of 1991" are from "Film Comment: Higher Anxiety" by Jack Mathews, *Los Angeles Times* (Aug. 4, 1991). "I was crucified" is from "Mel Gets Last Laugh." "There are three pillars . . ." is from "Mel Laughs It Off" by Lindsay Mackie, *The Guardian* (UK) (Sept. 19, 1991). "Gorgeously staged by me" is from "Mel Brooks Picks Five-ish Favorite Scenes Ahead of AFI Honor" by Susan King, *Los Angeles Times* (June 6, 2013). "Decreasingly important parts . . ." is William Gibson from *Anne Bancroft: A Life*. Carrie Fisher wrote about Dr. Evan Chandler in her book *Shockaholic* (Simon & Schuster, 2011). I also paid attention to Raymond Chandler's book exploring his nephew Jordan Chandler's accusations against Michael Jackson, *All That Glitters: The Crime and the Cover-up* (Windsong Press, 2004), which comments on his brother Dr. Evan Chandler, Mel Brooks, and the *Robin Hood: Men in Tights* credits. "I'm always questioning . . ." is from "Pell-Mel." Bernard Weinraub declared *Robin Hood: Men in Tights* "a modest success" in his roundup in the *New York Times* (Sept. 5, 1993). "I wasn't happy at all" (Jean-Marie Poire) and "It was an experiment . . ." (MB) are from "French Fume as Yanks Snub a Dub" by Michael Williams, *Variety* (Oct. 23, 1995).

CHAPTER 16: 1995: HE WHO LAUGHS LAST

*"Demolition Man . . ."* is from "Sentimental Journey: Boy, Can Mel Talk." "Dracula is too fantastical . . ." is from the *Film Talk* program

with Colin Grimshaw (UK), April 15, 1975. "I was amazed at the comic skill . . ." is from "Sneak Reviews: Funny You Should Ask" by Ray Greene, *Boxoffice* (Dec. 1, 1995). "If anybody hears of any . . ." is from "Brooks Still Rubs Critics the Wrong Way" by Andy Seiler, *USA Today* (Jan. 3, 1996). The anecdote about Brooks confronting Roger Ebert is from "10 Smart Questions for Mel Brooks" by Kate Meyers, ew.com (June 28, 1996). Ebert's response was published at https://www.rogerebert.com/answer-man/movie-answer -man-07211996 (July 21, 1996). "It, I think, felt more like . . ." is Steven Weber from *Mel Brooks: Make a Noise*.

"Pathos and real life," Sid Caesar's credo, is from an NBC inter- departmental memo (March 5, 1954). "Fantasy of success . . ." is CR from "Brooks' Bookshop." MB and Joseph Heller were jointly interviewed by David L. Ulin for the *Los Angeles Times* (Feb. 27, 1998). "He seemed to like that" is Helen Hunt from *Mel Brooks: Make a Noise*. "At the end of a day with Mel . . ." is Thomas Meehan from "Shtick Shift at 76: Mel Brooks Is Red-Hot" by Lynda Gorov, *Boston Globe* (June 15, 2003). "My main job . . ." is Meehan from "Without You, I'm Nothing" by Winnie McCroy, *Gay City News*, Nov. 18–24, 2004. "Doesn't like to do Scene II until . . ." is Meehan from the show business roundup (multiple bylines) in the *Daily News* (New York) (June 9, 2003). "Mel Brooks is a fountain . . ." is from "Musical Moment: An Interview with Book Writer Thomas Meehan," www.makemusicals.com (2011). The lunches at Or- so's are described from "The Return of Power Dining" by Merle Ginsberg, *Hollywood Reporter* (April 5, 2011); "Mel Brooks, Actors Carry on Tradition" by Bob Verini, *Variety* (Sept. 27, 2007); and "The Table at Orso" by Paul Mazursky, www.salon.com (Nov. 8, 2007). "Owner of most . . ." (referring to Robert F. X. Sillerman), "Local critics were kept away . . . ," and "theater pundits . . ." are from "Hitler Sings! Mel Kvells!" by Chris Jones, *Variety* (Feb. 19–25, 2001). "Mel was a hero . . ." is Nathan Lane from "Almost a One-Man Show" by Patricia O'Haire, *Daily News* (New York) (June 4, 2001).

"Producers and moneymen . . ." (Meehan) and the chronology and evolution of *The Producers* musical are drawn from Mel Brooks and Tom Meehan's *The Producers: How We Did It* (Hyperion, 2001). "In Pittsburgh, however . . ." is from "History of 'The Producers': Part III" by Adam Sternbergh, *New York* (Dec. 12, 2005).

"A fantastical third act" is from "Shtick Shift at 76." "Come [to New York] and spend money . . ." is Mayor Rudolph Giuliani from "Lower Manhattan Goes Back on the Job Today" by Greg Gittrich and Corky Siemaszko, *Daily News* (New York) (Sept. 27, 2001). "While Mr. Brooks said . . ." (footnote) is from John Morris's obituary by Richard Sandomir, *New York Times* (Jan. 28, 2018). "A familiar grinning face . . ." is from "Tony, Meet Mel: Record Sweep for Brooks' *The Producers*" by Blake Green, *Newsday* (June 4, 2001). "We may be in for some flak . . ." is from "$480 Seats Music to Producers' Ears" by Patricia O'Haire and Robert Dominguez, *Daily News* (New York) (Oct. 27, 2001).

### CHAPTER 17: 2001: UNSTOPPABLE

"Feels no competition . . ." is Charles H. Joffe from "Play It Alone, Brickman" by Jesse Kornbluth, *New York Times* (Feb. 24, 1980). "I admire Woody Allen . . ." is from "Mel Gets Last Laugh." "Productions in Toronto and Australia . . ." and "cleaned up for heartland families" are from "History of *The Producers*: Part III." "Every stray thought I get . . ." is from "Shtick Shift at 76." MB's forthcoming "anecdotal book" was announced in the Jan. 20, 2003, *Publishers Weekly*. "My dad was disappointed . . ." is Max Brooks from "The Brooks Family of Writers: Michelle, Max and Mel" by Steve Julian, *This Stage Magazine* (Nov. 9, 2010). "Just a teeny bit less . . ." is from "Shtick Shift: Bawdy Producers Tamed for H'Wood" by Sara Stewart, *New York Post* (Dec. 11, 2005).

"Marvelous inventions of texture and color" is from Alan Alda, *Things I Overheard While Talking to Myself* (Hutchinson, 2007). Jonathan Sanger is quoted in this chapter from Douglass K. Daniel's interview with him in *Anne Bancroft: A Life*. "Waking up in the afternoon . . ." is from "The Brooks Family of Writers: Michelle, Max, and Mel." "He'd been her shield . . . ," "my father's keeper . . . ," "What am I going to do? . . . ," "My dad liked going to the same . . . ," and "I'd always been jealous . . ." are from "Saving Mel Brooks" by Max Brooks, *Men's Health* (March 2007). Dick Van Patten meeting MB at the racetrack is from Van Patten's memoir *Eighty Is Not Enough: One Actor's Journey Through American Entertainment* (Phoenix, 2009). The French Roast coffee shop anecdote is from the "Rally for Doomed *Alias* Star" roundup in the *New York Post* (Aug. 23, 2005). "Memorialized . . ." is from "Q. and A.: Mel Brooks," *Hollywood Reporter* (Dec. 8, 2005). "Be sure to save this . . ." is from "Produce This," *New York Post* (Dec. 21, 2005). "Grief therapist" and "the worst year . . ." are Thomas Meehan from "History of 'The Producers': Part III." Buck Henry blamed Kenneth Tynan for exaggerating his feud with MB in "Buck Henry Gets Cagey" by Jon S. Denny, *American Film* (December 1980).

"Showstopper if you've got . . ." is Gene Wilder from "I Like Show but I Don't Like the Business" by Susan Dominus, *The Telegraph* (UK) (April 22, 2007). "Mel was always driven . . ." is from "The Robert Chalmers Interview: Gene Wilder: An Angel in America," *The Independent on Sunday* (UK) (June 19, 2005). MB's rant against *Young Frankenstein*'s critics was reported in Michael Riedel's column in the *New York Post* (Jan. 18, 2008). "A lot of people have the money . . ." is from "It's Alive, and It's on Broadway: Madcap Producer Mel Brooks" by Robert Kahn, *Newsday* (Nov. 4, 2007). "I was there last night . . ." is from "Monster Work of Art Is Never Really Done" by Cindy Adams, *New York Post* (Jan. 22, 2008). "So keyed up . . ." is from "Come On, Feel the Noise" by Jeremy McCarter, *New York* (Nov. 9, 2007). "Said to earn nearly . . ." is from "Monster Cuts" by Michael Riedel, *New York Post* (June 6, 2008). "It still smarts . . ." is from "He Keeps on Joking" by Steven Zeitchik, *Los Angeles Times* (Dec. 10, 2012).

"I was never recognized . . ." is from "Delightful Banter with Boundless Brooks" by Kam Williams, *The Aquarian Weekly* (June 7, 2013). "Impressive crew" (President Obama) and "as something to put . . ." (MB) are from "Presenting America's Newest Comedy Team: Mel Brooks and Obama" by Julie Hirschfeld Davis, *New York Times* (Sept. 22, 2016). "I had the three thirds . . ." is from "The History of Mel Brooks: Part I." "Painful" and "there will be hundreds of thousands . . ." are from David Bianculli's interview with MB. "Seems to have made peace . . ." and Max Brooks's comments about lost time are from "I Am a National Treasure." "It's not easy being a father . . ." is from "Mel Brooks: What I Know Now." "He can't feed himself . . ." is from "The History of Mel Brooks: Part I" by Curt Schleier, *The Forward* (May 13, 2013). "It's empty spaces . . ." is from "Schmoozing with Mel Brooks, the 88-Year-Old Man" by Danielle Berrin, *Jewish Journal* (Jan. 29, 2015). "Mel sometimes doesn't like . . ." is CR from "I Am a National Treasure." "A market value . . ." and other details of MB's financial portfolio are from "Talking Money with Mel Brooks" by Geraldine Fabrikant, *New York Times* (Oct. 26, 1997). "A leaner, meaner *Young Frankenstein* . . ." is Susan Stroman from her BBC World Service interview with MB (Oct. 13, 2007). "I've kind of cockneyed it up . . ." is from "Frankenstein Musical Gets Cockneyed Up" by Robert Dex, *Evening Standard* (UK) (Feb. 9, 2017). "A whole new opening" and "Her name is Sheila . . ." are from Graham Norton's show on BBC Radio 2 (Sept. 16, 2007).

## PERMISSIONS

Michael and Stephen Tolkin have graciously given permission for quoting from Mel Tolkin's unpublished memoir and his letters to Lucille Kallen.

Licensed photographs used with permission of the New York Public Library; *Photofest*; and ZumaPress.com.

# Filmography

(Major films with Brooks as credited writer, composer, director, producer, and/or star)

1954
*NEW FACES*

1963
*THE CRITIC*
(animated short)

1968
*THE PRODUCERS*

1970
*THE TWELVE CHAIRS*

1974
*BLAZING SADDLES*

1974
*YOUNG FRANKENSTEIN*

1976
*SILENT MOVIE*

1977
*HIGH ANXIETY*

1981

*HISTORY OF THE WORLD, PART I*

1983

*TO BE OR NOT TO BE*

1987

*SPACEBALLS*

1991

*LIFE STINKS*

1993

*ROBIN HOOD: MEN IN TIGHTS*

1995

*DRACULA: DEAD AND LOVING IT*

1999

*SCREW LOOSE*

2005

*THE PRODUCERS*

More details and a complete listing of all of Brooks's credits and his numerous small- and big-screen cameo appearances can be found at www.imdb.com.

# Index

# About the Author

Patrick McGilligan is the author of the *New York Times* Notable Books *George Cukor: A Double Life* and *Fritz Lang: The Nature of the Beast.* His biography *Alfred Hitchcock: A Life in Darkness and Light* was nominated for an Edgar Award and won the prize for the best foreign book translated into French given by the national association of French film critics. His most recent book, *Young Orson: The Years of Luck and Genius on the Path to* Citizen Kane, was a finalist for the *Los Angeles Times* biography of the year in 2015. His other works include the life stories of directors Nicholas Ray, Robert Altman, and Oscar Micheaux, and actors James Cagney, Jack Nicholson, and Clint Eastwood. He edited the acclaimed five-volume *Backstory* series of interviews with Hollywood screenwriters and (with Paul Buhle) the definitive *Tender Comrades: A Backstory of the Hollywood Blacklist.* His books have been translated into ten foreign languages. He lives in Milwaukee, Wisconsin.